Lecture Notes in Artificial Intelligence   10454

Subseries of Lecture Notes in Computer Science

More information about this series at http://www.springer.com/series/1244

Yang Gao · Saber Fallah
Yaochu Jin · Constantina Lekakou (Eds.)

Towards Autonomous Robotic Systems

18th Annual Conference, TAROS 2017
Guildford, UK, July 19–21, 2017
Proceedings

 Springer

Editors
Yang Gao
University of Surrey
Guildford
UK

Saber Fallah
University of Surrey
Guildford
UK

Yaochu Jin
University of Surrey
Guildford
UK

Constantina Lekakou
University of Surrey
Guildford
UK

ISSN 0302-9743   ISSN 1611-3349   (electronic)
Lecture Notes in Artificial Intelligence
ISBN 978-3-319-64106-5   ISBN 978-3-319-64107-2   (eBook)
DOI 10.1007/978-3-319-64107-2

Library of Congress Control Number: 2017947038

LNCS Sublibrary: SL7 – Artificial Intelligence

Printed on acid-free paper

This Springer imprint is published by Springer Nature
The registered company is Springer International Publishing AG
The registered company address is: Gewerbestrasse 11, 6330 Cham, Switzerland

Preface

This volume contains the papers presented at TAROS 2017, the 18th Towards Autonomous Robotic Systems (TAROS) Conference, held at the University of Surrey, Guildford, UK, during July 19–21, 2017 (https://www.surrey.ac.uk/taros2017).

TAROS is the longest running UK-hosted international conference on robotics and autonomous systems (RAS), which is aimed at the presentation and discussion of the latest results and methods in autonomous robotics research and applications. The conference offers a friendly environment for robotics researchers and industry to take stock and plan future progress. It welcomes senior researchers and research students alike, and specifically provides opportunities for research students and young research scientists to present their work to the scientific community.

Being a featured event of the UK Robotics Week 2017, TAROS 2017 was held at the University of Surrey to include an academic conference, industry exhibitions, robot demonstrations, and other satellite events. The program highlights include:

- Keynote lectures, given by world leaders in AI robotics from Google, Chinese Academy of Sciences, and UK Atomic Energy Authority.
- Oral presentations, covering topics of swarm and multi-robotic systems, human–robot interaction, robotic learning and imitation, robot navigation, planning and safety, soft and reconfigurable robots, service and industrial robots.
- Poster presentations, covering topics of humanoid and bio-inspired robots, mobile robots and vehicles, robot design and testing, detection and recognition, learning and adaptive behaviors, human–robot and robot–robot interaction.
- Industrial and academic exhibition stands and live demos.
- IET-sponsored evening lecture on the first European Mars rover given by Airbus.

TAROS also offers several prizes on papers and exhibitions. This year the following papers were nominated by the international Program Committee (IPC):

Nominees for Best Paper Prize sponsored by Springer

- Junshen Chen, Marc Glover, Chenguang Yang, Chunxu Li and Zhijun Li, "Development of an Immersive Interface for Robot Teleoperation"
- Jens Lundell, Murtaza Hazara and Ville Kyrki, "Generalizing Movement Primitives to New Situations"
- Ali Narenji Sheshkalani, Ramtin Khosravi and Mayssam Mohammadi, "Verification of Visibility-Based Properties on Multiple Moving Robots"
- Alan Winfield and Marina Jirotka, "The Case for an Ethical Black Box"
- Stefan Schubert, Peer Neubert, and Peter Protzel, "Towards Camera-Based Navigation in 3D Maps by Synthesizing Depth Images"

Nominees for Best Student Paper Prize in memory of Professor Ulrich Nehmzow

- Tom Bridgwater, Alan Winfield, and Tony Pipe, "Reactive Virtual Forces for Heterogeneous Swarm Exploration and Mapping"

- Pedro Proença and Yang Gao, "Probabilistic Combination of Noisy Points and Planes for RGB-D Odometry"
- James O'Keeffe, Danesh Tarapore, Alan Millard, and Jon Timmis, "Towards Fault Diagnosis in Swarm Robotic Systems via Characterization of Robot Behavior"

Nominees for Best Poster Prize sponsored by the UK-RAS Network

- Erwin Lopez, Guido Herrmann, and Ute Leonards, "Drivers' Manoeuvre Classification for Safe HRI"
- Josie Hughes and Fumiya Iida, "3D Printed Sensorized Soft Robotic Manipulator Design"

The IPC's Award Panel evaluate the presentations given by the shortlisted candidates during the conference and announced the winners at the Award Ceremony.

The TAROS 2017 Organizing Committee would like to thank all the authors, IPC members, and the conference sponsors including Airbus Defence and Space, Chinese Academy of Sciences, IET, Springer, and the UK-RAS Network.

June 2017

Yang Gao
Saber Fallah
Yaochu Jin
Constantina Lekakou

Organization

Program Committee

Rob Alexander	University of York, UK
Ronald Arkin	Georgia Institute of Technology, USA
Robert Babuska	TU Delft, The Netherlands
Nicola Bellotto	University of Lincoln, UK
Rob Buckingham	UKAEA - RACE
Stephen Cameron	Oxford University, UK
Alessandro Di Nuovo	Sheffield Hallam University, UK
Liang Ding	Harbin Institute of Technology, China
Stéphane Doncieux	ISIR/UPMC
Marco Dorigo	Université Libre de Bruxelles, Belgium
Kerstin Eder	University of Bristol, UK
Saber Fallah	University of Surrey, UK
Yang Gao	University of Surrey, UK
Antonios Gasteratos	Democritus University of Thrace, Greece
Dongbing Gu	University of Essex, UK
Heiko Hamann	University of Paderborn, Germany
Fumiya Iida	University of Cambridge, UK
Yaochu Jin	University of Surrey, UK
David Lane	Heriot-Watt University, Institute for Sensors Signals and Systems, UK
Stanislao Lauria	Brunel University, UK
Mark Lee	Aberystwyth University, UK
Tina Lekakou	University of Surrey, UK
Marco Leo	Institute of Optics
Jin-Guo Liu	Shenyang Institute of Automation, Chinese Academy of Sciences, China
Poramate Manoonpong	University of Southern Denmark
Raul Marin	Jaume I University, Spain
Xiaolin Meng	University of Nottingham, UK
Daniel Mège	Space Research Centre, Polish Academy of Science, Poland
António J.R. Neves	DETI-IEETA-University of Aveiro, Portugal
Andrew Philippides	CCNR, University of Sussex, UK
Robert Richardson	University of Leeds, UK
Tobias Seidl	Westfälische Hochschule, Germany
Paul Siebert	Unversity of Glasgow, UK
Panagiotis Tsiotras	Georgia Institute of Technology, USA
Oskar von Stryk	Technische Universität Darmstadt, Germany

Alan Winfield   Bristol Robotics Lab
Ulf Witkowski   South Westphalia of Applied Sciences, Germany

Additional Reviewers

Annamalai, Andy	Kiel, Henning	Pan, Yunpeng
Bennemann, Michael	Kim, Seungsu	Proença, Pedro
Boutselis, Georgios	Kohlbrecher, Stefan	Rogers, Jonathan
Chen, Fei	Kumar, Suresh	Ruotsalainen, Laura
Dor, Mehregan	Loianno, Giuseppe	Schloegl, Barbara
Gas, Bruno	Matsubara, Takamitsu	Seweryn, Karol
Heßing, Christian	Morin, Pascal	Shaikh, Danish
Just, Olaf	Pan, Yongping	Vidoni, Renato

Contents

Development of an Immersive Interface for Robot Teleoperation

Junshen Chen[1], Marc Glover[2], Chenguang Yang[1,2(✉)], Chunxu Li[1], Zhijun Li[3], and Angelo Cangelosi[2]

[1] Zienkiewicz Centre for Computational Engineering,
Swansea University, Swansea SA1 8EN, UK
cyang@theiet.org
[2] Center for Robotics and Neural Systems, Plymouth University,
Plymouth PL4 8AA, UK
[3] College of Automation Science and Engineering,
South China University of Technology, Guangzhou 510640, China

Abstract. In this paper, a novel interface of human-robot interaction has been developed to provide enhanced user experience for teleoperators. The interface has been implemented and tested on a Baxter robot platform and it can be easily adapted to other robot platforms. The main objective of this work is to provide a teleoperator immersive experience when controlling a telerobot arm by enabling the user to see and feel what the robot sees and feels from a first person point of view. This objective has been achieved by our designed interface integrating a haptic feedback device, a virtual reality headset, and an RGB-D camera. An operator can manipulate a robotic arm and receive force feedback information about interactions between the robot's grippers, as well as the robot's environment, whilst viewing the captured visual information of the robot's workspace, on the screen of the virtual reality headset. A servo motor driving platform has been designed as a new robot head to manipulate the camera on top of it, such that a teleoperator is able to control the pose of the camera in a natural manner via the wearable virtual reality headset. The orientation of the built-in inertial measurement unit (IMU) of the virtual reality headset is used to directly command the angles of the head platform on which the camera is mounted. The operator will have an immersive and in-depth experience when manipulating the robotic arm. Extensive tests with a variety of users have been carried out to evaluate the design in this work with quantified analysis.

Keywords: Teleoperation · Immersive virtual feedback · Human-robot interaction

1 Introduction

With the advance of automation technologies, robots have become increasingly prominent in our everyday lives [1]. Autonomous robots have become in com-

This work was supported in part by EPSRC grants EP/L026856/1 and EP/J004561/1 (BABEL) as well as Royal Society Newton Mobility Grant IE150858.

Y. Gao et al. (Eds.): TAROS 2017, LNAI 10454, pp. 1–15, 2017.
DOI: 10.1007/978-3-319-64107-2_1

mon use in industrial, as these robots are able to complete high precision tasks with minimal completion time, especially within hazard environments. However, specialised tasks that require extensive interactions with uncertain environment, e.g., it is not suitable for fully-autonomous robots to complete medical operation. A tele-controlled robot with human operator may be desired for these tasks [2], i.e., teleoperation. Works demonstrated in [3] showed how stereo vision contributes to improve the performance of applications in mobile robot teleguide. [4] presents a non-contacting vision-based method of robot teleoperation which improves accuracy of object gripping tasks. Teleoperation has progressed to the point, where human operators can easily control a multi-jointed robotic arm [5–8], via a haptic feedback device. As introduced in [9], with haptic force feedback, a pilot can have a natural representation when approaching obstacles. Force feedback was also added in [10] to aid camera system avoiding obstacle in mobile robot teleoperation. It is natural to combine haptic information with visual information for coordinated information feedback. However, conventional means of visual feedback using a monitor do not provides to an operator an immersive user experience. To enhance the telepresence, in this work, an immersive visual feedback device Oculus Rift DK2 is employed, together with a Kinect v2 RGB-D imaging device, and haptic device Geomagic Touch, to teleoperate a Baxter robot arm (Fig. 1).

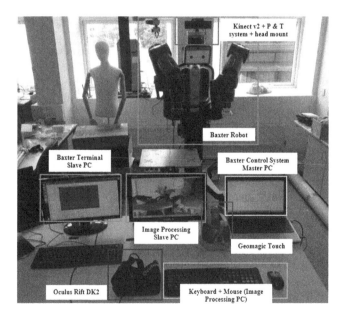

Fig. 1. Illustration of the teleoperation setup, with each key component labelled, including a Kinect head mount system, a Baxter robot, a Geomagic Touch and an Oculus Rift DK2. [photo taken at Plymouth University]

Haptic feedback devices which give an operator force feedback from a tele-robot have been utilised by numerous researchers [11,12]. In this work, using IR sensor at the cuff of Baxter's end effector (Fig. 2), the haptic feedback information is provided as the distance between an object/surface and the baxter's gripper. This haptic force feedback is also bonded with two other customised force feedbacks, tactile force, and restoration force. Tactile force is derived from a force sensing resistor (FSR) mounted onto one of the pincers of Baxter's end effector gripper (referred to as the FSR pincer, Fig. 2), which allows an operator to sense the firmness of objects picked up with the gripper. Restoration force tends to return the haptic joystick back to the preset original pose, after an operator has used the haptic joystick to change the position of the robot's gripper's pincers. Force feedback is presented to an operator via a Geomagic Touch haptic feedback joystick (Fig. 1), which is also used by the operator to control the position of Baxter's end effector.

Fig. 2. Illustration of one of the Baxter robot's end effectors. A: the cuff camera; B: the IR range sensor; C: active, gripper attachment [20]; D: VR headset capture of the operators view of the robot workspace, captured by the cuff camera

Immersive visual feedback technique which provides an operator a sense of telepresence has been implemented in many research projects [13,14]. In [15], a panoramic display system was used for improving teleoperation performance of a mining robot. An virtual reality (VR) headset, Oculus Rift, was used in [16] to control a simulated robot in a combat scenario. An intuitive 3D interface was designed to allow operator immersed in a virtual environment while teleoperating [17]. Rather than using the conventional interface composed of a monitor and a keyboard [18], immersive visual feedback technique can give operators a feeling that they are controlling robot as sitting inside robot. In this paper, the output image stream after image processing is displayed on the Oculus Rift DK2 headset. The operator is be able to manipulate the gaze of the Kinect camera's field of view (via a servo pan and tilt kit), as they move their head in a manner which is naturally similar, towards a certain direction for a better view. The IMU unit built into the Oculus Rift headset tracks the operator's head motion, and this subsequently turns the developed pan and tilt servo platform on which the Kinect camera is mounted. The Kinect pan and tilt servo platform is mounted onto the head of Baxter, and enables an operator to feel as though they are looking at the robot's workspace from a static position, in place of the robot.

In order for the operator to control the gaze of visual feedback camera, i.e., Kinect v2, a pan and tilt servo mount has been designed and manufactured, and fixed on top of Baxter's head. This also could be beneficial to other research carried out on the Baxter robot platform in the future. Baxter is a robust, reliable research robot platform which has only been available for nearly three years, and research already conducted on this platform has shown very promising and interesting results, this project will be the first of its kind to implement a system which combines haptic, immersive visual feedback on this platform. Extensive tests have been carried out, based on our previous work [19], to compare the user experiences of non-immersive and immersive teleoperation interfaces and their performances.

2   System Communications

Commands/data are sent/received via User Datagram Protocol (UDP) sockets, over a local wireless network as shown in Fig. 3, between the slave (Baxter terminal) computer and the Baxter robot. Two additional computers are employed, namely, a master computer, which is connected to the Geomagic Touch haptic joystick and controls the position of the Baxter's end effector, and a slave computer, which captures and processes images from the Kinect v2 device and from the cuff camera of Baxter's right arm (Fig. 2), as well as rendering, and serving these images to the Oculus Rift headset. This computer also sends the orientation of the Oculus Rift to the Arduino microcontroller which controls the pose of the head platform. All communications between the single master, the two slave computers, the Arduino microcontroller system, the and Baxter robot, are transmitted over the local wireless network. A Baxter control system model, interfaces with the Geomagic Touch haptic feedback controller, to apply force

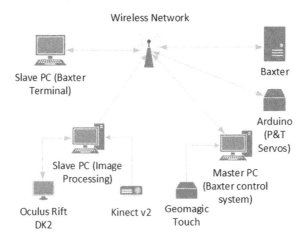

Fig. 3. Network diagram, representing each PC/terminal as a node on the local wireless network

feedback to the operator via the controller, and sets the position of the Baxter's end effector from the position of the haptic feedback controller's end effector (via the slave/Baxter terminal computer). This model is executed on the master computer. In order to control the orientation and position of the Baxter's end effector, the master computer must send the end effector orientation and position data to the slave (Baxter terminal) computer, which is subsequently sent to the Baxter robot. A Baxter control script written in *Python* is running on the slave computer (Baxter terminal), listening for commands from the master computer, interpreting them, and then sending the commands to the Baxter (sent as ROS commands). The overall communications system is shown in Fig. 3.

3   Haptic Feedback and Teleoperation Control

3.1   Position and Orientation Control

The position of the Baxter's end effector is determined by the position of the first three joints of the Geomagic Touch haptic feedback controller. A Simulink program developed in our previous work [5] is used to interface between the master computer and the Geomagic Touch controller. The Baxter's end effector position commanded by the Geomagic Touch, must first be modified to match the Baxter's frame as detailed in [5]. This position is then sent to the Baxter robot, via the slave Baxter terminal PC. To control the orientation of the Baxter's end effector, the transformation matrix, which include the rotation and translation of the 4th, 5th and 6th joints of the Geomagic Touch controller is used to calculate the Euler angles of the roll, pitch, and yaw of the Baxter's end effector.

3.2   Haptic Feedback

Tactile Force. Using IR sensor at the cuff of Baxter's end effector, the haptic feedback information is provided as the distance between an object and the baxter's gripper. The operator receives haptic feedback continuously while controlling the position and orientation of the Baxter's end effector. The haptic joystick provides to the operator feedback information about the workspace environment, which can be noticed both consciously and subconsciously by the operator. Operator using only a joystick is not able to receive tactile feedback when grasping an object with the robot arm's gripper. Tactile feedback whilst grasping an object is important for enhanced user experience of natural feeling and delicate manipulation of soft objects. Therefore, a simple one dimensional force sensor is added one of the pincer pads, on the end effector's gripper.

The operator can change the position of both pincers of the robot arm gripper's end effector, by pressing the second button on the joystick stylus (Fig. 4a). Changing the position of the feedback joystick's first joint will now open or close the gripper (Fig. 4c, d), with a resolution of 256 divisions (8-bit unsigned). The position of the robot arm and the end effector will also be fixed, so that only the gripper's pincers may move. The operator only feels force feedback through the haptic joystick when the FSR has some force applied to it, and when the operator has pressed the second stylus button to fix the position of the robot arm, in order to change the position of the gripper's pincers. The operator can now feel the firmness/consistency of an object, which is in-between the gripper's pincers; through force feedback. The force exerted by the gripper's pincers on the object is however constant, therefore the operator does not receive true (natural feeling) haptic information about the firmness/consistency of an object.

Algorithm 1. Haptic force feedback function

1: Sending reference trajectories
2: **if** second button pressed **then**
3:     Initial pose recorded
4:     Arm position fixed
5:     Joint 1 can be moved to close gripper
6:     Tactile force **on**
7: **end if**
8: **if** second button pressed again **then**
9:     Restoration force **on**
10:     Joints restore to initial pose
11:     **while** joint reaches acceptance zone **do**
12:         Arm position fixed
13:     **end while**
14: **end if**

Restoration Force. When the operator has changed the position of the gripper's pincers, the operator then presses the second stylus button to release the position of the robot arm. However, since the angle of the haptic joystick's joints has changed (Fig. 4c), the position of the robot arm will stay in the fixed position (Fig. 4f), until the angles of the haptic joystick's joints match the angles of the haptic joystick's joints when the second stylus button was initially pressed (Fig. 4g); an acceptance zone of roughly ±5% of the initial haptic joystick's joint angles is used.

To force the angles of the haptic joystick's joints to go back to their respective angles when the second stylus button was initially pressed (Fig. 4e), the angle of each of the haptic joystick's joint at the time of the initial button pressed is respectively fed into a separate PD controller as the desired angle, and the current haptic joystick's joint angles as the process variable; the output of each PD controller is used to create a 3 dimensional joint torque vector, which is then supplied to the Geomagic Touch joystick and given to the operator as force feedback (which exhibits spring-like behaviour, Fig. 4e):

$$T = K_p \left(P_{SP} - P_{PV} \right) + K_d \left(\dot{P}_{SP} - \dot{P}_{PV} \right) \tag{1}$$

where haptic feedback controller joint torques $T = \left[T_{J1} \; T_{J2} \; T_{J3} \right]^T \in R^{3 \times 1}$, K_p and K_d are properly chosen gains, P_{SP} is the preset point, and P_{PV} is

(a) Second button pressed, initial joint positions recorded

(b) Arm joints positions are fixed

(c) Moving joint 1, to close grippers

(d) Gripper closed

(e) Press the button again, joints back to initial pose (controllers enabled)

(f) Arm pose is fixed until Geomagic joints have each reached the acceptance zone

(g) Geomagic joints have reached the acceptance haptic feedback stops (controllers disabled)

(h) Arm joints released, normal position control resumes

Fig. 4. Illustrates the function of the haptic feedback PD controllers, returning the Geomagic joints to their initial angles, after the operator grasps an object with the end effector gripper. The light grey button nearest the operators hand is referred to as the second button, and the dark grey button is referred to as the first button, respectively

the process variable point. These PD controllers are disabled when each of the joystick's joints have reached their respective acceptance zone.

Changing Perspective. The operator has the option to display the Kinect colour images, or camera images captured from the end effector camera of the robot arm (Fig. 2). When the operator switches views to the end effector camera, a gain of K is applied to all end effector position movements transmitted to the Baxter robot (Eq. 2):

$$P_{pm} = P_{ini} + K \left(P_{cur} - P_{ini} \right) \tag{2}$$

where P_{pm} is the end effector position, P_{ini} is the initial end effector position, in precision mode, P_{cur} is the end effector position calculated by the Geomagic Touch controller block, using standard position mapping [5]. Since the position mapping between the Geomagic and robot arm has changed, the angles of the Geomagic's joints are returned to their respective initial angles.

4   Visual Feedback System

4.1   Mounting Kinect V2 on Baxter

The head platform was purposely designed to fit directly onto the head of Baxter in SolidWorks, and 3D printed (Fig. 5). This head platform does not require any modifications to be made to the existing Baxter robot, since the platform attaches directly to the head of Baxter (as shown in Fig. 6a). The legs of the head platform allow the platform to be fixed around the head of the Baxter robot, whilst not interfering with the field of view of the robot's sonar ring (Fig. 6a).

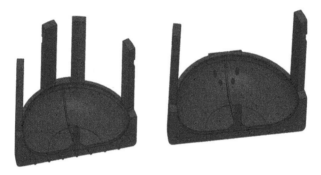

Fig. 5. The two halves of the Kinect - Baxter head mounting base; back half (left, and front half (right). The cross section shows the profile of the Baxter head cap, and central peg. The legs (with notches), fix the head mounting base, to the head of Baxter

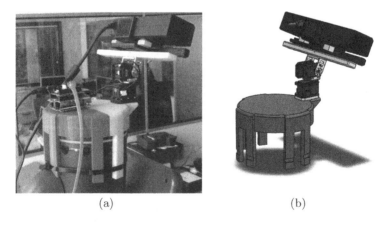

(a)   (b)

Fig. 6. (a) The 3D printed head platform attached directly to the head cap of the Baxter robot (grey ABS dish, above green LED ring); the platform's six legs fit around the head of the Baxter. (b) The complete pan and tilt servoing platform with Kinect amounted; 3D printed support bar (green) attaches the Kinect to the tilt servo bracket, MDF pan servo spacer (green) mounts the servo assembly to the Baxter head mount. (Color figure online)

Small notches in each of the platform's legs (Fig. 6b), guide a zip tie which is used to fix the head platform laterally to the robot. Two Dynamixel MX28R servo, one tilt servo and one pan servo, was directly attached to the edge of the head platform. It can hold the Kinect v2 with a 3D printed support bar attached to the tilt servo. This gives us the view from Baxter's head.

4.2   Viewing the Robot Workspace

Controlling Kinect's View. We used an Arduino Microcontroller Development board to control the both pan and tilt positions of MX-28R servos. Servo data packets containing the desired servo setting position are output via the Arduino's USART peripheral, to a TTL to RS485 converter, in order to convert TTL logic level signals to RS485 levels (MX-28R utilise the RS485 communications protocol). The Arduino is connected to a Wi-Fi shield, from which the Arduino can receive UDP packets, which contain encoded servo position strings, constructed as follows: Servo ID, separating character, desired servo position, and finally an end-of-file character. The broadcast string "S1,1023\0", will set servo ID 1 (pan servo), to position 1023 (90°). The Arduino decodes the received strings, and sets the pan and tilt servo positions appropriately. Using the image processing slave PC (Fig. 3), pitch and yaw angles of the Oculus Rift are acquired, encoded into a position string, and subsequently sent as an UDP packet via Wi-Fi to the Arduino Wi-Fi shield. Pitch and yaw angles are given as Euler angles by the Oculus Rift Software Development Kit (SDK). So that the Kinect sensor will follow the operator's head motion when they turn or tilt their head.

Rendering on Oculus Rift. To give the most immersive experience possible to the operator, the output of the Kinect v2s colour camera (the view from Baxter), is displayed on the screen of the Oculus Rift DK2. This gives the operator the sensation that they are looking at the workspace through the eyes of Baxter. To do this, the current colour and depth frames are captured from the Kinect v2. A distortion was applied to original image (as shown in Fig. 7) to cancel Oculus Rift's lenses' distortion. A flat image of Oculus's capture will present to operator as final image (unless stereoscopic effects are used to create a 3 dimensional view of the environment). The captured 1920×1080 pixels colour image from the Kinect v2 is presented to each eye of the Oculus Rift; the Oculus SDK then internally rescales the size of each image to match the resolution of each eye.

A Natural View of the Workspace. Oculus Rift DK2 features a built-in 9-axis IMU (Inertial Measurement Unit); a 6-axis MEMS gyroscope and accelerometer (Invensense MPU-6500), and a 3-axis MEMS magnetometer (undisclosed manufacturer and model). The Oculus SDK can be used to extract the Euler angles of the Oculus Rift, from the IMU; the IMU applies digital low pass filtering to the output gyroscope and accelerometer on-chip, the SDK reads these outputs and converts the accelerometer and gyroscope data from Quaternion notation to Euler angle notation. Euler showed that any rotation in a 3

Fig. 7. Radial distortion is added to the input image before it is displayed on the Oculus Rift, to compensate for radial distortion due to the headset's lenses

dimensional space, can be described as 3 rotation about each axis (x, y, and z). Therefore, obtaining the Euler angles of the Oculus Rift via the Oculus SDK, represents the orientation of the operator's head as roll (about the z axis), pitch (about the x axis), and yaw (about the y axis). However, the orientation of the Kinect v2 can only be altered for the yaw and pitch (pan and tilt servos), therefore the roll in this case is fixed; this extra degree of freedom could be added later by mounting the current Kinect pan tilt servo assembly, on top of a servo which will control the roll of the Kinect v2. The obtained Euler angles of the Oculus's pitch and yaw, are given in radians; these are converted into degrees to simplify the process of converting the pitch and yaw angles into the tilt and pan servo positions respectively. The conversion is given as follows:

$$R_s = \frac{R_O}{R_a} \tag{3}$$

where R_s is the position of the tilt or pan of servo, R_O is the pitch or yaw angle of the Oculus and $R_a = 0.088°$ is the angular resolution of servo. The clockwise rotations have been set as a positive rotation.

Changing Perspectives. During system testing, it is difficult for the operator to gain a sense of depth within Baxter's workspace; this is due to a significant distance between the Kinect's camera and the target object; when controlling Baxter to complete a pick and place operation. Due to the lack of the operator's sense of depth, a method was devised to change the images rendered of the Oculus Rift's display from the Kinect's colour video stream, to the camera built into the cuff of Baxter's right arm (as shown in Fig. 8).

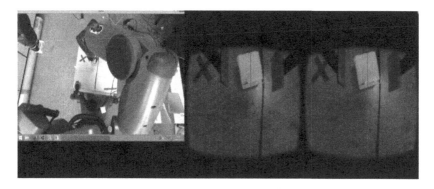

Fig. 8. Monitor outputs: left image is the image captured by Kinect on the top of Baxter, and the two distorted images on the right, are the right arm, cuff camera. A pink line represents the centre of the frame to make aligning the gripper with objects easier. (Color figure online)

5 Test and Evaluation

5.1 Testing Scenario

Twelve subjects were asked to pick up one Lego block each time and stack it on top of one another. Three different settings of the teleoperation system were tested: VR system plus force feedback on the haptic device; VR system only (without force feedback); and on-screen visual feedback with keyboard control of Kinect's position plus force feedback on the haptic device. The gain K for the force feedback in Eq. 2 was set at 0.25 due to the designer's experience.

Number of collisions that the end-effector collided with the table was recorded while operator performing each task. The result was shown in Fig. 9. All the operators were asked to fill in a questionnaire after they completed all three tasks, the questionnaire is attached in Appendix A.

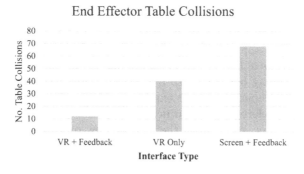

Fig. 9. Total number of collisions that the end-effector collided with the table while twelve operators performing each task.

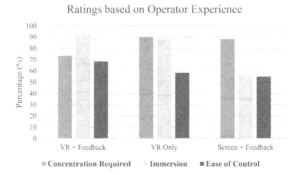

Fig. 10. Average user experience ratings of each system setting, including concentration required, immersion and ease of control.

It is illustrated from Fig. 9 that there is a relationship between the level of the immersion experienced by the operator and the collision times of robot's end effector. Since the number of the collision times increased significantly when the operators' immersion level decreased. The sensation of viewing the robot workspace in a way which is close to the natural humans view (as well as control of view), could be considered as the cause of this result.

The ratings of the three different teleoperation experiences is shown in Fig. 10. The least concentration level during teleoperation was required when both VR and force feedback applied. The level of immersion decreased dramatically between VR systems and screen visual feedback system. And it also became harder for the users to complete the task while the level of immersion decreased.

6   Conclusion

A novel human-robot interaction interface for teleoperation has been developed in this paper. The interface integrated both visual feedback and haptic feedback technologies to provide immersive user experience. The visual feedback is provided by a vision system mounted on a custom-built head platform, which is naturally controlled to track the head's motion of human operator. The designed interface provides operator an immersive sensation of viewing from robot's perspective, aiding operator in concentrating on completing a given task. In the meantime, operator is able to manipulate the position of the Kinect device in a natural way by moving his/her head. It can reduce the cognitive load on user while performing teleoperation. User experience investigation results show that the invited testers preferred using our designed interface to view visual feedback of the robot workspace and control the field of view of visual feedback, rather than using the conventional interface composed of a monitor and a keyboard. The use of virtual reality based interfaces in teleoperation projects is a solution which may become more apparent in the near future, since these interfaces offer immersive platforms for visual feedback to the operator, that can only be experienced on these types of devices.

Appendix

A   Participant Questionnaire

Baxter Teleoperation - Questionnaire

Gender:		Age:	
Q1.			
Have you controlled any kind of robot before?			
If yes, please give details:			
Q2.			
Have you used a virtual reality headset before?			
If yes, please give details:			

After completing the series of simple pick and place tasks, please complete the following questions, by either highlighting, or circling your choices; 0 very poor, 5 excellent:

	Screen + Keyboard	VR Only	VR + Haptic Feedback
System Responsiveness	0 1 2 3 4 5	0 1 2 3 4 5	0 1 2 3 4 5
Concentration Required	0 1 2 3 4 5	0 1 2 3 4 5	0 1 2 3 4 5
Immersive Experience	0 1 2 3 4 5	0 1 2 3 4 5	0 1 2 3 4 5
Ease of Control	0 1 2 3 4 5	0 1 2 3 4 5	0 1 2 3 4 5
Task Difficulty	0 1 2 3 4 5	0 1 2 3 4 5	0 1 2 3 4 5
Time to complete task	0 1 2 3 4 5	0 1 2 3 4 5	0 1 2 3 4 5
Task Completed	Yes No	Yes No	Yes No

Q3.
In terms of how immersive your experience was, how did controlling the robot while looking at the PC monitor, compare with controlling the robot while looking through the virtual reality headset? Which did you prefer? Please give reason(s) why:
Q4.
Did you face any challenges when using the Kinect camera or the cuff camera? Was the ability to switch between cameras helpful?
Q5.
Was the received haptic feedback helpful? Was the force feedback you received what you were expecting? Please give details:
Q6.
Any suggestions how the VR + Haptic Feedback system could be improved?

References

1. Billard, A., Calinon, S., Dillmann, R., Schaal, S.: Robot programming by demonstration. In: Siciliano, B., Khatib, O. (eds.) Springer Handbook of Robotics, pp. 1371–1394. Springer, Heidelberg (2008)
2. Sarmah, A., Gulhane, U.: Surgical robot teleoperated laparoscopic grasper with haptics feedback system. In: 2010 International Conference on Emerging Trends in Robotics and Communication Technologies, pp. 288–291, December 2010
3. Livatino, S., Muscato, G., Privitera, F.: Stereo viewing and virtual reality technologies in mobile robot teleguide. IEEE Trans. Robot. **25**, 1343–1355 (2009)
4. Kofman, J., Wu, X., Luu, T.J., Verma, S.: Teleoperation of a robot manipulator using a vision-based human-robot interface. IEEE Trans. Industr. Electron. **52**, 1206–1219 (2005)
5. Ju, Z., Yang, C., Li, Z., Cheng, L., Ma, H.: Teleoperation of humanoid Baxter robot using haptic feedback. In: 2014 International Conference on Multisensor Fusion and Information Integration for Intelligent Systems, pp. 1–6, September 2014
6. Reddivari, H., Yang, C., Ju, Z., Liang, P., Li, Z., Xu, B.: Teleoperation control of Baxter robot using body motion tracking. In: 2014 International Conference on Multisensor Fusion and Information Integration for Intelligent Systems, pp. 1–6, September 2014
7. Wang, X., Yang, C., Ma, H.: Automatic obstacle avoidance using redundancy for shared controlled telerobot manipulator. In: The 5th Annual IEEE International Conference on Cyber Technology in Automation, Control and Intelligent Systems, pp. 1338–1343, 8–12 June 2015
8. Liang, P., Yang, C., Li, Z., Li, R.: Writing skills transfer from human to robot using stiffness extracted from sEMG. In: The 5th Annual IEEE International Conference on Cyber Technology in Automation, Control and Intelligent Systems, pp. 19–24, 8–12 June 2015
9. Hou, X., Mahony, R.: Dynamic kinesthetic boundary for haptic teleoperation of vtol aerial robots in complex environments. IEEE Trans. Syst. Man Cybern. Syst. **46**, 694–705 (2016)
10. Cho, S.K., Jin, H.Z., Lee, J.M., Yao, B.: Teleoperation of a mobile robot using a force-reflection joystick with sensing mechanism of rotating magnetic field. IEEE/ASME Trans. Mechatron. **15**, 17–26 (2010)
11. Romano, J., Hsiao, K., Niemeyer, G., Chitta, S., Kuchenbecker, K.: Human-inspired robotic grasp control with tactile sensing. IEEE Trans. Robot. **27**, 1–10 (2011)
12. Lee, S., Sukhatme, G., Kim, G.J., Park, C.M.: Haptic teleoperation of a mobile robot: a user study. Presence **14**, 345–365 (2005)
13. Tachi, S., Komoriya, K., Sawada, K., Nishiyama, T., Itoko, T., Kobayashi, M., Inoue, K.: Telexistence cockpit for humanoid robot control. Adv. Robot. **17**(3), 199–217 (2003)
14. Kim, D.Y., Lee, M.S., Choi, S.H., Koo, K.-J., Hwang, I., Kim, Y.J.: An immersive telepresence platform based on distributed architecture. In: 2013 International Conference on ICT Convergence, pp. 465–467, October 2013
15. James, C.A., Bednarz, T.P., Haustein, K., Alem, L., Caris, C., Castleden, A.: Teleoperation of a mobile mining robot using a panoramic display: an exploration of operators sense of presence. In: 2011 IEEE International Conference on Automation Science and Engineering, pp. 279–284, August 2011

16. Conn, M.A., Sharma, S.: Immersive telerobotics using the oculus rift and the 5DT ultra data glove. In: 2016 International Conference on Collaboration Technologies and Systems, pp. 387–391, October 2016
17. Regenbrecht, J., Tavakkoli, A., Loffredo, D.: A robust and intuitive 3d interface for teleoperation of autonomous robotic agents through immersive virtual reality environments. In: 2017 IEEE Symposium on 3D User Interfaces, pp. 199–200, March 2017
18. Dünser, A., Lochner, M., Engelke, U., Fernández, D.R.: Visual and manual control for human-robot teleoperation. IEEE Comput. Graph. Appl. **35**, 22–32 (2015)
19. Chen, J., Glover, M., Li, C., Yang, C.: Development of a user experience enhanced teleoperation approach. In: 2016 International Conference on Advanced Robotics and Mechatronics, pp. 171–177, August 2016
20. Rethink Robotics, May 2014. http://sdk.rethinkrobotics.com/mediawiki-1.22.2/images/thumb/4/48/Hand_sensors.png/425px-Hand_sensors.png. Accessed 01 July 2015

Generalizing Movement Primitives
to New Situations

Jens Lundell[1], Murtaza Hazara[2(✉)], and Ville Kyrki[2]

[1] AASS Research Center, Örebro University, Örebro, Sweden
jens.lundell@oru.se
[2] School of Electrical Engineering, Aalto University, Espoo, Finland
{murtaza.hazara,ville.kyrki}@aalto.fi

Abstract. Although motor primitives (MPs) have been studied extensively, much less attention has been devoted to studying their generalization to new situations. To cope with varying conditions, a MP's policy encoding must support generalization over task parameters to avoid learning separate primitives for each condition. Local and linear parameterized models have been proposed to interpolate over task parameters to provide limited generalization.

In this paper, we present a global parametric motion primitive (GPDMP) which allows generalization beyond local or linear models. Primitives are modeled using a linear basis function model with global non-linear basis functions. The model is constructed from initial non-parametric primitives found using a single human demonstration and subsequent episodes of reinforcement learning to adapt the demonstrated skill to other task parameters. The initial models are then used to optimize the parameters of the global parametric model. Experiments with a ball-in-a-cup task with varying string lengths show that GPDMP allows greatly improved extrapolation compared to earlier local or linear models.

1 Introduction

Learning from demonstration (LfD) is a parametric supervised learning framework; the parameters of a model [1–5] are fine-tuned, thus fitting the model to the training data (demonstrations). Developing a model capable of adapting and generalizing to new unseen situations is one of the main challenges and objectives of supervised learning. In the context of motor primitives (MPs), a generalizable model can be translated into a model achieving a successful reproduction of an imitated task in a perturbed environment. For example, a generalizing model can reproduce a ball-in-a-cup task for a different string length unseen in the demonstrations; the model is interpolating when this new string length is in the range of demonstrations set; otherwise, it is extrapolating.

Recently, researchers have shown interest in generalizing MPs to new situations [6–9]. Such a generalization is achieved by parametrizing a policy encoding with respect to an evaluated environment condition. Although these parametric models are capable of interpolation, they are not guaranteed to extrapolate.

© Springer International Publishing AG 2017
Y. Gao et al. (Eds.): TAROS 2017, LNAI 10454, pp. 16–31, 2017.
DOI: 10.1007/978-3-319-64107-2_2

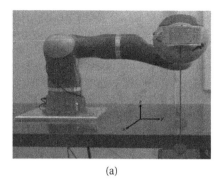
(a)

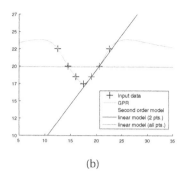
(b)

Fig. 1. (a) Ball-in-a-cup game with two different string lengths. (b) Models fit to 7 points of a non-linear function. Only the second order model captures the global pattern, while the GPR model tends to the mean when extrapolating, and the linear model is either (when trained with all samples) leaning toward the mean, or finds only the local pattern when fit to only two points marked by the green color. (Color figure online)

In fact, very few researchers have considered global policy encoding capable of extrapolation [10,11].

In this paper, we propose a new parametric LfD approach for generalizing an imitated task to new unseen situations. We selected the ball-in-a-cup task to assess how effective our method is in generalizing from initial demonstration with certain string length to changed lengths. The kinematics of the initial demonstration are encoded using a Dynamic Movement Primitive (DMP). Afterwards, the shape parameters of the DMP are optimized using PoWER [12] to adapt the skill to a few other string lengths. These training data are then used to build a global parametric model of the skill. Then, the global model can be used for generalizing model parameters (e.g. shape parameters of DMP) to new task parameters (e.g. string lengths) without re-learning the generalized model.

The main contribution of this paper is a novel global parametric MP model (GPDMP) based on DMPs which employs a linear basis function model with global non-linear basis functions. The representative power of the model can be controlled to avoid the over-fitting problem. We also show that the PDMP method proposed by Matsubara et al. [10] can be reduced to a linear special case of our parametric model. Furthermore, we propose a new mechanism for exploring the DMP's policy space. Experiments with a ball-in-a-cup task show that the proposed model greatly improves extrapolation capability over the existing local or linear models.

2   Related Work

To adapt LfD models to new environments, the model parameters need to be adjusted according to parameters characterizing the new environment or task.

Existing generalizable LfD models can be categorized as (i) generalization by design where the parameters are explicit in the model structure such as the goal of a DMP; (ii) generalization based on interpolation which uses a weighted combination of training models; and (iii) generalization by global linear models where the model parameters depend linearly on the environment/task parameters.

Kober et al. [13] utilized a cost regularized kernel regression (based on Gaussian process regression) for learning the mapping of new situations to meta-parameters including the initial position, goal, amplitude and the duration of the MPs; they model the automatic adjustment of the meta-parameters as a RL problem. The approach allows then adjusting these designed aspects of motion based on the task but does not enable modifying other characteristics of the trajectory (policy), making the approach suitable for learning tasks where the DMPs are adapted spatially and temporally without changing the overall shape of the motion, but unsuitable for tasks where the dynamics during motion are changed such as in this paper.

Researchers have recently shown interest also in generalizing DMP shape parameters to new situations [7–9,14–16]. The approaches are primarily based on local regression methods. For example, Da Silva et al. [7] extract lower dimensional manifolds (latent space) from learned policies using ISOMAP algorithm; they achieve a generalizable policy by mapping the manifolds (representing task parameters) to DMPs shape parameters. Support Vector Machines with local Gaussian kernels are used for learning the mapping. Similarly, Forte et al. [8] utilize Gaussian process regression (GPR) to learn the mapping of task parameters to DMP shape parameters. Ude et al. [9] and Nemec et al. [15] utilize Locally Weighted Regression (LWR) and kernels with positive weights for learning the mapping. Stulp et al. [14] learn the original shape parameters and generalize it with one single regression using Gaussian kernels. Mülling et al. [16] propose a linear mixture of MPs for generalization and refine the generalized behavior using RL.

Although the local regression approaches might interpolate within the range of demonstrations, their extrapolation capability is not guaranteed, which is mainly because of the kernels learning the local structure; thus they typically tend towards the mean of training data when extrapolating. This problem is illustrated using a simple example in Fig. 1(b) which shows local (GPR) and global (linear, second order) models fit to a set of points. When a line is fit to two points close to each other, it learns the local pattern allowing interpolation and extrapolation in a small neighborhood. If the line fit is made using all points, the fit tends to become poor everywhere. A local regression such as GPR performs well in interpolation, but not in extrapolation. When a well fitting higher order global model can be found, it typically outperforms the others in extrapolation.

Carrera et al. [6] developed a parametric MPs model based on a mixture of several DMPs. First, they record multiple demonstrations. A DMP model is fit to each demonstration, and a parametric value is assigned to it representing the task environment in which the demonstration was recorded. Then, they calculate the influence of each model using a distance function between the model parameters and the parametric value describing the current environment perturbation. Using the influence of each model as its mixing coefficient, the mixture of models is computed at the acceleration level. Since it is a linear combination with positive coefficients, the mixture model is not expected to be capable of extrapolation. In fact, we have observed in our experiments (see Sect. 4.3) that this model is incapable of extrapolation in a Ball-in-a-Cup task.

Calinon et al. [11] proposed an MPs model based on a Gaussian mixture model and generalize it to new situations using expectation maximization. Although their model is capable of linear extrapolation, it is only applicable when the task parameters can be represented in the form of coordinate systems.

All things considered, few researchers [10] have considered the extrapolation capability in generalizing task parameters to model parameters, which is the main focus of this paper. We show (see Sect. 3.3) that the model proposed by Matsubara et al. [10] is a linear special case of the proposed parametric model.

3 Method

In this section, we review dynamic movement primitives (DMPs). After that, we clarify our global parametric dynamic movement primitives (GPDMPs) method which incorporates both linear and non-linear parametric models. Besides that, we reformulate the parametric DMP method proposed by Matsubara et al. [10] and demonstrate how it can be reduced to a linear special case of the proposed approach.

3.1 Dynamic Movement Primitives

DMPs encode a policy for a one-dimensional system using two differential equations. The first differential equation

$$\dot{z} = -\tau \alpha_z z \tag{1}$$

formulates a canonical system where z denotes the phase of a movement; $\tau = \frac{1}{T}$ represents the time constant where T is the duration of a demonstrated motion, and α_z is a constant controlling the speed of the canonical system. This first order system resembles an adjustable clock driving the transform system

$$\frac{1}{\tau}\ddot{x} = \alpha_x(\beta_x(g - x) - \dot{x}) + f(z; \mathbf{w}) \tag{2}$$

consisting of a simple linear dynamical system acting like a spring damper perturbed by a non-linear component (forcing function) $f(z; \mathbf{w})$. x denotes the state of the system, and g represents the goal. The linear system is critically damped by setting the gains as $\alpha_x = \frac{1}{4}\beta_x$. The forcing function

$$f(z; \mathbf{w}) = \mathbf{w}^T \mathbf{g} \tag{3}$$

controls the trajectory of the system using a time-parameterized kernel vector $\mathbf{g}$ and a modifiable policy parameter vector (shape parameters) $\mathbf{w}$. Each element of the kernel vector

$$[\mathbf{g}]_n = \frac{\psi^n(z)z}{\sum_{n=1}^N \psi^n(z)}(g - x_0) \tag{4}$$

is determined by a normalized basis function $\psi^n(z)$ multiplied by the phase variable z and the scaling factor $(g - x_0)$ allowing for the spatial scaling of the resulting trajectory. Normally, a radial basis function (RBF) kernel

$$\psi^n(z) = \exp(-h_n(z - c_n)^2) \tag{5}$$

is selected as the basis function. The centres of kernels (c_n) are usually equispaced in time spanning the whole demonstrated trajectory. It is also a common practice to choose the same temporal width ($h_n = \frac{2}{3}|c_n - c_{n-1}|$) for all kernels. Furthermore, the contribution of the non-linear component (3) decays exponentially by including the phase variable z in the kernels. Hence, the transform system (2) converges to the goal g.

The shape parameter vector $\mathbf{w}$ can be learned using weighted linear regression (LWR) [17]; firstly, the nominal forcing function f^{ref} is retrieved by integrating the transform system (2) with respect a human demonstration x^{demo}; next, the shape parameter for every kernel is estimated using

$$[\mathbf{w}]_n = (\mathbf{Z}^T \Psi \mathbf{Z})^{-1} \mathbf{Z}^T \Psi \mathbf{f}^{ref} \tag{6}$$

where $[\mathbf{f}^{ref}]_t = f_t^{ref}$, $[\mathbf{Z}]_t = z_t$, and $\Psi = \text{diag}(\psi_1^n, ..., \psi_t^n, ..., \psi_T^n)$.

3.2   Global Parametric Dynamic Movement Primitives

Using DMPs, a task can be imitated from a human demonstration; however, the reproduced task cannot be adapted to different environment conditions. To overcome this limitation, we have integrated a parametric model to DMPs capturing the variability of a task from multiple demonstrations. We transform the basic forcing function (3) into a parametric forcing function

$$f(z, \mathbf{l}; \mathbf{w}) = \mathbf{w}^T(\mathbf{l})\mathbf{g} \tag{7}$$

where the kernel weight vector $\mathbf{w}$ is parametrized using a parameter vector $\mathbf{l}$ of measurable environment factors.

We model the dependency of the weights with respect to parameters as a linear combination of J basis vectors $\mathbf{v}_i$ with coefficients depending on parameters in a non-linear fashion,

$$\mathbf{w}(\mathbf{l}) = \sum_{i=0}^J \phi_i(\mathbf{l})\mathbf{v}_i \tag{8}$$

where $\phi_i(\mathbf{l})$ is a function describing the coefficient of the ith basis vector $\mathbf{v}_i$.

For a chosen non-linear basis (known functions ϕ_i), the basis vectors can be chosen by minimizing the difference between modeled and initial non-parametric DMP shape parameters,

$$\arg\min_{\mathbf{v}_{0,\ldots,J}} \sum_{k=1}^{K} \left\| \mathbf{w}(\mathbf{l}_k) - \mathbf{w}^k \right\|_2 \tag{9}$$

where $\mathbf{w}^k$ denotes the weight vector of a non-parametric DMP optimized for parameter values $\mathbf{l}_k$. The initial weights can be merely imitated from a human demonstration using (6) or improved using a policy search method [18]. In either case, reproducing an imitated task using $\mathbf{w}^k$ should lead to a successful performance in an environment parametrized by $\mathbf{l}_k$.

The formulation captures linear models such as [10] as a special case. Considering a single parameter l for presentational simplicity, the linear model can be written

$$\mathbf{w}(l) = l\mathbf{v}_1 + \mathbf{v}_0. \tag{10}$$

In the next section we show the equivalence of (10) to the mode presented in [10].

To optimize the linear model using DMPs for two parameter values, each element of the weight vectors $[\hat{\mathbf{v}}_1]_i$ and $[\hat{\mathbf{v}}_0]_i$ can be estimated independently using

$$[\hat{\mathbf{v}}_1]_i = \frac{[\mathbf{w}^1]_i - [\mathbf{w}^2]_i}{l_1 - l_2} \tag{11}$$

$$[\hat{\mathbf{v}}_0]_i = [\mathbf{w}^1]_i - l_i[\hat{\mathbf{v}}_1]_i \tag{12}$$

The linear model requires thus $2N$ parameters where N refers to the number of kernels $\mathbf{g}$.

For a general polynomial model in one parameter, the non-linear basis is

$$\phi(l) = (1\ l\ l^2 \ldots\ l^J). \tag{13}$$

The number of initial DMPs must then be at least equal to or greater than the order of the model to avoid unconstrained optimization problems. In the experimental part of the paper, we consider a second order model in one parameter, so that

$$\mathbf{w}(l) = l^2\mathbf{v}_2 + l\mathbf{v}_1 + \mathbf{v}_0. \tag{14}$$

The model choice for a particular application is a compromise between complexity of the attractor landscape that can be modeled and overfitting due to insufficient data.

3.3   Relationship to Matsubara's PDMP

Matsubara et al. [10] have proposed a PDMP method for learning parametric attractor landscape by extracting a small number of common factors from M

demonstrations. Firstly, these M demonstrations are aligned so that they have the same size. Then, the nominal forcing function matrix is generated using

$$\mathbf{F}_{all}^{ref} = \left(\mathbf{f}_1^{ref} \; \mathbf{f}_2^{ref} \; ... \; \mathbf{f}_M^{ref}\right) \tag{15}$$

where $\mathbf{f}_m^{ref}$ represents the reference forcing function calculated for the m-th demonstration $\mathbf{x}_m^{demo}$. Next, using the singular value decomposition of the nominal forcing functions matrix

$$\mathbf{F}_{all}^{ref} = \mathbf{U\Sigma V}^T \tag{16}$$

the matrix of desired basis $\mathbf{F}^{basis}$ function is created from the first J columns of $\mathbf{V}$. They estimate the forcing function using

$$\hat{f}(z, s; \mathbf{w}) = \Sigma_{j=1}^J s_j b_j(z; \mathbf{w}) \tag{17}$$

where the basis function

$$b_j = \mathbf{w}_j^T \mathbf{g} \tag{18}$$

is a weighted sum of kernels $[\mathbf{g}]_n$ (4). The weight vector $\mathbf{w}$ can be calculated using least square fitting or LWR as

$$[\mathbf{w}_j]_n = (\mathbf{Z}^T \mathbf{\Psi Z})^{-1} \mathbf{Z}^T \mathbf{\Psi F}^{basis} \tag{19}$$

In addition, the hyper parameter is calculated using

$$s_j = \beta_{j,1} l + \beta_{j,2} \tag{20}$$

where l represents an environment parameter. The structure of the basis function (18) allows for further simplification of the forcing function (17). In fact, by substituting (20) into (17), we get

$$\begin{aligned}
\hat{f}(z, s; \mathbf{w}) &= \Sigma_{j=1}^J (\beta_{j,1} l + \beta_{j,2}) b_j(z; \mathbf{w}) \\
&= \Sigma_{j=1}^J (\beta_{j,1} l \mathbf{w}_j^T \mathbf{g}) + \Sigma_{j=1}^J (\beta_{j,2} \mathbf{w}_j^T \mathbf{g}) \\
&= (\Sigma_{j=1}^J \beta_{j,1} \mathbf{w}_j^T) l \mathbf{g} + (\Sigma_{j=1}^J \beta_{j,2} \mathbf{w}_j^T) \mathbf{g} \\
&= \mathbf{v}_1^T l \mathbf{g} + \mathbf{v}_0^T \mathbf{g} \\
&= (\mathbf{v}_1 l + \mathbf{v}_0)^T \mathbf{g}
\end{aligned} \tag{21}$$

which is equivalent to our linear parametric model (10). However, Matsubara's approach is computationally more complex. In fact, their method involves three main processes: an SVD decomposition of the matrix F^{basis} of desired basis functions, calculating J kernel vectors $\mathbf{w}$ for basis functions b_j, and computing J style parameters $\beta_{j,1}$ and $\beta_{j,1}$. The complexity of the SVD (16) is $O(s_d^2 M + M^3)$ where s_d refers to the size of each one of M demonstrations. Moreover, $J \times N$ basis function parameters and $J \times 2$ style parameters need to be estimated using least square fitting. The number of desired basis functions $J \geq 2$ should be at least two; otherwise, the learned model will be too general failing to capture the variability of a task. On the other hand, our linear parametric model (8) requires only the estimation of $2 \times N$ parameters. Hence, our approach is simpler, less computationally complex, and at least as representative as the Mastubara's method. Furthermore, our GPDMP approach accommodates higher order parametric models (8), thus allowing the generalization of skills with more complex dependencies.

3.4   Reinforcement Learning

Executing a DMP with imitated shape parameters might not lead to a successful reproduction of a task. One way to refine the shape parameters is to learn them through trial-and-error using policy search reinforcement learning (RL). Next, we briefly review the state-of-the-art policy search method PoWER [12] which was used in this work to optimize individual primitives.

PoWER (see Algorithm 1) updates the DMP shape parameters $\theta \equiv \mathbf{w}$ iteratively. In each iteration, (several) stochastic roll-out(s) of the task is performed, each of which is achieved by adding random (Gaussian) noise to the DMPs shape parameters. Each noisy vector is weighted by the returned accumulated reward. Hence, the higher the returned reward, the more the noisy vector contribute to the updated policy parameters. This exploration process continues until the algorithm converges to the optimal policy.

Algorithm 1. Pseudocode of the PoWER [12] algorithm for a one-dimensional policy.

Input: The initial policy parameters θ, the exploration variance Σ

1: **repeat**
2:    *Sample*: Perform rollout(s) using $\mathbf{a} = (\theta + \epsilon_\mathbf{t})^\mathbf{T} \phi(\mathbf{s}, \mathbf{t})$ with $\epsilon_\mathbf{t}^\mathbf{T} \phi(\mathbf{s}, \mathbf{t}) \sim \mathcal{N}(\mathbf{0}, \phi(\mathbf{s}, \mathbf{t})^\mathbf{T} \hat{\Sigma} \phi(\mathbf{s}, \mathbf{t}))$ as stochastic policy and collect all $(\mathbf{t}, \mathbf{s_t^h}, \mathbf{a_t^h}, \mathbf{s_{t+1}^h}, \epsilon_\mathbf{t}^\mathbf{h}, \mathbf{r_{t+1}^h})$ for $\mathbf{t} = \{\mathbf{1}, \mathbf{2}, \dots, \mathbf{T} + \mathbf{1}\}$.
3:    *Estimate*: Use unbiased estimate

$$\hat{Q}^\pi(s, a, t) = \sum_{\tilde{t}=t}^T r(s_{\tilde{t}}, a_{\tilde{t}}, s_{\tilde{t}+1}, \tilde{t}).$$

4:    *Reweight*: Compute importance weights and reweigh rollouts, discard low-importance rollouts.
5:    *Update* policy using

$$\theta_{k+1} = \theta_k + \frac{\langle \sum_{t=1}^T \epsilon_t Q^\pi(\mathbf{s}, \mathbf{a}, t) \rangle_{w(\tau)}}{\langle \sum_{t=1}^T Q^\pi(\mathbf{s}, \mathbf{a}, t) \rangle_{w(\tau)}}$$

6: **until** convergence $\theta_{k+1} \approx \theta_k$

The structure of the noise is a key element influencing the convergence speed of a policy search method but the choice is a trade-off. In the case of DMP shape parameters and uncorrelated noise, high noise variance causes large accelerations of the system, causing a safety hazard and possibly surpassing the physical capabilities of the robot. In contrast, low noise variance makes the learning process slow.

To address this trade-off, we propose to use correlated noise instead of the earlier works employing uncorrelated noise. Since the elements of a DMP parameter vector correspond to temporally ordered perturbing forces, we want to control their temporal statistics. To achieve this, an intuitive structure for the covariance matrix $\Sigma = \mathbf{R}^{-1}$ can be used where the quadratic control cost matrix

$$\mathbf{R} = \sum_{k=1}^{K} w_k \mathbf{A}_k^T \mathbf{A}_k \tag{22}$$

is a weighted combination of quadratic costs related to finite difference matrices $\mathbf{A}_1 \cdots \mathbf{A}_K$. w_k denotes the weight of the k-th finite difference matrix, and k is the order of differentiation. This structure allows us then to control statistics of any order. In experiments, we consider variation only in acceleration (second order). Thus, $w_2 = 1$ and all other weights $w_k = 0, k \neq 2$, and the second order finite difference matrix $\mathbf{A}_2$ can be written

$$\mathbf{A}_2 = \begin{bmatrix} 1 & 0 & 0 & & 0 & 0 & 0 \\ -2 & 1 & 0 & \cdots & 0 & 0 & 0 \\ 1 & -2 & 1 & & 0 & 0 & 0 \\ \vdots & & \ddots & & & \vdots \\ 0 & 0 & 0 & & 1 & -2 & 1 \\ 0 & 0 & 0 & \cdots & 0 & 1 & -2 \\ 0 & 0 & 0 & & 0 & 0 & 1 \end{bmatrix}. \tag{23}$$

With this covariance matrix, the noise signal is smooth (see Fig. 2(a) due to limited acceleration and it has small magnitude in the beginning and at the end of the trajectory. Hence, safe exploration is provided. It is worth mentioning that a similar covariance matrix has been applied in [19,20] for direct trajectory encoding.

In order to control the magnitude of noise, we used a further modified covariance matrix $\Sigma = \gamma \beta \mathbf{R}^{-1}$ where γ is a constant controlling the initial magnitude and convergence factor

$$\beta = \frac{1}{\sum_{i=1}^{I} r_i^2}, \tag{24}$$

reduces the magnitude of noise as the policy search algorithm is converging to the optimal policy.

4   Experimental Evaluation

We studied experimentally the generalization performance of the proposed model using a Ball-in-a-Cup task taught to KUKA LBR 4+ initially using

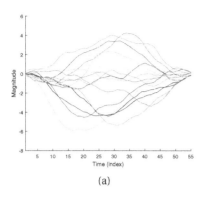
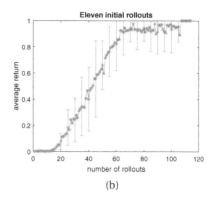

(a)   (b)

Fig. 2. (a) Noises ϵ sampled from a zero mean multivariate Gaussian distribution $\mathcal{N}(0, \Sigma)$ with $\gamma = 1$ and $\beta = 0.01$. (b) Mean and variance of returns over 12 trials.

kinesthetic teaching. In this section, we explain the scenario, compare the proposed noise (proposal) generation to standard uncorrelated noise in terms of convergence speed, and study the extrapolation capability of the model.

4.1 Ball-in-a-Cup Task

The Ball-in-a-Cup game consists of a cup, a string, and a ball; the ball is attached to the cup by the string (see Fig. 1(a)). The objective of the game is to get the ball in the cup by moving the cup in a suitable fashion. In practice, the cup needs to be moved back and forth at first; then, a movement is induced on the cup, thus pulling the ball up and catching it with the cup.

We chose the Ball-in-a-Cup game because variation in the environment can be generated simply by changing the string length. The string length is observable and easy to evaluate, thus providing a suitable parameter representing the environment variation. Nevertheless, changing the length requires a complex change in the motion to succeed in the game. Hence, the generalization capability of a parametric LfD model can be easily assessed using this game.

The state of the robot is defined in a seven dimensional space $\mathbf{X} = \{x, y, z, q_x, q_y, q_z, q_w\}$, where $\mathbf{X}_p = \{x, y, z\}$ represents the position of the robot end effector (cup), and $\mathbf{X}_q = \{q_x, q_y, q_z, q_w\}$ formulates its orientation using a quaternion. The ball-in-a-cup is essentially a two-dimensional game and thus only motion along two axes, y and z was used. In the demonstration phase, the robot was set compliant along y and z, while it was set stiff rotationally and along x, which were considered as constant states. The plane spanning y and z was orthogonal with respect to the table upon which the robot was mounted (see Fig. 1(a)).

The trajectories along y and z were encoded using separate DMPs with same number of parameters. We found experimentally that 55 kernels (shape parameters) were required so that the reproduced movement was able to put the ball above the rim of the cup in the execution phase. In total, 110 shape parameters were then learned using LWR (6). However, using these initial shape parameters, the reproduced movement did not put the ball back into the cup. Hence, the shape parameters were optimized in a trial-and-error fashion using RL as described in Sect. 3.4.

Reward function is the most fundamental ingredient of RL. We formulated the reward function similar to [12] as

$$r(t) = \begin{cases} e^{-\alpha d^2}, & \text{if } t = t_c, \\ 0, & \text{otherwise} \end{cases} \tag{25}$$

where t_c denotes the time instant when the ball crosses the rim of the cup with a downward motion; d represents the horizontal distance between the rim of the cup and the centre of the ball; and α is a scaling parameter set to 100 in our experiments. The closer the ball is to the rim of the cup, the higher the reward will be. As the shape parameters are fine-tuned in a trial-and-error approach, the ball would get closer to the cup. Furthermore, the reward is zero if the ball does not reach above the rim of the cup. Without such a constraint, the RL algorithm might converge to a policy where the ball is tossed to the bottom of the cup.

4.2 RL Convergence Rate

Figure 2(b) depicts the convergence rate for the RL algorithm with the proposed method starting from an imitated trajectory. Figure 2(b) shows both mean and variance of returns over 12 trials. On average a total of 80 rollouts (including 11 initial rollouts) are required for the policy to converge to an optimal one where the robot repeatedly succeeds at bringing the ball into the cup. After the ball went into the cup for the first time, on average 11 additional rollouts were required for the policy to converge. The convergence rate is similar to [12] where 75 rollouts were typically required for convergence. However, the results are not directly comparable due to differences in hardware realizations and human demonstration quality.

Figure 3 shows a comparison between the proposed correlated (blue) and earlier uncorrelated (red) exploration noises. The graph on left (Fig. 3(a)) shows that the proposed correlated noise improves the convergence rate significantly. The slow learning rate of uncorrelated noise is partially due to the small variance of the sampled noise in comparison to the correlated noise as shown in Fig. 3(b). However, larger noise variance was not feasible in the uncorrelated case because of the required accelerations were not physically realizable. This is demonstrated in Fig. 3(c) which shows accelerations in three cases: original demonstration, correlated noise and uncorrelated noise. Figure 3 shows that although the magnitude of the noise is smaller in the uncorrelated case, the learned policy requires much larger accelerations. After 36 iterations, the learned policy with uncorrelated exploration became infeasible to be executed on the real robot as it required more acceleration than the robot was physically able to realize.

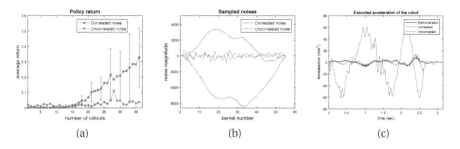

Fig. 3. (a) Returns for uncorrelated (red) and correlated (blue) exploration noise. (b) Two samples of correlated and uncorrelated noise. (c) Acceleration of end-effector in y-direction for demonstration (black), and policies after 36 roll-outs with uncorrelated (red) and correlated (blue) exploration noise. (Color figure online)

4.3   Generalization Capability

We evaluated both the proposed linear 10 and second order (14) GPDMP models for generalizing the DMP policy (shape) parameters. As a comparison, we used the parametric model by Carrera et al. [6] as a recent example of a data-driven local regression model.

All models require training data with varying string lengths. The training data was collected from a single demonstration with a string length of 40 cm. Starting from the shape parameters derived from this demonstration, the parameters were then learned using PoWER for string lengths of $32, 35, 38, 40$ and 41 cm. It should be noted that during the RL, executing the task with shape parameters learned for a specific length did not lead to a successful reproduction for another string length in the training set.

We performed two experiments, both studying the range of interpolation and extrapolation obtained by the models, with varying number of training data. In both experiments, a reproduction was considered to be successful if 5 consecutive replications of the Ball-in-a-Cup task with the same shape parameters put the ball into the cup.

Generalization over Minor Variations. In the first experiment, we studied generalization over minor variations by extracting parametric models from two training samples with string lengths of 38 and 41 cm. As there were only two training samples, only the linear variant 10 and the locally interpolating model of Carrera et al. [6] were used. The range of validity for these is shown in Fig. 4, the red line showing the range of validity, and (a) and (b) denoting Carrera et al. and the linear GPDMP, correspondingly. The training samples are shown with crosses. Both models were capable of interpolating successfully within the range of the training samples. In addition, the proposed linear model was able to extrapolate within ± 2 cm from the training samples. The result demonstrates that models using a positive linear combination of training models, such as Carrera's and others in the literature, are not well suited for extrapolation as they

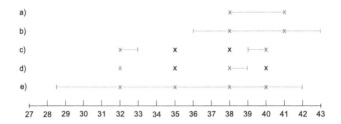

Fig. 4. Validity ranges for different models (red lines). Input data indicated as X. (a)–(b) small task variation: (a) Carrera et al. [6]; (b) linear GPDMP; (c)-(e) larger task variation: (c) Carrera et al.; (d) linear GPDMP; (e) second order GPDMP. (Color figure online)

tend towards the mean of training data when extrapolating as discussed in Sec. 2. However, a simple linear model is global and capable of extrapolation when the variation in the task is minor.

Generalization over Larger Variations. In the second experiment, we studied larger variations by extracting Carrera's PDMP [6], the linear GPDMP model 10, and the second order GPDMP (14) using a dataset of four samples with string lengths of 32, 35, 38, and 40 cm. The range of validity for each of these is shown in Fig. 4, (c) denoting Carrera et al., (d) the linear GPDMP, and (e) the second-order GPDMP.

Both Carrera's and the linear GPDMP show poor performance, capable of limited interpolation and missing also some of the training samples. The reasons for the failures appear to be different: Carrera's model uses a positive linear combination of the training data weighted inversely proportional to a distance metric in the task parameter space. With an optimal distance metric, the model should at least be able to replicate the training samples. We used the metric proposed in the original paper in our experiment but believe that with a more suitable metric the model would be likely to be able to interpolate successfully in this experiment. Nevertheless, success in extrapolation would be unlikely as explained earlier. Similarly, models employing Gaussian process regression or support vector machines would be unlikely to perform better in extrapolation. The failure of the linear GPDMP is likely due to the fact that the linear model is simply incapable of representing the complex relationship between the task and policy parameters. The linear approach by Matsubara et al. [10] would be likely to suffer from the same problem.

In contrast to the above, the proposed second order GPDMP (e in Fig. 4) is capable of both interpolation over the whole range and a surprising range of extrapolation within the range of $[-3.5\,\text{cm}, +2\,\text{cm}]$. It thus greatly outperforms the others. This demonstrates that global non-linear models are clearly beneficial for representing parametric policies. The choice of a model complexity for a particular application is not trivial, but model selection criteria based on e.g. information theoretic metrics could be used. In our experiments, the achieved range of extrapolation already approached the performance limits of the physical system and therefore we did not study how higher order models could have increased the extrapolation capability even further.

Extrapolation Using a One-Dimensional Basis for Policy. To further study the complexity of policies needed for extrapolation, we performed a separate experiment with a linear GPDMP fit to demonstrations with lengths 38 and 41 cm, identical to the first experiment. Instead of using the model as such, we searched experimentally, if a task parameter value other than the real one would lead to success. Thus, in effect we studied if non-linear coefficients for the one-dimensional basis 10 would allow generalization, and found that this is indeed the case. Figure 5 shows the found task parameter values (string lengths) that lead to success versus their actual values. The two training points used to determine the basis using (11–12) are shown in red. As seen in Fig. 5, in the neighborhood of the training points, a line fit would have small residual error, showing that in that neighborhood a linear model is valid, as also apparent from the earlier Fig. 4. However, the one-dimensional basis ($\mathbf{v}_1$) is sufficient for significant further generalization (up to -8 cm) if non-linear coefficients are used. This extended range of validity is shown with green dashed line in Fig. 4 and is only slightly less than that of the second order model. It should be noted, however, that this is not a free lunch; the linear space coefficients were found by trial and error and the two training points do not allow to determine the non-linearity. Nevertheless, low dimensional vector spaces appear surprisingly powerful in policy representation, but simple linear transforms of task variables are not sufficient for coefficients.

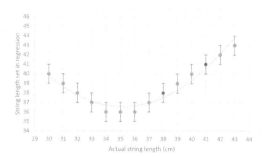

Fig. 5. One-dimensional linear space coefficients found by trial and error.

5   Conclusion and Future Work

In this paper, we proposed a global model for mapping a task parameter to policy parameters. The training examples for constructing the global model were obtained from a single human demonstration and optimized using reinforcement learning. The trained global model is capable of both inter- and extrapolating policy parameters from new task parameters unseen in the examples. In fact, policy parameters are generalized without re-learning. The global model is simple and can easily be scaled to accommodate for non-linearities in the task space. Experiments showed a significant improvement in extrapolation capabilities over current state-of-the-art. This is due to inherent structures of existing methods which are based either on linear or local regression type relationships between task and policy parameters. Studying the extension of the other available models towards more global regression would open interesting research venues. For example, Gaussian process regression models are capable of representing global relationships, however, the typically used covariance structures (kernels) are local.

Our experiments were limited to a single task parameter and future work should address generalization over more parameters. In addition, we will consider the choice of basis function and model complexity using multiple tasks. Both of these research questions are addressed in model selection methods based on either cross validation or information criteria such as BIC or AIC. Nevertheless, experimental evidence in this paper indicates that the current local and linear models have limited extrapolation powers which needs to be addressed by models able to capture more global relationships despite the number of task parameters.

References

1. Argall, B.D., Chernova, S., Veloso, M., Browning, B.: A survey of robot learning from demonstration. Robot. Autonom. Syst. **57**(5), 469–483 (2009)
2. Chernova, S., Veloso, M.: Confidence-based policy learning from demonstration using Gaussian mixture models. In: Proceedings of the 6th International Joint Conference on Autonomous Agents and Multiagent Systems, p. 233. ACM (2007)
3. Sammut, C., Hurst, S., Kedzier, D., Michie, D., et al.: Learning to fly. In: Proceedings of the Ninth International Workshop on Machine Learning, pp. 385–393 (1992)
4. Hovland, G.E., Sikka, P., McCarragher, B.J.: Skill acquisition from human demonstration using a hidden Markov model. In: IEEE International Conference on Robotics and Automation, Proceedings, vol. 3, pp. 2706–2711. IEEE (1996)
5. Calinon, S., D'halluin, F., Sauser, E.L., Caldwell, D.G., Billard, A.G.: Learning and reproduction of gestures by imitation. IEEE Robot. Autom. Mag. **17**(2), 44–54 (2010)
6. Carrera, A., Palomeras, N., Hurtós, N., Kormushev, P., Carreras, M.: Learning multiple strategies to perform a valve turning with underwater currents using an I-AUV. In: OCEANS 2015-Genova, pp. 1–8. IEEE (2015)
7. Da Silva, B., Konidaris, G., Barto, A.: Learning parameterized skills. arXiv preprint arXiv:1206.6398 (2012)
8. Forte, D., Gams, A., Morimoto, J., Ude, A.: On-line motion synthesis and adaptation using a trajectory database. Robot. Autonom. Syst. **60**(10), 1327–1339 (2012)
9. Ude, A., Gams, A., Asfour, T., Morimoto, J.: Task-specific generalization of discrete and periodic dynamic movement primitives. IEEE Trans. Robot. **26**(5), 800–815 (2010)

10. Matsubara, T., Hyon, S.-H., Morimoto, J.: Learning parametric dynamic movement primitives from multiple demonstrations. Neural Netw. **24**(5), 493–500 (2011)
11. Calinon, S., Alizadeh, T., Caldwell, D.G.: On improving the extrapolation capability of task-parameterized movement models. In: 2013 IEEE/RSJ International Conference on Intelligent Robots and Systems, pp. 610–616. IEEE (2013)
12. Kober, J., Peters, J.R.: Policy search for motor primitives in robotics. In: Advances in Neural Information Processing Systems, pp. 849–856 (2009)
13. Kober, J., Oztop, E., Peters, J.: Reinforcement learning to adjust robot movements to new situations. In: IJCAI Proceedings-International Joint Conference on Artificial Intelligence, vol. 22, p. 2650 (2011)
14. Stulp, F., Raiola, G., Hoarau, A., Ivaldi, S., Sigaud, O.: Learning compact parameterized skills with a single regression. In: 2013 13th IEEE-RAS International Conference on Humanoid Robots (Humanoids), pp. 417–422. IEEE (2013)
15. Nemec, B., Vuga, R., Ude, A.: Efficient sensorimotor learning from multiple demonstrations. Adv. Robot. **27**(13), 1023–1031 (2013)
16. Mülling, K., Kober, J., Kroemer, O., Peters, J.: Learning to select and generalize striking movements in robot table tennis. Int. J. Robot. Res. **32**(3), 263–279 (2013)
17. Ijspeert, A.J., Nakanishi, J., Schaal, S.: Movement imitation with nonlinear dynamical systems in humanoid robots. In: IEEE International Conference on Robotics and Automation, Proceedings, ICRA 2002, vol. 2, pp. 1398–1403. IEEE (2002)
18. Peters, J.R.: Machine learning of motor skills for robotics. Ph.D. thesis, University of Southern California (2007)
19. Kalakrishnan, M., Righetti, L., Pastor, P., Schaal, S.: Learning force control policies for compliant manipulation. In: 2011 IEEE/RSJ International Conference on Intelligent Robots and Systems (IROS), pp. 4639–4644. IEEE (2011)
20. Kalakrishnan, M., Chitta, S., Theodorou, E., Pastor, P., Schaal, S.: STOMP: stochastic trajectory optimization for motion planning. In: 2011 IEEE International Conference on Robotics and Automation (ICRA), pp. 4569–4574. IEEE (2011)

Recovery of a Humanoid Robot from a Destabilising Impact

Christopher D. Wallbridge[(⊠)] and Guido Bugmann

Plymouth University, Plymouth PL4 8AA, UK
{Christopher.Wallbridge,G.Bugmann}@plymouth.ac.uk

Abstract. This paper examines the case of a bipedal robot under an external impact along the axis of the two supporting feet. The dynamics of the robot is modelled using the 3-Mass Linear Inverted Pendulum Model. The model shows that, for impacts below a given threshold, the robot recovers naturally and no corrective action is required. For larger, destabilising impacts, this paper described how to calculate a single or a sequence of corrective steps. The key information used for the calculations is the initial velocity generated by the impact. The behaviour of the model for various initial configurations and impact parameters is illustrated by simulations.

Keywords: Humanoid · Robot · Dynamics · Impact · Corrective stepping · Bipedal · LIPM

1 Introduction

The detection of destabilising events and the prevention of falls is a crucial functionality of future real-world walking robots. Notably, the IEEE International Conference on Robotics and Automation 2016 had a workshop devoted to "Legged Robot Falling: Fall Detection, Damage Prevention, and Recovery Actions"[1]. The work presented here focuses on bipedal Humanoid robots. These robots are unstable when compared to other robots with wheels, or additional legs. Falls can be costly, both in the time taken for the robot to recover and in potential repairs for any damage sustained. To allow humanoid robots to be deployed in a real world requires that they be able to take corrective action to unforeseen impacts.

2 The 3-Mass Linear Inverted Pendulum Model

Initial work on modelling gait used an Inverted Pendulum Model (IPM) with a single mass located on top of a massless pole [1]. The IPM has been further developed into a Linear Inverted Pendulum Model (LIPM) for use in robot controllers [3]. The LIPM adds a constraint into the motion of the pendulum,

---

[1] http://www.icra2016.org/.

© Springer International Publishing AG 2017
Y. Gao et al. (Eds.): TAROS 2017, LNAI 10454, pp. 32–40, 2017.
DOI: 10.1007/978-3-319-64107-2_3

keeping the height of the mass above the plane of motion at a constant distance. This simplifies computation by decoupling the forward and lateral motions.

While functional, this model proved to be insufficient when used in a robot controller. Work by Yuping et al. [4] showed the importance of the mass distribution in a walking system. Therefore, an improvement to the model would also be modelling the mass distribution in the system.

Bugmann [2] expanded upon the LIPM to create a 3-Mass Linear Inverted Pendulum Model (3-MLIPM). By looking at torques created by gravity and how they relate to propulsion torques, the following formula can be found for a system of n number of joints and masses:

$$\sum_{i=1}^{n} m_i \ddot{x}_i z_i = \sum_{i=1}^{n} g m_i x_i \qquad \sum_{i=1}^{n} m_i \ddot{y}_i z_i = \sum_{i=1}^{n} g m_i y_i \qquad (1)$$

This torque equation (1) can then be further used in an equation for the forward walking gait of the robot.

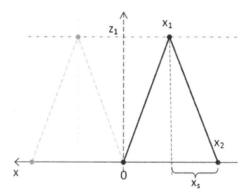

Fig. 1. 3-Mass robot model for a walking gait, with the motion going towards the left. The masses are linked together by virtual poles that maintain a constant height (z_1). Note that in a real robot the height constance is achieved by using articulated knee joints. The masses m_1 and m_2 are at (x_1, z_1) and ($x_2, 0$) respectively. m_3 is located at (0,0) and does not affect the dynamics of the system [2].

Using these torque equations to work out accelerations, it is possible to work out the upper-body (m_1) motion for a walking gait. The swinging foot (m_2) is assumed to have a sinusoidal motion where T is the time to complete one whole cycle of the gait:

$$x_{2,t} = -2x_s \cdot cos(\frac{2\pi}{T}t) \qquad (2)$$

The equation for motion for m_1 is then:

$$x_{1,t} = C_1 cosh(a_1 t) + C_2 sinh(a_1 t) + C_3 cos(\omega t) \qquad (3)$$

Where:

$$C_1 = x_{1,0} - C_3 \qquad C_2 = \frac{v_{1,0}}{a_1}$$

$$C_3 = \frac{m_2 g 2 x_s}{m_1 z_1 (a_1^2 + w)} \qquad w = \frac{2\pi}{T}$$

$$\alpha_1 = \sqrt{\frac{g}{z_1}} \tag{4}$$

The 3-MLIPM appears to provide a much more accurate model of the motion of a robot while walking compared to the IPM, showing that the swinging leg has the effect of pulling on the central mass (m_1) of the body. From Eq. (3) we are able to work out the position of the main body mass with an initial velocity and initial position. So far we have used this to generate a walking gait.

3 Identifying a De-stabilising Impact

To identify shorty after impact whether a corrective action is needed, a model of the stability of the robot needs to be created. Here, the 3-MLIPM will be expanded upon. Unlike Eq. (3) we are not looking at the leg already in motion, as during a normal walking gait. Here, all masses are initially static. The masses m_1 for the mass of the main body of the robot, and m_2 for the mass of the leg that is not being used as the pivot will be considered. These are at positions (x_1, z_1) and $(x_2, 0)$ respectively (Fig. 1). Using Eq. (1) we get the formula:

$$m_1 \ddot{x}_1 z_1 = m_1 x_1 g + m_2 x_2 g \qquad \rightarrow \qquad \ddot{x}_1 = x_1 \frac{g}{z_1} + \frac{m_2 x_2 g}{m_1 z_1} \tag{5}$$

For simplicity the equation is re-written as:

$$\ddot{x}_1 = \alpha_1^2 \cdot x_1 - \alpha_2 \tag{6}$$

Where α_1 remains the same as in Eq. (4) and:

$$\alpha_2 = \frac{-m_2 x_2 g}{m_1 z_1} \tag{7}$$

As an estimate based on Eq. (3) the formula for motion should be able to be represented as an equation in the form:

$$x_{1,t} = D_1 \cosh(\alpha_1 t) + D_2 \sinh(\alpha_1 t) + D_3 \tag{8}$$

From this the first and second derivatives are then calculated:

$$\dot{x}_{1,t} = D_1 \alpha_1 \sinh(\alpha_1 t) + D_2 \alpha_1 \cosh(\alpha_1 t) \tag{9}$$
$$\ddot{x}_{1,t} = D_1 \alpha_1^2 \cosh(\alpha_1 t) + D_2 \alpha_1^2 \sinh(\alpha_1 t) \tag{10}$$
$$= \alpha_1^2 \cdot x_1 - D_3 \alpha_1^2 \tag{11}$$

For (8) to be correct, (11) should be equal to (6). This is the case if:

$$D_3 \alpha_1^2 = \alpha_2 \tag{12}$$

Therefore:

$$D_3 = \frac{\alpha_2}{\alpha_1^2} \tag{13}$$

To workout D_1 and D_2 we take the case where time is set to zero $(t = 0)$. Using Eq. (8):

$$D_1 = x_{1,0} - D_3 \tag{14}$$

Using Eq. (9):

$$\dot{x}_{1,0} = v_0 \qquad D_2 = \frac{v_0}{\alpha_1} \tag{15}$$

This means that it is possible to predict the motion of the robot based on an initial position $(x_{1,0})$ and an initial velocity (v_0) resulting from the impact (Fig. 2).

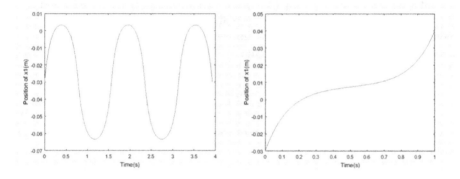

Fig. 2. Graphs showing model of position of x_1. On the left, the motion of x_1 in a stable system. On the right the motion of x_1 in an unstable system.

If the initial velocity is low enough then x_1 will oscillate between a front and back excursion amplitude, eventually coming to a stop due to friction. For an amplitude beyond a given tipping point the position of x_1 will continue to accelerate. The model assumes that the height stays constant which allows the speed to increase infinitely. However, in reality, the legs will no longer be able to maintain this height and the robot will fall over. The tipping point of the robot is slightly beyond the pivot leg. This position can be worked out by calculating when acceleration is zero by using Eq. (10), which resolves to the value of D_3.

So for the robot to remain stable, the velocity of the position of x_1 must reach zero. By using Eq. (9) the robot can be determined to be stable if the following equation is true at some value of time:

$$\frac{v_0}{a_1(D_3 - x_{1,0})} = tanh(a_1 t) \tag{16}$$

As the function $tanh$ has two horizontal asymptotes at $y = -1$ and $y = 1$, and time can only have a positive value the following constraint can be made if Eq. (16) is to evaluate to true at some point in time, thereby showing that the system is stable:

$$0 \leq \frac{v_0}{a_1(D_3 - x_{1,0})} < 1 \tag{17}$$

This constraint means that by looking at the initial velocity, and the initial position it is possible to immediately decide if the robot will become unstable and fall, thereby being able to start the corrective action as soon as possible.

4   Calculating a Stabilizing Response

Once a de-stabilising event has been detected, the robot controller needs to react quickly and efficiently. To do this we need to calculate the new position for the robot to move one of its feet to stabilise itself. To calculate this, the motion needs to be re-calculated considering the fact that the robot now has a swinging foot with a non-zero mass. It is assumed that the swinging foot has a sinusoidal motion, similar to Eq. (2). However, unlike the previous equation the new position of x_2 is not a fixed distance ahead of the previous pivot point but needs to be determined based on the impact. This position will be called $x_{2,t'}$, where t' is the time where the swinging foot touches the ground, becoming the new pivot foot:

$$x_{2,t'} = x_{2,0} + \frac{1}{2}(x_{2,t'} - x_{2,0}) \cdot (1 - cos(\omega t)) \tag{18}$$

The new equations for the motion of the robot based on the torque Eq. (1) and motion of the foot becomes:

$$\ddot{x}_1 = x_1 \frac{g}{z_1} + \frac{m_2 g}{m_1 z_1}(x_{2,0} + \frac{1}{2}(x_{2,t'} - x_{2,0}) \cdot (1 - cos(\omega t))) \tag{19}$$

$$= \alpha_1^2 x_1 + \alpha_3 x_{2,0} + \frac{\alpha_3 \alpha_4}{2} - \frac{\alpha_3 \alpha_4}{2}cos(\omega t) \tag{20}$$

Where α_1 remains the same as in Eq. (4), ω represents the angular velocity, and:

$$\alpha_3 = \frac{m_2 g}{m_1 z_1} \qquad \alpha_4 = x_{2,t'} - x_{2,0} \tag{21}$$

Again the model for the position of the robot is estimated based on Eq. (3):

$$x_{1,t} = E_1 cosh(\alpha_1 t) + E_2 sinh(\alpha_1 t) + E_3 cos(\omega t) + E_4 \tag{22}$$

The first and second derivatives are calculated:

$$\dot{x}_{1,t} = E_1 \alpha_1 sinh(\alpha_1 t) + E_2 \alpha_1 cosh(\alpha_1 t) - E_3 \omega sin(\omega t) \tag{23}$$

$$\ddot{x}_{1,t} = E_1 \alpha_1^2 cosh(\alpha_1 t) + E_2 \alpha_1^2 sinh(\alpha_1 t) - E_3 \omega^2 cos(\omega t) \tag{24}$$

$$= \alpha_1^2 x_{1,t} - \alpha_1^2 E_4 - (\alpha_1^2 E_3 + E_3 \omega^2) \cdot cos(\omega t) \tag{25}$$

For Eq. (22) to be correct, Eq. (25) should be equal to Eq. (20). This is the case if:

$$E_3 = \frac{\alpha_3\alpha_4}{2(\alpha_1^2 + \omega^2)} \qquad E_4 = \frac{2\alpha_3 x_{2,0} + \alpha_3\alpha_4}{-2\alpha_1^2} \tag{26}$$

E_1 and E_2 are worked out by looking at the case where time is set to zero $(t = 0)$. Using Eq. (22) for E_1 and (23) for E_2:

$$E_1 = x_{1,0} - E_3 - E_4 \qquad E_2 = \frac{v_0}{\alpha_1} \tag{27}$$

The position needs to be calculated based on the swinging foot having reached its front position (t'). This occurs when:

$$cos(\omega t') = -1 \tag{28}$$

The position and velocity is now calculated based on this:

$$x_{1,t'} = E_1 cosh(\alpha_1 t') + E_2 sinh(a_1 t') - E_3 + E_4 \tag{29}$$
$$v_{t'} = E_1\alpha_1 sinh(\alpha_1 t') + E_2\alpha_1 cosh(\alpha_1 t') \tag{30}$$

By adjusting Eq. (17) to look at the new position of the robot an analysis can be made for the position and velocity to see if this will stabilise the robot:

$$0 \le \frac{v_{t'}}{\alpha_1\left(\frac{\alpha_3 x_{2,t'}}{\alpha_1^2} - x_{1,0'}\right)} < 1 \tag{31}$$

As the position used in these equations is relative to the position of the pivot foot:

$$x_{1,0'} = x_{1,t'} - x_{2,t'} \tag{32}$$

Using these equations and expanding out all the terms that contain $x_{2,t'}$ the minimum movement required to stabilise the robot can be found:

$$x_{2,t'} > \frac{\alpha_7(E_2 + x_{1,0}) + \alpha_3 x_{2,0}\left(\frac{1+\alpha_7}{\alpha_5} + \frac{1-\alpha_7}{\alpha_6}\right)}{1 + \alpha_3\left(\frac{1}{\alpha_1^2} + \frac{1+\alpha_7}{\alpha_5} + \frac{\alpha_7-1}{\alpha_6}\right)} \tag{33}$$

Where:

$$\alpha_5 = 2(\alpha_1^2 + \omega^2) \qquad \alpha_6 = -2\alpha_1^2$$
$$\alpha_7 = cosh(\alpha_{1t'}) + sinh(\alpha_{1t'}) \tag{34}$$

With a calculation for the minimum step, and knowledge of the maximum speed and reach of the leg, a region of coordinates in time and space can be shown. Figure 3 shows an example of this region below the marked lines representing the position the leg can reach and the speed it can reach the position at, and above the unmarked line showing the minimum step required. This region then represents the possible movements of the leg that will balance the robot in a single step.

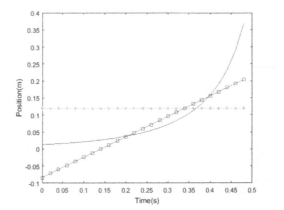

Fig. 3. A graph showing an example of the balance region for a robot. The line without a marker shows the minimum step required defined by Eq. (33). The square marked line shows the maximum position reachable by the foot based on it having a simple linear speed, in reality this would need to be calculated based on the configuration of the leg and servos. The star marked line shows an example of the maximum position the foot can reach.

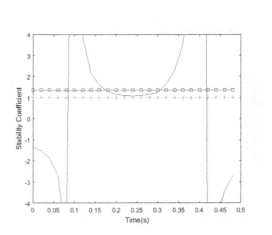

Fig. 4. A graph showing the stability coefficient of the robot. The square marked line represents the initial stability calculated using Eq. (17). The line without a marker is the stability coefficient assuming the robot moves the leg at an assumed maximum possible speed using Eq. (30). The star marked line shows the stability that needs to be reached. Note the lines at 0.08 and 0.42 are caused by asymptotes and do not reflect true values.

In many cases it is likely that a single step will not be enough to stabilise the robot. In this case the robot needs to take a sequence of corrective steps. Each step should have the effect of reducing the overall speed that has been created by the impact. This can be done by analysing the stability coefficient of a potential step and seeing if this can be made smaller than the previous stability coefficient, while remaining over 0 (Fig. 4).

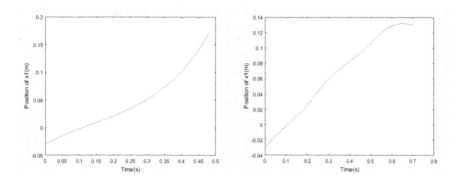

Fig. 5. Graphs showing a simulated impact and reaction of a robot. On the left the position if the robot takes no action, showing a fall. On the right the robot takes two steps. Step 1 is completed at 0.24 s and step 2 is completed at 0.52 s.

If this reduction of the stability coefficient continues then the robot reaches a state where one more step will lead to a balanced state of the robot as shown in Fig. 5. This shows that it is possible to balance the robot if an initial speed and position of the main mass of the robot can be calculated compared to the position of the leg.

5   Conclusion

This model shows that knowing the position of the robot and the velocity created by the impact, an immediate decision can be made as to whether a reaction is necessary, and the stepping sequence that will correct the instability.

To actually implement this in a robot there are two main challenges that need to be resolved. The first is to measure the velocity resulting from the impact. Using an accelerometer and integrating the values to get a measurement for speed seems the most likely solution but the accelerometer needs to be able to sample at a high enough frequency, and drift accounted for.

The second challenge that needs to be overcome is the lateral motion of the robot required to lift the leg. Bugmann's [2] paper on the 3-MLIPM describes the lateral motion during a walking gait, where the lateral motion is at maximum velocity when both feet are on the ground, and acceleration is minimal. However, in the case of a robot suddenly reacting to an external impact the opposite is true, the robot has no velocity, and needs maximum acceleration to account for this.

References

1. Buczek, F.L., Cooney, K.M., Walker, M.R., Rainbow, M.J., Concha, M.C., Sanders, J.O.: Performance of an inverted pendulum model directly applied to normal human gait. Clin. Biomech. **21**(3), 288–296 (2006)
2. Bugmann, G.: Joint torques and velocities in a 3-mass linear inverted pendulum model of bipedal gait. In: Dixon, C., Tuyls, K. (eds.) TAROS 2015. LNCS, vol. 9287, pp. 82–93. Springer, Cham (2015). doi:10.1007/978-3-319-22416-9_10
3. Kajita, S., Kanehiro, F., Kaneko, K., Yokoi, K., Hirukawa, H.: The 3d linear inverted pendulum mode: a simple modeling for a biped walking pattern generation. In: Proceedings of 2001 IEEE/RSJ International Conference on Intelligent Robots and Systems, vol. 1, pp. 239–246. IEEE (2001)
4. Yunping, L., Lipeng, W., Ping, M., Kai, H.: Stability analysis of bipedal robots using the concept of Lyapunov exponents. Math. Prob. Eng. **2013** (2013). Article ID 546520, 4 pages

Using Robot Operating System (ROS) and Single Board Computer to Control Bioloid Robot Motion

Ganesh Kumar Kalyani, Zhijun Yang,
Vaibhav Gandhi$^{(\boxtimes)}$, and Tao Geng

Design Engineering and Mathematics Department,
Faculty of Science and Technology,
Middlesex University, London NW4 4BT, UK
Gk434@live.mdx.ac.uk,
{Z.Yang, V.Gandhi, T.Geng}@mdx.ac.uk

Abstract. This paper presents a research study on the adaptation of a novel technique for placing a programmable component over the structural component of a Robotics Bioloid humanoid robot. Assimilating intelligence plays an important role in the field of robotics that enables a computer to model or replicate some of the intelligent behaviors of human beings but with minimal human intervention. As a part of this effort, this paper revises the Bioloid robot structure to be able to control the robotic movement via a single board computer BeagleBone Black (BBB) and Robot operating system (ROS). ROS as the development framework in conjunction with the main BBB controller that integrates robotic functions is an important aspect of this research, and is a first of its kind approach as far as the authors knowledge. A full ROS computation has been developed by which an API that will be usable by high level software using ROS services has also been developed. The experiments demonstrate that the human like body structure of the Bioloid robot and BeagleBone Black running ROS along with the intellectual components can make the robot walk efficiently.

Keywords: Robot · Robot Operating System (ROS) · Single Board Computer (SBC) · System integration

1 Introduction

There are different facets of a walking robot namely; structural components, sensing components and decision making components. The structural components include a manipulator (links, joints, etc.), the end-effector and actuators (servo motor, stepper motor, pneumatic and hydraulic cylinder etc.). Sensing components are devices that are meant to gather information about the internal state of the robot or to communicate with the outside world. The robot's decision making components include a processor (which is the brain of a robot that calculates the motion and velocity of the robot's joints), controllers that control and correlate the motion of actuators, and software (tools and libraries for conveying and collection of routine information) [1].

© Springer International Publishing AG 2017
Y. Gao et al. (Eds.): TAROS 2017, LNAI 10454, pp. 41–50, 2017.
DOI: 10.1007/978-3-319-64107-2_4

The walking humanoid robot requires the provision of a system integration arrangement within its decision making, sensing, and structural components. There must be a centralized or a distributed control system which can be used in such cases. In the centralized setup, the main computer is normally aware of the sensory information around the robot body. At the same time, it becomes inconvenient to increase the number of joints as the main computer must bear much calculation burden. A distributed system may comprise of many more joints and many peripheral devices such as cameras, wireless LAN, and control area network module [2]. However, the sub-controllers and the communication bus lines between the main computer and the sub-controllers need to be provided. In cases where the main controller used is not a real-time operating system (RTOS) but only a general-purpose operating system (GPOS), a Real-Time Extension (RTX) which is a commercial program capable of accessing the hardware directly must be provided [2]. In this case, the number of joint motor controllers of the robot must be worked out which depends on the degrees of freedom (DOF).

Generally, a walking humanoid robot is required to be configured with an autonomous motion controller, which takes care of the autonomous motion processing, e.g., integrating the odometer and the map information to guide the robot. Apart from this, the autonomous processor controls and directs the hardware while image processing tools like Open CV (intel C/C++ libraries for computer vision) or Direct show (Microsoft Multi-Media Development Tool) can be used for accessing images from the camera connected to the USB, and the program provided in the tools can carry out image processing [2]. The motion controller includes walking program and special action program written in suitable programming languages for e.g., C, C++. In the work presented in this paper, a robot's autonomous motion controller is designed using Robot Operating System (ROS) while keeping the basic and fundamental requirements of a prototype humanoid robot, the bioloid humanoid robot. The adapting strategy of the decision-making component and ROS with BBB in the structural body of humanoid robot has been redesigned and implemented in this paper. ROS gives standard robot services such as hardware abstraction, low-level device control, implementation of commonly used functionality, topics and message services between processes, and package management. ROS based topic transmission and frame transform procedures are represented in a graph architecture where processing takes place in nodes that may subscribe and publish the sensor, pose, control, state, planning and other messages. Despite the significance of unified software structure in robot control, ROS itself is not a real-time software package. However, it is possible to combine ROS with real time hardware ROS is running on to form a real-time framework. This framework can serve as an operating system and middleware for service robots. It gives not just standard operating services (hardware abstraction, contention management, process management) but in addition high level system functionalities (asynchronous and synchronous operations, centralized data base, a configured robot system etc.) [3].

A collection of nodes and programs called roscore are the pre-requisites of any ROS-based system. There must be a roscore running for ROS nodes to communicate [4]. Communication buses named ROS Topics are used while using the ROS modules. These comprise of anonymous publish/subscribe semantics that in-turn decouple the production of information from its consumption. Generally, the nodes are unaware of the extremities with which they are communicating. The nodes that are in search of data subscribe to the relevant topics i.e. the nodes that generate data publish to relevant topics. Thus, there can be multiple subscribers and publishers to a topic [5]. An rqt_graph is commonly used as a GUI plugin for visualizing the ROS computation graph [6].

The remainder of the paper is organized into three sections. Section 2 describes the theoretical considerations to be kept in mind while formulating the scheme for adaptability of installing ROS based autonomous motion controller into a walking humanoid robot. Section 3 describes the original decision making components of a walking humanoid robot (Robotis Bioloid) as well as that of the replaced robot autonomous motion controller (BeagleBone Black). In this section, the details of a ROS based motion control strategy are given. Section 4 narrates the exchanging strategy that was adopted to address the motion control issue. Section 5 concludes the paper.

2   Theoretical Considerations

2.1   General Points Regarding Controllers

1. Powerful processor for providing Artificial Intelligence and overall control, while basic microprocessor as I/O managers must be used in walking humanoid robots.
2. Preferably use three-layer configuration:
   (a) Top layer - Powerful PC as the "brain" of the robot.
   (b) Middle layer - Multiple sub-system managers for motion control, sensor management and processing.
   (c) Lower layer - Large number of low performance microprocessors for managing miscellaneous tasks.
3. Basic microprocessor can be plugged in to a USB on the computer and it can send and receive commands over serial port and all other higher-level instructions could run on the computer. The computer could issue commands by taking decisions and the other processor could control the motors to perform the required tasks.
4. Decisions on processor can be taken considering the following:

   (d) Processing Power - If controlling the motors is only required i.e. all processing is done on an external PC, then a motor driver circuit may be enough. For basic on-board processing like transformation of coordinates, simple command loops and inverse kinematics, a basic microprocessor may be sufficient. If automating the robot and implementing advanced features is desired, BeagleBone Black, Raspberry Pi or Intel Atom may be sufficient.
   (e) Programming ability - Basic Python and C/C++ is required for BeagleBone Black, Raspberry Pi and Intel programming. However, wherever necessary, libraries must be included in addition.
   (f) Compatibility - The chosen processor should support (both number and type) the motors used [7].

2.2 General Points Regarding the Software

1. ROS, a comprehensive robot-related software framework depends on the machine controller that integrates robotic functions [8].
2. Python API allows either to use all the C++ from a remote machine or create Python Modules that can run remotely or on the robots.
3. Embedded software, running on a motherboard located in the head of the robot allows autonomous behaviour. Desktop software running on a computer located outside the robot, allows creation of new behaviours and the remote control of the robot [9].

2.3 Preliminary Adaptability Analysis

The above theoretical considerations have been carefully considered and a ROS based architecture is used for data acquisition for motor actuation and decision making processes of the robot. The BeagleBone Black single board computer (SBC) is used in place of the CM530 decision making component of the Bioloid humanoid walking robot (see Table 1).

3 Decision Making Component

The original main control unit of the humanoid robot kit is CM-530 controller. AX 12A Dynamixel servo motors, the gyro/accelerometer sensor, infra-red and distance measuring sensors also all communication devices needed (RoboPlus software) are easily connected to CM-530 (see Fig. 4). Different components in the system have their own identifications (IDs) so that the topics or messages can be addressed to specific target components. Position and speed of walking can be easily obtained from the integral motor Dynamixel AX 12A and its encoders. This robot can provide feedback for angular position, angular velocity and load torque. Several Dynamixel units can be connected through daisy chain to save resources [10].

3.1 BeagleBone Black Processor

BeagleBone Black is a powerful processor that is used in the humanoid robot presented in this paper. The structural platform of the robot is constructed using 2 legs and 12 servos to have 12 DOFs. The BeagleBone Black is connected to the robot through software for controlling its motion and function [9, 11]. The complete interface of the BeagleBone Black with robot and computer is shown in Fig. 1.

Gyro/accelerometer sensors are mounted around the middle portion of the body. This senses the robot's position and controls its balance for walking, thus preventing it from falling. A wireless network is used to provide communication between the computer and the robot. The robot is controlled through the computer instructions and feeds back the data streams from the IR sensor for detection of obstacles in the front of the robot. Thus, the IR sensor acts as a guide for the robot in assisting it in its forward

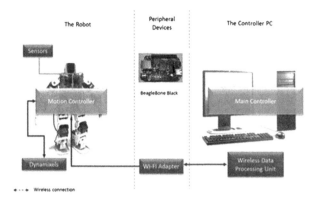

Fig. 1. Interfacing of the robot with computer [8]

movement and avoiding collision with potential obstacles. This approach can be further used in Brain-computer interface related applications [12].

4   Exchange Strategy for the Adaptation Process

4.1   System Modification and Walking Methodology

In this paper, a Debian image with ROS indigo version implementation is installed on the BeagleBone Black. To maneuver the robot without interruption, a Wi-Fi module is enabled in the BeagleBone Black using necessary libraries and repositories. A USB hub is connected to the serial port of the BeagleBone Black to which all peripherals are connected. USB2Dynamixel [10] is a device to operate the dynamixel actuators which is connected through the Wi-Fi interface of the BeagleBone Black. Gyro/accelerometer sensor is connected to serial clock and serial data pins while infra-red sensor is connected to the analog to digital converting pins (ADC) of the BeagleBone Black. Wi-Fi adapter is mounted on the humanoid robot and is connected through the serial interface of the BeagleBone Black. The interfacing of the sensors with robot movement is shown in the Figs. 2 and 3.

For controlling the robot movement, software code is written in python to control each servo. The humanoid robot is made to move forward at a desired speed as per the operator's instructions. The walking pattern of the robot is fine- tuned so that the robot maneuvers in small steps and take care of the balancing strategy [13]. The most important challenge in walking the robot is to prevent it from toppling over when one leg is lifted. This is overcome by using the accelerometer sensor. The robot is made to tilt on one side such that its center of gravity is in correct position to prevent it from falling.

The IR sensor detects an obstacle and send a feedback to the robot actuators to stop the robot in a balanced standing position. This is another important improvisation in the robot where it does not stop abruptly, and thus any chances of falling while executing the halt operation are avoided. Keeping these basic and fundamental design

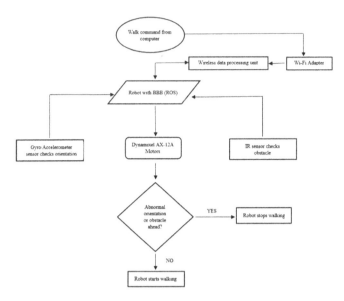

Fig. 2. Sensor interface for robot movement

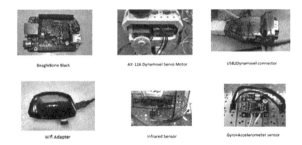

Fig. 3. Figure showing the BBB, AX-12A motors, USB2Dynamixel connector, Wifi Adapter, IR Sensor and the Gyro+Accelerometer sensor used in the experiment.

requirements of the humanoid robot, the adapting strategy is evolved. Deciding cum enforcing components of the bioloid robot are replaced under this strategy with the BBB such that the biped robot performs walking, which was not present earlier. This enhancement was made possible using ROS and Python.

In the bioloid robot, the CM530 controller was the key for governing all the robotic movements and the control of the motors (see Fig. 4). The idea was to replace this default controller with a different controller which can be easily programmable and can make the working of the robot more efficient. The deciding cum enforcing intelligence providing components of the BBB Board (incorporating Robot Operating System (ROS) and Python libraries and walking control) are implanted in the bioloid robot. While carrying out this process the original decision making components are removed from the bioloid robot. This approach has been implemented and shown in this paper.

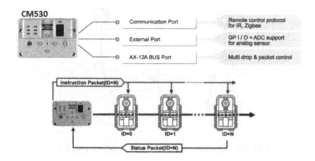

Fig. 4. Decision making components of Bioloid humanoid [10]

Table 1. Exchange of components [10, 11]

Sr. no.	Particulars	Existing component	Replacing component
1	CPU	STM32F103	AM33588
2	Controller	CM530	BeagleBone Black
3	Remote controller	RC100	Wi-Fi
4	Software	RoboPlus with C++	ROS with Python

Such an installation procedure has been undertaken for the first time as far as the researchers' knowledge goes. The main components replacement is shown in Table 1.

The Bioloid robot gaits are re-designed in the way that the robot body leans to the left/right direction when its right/left leg lifts and move forward. This simple design effectively avoids the collision between the robot feet with the ground. A check is also made to see that the robot is in a stable position, which makes it to avoid falling. If the parameter values are more than the prescribed limits inscribed in an accelerometer sensor, then the robot is made to tilt the other side to counter balance in order not to fall. The angle to which the robot leans is governed with the feedback from the accelerometer sensor. This angle is 20°. If the robot tilts beyond 25°, then it would come back to its standstill position and stops further movement. When the robot moves forward, the IR sensors sense obstacles in front of the robot. If an obstacle is detected to be present at around 35 cm then the robot stops moving further and comes to its standstill position. This dynamic model can be used, as a building block, to actuate the motors on legs and joints for a swing-stance period of the legs for its further movement [3]. At the same time, the robot stops further movement, and when the obstacle is removed, the robot continues its motion. Using the onboard IR sensor, the robot can navigate in places and a continuous feedback is sent from the IR sensor. The position of the pelvis center and the ankle in the view point of sagittal plane is as shown in Figs. 5 and 6. For the moment, the maximum walking speed of the robot is 0.5 foot/second. Beyond this limit the robot may get unstable and falls. Slippery or uneven surfaces also affects the robot and possibly make it fall.

The RoboPlus software of the Robotis Bioloid robot is an icon type C-language based software meant for easy programming and managing motion and behavior. In the work presented in this paper, this component has been replaced with ROS and Python

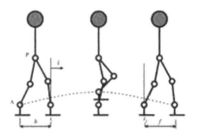

Fig. 5. Sagittal view for the walking pattern

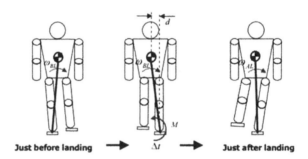

Fig. 6. Schematics of landing position control

scripts for a more flexible control of the autonomous robot movement. ROS is a promising robot software environment due largely to its rich open source repository and innovative compilation and operating structure. This demo work provides a proof of the concept framework in which a simple ROS motion control scheme is used. One Python ROS node is created to control the robot motion and publish one topic on the robot status. Based on this work, more potential nodes can be added for signal processing and motion control.

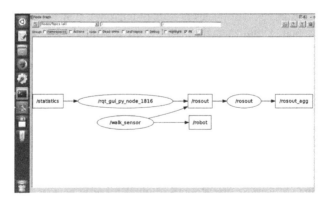

Fig. 7. Rqt_graph representing the dynamics of the system where the rosnode '/walk_sensor' communicating on the ROS topic '/robot'.

The biped walking gaits are imbibed to this revised hybrid humanoid robot using ROS and Python libraries, walking algorithmic codes and controls for the first time in this research study. During robot walking, ROS acts as the intermediate communication between the computer and the BBB. ROSCORE is the first program that had been run in one terminal when using ROS. ROSRUN is the command that instructs ROSNODE (rosnode displays information about the ROS nodes); which is the '/walk_sensor' here to publish on the ROStopic '/robot' (see Fig. 7). Thus, dynamic and stable walking is achieved.

4.2 Performance Trials

Trials have been carried out using BeagleBone Black to access and control the motion of individual AX-12 Dynamixel servo motors. The accelerometer sensor is added to the interface to control the servo motors. The Bioloid humanoid robot structure that is incorporated with BeagleBone Black and ROS accesses individual servos and accelerometer sensor to make the robot walk with perfect balance and gait. Additional libraries are added to enable the BeagleBone Black with Wi-Fi adapter and IR sensor. IR sensor is mounted in front of the robot to send real time information to the computer. An obstacle in front of the robot is sensed using IR sensors, which stops further movement of the robot. Trials have been carried out on all these sensor functions, to enhance the capability of the Bioloid humanoid robot.

A video showing a demonstration of the work presented in this paper can be accessed in [14]. As perceived in the video, the robot is seen walking as described theoretically and makes good use of its sensors for walking and navigation, and does not trip over. Also, different walking speeds for the robot have been implemented namely, fast and slow. The robot maintains its balance very well in both the mentioned walking speeds.

5 Conclusion

As far as the authors are aware, this project study is the first of its kind, wherein a biped robot is controlled using ROS and BBB. In what is referred to as the robot brain, the main BBB controller, and the ROS software has been successfully implemented in the structural body of the bioloid walking humanoid robot. The initial performance of the Bioloid robot, with its revised brain i.e., the controller and the software seems promising. This transformed Bioloid humanoid walking robot is much enhanced in terms of its autonomous behavior based on the sensed data.

Although, initial tests prove the approach to be reasonably robust, and integration of the hardware with the software is successful, further room for improved performance still exists. One of the improvements that can be proposed here is the implementation of a USB camera along with some image processing in the software. This improvisation would further enhance the performance of the robot.

Acknowledgment. The project is funded by an EPSRC grant EP/P00542X. The authors would also like to thank the Faculty of Science and Technology, Middlesex University for partly funding this project.

References

1. Morecki, A., Knapczyk, J.: Basics of Robotics: Theory and Components of Manipulators and Robots. International Centre for Mechanical Sciences, vol. 402. Springer, Heidelberg (1999)
2. Kim, J.H., Park, I.W., Oh, J.H.: Design and walking control of the Humanoid Robot KHR-2 KAIST Humanoid Robot 2. In: ICCAS-2004, Bangkok, 25–27 August 2004
3. Jackie, K.: Proposal for implementation of real-time systems in ROS 2. http://design.ros2.org/articles/realtime_proposal.html
4. ROSCORE, October 2016. http://wiki.ros.org/roscore
5. ROS TOPIC, October 2016. http://wiki.ros.org/Topics
6. Rqt_graph, November 2016. http://wiki.ros.org/rqt_graph
7. Paramkusam, D.: Things to consider before deciding on the processor, 25 March 2016
8. Foote, T.: Visualizer of delta robots using ROS and EtherCAT, ROS Robotics News, 15 April 2015
9. NAO Software 1.14.5: 2013 Documentation. Python SDK and software in and out of the robots, 27 June 2013
10. ROBOTIS e-Manual v1.25.00, v1.27.00, ROBOTIS, 27 June 2015
11. Grimmett, R.: Mastering BeagleBone Robotics. Packt Publishing Ltd., Birmingham (2014)
12. Gandhi, V., Prasad, G., Coyle, D., Behera, L., McGinnity, T.M.: EEG-based mobile robot control through an adaptive brain–robot interface. IEEE Trans. Syst. Man Cybern. Syst. **44** (9), 1278–1285 (2014)
13. Yang, Z.: Dynamic control of walking leg joints: a building block model perspective. In: ICNC-2011, pp. 459–463 (2011)
14. Video link. https://www.youtube.com/watch?v=f4AoTJh2cXg. Accessed 11 May 2017

Verification of Visibility-Based Properties on Multiple Moving Robots

Ali Narenji Sheshkalani[(⊠)], Ramtin Khosravi, and Mayssam Mohammadi

School of Electrical and Computer Engineering, University of Tehran, Tehran, Iran
{narenji,r.khosravi}@ut.ac.ir, mayssam.moh@gmail.com

Abstract. In a multi-robot system, a number of autonomous robots sense, communicate, and decide to move within a given domain to achieve a common goal. To prove such a system satisfies certain properties, one must either provide an analytical proof, or use an automated verification method. To enable the second approach, we propose a method to automatically generate a discrete state space of a given robot system. This allows using existing model checking tools and algorithms. We construct the state space of a number of robots, each arbitrarily moving along a certain path within a bounded polygonal area. This state space is then used to verify visibility properties (e.g., if the communication graph of the robots is connected) by means of model-checking tools. Using our method, there is no need to analytically prove that the properties are preserved with every change in the motion strategy of the robots. We have provided a theoretical upper bound on the complexity of the state space, and also implemented a tool to automatically generate the state space and verify some properties to demonstrate the applicability of our method in various environments.

Keywords: Formal methods for robotics · Distributed robot systems · Verification

1 Introduction

Mobile robots are able to sense, communicate, and interact with the physical world, and are able to collaboratively solve problems in a wide range of applications. In many applications within the general area of robot motion planning, visibility problems play an important role.

There has been a close relationship between robot motion planning and computational geometry in the applications where the robots are constrained to move within a geometric domain. Traditionally, there has been a research area with the goal of minimizing the number of (stationary) guards or surveillance cameras to guard an area in the shape of a certain geometric domain like extensions of art-gallery problems [21]. Moving to the area of mobile guards, Durocher et al. [7] considered the sliding cameras problem in which the cameras travel back and forth along an axis-aligned line segments inside an orthogonal polygon. In the Minimum Sliding Cameras (MSC) problem, the objective is to guard the polygon

© Springer International Publishing AG 2017
Y. Gao et al. (Eds.): TAROS 2017, LNAI 10454, pp. 51–65, 2017.
DOI: 10.1007/978-3-319-64107-2_5

with the minimum number of sliding cameras. In MSC problem, it is assumed that the polygon is covered by the cameras if the union of the visibility polygons of the axis-aligned segments equals the polygon. One of the original works on the subject of mobile guards is studied by Efrat et al. [8] considering the problem of sweeping simple polygons with a chain of guards. They developed an algorithm to compute the minimum number of guards needed to sweep a simple polygon.

Traditionally, the correctness of robot motion planning algorithms within the context of computational geometry such as the ones mentioned above is investigated by manual proofs. It may be hard for certain types of planning algorithms to prove they correctly satisfy the problem's constraints (such as connectivity among the robots or covering of the whole area). On the other hand, when it comes to practical applications of motion planning algorithms, the designer may heuristically tune the algorithm's parameters or even the whole strategy in order to find the best solution that fits both the problem constraints and practical restrictions. In these cases, manually proving the algorithm with every change may be impractical.

An alternative and more reliable approach to examine the correctness of the planning algorithms is formal verification, and more specifically, model-checking [5] which has become more popular in recent years. Here, a mathematical model of all possible behaviors of the system is constructed, often as a state transition system, and is automatically verified against the desired correctness properties over all possible paths. The properties are often expressed in temporal logic formulas.

In a few existing works, model checking has been employed to verify motion planning algorithms. In [10], the authors used a discrete representation of the continuous space of the movement of a single robot, producing a finite state transition system. Later, [9] extended the previous framework to multiple robots. These frameworks generate a motion plan for the robot to meet some regions of interest inside a polygon in order to satisfy a given Linear Temporal Logic (LTL) [22] formula.

Another related area to which model-checking techniques have been applied are robot swarms. In [18] a swarm of foraging robots is presented and in [17] is analyzed using the probabilistic model-checker PRISM [15]. A hierarchical framework for model-checking of planning and controlling robot swarms is suggested in [16] to make some abstraction of the problem including the location of the individual robots. Dixon et al. [6] used model-checking techniques to check whether temporal properties are satisfied in order to analyze emergent behaviors of robotic swarms. Moreover, [4] presented property-driven design, a novel top-down design method for robot swarms based on prescriptive modeling and model checking. In 2014, Guo and Dimarogonas [13] proposed a knowledge transfer scheme for cooperative motion planning of multi-agent systems. They assumed that the workspace is partially known by the agents where the agents have independently-assigned local tasks, specified as LTL formulas.

More recently, Sheshkalani et al. [25] focused on the verification of certain properties on a multi-robot system where each robot was programmed with an arbitrary navigation algorithm. The robots were assumed to move along the boundaries of a given polygon. They constructed a transition system on which the visibility properties can be investigated.

We believe that the result presented in [25] is restrictive in the sense that the robots are only allowed to move along the boundary of the environment. On the other hand, allowing the robots to freely move inside the polygon causes the state space to grow considerably. To remedy these problems, we define a generalized version of the problem of [25] by assuming that each robot is able to move freely along a simple path inside the environment. In addition to making the problem much more general, we have improved the result of the mentioned paper in terms of state space complexity.

As an application of the problem studied in this paper, the problem of guarding a bounded environment with a number of sliding cameras can be viewed as a special case of our problem. This way, our method is related to the previous study of [7]. Note that the mentioned study address the combinatorial optimization problem of minimizing the number of cameras. On the other hand, we address the problem of verifying correctness of the motion strategies for the given system. Another, more interesting, application of the problem is to consider the connectivity preserving (global connectivity maintenance) of the communication graph. Sabattini et al. [23] proposed a method to preserve the strong connectivity by estimating the algebraic connectivity of the communication graph in a decentralized manner. This way, our method can be used to guarantee the correctness of the desired requirements related to the *Connectivity* property.

The inputs to our method are comprised of (1) the environment, in the form of a simple polygon, (2) the algorithms controlling the motions of the robots, (3) the paths on which the robots are allowed to move, along with their initial positions, and (4) the requirement, expressed as a LTL formula. The output of the method is a True/False answer to the desired requirement as well as a transition system, labeled by two visibility-related atomic proposition: *Connectivity* (the communication graph of the robots is connected) and *Coverage* (the robots can collectively see the entire environment). The generated transition system is used to model check the visibility properties expressed in temporal logic formulas over the mentioned atomic propositions. The problem is defined more elaborately in Sect. 2.

We define a notion of state for such a system to construct a transition system on which the properties can be verified using the conventional model-checking algorithms (Sect. 3). Our method is abstract from specific motion planning algorithms in the sense that each robot may be programmed with a separate algorithm which during execution may cause the robot to sense the surroundings through various sensors or perform communications with other robots. In the end, all the sensing, communication, and internal logic leads to (possibly several) movement steps which is treated as actions by our method, causing transitions between states. Additionally, we provide a theoretical upper bound on the complexity of the state space (Sect. 4). Finally, we have implemented a tool to automatically generate the state space and verify the correctness of some sample requirements using CADP [11] tool to demonstrate the applicability of our method in various environments (Sect. 5).

2   Preliminaries and Problem Definition

The following definitions are borrowed from [12]. A simple polygon P is defined as a closed region in the plane bounded by a finite set of line segments (called edges of P) such that there exists a path between any two points inside P which intersects no edge of P. Each endpoint of an edge of P is called a vertex of P. A vertex of P is called *convex* if the interior angle at the vertex formed by two edges of that vertex is at most $180°$; otherwise it is called *reflex*.

Definition 1 (Visibility [12]). *Two points p and q in P are said to be* visible *if the line segment joining p and q contains no point on the exterior of P. This means that the segment pq lies totally inside P. This definition allows the segment pq to pass through a reflex vertex or graze along a polygonal edge. We also say that p sees q if p and q are visible in P. It is obvious that if p sees q, q also sees p.*

For a simple polygon P, we use the notation V_p for the visibility polygon of a point $p \in P$. Removing V_p from P may result in a number of disconnected regions called *invisible regions*. Any invisible region has exactly one edge in common with V_p, called a *window* of p, which is characterized by a reflex vertex of P visible from p, like p'. The window is defined as the extension of the (directed) segment pp' from p' to the boundary of P say p''. We denote such a window which consists of two endpoints p' and p'' by $w(p, p')$ (Fig. 1).

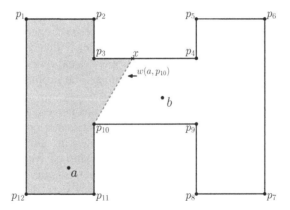

Fig. 1. The shaded area indicates the visibility polygon of point a (V_a). Point b is invisible from a, and its containing invisible region is characterized by the reflex vertex p_{10} which is separated from V_a by segment $p_{10}x$.

Consider a simple polygon P whose boundary is specified by the sequence of n vertices $<p_1, p_2, \ldots, p_n>$ including the set of reflex vertices P_{ref} and convex vertices P_{conv}, a set of robots $R = \{r_1, r_2, \ldots, r_k\}$, the corresponding navigation algorithms $Alg = \{a_1, a_2, \ldots, a_k\}$ (a_i is the navigation algorithm of robot r_i), and the corresponding paths $Paths = \{path_1, path_2, \ldots, path_k\}$ inside P are given with the following properties:

1. Robot r_i can only move along its corresponding path $path_i$,
2. Each step in the movement of each robot is specified by two parameters: direction (one of the two directions) and distance (a real positive number).

To discretize the state space of the system, we assume that the robots have turn taking movements as described in [1,6]. It means that during the movement of a robot, the position of other robots is fixed. Since our method is abstract from specific motion planning algorithms (each algorithm in set Alg is seen as a black-box) and the algorithms may be non-terminating (there might be no end goal), there is no way to determine if the state space has been constructed completely (especially for the cases in which the robots have time-sensitive behavior, e.g., take an action at a certain point in time). Hence, we take a time-bounded approach to state-space generation, and let the modeler determine how long the search for new states must take (using her knowledge of the navigation algorithms). As can be seen from our experimental results stated in Sect. 5, the growth rate of the number of generated states decreases significantly as time goes by, because in our case study the robots have a specific common goal which prevents the robots from making arbitrary actions.

The correctness properties may be built using temporal logics which are formalisms to describe temporal properties of reactive systems [2]. Apart from the logical operators, temporal logic formulas are constructed over a set of atomic propositions which may be true or false in each state of the system. Since our goal is to verify visibility properties, we need to define the two following properties:

Definition 2 (Connectivity). *The set of robots are connected if the graph induced by the visibility relation between pairs of robots is connected.*

Definition 3 (Coverage). *The robots cover P if the union of the visibility polygons of all robots ($\underset{r \in R}{\cup} V_r$) covers the whole P.*

Since we do not deal with the details of model-checking algorithms directly in this paper, we refer the reader for a detailed description of temporal logics to [2]. However, to bring an example, the LTL formula $\Box((Connectivity \wedge \neg Coverage) \rightarrow \Diamond(Connectivity \wedge Coverage))$ describes the property that whenever (represented by $\Box$) the visibility graph of robots is connected but the environment is not covered, eventually (represented by $\Diamond$) the system reaches a state in which both *Connectivity* and *Coverage* properties are satisfied (robots will eventually cover the environment by collaborating with each other).

We define a robot system RS as the tuple $(P, R, Alg, Paths, init)$ in which P indicates the environment of robots to navigate, R is the set of moving robots,

Alg is the set of navigation algorithms of robots, *Paths* is the position of paths in which the corresponding robots can move along them, and *init* specifies the initial position of robots over *Paths*. Our goal is to define the transition system equivalent of *RS*, over which temporal logic formulas may be model-checked.

To simplify our presentation of the method, we assume that the paths used throughout the examples in this paper are line segments.

3 Constructing the Discrete State Space

With the ultimate goal of verifying a temporal logic formula over a robot system $RS = (P, R, Alg, Paths, init)$, we must first construct the equivalent transition system of RS. As mentioned before, the states are labeled with the atomic propositions, hence, the transition system is called a Labeled Transition System (LTS) [2].

We define the LTS of RS as the tuple $(S, Act, \hookrightarrow, s_0, AP, L)$ where

- S is the set of states (defined below),
- $Act = \{\overleftarrow{move}_{r_i}, \overrightarrow{move}_{r_i} | 1 \leq i \leq k\}$ is the set of actions denoting the movement of robot r_i in its two possible directions,
- $\hookrightarrow \subseteq S \times Act \times S$ is the transition relation, (we use the notation $s \xrightarrow{\alpha} s'$ whenever $(s, \alpha, s') \in \hookrightarrow$),
- $s_0 \in S$ is the initial state (determined based on *init*),
- $AP = \{Connectivity, Coverage\}$ is the set of atomic propositions,
- $L : S \to 2^{AP}$ is the labeling function.

3.1 System States

The satisfaction of AP depends on the distribution of robots' position over *Paths*. We model each state of the system based on the topology of the robots and vertices of P. Additionally, we may need to store some extra information in order to identify the next states.

Consider the union of all the windows of the robots $W = \{w(p, p') | p \in R, p' \in P_{ref}, p' \in V_p\}$. The intersection of the line segments in W results in a subdivision inside P which is denoted by Sub_P (Fig. 2).

Definition 4 (Dual graph). *Let Sub_P be a subdivision of P. The dual graph of Sub_P that is represented by $DG(Sub_P)$ is a graph which has a node corresponding to each cell, and each pair of nodes are connected with an edge, if their related cells have an edge in common [12].*

Each node of $DG(Sub_P)$ is determined by the windows and the polygon edges which define the boundary of the corresponding cell in Sub_P. In Fig. 2, the corresponding node of cell c_i in $DG(Sub_P)$ is associated with the set of edges $\{w(d, p_{10}), w(b, p_4), (p_9, p_{10})\}$. $DG(Sub_P)$ does not change unless some cells are removed from or added to Sub_P. Therefore, we may use the dual graph of P to represent Sub_P. Since the satisfaction of AP can be determined by considering

Sub_P, we can store $DG(Sub_P)$ as a part of each state. Suppose robot r_i moves in one of its two possible directions (actions $\overleftarrow{move}_{r_i}$ or $\overrightarrow{move}_{r_i}$). The corresponding windows of r_i ($W_{r_i} = \{w(r_i, p') | r_i \in R, p' \in P_{ref}, p' \in V_{r_i}\}$) may move radially around p' during the movement of r_i respectively. Line segments W_{r_i} may construct new cells or destruct existing cells of Sub_P during the movement. Construction or destruction of cells may happen if and only if some line segments in W_{r_i} intersect some vertices of Sub_P. As mentioned before, we may need to store some extra information to correctly determine the next states to be encountered in the future as each robot moves. Let $Seq_{\overleftarrow{move}_{r_i}}$ indicates the sequence of intersection points of W_{r_i} with vertices of Sub_P and the robots during the movement of r_i in $\leftarrow$ direction (the same definition for $Seq_{\overrightarrow{move}_{r_i}}$ can hold as well - e.g., $Seq_{\overrightarrow{move}_d} = <i_3, p_4, i_7>$ in Fig. 2). Storing $Seq_{\overleftarrow{move}_{r_i}}$ and $Seq_{\overrightarrow{move}_{r_i}}$ in states enables efficient computation of the successor states regarding the transition types described in the next section.

We define a state of k robots inside the polygon P as:

1. $DG(Sub_P)$ along with the robots each cell of Sub_P contains,
2. $Seq_{\overleftarrow{move}_{r_i}}$ for all $1 \leq i \leq k$,
3. $Seq_{\overrightarrow{move}_{r_i}}$ for all $1 \leq i \leq k$.

By the definition of LTS, we assume each atomic proposition is either true or false in a state. The following lemma states that moving of the robots does not change the validity of the propositions *Connectivity* and *Coverage*, as long as the state defined above remains the same.

Lemma 1. *Each state s can be uniquely labeled with the atomic propositions $AP = \{Connectivity, Coverage\}$.*

Proof. Assume that the labeling $L(s) \in 2^{AP}$ is satisfied by the current state s. It is sufficient to prove that by moving the robots, $L(s)$ is valid while s does not change. We discuss the two atomic propositions separately.

Connectivity. Two robots r_i and r_j are connected, if one lies in the visible area of the other ($r_i \in V_{r_j}$). Since the boundaries of visible areas for each robot are determined by its corresponding windows (W_{r_j}) which are stored as the line segments in Sub_P, we can decide whether robot r_i locates inside V_{r_j}, by inspecting $DG(Sub_P)$. Assume that robots r_i and r_j are connected, and they are located in cells c_i and c_j respectively (based on Sub_P). If r_i moves in order to get disconnected, it must cross one of the line segments in W_{r_j}. In this case, r_j does not belong to c_j anymore. So, the current state s changes based on the definition of state.

Coverage. Polygon P is covered if and only if all the cells in Sub_P are covered by the robots. Assume that there exists at least one cell say c_i which is visible from none of the k robots (Fig. 2). The polygon remains uncovered as long as c_i is not destructed. More precisely, the polygon may get covered if the uncovered cells destructed. On the other side, assume that all the cells of Sub_P are covered by the robots. In order to make P uncovered, it is needed a new cell which is not visible from the robots to be constructed in Sub_P. Since any changes in validity of *Coverage* needs to make Sub_P different from its previous structure, *Coverage* is valid while s does not change. □

3.2   Transitions Events

A movement step of robot r_i is specified by the pair $move_{r_i} = (dir, dist)$ where:

  – $dir \in \{\leftarrow, \rightarrow\}$ is the direction of the movement along $path_i$,
  – $dist$ indicates the length of the movement.

We define $\overleftarrow{move}_{r_i}$ as the tuple $(\leftarrow, \delta)$, where δ is the smallest distance robot r_i can move in that direction along $path_i$ which causes a change in state. Also, we define $\overrightarrow{move}_{r_i}$ for the other direction similarly. We illustrate $\hookrightarrow$ as the smallest relation containing the tuples (s, α, s'), where $s, s' \in S$, $\alpha \in \bigcup_{1 \le i \le k} \{\overleftarrow{move}_{r_i}, \overrightarrow{move}_{r_i}\}$, and s' is the state obtained from s by taking action α. While r_i is making its movement, a transition $s \overset{\alpha}{\hookrightarrow} s'$ can occur in the following transition types:

(a) Some cells constructed or destructed in Sub_P which leads to changes in $DG(Sub_P)$,
(b) A robot crosses a window, and moves into another cell of Sub_P,
(c) If none of the two above types have occurred after the movement of the robot, it must be checked whether the order of points in $Seq_{\overleftarrow{move}_{r_j}}$ or $Seq_{\overrightarrow{move}_{r_j}}$ for some $1 \le j \ne i \le k$ has changed. If that is the case, we need to have a transition to s' with the same $DG(Sub_P)$ as of s, but having $Seq_{\overleftarrow{move}_{r_i}}$ and $Seq_{\overrightarrow{move}_{r_i}}$ updated for all $1 \le j \ne i \le k$.

As an example, consider Fig. 2 (both *Connectivity* and *Coverage* properties are not satisfied). Assume that robot b moves to the right. First, it destructs cells c_i, c_x and c_y, and constructs two new cells c_m and c_n (transition type (a)) before reaching $w(d, p_4)$ (Fig. 3). The *Coverage* property is satisfied in the generated state. Second, it constructs three other new cells c_j, c_k and c_l (Fig. 4). The validity of the properties are preserved in the generated state. Finally, it reaches $w(d, p_4)$, and makes robots b and d visible to each other (transition type (b)) which satisfies the *Connectivity* property as well (Fig. 5).

We may use the plane sweep algorithm [24] in order to find out whenever r_i reaches an intersecting point in Sub_P for type (a). More precisely, radial sweep algorithm [19] may be used to rotate $w(r_i, p')$ about p' in order to discover the intersection points of Sub_P. So, robot r_i may move towards its two possible directions ($\leftarrow$ or $\rightarrow$) until it reaches the end of c_i in order to compute $Seq_{\overleftarrow{move}_{r_i}}$ and $Seq_{\overrightarrow{move}_{r_i}}$ for type (c). Since AP may change only in transition types (a) or (b) based on Lemma 1, the validity of AP remains the same in type (c). Assume that robot r_i moves from its current position pos_i to a new position pos'_i, and a transition from s to s' occurred, in such a way that type (c) happened. Since none of the transition types (a) and (b) has happened, the dual graph of Sub_P and the

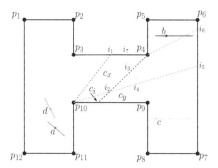

Fig. 2. A subdivision which consists of the intersection of line segments in W inside P.

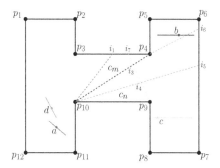

Fig. 3. The subdivision changes after moving b to the right before reaching $w(d, p_4)$. The *Covering* property is satisfied.

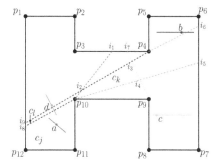

Fig. 4. Construction of two new cells c_k and c_l during the movement of b to the right before reaching $w(d, p_4)$.

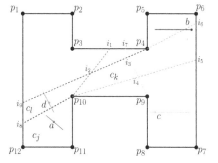

Fig. 5. The *Connectivity* property is satisfied. Transition type (c) happens after taking the action of robot b.

cells which the robots belong to remain the same as in s. It means that $Seq_{\overrightarrow{move}_{r_j}}$ or $Seq_{\overrightarrow{move}_{r_j}}$ for some $1 \leq j \neq i \leq k$ are changed during the movement of r_i. Precisely, the sequences in $Seq_{\overrightarrow{move}_{r_l}}$ or $Seq_{\overrightarrow{move}_{r_l}}$ for some $1 \leq l \leq k$ may change during the movement of r_i before reaching pos'_i, but the corresponding states are not generated. Since AP may change only in transition types (a) or (b), the states which are not generated during the movement have the same labels as in s. In the previous example, the obtained dual graph when robots b and d get visible to each other does not change while robot b reaches the right endpoint of the corresponding path (Fig. 5). On the other hand, $Seq_{\overrightarrow{move}_c}$ changes from $<i_1, p_3>$ to $<i_1, p_3, i_2>$ during the movement of b (after crossing $w(d, p_4)$) till reaching the right endpoint of its path which does not make any transitions of types (a) or (b). After taking the action of robot b, a state is generated (transition type (c)) with the same $DG(Sub_P)$ but different $Seq_{\overrightarrow{move}_c}$. Preventing the construction of type (c) transitions (during the movement) leads us to achieve a significant reduction in the size of the state space.

4 Analysis

In Sect. 3, the method of constructing an LTS on a given robot system $RS = (P, R, Alg, Paths, init)$ is described. In this section, we prove that the definition of the states and the transition events are consistent. Next, we discuss the state space complexity of our method.

4.1 Proof of Correctness

The following lemma states that for each state, the set of next sates can be uniquely determined independent of the exact position of the robots as long as the current state does not change.

Lemma 2. *Let $A = (S, Act, \hookrightarrow, s_0, AP, L)$ be the LTS of robot system $RS = (P, R, Alg, Paths, init)$. For each state $s \in S$, the set of next sates can be uniquely determined independent of the exact position of the robots as long as the configuration of the system is identical to state s.*

Proof. The transition events may only occur in the three types as explained in Sect. 3.2. Assume that robot r_i wants to move, and the current state of the system is s. The set of next states which belong to transition types (a) or (b) can be uniquely determined:

1. Robot r_i crosses one of the boundary line segments of its cell (type (b)): since the boundary line segments of each cell are unique for each state, the corresponding next states are unique respectively.
2. A window belonging to W_{r_i} crosses an intersection point of Sub_P (type (a)): the sequence of intersection points crossed by a window of W_{r_i} may vary while the corresponding Sub_P does not change. Since the sequence of intersection points ($Seq_{\overleftarrow{move}_{r_i}}$ or $Seq_{\overrightarrow{move}_{r_i}}$) are stored as a part of state s, the first intersection points of the two possible directions ($\leftarrow$ or $\rightarrow$) are unique respectively. It is important to note that the windows which are constructed or destructed during the movement of the robot are taken into account in order to compute $Seq_{\overleftarrow{move}_{r_i}}$ and $Seq_{\overrightarrow{move}_{r_i}}$, as well.

As mentioned in Sect. 3.2, the next state (s') which belongs to type (c) may be constructed at the end of the movement of r_i (none of the transition types (a) or (b) has happened during the movement). It means that there may exist a chain of intermediate states between s and s', but only s' is constructed. All of the intermediate states may be reached if the distance parameter in $move_{r_i} = (dir, dist)$ gets smaller. Since the proximity of all the windows to each other can be determined by $Seq_{\overleftarrow{move}_{r_i}}$ and $Seq_{\overrightarrow{move}_{r_i}}$ for all $1 \leq i \leq k$, the sequence of the intermediate states from s to s' are unique. Hence, the set of next states of s can be uniquely determined as long as the configuration of the system is equal to state s. □

4.2   Complexity

Lemma 3 states an upper bound on the maximum number of states for the robot system RS. The upper bound obtained in the lemma is not tight. In other words, the geometrical properties of the polygon, and therefore the resulting position of windows highly affect the size of the state space.

Lemma 3. *The maximum number of states in order to verify the given robot system $RS = (P, R, Alg, Paths, init)$ has the complexity of $O(n^{k^3})$ in which n and k denote the number of vertices of P and the number of robots.*

Proof. Consider a simple polygon P with n vertices and k robots inside. In order to compute the complexity of the state space, it is essential to obtain an upper bound on the maximum number of different subdivisions ($DG(Sub_P)$) shown as $C(DG(Sub_P))$ as well as the maximum number of different sequences of the robots ($Seq_{\overline{move}_{r_i}}$ and $Seq_{\overrightarrow{move}_{r_i}}$) shown as $C(Seq)$. Consider the current state s_i with the sequences $Seq_{\overline{move}_{r_i}}$ and $Seq_{\overrightarrow{move}_{r_i}}$ for $1 \leq i \leq k$ and $DG(Sub_P)$. As stated in Sect. 3.2 about type (c) transitions, there may exist more than one state with the same $DG(Sub_P)$ as in s_i, but with different sequences. So, each $DG(Sub_P)$ may correspond to more than one group of sequences belonging to the k robots ($C(DG(Sub_P)) \leq C(Seq)$). This way, it suffices to enumerate the number of different sequences for all the k robots as the parts of a state to obtain the maximum number of different states.

Consider a line segment in Sub_P which corresponds to $w(r_i, p')$. Line segment $w(r_i, p')$ may intersect some windows of the set W_{r_j} for some $1 \leq j \neq i \leq k$. In the worst-case scenario, $w(r_i, p')$ may intersect some windows of all $k - 1$ robots. Since the polygon is simple (it has no hole inside), at most two windows of W_{r_j} may intersect $w(r_i, p')$ simultaneously [3]. Therefore, the window $w(r_i, p')$ may intersect at most $2(k - 1) \in O(k)$ other windows at the same time. Based on the above discussion, the sequence say $Seq_{\overline{move}_{r_i}}$ may have at most $O(k^2)$ members which specify that robot r_i meets which intersection points of Sub_P during the movement to the left. Since the number of reflex vertices $|P_{ref}| \in O(n)$, each member of $Seq_{\overline{move}_{r_i}}$ may have $O(k^2 n^2)$ options. Additionally, as the sequence has $O(k^2)$ members, we may have $O((k^2)!)$ permutations. Hence, there exist at most $O((k^2)!(k^2 n^2)^{k^2})$ different sequences for $Seq_{\overline{move}_{r_i}}$.

Taking the sequences of all the k robots into account, we obtain complexity $O(((k^2)!(k^2 n^2)^{k^2})^k) \in O(n^{k^3})$ as an upper bound on the maximum number of different sequences ($C(Seq)$) which is an upper bound on the maximum number of states as well (assuming $k \leq n$).   □

Lemma 3 proves that the complexity of the state space is polynomial in terms of the complexity of the environment. Although the maximum number of states grows exponentially as the number of robots increases, in many applications like the one presented in Sect. 5, there may exist a global goal, so the robots avoid making arbitrary actions. As a comparison with the previous work of [25], they achieved the complexity of $O(n^{2^k})$ which is much greater than the complexity obtained by our method.

5   Experimental Results

We have used Computational Geometry Algorithms Library (CGAL) [14] to implement the proposed method in C++. The program automatically constructs the state space of the robot system $RS = (P, R, Alg, Paths, init)$ during the movement of the robots. Precisely, the states and the transitions are constructed with respect to the decisions made by the robots during their movements (determined by the motion algorithms). The implementation is available online via http://ramtung.ir/visification-1.0.zip which contains the source code as well as a Debian-based package.

As a case study, we consider robot swarms algorithms in which the robots use only local wireless connectivity information to achieve swarm aggregation. Particularly, we use the simplest *Alpha* algorithm which is examined using simulations and real robot experiments in [6, 20, 26] as the navigation algorithms of the robots in this experiment. It is assumed that the initial position of the robots are on the middle of the corresponding paths. Our experimental environment is an Ubuntu 14.04 machine, Intel Pentium (AMD64) CPU 2.6 GHz with 4 GB RAM.

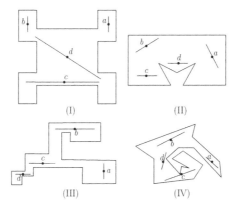

Fig. 6. The polygons used for the experimental results.

Figure 7 shows the growth rate of the size of the state space against the construction time for $k = 3$ (robots a, b and c) and $k = 4$ in different environments shown in Fig. 6 respectively. We executed the state space generation algorithm for 360 min ($timeBound = 360$). It shows that the number of investigated states converge quickly for all the polygons except for (I) when $k = 4$.

We used CADP [11] model-checker to verify the requirements (e.g., expressed in LTL formula) regarding the generated state space. Table 1 shows the results of the verification process after 360 min of running the state space generation algorithm with respect to the mentioned LTL formulas. The first formula $\Box\Diamond Connectivity$ is true, if the robots are infinitely often connected. The second formula $\Diamond(Connectivity \land Coverage)$ is true, if the system eventually reaches a

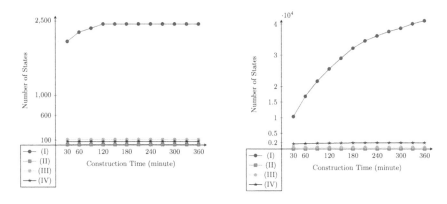

Fig. 7. The number of discovered states for $k = 3$ (left) and $k = 4$ (right).

state in which the communication graph is connected and the environment is fully covered by the robots which may be considered as a goal state. CADP evaluated each formula in less than two seconds for the polygons which shows the applicability of the proposed method. Since the robots are implementing the *Alpha* algorithm (which focuses on maintaining the connectivity) with $\alpha = 1$ (the decision in which the robot continues the previous direction or make a $180°$ turn depends on the value of α - number of visible robots), the robots in the polygons (III) and (IV) in Fig. 6 cannot reach a state in which the environment is covered. More precisely, consider Polygon (IV) with $k = 4$. Assume that robots c and d are visible to each other. Since robot c wants to keep the connection with d, it cannot cover some portion of the environment. If we increase the value of α by one ($\alpha = 2$), the number of visible robots for c (which is one) falls below the threshold. This way, based on the Alpha algorithm, robot c makes a $180°$ turn in order to avoid moving out the swarm. So, it may lead to cover the uncovered area.

As a comparison with a previous work, Dixon et al. [6] implemented the *Alpha* algorithm for three robots ($k = 3$) within grid sizes of 6×6 and 7×7, and

Table 1. The results of the verification of two LTL formulas.

LTL formula			$\Box\Diamond Connectivity$	$\Diamond (Connectivity \wedge Coverage)$
Polygon (I)	$k = 3$		True	False
	$k = 4$		True	False
Polygon (II)	$k = 3$		True	True
	$k = 4$		True	True
Polygon (III)	$k = 3$		False	False
	$k = 4$		False	False
Polygon (IV)	$k = 3$		False	True
	$k = 4$		False	False

obtained 168×10^6 and 501×10^6 number of states respectively. Even though they completely abstracted out the geometry of the environment, the number of states achieved are considerably greater than the number of states computed by our method which let the robots move continuously in a geometric domain.

6   Conclusion

We presented a method to construct a discrete state space for a multi-robot system and then verify the correctness properties by means of model-checking techniques. The notion of state has been defined in such a way that each state can be uniquely labeled with the atomic propositions *Connectivity* and *Coverage*. An important aspect of our method is that it treats the navigation algorithms as black-boxes. Iteratively searching for new states, at each step, our algorithm asks the black-box for its next action and creates the states caused by the action based on a precise definition of transitions. Using our provided implementation, the modeler can code the navigation algorithms and generate the state space. The generated state space is used to verify temporal formulas constructed over the mentioned propositions using CADP tool. An important benefit of this approach is to eliminate the need for analytical proof of correctness upon changes to the navigation algorithms.

From a geometric perspective, our method can be easily applied to more complicated cases, e.g., when the robots can move along possibly non-simplified paths (e.g., paths containing points in which a robot has more than two directions to choose). Furthermore, the geometric domain of simple polygons can be extended to polygonal domains, i.e., simple polygons having a number of holes inside. This makes our method applicable to more realistic situations.

References

1. Antuña, L., Araiza-Illan, D., Campos, S., Eder, K.: Symmetry reduction enables model checking of more complex emergent behaviours of swarm navigation algorithms. In: Proceedings of 16th Annual Conference on Towards Autonomous Robotic Systems, pp. 26–37 (2015)
2. Baier, C., Katoen, J.: Principles of Model Checking. MIT Press, Cambridge (2008)
3. Bose, P., Lubiw, A., Munro, J.I.: Efficient visibility queries in simple polygons. Comput. Geom. Theory Appl. **23**(3), 313–335 (2002)
4. Brambilla, M., Brutschy, A., Dorigo, M., Birattari, M.: Property-driven design for robot swarms: a design method based on prescriptive modeling and model checking. ACM Trans. Auton. Adapt. Syst. **9**(4), 17 (2014)
5. Clarke, E., Grumberg, O., Peled, D.: Model Checking. MIT Press, Cambridge (1999)
6. Dixon, C., Winfield, A.F., Fisher, M., Zeng, C.: Towards temporal verification of swarm robotic systems. Rob. Auton. Syst. **60**(11), 1429–1441 (2012)
7. Durocher, S., Filtser, O., Fraser, R., Mehrabi, A.D., Mehrabi, S.: A (7/2)-approximation algorithm for guarding orthogonal art galleries with sliding cameras. In: Pardo, A., Viola, A. (eds.) LATIN 2014. LNCS, vol. 8392, pp. 294–305. Springer, Heidelberg (2014). doi:10.1007/978-3-642-54423-1_26

8. Efrat, A., Leonidas, J.G., Har-Peled, S., Lin, D.C., Mitchell, J.S.B., Murali, T.M.: Sweeping simple polygons with a chain of guards. In: SODA 2000, pp. 927–936 (2000)
9. Fainekos, G.E., Girard, A., Kress-Gazit, H., Pappas, G.J.: Temporal logic motion planning for dynamic robots. Automatica **45**(2), 343–352 (2009)
10. Fainekos, G.E., Kress-Gazit, H., Pappas, G.: Temporal logic motion planning for mobile robots. In: Proceedings of the IEEE International Conference on Robotics and Automation, pp. 2020–2025 (2005)
11. Garavel, H., Lang, F., Mateescu, R., Serwe, W.: CADP 2010: a toolbox for the construction and analysis of distributed processes. In: Abdulla, P.A., Leino, K.R.M. (eds.) TACAS 2011. LNCS, vol. 6605, pp. 372–387. Springer, Heidelberg (2011). doi:10.1007/978-3-642-19835-9_33
12. Ghosh, S.K.: Visibility Algorithms in the Plane. Cambridge University Press, Cambridge (2007)
13. Guo, M., Dimarogonas, D.: Distributed plan reconfiguration via knowledge transfer in multi-agent systems under local LTL specifications. In: 2014 IEEE International Conference on Robotics and Automation (ICRA), pp. 4304–4309 (2014)
14. Hemmer, M., Huang, K., Bungiu, F., Xu, N.: 2D visibility computation. In: CGAL User and Reference Manual, 4.7 edn. CGAL Editorial Board (2015)
15. Hinton, A., Kwiatkowska, M., Norman, G., Parker, D.: PRISM: a tool for automatic verification of probabilistic systems. In: Hermanns, H., Palsberg, J. (eds.) TACAS 2006. LNCS, vol. 3920, pp. 441–444. Springer, Heidelberg (2006). doi:10.1007/11691372_29
16. Kloetzer, M., Belta, C.: Temporal logic planning and control of robotic swarms by hierarchical abstractions. IEEE Trans. Rob. **23**, 320–330 (2007)
17. Konur, S., Dixon, C., Fisher, M.: Analysis robot swarm behaviour via probabilistic model checking. Rob. Auton. Syst. **60**(2), 199–213 (2012)
18. Liu, W., Winfield, A.F.T.: Modeling and optimization of adaptive foraging in swarm robotic systems. Int. J. Rob. Res. **29**(14), 1743–1760 (2010)
19. Mirante, A., Weingarten, N.: The radial sweep algorithm for constructing triangulated irregular networks. IEEE Comput. Graph. Appl. **2**(3), 11–21 (1982)
20. Nembrini, J., Winfield, A., Melhuish, C.: Minimalist coherent swarming of wireless networked autonomous mobile robots. In: Proceedings of the Seventh International Conference on Simulation of Adaptive Behavior on From Animals to Animats, pp. 373–382. ICSAB, MIT Press (2002)
21. O'rourke, J.: Art Gallery Theorems and Algorithms. Oxford University Press, Oxford (1987)
22. Pnueli, A.: The temporal logic of programs. In: 18th Annual Symposium on Foundations of Computer Science, pp. 46–57. IEEE (1977)
23. Sabattini, L., Secchi, C., Chopra, N.: Decentralized estimation and control for preserving the strong connectivity of directed graphs. IEEE Trans. Cybern. **45**(10), 2273–2286 (2015)
24. Shamos, M.I., Hoey, D.: Geometric intersection problems. In: 17th Annual Symposium on Foundations of Computer Science, pp. 208–215. IEEE (1976)
25. Sheshkalani, A.N., Khosravi, R., Fallah, M.K.: Discretizing the state space of multiple moving robots to verify visibility properties. In: Proceedings of 16th Annual Conference on Towards Autonomous Robotic Systems, pp. 186–191 (2015)
26. Winfield, A.F., Liu, W., Nembrini, J., Martinoli, A.: Modelling a wireless connected swarm of mobile robots. Swarm Intelligence **2**(2–4), 241–266 (2008)

Self-adaptive Context Aware Audio Localization for Robots Using Parallel Cerebellar Models

M.D. Baxendale[1,3]([✉]), M.J. Pearson[2], M. Nibouche[1],
E.L. Secco[3], and A.G. Pipe[2]

[1] University of the West of England, Bristol, England
mark2.baxendale@live.uwe.ac.uk
[2] Bristol Robotics Laboratory, Bristol, England
[3] Liverpool Hope University, Liverpool, England

Abstract. An audio sensor system is presented that uses multiple cerebellar models to determine the acoustic environment in which a robot is operating, allowing the robot to select appropriate models to calibrate its audio-motor map for the detected environment. There are two key areas of novelty here. One is the application of cerebellar models in a new context, that is auditory sensory input. The second is the idea of applying a multiple models approach to motor control to a sensory problem rather than a motor problem. The use of the adaptive filter model of the cerebellum in a variety of robotics applications has demonstrated the utility of the so-called *cerebellar chip*. This paper combines the notion of cerebellar calibration of a distorted audio-motor map with the use of multiple parallel models to predict the context (acoustic environment) within which the robot is operating. The system was able to correctly predict seven different acoustic contexts in almost 70% of cases tested.

1 Introduction

There is a need for autonomous mobile robots to use a variety of senses to navigate in unstructured environments. Typically, vision is used to locate objects in the robot's environment, however, this can break down where vision is obscured. A number of attempts have been made to allow a robot to navigate by sound (see [1] for a review), however these systems are typically set up in a specific acoustic environment and break down when the robot moves to a new environment. We propose an audio sensor system that uses parallel models of cerebellar microcircuits to learn the different acoustic environments in which a robot is operating, allowing the robot to select an appropriate model and to calibrate its audio-motor map for the detected environment. The adaptive filter model of cerebellum [2] has shown itself to be a robust algorithm in a variety of robotics applications which have been demonstrated through the idea and application of the so called "cerebellar chip" [3–5]. This paper combines the notion of cerebellar calibration of a distorted audio-motor map with the use of multiple models to predict the context (acoustic environment) within which the robot is operating. The paper extends the idea of applying a multiple models approach, which is

© Springer International Publishing AG 2017
Y. Gao et al. (Eds.): TAROS 2017, LNAI 10454, pp. 66–78, 2017.
DOI: 10.1007/978-3-319-64107-2_6

usually employed in the solution to motor control problems, to a sensory problem, and in particular, the application of multiple cerebellar models to auditory input.

In the next section we describe the problem faced in audio localization and how our proposed cerebellar inspired solution could be applied in theory to reduce the error. This is followed by a description of an experiment to test the performance of this architecture in a real-world setting (Sect. 4). Finally, the results from this experiment are presented (Sect. 5) and discussed with conclusions drawn and future work presented (Sect. 6).

2 Background and Motivation

2.1 Audio Localization

The primary auditory cues used in the passive, binaural localisation of sound sources are Inter-aural Time Difference (ITD) of arrival of sounds and Inter-aural Level Difference (ILD) [6]. ILD relies on acoustic shadowing caused by the head of the animal; as such it is frequency dependent, and is effective for higher frequencies (greater than around 1500 Hz). On the other hand, ITD cues are limited to lower frequencies due to phase ambiguity as the period of the sound wave becomes comparable to the maximum ITD available for a given sensor or ear separation [6]. Sound from a source to either side of the median plane will reach one or other sensor or ear at different times (e.g. a sound originating from a source to the right of the median plane will reach the right ear or sensor before the left). The ITD has a maximum value of around 660 μs at an azimuth of 90° in humans [6], representing an inter-aural distance of around 15 cm. This is subject to uncertainty due to environmental influences such as obstruction of the sound source, the acoustic properties of surfaces or damage to or displacement of audio sensors.

This study uses a localization module based on the ITD with microphones mounted in free field, corresponding to Auditory Epipolar Geometry (AEG) described in [1], and does not take the Head Related Transfer Function (HRTF) into account. The robot head and ITD method are described more fully in Sect. 4.

2.2 Cerebellar Calibration of Audio-Motor Map

The previous two decades have seen the acceptance that the brain makes use of internal models for motor control and that they are likely to be located in the cerebellar cortex [7]. More recently, it has emerged that internal models play a role in non-motor functions and that the cerebellum plays a role in perceptual processes [8].

The cerebellum is a highly regular structure whose output is via Purkinje cells. Granule cells receive input from mossy fibres, which provide one of two main afferent pathways. Axons of the granule cells form parallel fibres which synapse onto the Purkinje cells. The second main afferent pathway is the climbing fibres that also synapse onto the Purkinje cells. The firing rate of the climbing fibres is orders of magnitude lower than that of the Purkinje cells so that it has no direct influence on the sensory signal yet does influence the weights of the parallel fibre-Purkinje cell synapses.

The adaptive filter model of the cerebellum was proposed by Fujita [9] as a variation on the Marr-Albus model [10,11]. This model emphasises the resemblance of the cerebellar microcircuit to an adaptive filter [2]. Sensory input is to granule cells via the mossy fibres. Granule cell axons form parallel fibre inputs to Purkinje cells. Hence, mossy fibre input is analysed into multiple filter pathways and synthesized at the Purkinje cell with weights that are affected by the climbing fibre input to the Purkinje cell. Whereas the parallel fibres convey sensory input signals, the climbing fibre conveys a teaching signal.

The cerebellar calibration model is an adaptation of that used in a precursory study to that reported here to calibrate whisker input to a robot platform [5], which draws on the adaptive filter model of the cerebellum as shown in Fig. 1a. An audio stimulus results in activation of the audio-motor map, which stores a probabilistic representation of the estimated sound source azimuth, generated by the ITD module, in robot head-centric space. The map is divided into a regular grid with activity in each cell of the grid forming one input (i.e. the mossy fibre/parallel fibre) into the cerebellar model. A course-coded version of the map transmits activity at each place on the map to the cerebellum via the parallel fibres. The Purkinje cell, represented by the summing element in Fig. 1a, synthesizes the parallel fibre signals modulated by the synaptic weights into a (positive- toward the right, or negative- toward the left) map shift signal that is applied as a bias to the motor output from the audio-motor map. The amount of bias is the weighted sum of the parallel fibre inputs:

$$\delta\theta = \sum_{i=0}^{n} w_i p_i \tag{1}$$

where n is the number of parallel fibres. The weights w_i of the parallel fibre-Purkinje cell synapses, initially zero, are learnt using the covariance learning rule [12], and updated as in [5]:

$$\Delta w_i = -\beta e p_i \tag{2}$$

where β is the learning rate, p_i the activity on each parallel fibre and e is the orient error, that is, the difference between the ground truth azimuth of the sound source and the calibrated audio-motor map output.

The cerebellar model is shown in situ in Fig. 1b. The map is divided into a regular grid with activity in each cell of the grid forming one input (i.e. the mossy fibre/parallel fibre input) into the cerebellar model. In the full system, the calibrated output from the audio-motor map is used to orient the robot head toward the sound source, and a visually derived error after orientation is used as a teaching signal to adjust the weights of parallel fibre/Purkinje cell synapses, which are initially set at zero, although this visually derived error was not used in the current study (see Sect. 4). Post learning, the cerebellar model applies a shift to compensate for distortion in the auditory map.

(a)

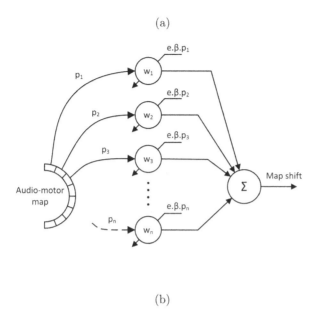

(b)

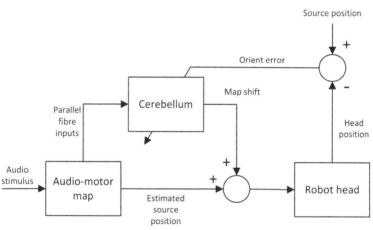

Fig. 1. Cerebellar calibration of audio-motor map. (a) Adaptive filter model of the cerebellum. The audio-motor map stores a probabilistic representation of sound source azimuth in robot head-centric space. A course-coded version of the map transmits activity at each place on the map to the cerebellum via the parallel fibres. The weights w_i of the parallel fibre-Purkinje cell synapses are updated by the covariance learning rule. (b) Cerebellar model in learning mode. Audio stimulus results in activation of the audio-motor map of sound source azimuth in robot head-centric space. Output from the audio-motor map is a motor command to orient the robot head in the direction of the sound source. The orient error is used as a teaching signal such that the cerebellum learns to compensate for distortion of the audio-motor map.

2.3   Multiple Models

A single internal model would need to be very complex in order to capture the range of contexts within which the organism or robot is required to operate as described in Sect. 2.1. This leads to the proposal that the central nervous system makes use of multiple models each specialized for different contexts [13]. A bio-inspired approach to implementing such models would need a means to select the appropriate model for a particular context. A candidate solution to this problem is the MOdular Selection and Identification for Control [MOSAIC] framework [14,15]. In this scheme, multiple forward models concurrently predict the consequences of an action (e.g. motor command) and a responsibility predictor attached to the module generates a signal that indicates the degree to which its model is appropriate for the context. The system needs to select the module appropriate to the context by switching the outputs of inverse models on or off. This switching involves two processes [13]:

- the generation of motor commands through the selection of the most appropriate controller (inverse model) for the estimated context based on sensory input
- a switching process using sensory feedback of the consequences of the action to select a more appropriate model if necessary.

In the original MOSAIC scheme, the inverse models' contribution is determined through a responsibility signal. This is derived through two further processes [13]: first, each forward model's prediction of the next state of the controlled system can be compared to the actual state through sensory feedback, but only after the action has taken place (or during action). The second process estimates responsibility from sensory contextual information, providing the potential to select modules before action.

3   Proposed System

The proposed system is shown in Fig. 2. This is a simplification of the multiple models framework, implementing only the models and the responsibility estimator, which simply attempts to identify the most appropriate model for a given context. A more complete system is the subject of current work (Sect. 6). The system has a single ITD module that produces an estimate of sound source azimuth. For the purposes of this study, the ITD module uses a cross-correlation algorithm as described in Sect. 4.2.

Each cerebellar model, having been trained in a particular context (Sect. 4.3) produces a map-shift signal based on the output of the ITD module, which should depend on the context within which the model was trained. Models are pre-trained in this study. Each map shift is then added to the estimated position produced by the ITD module and this becomes a prediction of the sound source location- one prediction for each model. Hence, a set of azimuth estimates are produced from a single ITD, and the idea is that the different environments in which the models learned will be reflected in the different estimates produced. The problem is then one of how to identify the correct context. It is assumed that the model trained in the current context will produce the lowest error in azimuth estimation (of course, this is not always the case, as discussed in Sect. 6). In this study, each prediction is compared to the ground truth position, which is already known from the positioning of the sound source. Although, of course, in the real system, the ground truth cannot be found until the robot head orients toward the sound source, it has been used here merely for convenience to test the efficacy of the approach, and would ultimately be used with visual feedback on a mobile platform. The resulting prediction error is transformed by a psuedo-likelihood function before being normalised across all models using a *softmax* function as in [13]:

$$\frac{e^{-|\theta_t - \theta_i|^2/\sigma^2}}{\sum_{j=1}^{n} e^{-|\theta_t - \theta_j|^2/\sigma^2}} \tag{3}$$

where θ_t is the ground truth azimuth, θ_i is the estimate produced by the ith model, n is the number of estimates (models) and σ is a scaling factor which is equivalent to the standard deviation assuming a Gaussian distribution of estimates, and is set to unity in this specific configuration. The maximum softmax value corresponds to the lowest error in estimation and is assumed to correctly identify the context. The value of σ determines the distribution of responsibilities across models and has no affect on this identification, and so its value is not important in this particular study (however, it will be important in studies where the outputs of models are to be combined in some way).

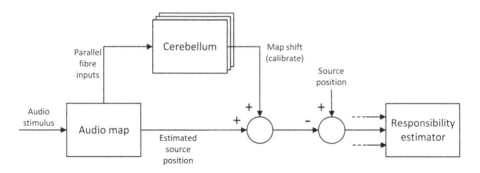

Fig. 2. multiple-models- inspired context estimation as it has been implemented in this study. For a given context, each model provides an estimate of source position. Each estimate is then compared to the ground truth source position and the responsibility estimator classifies the acoustic context based on the estimation errors. In the real system, the head would orient toward the sound source based on the currently selected cerebellar model and a posterior estimate of likelihood calculated for each model.

4   Method

4.1   Experimental Setup

Experiments were automated and controlled using a computer running the Matlab environment (The Mathworks Inc.). Algorithms were implemented in the same environment.

Two microphones (Audio-Technica ATR-3350 omnidirectional condenser lavalier) were mounted on a horizontal bar with a spacing between centres of 25 cm (Fig. 3). A relatively large inter-microphone distance was used for the purposes of this study in order to achieve a high resolution in the ITD estimation. The microphone bar also had a USB webcam mounted in the centre and was itself mounted on a stepper motor such that it could be oriented toward the estimated sound source azimuth to generate visual feedback of the ground truth position. In the full system, the robot head orients to the estimated azimuth and visual feedback is used to generate the ground truth azimuth. As spatial coordinates have an origin at the robot head the system can be transferred to a mobile platform and it is anticipated that such a mobile platform would rotate on a head-centric axis toward the estimated azimuth. However, in this study, for convenience, the ground truth was taken simply as the randomised set of positions generated for training of the cerebellar models, and the microphone/camera bar remained facing directly ahead.

The sound source was mounted on a motorised platform that could traverse a circular track such that it could be placed (under computer control) at any azimuth between $-90°$ (left with respect to the robot head) and $+90°$ at a constant distance from the robot head (Fig. 3). A geared stepper motor was used to move the platform and this allowed the source to be placed with a high level of accuracy. $1°$ increments were used in this study although results are limited by the resolution of the ITD module, which varies from $\pm 1.7°$ at zero azimuth to $\pm 5°$ at $\pm 70°$ azimuth. The resolution is affected by the sampling frequency and inter-microphone distance. The microphones were connected to a computer using a M-Audio MobilePre USB audio capture unit.

The sound source was also mounted on a further stepper motor such that it could be rotated in the transverse plane through an angle ϕ as shown in Fig. 3a. This allowed the alteration of the acoustic context by rotation of the sound source so that it might face away at angle ϕ from the robot head. The experimental arena was surrounded by a semi-circular screen that, combined with different orientations of the sound source, produced different acoustic contexts.

4.2   ITD Module

The captured audio was processed by the ITD module which used a cross-correlation algorithm to provide an estimate of the azimuth of the location of a sound source:

$$r_{lr} = \sum_{k=0}^{n} R(k)L(k - \tau) \qquad (4)$$

(a)

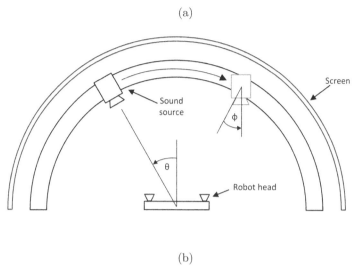

(b)

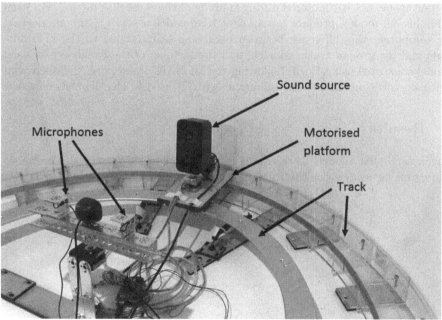

Fig. 3. Experimental apparatus. (a) Plan view of the experimental arena. For a given context, the sound source was placed at various azimuths (θ), and oriented at a fixed angle (φ) on its vertical axis. (b) Photograph of the experimental arena.

where R is the right- and L the left channel audio signal, k is the sample number, n is the current sample and τ is the time lag between left and right channel. The algorithm finds that time difference which results in maximum similarity between the two channels (maximum correlation value), which corresponds to the time difference of arrival of the sound. This was then converted into an estimated azimuth:

$$\theta = \frac{180}{\pi} \sin^{-1}(\frac{c\tau}{df_s})$$ (5)

where c is the velocity of sound, τ is the estimated ITD, d is the inter-aural distance and f_s is the audio sampling frequency.

4.3   Cerebellar Models

The cerebellar models were trained in different acoustic contexts. During learning, the robot head was presented with audio from randomised positions along the circular track, such that the direction of arrival of sound was from various azimuths (θ in Fig. 3a). 60 iterations were used to train a model.

Post learning, all models were presented with the same set of audio stimuli at azimuths from $-45°$ to $45°$ in $15°$ increments (some of which may be novel azimuths- i.e. not encountered during training of the cerebellar model). For each stimulus, all models produce a map shift from which a set of errors are derived by computing the difference between each map shift (added to the ITD output) and the ground truth azimuth, and the softmax of the likelihood for each model computed using Eq. 3. Following the MOSAIC framework, the maximum softmax, corresponding to the minimum error, is used to identify the context.

5   Results

Seven cerebellar models were trained, as described in Sect. 4 with the sound source facing away from the robot head at a different angle (ϕ in Fig. 3a) for

Table 1. Context identification

Context	Context (source orientation ϕ)	Correct identifications (n $= 7$ azimuths θ)
1	135° left	85.7%
2	90° left	71.4%
3	45° left	42.9%
4	0° facing the robot	14.3%
5	45° right	71.4%
6	90° right	100.0%
7	135° right	100.0%

Confusion Matrix

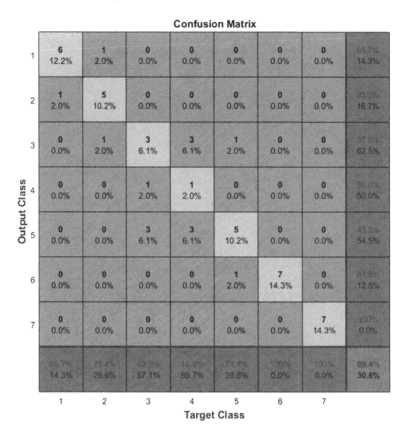

Fig. 4. Confusion matrix. Green cells show proportion of correct context identification (14.3% indicates context was always correctly identified. Red cells show incorrect identification. For example, Target (true) context 1 was correctly identified in 6 out of 7 cases (source azimuth) and mis-identified as context 2 in one case. (Color figure online)

each model (135° left; 90° left; 45° left; 0°; 45° right, 90° right and 135° right with respect to the robot head). After training, the robot head was presented with sound source azimuths (θ in Fig. 3a) of −45° (left with respect to the robot head) to +45° (right with respect to the robot head) in 15° increments in each of the seven contexts. Therefore an overall set of 49 (7 contexts, φ each with 7 azimuths, θ) different configurations where explored. For each source azimuth/context combination, the seven cerebellar models generated estimates of the context as described in Sect. 3, and the model with the lowest error was used to identify the context. Table 1 shows the rate of context identification. Each row in Table 1 represents seven different source azimuths in the same context. Figure 4 shows a confusion matrix summarising the performance of the context estimation. The green cells in Fig. 4 represent correct identification of a context and ideally, each would display the number 7 indicating that all 7 contexts were successfully identified, and red cells would display zero. Figure 5 shows plots of

(a)

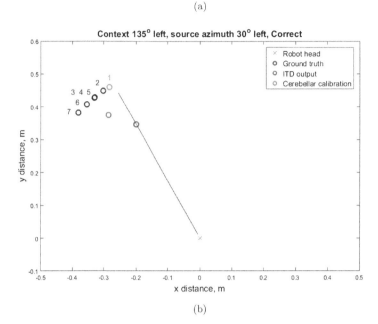

(b)

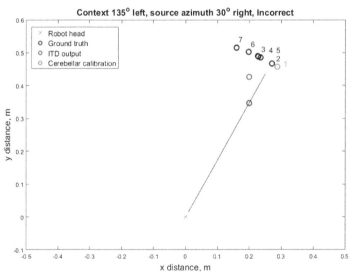

Fig. 5. Plots of sound source azimuth for a context/azimuth pair. The context is that the sound source is rotated (ϕ in Fig. 3a) $135°$ to the left away from the robot. The sound source azimuth (θ in Fig. 3a) is $45°$ left and right. Blue circles represent the ground truth azimuth. Red circles represent the ITD estimate. The green circle represents the estimate for the model that was trained in this context. The black circles represent the estimates of the remaining six models. ITD estimate and calibrated points are offset for clarity. (a) Correct identification. (b) Incorrect identification. (Color figure online)

sound source azimuths along with ITD estimates and cerebellar calibration by each of the seven models in one case in which context identification was correct (Fig. 5a) and one case where context identification was incorrect (Fig. 5b).

6 Discussion and Future Work

This paper has presented a simple context estimation system which is able to identify the robot's acoustic context (albeit in a highly constrained way) with a high degree of success, correctly identifying the acoustic context in 69.4% of 49 cases tested. Figure 4 shows that the majority of contexts were correctly identified, and, where mis-classification occurred, this was mostly of a neighbouring (similar) context. The performance of the responsibility estimator varies with the nature of the context. Mis-identification of the context more often occurs where there is little distortion and hence little difference between the model estimates. This is evident where the sound source directly faced the robot head, so that all models produced similar estimates. The identification rate in this case was only 14.3%, no better than chance. Confusion can also occur where the incorrect model happens to produce a smaller error than the correct model as seen in Fig. 5b. Success was greatest where the sound source faced away from the robot head, and there was a clearer distinction between contexts. In terms of localization of the sound source, however, this may not matter, as the goal is to identify the most appropriate model- even if that model did not learn in the presented context. It is anticipated that this technique could be used to augment more classical approaches to sound source localization (including the simple version of ITD used here).

Future work will include mixing model outputs in proportion to their responsibility estimates, and it is anticipated that this will in particular facilitate the adaptation to novel contexts and improve the overall accuracy of the sound source azimuth estimate. This system can only confirm correct model selection after orientation of the robot head (in the real system) to produce a posterior likelihood that the selected model is appropriate. Future work may also include investigation of a responsibility predictor which generates a prior responsibility based on contextual signals. Finally, we wish to investigate to what extent the system could learn de novo, as described in [14].

Acknowledgement. The authors wish to thank Ahmad Sheikh for his contribution to developing the moving sound source apparatus.

References

1. Argentieri, S., Danès, P., Souères, P.: A survey on sound source localization in robotics: from binaural to array processing methods. Comput. Speech Lang. **34**(1), 87–112 (2015)
2. Dean, P., Porrill, J., Ekerot, C.F., Jorntell, H., Ekerot, C.-F.: The cerebellar microcircuit as an adaptive filter: experimental and computational evidence (report). Nat. Rev. Neurosci. **11**(1), 30 (2010)

3. Porrill, J., Dean, P., Anderson, S.R.: Adaptive filters and internal models: multi-level description of cerebellar function. Neural Netw. **47**, 134–149 (2013)
4. Porrill, J., Dean, P., Stone, J.V.: Recurrent cerebellar architecture solves the motor-error problem. Proc. Royal Soc. B Biol. Sci. **271**(1541), 789–796 (2004)
5. Assaf, T., Wilson, E.D., Anderson, S., Dean, P., Porrill, J., Pearson, M.J.: Visual-tactile sensory map calibration of a biomimetic whiskered robot. In: 2016 IEEE International Conference on Robotics and Automation (ICRA), pp. 967–972. IEEE (2016)
6. Blauert, J.: Spatial Hearing: The Psychophysics of Human Sound Localization, vol. Rev. MIT Press, Cambridge, Mass, London (1997)
7. Imamizu, H., Kawato, M.: Cerebellar internal models: implications for the dexterous use of tools. Cerebellum **11**(2), 325–335 (2012). (London, England)
8. Baumann, O., Borra, R., Bower, J., Cullen, K., Habas, C., Ivry, R., Leggio, M., Mattingley, J., Molinari, M., Moulton, E., Paulin, M., Pavlova, M., Schmahmann, J., Sokolov, A.: Consensus paper: the role of the cerebellum in perceptual processes. Cerebellum **14**(2), 197–220 (2015)
9. Fujita, M.: Adaptive filter model of the cerebellum. Biol. Cybern. **45**(3), 195–206 (1982)
10. Marr, D.: A theory of cerebellar cortex. J. Physiol. **202**(2), 437–470 (1969)
11. Albus, J.S.: A theory of cerebellar function. Math. Biosci. **10**(12), 25–61 (1971)
12. Sejnowski, T.J.: Storing covariance with nonlinearly interacting neurons. J. Math. Biol. **4**(4), 303–321 (1977)
13. Wolpert, D.M., Kawato, M.: Multiple paired forward and inverse models for motor control. Neural Netw. **11**(78), 1317–1329 (1998)
14. Haruno, M., Wolpert, D.M., Kawato, M.: Mosaic model for sensorimotor learning and control. Neural Comput. **13**(10), 2201–2220 (2001)
15. Sugimoto, N., Haruno, M., Doya, K., Kawato, M.: Mosaic for multiple-reward environments. Neural Comput. **24**(3), 577–606 (2012)

A Comparison of Analytical and Empirical Controllers for the SLIP Hopper

Matthew F. Hale$^{(\boxtimes)}$, Jonathan L. du Bois, and Pejman Iravani

University of Bath, Bath BA2 7AY, UK
m.hale2@bath.ac.uk

Abstract. The Spring-Loaded Inverted Pendulum (SLIP) model poses a challenging control problem, important for the development of legged robots, due to the difficultly in solving the stance phase of the dynamics. Multiple attempts have been made to approximate these dynamics to allow for an analytical control method; here four of these methods have been compared for controlling agile hopping, where there are large changes in forward velocity across a single stance. In addition, a new, empirical, approach has been demonstrated. In this, a simple control law is formulated, based on some simple approximations, which allows the parameters to be selected empirically through simulation. This has led to a controller able to offer similar performance to the best analytical approximation but with a much simpler form. This empirical controller may present new opportunities for controlling more complex dynamics and the development of a self-tuning method in future work.

1 Introduction and Related Work

The use of legs for transport is almost universal in the animal kingdom, and yet very rare in man-made machines. Legs can potentially allow robots to traverse difficult, discontinuous terrain and negotiate environments designed for people, such as inside buildings and climbing staircases. However, progress has been hindered by two major shortcomings: low efficiency and difficulty of control.

These two problems are not unrelated; the difficulties in controlling dynamic motions have lead to a reliance on high-gain control and limiting motion to slow, static gaits which are inherently inefficient. By contrast, animals move with a dynamic motion which allows energy to be maintained from one step to the next, increasing efficiency.

The Spring-Loaded Inverted Pendulum (SLIP) model for legged locomotion, first described in the 1980s [1], has become the standard model for studying the stability and control of dynamic gaits. As illustrated in Fig. 1, the model consists of a point mass body and a massless leg. During the flight phase, when the foot is not in contact with the ground, the motion is ballistic, with gravity the only force. However, when the foot hits the ground, the stance phase, the spring-like leg is compressed. Although this model appears very simple, there exist no closed form analytical solution to the stance phase dynamics. This fact has motivated

© Springer International Publishing AG 2017
Y. Gao et al. (Eds.): TAROS 2017, LNAI 10454, pp. 79–85, 2017.
DOI: 10.1007/978-3-319-64107-2_7

the search for approximate solutions which can be computed analytically and used to control the full dynamics.

Early work in robotic leg locomotion made no attempt to solve the SLIP stance dynamics. For example, classic work by Raibert used simple manually tuned proportional controllers [4], and Zeglin and Brown instead used the "ball-hopper" model, which assumes an instantaneous stance like that of a bouncing ball [8]. In the last few decades, there have been several attempts to approximate the stance phase of the SLIP hopper, with the objective of controlling its motion. These will be described in Sect. 3, but follow a general pattern of increasing accuracy at the cost of greater algebraic complexity. Geyer [3] began this with a simple approximation assuming small angles and small leg displacement, which was extended by Saranli [5] with an explicit correction for the asymmetric effects of gravity. Most recently, Yu [7] used a Taylor series truncation to produce a more accurate approximation. Schwind's approach [6] was somewhat different, providing an iterative solution produced applying the mean value theorem to a Hamiltonian dynamics based solution.

The objective of this simulation study is to compare these approximations for controlling the forward velocity of a 2D SLIP hopper under agile motion, where the variations in velocity may be large. These will also be compared against a simple, pre-tuned, empirical controller, taking the somewhat more pragmatic approach that the exact stance phase motion is not needed, so long as the relationship between the control input and the desired output can be captured. A biped runner, such as a human, is generally capable of stopping in a single step from a slow run; it seems both desirable and reasonable that when controlling a robotic runner such an action should also be possible.

2   SLIP Dynamics

From the system in Fig. 1, a reference length is defined as the rest leg length, r_0, and a reference time scale as $s = \sqrt{r_0/g}$. Dimensionless lengths, represented with

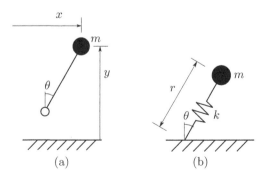

Fig. 1. SLIP model for (a) flight phase and (b) stance phase.

a bar, are defined as a multiple of r_0 and all derivatives, $\bar{(\,)}'$, in terms of the dimensionless time, $\bar{t} = t/s$. The flight dynamics are simple ballistic motion under gravity, which is trivial to solve. The stance phase dynamics are interesting, with no closed form solution:

$$\bar{r}'' = k^*(1 - \bar{r}) - \cos(\bar{\theta}) + \bar{r}(\bar{\theta}')^2 \tag{1a}$$

$$\bar{\theta}'' = \frac{1}{\bar{r}}\sin\bar{\theta} - \frac{2\bar{\theta}'\bar{r}'}{\bar{r}} \tag{1b}$$

The dimensionless stiffness $k^* = \frac{kr_0}{mg}$ describes similar systems, chosen for this simulation study as $k^* = 10$, a typical value for bipedal running [2].

3   Existing Analytical Approximations

The flight phase can easily be solved analytically, but the stance phase dynamics require approximation, either by numerical methods or using assumptions to allow for an analytical solution. Ideally, this approximation should be both fast and accurate to allow good real time control of a robot. This section will outline some such approximations from the literature, which will be compared in this paper; the full derivations and details can be found in the relevant references.

Schwind (2000): In a different approach from the others considered here, the system is modelled using Hamiltonian dynamics, with the mean value theorem being applied to produce iterative solutions [6].

Geyer (2005): This is a much used approximation, which has the benefit of a simple, easy to calculate algebraic form. The main assumptions are small angles and small leg compression [3].

Saranli (2010): Here the approximation based on Geyer's approach is improved with the addition of explicit improvements to compensate for the asymmetric effects of gravity, which should improve performance. Also included is a correction for damping, although these are not applicable here as the model is lossless [5].

Yu (2012): A more algebraically complex approximation to the stance dynamics, using a perturbation solution [7].

4   Empirical Controller

This section will develop a novel alternative to analytical approximations, by taking an empirical approach. The approximations in Sect. 3 give the liftoff conditions as function of touchdown conditions. However, to control the SLIP hopper the reverse is required: the touchdown angle must be chosen to meet a desired liftoff condition, such as forward speed. Consider Fig. 2; at the nth apex, the current forward velocity ($\bar{x}'_n$) is measured. At this point, the nth touchdown angle (θ_n^{td}) must be chosen, with the aim of making the the forward velocity of the next apex ($\bar{x}'_{n+1}$) equal to some target velocity ($\bar{x}'_{tgt}$), which may be different from the current velocity.

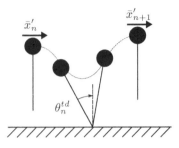

Fig. 2. The problem being considered: the relationship from the nth apex velocity to the $(n+1)^{th}$, as a function of the touchdown angle. Note that angles are defined as positive clockwise, so in the example shown θ_n^{td} is negative.

4.1 Controller Formulation

The objective of here is to find an expression for the required touchdown angle, with only a few constants which can then be empirically tuned through simulations. Firstly, consider the steady state case where $\bar{x}'_n = \bar{x}'_{n+1} = \bar{x}'_{ss}$ and $\bar{\theta}_n^{td} = -\bar{\theta}^{ss}$. If gravity is neglected during stance, the system will oscillate at its natural frequency and the dimensionless stance time will be approximately $\pi\sqrt{1/k^*}$. Also assuming a constant horizontal velocity and small angles, the horizontal displacement during stance phase is:

$$\Delta\bar{x} \approx 2\bar{\theta}^{ss} \approx \bar{x}'_{ss}\pi\sqrt{1/k^*} \tag{2}$$

Rearranging yields:

$$\bar{\theta}_n^{td} = -\bar{\theta}^{ss} \approx -\left(\frac{\pi}{2\sqrt{k^*}}\right)\bar{x}'_{ss} \tag{3}$$

Now the effect of deviating from this neutral angle will be considered; a trivial case is where $\bar{x}' = 0$, $\bar{\theta}_{ss} = 0$. Assuming small angles and an instantaneous stance phase, the change in forward velocity, $\Delta\bar{x}'$, is found to be:

$$\Delta\bar{x}' \approx 2\sqrt{2\bar{y}^{apex}}\,\bar{\theta}^\Delta \tag{4}$$

Combining (3) and (4) and collecting constants, we have achieved an equation for touchdown angle with two tunable parameters, K_1 and K_2:

$$\bar{\theta}_n^{td} = \underbrace{-K_1\bar{x}'_n}_{\bar{\theta}^{ss}} + \underbrace{K_2\Delta\bar{x}'}_{\bar{\theta}^\Delta} \tag{5}$$

4.2 Numerical Tuning

The values of K_1 and K_2 from (5) could be chosen using the approximations described. However, the inaccuracies introduced by the crude assumptions can be reduced by instead choosing these gains empirically through simulations.

Figures 3 and 4 show the estimation of K_1 and K_2 for the chosen parameters of $k^* = 10$ and $\bar{y}_n^{apex} = 1.1$. It can be seen that the linear relationships predicted by Eq. 5 holds well for finding K_1, where $\Delta\bar{x}' = 0$, and from finding K_2 when $\bar{x}'_n = 0$.

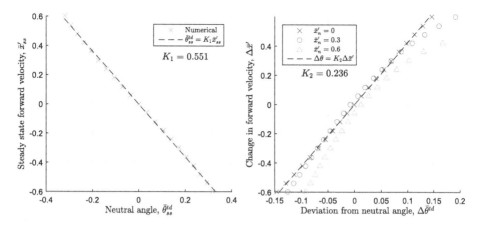

Fig. 3. Finding K_1.   **Fig. 4.** Finding K_2.

4.3 Additional Correction Term

It can be seen in Fig. 4 that as the initial speed, $\bar{x}'_n$, increases, the approximation for $\bar{\theta}^{\Delta}$ degrades. It has been found that this can be improved by adding a correction to K_2 proportional to $(1 - \cos\bar{\theta}_{ss})$, so:

$$\bar{\theta}^{td}_n = \underbrace{-K_1\bar{x}'_n}_{\bar{\theta}^{ss}} + \underbrace{\left[K_2 + K_3(1 - \cos(K_1\bar{x}'_n))\right]\Delta\bar{x}'}_{\bar{\theta}^{\Delta}} \tag{6}$$

This relationship is plotted in Fig. 5, which can be used to find an estimate for K_3. When this additional term is added to the controller, it will be described as the "three part empirical" controller, to distinguish it from the original "two part empirical" controller from (5).

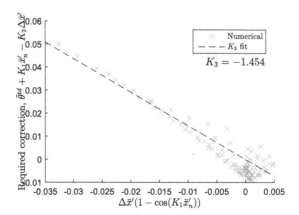

Fig. 5. Finding K_3.

5   Simulation Results

Controllers have been implemented based on each of the approaches in Sects. 3 and 4 and used to control a numerical simulation of the full SLIP dynamics using Matlab. These simulations aim to test the controllers' ability to make large changes in forward velocity over a single stance phase. In particular, a range of starting velocities of $\bar{x}'_n = [0, 0.6]$ and target velocities of $\bar{x}'_{n+1} = [0, 0.6]$ have been chosen. This corresponds to stopping or staring a jogging pace in a single step for a human or human-sized robot.

The results are compared in Fig. 6, plotted against the desired change in velocity ($\Delta\bar{x}' = \bar{x}'_{tgt} - \bar{x}'_n$); the magnitude of this value corresponds to how far from a symmetric stance the motion is. As starting velocity is always positive, positive values $\Delta\bar{x}'$ mean a increase in speed, and negative values slowing down or stopping.

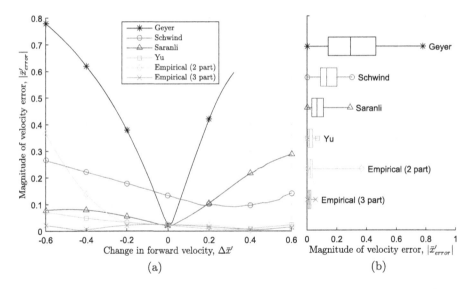

Fig. 6. The average velocity error for each controller, plotted (a) against $\Delta\bar{x}'$ and (b) as a box plot, showing the minimum, lower quartile, median, upper quartile and maximum of the error for each controller.

6   Conclusions

The analytical approximations compared here follow a pattern of, over time, increasingly algebraically complex formulations which are able to better capture the non-integrable stance phase dynamics. The novel empirical approach proposed shows comparable performance to the best approximation (Yu 2012). Although prior tuning is required, here done through systematic simulations, this approach offers several potential advantages. Firstly, although the empirical parameters K_1 and K_2 must be found, there is no need to explicitly find the physical system parameters, such as leg stiffness or body mass. For more complex or realistic model, with non-linear spring and frictional effects, body inertia and foot mass, finding these system parameters may be more involved than finding the required empirical gains. Secondly, the small number of controller gains suggests the possibility that these could be self-tuned, on-line during hopping. This would allow the controller to adapt to changing conditions, such as soft ground or a change in mass. Applying this controller to a hardware prototype and investigating self-tuning are areas of ongoing and future work.

References

1. Blickhan, R.: The spring-mass model for running and hopping. J. Biomech. **22**(11–12), 1217–1227 (1989)
2. Blickhan, R., Full, R.J.: Similarity in multilegged locomotion: bouncing like a monopode. J. Comp. Physiol. A **173**(5), 509–517 (1993)
3. Geyer, H., Seyfarth, A., Blickhan, R.: Spring-mass running: simple approximate solution and application to gait stability. J. Theoret. Biol. **232**(3), 315–328 (2005)
4. Raibert, M.H.: Legged Robots That Balance. MIT Press, Cambridge (1986)
5. Saranli, U., Arslan, Ö., Ankarali, M.M., Morgül, Ö.: Approximate analytic solutions to non-symmetric stance trajectories of the passive spring-loaded inverted pendulum with damping. Nonlinear Dyn. **62**(4), 729–742 (2010)
6. Schwind, W.J., Koditschek, D.: Approximating the stance map of a 2-DOF monoped runner. J. Nonlinear Sci. **10**(5), 533–568 (2000)
7. Yu, H., Li, M., Wang, P., Cai, H.: Approximate perturbation stance map of the SLIP runner and application to locomotion control. J. Bionic Eng. **9**(4), 411–422 (2012)
8. Zeglin, G., Brown, B.: Control of a bow leg hopping robot. In: Proceedings of 1998 IEEE International Conference on Robotics and Automation (Cat. No. 98CH36146), 1 May, pp. 793–798 (1998)

Design and Testing of a Parallel Manipulator for Space Micro-vibration Simulation

Shuai He[1,2], Zhenbang Xu[1,2(✉)], Xiaoming Wang[1,2], Ang Li[1,2], and Qi Huo[1,2]

[1] Innovation Lab of Space Robot System, Changchun Institute of Optics,
Fine Mechanics and Physics, Chinese Academy of Sciences,
No. 3888 Dong Nanhu Road, Changchun 130033, China
xiaoxiao4032@126.com, xuzhenbang@gmail.com, wangxm9301@163.com,
bcleon@126.com, 514590249@qq.com
[2] University of Chinese Academy of Sciences, Beijing 100049, China

Abstract. A micro-vibration shaking platform is required for performance testing of sensitive instruments in a micro-vibration environment on-board spacecraft before launch. In this study, a parallel manipulator is designed, which can reproduce 6-DOF space micro-vibrations. The important parts of the manipulator are optimized. Controlling the parallel manipulator is based on transfer function. The control principle and the transfer function testing are introduced. Because of the small structural damping coefficient of the system, the transfer function is simplified from a complex matrix to real matrix. Since the parallel manipulator be-haves slightly nonlinearly, an iterative control strategy is used to approach the desired acceleration step by step. The results from micro-vibrations testing show that the parallel manipulator can simulate 6-DOF space micro-vibrations and the iterative control strategy has better precision for the micro-vibrations control.

Keywords: Parallel manipulator · Micro-vibrations · Transfer function

1 Introduction

Devices, such as reaction wheel assemblies (RWAs) and control momentum gyroscopes (CMGs), mounted on spacecraft cause micro-vibrations of the spacecrafts main body during in-orbit operations [1]. The space micro-vibrations significantly affect accuracy in pointing, stability, and other important performance indices for large-caliber, high-resolution optical loads (James Webb space telescope, Space Inter-ferometry Mission et al.), and therefore ground testing is needed to test imaging quality under micro-vibration. Since current shake tables are unable to reproduce the space micro-vibrations which have the characteristics of low amplitude, a wide frequency range, and multiple directions, development of a micro-vibration shaking platform is needed.

Kamesh, Zhou Weiyong et al. [2–4] analyzed the micro-vibrations generated from a RWA to verify its performance as a vibration isolation system. The RWA

© Springer International Publishing AG 2017
Y. Gao et al. (Eds.): TAROS 2017, LNAI 10454, pp. 86–100, 2017.
DOI: 10.1007/978-3-319-64107-2_8

simulator was used to simulate micro-vibrations. Park et al. [5, 6] proposed two different kinds of multi-dimensional micro-vibration simulators. One simulator consisted of six identical single-axis micro-vibration actuators, configured as a "Cube", and the performance of the single-axis actuator was tested. The other simulator generated multi-dimensional disturbances using three actuators mounted on three mutually perpendicular plate surfaces. Vose et al. [7] designed a simulator comprising a moving platform, a base, six voice coil motors, and flexible connecting pipes, which can produce a micro-vibration velocity field. They developed a theoretical model of the simulation platform and tested the platforms performance. With the aim of overcoming drawbacks of small work space and slow vibration from the first generation, the second generation of simulators designed following the GoughC-Stewart configuration greatly increased the working space and vibration speed [8]. The parallel structure is used in most of the above micro-vibration platforms.

Because of the advantages of high maneuverability, precision, and high stiffness, parallel manipulators such as the Gough-Stewart platform (GSP) have been recently employed in various applications. The control strategy of parallel manipulator is crucial in achieving good performance. Strategies can be divided into two types [9, 10]: joint space control and task space control. The hinge space control method regards each branch of the parallel manipulator as a single-inputCsingle-output system. The influence between the branches is treated as disturbance so that the most widely used PID control can be transferred to parallel manipulator control. This method neglects the dynamic characteristics of the parallel manipulator; without a dynamic model, high-precision control cannot be achieved. The task space control method is currently the developing trend in parallel manipulator control, with the computed torque control method in task space control being especially favored by researchers [11]. The computed torque control method decouples the dynamic equations of the parallel manipulator and is essentially a special application of feedback linearization for nonlinearity. Nevertheless, poor robustness is its main disadvantage. Because of uncertainties in parameters and modeling errors, the system cannot achieve accurate cancellation, and hence the controller is sometimes unstable. The above control strategy is mainly concerned with the displacement and velocity trajectory recovery and tracking of the upper platform. Although [12, 13] describe the parallel manipulators acceleration control methods, while they are only suitable for shake tables with a single degree of freedom. A robust proportional-integral (PI) controller [14] considering the effects of uncertainties (such as modeling errors et al.) was designed for the acceleration control of the parallel manipulator, while it needs high-precision feedback displacement (The displacement amplitude of the upper platform is about 0.1 m when 1 mg acceleration disturbance at 50 Hz is needed.).

In order to simulate the micro-vibration environment of the optical load, a parallel manipulator design scheme is proposed and the structure design is carried out. The iterative control strategy based on transfer function is used to control the accelerations of the parallel manipulator. This method does not need to deduce the dynamic equation of the parallel manipulator and has the advantages of simple principle and convenient realization. The rest of the paper is laid out as follows. In Sect. 2, the structure of each part of the parallel manipulator are designed and described in detail. In Sect. 3, the control principle based on the transfer function, the transfer-function test, and the iterative control strategy are introduced. In Sect. 4, the results of the micro-vibration test performed on the parallel manipulator are presented. Conclusions are discussed in Sect. 5.

2   Structure

The parallel manipulator under study improves on the first-generation generator for which the 7th-order mode was low and the vibration mode was mainly driven by the bending of the support leg [15]. The redesign of the driving leg was key in improving the parallel manipulator mode and effective working bandwidth. Concurrently, while targeting the resistance to electrical flow, hinge bearing block, and other problems of the first-generation generator, the hinge and both the upper and lower platforms were also redesigned. In essence, the parallel manipulator consists of upper and lower platforms, and six legs. The legs are connected to both platforms using hinges. All upper hinges each have three degrees of freedom whereas the lower hinges each have two degrees of freedom (Fig. 1).

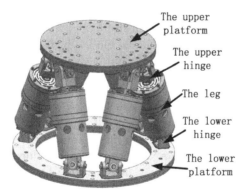

Fig. 1. Structure of the parallel manipulator

2.1   Driving Legs

Each driving leg (Fig. 2) has a voice motor which is the dynamic component. The sleeve protects the motor and forms the connection between the motor and the spring pieces. The spring pieces provide support for the motors mover and the legs superstructure. The stop plates are used to prevent the axial displacement of the leg from exceeding design specifications (2 mm) and avoid damage to the structure. The spacing in the spring pieces without changing the platforms geometric configuration is increased to increase the bending stiffness of the two parallel spring pieces.

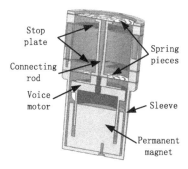

Fig. 2. Structure of the leg

The springs bending stiffness affects the effective working bandwidth just like the first-generation parallel manipulator. Therefore, it is necessary to redesign the spring. The new spring is made up of six sets of grooved arcs and the number of connections between the internal and the periphery increased to 6 (Fig. 3). The outer diameter (90 mm), thickness (0.4 mm) and material (Q-Be2) of the two generations of springs are kept unchanged. The bending stiffness of the new spring and the old one are 6060.6N.mm/rad, 2252.2N.mm/rad and the new springs bending stiffness has been significantly improved.

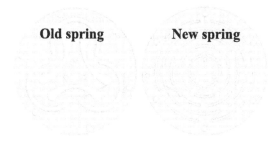

Fig. 3. Structure of the two generations of springs

2.2   Hinges

The upper and lower platforms are connected to the legs by hinges. An angular contact bearing is used in each hinge; the method of setting the bearing preload is compression of the inner ring, which ensures the deformation of the inner and outer rings of the bearing and eliminate bearing clearance. Each bearing is arranged in back-to-back form so that the hinge can bear a large axial force. To enhance the stiffness of the hinge, the bearing support is designed as a one-piece U-shaped structure (Fig. 4).

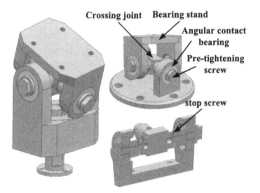

Fig. 4. Structure of the hinge

2.3 Upper and Lower Platforms

The dynamic component of the parallel manipulator is the voice motor, which consists of a mover, a stator, and a permanent magnet. The mover moves in the stators magnetic field and generates an induced electromotive force. Because there was no insulation between the six driving legs in the first-generation parallel manipulator, the induced electromotive forces generated between the legs interacted with each other, affecting the control. To solve this problem, the upper and lower platforms were designed with a three-layer structure. The middle layer is made of an insulating phenolic resin and is connected to the legs, whereas the other layers are made of steel, which improves the platforms stiffness (Fig. 5).

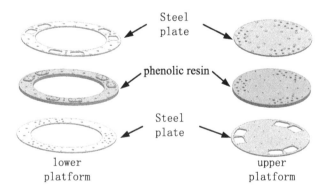

Fig. 5. Structure of the lower platform

3   Control Strategy

3.1   Control Principle Based on the Transfer Function

The actuator forces are control inputs of the system and the linear and angular accelerations of the upper platform are outputs of the system. We assume the system is linear (a sinusoidal input of frequency ω produces a sinusoidal output of the same frequency). A sinusoidal actuator force is applied to the first leg and the acceleration responses of the upper platform are measured. Let the Fourier transform of the actuator force be $F_1 = f_1 e^{j\omega}$ and the Fourier transform of the accelerations of the upper platform be

$$A_1 = e^{j\omega} \left[a_{11} e^{j\varphi_{11}}, a_{21} e^{j\varphi_{21}}, a_{31} e^{j\varphi_{31}}, a_{41} e^{j\varphi_{41}}, a_{51} e^{j\varphi_{51}}, a_{61} e^{j\varphi_{61}} \right]^T$$

then the transfer function of the output accelerations relative to the actuator force of this leg is:

$$
\begin{aligned}
H_1 &= [H_{11}, H_{21}, H_{31}, H_{41}, H_{51}, H_{61}]^T \\
&= \frac{\left[a_{11} e^{j\varphi_{11}}, a_{21} e^{j\varphi_{21}}, a_{31} e^{j\varphi_{31}}, a_{41} e^{j\varphi_{41}}, a_{51} e^{j\varphi_{51}}, a_{61} e^{j\varphi_{61}} \right]^T}{f_1}
\end{aligned}
\tag{1}
$$

The transfer functions of the output accelerations relative to the actuator forces of other legs are similarly obtained. Let the transfer function of the output accelerations relative to the actuator forces of all six legs at frequency ω be $H(\omega)$, then the relationship between the Fourier transform $F(\omega)$ of the actuator forces and the Fourier transform $A(\omega)$ of the output accelerations is:

$$H(\omega)F(\omega) = A(\omega) \tag{2}$$

where $H(\omega)$, $F(\omega)$, and $A(\omega)$ expressions are:

$$
H(\omega) = \begin{bmatrix}
H_{11} & H_{12} & H_{13} & H_{14} & H_{15} & H_{16} \\
H_{21} & H_{22} & H_{23} & H_{24} & H_{25} & H_{26} \\
H_{31} & H_{32} & H_{33} & H_{34} & H_{35} & H_{36} \\
H_{41} & H_{42} & H_{43} & H_{44} & H_{45} & H_{46} \\
H_{51} & H_{52} & H_{53} & H_{54} & H_{55} & H_{56} \\
H_{61} & H_{62} & H_{63} & H_{64} & H_{65} & H_{66}
\end{bmatrix}
\tag{3}
$$

$$F(\omega) = \left[f_1 e^{j\theta_1}, f_2 e^{j\theta_2}, f_3 e^{j\theta_3}, f_4 e^{j\theta_4}, f_5 e^{j\theta_5}, f_6 e^{j\theta_6} \right]^T e^{j\omega} \tag{4}$$

$$A(\omega) = \left[a_1 e^{j\alpha_1}, a_2 e^{j\alpha_2}, a_3 e^{j\alpha_3}, a_4 e^{j\alpha_4}, a_5 e^{j\alpha_5}, a_6 e^{j\alpha_6} \right]^T e^{j\omega} \tag{5}$$

The actuator forces $F(\omega)$ can be obtained using $F(\omega) = H(\omega)^{-1}A(\omega)$ and the time domain function $f(t)$ of the actuator forces can be obtained applying the inverse Fourier transform of $F(\omega)$.

3.2 Transfer Function Testing

Following [16], we determine the six-dimensional attitude through the outputs of six acceleration sensors installed at six locations. Therefore the testing later in this paper is to control the responses of the six acceleration sensors. Less accuracy in sensor installing is needed if we use an improved configuration (Fig. 6). The accelerations at point O are as follows:

$$
\begin{aligned}
a_x &= (2A_3 - A_1 - A_2)/3 \\
a_y &= \sqrt{3}(A_1 - A_2)/3 \\
a_z &= (A_4 + A_5 + A_6)/3 \\
\dot{\omega}_x &= (A_4 + A_5 - 2A_6)/(3R) \\
\dot{\omega}_y &= \sqrt{3}(A_5 - A_4)/(3R) \\
\dot{\omega}_z &= (A_1 + A_2 + A_3)/(3R)
\end{aligned}
\tag{6}
$$

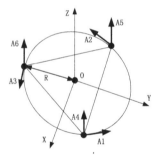

Fig. 6. Positional configuration of the acceleration sensors

The input force of each leg and the input current are directly proportional, and therefore the input force of each leg can be measured from its input current. By collecting simultaneously the drive currents and the acceleration signals of the sensors, the phase relationship between the input forces and the output accelerations is established and the transfer function can be obtained using the method described in Sect. 2.2. The transfer function testing flow is shown in Fig. 7. To achieve automatic control, the data acquisition device needs at least twelve input channels (for the six acceleration sensors and for the six input forces of the legs).

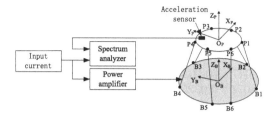

Fig. 7. Procedures for transfer function test method

When we used the method described above to measure the transfer functions, the absolute values of the phase differences between input forces and output accelerations were found to be near $0°$, $180°$ or $360°$, which indicates that the coefficient of damping for the structure is small and enables a simpler testing method for the transfer functions to be applied.

This new testing method is as follows: when the coefficient of damping for the structure is small, the transfer function can be represented as a matrix of real numbers; the positive and negative numbers represents phase differences of $0°$ and $180°$ respectively. The sign of each value in the transfer function matrix needs to be calibrated before commencing automatic control and the calibration matrix can be obtained experimentally. The experimental method for determining the calibration matrix is to drive a single leg using a sinusoidal vibration and measure the phase difference between the input force and the acceleration responses. If the absolute value of the phase difference is close to $0°$ or $360°$, the corresponding term of the calibration matrix is $+1$. If the absolute value of the phase difference is close to $180°$, the corresponding term of the calibration matrix is -1. The calibration matrix we obtained was:

$$
sign = \begin{bmatrix}
-1 & -1 & 1 & -1 & 1 & 1 \\
1 & 1 & -1 & -1 & 1 & -1 \\
1 & -1 & 1 & 1 & -1 & -1 \\
1 & 1 & 1 & 1 & 1 & 1 \\
1 & 1 & 1 & 1 & 1 & 1 \\
1 & 1 & 1 & 1 & 1 & 1
\end{bmatrix} \tag{7}
$$

Let H_{ij} be the ratio of the response acceleration amplitude to the input force amplitude for Sensor j when only Leg i is driven by a sinusoidal vibration. The transfer function H is then

$$
H = sign. \times \begin{bmatrix}
H_{11} & H_{12} & H_{13} & H_{14} & H_{15} & H_{16} \\
H_{21} & H_{22} & H_{23} & H_{24} & H_{25} & H_{26} \\
H_{31} & H_{32} & H_{33} & H_{34} & H_{35} & H_{36} \\
H_{41} & H_{42} & H_{43} & H_{44} & H_{45} & H_{46} \\
H_{51} & H_{52} & H_{53} & H_{54} & H_{55} & H_{56} \\
H_{61} & H_{62} & H_{63} & H_{64} & H_{65} & H_{66}
\end{bmatrix} \tag{8}
$$

To achieve automatic control, the data acquisition device only needs six input channels (for the six acceleration sensors). The transfer function matrices obtained from the testing at 40 Hz, 60 Hz, and 80 Hz are as follows:

$$
H_{40} = \begin{bmatrix}
-0.0475 & -0.1025 & 0.0725 & -0.0193 & 0.07 & 0.0035 \\
0.07 & 0.0325 & -0.0525 & -0.1025 & 0.075 & -0.014 \\
0.0775 & -0.011 & 0.075 & 0.035 & -0.0575 & -0.1075 \\
0.0575 & 0.3 & 0.2975 & 0.22 & 0.24 & 0.075 \\
0.2275 & 0.0675 & 0.055 & 0.2925 & 0.2925 & 0.21 \\
0.2875 & 0.2175 & 0.235 & 0.07 & 0.0725 & 0.305
\end{bmatrix}
\tag{9}
$$

$$
H_{60} = \begin{bmatrix}
-0.0375 & -0.0925 & 0.08 & -0.0148 & 0.075 & 0.04 \\
0.0675 & 0.03 & -0.0525 & -0.1025 & 0.0725 & -0.0198 \\
0.085 & -0.0052 & 0.08 & 0.035 & -0.055 & -0.1025 \\
0.05 & 0.295 & 0.2925 & 0.2175 & 0.2375 & 0.07 \\
0.2175 & 0.0625 & 0.0475 & 0.2825 & 0.2875 & 0.1975 \\
0.28 & 0.22 & 0.24 & 0.065 & 0.07 & 0.3075
\end{bmatrix}
\tag{10}
$$

$$
H_{80} = \begin{bmatrix}
-0.0375 & -0.0925 & 0.0875 & -0.0133 & 0.08 & 0.0475 \\
0.06 & 0.025 & -0.0525 & -0.1075 & 0.065 & -0.0325 \\
0.1 & -0.0073 & 0.0875 & 0.04 & -0.05 & -0.095 \\
0.0875 & 0.34 & 0.325 & 0.2425 & 0.265 & 0.0925 \\
0.2175 & 0.07 & 0.0375 & 0.2875 & 0.3 & 0.1925 \\
0.275 & 0.245 & 0.2675 & 0.0675 & 0.08 & 0.3125
\end{bmatrix}
\tag{11}
$$

3.3 Control Strategy

The initial forces are obtained from $F_0(\omega_i) = H(\omega_i)^{-1}A(\omega_i)$. Because of non-linearity, there is a difference between the actual response accelerations and the desired accelerations, and a control strategy must be adopted so that the deviation range between the actual response accelerations and the desired accelerations is with-in an acceptable range. For this study, we used the iterative control strategy [8].

Let $F_j(\omega_i)$ be the control forces at step j, $A_j(\omega_i)$ the actual output accelerations at step j, and $e_j(\omega_i) = A_j(\omega_i) - A(\omega_i)$ the deviation of actual output accelerations from the desired accelerations. Then the control input forces of step $j + 1$ is updated using the iterative control penalty as follows:

$$
F_{j+1}(\omega_i) = F_j(\omega_i) + K_j(\omega_i)H(\omega_i)^{-1}e_j(\omega_i)
\tag{12}
$$

where $K_j(\omega_i)$ is the controller gain at frequency ω_i. In this study, $K_j(\omega_i)$ was set to 1.0 to achieve the desired control effect.

To diminish the deviation further, let $K_j(\omega_i)$ take values within a certain range (for example, 0.1 to 1, at intervals of 0.1) and set $K_j(\omega_i)$ to the value giving a minimum for the deviation. When the systems nonlinearity is significant and the transfer function of the iterative control is always the same, the error of the final control may become unacceptable. When this situation occurs, the iteration can be continued by updating the transfer function, the basic idea of which is as follows:

An extra input force $\Delta f_k(1 \times 1)$ at frequency ω_i is sent to Leg k at step j and the change of the output accelerations $\Delta a_k(6 \times 1)$ is measured. Then $\frac{\Delta a_k(6\times1)}{\Delta f_k(1\times1)}$ is the k-th column of the updated transfer function matrix.

A flow chart of the control strategy is shown in Fig. 8, where ε_1, ε_2 is the control precision tolerance, k the number of updating the transfer function, num the maximum number of iterations after updating the transfer function.

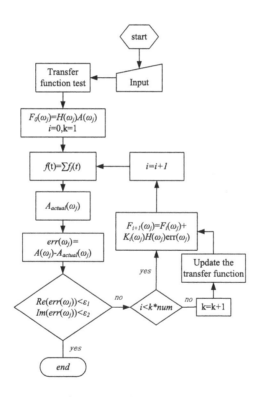

Fig. 8. Flow chart of the control strategy

Fig. 9. Micro-vibration testing devices

Table 1. Output accelerations at each iteration step for the single-frequency acceleration test

Conditions			A1 (mg)	A2 (mg)	A3 (mg)	A4 (mg)	A5 (mg)	A6 (mg)
1	40 Hz	Target	0.4	0.5	0.6	0.6	0.5	0.4
		Final output	0.4	0.5	0.6	0.6	0.5	0.39
		Errors	0%	0%	0%	0%	0%	2.5%
	60 Hz	Target	0.3	0.5	0.6	0.4	0.3	0.5
		Final output	0.3	0.49	0.61	0.41	0.31	0.49
		Errors	0%	2%	1.67%	2.5%	3.33%	2.0%
2	40 Hz	Target	0.3	0.3	0.5	0.6	0.7	0.6
		Final output	0.3	0.3	0.5	0.6	0.71	0.60
		Errors	0%	0%	0%	0%	1.43%	1.67%
	60 Hz	Target	0.4	0.3	0.6	0.5	0.7	0.7
		Final output	0.41	0.29	0.60	0.49	0.70	0.69
		Errors	2.5%	3.33%	0%	2%	0%	1.43%
	80 Hz	Target	0.5	0.5	0.3	0.2	0.3	0.4
		Final output	0.50	0.50	0.29	0.21	0.30	0.40
		Errors	0%	0%	3.33%	5%	0%	0%

4   Experimental Testing

The micro-vibration testing devices (Fig. 9) are composed of: (1) a power supply of the power amplifier, (2) a circuit board, (3) a power amplifier, (4) a power supply for the circuit board, (5) a spectrum analyzer, (6) a data acquisition computer, (7) a micro-vibration parallel manipulator, (8) a heavy load, (9) lifting ropes, (10) acceleration sensor, and (11) a support frame.

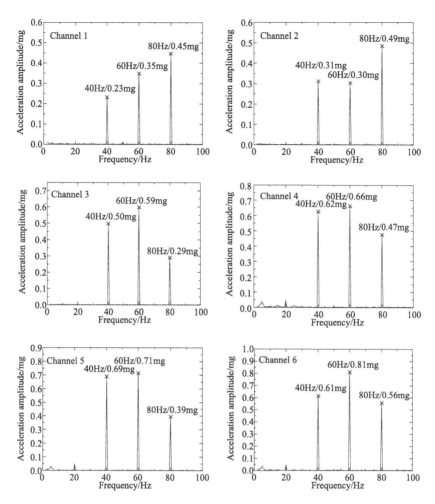

Fig. 10. Output accelerations at 1st iteration in Run 2

Two conditions are selected to test the micro-vibration parallel manipulator. Condition 1 simulates 40-Hz and 60-Hz acceleration disturbances and condition 2 simulates 40-Hz, 60-Hz and 80-Hz acceleration disturbances. Table 1 gives the target accelerations and the final output accelerations; Figs. 10 and 11 give the accelerations amplitude-frequency response curve at each iteration step in condition 2. The error of the actual output accelerations from the target accelerations (Table 1) is less than 5% after several iterations, which indicates that the parallel manipulator can simulate 6-DOF space micro-vibrations and the control strategy has better precision for the micro-vibrations control.

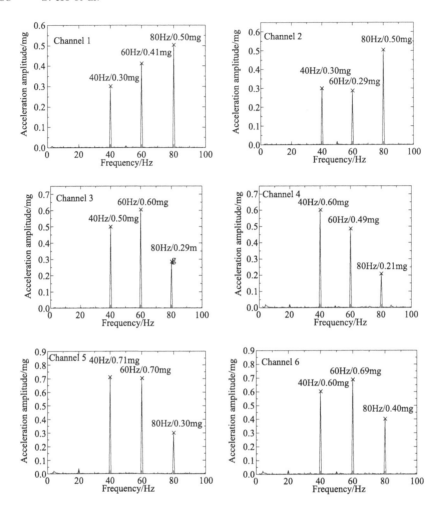

Fig. 11. Output accelerations at 2nd iteration in Run 2

5   Conclusions

This study presents the structural design, control, and testing of a parallel manipulator which can reproduce 6-DOF space micro-vibrations within 100 Hz. Controlling the parallel manipulator is based on transfer function. In transfer-function testing, the coefficient of damping of the system was found to be small, enabling the transfer function to be simplified from a complex to real matrix. Because the parallel manipulator behaves slightly nonlinearly, the iterative control based on the transfer function are used to approach the desired acceleration step by step. The results from micro-vibrations testing show that after several iterations the errors were less than 5%, showing that the parallel manipulator can simulate 6-DOF space micro-vibrations and the iterative control strategy has better precision for the micro-vibrations control.

Acknowledgments. This work was supported by the National Natural Science Foundation of China under Grant no. 11672290, the Jilin Scientific and Technological Development Program under Grant no. 20160520074JH, and the Youth Innovation Promotion Association, Chinese Academy of Sciences under Grant no. 2014195.

References

1. Laskin, R.A., Martin, M.S.: Control/structure system design of a spaceborne optical interferometer. In: Proceedings of the AAS/AIAA Astrodynamics Specialist Conference, pp. 369–395 (1989)
2. Kamesh, D., Pandiyan, R., Ghosal, A.: Passive vibration isolation of reaction wheel disturbances using a low frequency flexible space platform. J. Sound Vib. **331**, 1310–1330 (2012)
3. Zhou, W.Y., Li, D.X., Luo, Q., Jiang, J.P.: Design and test of a soft suspension system for cantilevered momentum wheel assembly. J. Aerosp. Eng. **227**(7), 1144–1160 (2012). doi:10.1177/0954410012451415
4. Zhou, W.Y., Li, D.X.: Experimental research on a vibration isolation platform for momentum wheel assembly. J. Sound Vib. **332**(5), 1157–1171 (2013)
5. Park, G., Lee, D.O., Han, J.H.: Development of multi-DOF active microvibration emula-tor. In: ASME Conference on Smart Materials, pp. 477–483 (2012)
6. Park, G., Lee, D.O., Han, J.H.: Development of multi-degree-of-freedom microvibration emulator for efficient Jitter test of spacecraft. J. Intell. Mater. Syst. Struct. **25**(9), 1069–1081 (2014)
7. Vose, T.H., Umbanhowar, P., Lynch, K.M.: Friction-induced velocity fields for point parts sliding on a rigid oscillated plate. Int. J. Manipulatorics Res. **28**(8), 1020–1039
8. Vose, T.H., Turpin, M.H., Dames, P.M.: Modeling, design, and control of 6-DOF flexure-based parallel mechanisms for vibratory manipulation. Mech. Mach. Theor. **64**, 111–130 (2013)
9. Paccot, F., Andreff, N., Martinet, P.: A review on the dynamic control of parallel kinematic machines: theory and experiments. Int. J. Manipulatorics Res. **28**(3), 395–416 (2009)
10. Kim, H.S., Cho, Y.M., Lee, K.: Robust nonlinear task space control for 6 DOF parallel manipulator. Automatica **41**(9), 1591–1600 (2005)
11. Yang, C.F., Huang, Q.T., Han, J.W.: Computed force and velocity control for spatial multi-DOF electro-hydraulic parallel manipulator. Mechatronics **22**, 715–722 (2012)
12. Stehman, M., Nakata, N.: Direct acceleration feedback control of shake tables with force stabilizaiton. J. Earthq. Eng. **17**, 736–749 (2013)
13. Nakata, N.: Acceleration trajectory tracking control for earthquake simulators. Eng. Struct. **32**(8), 2229–2236 (2005)
14. Yang, J.F., Xu, Z.B., Wu, Q.W., Zhu, M.C., He, S., Qin, C.: Dynamic modeling and control of a 6-DOF micro-vibration simulator. Mech. Mach. Theor. **104**, 350C369

15. Xin, J.: Optimization design of space multi-dimensional micro-vibration simulator based on six dimensional parallel mechianism. M.D thesis, Changchun Institute of Optics, Fine Mechanics and Physics, Chinese Academy of Sciences (2015). (Chinese)
16. Li, Z.F., Ren, W.J., Wang, A.P.: Study on acceleration measurement in space high quality microgravity active vibration isolation system. J. Vib. Shock **29**(12), 211–215 (2010). (Chinese)

The Automated Box and Blocks Test
an Autonomous Assessment Method of Gross
Manual Dexterity in Stroke Rehabilitation

Edwin Daniel Oña$^{(\boxtimes)}$, Alberto Jardón, and Carlos Balaguer

Robotics Lab, University Carlos III of Madrid, Avda. de la Universidad, 30,
28911 Leganés, Madrid, Spain
{eona,ajardon,balaguer}@ing.uc3m.es
http://www.roboticslab.uc3m.es

Abstract. Traditional motor assessment is carried out by clinicians using standard clinical tests in order to have objectivity in the evaluation, but this manual procedure is liable to the observer subjectivity. In this article, an automatic assessment system based on the Box and Blocks Test (BBT) of manual dexterity is presented. Also, the automatic test administration and the motor performance of the user is addressed. Through cameras RGB-D the execution of the test and the patient's movements are monitored. Based on colour segmentation, the cubes displaced by the user are detected and the traditional scoring is automatically calculated. Furthermore, a pilot trial in a hospital environment was conducted, to compare the automatic system and its effectiveness with respect to the traditional one. The results support the use of automatic assessment methods of motor functionality, which in combination with robotic rehabilitation systems, could address an autonomous and objective rehabilitation process.

Keywords: Automated · Assessment · Assistive · Manual dexterity · Rehabilitation · Stroke

1 Introduction

Since rehabilitation is a laborious process of expensive intervention, evaluating its therapeutic effectiveness is particularly important [12]. This assessment is commonly performed by health professionals themselves, using standardized tests in order to have objectivity in the evaluation, but which are susceptible to the subjectivity of the clinicians. In some cases, the evaluation methods are made up of well-defined exercises based on numerical tests (task-specific), which may be susceptible to be automated. Thus, an objective assessment of the physical condition of the subject will be obtained. Also, more time to evaluate the results will be provided to the therapist, who could correct the therapy method applied, change the level of difficulty or analyse in deep the process.

Currently, in addition to projects focused on the development of support robotic systems for rehabilitation, several research projects are also focused on

© Springer International Publishing AG 2017
Y. Gao et al. (Eds.): TAROS 2017, LNAI 10454, pp. 101–114, 2017.
DOI: 10.1007/978-3-319-64107-2_9

automating assessment methods based on neuromotor tests commonly used in hospitals. These traditional tests can be grouped by outcomes to be measured at any of these levels: Body functions/structure (impairment); Activities (refers to the whole person - formerly conceived as disability in the old ICIDH framework) and Participation (formerly referred to as handicap) [14]. According to this classification, some projects are developed within the *Body functions* category. In Otten et al. [10], an evaluation method based on low-cost sensors that record data of the user's movements is proposed. Their outcomes were compared with those obtained using the usual Fugl-Meyer Assessment (FMA) with similar results. Their conclusions suggest that the FMA is capable of being automated. Other attempt to automate part of the FMA is presented in Wang et al. study [16], in this case it is achieved using accelerometers and focusing on scores for shoulder and elbow movements.

Other studies seek to automate tests within the *Activity* category. In [11] a new system is proposed, called Rejoyce Arm and Hand Function Test (RAHFT), focused on the assessment of manual dexterity. This system uses the Rejoyce work station in which the participants perform manual dexterity tasks with the help of computer games. The authors state that this is the first manual dexterity test that does not rely on human judgement, offering a quantitative, standardised and remotely manageable assessment of the results. In [5] an automatic system is implemented, that objectively assess the upper limb functionality in post stroke rehabilitation. This system performs a post-processing of experimental data obtained whike performing reach tasks using the KINARM robotic system. In this case, the results are compared using the Chedoke-McMaster Stroke Assessment Scale (CMSA). In [15] an automatic evaluation based on the Wolf Motor Function Test (WMFT) is proposed. By using sensors which the users should be wearing, the time needed to complete 7 of the 17 tasks of the test is estimated. Other ongoing work is presented in [6], which aims to automate the Action Research Arm Test (ARAT). This paper has developed the automation of the ARATs grasp subtest, through the sensorizing of one of the objects used in the task, in this case a 7.5 cm cube. Finally, in [2] the Digital Box and Blocks Test (DBBT) is presented. It aims to automate the traditional BBT. The authors, using a Kinect® sensor, determine the number of transported blocks with a 90% success rate for 80 blocks. The system also detects the hand and its movements. However, the test administration is not addressed.

Of all the studies reviewed, several works are focused on detecting upper limb movements; either by using sensors the subject should wear; by sensorizing objects used in the test; or through computer vision systems. A common goal is to obtain automatic evaluation platforms that are objective, dynamic, that show repeatability, diagnostic capabilities and that can provide more information than the traditional scale. However, a complete automated system has not been implemented yet, and therefore, a system to be administered without any intervention of clinicians.

In this paper, the automation of the BBT scoring and the automatic administration of the test are studied. In Sect. 2, the methodology towards an automated assessment is presented. The method to count the blocks and the graphical interface functionality are described. The data analysis of a pilot trial results are shown in Sect. 3. Finally, the conclusions and future works are summarized in Sect. 4.

2 Methodology

For a rehabilitation process to be automated, the method to extract metrics and the degree of acceptance by both users and health professionals should be properly assessed. To design assistance rehabilitation systems, although the focus is on the subject to be treated, it is important to systematize the understanding of the requirements demanded by therapists in order to enable an easier integration of technology in their daily activities [13]. Regarding the method, those tests that are administered without direct contact of the professional are more susceptible to be automated. But it requires a proper patient performance, so a previous explanation of the procedure or a wizard to assist them is needed. Concerning metrics, it is essential to assess which ones give relevant information and are less invasive for the subject to be evaluated [1].

Thus, the BBT study is considered on the basis that the outcome is simple (total cubes transferred), the instructions test are systematic and clear, and the test development is well defined (three stages: training, dominant hand, and non-dominant hand). Also, for its wide use in clinical settings as an evaluation system in rehabilitation processes of people who have suffered a stroke. Complete BBT description is shown in [7].

The proposed system, named as the Automated Box and Blocks Test (ABBT) has two targets: to automate the scoring of the traditional BBT, and to enable the test administration, with the minimal participation of clinicians or without it. Thereby, two elements have been developed:

(a) *Automatic test scoring:* to automate the counting of cubes, and also obtaining additional information of the subject movements.
(b) *User interface:* to allow the therapist to administer the test at either the same or a remote place, to store the data obtained, to get an updated database, and to generate a historical report of previous sessions.

Based on that, the ABBT goes a step further than both the traditional test and the related study of DBBT [2], since the automatic test administration is addressed. The ABBT is made up of a portable and lightweight cube-shaped structure placed on a standard desk, as shown in Fig. 1. At the top of the structure, a Kinect® for Windows® V1 sensor is fixed. This is used for detecting the number of cubes displaced, as well as the hand movements while the subject performs the test. The BBT box is located on the desk and in the center of the structure.

The ABBT is implemented on Windows® 10, by using the Matlab® R2015b software. It provides, hardware support packages for devices such as Kinect® for Windows®. Besides, Matlab® software includes a set of toolboxes and libraries

Fig. 1. Proposed structure for the BBT automation at the Assistive Robotics Laboratory at the UC3M.

for image processing, and it also offers the graphical user interface development environment GUIDE to create a graphical user interface.

2.1 Automatic Test Scoring

The automatic counting process is developed in three stages:

(a) Detection of box edge,
(b) Segmentation by colour, and
(c) Score validation.

When test starts, the algorithm looks for the edge of the box. For that purpose, the depth data of Kinect® sensor is used. As result, both the left and the right compartments of the box are identified. Based on that, a region of interest (ROI) on the RGB image is defined to be processed. According to the hand to be evaluated (dominant or non-dominant), the corresponding ROI (left or right) is selected for the cubes counting. While the test period time is not complete, the counting process is executed. When the 60 s are over, the results are displayed through the interface. This above sequence is used on the three stages of the test. This method, combined with voice messages allows to administer the ABBT in an automatic way.

Detection of Box Edge. Kinect® sensor is placed on the top of the structure (see Fig. 1), and there is a distance of one meter up to the desk surface. Its position is fixed by using a holder made on ABS plastic in a low-cost 3D Printer.

Since the Kinect⊕ position remains unchanged, the distance from the sensor to the border of the BBT remains constant too. The process to detect the edge of the box, and differentiate between the two compartments is shown in Fig. 2. First, depth data are captured (see Fig. 2(a)), and after, a height threshold is applied, in this case 90 cm (distance from the box edge to the sensor). The points under this threshold are discarded, including the desk and the BBT bottom (see Fig. 2(b)). Morphological operations to reduce noise and to label the detected areas are applied to the thresholded image. Features based on several algorithms can be extracted from the processed image. In this case, using the *'BoundingBox'* function in Matlab⊕, the detected rectangles and its centroids are obtained from the image. According to the centroid coordinates, it is possible to identify both the left and the right compartments (see Fig. 2(c)). Finally, in Fig. 2(d) the ROI on the colour image are overlapped.

The left and right compartments identification is quite important, because it is the base to define the ROI in the colour image to be processed. Also, as this ROI changes according to the evaluation of the either dominant or non-dominant hand.

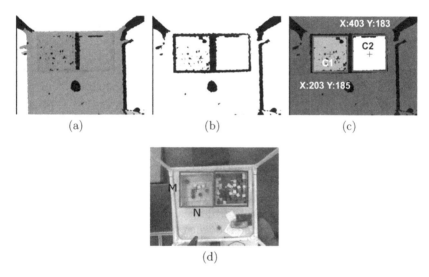

Fig. 2. Sequence for compartments identification: (a) depth image captured, (b) image after height threshold, (c) compartments detection with the position of centroids and, (d) ROI over the colour image.

Segmentation by Colour. To detect and to count cubes, the captured RGB images are segmented by colour, see Fig. 3. This is based on, the high contrast existing among the cubes colours of the BBT (red, green, blue and yellow), and also between them and the bottom of the box in beech colour. The colour images are captured with a resolution of 640×480 pixels. According to the compartments identification, a colour ROI (where the BBT is placed) is cropped

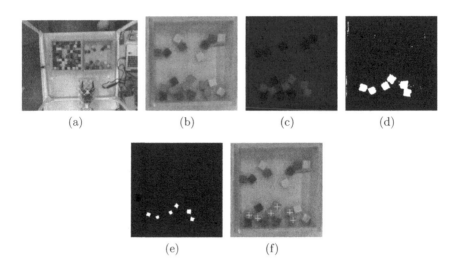

Fig. 3. Image processing for detecting red cubes: (a) captured colour image (640 × 480), (b) ROI cropped (left compartment in this case), (c) grayscale image, (d) binary map, (e) image after morphological operations and, (f) cubes detected in the colour image. (Color figure online)

from the whole image. The colour ROI is considered as a matrix of size M × N × 3 (see Fig. 2(d)), and each colour is processed separately. First, the colour ROI is resized up to three times more to improve the sample acquired. This region corresponds to the empty side of the box, and it depends on whether the test is performed for the non-dominant or dominant hand of the subject. Then, this dilated image is converted to grayscale first and to a binary map after (black and white), by tuning each colour considering the corresponding thresholds. These parameters are set automatically after the calibration of light (intensity of the scene), for which 3 cubes of each colour are deposited in one of the compartments of the box. Then a series of morphological operations (opening, closing, erosion and labelling) are applied. The same sequence (without the image capture, the cropped and the resize of image) it is repeated for each colour separately. Finally, a first count of cubes is made, depending on the colour, in the captured image. The above procedure is repeated for each captured RGB frame while the test is running.

Score Validation. Due to the lack of sensitivity and to the high spasticity on the hands, it is possible that some individuals have trouble grabbing a single cube, and they can take two at a time. In these cases, and according to the test rules [7], the additional cubes must be discarded and must be counted as one.

Having in mind this approach, a time vector to compare very close events is used, during the performance of the test. On the basis, that a healthy individual takes about a second to move a cube, it is detected if two or more cubes have appeared in very close time instants and in periods lower than a second. In that case, the additional cubes are discarded and it is only added one to the global counter.

2.2   User Interface

Graphical interface and its elements are shown in Fig. 4. The full view of Kinect® colour sensor is presented in a small window (see Fig. 4 upper left-hand corner). The scoring of cubes obtained by each colour is also shown in the middle of the image. Furthermore, in addition to the count of the cubes by colour, there are two windows to display the results. In the first one, the cubes obtained and its times of detection for the second stage (dominant hand) are plotted (see Fig. 4 upper right corner). In the second one, and after the third test stage is completed (non-dominant hand), a comparative graph of the current session along with the previous sessions is presented (see Fig. 4 lower right corner).

In order to face the automatic test administration, the ABBT plays the test instructions through a voice synthesizer to guide the subjects during the test execution. These instructions are the same as those provided by a therapist with the traditional BBT. Respect to the patient, the interface eases the test administration. Respect to the therapist, it enables to visualize the development of cubes detection (see Fig. 4 lower left-hand corner), to offer the user's profile options (see Fig. 4 upper left-hand corner), or to load automatically subject information stored in a local database. Among the stored information, the affected hand can be found, and therefore the ABBT select the appropriate ROI (empty region of the box).

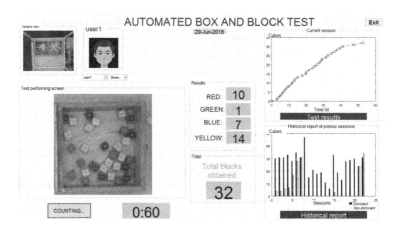

Fig. 4. ABBT graphical interface.

3 Results

The ABBT system is built based on an Intel® Core i7 computer, with a Kinect® for Windows® V1 sensor. The implemented algorithm is able to process 4.22 images per second (235 ms). Counting success rate was estimated at laboratory. Since the algorithm uses the segmentation by colour for the block-counting estimation, it could lose some blocks due to changes in light conditions. After several times of test, it is found that the system has 100% of accuracy when 30 blocks are transferred [9].

3.1 Pilot Study

A pilot study to investigate the ABBT effectiveness and impressions of individuals using the automated method was conducted at a healthcare facility. The test was administrated automatically. Healthcare professionals took part only to place the BBT at different stages, and to count the total of cubes transferred. The manual blocks counting were compared with the total obtained by the ABBT.

The trial was conducted at Fuenlabrada University Hospital, considering the good experiences accomplished while testing another robotic assistive system in hospital environments [3]. System settings are the same as the one shown in the above Fig. 1. Trials were carried out in different days in the same week. ABBT reproduces the test instructions through a voice synthesizer to guide the subjects during the test execution. These instructions are the same as the ones provided by a healthcare professional with the traditional BBT.

As the BBT rules shown, after the training period, the individuals proceeded to perform the test, by starting with their not affected hand (dominant). Then, the trials were carried out with their affected hand (non-dominant). At the end of each stage, one of the therapists proceeded to count the total of cubes displaced.

3.2 Participants

Four subjects with different levels of upper limb impairments were selected by medical professionals. The participants were chosen according to the following inclusion criteria: (a) Affectation of the upper extremity, (b) Gripping ability, (c) Spasticity according to Modified Ashworth Scale ≤ 2, and (d) Ability to understand Mini-mental test instructions ≥ 24. Demographics data of the participants in the trial are shown in Table 1.

3.3 Pilot Trial Results

The trial results were grouped by the relevance of the information provided to the therapist, such as: traditional scoring, additional outcome (more objectives and based on user's performance), and clinical outcome (whose interpretation can improve the clinical evaluation). A preliminary data analysis is shown in [8].

Table 1. Demographics of the participants and trial results

Participant	Age	Affectation	Gender	Total score[a]	
				Dominant	Non-dominant
Subject 1	23	Left-sided hemiparesis	Male	35/**44**	28/**32**
Subject 2	54	Akinetic-rigid syndrome	Female	45/**56**	37/**49**
Subject 3	55	Right-sided hemiparesis	Female	36/**50**	11/**11**
Subject 4	58	Right-sided hemiparesis	Male	33/**54**	3/**3**
Average of ABBT detection success rate:				73%	91%

[a]Scoring for the ABBT and the BBT (bold)

Traditional Scoring. The results obtained by using the ABBT have been different for the case of the dominant and the non-dominant hand. The average success ratio was of 90.75% for the non-dominant hand case, and of 74% for the dominant hand case. The scoring obtained by using the ABBT and the manual counting of blocks are also summarized in Table 1, according to each subject and in the case of both the dominant and the non-dominant hand. It can be seen that the success rate was different depending on whether the exercise is performed with the unaffected or the affected hand. This variation in the rate of success is due to the greater speed of movement with the healthy hand, and that makes difficult the detection of the cubes. Other factor is attributed to changes in light conditions, that were different during the test days.

Additional Outcome. The total counting of blocks and the time instant in which the cubes were detected is shown in Fig. 5. The results are grouped by dominant and non-dominant hand for each subject. A fairly linear trend in the displacement of cubes can be appreciated, but with different slopes. Besides, from the results obtained, it is a fact that the variation among the slopes is related to the subjects health condition. For example, a major slope is observed for the case of Subject 2, with akinetic-rigid syndrome. A minor slope is obtained for Subject 4, that suggests a major affectation level with respect to the other individuals who had hemiparesis.

The linear trend, can be estimated by using the simple linear regression (SLR) method. SLR considers only one independent variable employing the relation:

$$y = \beta_0 + \beta_1 x + \epsilon \tag{1}$$

where β_0 is the y-intercept, β_1 is the slope (or regression coefficient), and ϵ is the error term. Starting with a set of n observed values of x and y given by (x_1, y_1), (x_2, y_2), ..., (x_n, y_n). Using the SLR relation, these values form a system of linear equations. If the line is forced to start at zero, then the system could be simplified as:

$$Y = B \cdot X \tag{2}$$

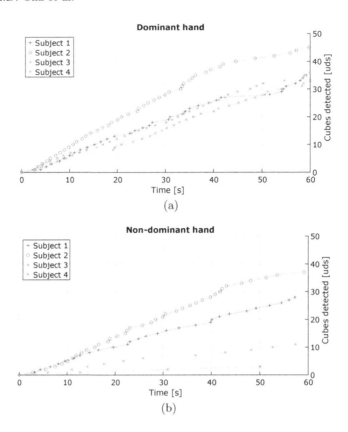

Fig. 5. Results of counting blocks and the time period detection during pilot trial: (a) Dominant hand, (b) Non-dominant hand.

where B is the slope or regression coefficient. Then, if X is the time axis, and Y is the number of cubes detected in the Eq. (2), by applying the SLR to the results obtained with ABBT, the relation is:

$$N_d = V_d \cdot t$$
$$N_{nd} = V_{nd} \cdot t \tag{3}$$

where, V_d and V_{nd} are the slopes by the linear fit, and it represents the average speed of blocks displacement for both the dominant and the non-dominant hand, respectively.

In Fig. 6, the analysis of data obtained for Subject 2 case are presented. In this case, the average speeds in transferring blocks are calculated by using Eq. (3). The results achieved with the BBT (see blue and yellow columns on Fig. 6 right-hand side) are compared with the ABBT results.

Clinical Outcome. Despite of not getting a higher rate of success on blocks estimation, the results can also be assessed in order to evaluate if the additional

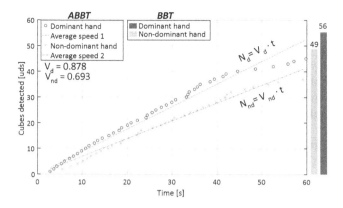

Fig. 6. Comparative between the ABBT and the BBT by its information provided for Subject 2 data. (Color figure online)

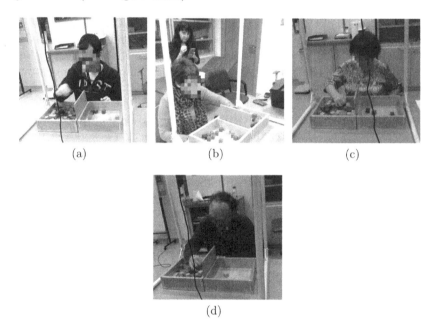

Fig. 7. Individuals performing the ABBT: (a) Subject 1, (b) Subject 2 with therapist, (c) Subject 3 and, (d) Subject 4.

information provided, is relevant to the health professionals. For example, the time information of the subjects for the non-dominant hand case (see Fig. 5(b)), suggests a reaction to fatigue during the test, and is a relevant factor for therapists as an indicator of spasticity, according to the local slope changes in the time intervals (elapsed time from one block to another) of cubes transferred.

Since, the average speed of cubes displacement for both the affected and the non affected hand is obtained (as V_d and V_{nd} coefficients given by making a linear fit), when the value of the two coefficients are close, it could mean that the therapy will have been effective. Also, taking a look at Eq. (1), it can be appreciated that the ϵ introduce a factor of non linearity. Then, the instantaneous speeds, that depends on the time periods elapsed to transfer a block and the next one, while running the test, are not constants. It could be used as an indicator of coordination in the arm movements, related to the dispersion of the samples.

Some pictures of participants during the performance of the pilot trials are shown in Fig. 7.

4   Discussion and Conclusions

In this paper, the procedure to automate the assessment method of BBT, including the hardware and software development, is presented. Besides, the automatically administration of the test, without intervention of healthcare professionals, is evaluated. In this way, a pilot study was designed and conducted to investigate the ABBT effectiveness in a real situation. Also, to assess the clinical viability, with a minimal or null intervention of clinicians, of the automatic administration of the ABBT is intended.

In addition, the sensorization of the system is appropriate and it provides additional information respect to the traditional BBT. This information, is stored on the patient's register directly, making easier to generate a medical history updated. In this way, the cubes colour and the time instant when they were detected are obtained and registered by the ABBT. The linearity in the timeline of cubes detection, suggest an indicator of a major level of coordination, according to the data dispersion with respect to the linear fit; and the average speeds, given by the trend slopes, can be related with the effectiveness of therapy. This approach, requires more trials to be consolidated, but it is encouraging. Additionally, a minimum of 5 participants will be required to conduct an usability study [4].

Regarding to the DBBT [2], not only an algorithm for counting cubes was developed, but also an interface which allows to perform all stages (training, dominant hand and non-dominant hand) of the test. Through this interface the test instructions are provided to users by voice messages, and it allows to administer the test automatically. In case of failure or user distraction, due to simplicity of the interface, it allows the user to repeat the test easily. The accuracy of counting the cubes is improved too, by obtaining a success rate of 100% up to 30 cubes transferred. It is appreciated too, that the algorithm effectiveness in clinical trials has been reduced with respect to that obtained in the laboratory. This decrease is attributed on the one hand, by failure in counting all cubes due to the higher speed in the case of dominant hand, and on the other hand, by influence of ambient light conditions that it introduced false positives in the cubes detection while performing the tests. The calibration process must be improved in future developments.

After the pilot study, the interface, the instructions provided by the interface and the results were evaluated by the users and the therapists. They positively accepted the approach to automate the test, and raised suggestions and comments. Since ABBT is a low-cost system, by its few required elements, the possibility of performing the rehabilitation assessment at home was highlighted by the participants. Their opinions and the obtained results, further supports the feasibility of the use of automated systems in assessment of stroke physical rehabilitation. This fact combined with an adequate robotic rehabilitation system, will lead to an autonomous and objective rehabilitation process.

Acknowledgments. The research leading to these results has received funding from the ROBOHEALTH-A project (DPI2013-47944-C4-1-R) funded by Spanish Ministry of Economy and Competitiveness and from the RoboCity2030-III-CM project (S2013/MIT-2748), funded by Programas de Actividades I+D en la Comunidad de Madrid and cofunded by Structural Funds of the EU.

References

1. Coster, W.J.: Making the best match: selecting outcome measures for clinical trials and outcome studies. Am. J. Occup. Ther. **67**(2), 162–170 (2013)
2. Hsiao, C.P., Zhao, C., Do, E.Y.L.: The digital box and block test automating traditional post-stroke rehabilitation assessment. In: 2013 IEEE International Conference on Pervasive Computing and Communications Workshops (PERCOM Workshops), pp. 360–363. IEEE (2013)
3. Huete, A.J., Victores, J.G., Martinez, S., Gimenez, A., Balaguer, C.: Personal autonomy rehabilitation in home environments by a portable assistive robot. IEEE Trans. Syst. Man Cybern. Part C Appl. Rev. **42**(4), 561–570 (2012)
4. Jardón, A., Gil, A.M., de la Peña, A.I., Monje, C.A., Balaguer, C.: Usability assessment of asibot: a portable robot to aid patients with spinal cord injury. Disabil. Rehabil. Assist. Technol. **6**(4), 320–330 (2011). http://dx.doi.org/10.3109/17483107.2010.528144
5. Jung, J.Y., Glasgow, J.I., Scott, S.H.: A hierarchical ensemble model for automated assessment of stroke impairment. In: 2008 IEEE International Joint Conference on Neural Networks (IEEE World Congress on Computational Intelligence), pp. 3187–3191, June 2008
6. Lee, T.K., Leo, K., Sanei, S., Chew, E.: Automated scoring of rehabilitative tests with singular spectrum analysis. In: 2015 23rd European Signal Processing Conference (EUSIPCO), pp. 2571–2575. IEEE (2015)
7. Mathiowetz, V., Volland, G., Kashman, N., Weber, K.: Adult norms for the box and block test of manual dexterity. Am. J. Occup. Ther. **39**(6), 386–391 (1985)
8. Oña, E., Jardón, A., Balaguer, C.: Toward an automated assessment method of manual dexterity. In: 2016 International Workshop on Assistive and Rehabilitation Technology (IWART), pp. 1–2. nBio-UMH (2016)
9. Oña, E., Jardón, A., Balaguer, C., Cuesta, A., Carratalá, M., Monge, E.: El 'automatizado box & blocks test' sistema automático de evaluación de destreza manual gruesa. In: XXXVII Jornadas de Automática, pp. 619–626. CEA, Áccesit to the best works of Computer Vision (2016)

10. Otten, P., Kim, J., Son, S.H.: A framework to automate assessment of upper-limb motor function impairment: a feasibility study. Sensors **15**(8), 20097 (2015). http://www.mdpi.com/1424-8220/15/8/20097
11. Prochazka, A., Kowalczewski, J.: A fully automated, quantitative test of upper limb function. J. Mot. Behav. **47**(1), 19–28 (2015)
12. van der Putten, J., Hobart, J.C., Freeman, J.A., Thompson, A.J.: Measuring change in disability after inpatient rehabilitation: comparison of the responsiveness of the barthel index and the functional independence measure. J. Neurol. Neurosurg. Psychiat. **66**(4), 480–484 (1999). http://jnnp.bmj.com/content/66/4/480.abstract
13. Saborowski, M., Kollak, I.: How do you care for technology? Care professionals' experiences with assistive technology in care of the elderly. Technol. Forecast. Soc. Change **93**, 133–140 (2015). http://www.sciencedirect.com/science/article/pii/S0040162514001632
14. Salter, K., Campbell, N., Richardson, M., Mehta, S., Jutai, J., Zettler, L., Moses, M., McClure, A., Mays, R., Foley, N., Teasell, R.: Outcome measures in stroke rehabilitation. Evidence-based review of stroke rehabilitation, 16th edn., London, Ontario, Canada, pp. 1–144 (2013)
15. Wade, E., Parnandi, A.R., Matarić, M.J.: Automated administration of the wolf motor function test for post-stroke assessment. In: 2010 4th International Conference on-NO PERMISSIONS, Pervasive Computing Technologies for Healthcare (PervasiveHealth), pp. 1–7. IEEE (2010)
16. Wang, J., Yu, L., Wang, J., Guo, L., Gu, X., Fang, Q.: Automated Fugl-Meyer assessment using SVR model. In: 2014 IEEE International Symposium on Bioelectronics and Bioinformatics (ISBB), pp. 1–4. IEEE (2014)

Combining Depth and Intensity Images to Produce Enhanced Object Detection for Use in a Robotic Colony

Steven Balding[(✉)] and Darryl N. Davis

Faculty of Engineering and Computer Science, University of Hull, Hull, England
S.Balding@2013.hull.ac.uk, D.N.Davis@hull.ac.uk

Abstract. Robotic colonies that can communicate with each other and interact with their ambient environments can be utilized for a wide range of research and industrial applications. However amongst the problems that these colonies face is that of the isolating objects within an environment. Robotic colonies that can isolate objects within the environment can not only map that environment in detail, but interact with that ambient space. Many object recognition techniques exist, however these are often complex and computationally expensive, leading to overly complex implementations. In this paper a simple model is proposed to isolate objects, these can then be recognize and tagged. The model will be using 2D and 3D perspectives of the perceptual data to produce a probability map of the outline of an object, therefore addressing the defects that exist with 2D and 3D image techniques. Some of the defects that will be addressed are; low level illumination and objects at similar depths. These issues may not be completely solved, however, the model provided will provide results confident enough for use in a robotic colony.

Keywords: Anchoring · Robotic vision · Sobel · Depth map · Robotic colony

1 Introduction

Robotic colonies are an important part of modern robotics research and are becoming used more and more in industry. A robotic colony provides a collection of agents that can work uniformly and autonomously to survey and interact with their environment [1]. However for a robot to interact with other agents and the ambient environment the robot must find a relationship between the perceptual data it gathers and a symbolic representation of objects within the environment [2–4]. The perceptual data gathered is only useful for anchoring, however, if an object can be isolated within the data. Methods proposed for isolating object within an image are often computational expensive and complex, with techniques such as Convolution Neural Networks becoming popular [5]. However for a robotic agent to detect objects within the environment simpler methods, such as kernel filters, can be used to separate and classify objects by features or light intensity. These less complex methods have issues which are addressed in the paper.

© Springer International Publishing AG 2017
Y. Gao et al. (Eds.): TAROS 2017, LNAI 10454, pp. 115–125, 2017.
DOI: 10.1007/978-3-319-64107-2_10

Detecting objects within a 2D image is a common practice with good results [6, 7] achieved using Kernel filters such as Sobel operators providing not just edge detection but also the orientation of the edge [7, 8]. Vision processing using just Sobel filters can handle image noise relatively well, and as such, have been commonly used for quick moving detection, such as license plate recognition [9]. Canny edge detection is another popular method that gives a more refined edge information at the expense of computational time [10, 11]. This technique has been used in conjunction with convex hulls to remove isolate objects form the background [12]. More expansive techniques allow an object to be described in 3D, using binocular images to estimate distance. However both 2D and 3D techniques suffer from similar problems. The images need to have a contrast on the edge for an edge to be found. The images being analysed might not yield edges due to images with little to no definition or object occlusion and even reducing noise with a Gaussian distribution filter could leave the image with edges that are not identified. There have been 2D and laser range finder combinations [1] used to success, however this will still leave problems with object occlusion and does not account for the 3D world.

In contrast 3D cameras, such as the Kinect, are being used commonly for computer vision [13]. The resulting image form a 3D camera can still be a 2D matrix but rather than an intensity or a colour, instead there is the depth of any given x, y pixel. Plotting this result as a 3D point cloud, objects can be identified and mapped using the resulting vectors. However, problems still arise when considering an image that is contains multiple objects at the same depth, classifying these with depth alone is a rather difficult task that requires high resolution equipment.

In this paper, a model is proposed incorporating simple 2D and 3D techniques for producing a probability mapping of an objects outline, this data can then be used to isolate an object and tag that isolated object. The model will achieve this by normalize the colour based image and the depth image and run separate filters on the receptive image to detect edges within each image, the intensity of the edge will also act as our probability of an object at that point. Analysing the results of both image filters will produce a probability map that will show where an object or its boundary is likely to be regardless of stacked objects or poor lighting, while being computationally inexpensive and simple to implement. The object can then be classified based on simple pre-defined characteristics such as volume or color.

2 Sobel Operator

2.1 Overview of Sobel Operator

When detecting edges in an image, often the process is approximating the first order derivatives by convolving a set kernel with the original image. With a Sobel operator (or filter) [14], kernels are used for both the horizontal and vertical plane, as shown in Fig. 1. This will return the local derivative of that kernel for vertical and horizontal respectively. To obtain the absolute magnitude edge gradient of that pixel:

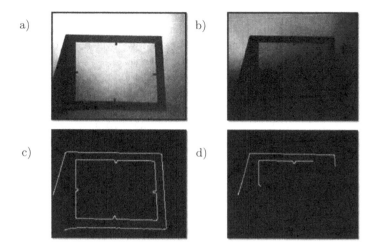

Fig. 1. (a) Good lighting (b) Poor lighting (c) Good edge detection (d) Poor edge detection

Table 1. Kernel for vertical (left) and kernel for horizontal (right)

-1	0	1
-2	0	2
-1	0	1

-1	-2	-1
0	0	0
1	2	1

$$G = \sqrt{G_x^2 + G_y^2}$$

Gx =   Left Sobel filter.
Gy =   Right Sobel filter.

Because the horizontal and vertical plane are observed it is possible to also find the orientation of that edge pixel with:

$$\theta = \tan^{-1}\frac{G_y}{G_x}$$

After these operations, there will be a maximum response from the vertical and horizontal plane, a final edge gradient and angle of orientation. This spatial information is very useful for identifying an object. Not only do these operations leave us with a clear edge, the angle of neighboring pixels can be observed to find recognizable shapes and curves; this will further help isolate object in a picture. This operation also includes average factoring which helps reduce some of the low level noise of the image by taking a more balanced view of the entire image (Table 1).

For any modern robot this will also not prove to be too computationally expensive as the kernels can be decomposed as products of an interpolation and a differentiation kernel, and could even be possible from a video feed.

There are issues however, and these issues fall into two main categories; the first being image noise and the second being intensity of edge being detected.

2.2   Problems of Sobel Operators

The problem of noise in images is a common one - image noise can come in many forms, usually coming down to white noise or salt and pepper noise. Sobel operators, as stated before, can naturally deal with some amount of noise and post-processing with filters such as Gaussian which can further reduce the image noise and better detect edges. Methods for Sobel noise reductions have been proposed [15], but these can be computationally expensive with a lot of post or pre-processing. In the model proposed, noise will be reduced by comparing edges from 2D and 3D images.

Edge detection, at its core, is looking at the difference of intensity of neighboring pixels in order to find an edge. For this to be successful, a clear change in light intensity is required. Considering an image that is only partial lighted, will show sections of the object within the image that produce a false edge.

There are ways to deal with this in the context of robotic agents identifying the object, for example using neural networks or convolution networks might mean training an image to be recognised from a partial image. However this could take a lot of sample images and long training time, more over this could still be inaccurate if there is a large percentage of the image covered in darkness or the shape left behind could look like another object.

It should also be noted that it is not just light that can cause edge detection to be unreliable, stacked objects of the same or similar colour can sometimes cause issues.

The system proposed will not intrinsically solve this problem, although dues to its probabilistic nature, it could highlight areas of potential for a more thorough inspection. It should be considered, however, that two object at the same distance same colour and out of reach of haptic feedback would be difficult for us as humans to differentiate between, so expecting a robot to perform that type of recognition would be very difficult.

3   Depth Image Mapping

3.1   Depth Image Overview

3D depth cameras offers robotics sight with reasonably accurate depth analysis. This one of a few major branches in robotics and AI that does not consider how a human perceives the world, but rather uses technology to surpass that of our vision. It is still a relatively new field for computer vision, with most offers in the past favoring 2D images, but with the reduction of price of the cameras, more and more example of vision processing with RBG-D images are occurring.

3D cameras will return a depth value fort each x and y in an image, this is usually converted to either an intensity value, giving a grayscale image of depth or a point cloud, where by the pixels are mapped in 3D Cartesian space.

In a paper regarding depth kernels [16],one of the feature detection methods mentioned is edge detection over depth maps, and although the results are good, the problem of object occlusion and same depth objects is not covered.

There are other examples of 3D object classification that use point could data to good effect. Some opting for measuring similarities between point descriptors of curated 3D models and real world point cloud data [17] and some using custom 3D Convolution Neural Networks (CNN) [5]. These approaches are very successful, however they are computationally complex, and, in the case of the CNN, they lack information contained within the pixel.

It is proposed that the model in this paper will help reduce computational complexity, store angular and spatial information of a given pixel and produce a strong probabilistic assessment of an objects border. It is also still unclear in these results if this type of network or feature descriptors can separate and classify stacked and same depth objects (Fig. 2).

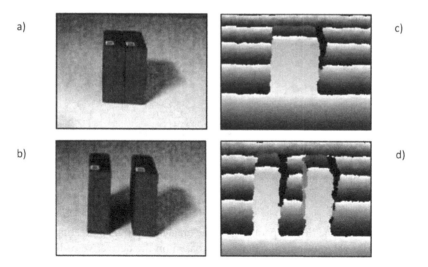

Fig. 2. (a) Colour picture of two stacked objects (b) Depth map of two stacked objects (c) Colour picture of two separated objects (d) Depth map of two separated objects

3.2   Sobel Filter with Depth Map

In this paper the model that is proposed will take edge detection values from a 2D image using a Sobel filter, but also values from an RGB-D image of the same perspective of the original 2D image. To achieve this there are 3 stages;

First is to downsize the image from the camera to the same resolution of the RBG-D images. In the case of a Kinect V2 camera (V1 performs poorly in low light conditions) this is 512×424. The colour image can be recorded at 1920×1080. The Kinect has a built in function to deal with this conversion called the 'ICoordinateMapper', other cameras might have to manually preform registration.

Then a grey scale images will be produced where by the intensity of light (from 0–255) of any given pixel will be the value of the depth of that pixel. The Kinect gives precision of 11 bits ($2^{11} = 2048$), this means that the pixel depth can be scaled to the light intensity value which is 0–255. When this has been processed, the resulting image will be a depth map similar to that of a grey sale image, but rather than considering light, depth is the focus (Fig. 3).

Fig. 3. Image of grayscale depth map

Finally, running the Sobel operator over the created depth map, treating it as before. This will yield a value of an edge that is not based on the derivative of light intensity (although we are creating an artificial grey scale for the Sobel filter), but rather a response to the difference on the depth of an image. The values given back from this operation that highlight edges on object that are not illuminated, something that cannot be ascertained from just processing a 2D image (Fig. 4).

After obtaining an edge detection image on both a 2D light intensity image and 3D depth map, the data points for both images can be combined to ascertain the probability space.

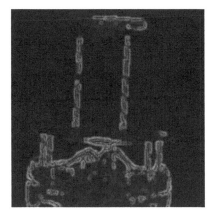

Fig. 4. Image of filter over depth map

4 Probability Mapping

4.1 Probability Weighting

At the point of obtaining the two images of the same resolution, it is possible to take the newly found edge intensity value and combine both value to form the likelihood of that edge existing. However, the higher the intensity the more weight should be placed on its value, moreover, if the light source for the image is good then weighting more towards these probabilities would act as more realistic impression of an objects edge, as using the difference in light intensity is more reliable than just depth detection.

Object in a real dynamic environment tend to collide and often exists at very similar depths (for example, a shelf of books). A rudimentary approach is proposed to account for the quality of the light source and weight the values in favour of well illuminated images.

To determine the weighting of the probability map the over quality of the light source must be determined. In this paper, the proposed method is basic, more complex methods could be implemented for better accuracy. To obtain the light source rating a relative luminance calculation will be performed on each pixel in the original colour 2D image, these values will then find the arithmetic mean to find a finale weighting for the probability mapping.

$$L = \frac{\sum_{i=1}^{q} \left(\sum_{j=1}^{q} 0.2126R_{ij} + 0.0722B_{ij} + 0.7152G_{ij} \right)}{q}$$

q =   Pixel count of the image.
R =   Red pixel intensity for given x, y coordinate.
B =   Blue pixel intensity for given x, y coordinate.
G =   Green pixel intensity for given x, y coordinate.

After the calculating the coefficient for the weighting, it is possible to produce the probability map using the following to give a scaled balanced return.

$$\frac{a * \left(\frac{l}{255}\right)^2 + b * \left(\frac{d}{255}\right)^2}{a+b}$$

a =   weighting for 2D image.
b =   weighting for 3D image.
l =   pixel intensity for 2D (light based) image.
d =   pixel intensity for 3D (depth based) image.

The weighting on the combined probability calculation will be set for 5 for depth map images and scaled from 1–10 for the relative luminance, this will account for an image with high and low quality light sources. The depth could be called higher, maybe as a result of objects distance from the camera (Fig. 5).

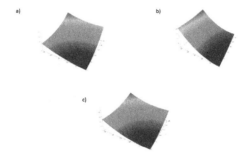

Fig. 5. (a) Graph of probability map a = 5, b = 5 (b) Graph of probability map a = 10, b = 5 (c) Graph of probability map a = 1, b = 5

4.2   Object Detection

There are many different methods for recognizing an object from edge detection [18] and more complex methods that will deal with partial and complex outlines [19], the output from the model proposed in this paper could also fit into other models, using the probability map instead of an edge intensity map. However, because the spatial and orientation data is kept (due to the Sobel operator) for each pixel in both the light and depth map image, a 5 dimensional set can be produced for any given pixel in the image:

$$S = \{p, l, l\theta, d, d\theta\}$$

S =   Set of values stored within each pixel.
p =   Value from probability map at given X, Y.

l =   Value from 2D Sobel filter map at given X, Y.
lθ =   Orientation angle from 2D Sobel filter at given X, Y.
d =   Value from 3D Sobel filter map at given X, Y.
dθ =   Orientation angle from 3D Sobel filter at given X, Y.

With this complete information about any given pixel it is possible to classify an object in an image more clearly. An example; a football is taken as the object, the ball is white and written in the center, in black, is the name of the manufacturer.

Given only 2D edge detection producing a convex hull of this image might produce one for the outline of the ball and another for the writing, with the information given in this model it is possible to ask, is this writing the same depth as the object it is placed on. This extra level of information can further help isolate, classify and tag an object in an image and further more reduce high level noise.

5 Results

The probability map that is returned from the depth and colour images can be placed through a threshold operator, in this case hysteresis, to return an images that gives a solid line that represents the object. An advantage of this probability map is that the thresholds can be adjusted to suit the needs, using the probability of a line becoming the threshold. This final image can then be classified from features such as convex hull area, corners, histogram features or many other feature descriptors, in this case we use a simple convex hull area technique (Fig. 6).

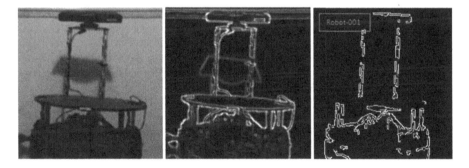

Fig. 6. Left: colour image. **Middle**: Probability mapping. **Right**: Finally tagged image.

Another aspect of this model was it simplicity, not only to implement, but for computational speed. Below are the results of a timed run using a simple Sobel operator as the benchmark (Table 2).

Table 2. Showing task *complete times, measure*d with the chrono library

	Test 1 (Microseconds)	Test2 (Microseconds)	Average (Microseconds)
Benchmark (just Sobel)	359,329	341,335	350,332
Depth map	296,546	278,512	287,529
Probability mapping	362596	382596	372,596
Fully classified	420,923	413,519	417,221

6   Conclusion

The model presented in this paper should find use as a simple and quick to implement solution for multi agent swarm. This model can classify images quickly and loosely, whilst making up for some of the issues of the incorporated techniques.

One of the advantages that this system conveys is, each pixel can still contain depth, light intensity and orientation within each pixel. This in turn meant that classification algorithm can work with more than just the outline of an image.

In further work objects will not just be classified as simple objects, but rather, account for the potential of sentience in the perceived data. This would add another dimension of functionality, as well as adding further accuracy to the classification.

References

1. Milella, A., Di Paola, D., Mazzeo, P.L., Spagnolo, P., Leo, M., Cicirelli, G., D'Orazio, T.: Active surveillance of dynamic environments using a multi-agent system. IFAC Proc. **43**, 13–18 (2010)
2. Harnad, S.: The symbol grounding problem. Symb. Grounding Probl. D. **42**, 335 (1990)
3. Coradeschi, S., Saffiotti, A.: An introduction to the anchoring problem. In: Robotics and Autonomous Systems, pp. 85–96 (2003)
4. Gwatkin, J.: Robo-CAMAL: anchoring in a cognitive robot. Doctoral dissertation, University of Hull, Kingston upon Hull, UK (2009)
5. Maturana, D., Scherer, S.: VoxNet: a 3D convolutional neural network for real-time object recognition. In: IROS, pp. 922–928 (2015)
6. Sharifzadeh, S., Centre, E., Manufacturing, I.: Edge detection techniques : evaluations and comparisons, vol. 2, pp. 1507–1520 (2008)
7. Kim, D.: Sobel operator and canny edge detector ECE 480 Fall 2013 Team 4, pp. 1–10 (2013)
8. Anusha, G.: Implementation of SOBEL edge detection on FPGA. Int. J. Comput. Trends Technol. **3**, 472–475 (2012)
9. Israni, S.: Edge detection of license plate, pp. 3561–3563 (2016)
10. Lakshmi, S., Sankaranarayanan, D.V.: A study of edge detection techniques for segmentation computing approaches. Int. J. Comput. Appl. CASCT, pp. 35–41 (2010)

11. Pavithra, C., Kavitha, M., Kannan, E.: An efficient edge detection algorithm for 2D-3D conversion. In: 2014 International Conference on Computation of Power, Energy, Information and Communication (ICCPEIC), pp. 434–436. IEEE (2014)
12. Adhikari, S., Kar, J., Dastidar, J.G.: An automatic and efficient foreground object extraction scheme. Int. J. Sci. Adv. Inf. Technol. **3**, 40–43 (2015)
13. Abdulmajeed, R., Mansoor, R.Z.: Implementing kinect sensor for building 3D maps of indoor environments. Int. J. Comput. Appl. **86**, 18–22 (2014)
14. Kanopoulos, N., Vasanthavada, N., Baker, R.L.: Design of an image edge detection filter using the sobel operator. IEEE J. Solid-State Circ. **23**, 358–367 (1988)
15. Gao, W., Yang, L., Zhang, X., Liu, H.: An improved Sobel edge detection. In: Proceedings of 2010 3rd IEEE International Conference on Computer Science and Information Technology, ICCSIT 2010. vol. 5, pp. 67–71 (2010)
16. Bo, L., Ren, X., Fox, D.: Depth kernel descriptors for object recognition. In: 2011 IEEE/RSJ International Conference on Intelligent Robots and Systems, pp. 821–826. IEEE (2011)
17. Frome, A., Huber, D., Kolluri, R., Bülow, T., Malik, J.: Recognizing objects in range data using regional point descriptors. In: 8th European Conference on Computer Vision, Prague, Czech Republic, Proceedings, Part III, 11–14 May 200, vol. 3023, pp. 224–237 (2004)
18. Ushma, A., Scholar, M., Shanavas, P.A.R.M.: Object detection in image processing using edge detection techniques. IOSR J. Eng. **4**, 10–13 (2014)
19. Mikolajczyk, K., Zisserman, A., Schmid, C.: Shape recognition with edge-based feactures, pp. 1–10. Brit. Mach. Vis. Conf, Norwich (2003)

Investigation of Hardware-in-the-Loop Walking/Running Test with Spring Mass System

Zhanye Yang$^{(\boxtimes)}$, Pejman Iravani, Andrew Plummer, and Min Pan

University of Bath, Bath, UK
zy339@bath.ac.uk

Abstract. Hardware-in-the-Loop (HIL) testing has been used successfully for a number of years on a wide range of applications. Any delay in actuation systems will increase the system energy if it is not properly compensated for due to the negative damping effect. A HIL walking/running testing system has advantages for testing lower-limb prosthetics over traditional human-based testing, i.e. safer, more objective. However, the stiff ground contact discontinuity is hard to compensate. This paper investigates the effect of introducing nonlinearity and discontinuity into a HIL system by comparing three types of Spring Mass System. Also, a requirement on the HIL testing actuation system is concluded that the actuation system delay frequency should be 20 times greater than the system natural frequency in order to keep the system simulation stable.

Keywords: Hardware-in-the-Loop · Delay compensation · Prosthetic test

1 Introduction

Hardware-in-the-Loop (HIL) technology is known as Hybrid testing or Model-in-the-Loop Simulation (MIL). There are various definitions of HIL simulations [2,4]. Here, HIL testing is defined as a test system which is implemented with both a numerical model and a physical system. Hybrid testing technology has a wide range of applications in the aircraft, automotive, seismic and defence industries [1,3,5]. These applications benefit from the advantages of HIL testing: (1) High fidelity (2) Low cost (3) Flexibility (4) Concurrent systems engineering.

To authors' best knowledge, no one has implemented walking simulation with HIL. A HIL walking simulation could be used to develop walking robot parts and testing lower limb prosthetics.

An example HIL testing with an industrial robot on a lower leg prosthesis is shown in Fig. 1. The testing system consists of a virtual system, a transfer system and a physical system. In the virtual system, a human walking model is simulated. Different from a normal walking simulation, an interface point is created and located at one of the lower legs just like an amputee. The simulation is outputting the interface point position to a robot controller. In the

© Springer International Publishing AG 2017
Y. Gao et al. (Eds.): TAROS 2017, LNAI 10454, pp. 126–133, 2017.
DOI: 10.1007/978-3-319-64107-2_11

transfer system, an industrial robot is position controlled to move the prosthetic foot to the position demand from the simulation. In the physical system, a real prosthetic foot makes contact with ground. A force sensor is used to connect the end-effector of the robot and the top of the prosthetic foot. It measures torques and forces at the physical interface and feeds them back to the walking simulation.

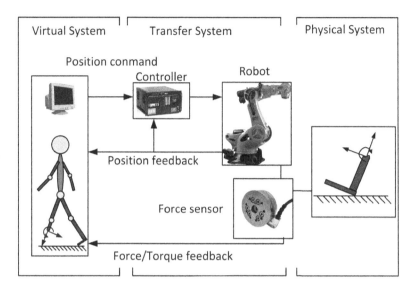

Fig. 1. An example of Hardware-in-the-Loop walking simulation architecture for testing a foot prosthetic.

For HIL testing, a delay in the actuation system is inevitable. Such a feature will lead to an effect equivalent to negative damping [3]. If the negative damping is larger than system damping, a system will be unstable. To solve this problem, compensation of delay is necessary. Walking is a dynamic process with nonlinearity and discontinuity. Ground contact can be regarded as a high natural frequency system due to very large stiffness of the ground. Therefore, HIL testing for such a system is challenging. This might be one of the reasons why no one has developed a HIL in walking or running test system before. In this paper, a Spring Mass System (SMS) is used as a simple example to study a HIL hopping or running system.

In the remainder of this paper, a lead compensation and Horiuchi compensation [3] are implemented on a HIL SMS with different properties to investigate system stability.

2   Preliminary Analysis with Spring Mass System

2.1   Three Types of Spring Mass System

Figure 2 shows three simple SMS. The SMS consists of a mass and a spring under the mass. The mass is able to move vertically. y is the displacement of the point mass starting from the spring in equilibrium.

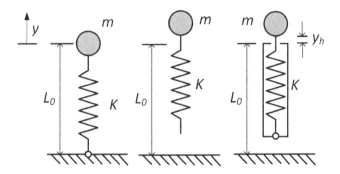

Fig. 2. Left: SMS with fixed foot. Middle: SMS hopper. Right: SMS hopper with a hard stop

The initial parameters of these SMS are shown in Table 1. This gives the system normalised system energy and normalised stiffness:

$$\begin{cases} E_n = \frac{E}{L_0 mg} = 1.05 \\ K_n = \frac{KL_0}{mg} = 20 \end{cases} \quad (1)$$

This set of parameters gives a human-like characteristic in the Spring Loaded Inverted Pendulum (SLIP) walker [6]. The natural frequency of the system is similar to human walking body frequency so that we consider it as a starting point for the investigation of HIL walking testing.

Table 1. SMS simulation parameters

m (Mass)	L_0 (Length of Spring)	K (Stiffness)	f_n (Natural frequency)	E (Total Energy)
70 kg	1 m	13 734 N m^{-1}	2.23 Hz	721.03 J

Linear, Continuous SMS (LCSMS): In the left of Fig. 2, the SMS has a fixed foot on the ground. The force applied on the system is linear and continuous. The dynamic equation of the SMS is:

$$(\ddot{y} + g)m = F_s = -yK \quad (2)$$

Nonlinear, Continuous SMS (NCSMS): Unlike the left SMS, the middle SMS is free to hop. Thus, it will have two phases i.e. air phase and stance phase. In the air phase, the mass takes zero spring force. In the stance phase, the mass takes spring force proportionally to the compression of spring. The combined force of both phases that is nonlinear and continuous. The dynamic equation of the SMS is:

$$(\ddot{y} + g)m = \begin{cases} 0 & \text{for } y \geq 0 \\ -yK & \text{for } y < 0 \end{cases} \tag{3}$$

Nonlinear, Discontinuous SMS (NDSMS): The last one in the right has a "hard stop" on the spring when the spring is compressed over y_h, $i.e. y < -y_h$. The "hard stop" is simulated as another very stiff spring. This means the total force is nonlinear and close to discontinuous. This "hard stop" is considered to be close to a sudden hard contact with ground. The dynamic equation of the SMS system is:

$$(\ddot{y} + g)m = \begin{cases} 0 & \text{for } y \geq 0 \\ -yK & \text{for } -y_h \leq y < 0 \\ -y_h K + (y - y_h)K_h & \text{for } y < -y_h \end{cases} \tag{4}$$

y_h is assumed to be $0.05\,\text{m}$. K_h is calculated as $20\,K$ to create the discontinuous force. We consider it is good enough to represent a "hard stop" from the ground.

2.2 HIL Testing of SMS and Compensation Method

In Fig. 3, HIL testing of SMS configuration is shown. It has a similar configuration with the HIL prosthetic foot testing in Fig. 1. All parts of this system are simulated in a computer to do preliminary analysis. In this initial investigation, the actuation system is defined as a pure time delay:

$$A(s) = e^{-s\tau} \tag{5}$$

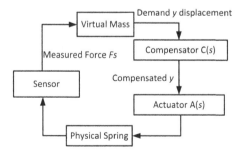

Fig. 3. HIL testing of SMS configuration. Note: all parts are simulated in this investigation.

The delay frequency is then calculated as $f_d = 1/\tau$. The frequency ratio of delay frequency f_d and system natural frequency f_n is defined as:

$$R_f = \frac{f_d}{f_n} \tag{6}$$

Without compensation, due to the lack of damping in this system, SMS will often be unstable. In Fig. 4, an example of LCSMS is shown. With $R_f = 45$, roughly $0.01\ s$ delay, the system is unstable. Therefore, compensations are needed.

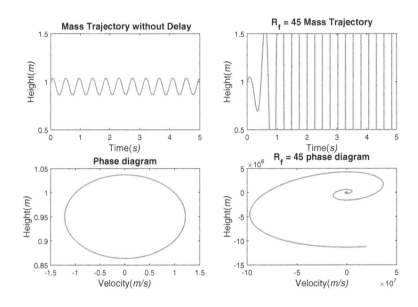

Fig. 4. An example of delay effect in HIL testing of the linear continuous SMS.

Two types of compensation are tested in this paper:

(1) Lead Compensation: Fundamentally Lead compensation predicts the signal with Euler Method explicitly. First order lead compensation with the time constant τ can be represented as:

$$C(s) = \frac{\tau s + 1}{D s + 1} \tag{7}$$

A very large pole, $1/D$ is added to make the lead compensation implementable, which has little effect of the system.

(2) Horiuchi Compensation: Horiuchi proposed a delay compensation using a polynomial function [3]. A 3rd order Horiuchi Compensator implemented in this paper is:

$$x_{new} = \sum_{i=0}^{3} a_i x_i \tag{8}$$

where a_i are coefficient constants. x_i is the measured position i samples previously. x_{new} is compensated position signal that feeds into the actuation system.

2.3   Results

The simulation is implemented in the MATLAB/Simulink environment. The solver is $ode8$. The time step is 10^{-4} s. R_f is selected to be 40, which means 0.011 s delay in actuation system. The model is executed for 15 cycles. The phase diagrams of the simulations are shown in Fig. 5.

Without compensation, three systems all go unstable very quickly. The Lead compensation and the Horiuchi Compensation work fine for LCSMS and NCSMS despite the lead compensation causing a slight energy increase. However, both compensations fail in DCSMS due to the "hard stop" from the very stiff ground

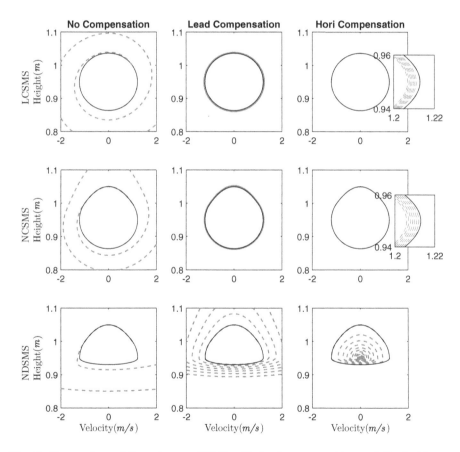

Fig. 5. Comparison of three types of SMS with lead compensation and Horiuchi compensation phase diagram. Black solid curves represent expected original phase curve. Magenta dashed curves represent actual simulated phase curve. Two partial enlarged diagrams are displayed in the boxes on the right side. (Color figure online)

spring. The ground stiffness, K_h, leads to a high natural frequency system. The delay frequency and natural frequency ratio R_f for the ground in this case is calculated to be 8.95, which seems too small. It is necessary to determine the accepted range for R_f.

3 R_f Limit Test on the LCSMS

The "hard stop" from the ground in the DCSMS is equivalent to a high stiffness LCSMS. An investigation on LCSMS can be useful to tell the reason why the compensations fail in DCSMS. SMS is expected to be energy conservative. It is a good way to evaluate system stability by examining system energy. In this section, different R_f values are tested on LCSMS. After the simulation being executed for 15 cycles, system energy is recorded. In Fig. 6, the test results are shown.

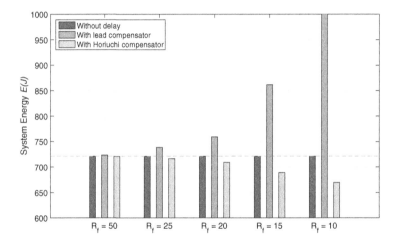

Fig. 6. LCSMS system energy with different R_f values and different compensations. The original system energy is shown with red dashed line. The left dark blue bars also represent original energy of the systems. (Color figure online)

From the bar graph, one can notice system energy change increases as R_f decreases. This means HIL emulation of HIL is less accurate when the delay is longer, which meets our expectation. Also, Lead Compensation increases energy while Horiuchi Compensation decreases energy.

Assume that about 1% of energy change for every cycle is acceptable. After 15 cycles, energy change is required to be roughly smaller than 100 J. Up to now, we can say that $R_f = 20$ is currently the lowest value to meet our requirement. For the "hard stop" from Sect. 2, $R_f = 8.95$ is much smaller than the requirement, that is why the phase diagram was not close to the expectation. A further analysis is needed to give a clearer idea of the accepted range.

4   Conclusion

This paper proposed a new potential HIL application for prosthetic testing. Three types of Spring Mass System (SMS) were tested in simulation to investigate the main obstacle of such an application. It was found that the very large stiffness from the ground caused a loss of fidelity in the Nonlinear Discontinuous Spring Mass System (NDSMS). Then, the acceptable frequency ratio R_f was analyzed and determined to be larger than 20. This will inform the actuation system selection and design in future.

For a Spring Loaded Inverted Pendulum (SLIP) walker model, there is no real "hard stop" from the ground, and so is similar to NCSMS. In this case, the dominant factor is the body or leg swing frequency (about 2 Hz). HIL testing should be easier to implement. However, in experimental testing, walking system with HIL may also exhibit a high frequency mode due to the impact from the ground, which will lead to a loss of fidelity in testing. If this proves to be the case, future work may include the investigation of other compensation methods to solve the "hard stop" problem, or the use of a different HIL testing approach like pseudo dynamics HIL testing.

References

1. Cai, G., Chen, B.M., Lee, T.H., Dong, M.: Design and implementation of a hardware-in-the-loop simulation system for small-scale UAV helicopters. Mechatronics **19**(7), 1057–1066 (2009)
2. Fathy, H.K., Filipi, Z.S., Hagena, J., Stein, J.L.: Review of hardware-in-the-loop simulation and its prospects in the automotive area. Model. Simul. Mil. Appl. **6228**, 62280E-1–62280E-20 (2006)
3. Horiuchi, T., Nakagawa, M.: Development of a real-time hybrid experimental system with actuator delay compensation. In: Eleventh World Conference on Earthquake Engineering (1996)
4. Plummer, A.R.: Model-in-the-loop testing. Proc. Inst. Mech. Eng. Part I J. Syst. Control Eng. **220**(3), 183–199 (2006)
5. Rajaram, V., Subramanian, S.C.: Design and hardware-in-loop implementation of collision avoidance algorithms for heavy commercial road vehicles. Veh. Syst. Dyn. **54**(7), 871–901 (2016)
6. Rummel, J., Blum, Y., Seyfarth, A.: Robust and efficient walking with spring-like legs. Bioinspiration Biomim. **5**(4), 046004 (2010)

Surface Inspection via Hitting Sets and Multi-goal Motion Planning

Stefan Edelkamp[1], Baris Can Secim[2], and Erion Plaku[2(✉)]

[1] Faculty of Computer Science and Mathematics, University of Bremen, Bremen, Germany
[2] Department of Electrical Engineering and Computer Science, Catholic University of America, Washington, DC, USA
plaku@cua.edu

Abstract. This paper develops an approach that enables an aerial vehicle to carry out 3D surface inspections. Given a 3D environment with a set of objects that need to be inspected, and an inspection quality $0 < \alpha < 1$, the objective is to compute a set of waypoints whose joint visibility ratio is at least α and a dynamically-feasible and collision-free trajectory that enables the aerial vehicle to reach all the waypoints. The approach seeks to minimize the number of the waypoints and the overall distance traveled by the aerial vehicle.

A superset of the waypoints is first generated by using random sampling or approximations of the medial axis via skeletonization algorithms. To reduce the number of the waypoints, the approach applies a visibility filtering mechanism based on a computation of a hitting set via Monte-Carlo search over an axis-aligned bounding box obstacle tree. After generating the waypoints, a multi-goal motion planning approach is applied to compute a collision-free and dynamically-feasible trajectory that visits all the waypoints while seeking to minimize the distance traveled. Experimental results in simulation with complex 3D models where the aerial vehicle carries out outside and inside inspection tasks demonstrate the effectiveness of the approach.

1 Introduction

Unmanned aerial vehicles (UAVs) provide a viable mechanism to automate the inspection of complex 3D environments and structures. As UAVs become an economically-feasible option for deployment, it is important to increase their autonomy. The inspection problem, however, poses significant challenges. It first requires determining a set of locations, referred to as guards or waypoints, whose combined visibility covers the entire or as much as possible of the surface area that needs to be inspected. Waypoint computations lead to NP-hard art-gallery problems when a minimal set is required [19]. Often approaches resort to approximations in order to remain efficient while still generating a small number of waypoints that cover the inspection area [1,12,15,18].

© Springer International Publishing AG 2017
Y. Gao et al. (Eds.): TAROS 2017, LNAI 10454, pp. 134–149, 2017.
DOI: 10.1007/978-3-319-64107-2_12

In addition, collision-free and dynamically-feasible motions need to be planned that enable the UAV to visit all the waypoints. The vehicle dynamics express physical constraints on the feasible motions, such as restricting the velocity, acceleration, steering, turning radius, and direction of motion. Failing to take the dynamics into account during planning could result in infeasible paths that cannot be followed by the vehicle. Motion planning with dynamics, however, is undecidable [4].

To address these challenges, we propose an approach for inspection of 3D surfaces that combines geometric processing with sampling-based motion planning. Geometric processing seeks to generate a set of waypoints whose combined visibility reaches a desired user-defined inspection quality $\alpha(0 < \alpha < 1)$. We rely on efficient medial-axis approximating skeletonizations of the 3D model being inspected and fast ray intersection tests based on accelerated axis-aligned bounding box (AABB) trees. An essential aspect of the proposed approach is the computation of a minimal set of waypoints by solving a *hitting-set* problem. It is based on an advanced implementation of the Nested Monte-Carlo Policy Adaptation (NRPA) algorithm [23], where we increased the diversity of the solutions

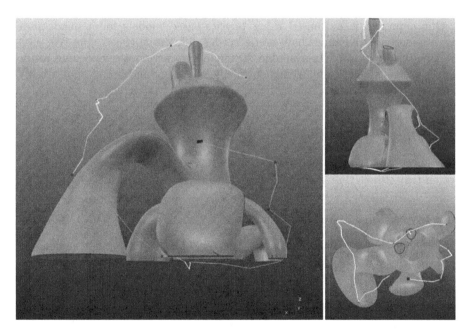

Fig. 1. Example of a 3D surface inspection task from different viewpoints. The combined visibility from the waypoints (shown in blue) generated by our approach reaches the desired inspection quality (set to $\alpha = 99\%$). The solution path (shown in yellow) obtained by our approach enables the quadcoptor to reach all the waypoints. Figure best viewed in color and on screen. Videos of the quadcoptor inspecting this and other 3D models from the outside or the inside can be found in the supplementary material. A more extensive list can be found at goo.gl/itjNKI.

in a beam [6]. Hitting sets are common in AI. In action planning, hitting sets are used to improve state-of-the-art heuristics [2], while in knowledge representation they help to compute diagnoses [22]. Our hitting-set solver is generic and so it can be used in these other settings as well.

After generating the waypoints, we rely on state-of-the-art multi-goal motion planning, such as DROMOS [21], to compute collision-free and dynamically-feasible motions that enable the UAV to reach each waypoint. The motion planner, starting from the initial state, incrementally expands a motion tree with collision-free and dynamically-feasible trajectories as branches. Short TSP tours are used to guide the motion-tree expansion and reduce the distance traveled by the UAV as it reaches the waypoints.

Waypoint generation combined with motion planning has been used to generate short inspection tours [8,11]. These methods, however, do not take the vehicle dynamics into account. As a result, the planned paths are not necessarily dynamically-feasible, so the robot might not be able to follow the planned paths. There has also been work that generates dynamically-feasible motion trajectories by using a motion-tree expansion [9,20]. These methods, however, have focused on 2D inspection. It remains open to effectively extend these approaches for 3D inspections.

Our approach is evaluated using physics-based models for a quadcoptor whose underlying dynamics have second-order differential constraints. We used an extensive set of publicly-available 3D models to carry out outside and inside inspection tasks. The result demonstrate the efficiency and broad applicability of the approach.

2   Problem Formulation

This section defines the inspection problem as well as the vehicle model and motion trajectories that enable the vehicle to carry out the inspection task.

2.1   Inspection via Waypoints

The world $\mathcal{W}$ contains objects $\mathcal{O} = \{\mathcal{O}_1, \ldots, \mathcal{O}_n\}$. The inspection region, denoted by $\mathcal{R}$, is defined as

$$\mathcal{R} \subseteq \bigcup_{i=1}^{n} \text{SURFACE}(\mathcal{O}_i). \tag{1}$$

where $\text{SURFACE}(\mathcal{O}_i)$ denotes the surface of $\mathcal{O}_i$. In 3D environments, the objects could be represented, for example, as triangle meshes and the inspection region as a set of triangle and object indices. Our framework also supports the specification of the inspection region by intersection as $\mathcal{R} = \bigcup_{i=1}^{n} \text{SURFACE}(\mathcal{O}_i) \cap \mathcal{M}_i$, where each $\mathcal{M}_i$ is a user-provided 3D object.

To inspect $\mathcal{R}$, the UAV takes snapshots from different locations. A point $q \in \mathcal{R}$ is considered visible from a location $p \in \mathcal{W}$ only when the segment $\overline{pq}$ from p to q does not intersect an object (except at the endpoint q). A point

$q \in \mathcal{R}$ is considered visible from $p \in \mathcal{W}$ iff $\overline{pq} \in \mathcal{W}$, i.e., the segment from p to q remains entirely in $\mathcal{W}$. Let $vis(\mathcal{R}, p)$ denote the area of $\mathcal{R}$ that is visible from $p \in \mathcal{W}$, i.e.,

$$vis(p) = \{q : q \in \mathcal{R} \wedge vis(p, q) = \texttt{true}\}. \tag{2}$$

The visible area from a set of points $p_1, \ldots, p_\ell \in \mathcal{W}$ is defined as

$$vis(p_1, \ldots, p_\ell) = \bigcup_{j=1}^{\ell} vis(p_j). \tag{3}$$

The quality of a set of points $p_1, \ldots, p_\ell \in \mathcal{W}$ is defined as the fraction of the area in $\mathcal{R}$ that is visible, i.e.,

$$quality(p_1, \ldots, p_\ell) = \frac{area(vis(p_1, \ldots, p_\ell))}{area(\mathcal{R})}. \tag{4}$$

The user defines an inspection quality α, $0 < \alpha < 1$, and the first objective is to generate a set of waypoints $p_1, \ldots, p_\ell$ such that $quality(p_1, \ldots, p_\ell) \geq \alpha$. As we cannot expect the vehicle to get arbitrarily close to the object, in some cases, e.g., a sphere connected to a wall, feasible inspection tours exist only if $\alpha < 1$.

2.2   Physics-Based Modeling of Vehicle Motions

The underlying vehicle dynamics are encapsulated by a function

$$s_{new} \leftarrow \text{SIMULATE}(s, a, dt), \tag{5}$$

Fig. 2. Physics-based model, implemented in V-REP and Bullet, of the quadcopter used for the aerial inspection tasks.

which computes the new state s_{new} when the control action a is applied to the state s for one time step dt. A state $s \in \mathcal{S}$, where $\mathcal{S}$ denotes the state space, describes the position, orientation, steering angle, velocity, and other components necessary to describe the vehicle motions. A control action $a \in \mathcal{A}$, where $\mathcal{A}$ denotes the action space, defines inputs that are used to drive the vehicle such as acceleration and steering angle.

Often the vehicle dynamics are described by a set of differential equations $\dot{s} = f(s, a)$. In such cases, SIMULATE can be implemented using numerical integration techniques, such as Runge-Kutta. For an increased level of realism, physics-based engines such as Bullet, V-REP, PhysX, Gazebo can also be used. Physics-based engines can efficiently simulate general rigid-body dynamics by computing the forces acting on the moving bodies and the motions that result from applying those forces. The experiments in this paper use V-REP in combination with Bullet to create a physics-based model of a quadcopter.

A motion trajectory $\zeta : \{1, \ldots, T\} \rightarrow \mathcal{S}$ is defined as a sequence of states. A dynamically-feasible trajectory is obtained by starting at a state s and applying a sequence of control actions $a_1, \ldots, a_{T-1}$ in succession. Such trajectory is defined as $\zeta(1) = s$ and $\forall i \in \{2, \ldots, T\} : \zeta(i) = \text{SIMULATE}(\zeta(i-1), a_{i-1}, dt)$. The trajectory ζ is collision-free when every state $\zeta(i)$ avoids collisions. We use PQP [17] to efficiently check for collisions.

2.3   Problem Statement

Surface inspection can now be stated as follows.

Definition 1. *Given a desired inspection quality* $0 < \alpha \leq 1$, *a world* $\mathcal{W}$, *objects* $\mathcal{O} = \{\mathcal{O}_1, \ldots, \mathcal{O}_n\}$, *a surface area* $\mathcal{R} \subseteq \bigcup_{i=1}^{n} \text{SURFACE}(\mathcal{O}_i)$, *a start point* $p_{start} \in \mathcal{W}$, *and a vehicle model* $\langle \mathcal{S}, \mathcal{A}, f, \text{SIMULATE} \rangle$ *compute*

- *a set of inspection points* $\mathcal{P} = \{p_1, \ldots, p_\ell\} \subset \mathcal{W}$,
- *a tour* $\Gamma = \text{tour}(p_{start}, p_1, \ldots, p_\ell)$, *which starts at* p_{start} *and specifies an ordering of* $p_1, \ldots, p_\ell$, *and*
- *a collision-free and dynamically-feasible trajectory* $\zeta : \{1, \ldots, T\} \rightarrow \mathcal{S}$ *which connects the inspection points in the order defined by* Γ

such that quality$(p_{start}, p_1, \ldots, p_\ell) \geq \alpha$.

The approach seeks to reduce the number of inspection points and the distance traveled by the vehicle.

3   Method

Our approach starts by generating a set of inspection points that achieve the desired inspection quality. Multi-goal motion planning is then used to find a collision-free and dynamically-feasible trajectory that enables the vehicle to reach all the waypoints while reducing the distance traveled. Figure 3 provides a schematic illustration.

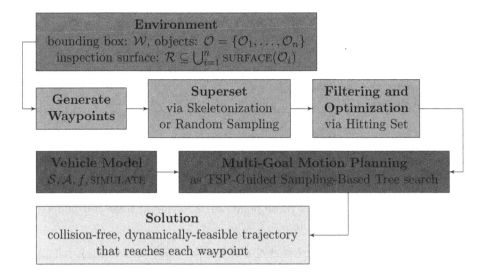

Fig. 3. A schematic illustration of our approach.

3.1   Generating the Inspection Points

Pseudocode for generating the inspection points is shown in Algorithm 1. The underlying idea is to start with a large set of points and then filter the set down while maintaining the desired inspection quality. We rely on skeletonizations to draw a good set of candidates since points on the skeleton of a 3D model tend to see large surface areas.

The vertices on the skeleton are filtered to determine viable candidates for the inspection points. Points that are too close to the obstacles are removed. The filtering mechanism is shown in Algorithm 2. The skeletonization step is optional, one can actually use any sampled set of points, whose joint visibility surface defines the region to be inspected. Especially if we inspect an object from the outside random sampling often is more robust than the skeletonization approaches.

Algorithm 1. GENERATEINSPECTIONPTS$(\mathcal{W}, \mathcal{O}, \mathcal{R}, \alpha)$

Input: $\mathcal{W}, \mathcal{O}, \mathcal{R}$ CAD objects
α: desired inspection quality, $0 < \alpha \leq 1$
Output: a set of inspection waypoints

1: $skeleton \leftarrow$ SKELETONIZE$(\mathcal{W})$
2: $V_1 \leftarrow$ SAMPLE$(skeleton)$
3: $V_2 \leftarrow$ SAMPLE$(\mathcal{R})$
4: $adjacent \leftarrow$ FILTERINSPECTION(V_1, V_2, α);
5: **return** HITTINGSET$(adjacent, \alpha)$

Algorithm 2. FILTERINSPECTIONPTS(V_1, V_2, α)

Input: V_1, V_2, α: desired inspection quality, $0 < \alpha \leq 1$
Output: a set of inspection points

1: **for** $(i, j) \in \{0, \ldots, |V_1| - 1\} \times \{0, \ldots, |V_2| - 1\}$ **do**
2:     $adjacent(i, j) \leftarrow$ VISIBLE(v_i, v_j)
3: **return** $adjacent$

3.2   Skeletonization

Skeletons are effective shape abstractions used in segmentation, shape matching, reconstruction, and virtual navigation. The surface skeleton Σ of a 3D object Ω with boundary Δ is defined as those points in Ω having at least two boundary points at minimum distance, i.e.,

$$\Sigma(\Omega) = \{x \in \Omega \mid \exists a, b \in \Delta \wedge a \neq b \wedge ||x - a||_2 = ||x - b||_2\}. \tag{6}$$

As the skeleton may contain hyperplanes (also called faces or sheets), a curve skeleton Θ can be defined based on shortest geodesics that consists of a (Jordan) curve. In fact, Θ is a 3D embedded graph $G = (V, E)$ where V is the set of intersections (nodes of degree > 2) and E is the set of curves. The skeleton nodes constitute a superset of the waypoints, which is then filtered via a hitting-set solver.

There are different ways of obtaining skeletonizations. We have implemented both a triangulated surface mesh skeletonization resulting in a curve skeleton and a voxel-based skeletonization resulting in a set of pixels.

3.3   Hitting-Set Solver

Hitting set is a well-known but computationally-demanding optimization problem, with a decision variant already mentioned in Karp's prototypical set of 21 NP-hard problems [14]. We use the following equivalent formulation:

> Given a bipartite graph $G = (V, E)$ with $V = V_1 \cup V_2$, $V_1 \cap V_2 = \emptyset$, and $E \subseteq (V_1 \times V_2)$, find a subset V' of V_1 of minimal cardinality, so that all nodes in V_2 are covered, i.e., for every $v_2 \in V_2$ there is a $v_1 \in V_1$ such that $(v_1, v_2) \in E$.

Mathematical Program. There is a simple mathematical IP problem encoding of the hitting-set problem. On the bipartite graph define Boolean variables $p_{i,j}$ that denote if the element $j \in V_2$ is adjacent to node $i \in V_1$, and x_i that denotes if a node in V_1 is selected. If $n = |V_1|$ and $m = |V_2|$ then the task is to minimize $\min \sum_{j=1}^{n} x_j$ subject to $\sum_{j=1}^{n} p_{i,j} x_j \geq 1$, for every $j \in \{1, \ldots, n\}$

and $x_i \in \{0, 1\}$ for every $i \in \{1, \ldots, m\}$. As the problem is hard and the values for n and m are considerably large, we are interested in computing approximate solutions with randomized search.

Related work on pyramid visibility [25] applies IP-solving for the dual set cover problem. It approximates the model in an iterated hierarchical refinement process, so that the IP solver is called over and over again.

In our setting, V_1 is the set of waypoints to be minimized and V_2 is the set of (possibly sampled) object surface points. In the hitting-set problem, the sampled points are located on the surface of the objects.

Monte-Carlo Hitting Set Solver. Different approaches to solving the hitting-set problem can be considered. Given an immediate formalization of the problem as an integer program, ILP solvers compute optimal solutions. However, considering the expected size of the input (hundreds of waypoints, thousands of object surface sampling points), ILP solvers becomes computationally impractical.

Monte-Carlo search is a set of randomized algorithms for solving combinatorial problems. While for two-player games including Go [24] tree exploring algorithm like UCT [16] are used, for single-agent games Nested Monte-Carlo search [5] has led to many recent high scores. Nestedness is used as a method to trade exploitation with exploration and exponentially condenses the information obtained in the recursive calls to the algorithm. All algorithms are based on the concept of a *rollout*, denoting a random play to the end of the game. Unless the end of the game, a set of successors for the current position is generated and one successor is randomly chosen with respect to some reinforcement strategy based on the outcome of preceedings runs.

We use an efficient game implementation for solving the above hitting set problem. The input is a bipartite graph in the form of a Boolean adjacency matrix *adjacent* of size $V_1 \times V_2$ (equivalently an adjacency list can be used in case RAM becomes exhausted). As a policy, we use a mapping from V_1 to $\mathbb{R}$. The code in Fig. 4 displays all domain-dependent hitting set code of our generic Monte-Carlo search framework.

For conducting a rollout that generates some valid cover V_2' for V_2 the algorithm maintains two Boolean vectors: *visited* for representing the current selection for V_1' of V_1 (to be minimized), and *chosen* for counting the current coverage of V_2 (to be maximized). As optimization objective we used the score function $|V_1'| - 100 \cdot |V_2'|$. A rollout is *valid*, if we have $\alpha \cdot |V_2| \leq |V_2'|$.

3.4 Connecting the Waypoints with Feasible Motions

After generating the inspection points, we rely on multi-goal sampling-based motion planning to compute a collision-free and dynamically-feasible trajectory that enables the vehicle to reach each waypoint. For this paper, we used DRO-MOS [21] due to its efficiency, scalability, and applicability to 3D environments.

```
class Game {
 public:
  int length, size;
  Move rollout[MaxPlayoutLength];
  Game () {
   for (int j=0; j<SET; j++) visited[j] = 0;
   for (int j=0; j<HITTING; j++) chosen[j] = 0;
   length = size = 0;
  }
  int code (Move m) { return m; }
  bool terminal() { return size >= SET*ALPHA; }
  double score() { return length - size*100; }
  void play(Move m) {
    rollout[length++] = m;
    chosen[m] = 1;
    for (int j = 0; j<SET; j++)
      if (visited[j] == 0 && adjacent[m][j]) {
        visited[j] = 1;
        size++;
      }
  }
  int legalMoves(Move moves[MaxLegalMoves]) {
    int succs = 0;
    for (int m = 0; m < HITTING; m++)
      if (chosen[m] == 0) moves[succs++] = m;
    return successors;
  }
};
```

Fig. 4. Monte-Carlo hitting set solver implementation.

DROMOS expands a motion tree in the state space by adding collision-free and dynamically-feasible motion trajectories as branches. It uses TSP tours over the waypoints to effectively guide the motion-tree expansion.

4   Experiments

To validate our approach, we use a physics-based model of a quadcopter based on V-REP and Bullet physics engines. Our code interfaces with the 4.8.1 version of the computational geometry algorithm library (CGAL), where skeletonization and ray intersection algorithms are implemented. All data files and programs will be made publicly available.

Implementation Notes. The newest version of CGAL offers an implementation of the mean curvature skeleton algorithm to compute the curve skeleton of a shape, which captures its essential topology. Figure 5 shows the initial CAD model and the curve skeleton together with some additional information (the nodes in the skeleton and some skeleton-to-mesh edges) to the right.

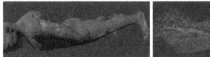

Fig. 5. (left) CAD model (right) Curve skeleton with vertices (shown as discs) and visibility information (indicated with lines).

For voxel-based skeletonization we first apply *binvox*[1] to obtain a voxelization of the 3D CAD model, followed by *thinvox*[2] for 3D voxel thinning. Depending on the resolution chosen (we used the default one) running time can increase to a couple of minutes. We view the model transformation as offline cost that belongs to the input. Moreover, it is well-known that voxelization can be done much faster on a GPU [10]. For running our program, we used a single core of a contemporary personal computer infrastructure (Ubuntu 14.04 LTS (64 Bit), Intel Core i7–4500U, 1.8 GHz, 16 GB).

4.1 Results

Table 1 shows the outcome of skeletonization and hitting set computation for many benchmark instances (mainly from the CGAL and partly from the Stanford libraries). The running time was limited to two minutes, but in many cases our waypoint generator converged much faster. We see that both skeletonization methods give similar results.

Inside and Outside Surface Inspections. Figures 6 and 7 show inside and outside surface inspections of complex 3D models carried out by the quadcopter. The waypoints generated by our approach were passed as input to the sampling-based motion planner, which computed a collision-free and dynamically-feasible motion trajectory that enabled the quadcopter to reach each waypoint. The running time for the motion planner was negligible, between 0.5 s and 3 s.

---

[1] http://www.patrickmin.com/binvox.
[2] http://www.patrickmin.com/thinvox.

Table 1. Results of Monte-Carlo hitting set filtering on two different skeletons; n is the number of vertices in the initial skeleton, $\alpha\%$ the number of generated waypoints wrt. visibility parameter α.

Model	Mesh	Skeleton (CGAL)			Skeleton (binvox)		
		n	99%	90%	n	99%	90%
Anchor	119	519	5	3	6143	10	6
Bones	137	2154	41	24	6449	50	22
Bull	335	6200	15	7	5912	21	7
Bunny	242	37706	4	2	4580	4	2
Couplingdown	216	1841	11	6	8657	10	4
Cross	2	40	1	1	1642	1	1
Cube	2	8	1	1	8	1	1
Dino	95920	143880	96	5	3948	10	6
Dragknob	7	161	1	1	5847	1	1
Eight	135	766	4	3	2609	5	3
Elephant	299	2775	15	8	4864	12	7
Elk	167	1645	9	5	4879	8	4
Ellipsoid	19	162	1	1	480	1	1
Fandisk	192	6475	2	1	6630	2	1
FPT	22	454	1	1	2472	1	1
Genus1	4	50	1	1	569	1	1
Handle	78	1165	2	1	5969	3	1
Hedra	2	6	1	1	308	1	1
Helmet	55	496	3	1	4952	4	2
Homer	267	4930	9	5	3068	10	5
Joint	18	221	1	1	23221	7	5
Knot1	471	3200	11	7	6242	10	7
Knot2	416	5700	17	9	5303	17	9
Lion-head	117	8356	4	2	6725	3	2
Man	434	17495	81	12	3450	57	10
Mushroom	2	2337	1	1	10255	2	1
Oblong	20	424	2	1	6860	5	3
Oni	50	1435	3	1	4724	6	2
Pinion	50	650	10	7	13514	8	5
Pipe	2	160	1	1	2577	4	3
Retinal	86	3643	2	2	1124	2	2
Rotor	62	600	1	1	6284	6	4
Sphere	2	162	1	1	8	1	1
Spool	10	649	2	2	6678	6	2
Star	3	14	1	1	3955	1	1
Tetra_12f	2	8	1	1	2791	1	1
Tetra_6f	2	5	1	1	6878	1	1
Tripod	3	24	1	1	4912	1	1
Turbine	422	9210	17	7	9138	13	6
Solve	5552	8328	97	9	21538	15	9

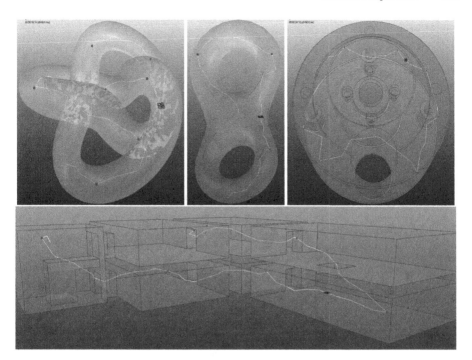

Fig. 6. Examples of scenes where the quadcopter is required to inspect the inside surface of the 3D model. The blue dots indicate the waypoints generated by our approach. The yellow dotted-line indicates the paths that the quadcopter needs to follow. After the waypoints were generated, the motion planner took 0.5 s–3 s to find a solution. Figures best viewed in color and on screen. Videos of the quadcoptor inspecting these and other models can be found in the supplementary material. A more extensive list can be found at goo.gl/itjNKI.

We note that sampling-based motion planning has been applied to complex structure inspection and tested on a probabilistic roadmap in one industrial ship hull inspection domain [11]. The approach connected and contracted the set of sampling RRT points in a TSP solution process. The runtime spent was considerable (2 h). We could not do a head-to-head comparison with [11] since the model they used is not publicly available. For our models, we apply skeletonizations in our framework to effectively generate a small set of inspection points and then use a fast multi-goal motion planner to find a solution. The runtimes were small (2–3 min to generate the inspection points and less than 3 s for the multi-goal motion planner).

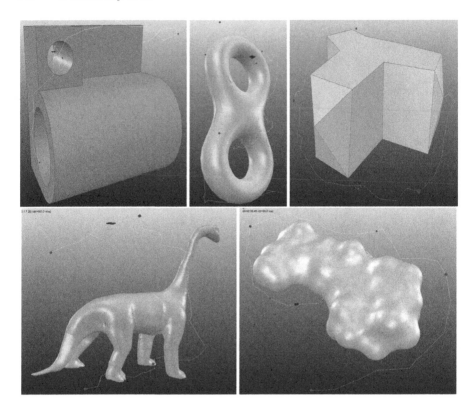

Fig. 7. Examples of scenes where the quadcopter is required to inspect the outside surface of the 3D model. The blue dots indicate the waypoints generated by our approach. The yellow dotted-line indicates the paths that the quadcopter needs to follow. Figures best viewed in color and on screen. After the waypoints were generated, the motion planner took 0.5 s–3 s to find a solution. Videos of the quadcoptor inspecting these and other models can be found in the supplementary material. A more extensive list can be found at goo.gl/itjNKI (anonimity maintained).

5 Discussion

We have developed a framework that enables an UAV to carry out surface inspection of 3D models. The premise of the paper was that such complex inspection tasks can be accomplished by (i) generating a set of waypoints whose joint visibility covers the inspection area at the desired inspection quality, and (ii) using multi-goal motion planning to compute feasible motions that connect the waypoints. Our approach is general – it can work with any 3D model and vehicle model whose motions can be simulated.

We noted that workspace decompositions into convex regions (such as triangulations or trapezodial maps) usually lead to a number of waypoints that is too large for starting the filtering process. Moreover, further experiments indicated that the outcome is often inferior to starting with the skeleton of the medial axis. The exact medial axis in 3D includes faces, so that a full skeleton was preferable. This way we bypassed known limitations to computing a minimized set of guards for full visibility [3].

Our work opens up several avenues for future research. One research direction is to extend the framework to the multi-agent inspection problem, that is given a fleet of vehicles and a set of inspection areas, concurrently perform the inspection task to the stated degree of satisfaction in the minimal amount of time (with minimal makespan). There are various multi-agent pathfinding algorithms [13], some of them already operating on industrial production floors [7], but they usually impose strong limitations on the vehicle dynamics and the freespace that can be used by the robots. As the Monte-Carlo search approach is quite flexible and applicable to both solving the vehicle routing and the hitting set problems, we think that further exploring this research avenue is a viable option.

Another research direction is to leverage online visibility. Visibility problems like shadow casting are often natively encoded on current graphics cards. Besides ray tracing, a standard and very fast geometric primitive is Z-buffering. While this approach is a good predictor of what part of the scene can be seen from one waypoint, the individual Z-buffering results have to be attached back to the objects of interest with the visibility union to be computed.

Finally, real-world optimization problems usually consist of several subproblems that interact with each other. In order to solve such problems, it is important to understand and deal with these interactions. So far, the research literature is lacking systematic approaches for dealing with such interdependent problems. For the inspection problem, there are three hard combinatorial problems that depend on each other: (i) generating the waypoints, (ii) finding an optimal order to visit the waypoints, and (iii) generating feasible motions to visit the waypoints in the order specified by the tour. An optimal solution to step (i) or even (ii) could turn out to be infeasible due to constraints imposed by the vehicle dynamics and obstacles in the environment. As such, one research direction is to combine all these problems and feedback information from one layer to the other.

Acknowledgment. The work of B. Can Secim and E. Plaku was supported by NSF IIS-1449505 and NSF IIS-1548406.

References

1. Ardiyanto, I., Toyohashi, M.J.: Visibility-based viewpoint planning for guard robot using skeletonization and geodesic motion model. In: IEEE International Conference on Robotics and Automation, Karlsruhe, Germany, pp. 660–666 (2013)
2. Bonet, B., Helmert, M.: Strengthening landmark heuristics via hitting sets. In: European Conference on Artificial Intelligence, Lisbon, Portugal, pp. 329–334 (2010)
3. Borrmann, D., De Rezende, P.J., De Souza, C.C., Fekete, S.P., Friedrichs, S., Kröller, A., Nüchter, A., Schmidt, C., Tozoni, D.C.: Point guards and point clouds: solving general art gallery problems. In: ACM Symposium on Computational Geometry, Rio de Janeiro, Brazil, pp. 347–348 (2013)

4. Branicky, M.S.: Universal computation and other capabilities of continuous and hybrid systems. Theor. Comput. Sci. **138**(1), 67–100 (1995)
5. Cazenave, T.: Nested Monte-Carlo search. In: International Joint Conference on Artificial Intelligence, Pasadena, CA, pp. 456–461 (2009)
6. Cazenave, T.: Monte Carlo beam search. IEEE Trans. Comput. Intell. AI Games **4**(1), 68–72 (2012)
7. D'Andrea, R.: A revolution in the warehouse: a retrospective on Kiva systems and the grand challenges ahead. IEEE Trans. Autom. Sci. Eng. **9**(4), 638–639 (2012)
8. Danner, T., Kavraki, L.E.: Randomized planning for short inspection paths. In: IEEE International Conference on Robotics and Automation, Washington, DC, pp. 971–976 (2000)
9. Edelkamp, S., Pomarlan, M., Plaku, E.: Multi-region inspection by combining clustered traveling salesman tours with sampling-based motion planning. IEEE Robot. Autom. Lett. **2**, 428–435 (2017)
10. Eisemann, E., Décoret, X.: Single-pass GPU solid voxelization for real-time applications. In: Graphics Interface, Ontario, Canada, pp. 73–80 (2008)
11. Englot, B., Hover, F.: Sampling-based coverage path planning for inspection of complex structures. In: International Conference on Automated Planning and Scheduling, Sao Paulo, Brazil, pp. 29–37 (2012)
12. Fabbri, R., Estrozi, L.F., Da, L., Costa, F.: On Voronoi diagrams and medial axes. J. Math. Imaging Vision **17**, 27–40 (2002)
13. Hönig, W., Kumar, T.K.S., Cohen, L., Ma, H., Xu, H., Ayanian, N., Koenig, S.: Multi-agent path finding with kinematic constraints. In: International Conference on Automated Planning and Scheduling, London, UK, pp. 477–485 (2016)
14. Karp, R.M.: Reducibility among combinatorial problems. In: Miller, R.E., Thatcher, J.W. (eds.) Complexity of Computer Computations, pp. 85–103. Plenum Press, New York (1972)
15. Kazazakis, G.D., Argyros, A.A.: Fast positioning of limited-visibility guards for the inspection of 2D workspaces. In: IEEE/RSJ International Conference on Intelligent Robots and Systems, Lausanne, Switzerland, pp. 2843–2848 (2002)
16. Kocsis, L., Szepesvári, C.: Bandit based Monte-Carlo planning. In: European Conference on Machine Learning, Berlin, Germany, pp. 282–293 (2006)
17. Larsen, E., Gottschalk, S., Lin, M.C., Manocha, D.: Fast proximity queries with swept sphere volumes. Tr99-18, Department of Computer Science, University of N. Carolina, Chapel Hill (1999). http://gamma.cs.unc.edu/SSV/
18. Li, X., Yu, W., Lin, X., Iyengar, S.S.: On optimizing autonomous pipeline inspection in 3D environment. IEEE Trans. Robot. **28**(1), 223–233 (2012)
19. O'Rourke, J.: Art Gallery Theorems and Algorithms, vol. 57. Oxford University Press, Oxford (1987)
20. Papadopoulos, G., Kurniawatia, H., Patrikalakis, N.M.: Asymptotically optimal inspection planning using systems with differential constraints. In: IEEE International Conference on Robotics and Automation, Karlsruhe, Germany, pp. 4126–4133 (2013)
21. Plaku, E., Rashidian, S., Edelkamp, S.: Multi-group motion planning in virtual environments. Comput. Anim. Virtual Worlds (2016, in press). doi:10.1002/cav.1688
22. Reiter, R.: A theory of diagnosis from first principles. Artif. Intell. **32**(1), 57–95 (1987)
23. Rosin, C.D.: Nested rollout policy adaptation for Monte Carlo tree search. In: International Joint Conference on Artificial Intelligence, Barcelona, Spain, pp. 649–654 (2011)

24. Silver, D., Huang, A., Maddison, C.J., Guez, A., Sifre, L., van den Driessche, G., Schrittwieser, J., Antonoglou, I., Panneershelvam, V., Lanctot, M., Dieleman, S., Grewe, D., Nham, J., Kalchbrenner, N., Sutskever, I., Lillicrap, T., Leach, M., Kavukcuoglu, K., Graepel, T., Hassabis, D.: Mastering the game of Go with deep neural networks and tree search. Nature **529**, 484–503 (2016)
25. Yu, W., Li, M., Li, X.: Optimizing pyramid visibiliy coverage for autonomous robots in 3D environment. In: International Conference on Computer Science and Education, Colombo, Sri Lanka, pp. 1023–1028 (2013)

Integrated and Adaptive Locomotion and Manipulation for Self-reconfigurable Robots

Thomas Joseph Collins[(✉)] and Wei-Min Shen

Information Sciences Institute, University of Southern California,
Los Angeles, CA, USA
collinst@usc.edu, shen@isi.edu

Abstract. Integrated and adaptive locomotion and manipulation (IALM) is a key capability for robots to perform real-world applications in challenging environments. It requires interleaving many tasks, sometimes simultaneously, and switching the functions and roles of body components on demand. For example, for autonomous assembly in space, a multiple-tentacle single body "octopus" may have to become a distributed group of "ant" robots, while a hand-like end-effector useful in one case may have to function as an anchor foot in a different situation. This paper presents a general control framework for coordinating high-dimensional dexterous locomotion and manipulation in self-reconfigurable robotic tree structures. The controller is implemented on the SuperBot robotic system and validated in real-time, high fidelity, physics-based simulation. The results have shown many promising capabilities in high-dimensional, dynamic kinematic control for locomotion, manipulation, and self-reconfiguration essential for future autonomous assembly applications.

Keywords: Self-reconfigurable robots · Manipulation · Autonomous assembly

1 Introduction

Real-world applications of robotic systems in challenging environments often demand extraordinary capabilities. For example, Fig. 1 shows a potential high-payoff and high-risk application for autonomous assembly in space.

To accomplish such challenging tasks, a robotic system must self-assemble large structures from modular components. It needs to plan its course of actions, transport pieces from storage to working sites, and manipulate components for alignment, docking, and secure assembly. To meet these challenges, self-reconfigurable robots may offer some critical advantages over fixed-shape robots. For example, self-reconfigurable robots may provide on-demand shape optimization, resilience to single-point failures, and flexible, low-cost launch options. In this paper, we will focus on the capability of interleaved and even simultaneous IALM.

© Springer International Publishing AG 2017
Y. Gao et al. (Eds.): TAROS 2017, LNAI 10454, pp. 150–165, 2017.
DOI: 10.1007/978-3-319-64107-2_13

Fig. 1. Autonomous assembly of large surfaces in space using self-reconfigurable robots.

There are several technical challenges to achieve IALM. Specifically, a robot must deal with the high numbers of degrees of freedom (DOF) required for dextrous and precise manipulation, the fact that global configuration information is not at a central location but distributed among the network of modules, and the fact that interaction points with the environment such as the location of a hand and a foot are dynamic and not completely known in advance. Such challenges make it difficult to directly apply any traditional manipulation techniques because we cannot assume a fixed "base" from which kinematics can be computed and, additionally, the roles of the modules change dynamically from situation to situation. For example, a "foot" for walking in one step may need to become a "hand" for grasping in the next step. Furthermore, self-reconfiguration changes the underlying kinematic structure of the tree itself, necessitating novel approaches.

The contributions of this paper include an integrated controller for adaptive and simultaneous locomotion and manipulation (named *loco-manipulation*). The configuration information of the robotic tree is distributed throughout the network of modules, and a "brain" module is elected dynamically from step to step using local message passing. High-dimensional and precision manipulation is accomplished via a combination of the provably-convergent Particle Swarm Optimization (PSO) variant called Branch and Bound Particle Swarm Optimization [18] (for inverse kinematics) and the RRT-Connect path planner [8]. This controller enables general tree structures of self-reconfigurable robotic modules to perform sophisticated locomotion and manipulation tasks simultaneously and safely (i.e., without collision). For self-reconfiguration, this controller computes the joint angles that enable the modules in the tree to self-reconfigure into a different tree for better performance in loco-manipulation tasks. An efficient, dynamic kinematic representation keeps track of the current kinematics of the tree. The proposed controller is implemented using the SuperBot [14] robotic system concept and validated in a high-fidelity physics-based simulation for autonomous assembly in a micro-gravity environment. The results are encouraging, demonstrating that a self-reconfigurable robotic system is able to change its configuration on-demand, transport components, and assemble a simple structure at a given working site.

The rest of the paper is organized as follows. Section 2 discusses related work. Section 3 details the proposed controller with system architecture and sub-system descriptions. Section 4 presents results for integrated and adaptive locomotion and manipulation with an application of autonomous assembly in mind, and finally Sect. 5 concludes the paper with future work.

2   Related Work

A number of modular and self-reconfigurable robot hardware systems have been proposed, including [3,10,13,14,17,20]. In many of these systems, distributed algorithms have been developed for locomotion, manipulation, and self-reconfiguration. These algorithms tend to be intimately tied to the modules in question and not broadly applicable. On the other hand, a number of general and powerful algorithms that have been developed to control modular and self-reconfigurable robot systems. In [9], Moll et al. proposed a distributed algorithm for controlling the center of mass of arbitrary kinematic trees of self-reconfigurable modules. Shen et al. proposed a digital hormone model for controlling self-reconfigurable, modular swarms of robots in [16]. However, general-purpose IALM is still an open problem.

Fig. 2. Sample locomotion results. A 6-module, 18-DOF tree structure of SuperBot modules locomotes on the planar ground surface in a given direction by repeatedly anchoring itself to the ground along the given direction.

Manipulation using physically-connected modular robots has been looked at primarily from a low-level control perspective, such as in [6], where control laws were automatically generated to follow a known reference trajectory, and

Fig. 3. Sample manipulation results. A 6-module 18-DOF tree structure of SuperBot modules picks up an object and passes it from one open end-effector to another. This is a behavior never before demonstrated, even in simulation, on a distributed system of modular robots.

a hardware perspective, such as in [22]. In [21], the self-assembly of robotic manipulators made of heterogeneous active and passive components is successfully demonstrated, and manipulation is performed with the assembled manipulators. Modules in this work move on a discrete grid which greatly simplifies locomotion. Additionally, in [1], the cooperative locomotion and manipulation (transport) of passive components by self-reconfigurable robot manipulators was successfully demonstrated. In this work, only serial manipulators were used, and locomotion took place on a discretized grid.

Some recent work outside the realm of modular robotics has focused on controlling robots with many arms and legs, such as [19]. However, such systems are centralized, and their kinematic structures are fixed.

The use of Particle Swarm Optimization, particularly to solve the inverse kinematics problem, has been studied in [5,11,12], with encouraging results. The use of PSO allows for the elimination of the well known pitfalls of traditional Jacobian inverse kinematic methods [2] (singularities, poor scaling with DOF, difficulty in applying them to dynamic situations with kinematic structure changes). This work represents the first application of Branch and Bound Particle Swarm Optimization [18].

3 Overview of the IALM Controller

3.1 Overview

The proposed controller, Algorithm 1, executes as a distributed behavior independently and in parallel on each module. Modules have no fixed ID numbers and can only communicate with modules physically docked to their connectors.

Algorithm 1. Overview of the tree control algorithm proposed in this work.

Input:
$Tasks$: a queue of tasks to perform

```
 1 Function CONTROLTREE()
 2 │   updateTree := ShouldUpdateTree();
 3 │   ProcessIncomingMessages();
 4 │   Brain = AmIConnectedToGround();
 5 │   if Brain == true then
 6 │   │   if updateTree == true then
 7 │   │   │   ClearAndReset(KinMap);
 8 │   │   │   KinMap := DiscoverKinematicStructure() ;    // Distributed
   │   │   │   BFS, Sect.3.2
 9 │   │   else if (Task := GetCurrentTask()) then
10 │   │   │   GoalA := FindGoalAngles(Task);           // BBPSOIK, Sect.3.3
11 │   │   │   Path := PlanPath(CurrentAngles(), GoalA); // Use RRT-Connect
12 │   │   │   ExecutePath(Path);
13 │   │   │   TransferBrainData(DidBrainChange(Task));
```

The overall system of modules is assumed to be a tree structure (no loops), in which a single module is attached to some fixed structure (e.g., the ground). A single module is elected at each step to (1) map the kinematic structure of the tree from its perspective (see Sect. 3.2), (2) compute a set of collision-free joint angles for the tree that solve the next task or subtask (e.g., picking up an object, see Sect. 3.3), and (3) plan a collision-free path from the current joint angles to the goal joint angles. In general, any module could be elected to be the leader. In this work, the leader is always chosen to be the module *currently* connected to the ground. This leader is called the *kinematic brain*. Note that this is purely for convenience of kinematics computations and more sophisticated leader election or task protocols, such as those presented in [15], could be used instead.

First, all messages are processed (Line 3). This happens at all modules. Modules relay state information (joint angles, connector statuses, etc.) to the current kinematic brain and listen to the brain's commands to set their joint angles or dock/undock with other modules. If the kinematic representation of the tree is out of date (Line 2) – which occurs, e.g., when the joint angles of any module move more some small pre-specified amount or a connector's state changes – then the kinematic representation of the tree is re-computed by the kinematic brain (Lines 7–8). Finally, with an up-to-date kinematic map of the structure, the next task or subtask (such as picking up a certain object, placing an object, locomoting in a certain direction, etc.) is determined based on some high-level goal (Line 9). These high-level goals are generally generated externally. The BBPSOIK procedure discussed below in Sect. 3.3 is used to find an optimal set of goal joint angles that would perform the desired subtask and meet the necessary error tolerance to enable successful docking (Line 10). The RRT-Connect path planner is then used (Line 11) to plan a collision-free motion path from the current joint angles of the tree to the computed goal angles. This path is then executed (Line 12). Finally, if the brain is to change based on the execution of the task – the brain changes at each locomotion step, as a new module connects to the ground – the state information of the current brain module is transmitted to the new brain module (Line 13).

As an example of generating subtasks from externally generated goals, consider Fig. 3. The externally generated goal is to pick up the object and switch it from one end-effector to the other open end-effector. The first time Line 9 is hit, the kinematic brain realizes the object has not been picked up. The generated subtask then becomes finding a set of joint angles that would align an open end-effector of the tree with the object to grasp it. Once the object has been grasped, the next subtask would be to find a set of joint angles that aligned the object precisely with the other open end-effector in the tree in order for the switch from one effector to the other to occur.

3.2   Kinematic Structure Discovery

The controller presented here assumes that a forward kinematics model of the module types involved in the tree are known to each module. It is convenient if this forward kinematics model is given in the form of two functions $to(C, \mathbf{q_i})$ and $from(C, \mathbf{q_i})$, where C is any connector face of the module in question, and $\mathbf{q_i}$ is a set of joint angles for module i. It is assumed that any pair of connectors can dock to one another at one pre-specified orientation. Then, these functions give the local homogeneous transformations to each connector from some specified center pose of the module and from each connector to the center of the module, respectively (and with respect to the same coordinate system). $\mathbf{q} = \{\mathbf{q_i}\}$ is reserved to denote the joint angles of the entire tree as a set of joint angles of each module.

Given these two functions, it is possible to compute the pose of any module i relative to some base frame for any tree joint angles $\mathbf{q}$ by post-multiplying an alternating sequence of these $to(C, \mathbf{q_i})$ and $from(C, \mathbf{q_i})$ transformations along the shortest path from the *brain* module – the single module connected to the ground and the most convenient base module of kinematics calculations – to module i. Assume T_G is the pose of the foot module's connector that is docked to the ground relative to some base frame (e.g., the center pose of the foot module). Let $L_C = \{C_1, C_2, ..., C_{2k}\}$ be the (even-numbered, as pairs of connectors are involved in docking modules together) list of connectors along the shortest path from base module 1 to module i in question. Let C_0 be the connector docked to the ground. Then, the relative pose of module 2's center, for example, is given by $T_2 = T_G from(C_0, \mathbf{q_1}) to(C_1, \mathbf{q_1}) from(C_2, \mathbf{q_2})$.

Once the poses of every module i, $\{T_i\}$ in the tree are specified relative to the same base frame, the pose of any connector of module i can be easily represented in the same base frame by post-multiplying to the module pose the corresponding $to(C, \mathbf{q_i})$ for the connector in question. This dual-layer kinematic representation makes it easy to use the poses of module centers for tasks like collision detection while simultaneously making it easy to generate the pose of any connector in the tree, some of which are being considered as end-effectors. If each module has these functions for each module type involved in the system, this can be easily extended to heterogeneous trees. Using this representation and a distributed breadth-first search procedure, the kinematic brain module builds a *kinematic map* of module nodes that represents the kinematic structure of the tree from the point of view of the current brain module. Each kinematic node discovered reports its current state values, including its joint angles, end-effector status, connector statuses, etc. The connector path from the kinematic brain module to each module in the tree is saved and used subsequently to communicate with specific modules as needed (e.g., to command them to set their joint angles or connect to an object). The kinematic map is used for both inverse kinematics calculations (Sect. 3.3) and path planning.

3.3   Inverse Kinematics (IK)

Inverse Kinematics as Optimization. Assuming, for the moment, that the modular robot tree in question is simply one centralized system, is quite simple to transform any IK problem into an optimization problem. Consider workspace goal pose T. Assume that a forward kinematics model $W = K(\mathbf{q})$ is given, where $\mathbf{q}$ is a vector of the tree's joint angles and W is the workspace pose of the end-effector corresponding to joint angles $\mathbf{q}$. Let $C(\mathbf{q})$ be a collision function which returns 0 if a set of joint angles is collision free and 1 otherwise. Then, the IK problem can be solved by minimizing:

$$F(\mathbf{q}) = a_p P_{error}(\mathbf{q}) + a_o O_{error}(\mathbf{q}) + a_c C(\mathbf{q}) \tag{1}$$

In the above equation P_{error} is the Euclidean position distance between T and W, while O_{error} is some measure of orientation error between T and W. a_p and a_o are optional constants weighing the differing importance of P_{error} and O_{error} (as they are measured on different scales). There are a number of ways to measure O_{error}, but, for this work, the magnitude of difference in Roll-Pitch-Yaw Euler Angles (in degrees) between T and W is minimized. Equation 1 can be generalized to the case of multiple end-effectors by summing up the P_{error}'s, O_{error}'s and collision errors for each end effector and minimizing one large sum. Multi-objective optimization methods could be used instead, but they are left for future work.

For the kinematic self-reconfiguration problem, in which a configuration must be found to align to modular robot connectors for docking, a very similar function can be minimized. In Eq. 1, P_{error} and O_{error} are error terms relative to a fixed target T. In the self-reconfiguration problem, there is no fixed target T. Rather, there are two end effector poses $\{W_1, W_2\} = K(\mathbf{q})$ returned by the forward kinematics model and the error between them must be minimized. By redefining P_{error} to be the Euclidean position distance between W_1 and W_2 and redefining O_{error} to be the magnitude of difference in Roll-Pitch-Yaw Euler Angles (in degrees) between W_1 and W_2, Eq. 1 can again be minimized.

Branch and Bound Particle Swarm Optimization. Simply put, Branch and Bound PSO (BBPSO, [18]) is an embedding of PSO within the branch and bound framework [7]. Assuming the global minimum of the function $F(S^n)$ to be minimized is known (where $S^n \subseteq R^n$, e.g., the space of possible joint angles subject to joint limits), PSO is used as a metaheuristic to find the current upper bound α_i of each partition, as the search space is recursively and exhaustively split. The only change required to the PSO algorithm is that each swarm must search only in the bounds of the partition element in which it is spawned. The known global minimum value of F is the β_i (lower bound) for each partition. The convergence of the above algorithm to the global minimum of F (assuming a known minimum value of F) and the convergence in a finite amount of time given *any* positive error ϵ is theoretically proved in [18].

By minimizing Eq. 1 using the BBPSO framework – note that traditional PSO could be used instead, but it does not provide global convergence guarantees – in the space of the joint angles of the tree of modules, one arrives at a globally convergent and optimal inverse kinematics and kinematic self-reconfiguration solution, which the authors of the present work call BBPSOIK. The is the first application of the BBPSO algorithm to the inverse kinematics (IK) problem, which results in the first globally convergent, optimal inverse kinematics solver applicable in general to modular robots that are physically connected in tree structures. Note that this claim is due to the fact that the function F in Eq. 1 has a known theoretical lower bound minimum of 0, regardless of the number of end-effectors (provided, of course, the problem has a solution).

4   Results, Validation, and Discussion

4.1   BBPSO as an IK/Self-reconfiguration Solver (BBPSOIK)

In previous work [4], we evaluated traditional PSO as a high-DOF IK solver. Though the results were highly encouraging, traditional PSO does not provably converge to globally optimal solutions. Though it often works well in practice, it is not possible to *guarantee* a solution of acceptable quality is produced in a finite amount of time using basic PSO. BBPSO, on the other hand, does provide these theoretical guarantees of solution quality, which is vitally important in the sort of dangerous environments being considered. Motivated by this, the authors performed another suite of tests, this time evaluating BBPSOIK as an inverse kinematics (and kinematic self-reconfiguration) solver. The configurations used (with end-effectors highlighted yellow) are visually shown in Fig. 4.

For clarity of presentation, the test cases are divided into the following categories (applicable tree configurations from Fig. 4 are given in parentheses):

1. Category I: Solve position and orientation IK for all end-effectors ((i)–(v)).
2. Category II: Solve position and orientation IK for one end-effector ((iv), (v)).
3. Category III: Solve position IK for all end-effectors ((i)–(v)).
4. Category IV: Solve position IK on one end-effector and position and orientation IK on the other (iv).

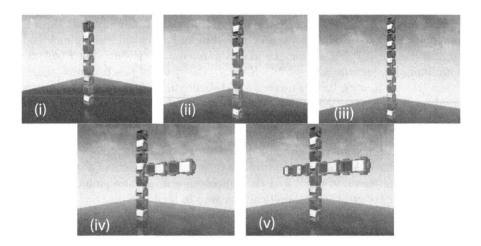

Fig. 4. The configurations of SuperBot modules used to validate the proposed BBP-SOIK solver. (i) A 4-SuperBot snake (12 DOF, 1 end-effector); (ii) A 5-SuperBot snake (15 DOF, 1 end-effector); (iii) A 6-SuperBot snake (18 DOF, 1 end-effector); (iv) A 6-SuperBot tree (18 DOF, 2 end-effectors); (v) A 9-SuperBot tree (27 DOF, 3 end-effectors). (Color figure online)

5. Category V: Solve kinematic self-reconfiguration problem to reconfigure from configuration (iii) to configuration (iv).
6. Category VI: Solve kinematic self-reconfiguration problem to reconfigure configuration (v) by randomly selecting two end-effectors to connect.
7. Category VII: Solve kinematic self-reconfiguration problem to reconfigure from configuration (iv) to configuration (iii).

For tests in category II, one tree end-effector was randomly selected during each of the 100 test runs. Figure 6 tabulates the results. Each row is a configuration/test category pair. For each such pair, the algorithm was run 100 times. ϵ represents the error tolerance given to the program. The column ϵ-Success is the percentage of the 100 test cases in which a solution of acceptable quality was found within a fixed time limit (200 s, leading to at most 27 partitions). The Avg. Partitions and Avg. Runtime columns gives the average number of branch and bound partitions and average runtime (over the 100 runs, including ϵ-failures). Since ϵ is a combined measure of position and orientation error (see Eq. 1), selecting it is not completely straightforward. If a_p an a_o are both 1 (as they are in this work), orientation error is much more heavily penalized than position error, and ϵ will primarily constitute position error (in meters). Based on experiments the authors have performed with new versions of the SINGO connector of SuperBot modules, the position tolerance of the connector is approximately 5–6 mm with very little tolerance for orientation error. Therefore, ϵ values in most of the tests above were chosen to be between 0.004 and 0.006. The cases in which ϵ is much greater correspond to cases where BBPSOIK has difficulty converging to such small ϵ values. Figure 5 shows sample numerical runs in which it is observed

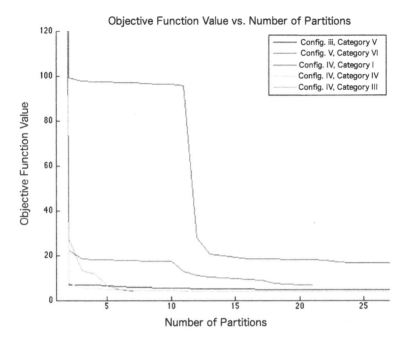

Fig. 5. Example algorithm runs showing monotonic error decreases with the number of active partitions.

Config.,Category	ε−Success	ε	Avg. Error	Avg. Partitions	Avg. Runtime
(i), I	96/100	0.004	0.00374	6.7	20.1s
(ii), I	99/100	0.004	0.00374	6.13	19.6s
(iii), I	95/100	0.004	0.00367	6.79	29.2s
(iv), I	46/100	0.05	0.069	18.12	126.1s
(i), III	100/100	0.004	0.00303	1	0.08s
(ii), III	100/100	0.004	0.00291	1	0.13s
(iii), III	100/100	0.004	0.00295	1	0.19s
(iv), III	99/100	0.004	0.00355	3.95	15.4s
(v), III	46/100	0.004	0.0221	15.49	139.1s
(iii), V	94/100	0.006	0.00624	4.91	24.2s
(iv), VII	97/100	0.006	0.00583	4.78	16.4s
(v), VI	87/100	0.006	0.00647	7.26	49.39s
(iv), IV	59/100	0.025	0.037	14.9	100.2s
(iv), II	93/100	0.004	0.00436	7.02	31.4s
(v), II	94/100	0.004	0.00363	5.73	33.5s

Fig. 6. BBPSOIK Results.

that the error monotonically decreases as a function of the number of partitions active. This provides validation that the spawning of partition elements in BBPSO forces PSO out of local minima, decreasing solution error as expected. In each partition, 20 particles were used with a maximum iteration count of 50. The authors observed that smaller particle swarms with smaller maximum iteration counts allowed for more branching, which more quickly forced PSO out of local minima, leading to better performance than with larger swarms. Figure 6 shows that the proposed algorithm converges well to optimal solutions for single-end-effector position and orientation IK problems, two-end-effector position IK problems, and problems in categories V-VII. It has difficulty consistently converging quickly when the position and orientation IK of multiple end effectors must be solved simultaneously and for tests in category IV. This makes intuitive sense, given that they are difficult multi-objective optimization problems. Future work will apply more advanced multi-objective PSO methods to such problems within a branch and bound framework.

4.2   Loco-manipulation Results

The controller proposed in this work is a novel combination of an efficient kinematic representation and discovery procedure, a novel application of BBPSOIK for solving inverse kinematics and kinematic self-reconfiguration problems, and a probabilistically complete path planner (RRT-connect). This combination, including the ability of the kinematic brain module to dynamically move from module to module, permits the controller to select optimal collision-free joint angles that solve tasks and then move in collision-free paths to those joint configurations, regardless of dynamic changes to the kinematic base frame or the structural configuration of the modules (i.e., their connections to one another). This facilitates adaptive loco-manipulation, including novel behaviors never before demonstrated on modular robotic systems. Note that, in the subsequent results, the end-effectors of the robots are assumed to be able to connect to the ground or objects at any orientation around the vector normal to the ground or the object. The environment, including the poses of the ground and objects, are assumed known to each module.

Locomotion. Figure 7 demonstrates locomotion using an 8-module (24-DOF) SuperBot tree with 4 extremities/end-effectors. At each step in the locomotion, a random free end-effector is selected, BBPSOIK is used to find a collision-free set of joint angles that aligns the end-effector with the ground in the direction of locomotion (the red arrow in the figure), and RRT-connect plans a collision-free path to the goal angles. Once the path is executed, the end-effector module attaches to the ground, becoming the new kinematic brain, and the process is repeated. Locomotion toward a target location is also possible. In such cases, the

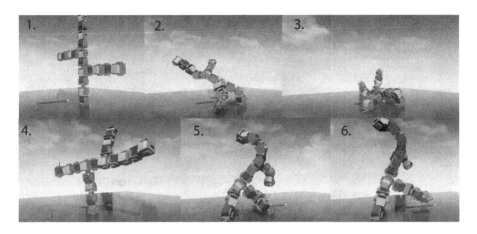

Fig. 7. Example locomotion results with an 8-module 24-DOF SuperBot tree with 4 extremities/end-effectors. (Color figure online)

direction of motion is dynamically determined based on the position difference between the current kinematic brain module and the target location. Though locomotion with modular robots has been demonstrated many times before, gaits to facilitate locomotion are most often tied intimately to the hardware and module configuration used. This represents one of the first general-purpose locomotion strategies theoretically applicable to any tree of modular or self-reconfigurable robots. This test was repeated for each configuration in Fig. 4 for 20 randomly selected motion directions.

Manipulation. Figure 8 demonstrates manipulation using an 8-module (24-DOF) SuperBot tree. The red object is picked up by one randomly-selected end-effector and passed to another open end-effector in the tree. This is a novel manipulation behavior never before demonstrated (even in simulation) using modular or self-reconfigurable robots. The kinematic brain keeps track of which end-effectors are connected to objects (of known geometry), so the object dynamically becomes part of the kinematic representation of the tree as long as it remains connected to one of the modules. This enables the controller to facilitate the transportation (simultaneous locomotion and manipulation) of passive objects from place to place while ensuring that the object being carried does not collide with the robot or its environment along the way. This test was repeated with configurations (iv) and (v) in Fig. 4 for 20 randomly selected (but reachable) object locations.

Fig. 8. Example manipulation results with an 8-module 24-DOF SuperBot tree with 4 extremities/end-effectors. The object is picked up by one end-effector before being passed from to another open end-effector.

Self-reconfiguration. Figure 9 demonstrates self-reconfiguration of a 6-module 18-DOF SuperBot tree into a long snake and vice versa. This is achieved by reducing the problem of lining up two end-effectors for self-reconfiguration to an optimization problem and efficiently solving using BBPSOIK. This allows the tree structures in question to change their structural configurations (connections) to best match the task at hand. The kinematic discovery procedure dynamically adapts to these changes, and, assuming the changes result in a new tree structure of modules, the kinematic brain can immediately use the new tree structure and its extremities for loco-manipulation.

Fig. 9. Top: A 6-module, 18-DOF SuperBot tree reconfiguring into a snake. Bottom: A 6-module, 18-DOF SuperBot snake manipulator reconfiguring into a 3-extremity tree.

Autonomous Building by Pick, Carry, Place. One of the goal usages of this framework is to enable trees of robots with multiple extremities to autonomously build structures. As a first step toward this type of behavior, Fig. 10 demonstrates a 6-module, 18-DOF SuperBot tree locomoting to, picking up, transporting, and placing the six red cylindrical objects in their respective

Fig. 10. Top left to bottom right: a demonstration of a 6-module, 18-DOF SuperBot tree performing a pick, carry, and place task. The six red cylinders are grabbed (in descending order of height) from the pile and placed in the goal areas. (Color figure online)

goal areas (blue). This is a novel demonstration of locomotion with manipulation never before performed by a system of modular robots (even in simulation). It differs from the collaborative manipulation in [1], as the proposed controller makes use of only a single tree of modules (rather than multiple serial manipulators) to perform the transportation and manipulation. Also, the robot is free to move anywhere on the ground plane, as its foot placements are not discretize. Future work will demonstrate the autonomous building of more complex structures with different sizes and shapes of building materials.

Limitations. The proposed controller has been shown to facilitate novel loco-manipulation using self-reconfigurable, modular robot trees. However, some points are worth mentioning. First, the framework currently assumes a single point of contact, with motors strong enough to support the entire structure during loco-manipulation activities. This assumption is more reasonable in environments such as outer space and under water, both of which are prime examples of dangerous and isolated environments, but it nevertheless provides a limitation.

Currently, the controller operates on a simulated distributed set of robotic modules in a hybrid distributed and centralized fashion, with the most important computations happening in a centralized place (the kinematic brain). The benefit of performing computations this way, particularly in dangerous environments, is that claims about the optimality and collision-freeness of solutions for inverse kinematics (IK) and kinematic self-reconfiguration can be made from a global perspective to ensure the safe operation of the system in the environment. However, a fully distributed methodology would provide increased robustness and fault-tolerance.

5 Conclusions and Future Work

This work proposed a novel, hybrid centralized and distributed controller based on Branch and Bound Particle Swarm Optimization (BBPSO) and

Rapidly-Exploring Random Trees (RRT-connect) that takes an important step in facilitating adaptive loco-manipulation in trees of modular and self-reconfigurable robots. This work represents the first application of BBPSO to the problems of inverse kinematics and kinematic self-reconfiguration.

Results in physics-based simulation demonstrate the generality and power of the proposed approach and include demonstrations of loco-manipulation behaviors never before shown on systems of modular or self-reconfigurable robots. Future work will aim to enable multi-contact support during loco-manipulation and parallel kinematic structures of modules (such as those with loops). A fully distributed implementation of the controller is also currently being developed. Further validation of the controller, including validation on different module types, more complex tree configurations, and more complex autonomous building tasks, will all be performed.

References

1. Bonardi, S., Vespignani, M., Moeckel, R., Ijspeert, A.J.: Collaborative manipulation and transport of passive pieces using the self-reconfigurable modular robots roombots. In: 2013 IEEE/RSJ International Conference on Intelligent Robots and Systems, pp. 2406–2412 (2013). doi:10.1109/IROS.2013.6696694
2. Buss, S.R.: Introduction to inverse kinematics with Jacobian transpose, pseudoinverse and damped least squares methods. IEEE J. Robot. Autom. 17(1–19), 16 (2004)
3. Castano, A., Shen, W.M., Will, P.: CONRO: towards deployable robots with inter-robots metamorphic capabilities. Autonom. Robots 8(3), 309–324 (2000)
4. Collins, T., Shen, W.M.: Particle swarm optimization for high-DOF inverse kinematics. In: 2017 IEEE International Conference on Control, Automation, and Robotics, Proceedings, vol. 2, pp. 1049–1054. IEEE (2017)
5. Durmus, B., Temurtas, H., Gun, A.: An inverse kinematics solution using particle swarm optimization. In: Proceedings of Sixth International Advanced Technologies Symposium, IATS 2011, Turkey, pp. 193–197 (2011)
6. Giusti, A., Althoff, M.: Automatic centralized controller design for modular and reconfigurable robot manipulators. In: 2015 IEEE/RSJ International Conference on Intelligent Robots and Systems (IROS), pp. 3268–3275. IEEE (2015)
7. Horst, R., Tuy, H.: Global Optimization: Deterministic Approaches. Springer, New York (2013)
8. Kuffner, J.J., LaValle, S.M.: RRT-connect: an efficient approach to single-query path planning. In: IEEE International Conference on Robotics and Automation, Proceedings, ICRA 2000, vol. 2, pp. 995–1001. IEEE (2000)
9. Moll, M., Will, P., Krivokon, M., Shen, W.M.: Distributed control of the center of mass of a modular robot. In: 2006 IEEE/RSJ International Conference on Intelligent Robots and Systems, pp. 4710–4715. IEEE (2006)
10. Murata, S., Yoshida, E., Kamimura, A., Kurokawa, H., Tomita, K., Kokaji, S.: M-TRAN: self-reconfigurable modular robotic system. IEEE/ASME Trans. Mechatron. 7(4), 431–441 (2002)
11. Rokbani, N., Alimi, A.: Inverse kinematics using particle swarm optimization, a statistical analysis. Procedia Eng. 64, 1602–1611 (2013). doi:10.1016/j.proeng.2013.09.242

12. Rokbani, N., Alimi, A.M.: IK-PSO, PSO inverse kinematics solver with application to biped gait generation. arXiv preprint arxiv:1212.1798 (2012)

13. Romanishin, J.W., Gilpin, K., Rus, D.: M-blocks: momentum-driven, magnetic modular robots. In: 2013 IEEE/RSJ International Conference on Intelligent Robots and Systems (IROS), pp. 4288–4295. IEEE (2013)

14. Salemi, B., Moll, M., Shen, W.M.: Superbot: a deployable, multi-functional, and modular self-reconfigurable robotic system. In: 2006 IEEE/RSJ International Conference on Intelligent Robots and Systems, pp. 3636–3641. doi:10.1109/IROS.2006. 281719 (2006)

15. Salemi, B., Will, P., Shen, W.M.: Autonomous discovery and functional response to topology change in self-reconfigurable robots. In: Braha, D., Minai, A.A., Bar-Yam, Y. (eds.) Complex Engineered Systems, pp. 364–384. Springer, Heidelberg (2006). doi:10.1007/3-540-32834-3_16

16. Shen, W.M., Will, P., Galstyan, A., Chuong, C.M.: Hormone-inspired self-organization and distributed control of robotic swarms. Autonom. Robots **17**(1), 93–105 (2004)

17. Sprowitz, A., Pouya, S., Bonardi, S., Van den Kieboom, J., Möckel, R., Billard, A., Dillenbourg, P., Ijspeert, A.J.: Roombots: reconfigurable robots for adaptive furniture. Comput. Intell. Mag. IEEE **5**(3), 20–32 (2010)

18. Tang, Z., Bagchi, K.K.: Globally convergent particle swarm optimization via branch-and-bound. Comput. Inf. Sci. **3**(4), 60 (2010)

19. Tonneau, S., Del Prete, A., Pettré, J., Park, C., Manocha, D. et al.: An efficient acyclic contact planner for multiped robots. Rpport LAAS n 16024. 2016. https://hal.archives-ouvertes.fr/hal-01267345v2/document

20. Yoon, Y., Rus, D.: Shady3D: a robot that climbs 3D trusses. In: 2007 IEEE International Conference on Robotics and Automation, pp. 4071–4076. IEEE (2007)

21. Yun, S., Rus, D.: Self assembly of modular manipulators with active and passive modules. In: IEEE International Conference on Robotics and Automation, ICRA 2008, pp. 1477–1482. IEEE (2008)

22. Zhu, W.H., Lamarche, T., Dupuis, E., Jameux, D., Barnard, P., Liu, G.: Precision control of modular robot manipulators: the VDC approach with embedded FPGA. IEEE Trans. Rob. **29**(5), 1162–1179 (2013). doi:10.1109/TRO.2013.2265631

Risk-Based Triggering of Bio-inspired Self-preservation to Protect Robots from Threats

Sing-Kai Chiu, Dejanira Araiza-Illan[(✉)], and Kerstin Eder

Department of Computer Science, University of Bristol, Bristol, UK
sc15316.2015@my.bristol.ac.uk,
{dejanira.araizaillan,kerstin.eder}@bristol.ac.uk

Abstract. Safety in autonomous systems has been mostly studied from a human-centered perspective. Besides the loads they may carry, autonomous systems are also valuable property, and self-preservation mechanisms are needed to protect them in the presence of external threats, including malicious robots and antagonistic humans. We present a biologically inspired risk-based triggering mechanism to initiate self-preservation strategies. This mechanism considers environmental and internal system factors to measure the overall risk at any moment in time, to decide whether behaviours such as fleeing or hiding are necessary, or whether the system should continue on its task. We integrated our risk-based triggering mechanism into a delivery rover that is being attacked by a drone and evaluated its effectiveness through systematic testing in a simulated environment in Robot Operating System (ROS) and Gazebo, with a variety of different randomly generated conditions. We compared the use of the triggering mechanism and different configurations of self-preservation behaviours to not having any of these. Our results show that triggering self-preservation increases the distance between the drone and the rover for many of these configurations, and, in some instances, the drone does not catch up with the rover. Our study demonstrates the benefits of embedding risk awareness and self-preservation into autonomous systems to increase their robustness, and the value of using bio-inspired engineering to find solutions in this area.

Keywords: Risk-based triggering mechanism · Bio-inspired self-preservation · ROS

1 Introduction

Autonomous systems such as delivery drones, self-driving cars and robotic assistants are becoming an affordable reality in our daily life. Safety aspects so far have been studied from a human-centered perspective, i.e. keeping people and people's property safe, exemplified by safety standards for robots that interact and collaborate with people (e.g. ISO/TS 15066:2016 Robots and robotic devices – Collaborative robots). Nonetheless, as robots and autonomous systems

© Springer International Publishing AG 2017
Y. Gao et al. (Eds.): TAROS 2017, LNAI 10454, pp. 166–181, 2017.
DOI: 10.1007/978-3-319-64107-2_14

are also valuable property, and so are the loads they carry, they will need to look after their own safety if possible; i.e. they will need self-preservation mechanisms in the presence of external threats, such as vandalism and theft [5,18].

Nature has evolved a range of strategies to survive in a dangerous environment, including morphological, ecological and behavioural adaptations. Animals utilize multiple environmental cues to assess whether they are at risk [20]. The plasticity to exhibit behaviours in response to a potential threat is crucial for survival. Anti-predatory strategies with no detrimental effects on the predator, such as taking refuge, and late resort fleeing mechanisms such a protean flight, provide a source of bio-inspired behaviour for robotic safe threat avoidance, as they ensure safety for both the robot and its antagonist.

Although many strategies such as stealth navigation [22] and fleeing behaviours have been designed and implemented for mobile autonomous systems [2,10] to avoid dangerous encounters, mechanisms to trigger one or several of these self-preservation strategies to achieve an adequate and timely response to the threats still need to be developed. In nature, the instant of evasion initiation depends on many biological and environmental factors [9,12]. How can we use this knowledge for the design of more competent and fully autonomous systems, able to respond to threats towards robust self-preservation?

In this paper, we propose a novel biologically inspired mechanism that emulates environmental and biological evasion initiation factors, to trigger self-preservation response behaviours based on a risk analysis of the dangerous situation. We demonstrate the construction and implementation of such a mechanism through a case study consisting of a delivery rover and an attacking drone. To evaluate the proposed risk-based triggering mechanism within a cost-effective realistic framework, we implemented a simulator in the Robot Operating System (ROS)[1] and the 3D physics simulator Gazebo[2]. In a simulation, the drone pursues the delivery rover either persistently or constrained within a time bound. The rover tries to avoid theft or damage by choosing from a variety of predefined response behaviours such as fleeing or seeking refuge, once it has evaluated the risk in the environment in the context of its internal state.

We compared the use of the triggering mechanism and different configurations of response behaviours to not using it at all, i.e. a rover that is unaware of the risk and cannot trigger self-preservation responses. Our results show that, overall, the triggering mechanism coupled with self-preservation responses has the potential to increase the rover's success on reaching a delivery location, or at least the distance between the threat and the rover. This demonstrates the benefits of embedding risk awareness and self-preservation strategies into autonomous systems to increase their robustness, and the usefulness of employing bio-inspired engineering solutions towards achieving true autonomy.

---

[1] http://www.ros.org/.

[2] http://gazebosim.org/.

2   Related Work

Anti-predator individual mechanisms are divided into different categories: detection avoidance, behavioural vigilance, warning signals, defensive adaptations, and last resort behaviours [6]. Detection avoidance and defensive adaptations comprise morphological behaviours such as crypsis (matching the background of the environment), weaponry in the body (e.g. spines), the release of chemicals [4] to conceal their presence, deceive and mislead predators [7], and also behaviours such as crouching for concealing the body, seeking refuge [15], mobbing and distraction. As warning signals, vocal signals warn other animals of predators' presence, whereas displays of coloration advertise potential chemical defence to dissuade predators. Morphological adaptations are difficult to implement within the design of robots, although some are emerging, e.g. robots that match their background [23]. Avoidance and defensive behaviours do not negatively impact on the safety of the antagonist.

Last resort behaviours involve increasing the distance between prey and predators. Examples are protean behaviour or fleeing away in a zigzag (irregular) manner [14], along with freezing (immobility) where extreme examples are thanatosis or feigning death, and autotomy or leaving a limb behind. Fleeing, freezing and proteanism are well suited to autonomous navigation tasks [2,10].

Animals need to recognize the risk of predation. Vigilance is a behavioural adaptation where animals alternate between foraging and scanning for potential threats [6]. Factors and cues such as predator size, approach velocity, perceived sounds, or physical weaponry, influence the choice of response behaviours once a threat has been detected [1,8,13,19–21]. As with animals, basic capabilities to assess risk from sensed environmental threats are necessary for robot autonomy.

Risk assessment procedures provide a systematic approach to guide developers in creating autonomous robots that are safe and dependable, from a human-centric perspective –i.e. for safe human-robot interactions–, at design time [11,16,17,24]. Environmental risk analyses can be adopted at runtime, e.g. as on-line risk monitors, to control the execution of self-preservation strategies, and even to trigger adaptation and learning towards dealing with threats in the environment as in [3]. These domains, nonetheless, could benefit from considering biologically inspired mechanisms for efficient self-preservation responses as well as risk measures and factors.

This paper proposes such a bio-inspired runtime self-preservation mechanism to trigger different response behaviours according to perceived threats from the environment. Selecting a response behaviour might mean giving up on other behaviours, such as the delivery of a package, or reaching a final destination, either in the short or the longer term. The decision to trigger self-preservation behaviours is critical. A device is needed to assess whether and when the danger from the environment implies a greater risk and consequently the potential for greater costs and loss, than not reacting to it.

3 Mechanism to Trigger Self-preservation Behaviours According to Threats

The threats and dangerous situations in the environment that may affect an autonomous system differ widely, depending on the system's application. Hazard analysis, as part of a rigorous and systematic risk assessment, involves customers, stakeholders and system designers in the identification and evaluation of the relevant threats and dangers, taking into consideration severity of the harm and the likelihood of it occurring, which results in a risk rating, from low, via moderate and high, to extreme. We assume that a set of possible threats has been identified using such a process, and that system designers have equipped the autonomous system with means, including sensing and real-time processing, to detect these in a timely manner.

For example, the analysis in Table 1 shows possible generic threats with their risk rating for a delivery rover, according to some hazard analysis, for different types of environments, together with the bio-inspired self-preservation response behaviours to mitigate these, such as fleeing, seeking refuge, thanatosis and autotomy. Physical harassment by small animals or children may not pose much of a threat, and adequate responses would include moving away or shutting down for some time (an implementation of thanatosis), in urban environments. If the rover is likely to be stolen with its contents, a distraction could be achieved by safely releasing the parcel it carries whilst fleeing (an implementation of autotomy). A cross is used to indicate a potentially beneficial response behaviour for the combination of threat and environment.

Qualitative processes to grade the risk of hazards provide metrics to classify their consequences, according to their severity and likelihood of occurrence [24]. For example, a risk classification matrix based on the one in the safety standard IEC 61508 'Functional Safety of Electrical/Electronic/Programmable Electronic Safety-related Systems', where four risk classes are possible, from the most severe (Class I) to the least severe (Class IV), as shown in [24]. In our proposed mechanism, we have adapted these qualitative processes to compute a measure to trigger pertinent response behaviours against threats in the environment.

Following an analysis like the one in Table 1, where adequate self-preservation behaviours are chosen as response to particular threats, the next step is the implementation of a mechanism to trigger the start of such responses, once the risk level is assessed and deemed to be at the corresponding level. We propose the computation of a quantitative measure of risk with respect to the hazards in the environment, and other system-related internal factors that should be accounted for in terms of system safety, the latter emulating internal biological that influence the process of initiating defensive mechanisms in animals. We consider the existence of N risk factors from environment sensing information collected by an autonomous system, which indicate the type of hazard or threat from the environment towards the system, and hence its risk rating, and M other factors that assess relevant data about the current state of the system (e.g. battery life, distance to the destination, proximity to good users). Each factor is evaluated through a metric $r_i, i = 1, \ldots, N, N+1, \ldots, N+M, r_i \in \mathbb{R}$,

Table 1. Analysis of environmental threats and suitable response behaviours in different environments for a delivery rover

Threats	Risk rating	Response behaviour	Environment		
			Urban	Open terrain	Indoor
Physical harassment by children or animals	Low	Fleeing		X	
		Seeking refuge	X	X	X
		Thanatosis	X	X	X
		Autotomy			
Close distance damage	Medium	Fleeing		X	
		Seeking refuge	X	X	X
		Thanatosis			
		Autotomy	X	X	
Long distance damage	Medium	Fleeing	X	X	
		Seeking refuge	X	X	X
		Thanatosis			
		Autotomy			
Theft and unauthorized access through physical means	High	Fleeing		X	
		Seeking refuge	X	X	X
		Thanatosis			
		Autotomy	X	X	X
Theft and unauthorized access through remote access (hacking)	High	Fleeing		X	
		Seeking refuge	X	X	X
		Thanatosis			
		Autotomy	X	X	X

a function over measured or sensed system variables $\bar{x} = [x_1, \ldots, x_j]$ that produces a score, i.e. $r_i : \bar{x} \to \mathbb{R}$. An overall risk score r_{TOTAL} can be computed as the (weighted) accumulation of all these r_i factors, e.g.

$$r_{TOTAL} = \sum_{i=1}^{N+M} w_i \cdot r_i \qquad (1)$$

to provide a mapping between a level of threat and a response $a \in \mathcal{A}$, i.e. $r : \mathbb{R} \to a$, where $\mathcal{A}$ is the set of all implemented possible response behaviours such as fleeing or freezing (thanatosis).

4   Case Study

As a case study to evaluate the proposed risk-based self-preservation response triggering mechanism, we continue with the delivery rover example, pursued by an autonomous drone. Three particular scenarios from Table 1 were employed to create a risk scoring model, for which environmental and internal factors to sense and measure were derived, to compute a risk rating as explained in Sect. 3. Additionally, these scenarios were used to choose and implement predefined response behaviours to be triggered according to the computed risk, by the response triggering mechanism:

1. The drone is at a long distance from the rover, where attempts to hack the rover's control towards stealing the delivery consignment can be made. Fleeing has been chosen as the rover's response behaviour by the designer.
2. The drone is harassing the rover at a closer distance, for which fleeing with proteanism could provide means to confuse the drone.
3. The drone is seeking to damage the rover, approaching until physical contact is made, for which refuge against the drone needs to be sought.

Note that as the distance between the rover and the drone decreases, the intentions of the drone might become more sinister and the perceived risk of damage to the rover increases accordingly.

After designing the risk scoring model for the triggering mechanism, a simulator was implemented in ROS and Gazebo. We used available robot models corresponding to real hardware platforms, to provide realism and validity to the experiments, at a computational cost.

4.1 Instantiation of the Triggering Mechanism for the Case Study

According to the scenarios, four main environmental and internal factors have been considered for the mechanism to trigger self-preservation responses: the perceived distance between the rover and the drone, the perceived drone sound, the perceived drone speed, and the rover's battery life, i.e. $N = 3$ and $M = 1$. Each of these cues is considered to have equal impact in the measured total risk r_{TOTAL}. In practice, different scenarios may require a different weighting of the risk factors, and different number of environmental and internal cues, depending on the environment and what an autonomous system can detect and sense. The total risk r_{TOTAL} is computed as the accumulation of the relevant individual risk metrics (from the distance r_d, sound r_p, speed r_v and battery life r_b respectively), each weighted by 0.25,

$$r_{TOTAL} = 0.25r_d + 0.25r_p + 0.25r_v + 0.25r_b. \qquad (2)$$

Consider the Euclidean distance between the rover in location (x, y, z) and the drone in location (x_d, y_d, z_d) (all in meters) in the 3D space at time t, defined as

$$d(t) = \sqrt{(x - x_d)^2 + (y - y_d)^2 + (z - z_d)^2}. \qquad (3)$$

We assign a score $s(t)$ that is inverse to the distance $d(t)$, which increases if the drone approaches the rover, and decreases if the rover moves away,

$$s(t) = \frac{100}{d(t)}. \qquad (4)$$

We then compute five consecutive distance scores, i.e. samples $i = 1, \ldots, 5$ at times $t_1, \ldots, t_5$ (e.g. every second). Consider the gradient of these samples,

$$\nabla s = \frac{\sum_{i=1}^{5} (s(t_i) - \mu_s)(t_i - \mu_t)}{\sum_{i=1}^{5} (s(t_i) - \mu_s)^2}, \tag{5}$$

where μ_s is the average of distance scores over the samples $i = 1, \ldots, 5$, $\mu_t = 3$ (the average of 5 s). If the gradient is positive, the rover is in greater risk of an attack, as the drone has moved closer. Whereas if the gradient is negative the robot is no longer in as high a risk as it was before. Consequently, we propose the computation of the risk given a distance change through the metric

$$r_d = \begin{cases} \beta_d \nabla s & \text{if the gradient is positive} \\ 0 & \text{if the gradient is negative} \end{cases}, \tag{6}$$

where β_d is a coefficient that normalizes r_d to a value between 0 and 1.

The sound pressure p at time t is calculated from the measured distance $d(t)$ defined in (3),

$$p(t) = \frac{60}{d(t)}. \tag{7}$$

The sound pressure increases if the drone gets closer to the rover. Note that this measure does not take into account how sound reflects from surfaces, nor the presence of objects in between the origin of sound and the sensor. The risk given the sound pressure change is also computed from the gradient of five pressure samples,

$$r_p = \begin{cases} \beta_p \frac{\sum_{i=1}^{5}(p(t_i)-\mu_p)(t_i-\mu_t)}{\sum_{i=1}^{5}(p(t_i)-\mu_p)^2} & \text{if the gradient is positive} \\ 0 & \text{if the gradient is negative} \end{cases}, \tag{8}$$

where μ_p is the average over the pressure samples, and β_p normalizes r_p to a value between 0 and 1.

To calculate an approximation of the relative approach velocity, a sample of the distance $d(t)$ in meters is taken every two seconds (where $d(t_2)$ is the most recent sample, and $d(t_1)$ is the previous sample), and we use the standard definition of the velocity as the difference of the distance over a period of time (in this case 2 s),

$$v(t) = \frac{d(t_2) - d(t_1)}{2}. \tag{9}$$

The risk, given the velocity change, is also computed from the gradient of five approximations,

$$r_v = \begin{cases} \beta_v \frac{\sum_{i=1}^{5}(v(t_i)-\mu_v)(t_i-\mu_t)}{\sum_{i=1}^{5}(v(t_i)-\mu_v)^2} & \text{if the gradient is positive} \\ 0 & \text{if the gradient is negative} \end{cases}, \tag{10}$$

where μ_v is the average over five velocity approximations, and β_v normalizes r_v to a value between 0 and 1. In general, the velocity of the drone remains constant once the maximum has been reached, with changes only at the initial lift from the ground, and when performing a rotation to face the rover's direction.

Monitoring the battery life is analogous to biological internal factors such as hunger or health status, which influence the kind of triggered anti-predator strategies. The remaining battery energy level at time t is computed considering a total capacity of B_{TOTAL}, and a linear discharge rate ϕ,

$$b(t) = 100 - \frac{B_{TOTAL} - t\phi}{6}. \tag{11}$$

The risk given the battery life is calculated according to the energy level,

$$r_b = \beta_b b(t). \tag{12}$$

where μ_b is the average over five computations, and β_b normalizes r_b to a value between 0 and 1.

Based on the computed total risk r_{TOTAL}, different sets of response behaviours can be programmed, to be triggered when risk thresholds are met. For example, the rover decides to pursue its delivery goal if $r_{TOTAL} < \gamma_{flee}$, flee towards the delivery goal if $r_{TOTAL} \geq \gamma_{flee}$, flee with proteanism if $r_{TOTAL} \geq \gamma_{prot}$, or seek refuge if $r_{TOTAL} \geq \gamma_{ref}$, with $\gamma_{flee} \leq \gamma_{prot} \leq \gamma_{ref}$ as thresholds of risk. Alternatively, the rover could perform only one response behaviour, e.g. fleeing when $r_{TOTAL} \geq \gamma_{flee}$.

This risk measuring model reflects the scenarios and the designer's intentions regarding response strategies to avoid financial loss and damage. After executing a response behaviour for some time, the total risk r_{TOTAL} is recomputed to determine if a change in behaviour is needed, i.e. if the rover should continue with the original task (e.g. reaching a delivery goal), try another response behaviour, or continue with the same response, as per the design.

4.2   Implementation of the Simulator in ROS and Gazebo

The ROS framework offers a platform to develop modular software for robots and autonomous systems, consisting of 'nodes' (concurrent programs in e.g. Python and C++), 'topics' (broadcast messages) and 'services' (one-to-one communication). ROS allows distributed computation through a server-client architecture. Gazebo is a 3D physics simulator compatible with ROS. Many robotic platforms are freely available in simulation for ROS and Gazebo. We constructed a simulator that uses the Clearpath Robotics Jackal as the rover[3], and the Hector quadrotor[4] as the drone. An example of both robots visualized in a Gazebo simulation is shown in Fig. 1.

The structure of our simulator is shown in Fig. 2. The Drone and Rover Model Nodes (in dark gray) comprise the Gazebo 3D models, and the low-level motion control for the actuators (e.g. rotation of the wheels). The implemented bio-inspired risk-based triggering mechanism (as a single node) is shown in light gray,

---

[3] http://wiki.ros.org/Robots/Jackal.
[4] http://wiki.ros.org/hector_quadrotor.

Fig. 1. Visualization of the 3D simulation of the Jackal rover and the Hector Quadrotor in Gazebo.

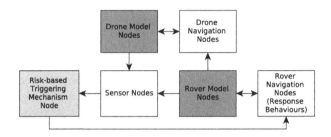

Fig. 2. Structure of the ROS and Gazebo simulator for the case study, comprising a delivery rover and a drone trying to steal from, or vandalize the rover. A bio-inspired risk-based triggering mechanism selects adequate self-preservation response behaviours in the rover.

with data inputs from the sensor nodes, and outputs to the Rover Navigation Nodes. Other developed nodes (Drone and Rover Navigation and Sensors) are shown in white. All the developed nodes were implemented in Python.

The Drone Navigation Nodes control the quadrotor's linear and angular velocity according to readings of the rover's current location in the Gazebo model, aiming to minimize the distance between itself and the rover, $d(t)$. The drone indicates if the rover has managed to hide or reach its delivery goal, or if it has been successfully reached, i.e. if the distance $d(t)$ is smaller than a minimal threshold, $d_{capture}$. The drone rotates over the vertical axis at an angular speed ω_d to change its orientation towards the rover, and at the linear speed of v_d to pursue the rover. A "persistent" drone has an infinite amount of battery charge, and will pursue the rover until a drone-rover interaction is finished. A "cautious" drone considers its finite battery charge, deciding to stop pursuit after some time has elapsed to be able to return to its base safely. Notice that the latter mode is more realistic than the former, as it represents a modelling refinement that considers individual costs that the threats in the environment would also need to consider.

The Jackal rover has been programmed to navigate autonomously towards a delivery goal, a location (x_g, y_g), by iteratively performing angle correction at a speed of ω, followed by a linear displacement at a speed v. If a self-preservation response behaviour is triggered by the risk-based mechanism, the

Rover Navigation Nodes execute a combination of fleeing (moving faster towards the delivery goal), fleeing with proteanism (following sub-goals with randomized orientation angles but avoiding the pursuer, as proposed in [2]), or seeking refuge (navigating towards a refuge in a fixed location), all of these at an increased linear speed of $2v$. By decoupling the navigation nodes from the triggering mechanism, the modular structure allows testing different complex self-preservation behaviours.

Sensors Nodes emulate real sensing by reading data from the Gazebo models, such as the location of the drone, and through models of the rover's internal state, such as the state of the battery charge. The sensing output is used by the risk-based metrics, embedded in the triggering mechanism node, to trigger adequate response behaviours.

5 Experiments and Results

Experiments in simulation were conducted to evaluate a self-preservation triggering mechanism presented in Sect. 3, and instantiated for the case study in Sect. 4.1.

5.1 Setup

Two different self-preservation configurations were tested in simulation. In the configuration A, the rover chooses fleeing, proteanism or seeking refuge, if r_{TOTAL} exceeds the risk thresholds $\gamma_{flee} \leq \gamma_{prot} \leq \gamma_{ref}$, respectively. In the configuration B, the rover chooses fleeing if $r_{TOTAL} \geq \gamma_{flee}$. Additionally, the rover does not have a triggering mechanism nor self-preservation behaviours in configuration C. Two drone pursuit modes were tested, persistent and cautious, in combination with the three configurations described before.

We generated (pseudorandomly) 150 sets of initial locations for the rover, the drone, the hideaway, and the rover's delivery goal. The initial locations were restricted so that the distances between the rover and the drone to be sufficiently apart at the start of a simulation. Each one of these initial location sets was applied to each configuration A to C, in combination with a persistent or cautious pursuer, for a total of 150 × 3 × 2 simulations. This allowed a fair comparison of all the configurations A to C, for the different kinds of pursuers. A simulation is run with each set, lasting an allowed maximum of 80 s (plus 20 s of launching overhead, and 45 of termination). The rover will stop moving if it is reached by the drone, or if it safely reaches the delivery location.

Other setup parameters for the triggering mechanism comprised $\beta_p = \frac{1}{8}$, $\beta_d = \frac{1}{14}$, $\beta_v = \frac{1}{4}$, $\beta_b = \frac{1}{100}$, $B_{TOTAL} = 600$, $\phi = 1$, $\gamma_{flee} = 0.2$, $\gamma_{prot} = 30$, and $\gamma_{ref} = 40$. For the drone, we used $\omega_d = 0.4$ rad/s, and $v_d = 0.5$ m/s, with a $d_{capture} = 0.15$ m. The rover navigates with $v = 0.5$ m/s and $\omega = 1.0$ rad/s.

The simulations ran on a PC with Intel 3230 M 2.60 GHz CPU, 8 GB of RAM, 64-bit Ubuntu 14.04, ROS Indigo, and Gazebo 2.2.5. For each simulation, we collected the sets of initial parameters, type of triggered self-preservation strategy according to r_{TOTAL}, and conclusion of the encounter (distances and elapsed simulation time). All the logged data and examples of simulations with varied initial conditions and observed behaviours are openly available online[5].

5.2   Results

We considered the following success criteria during a simulation: reaching the consignment delivery location before capture (strong success); increasing the distance between the drone and the rover when not captured (success); and changing the outcome to reaching the delivery location with configurations A and B, compared to being captured with configuration C, for the same initial condition (relative success). We expected that, in general, the first two types of success would be more frequent in the simulations when using the triggering mechanism and the self-preservation behaviours than without using any self-preservation at all. Using configurations A or B would make the rover reach the delivery goal in instances that it would not without self-preservation. Furthermore, we expected that using self-preservation would grant more success when the rover was pursued by a cautious drone than with a persistent one, as the rover would have the opportunity to reach the delivery goal once the drone gave up.

Table 2 shows the number of simulations that were successful (according to the success criteria), were inconclusive (i.e. by the end of the time limit per

Table 2. Results with and without the risk-based triggering mechanism, over 150 simulations with different initial conditions.

	Number of simulations		
Configuration	A	B	C
Self-preservation behaviour	All	Fleeing	None
Persistent pursuit mode			
Delivery goal reached (strong success)	116/150	138/150[†]	138/150[†]
Distance increased (success)	97/118[‡]	114/138[‡]	–
Rover was captured (strong failure)	32/150*	12/150	11/150
Not captured, goal not reached (inconclusive)	2/150	0/150	1/150
Goal reached, out of previously captured with C (rel. success)	8/11°	6/11°	–
Captured, out of previously reaching goal with C (rel. failure)	29/138•	7/138	–
Cautious pursuit mode			
Delivery goal reached (strong success)	143/150	145/150[†]	145/150[†]
Distance increased (success)	87/144[‡,°]	60/148[‡,°]	–
Rover was captured (strong failure)	6/150*	2/150$	5/150
Not captured, goal not reached (inconclusive)	1/150	3/150	0/150
Goal reached, out of previously captured with C (rel. success)	5/5	5/5#	–
Captured, out of previously reaching goal with C (rel. failure)	6/145	2/145#	–

---

[5] https://github.com/riveras/self-preservation.

simulation, the rover was not captured but did not reach the delivery goal either), failed (i.e. the rover was captured), for a drone in two pursuit modes (persistent or cautious), over 150 simulations with different initial locations (for the rover, drone, delivery goal and refuge), and with or without the triggering mechanism and different types of self-preservation behaviours. We also recorded which self-preservation strategies were triggered on each simulation, shown in Table 3, to confirm the correct functioning of the triggering mechanism.

The results show that, in general, the combination of the triggering mechanism and only fleeing (configuration B) is more successful than combining the triggering mechanism with the multiple anti-predator behaviours of configuration A, and than not reacting to the threat. We observed that seeking refuge sometimes lead the rover to move closer to the drone. Additionally, we observed an oscillation between navigation objectives due to the risk increasing and decreasing: moving towards a refuge or trying to reach the delivery goal, which in some cases caused the rover to be 'stuck' in a particular segment of the environment, and the drone was able to get closer. These issues are reflected in the strong failure results (see * in Table 2).

In terms of the different drone pursuit behaviours, persistent and cautious, the mechanism in configuration B was as strongly successful (i.e. it reached the delivery goal) as a rover without any self-preservation (see † in Table 2). Nonetheless, in terms of increased overall distance between the drone and the rover by the end of a simulation, any of the self-preservation configurations A or B achieved better results for a persistent drone, than for a cautious drone (see ‡ in Table 2), which was contrary to our expectations. The behaviours in configurations A or B are triggered for longer and at a higher frequency for a persistent drone, which leads to more instances of success than for a cautious drone. Furthermore, only fleeing (configuration B) for longer under a persistent drone threat is more efficient at increasing the distance between the rover and the drone, than a combination of self-preservation behaviours (configuration A). The opposite happens for a cautious drone, where configuration A outperforms configuration B (see ◇ in Table 2). This highlights the usefulness of self-preservation behaviours that momentarily change the navigation goals (proteanism or seeking refuge) when the threats in the environment are limited by the management of their own resources.

A rover with configuration A was more successful than one with configuration B at changing the simulation outcomes to reaching the delivery goal for a persistent drone, for the same starting conditions where the rover would be captured with configuration C (see ° in Table 2). Nonetheless, new and more capture instances were introduced with configuration A (see • in Table 2). Only configuration B achieved some relative success, for a cautious drone (see # in Table 2), coupled to the most reduced strong failure results (see $ in Table 2).

The results in Table 3 show that indeed the triggering of self-preservation behaviours takes place in the majority of the simulations. Note that, in the configuration A, different anti-predator behaviours were allowed per simulation.

Table 3. Triggering of self-preservation behaviours according to the measured total risk r_{TOTAL} over 150 simulations with different initial locations.

	Number of simulations	
Configuration	A	B
Self-preservation behaviour	All	Only fleeing
Persistent pursuit mode		
Use of simple fleeing	148/150	148/150
Use of fleeing with proteanism	59/150	–
Use of refuge seeking	25/150	–
No behaviours triggered	2/150	2/150
Cautious pursuit mode		
Use of simple fleeing	141/150	142/150
Use of fleeing with proteanism	41/150	–
Use of refuge seeking	2/150	–
No behaviours triggered	9/150	8/150

Fewer simulations where protean fleeing and seeking refuge were triggered evidence that performing fleeing beforehand helps reducing the risk.

5.3   Discussion

As shown by the results in the previous section, the use of the triggering mechanism in combination with self-preservation behaviours was successful (i.e. increased the distance between the rover and the pursuer in more than half of the simulations with a variety of initial conditions) for a persistent pursuer, and also was strongly successful (i.e. allowed the rover to get to the delivery goal in more instances) for a cautious pursuer, compared to not reacting to the threats. Nonetheless, particular combinations of self-preservation behaviours were less strongly successful against a persistent pursuer, whereas for a cautious pursuer only fleeing was not that successful. Also, relative success results were varied. These mixed results, according to our expectations, require further examination of combinations of fleeing and refuge seeking behaviours, to provide a more conclusive evaluation of the triggering mechanism. Furthermore, anti-predator behaviours coupled with the triggering mechanism should be designed so that they are more effective than 'doing nothing'.

An element that influences the functioning of the triggering mechanism is the number and inter-relationships of the risk factors. Variations of the risk models in Sect. 4.1, such as the use of different weights and coefficients, would need to be explored further. There are evidently trade-offs between avoiding an attack and achieving a successful delivery. Hence, suitable models and computation of the risk factors need to be explored further, e.g. multi-objective optimization.

Additionally, more sophisticated mechanisms could be used to enhance the risk computation, such as prediction models for the drone.

Threats to the validity of the case study used in this paper and the results include, besides a limited number of combination of self-preservation behaviours and risk factors, the definition of 'success' for the evaluation and result reporting. The selection of some success metrics or criteria over others has an impact on the reported results. Whereas only considering reaching the delivery goal as 'success' is intuitive, it leaves out other aspects of the encounter such as significantly increasing the distance between the drone and the rover, getting outside the line of view of the drone. These latter aspects can also be considered as successful encounters from the rover's perspective, and altogether provide a better picture of the effect of the use of the triggering mechanism and the self-preservation behaviours, towards a more holistic evaluation methodology.

6 Conclusions and Future Work

We presented a biologically inspired risk-based triggering mechanism to initiate self-preservation strategies. This mechanism considers environmental and internal system factors to measure the overall risk at any moment in time, to decide whether behaviours such as fleeing or hiding are necessary, or whether the system should continue with its task. This emulates animal anti-predator behaviour initiation. The mechanism's design is based on risk assessment methodologies for robotics design, complementing traditional human-centered safety analyses towards systems with more autonomy and self-preservation.

A case study was developed to evaluate such a triggering mechanism coupled with different self-preservation strategies, compared against not reacting to threats. In the case study, a delivery rover is attacked by a drone in a simulated environment in ROS and Gazebo, with a variety of different randomly generated conditions such as initial locations, and delivery goals.

Our study demonstrates the need for embedding risk awareness and self-preservation towards successful autonomous systems, and the usefulness of bio-inspired engineering solutions. In general, the triggering mechanism coupled with self-preservation strategies increases the distance between the threat of the drone and the rover. Nonetheless, some of the self-preservation behaviours lower the frequency of reaching the delivery goal.

As future work, an extensive study of combinations of adequate and optimized self-preservation behaviours is necessary to determine what actions lead to achieving a delivery objective while increasing the distance between the treat and the rover. Additionally, new risk metrics that consider more complex factors such as probable future actions (i.e. prediction) for the threats could be incorporated into the mechanism to obtain a more robust risk measure.

Acknowledgement. The work by D. Araiza-Illan and K. Eder was funded by the EPSRC project "Robust Integrated Verification of Autonomous Systems" (ref. EP/J01205X/1).

References

1. Amo, L., López, P., Martín, J.: Wall lizards combine chemical and visual cues of ambush snake predators to avoid overestimating risk inside refuges. Anim. Behav. **67**(4), 647–653 (2004)
2. Araiza-Illan, D., Dodd, T.J.: Bio-inspired autonomous navigation and escape from pursuers with potential functions. In: Herrmann, G., Studley, M., Pearson, M., Conn, A., Melhuish, C., Witkowski, M., Kim, J.-H., Vadakkepat, P. (eds.) TAROS 2012. LNCS, vol. 7429, pp. 84–95. Springer, Heidelberg (2012). doi:10. 1007/978-3-642-32527-4_8
3. Arcaini, P., Riccobene, E., Scandurra, P.: Modeling and analyzing MAPE-K feedback loops for self-adaptation. Proc. SEAMS **2015**, 13–23 (2015)
4. Barnett, C., Bateson, M., Rowe, C.: State-dependent decision making: educated predators strategically trade off the costs and benefits of consuming aposematic prey. Behav. Ecol. **18**(4), 645–651 (2007)
5. Brščić, D., Kidokoro, H., Suehiro, Y., Kanda, T.: Escaping from children's abuse of social robots. In: Proceedings HRI, pp. 59–66 (2015)
6. Caro, T.: Antipredator Defenses in Birds and Mammals. University of Chicago Press, Chicago (2005)
7. Caro, T.: Antipredator deception in terrestrial vertebrates. Curr. Zool. **60**(1), 16–25 (2014)
8. Chivers, D.P., McCormick, M.I., Mitchell, M.D., Ramasamy, R.A., Ferrari, M.C.O.: Background level of risk determines how prey categorize predators and non-predators. Proc. Roy. Soc. Lond. B Biol. Sci. **281**(1787), 1–6 (2014)
9. Cooper, W.E., Stankowich, T.: Prey or predator? Body size of an approaching animal affects decisions to attack or escape. Behav. Ecol. **21**(6), 1278–1284 (2010)
10. Curiac, D.I., Volosencu, C.: Imparting protean behavior to mobile robots accomplishing patrolling tasks in the presence of adversaries. Bioinspiration Biomimetics **10**, 1–10 (2015)
11. Dogramadzi, S., Giannaccini, M.E., Harper, C., Sobhani, M., Woodman, R., Choung, J.: Environmental hazard analysis - a variant of preliminary hazard analysis for autonomous mobile robots. J. Intell. Robot. Syst. **76**(1), 73–117 (2014)
12. Domenici, P., Blagburn, J.M., Bacon, J.P.: Animal escapology II: escape trajectory case studies. J. Exp. Biol. **214**(15), 2474–2494 (2011)
13. Helfman, G.S.: Threat-sensitive predator avoidance in damselfish-trumpetfish interactions. Behav. Ecol. Sociobiol. **24**(1), 47–58 (1989)
14. Humphries, D.A., Driver, P.M.: Protean defence by prey animals. Oecologia **5**(4), 285–302 (1970)
15. Martín, J., López, P.: When to come out from a refuge: risk-sensitive and state-dependent decisions in an alpine lizard. Behav. Ecol. **10**(5), 487–492 (1999)
16. Martin-Guillerez, D., Guiochet, J., Powell, D., Zanon, C.: A UML-based method for risk analysis of human-robot interactions. In: Proceedings SERENE, pp. 32–41 (2010)
17. Rezazadegan, F., Geng, J., Ghirardi, M., Menga, G., Murè, S., Camuncoli, G., Demichela, M.: Risk-based design for the physical human-robot interaction (pHRI): an overview. Chem. Eng. Trans. **43**, 1249–1254 (2015)
18. Salvini, P., Ciaravella, G., Yu, W., Ferri, G., Manzi, A., Mazzolai, B., Laschi, C., Oh, S., Dario, P.: How safe are service robots in urban environments? Bullying a robot. In: Proceedings of RO-MAN, pp. 1–7 (2010)

19. Smith, M.E., Belk, M.C.: Risk assessment in western mosquitofish (Gambusia affinis): do multiple cues have additive effects? Behav. Ecol. Sociobiol. **51**(1), 101–107 (2001)
20. Stankowich, T., Blumstein, D.T.: Fear in animals: a meta-analysis and review of risk assessment. Proc. Roy. Soc. Lond. B Biol. Sci. **272**(1581), 2627–2634 (2005)
21. Stankowich, T., Coss, R.G.: Effects of predator behavior and proximity on risk assessment by columbian black-tailed deer. Behav. Ecol. **17**(2), 246–254 (2006)
22. Tews, A., Mataric, M., Sukhatme, G.: Avoiding detection in a dynamic environment. In: Proceedings of IROS, pp. 3773–3778 (2004)
23. Wang, G., Chen, X., Liu, S., Wong, C., Chu, S.: Mechanical chameleon through dynamic real-time plasmonic tuning. ACS Nano **10**(2), 1788–1794 (2016)
24. Woodman, R., Winfield, A.F., Harper, C., Fraser, M.: Building safer robots: safety driven control. Int. J. Robot. Res. **31**(13), 1603–1626 (2012)

Shark-Inspired Target Approach Strategy for Foraging with Visual Clues

Juan M. Nogales$^{(\boxtimes)}$, Mauricio Cunha Escarpinati$^{(\boxtimes)}$,
and Gina Maira Barbosa de Oliveira$^{(\boxtimes)}$

Federal University of Uberlandia, Uberlândia, MG, Brazil
juanmnviedman@ufu.br, escarpinati@gmail.com, gina@facom.ufu.br

Abstract. Searching is one of the key activities to fulfill any foraging task. When working with robots, most searching strategies depend on image processing, which is one of the most time-consuming processes. In this work, white shark hunting behaviors inspired the proposed strategy for a team of foraging robots to search and approach the objects. Based on current perceptions, a robot can speed up the foraging process by switching between its sensors to approach its target, that is, by depending less on image processing. On the other hand, the visual clues or targets in the environment have different shapes and colors to indicate which task is available. Such targets are provided by a set of landmarks that change their color according to their availability. In particular, we can manipulate the delays to show a new available task in these landmarks. Each robot makes decisions about which type of target to search based on its experiences. Robots can double-check when they identify unclear images, which are also included in the image database. The proposed strategy for search and approach surpassed the hardware limitations allowing robot navigation with little visual information. A small improvement in the foraging mechanism allowed robots to achieve faster adaptations.

Keywords: Foraging · Task-partitioning · Adaptive learning · Visual orientation

1 Introduction

The incredible white shark is the largest predatory and feared shark in oceans. According to the department of Fish and Wildlife of California, white sharks can reach lengths up to 6.5 m and weight up to 2200 kg [1]. These animals exhibit interesting strategies for hunting (e.g., the ambush attack to a seal shown in Fig. 1). According to the marine biologist Dr. Gregory Skomal, white sharks switch between their sensory organs depending on their current perceptions. When a shark is far from any prey, smelling and hearing organs guide its navigation trajectory. Once a shark perceives something, it approaches cautiously to the target, commonly from beneath. When the shark is about a couple meters away its target, smelling and hearing organs are switched off and vision turns on.

© Springer International Publishing AG 2017
Y. Gao et al. (Eds.): TAROS 2017, LNAI 10454, pp. 182–198, 2017.
DOI: 10.1007/978-3-319-64107-2_15

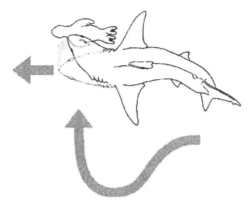

Fig. 1. White sharks' strategy for hunting seals: approach from beneath, confirm with sensory information and grasp the prey [3]

Based on visual clues, the shark identifies whether it is a prey or not, if it is not a prey, then the shark aborts the attack. Otherwise, the shark continues approaching guided by its vision. Once the shark is close enough its target, it relays more on electrosensory than its visual perceptions. Finally, the shark bites the prey and makes its final decision - either eat it or not [2].

Among senses, vision allows animals to acquire the richest information of current environmental conditions. In robotics, most of the work in computer vision is inspired by human vision [4–7]. Insect vision also inspired some works like [8,9]. Robots employ complex algorithms to process visual information, for instance, to identify an object among several clustered shapes by matching its patterns [4], to deal with different object-size conditions [5], or to track images even in oblique angles [6]. Unfortunately, besides image processing in robotics is time consuming, changes in illumination, shadows, or color turn the object identification still heavier computationally.

One of the most used techniques for object detection in robotics consists in to match patterns by windowing the size of them across the entire image [4,10]. The result from these techniques is a map of possible locations in the image where the target got more similarities. Then, robots may orientate their hardware toward the most probable location. Another common technique is thresholding; it has lower computational cost, but assumes a fixed illumination avoiding noticeable color variations. Under such condition, color thresholds segment the image for a later detection of targets among the segmented objects [8,11,12].

When robots base their navigation in environmental visual clues, they orientate themselves through embedded cameras [8,11–14], or through a global camera guidance working like a satellite [6]. Most of the authors prefer embedded cameras for scalability reasons. Generally, robotic visual search consists of four steps: segmentation, feature extraction and selection, target identification, and manipulation of the hardware to center and approach the target. In [12,14], a combination of lights provided visual clues that indicated the state of tasks.

Their testbed was a foraging activity where robots have to search, approach, and transport resources in unknown environments. In these works, foraging robots follow a global North Star light indicating the nest location. Other authors helped robots to navigate by including sensors of depth [15], specific application sensors [8], or cameras with optical zoom [16], which increases the cost as the number of robots increases. The proposed strategy intends to improve performance without boosting robots through hardware extensions.

In particular, we opted for the foraging testbed found in [12] to test our *Shark-approach* strategy for search and approach. We chose this model due to: navigation depends only on local information; robot decision-making is decentralized, i.e., each robot has to deal with its own perceptions and experiences; robots cannot share any information. There, robot navigation and task identification depend on visual clues, which are provided through TAMs (Task Abstraction Modules - smart color-changing landmarks proposed in [13]) and a global North Star light. However, changes in illumination and other robot colors, which may create false visual clues, were not considered in their model. In particular, embedded vision has to deal with occluded objects and with elongated visual perspectives, which get worst when they use a simple monocular camera.

Besides search and approach, our *Shark-approach* strategy allows robots to switch between their sensors to depend less on image processing and, therefore, they may increase the number of detected targets and improve their performance. In particular, robots can change their approaching behavior and to handle their embedded sensors by enabling and disabling them according to the perceptions - like a shark does. The *Shark-approach* strategy also allows robots to double check their target before approaching a false visual clue. We believe this strategy for search and approach can be employed in other activities where robots depend on visual information as security, monitoring, exploration, and search and rescue.

Here, we also modified lightly the model in [12]. The main differences are: (*i*) the *Shark-approach* enables robots to abandon any task after struggle for a while to complete it; (*ii*) we included a parameter to speed up decisions that compares both alternatives; (*iii*) we substituted the global North Star light that helped robots to find the nest with two fixed landmarks. Moreover, we combined geometric shapes and colors to surpass the bound of 6 colors of the embedded camera of our robotic platform (this bound was found in [13]).

The rest of this work is organized as follows: in Sect. 2, we provide a small description and details of some related works. Robots and the arena where they will execute the search and approach strategy while forage, our improvement in the decision-making mechanism, visual processing problems and proposed solutions are in Sect. 3. The experiments are discussed in Sect. 4, while Sect. 5 presents the conclusions and future works.

2   Related Works

The following cited works relay on image processing techniques to help robots to find targets and approach them or to navigate in the environment through visual clues. Since our robots cannot record any map information, they have to explore continually the environment. We discarded any SLAM mechanism.

Some techniques for object detection consist in to match a mask (target) across the entire image to find peaks of probability of the target location [4, 10]. In [4], the authors presented a method to locate objects by matching neighboring colors. This method indicates the likely of target locations according to the similarity between the target features and the explored region (window). Then, the mask is resized in order to re-analyze promising overlapping areas. However, due to we are working with so low computational resources, even a previous algorithm named *Backprojection* [10], which also use this matching of colors without the resizing steps, has a great complexity for our robots, $O((n+p)^2 \log(n+p))$, considering an $n \times n$ image with a mask of size $p \times p$.

The lightest technique for object detection found was thresholding [18], which works in conjunction with classifiers to distinguish between image descriptors (height, width, area, eccentricity, extent). This technique follows five stages: first, it creates a database of images; second, it segments and connects components using color thresholding; then, it extracts best descriptors; later, it trains a classifier using the descriptors of the images in the database; finally, it employs the classifier in different scenarios [17].

The training process requires heavy mathematical operations to find the best descriptors and to adjust the classifier. The training process has a computational complexity at least of $O(n^2 dpi)$, where n is the size of the image, d is the number of descriptors, p is the database size, and i is the number of iterations for training. Fortunately, these heavy processes can be done off-line and once the classifier is trained, it runs with lower complexity. The drawback of this technique resides in depending of color information, which is sensitive to illumination changes.

Next, when the intention is to navigate guided by visual clues, some authors have found interesting solutions. For instance, authors in [8] worked with autonomous mobile robots with visual capabilities to navigate in simple environments. Inspired in insect photoreceptors, which are spread across insect's body to increase their visual field, the authors positioned two CCD cameras in their robots such that they could handle noise and uncertainty in other sensor devices. These cameras worked as photoreceptors only differentiating between illuminated regions and dark walls. The information from cameras and bumper sensors fed the control-network architecture that regulated motor signals. The authors concluded that the key information for three different measurements of performance came from the visual sensors.

In [16], the authors combined cameras and depth sensors to help robots to navigate. Moreover, before start searching, robots create a list of places to visit based on the probability of finding an object in the rooms of the arena. Then, robots use their sensors to explore the arena: camera information helps robots to identify their targets, while depth sensor helps robots to estimate distance to targets and walls. Robots window the image with histogram patterns to identify their targets. The size of the window can be adjusted by using optical zoom camera capabilities. Once a robot recognize an object as a target, that is, an object belonging to its database, the robot centers its hardware toward the region of interest and computes the distance to the target. However, this method is computationally expensive; each cycle took the robots up to a couple of seconds, which may lengthen the search process. The authors mentioned that in comparison with the zoom strategy, to move the robot takes relatively little time and the adjustment of the visit plan carries a negligible cost.

Another implementation with limited resources was proposed in [19]. The authors provided landmarks with a combination of far and near distance clues, and turned on the Leds on the robots to distinguish them from other objects in the images. Robots may detect the searched landmarks from far distances and, when they approach, they can extract detailed information of the environment from near-distance clues (barcodes and QR-codes). Due to hardware limitations (small RAM and VGA monocular camera), the visual information was processed in a Java application running on a computer in order to extract near-distance clues information: barcodes and QR-codes printed in the bottom of the landmarks.

In [12], we found a model where image processing was not considered as critical as it is for search and approach objects. Their image processing solution was to detect colors in a perfect illuminated scenario, without shadows, and where robot bodies have only two colors (details in Fig. 2). In particular, their testbed is a foraging activity where robots are guided through TAMs. These TAMs are light-colored landmarks that indicate the state of a task through changes in color. They work as a stoplight: if there is an object (room) to pick up (drop), then the TAM exhibits a color indicating its availability. Once a robot enters, the TAM changes its color to indicate it is busy. After a while, which emulated a delivery (reception) of an object, the TAM changes again its color and the robot may depart.

Note that in foraging, only after a successful search, a robot may approach a target to pick up or drop an object, i.e., the success in distributed robotic foraging greatly depends on the search and approach strategy. Unlike [12], we worked in a more realistic simulator where robots might be confused with shadows or some parts of other robots, because robots have more colorful bodies. The image classifier was trained with two different light conditions and visual clues are coded by both shape and color. The following section details more about the tools we used and how the *Shark-approach* strategy overcame these visual problems.

3   Tools and Proposal

In this section, we described some tools like the robotic platform, the simulator, the arena. We also detail about the visual clues included in the arena, which compose the image database, the evaluation of the classifiers, and our *Shark-approach* strategy. Moreover, we provide information of the decision-making mechanisms and the controller.

Robotic Platform: We employed the e-puck robot, an open hardware robotic platform, which is not task-specific designed opening up opportunities for new strategies that may bring benefits to the team performance. Although there are many hardware extensions available for e-pucks, we wanted a solution without extra hardware. The standard version of e-puck robots is detailed in [20], whose available hardware includes 2 motors, 2 encoders, a dsPIC microcontroller of 40 MHz with 8 Kb of RAM and 144 Kb of flash memory, a VGA camera, 8 infrared sensors, Bluetooth, 10 Leds, 1 accelerometer, 3 microphones, and 1 speaker.

The embedded camera of the e-puck robot has a resolution of 640 × 480 pixels, allows digital zoom, and it is placed in the front of the robot at 2.5 cm from the floor. Despite this VGA camera can handle such resolution, the memory of the robot cannot. Therefore, we used images of 52 × 39 pixels as recommended by the manufacturer in [22] in order to run both the foraging code and the image processing in the robot itself. Working with this configuration, any object having a diameter above 4.5 cm and being closer than 5.5 cm from the camera will occupy the entire visual field.

Simulator: Recall that we opted for the foraging testbed found in [12] to test our *Shark-approach* strategy for search and approach. Authors in [12] employed ARGoS, which is a software for fast modeling in robotics. We employed Webots, which is a simulator created by the same design group of e-puck robots. Visual differences between e-pucks in ARGoS and Webots appear in Fig. 2.

Webots   Argos

Fig. 2. Visual appearance of e-puck robots in both simulators. The e-puck robot in Webots has all Leds on. In ARGoS, the robot has only one Led on

It is evident that Webots includes more details and features of the real e-puck robots. Moreover, it also has a smaller reality gap by including other physical details as sensor's noise, light effects, and inertia. By trying to replicate the model described in [12] using Webots, we found that: (*i*) using a more colorful scenario, robots can be deceived with false visual clues from another robots; (*ii*) sensor's noise and other external factors affect the performance of the team as a whole; (*iii*) execution times in robot's microcontroller must be slower when the camera is working. In fact, robots need to decrease or stop to obtain a good image.

Arena: It comprises one region for sources, another region for nests, and an alternate path. Each region includes a set of TAMs that indicate the available tasks. We followed a similar distribution as described in the arena of [12]. In particular, TAM landmarks indicate the available sources and nests in each region, but both regions are joined through caches (more details in Fig. 3).

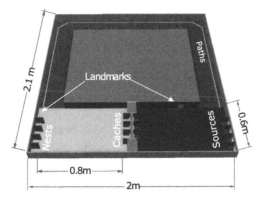

Fig. 3. Dimensions and regions of the arena employed to evaluate our proposal in foraging. The blue region includes 4 sources, while the red region includes 4 nests. Both regions are joined by 3 caches for transferring objects. Two cyan landmarks point out the beginning of the alternate paths (Color figure online)

The caches are a pair of TAMs such that one begins working as a nest in the region of sources and once an object is dropped there, it enables the other TAM to work as a source in the region of nests. In other words, caches work as an area for indirect transferences, where robots working in the region of sources may partition the transportation of the objects with robots in the region of nests.

Next, the alternate paths represent the option where robots do not partition, i.e., they carry the objects through this path, avoiding the transferences in caches, to deposit in the nests by themselves. To indicate the beginning of the alternate paths, the arena includes two fixed-color landmarks in each region. Since robots do not have any global North Star light for guidance, these local landmarks may be occluded as long as a robot approaches to it to begin its travel.

Visual Clues: We created a code for the tasks and their states by combining geometric shapes and colors in order to surpass the bound of 6 colors of the embedded camera of e-pucks (this bound was found in [13]). Due to the limited resources of e-puck robots, we used the color thresholding technique to segment the images and find the components in them. This technique depends on accurate color and illumination. However, we considered two light conditions to include little changes in color. From the histograms, we find out the thresholds of the colors that worked for both light conditions.

Next, tasks are abstracted through landmarks or TAMs, which can have triangle, circle, or square shapes in white, cyan, red, blue, and magenta colors. The height of each landmark or TAM is 6 cm, located at 3 cm from the floor. Only triangle landmarks have a different width of 5 cm. Consequently, when a robot is closer than 5.5 cm from the landmarks, its visual will be saturated. The visual range was defined using information from [23], where e-pucks could detect TAMs of 10 cm in a range of 90 cm. Since our TAMs have 6 cm, we defined a range of detection of 45 cm. The robot's field of view to detect a shape is in Fig. 4.

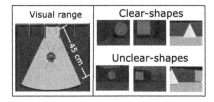

Fig. 4. Robot visual range (left). Samples of the geometric shapes from the image database (right)

The authors in [19] worked with e-pucks too and recommended to use RGB color model instead of HSL, because it is more stable and less complex computationally. Then, we too worked with RGB color model to create a database of images and their respective descriptors.

Image Database: Initially, our database included instances of targets and not-target shapes. Not-target shapes are segmented components big enough, but they are false visual clues. In most cases, it was due to a (colorful) robot near the visual field or a landmark partially occluded. For the descriptors, in order to be able to embed the code in the 144 Kb memory of the robots, we chose height, width, and area for both the shape and its bounding-box, eccentricity, and extent, which have low computational complexity.

Weka showed us that two descriptors, area of shape and width of the bounding-box, are enough to differentiate targets from the not-target shapes. Then, we decreased the number of instances in the database to 300 and included a second level of classification of targets: *clear-shapes* and *unclear-shapes*. *Clear-shapes* are trustable detections, while *unclear-shapes* require double-checking. Note that *unclear-shapess* came from perspectives in oblique angles and distances such that if the robot moves forward some distance, then it can distinguish them. Some samples of the image database are illustrated in Fig. 4.

Our simplified database consists of images obtained from simulations considering 2 different light positions, 6 classes for shapes (triangle, unclear-triangle, square, unclear-square, circle and unclear-circle), distinct angles and distances to the targets. For each light position, we took 25 images for *clear-shapes* and 25 with *unclear-shapes*. In this simplified database, Weka ranked the descriptors according to their *information gain ratio* and brought us the most contributive ones: eccentricity, extent, width of bounding-box, height of shape, width of shape.

Classifier Election: With these descriptors, we trained some supervised classifiers in Weka and compared the number of correctly classified instances (performance). In particular, we tested three classifiers: Decision table, Logistic regression, and J-48 Decision tree. The results of the training stage showed that the best classifier was Decision table (89.3%), but it needed 56 mathematical operations. While, the J-48 Decision tree was below with 84.8%, but it only needs 25 mathematical operations. Therefore, we opted for the J-48 Decision tree.

To summarize, our database of images considers not-target and targets. Targets can be *clear-shapes* or *unclear-shapes*. And *unclear-targets* cannot be distinguished due to distance or angle of perception, but once detected, the robot may approach and double-check them. The classifier answers imitates white shark's possible perceptions: not-prey or prey, if prey, go and taste it.

Shark-Inspired Strategy: Since sharks can switch between their sensory organs, we allowed robots to switch between their sensors. Moreover, since sharks can change their behavior of hunting depending on their perceptions, we also allowed robots to switch between behaviors too. When a robot is walking randomly in the arena, it stops periodically to obtain treatable images. In these images, the robot searches its target (a particular color and shape combination). If the robot detects a target and the classifier indicates that it is an *unclear-shape*, then the robot approaches to double-check. But, if the robot already double-checked this target, it return to the random exploration. Whenever the robot detects its target and the classifier indicates it is a *clear-shape*, then it turns off the camera, enables its distance sensors, and adjusts the speed on each wheel by using the descriptors' information. In particular, the speed of the robot is inversely proportional to the height of the shape, e.g., it goes faster for small images, because they are far.

After moving forward some distance or if the infrared sensors detected an obstacle, the robot stops again, moves back few steps to avoid shadowing the target, enables again its camera and takes another picture to adjust its trajectory or to identify the obstacle, respectively. If the robot considers it is close enough the target, it uses only color information. Because, when there is lacking almost 6 cm to reach its target, its visual field is saturated. Once the robot hits the target and detects an obstacle with the color of its target, then the search and approach is fulfilled successfully. Note that sharks need another sensory organ to make its final decision. Our strategy includes a final validation, but robots do not need more information to confirm their targets, just hit them. The chart

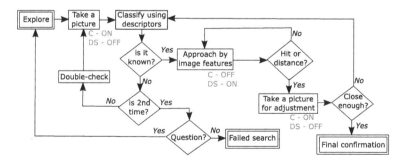

Fig. 5. Process for robot switch across its sensory systems inspired on white sharks [2]. The switch of sensors are in gray font, C for camera and DS for distance sensors. The Question? evaluation consider to abandon the search of that kind of target by declaring a failed search. The final target confirmation means a successful search and approach

showing the *Shark-approach* strategy, inspired by sharks hunting behaviors, is shown in Fig. 5.

Besides re-using previous image processing information, the *Shark-approach* strategy allows the following behaviors according to the classifier validation: (*i*) *clear-shape* confirmed, approaching speed depends on the descriptors; (*ii*) *unclear-shape* detected, cautious approach to double-check, and (*iii*) not-target (it was nothing), continue exploring. Note that the double-check step in the *Shark-approach* strategy can be compared to sharks' first detections, while the final confirmation is similar to the sharks' final decision: eat it.

Robots' Estimations: Each robot saves an estimation of the required time to complete each task. These estimations are compared through a probability function to help the robot to answer one of these questions: Partition? or Give up? However, congestions and cache delays to deliver/reception of objects affect these estimations and as a consequence, robot decisions are also influenced. After each successful target approach, the robot updates its estimations as follows:

$$\hat{t} \leftarrow (1 - \alpha)\hat{t} + \alpha t_i \tag{1}$$

where t_i is the time already invested to complete that task, α is the rate of learning. The bigger the alpha value, the more important is the time of the last experience. Hereby, robots follow Eq. (2) to decide whether partition or not (Partition?) and Eq. (3) to decide whether stop or continue waiting for a cache (Give up?).

Partition? - Decision-Making 1: Once a robot gets an object from a source, the robot can decide either to drop the object in a cache (to partition the transportation) or travel to store the object by itself (to not partition). In the region of nests, a robot can decide between picking an object from caches (to partition) or travel to the region of sources to harvest an object (to not partition). The partitioning probability function is given by

$$P_p = \begin{cases} 1/\left[1 + e^{R\left(\hat{t}_\Phi/(\hat{t}_{\phi_1} + \hat{t}_{\phi_2}) - 1\right)}\right], & \text{se } \hat{t}_\Phi > (\hat{t}_{\phi_1} + \hat{t}_{\phi_2}) \\ 1/\left[1 + e^{R\left(1 - (\hat{t}_{\phi_1} + \hat{t}_{\phi_2})/\hat{t}_\Phi\right)}\right], & \text{otherwise} \end{cases} \tag{2}$$

where P_p is the partitioning probability and R is a steepness factor, $\hat{t}_\Phi = \hat{t}_H + \hat{t}_S$ is the estimated time for the non-partitioning option, i.e., going to harvest an object in the region of sources ($\hat{t}_H$) and coming back to store it in a nest through the path ($\hat{t}_S$). While $\hat{t}_{\phi_1}$ is the estimated time to complete a task by partitioning at the region of sources, i.e., to pick an object from a source ($\hat{t}_{Ps}$) and drop it into a cache ($\hat{t}_{Dc}$); and $\hat{t}_{\phi_2}$ is the estimated time to complete a task by partitioning at the region of nests, i.e., to pick an object from a cache ($\hat{t}_{Pc}$) and store it in a nest ($\hat{t}_{Dn}$).

Give up? - Decision-Making 2: Due to a limited number of caches in the arena, robots may give up waiting an available cache. The *giving up* probability function follows:

$$P_g(\hat{t}, t_i) = \left(1 + e^{K\left[M\frac{t_i - \hat{t}}{t_{\phi_1} + t_{\phi_2}} + O\right]}\right)^{-1} \tag{3}$$

where K and M are steepness factors, t_i is the time already invested in a task, $\hat{t}$ can be the estimated time for dropping an object in a cache ($\hat{t}_{Dc}$) or for picking an object in a cache ($\hat{t}_{Pc}$), and O is the offset of the function. We modified the original function from [12] by adding the parameter M to speed up these decisions. M was adjusted such that when robots waited for a cache almost the same estimated time to travel through the paths, both stop or continue waiting for a cache are equally likely. Note that we are comparing both alternative through this parameter. By letting $M = 1$, it has no effect.

Controller: A hierarchical state machine defines the tasks (states) the robots can perform (see Fig. 6). Figure 6 shows the main states in the hierarchical state machine. Each state in a hierarchical state machine may nest simpler state machines describing the required activities to complete it. When a robot initializes, it first identifies the ground color to know which kind of TAM it must look for. For instance, if the robot begins in the blue region, its target will be a source of objects. On the other region, its target will be a cache. Next, whatever task the robot is working, it first executes the steps of the *Shark-approach* strategy.

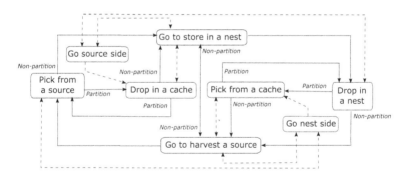

Fig. 6. Hierarchical state machine describing robot behaviors. Dashed lines represent the transitions where robots are able to abandon a task after failing its search

In Fig. 5, note that the proposed strategy has two possible outcomes: success or fail. Failed searches enable the transitions to abandon any task, dashed lines in Fig. 6. In particular, after leaving a TAM (i.e., a successful dropping/picking up of an object), the robot evaluates whether it will continue partitioning or not. This same question is evaluated after a failed search, but this time, the robot decides between abandon or continue searching that target (i.e., the current task).

Here, robots can reconsider all their decision, not only the task related to caches, but using the time already invested instead the estimation. For instance, if some robots are performing *Go storing to a nest* and one of them is struggling to find the landmark to travel. After a while, that robot may re-evaluate Eq. (2) to decide whether continue struggling with the non-partitioning option or change to the partition task, *Drop in a cache*. But, this time, the robot considers t_i instead of the estimated time for storing, $\hat{t}_S$.

In summary, the *Shark-approach* strategy allows robots to: (*i*) change their approaching behavior based on the classifier answers, (*ii*) speed up the search and approach by switching between their embedded sensors, (*iii*) re-used image processing by allowing double-check *unclear-shapes*. Since we worked with the standard equipment, our contributions may brought benefits to the team performance that are scalable by avoiding hardware-boosted solutions.

4   Simulations and Results

We analyzed the benefits and costs of the *Shark-approach* strategy for three configurations of decision-making. Finally, we compared the effect of the new transitions in the adaptability of the team through performance results. Recall that the *Shark-approach* strategy may enable these transitions after a failed search.

Configuration and Parameters: Since robots are competing among themselves for resources, we must analyze the optimal number of robots for each region. More robots do not mean greater performance; the traffic and the process to avoid collisions among robots decrease the performance. Here, we employ a diminishing returns analysis, which requires all variables to remain constant while the variable of interest is increased. Since the region of nests is symmetric to the region of sources, we only check the improvements by adding more robots in the region of sources and checking the number of stored objects within 10 min. These experiments informed us that 8 robots are optimal for our arena.

We used the values that offered the best results in [12] are $S = -2.5$, $K = -0.6$, and $O = -5$. Moreover, we let the parameter of learning estimations as $\alpha = 0.6$. We tested 4 values (in steps, each of 64 ms) for cache delays in delivery and reception of objects: 75 (good for partitioning), 350 (both options yield equal results), 700 (more robots will choose non-partitioning), and 1000 (good for non-partitioning). The estimated times were randomly initialized within these intervals: [200, 800] for partitioning and [1000, 2500] for non-partitioning tasks. These values were obtained from the reference settings: *Always* choose to partition with cache delays of 75 steps and *Never* choose to partition. Since all experiments initialized with estimated times from simulations with cache delays of 75 steps, then robots will begin favoring the partitioning option.

Benefits of Image Processing: To know how much profit yields the *Shark-approach* strategy, we let robots execute an exploration of 10 min in the environment to find a target, i.e., a triangle, square, or circle combined with task-related color. The geometric shape was randomly chosen before starting each simulation. Following the supervised training classification, robots saved an image of the shape, its descriptors, and the class. Then, we checked the number of correct classified shapes; results are in Table 1. Note that almost 36% of the targets were detected with the double-check step of the *Shark-approach*, i.e., by exploiting the *unclear-shape* images. This process brought significant improvements. Due to the descriptors passed through the same classifier, we expected similar errors.

Table 1. Performance on target detection of random shapes. Error percentages were computed by dividing the amount upon total of detected images

Simulation	Targets in	Targets by	Error	Error
	1st image	*Shark-approach*	1st image	*Shark-approach*
Sim1	61	40	13	7
Sim2	37	22	8	4
Sim3	37	25	10	9
Sim4	18	5	4	3
Sim5	36	18	9	7
Sim6	22	12	9	4
Sim7	36	16	9	6
Sim8	32	14	5	3
Sim9	61	40	13	11
Sim10	24	10	6	5
Total	364 (64.3%)	202 (35.7%)	86 (15.2%)	59 (10.4%)

Cost of Image Processing: Since each time a robot gets an image to search its target, it needs to stop 64 ms, we need to know how much time the image processing takes from foraging, we employed three settings of decision-making: *Never* partition, *Always* partition, and the *Model* of [12]. Cake charts in Fig. 7 illustrate the average distribution of time on the different tasks that robots can perform. It is important to mention that while robots wait inside a cache or travel through the alternative path, the image processing execution does not demand excessive computation, only a column or a row of the image was enough. Therefore, in this activities, it was not accounted as image processing steps.

Note that robots foraging with *Never* partition setting show a small percentage of time invested in image processing. While, robots foraging with *Always* partition setting has the greatest percentages of time for image processing and also the more objects transported to the nest. The adaptive *Model* setting returned an intermediated percentage for image processing analysis. Considering both *Always* and *Model* settings, it seems that robots require a greater amount of stops for image processing when partitioning. However, by comparing the amount

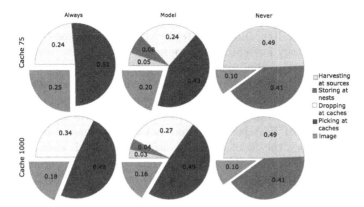

Fig. 7. Average of the distributions of time across the available tasks of foraging. Image processing is in separated piece

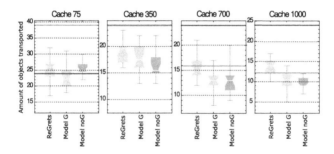

Fig. 8. Performance of foraging robots: the amount of objects stored in nests. The solid lines, red and blue, represent the average of the *Always* and *Never* partitioning settings, respectively (Color figure online)

of objects transported in Fig. 8, robots working with *Always* transported almost twice the amount of objects than with *Never* partition setting. Therefore, almost 10% of the time is invested into image processing. But, in the *Model* setting, robots need more time to learn which option is better.

Performance Analysis: We want to compare which model variation is faster to adapt to different delays from the ones they learned (initialized). The greater the cache delay, the faster must be the mechanism to adapt to new delays. We considered three variations: *Model noG*, which is the reference model working with $M = 1$ in Eq. 3 and where robots can only transition from tasks involving caches (*Drop in a cache* and *Pick up from a cache*); *Model G*, which validate the effect of changing $M = 5$ in the *Giving up* function; and *ReGrets*, which works with both $M = 5$ and all the transitions to reconsider any previous decisions, which were enabled by the *Shark-approach* strategy. The performance of the three variations and the *Never* and *Always* settings are illustrated in Fig. 8.

For each variation, we did 30 simulations of 30 min each with the following cache delays: 75, 350, 700, and 1000 steps. All the simulations employed the *Shark-approach* strategy for search and approach. Without the image classifier, robots detected shapes in other robots and followed them believing to be a target.

Model G brought small improvements when compared with *Model noG*, the reference model. On the other hand, t-test showed us that the new transitions brought significant improvements for almost all cache delays in *ReGrets*. It tied only for cache delays of 75 steps, which does not require adaptations. Therefore, new transitions, which the *Shark-approach* strategy enabled, were more important to the adaptability than the *M* parameter. Note that the greater was the need for adaptation, the faster was our proposal to overcome this need.

5   Conclusions

Due to the success for searching depends mostly on the image processing, the shark-inspired search and approach strategy worked efficiently by switching between sensors in order to improve the robot performance by focusing more on approach than processing images. The strategy overcame the complexity of the more realistic simulator and avoided any hardware extensions on the e-puck robot for the foraging testbed. Our strategy can also be employed in different activities as security patrolling, monitoring environments, exploration, and search and rescue, where vision is key to guide robot navigation.

Despite robots can only distinguish 6 colors, geometric shapes combined with colors can surpass this limitation. This solution does not require to link robots with to a computer to decode Barcodes. Also, the light image classifier considered *unclear-shape* images into the database for training, which combined with the *Shark-approach* mechanism increased the number of detected targets.

Our experiments confirm that the strategies proposed in [12] brought adaptability to the robots, which is required to overcome environmental changes, specially, due to congestions and cache delays. However, their model does not consider possible false visual clues due to colorful robots and light effects in the colors, which was critical for searching, and consequently, for foraging. Our results suggest that small changes in the decision-making mechanism allows for the group to speed up such an adaptation. However, the greater improvement was due to the new transitions (where robots reconsider any decision). These transitions were enabled by the failed searches of the *Shark-approach* strategy.

As future work, we want to explore which is the optimal number of steps for double checking detections, because we did an empirical adjustment based on trigonometry; we pick a number of steps such that the shape increased one pixel. We hope to begin to work with real e-pucks soon in order to implement the *Shark-approach* strategy. Moreover, we want to include sound in the sources for long distance clues as in [21].

Acknowledgments. We thank to CNPq, CAPES, and Fapemig for their financial support. JMN also is grateful with the OEA for the scholarship.

References

1. California department of fish and wildlife: white shark information. https://www. wildlife.ca.gov/Conservation/Marine/White-Shark. Accessed 11 Mar 2016
2. Sharkopedia: interview to Dr. Gregory Skomal. http://sharkopedia.discovery.com/ shark-topics/feeding-hunting-diet/\#great-white-hunting-tactics-an-interview- with-greg-skomal. Accessed 11 Mar 2016
3. Tricas, T., McCosker, J.E.: Predatory behavior of the white shark (Carcharodon carcharias), with notes on its biology. Proc. Calif. Acad. Sci. **43**(4), 221–238 (1982)
4. Ennesser, F., Medioni, G.: Finding Waldo, or focus attention using local color information. IEEE Trans. Pattern Anal. Mach. Intell. **17**(8), 805–809 (1995). doi:10. 1109/34.400571
5. Frintrop, S.: A visual attention system for object detection and goal-directed search. Dissertation, Rheinische Friedrich-Wilhelms Universitat Bonn, doi:10.1007/ 11682110(2006)
6. Baltes, J., Anderson, J.: Intelligent Global Vision for Teams of Mobile Robots. INTECH Open Access Publisher (2007). doi:10.5772/4773
7. Anderson, J., Baltes, J.: Doraemon user manual. http://robocup-video.sourceforge. net. Accessed 11 Mar 2016
8. Cliff, D., Husbands, P., Harvey, I.: Evolving visually guided robots. In: Proceedings of the Second International Conference on Simulation of Adaptive Behavior, pp. 374–383 (1993). doi:10.1.1.147.1548
9. Green, W.E., Oh, P.Y., Barrows, G.: Flying insect inspired vision for autonomous aerial robot maneuvers in near-earth environments. In: Proceedings of the International Conference on Robotics and Automation, pp. 2347–2352 (2004). doi:10. 1109/ROBOT.2004.1307412
10. Swain, M.J., Ballard, D.H.: Indexing via color histograms. In: Proceedings of the 3rd International Conference on Computer Vision (1990). doi:10.1109/ICCV.1990. 139558
11. Montinjano, E.M.: Distributed consensus in multi-robot systems with visual perception. Ph.d. thesis, Universidad de Zaragoza (2012)
12. Pini, G., Brutschy, A., Frison, M., et al.: Task partitioning in swarms of robots: an adaptive method for strategy selection. Swarm Intell. **5**(3–4), 283–304 (2011). doi:10.1007/s11721-011-0060-1
13. Brutschy, A., Pini, G., Baiboun, N., et al.: The IRIDIA TAM: a device for task abstraction for the e-puck robot. Technical report, TR/IRIDIA/2010-015, IRIDIA. Université Libre de Bruxelles, Brussels, Belgium (2010)
14. Sugawara, K., Sano, M.: Cooperative acceleration of task performance: foraging behavior of interacting multi-robots system. Phys. D Nonlinear Phenom. **100**(3), 343–354 (1997). doi:10.1016/S0167-2789(96)00195-9
15. Ye, Y., Tsotsos, J.K.: Where to look next in 3D object search. In: Proceedings of the International Symposium on Computer Vision (1995). doi:10.1109/ISCV.1995. 477057
16. Sjö, K., Glvez, D., Paul, C., et al.: Object search and localization for an indoor mobile robot. J. Comput. Inf. Tech. **17**(1), 67–80 (2009). doi:10.2498/cit.1001182
17. Gozanlez, R.C., Woods, R.E.: Digital Image Processing, 2nd edn. Prentice Hall, Upper Saddle River (2002)
18. Randen, T., Husoy, J.H.: Filtering for texture classification: a comparative study. IEEE Trans. Pattern Anal. Mach. Intell. **21**(4), 291–310 (1999). doi:10.1109/34. 761261

19. Sjriek, A., Ranjbar-Sahraei, B., May, S., et al.: An experimental framework for exploiting vision in swarm robotics. In: Proceedings of the European Conference on Artificial Life, vol. 83, pp. 775–782 (2013). doi:10.7551/978-0-262-31709-2-ch111
20. Mondada, F., Bonani, M., et al.: The e-puck, a robot designed for education in engineering. In: Proceedings of the 9th Conference on Autonomous Robot Systems and Competitions, vol. 1, no. 4, pp. 59–65 (2009). doi:10.1.1.180.8110
21. Montes-Gonzalez, F., Aldana-Franco, F.: The evolution of signal communication for the e-puck robot In: Proceedings of the 10th Mexican International Conference on Artificial Intelligence, pp. 466–477 (2011). doi:10.1007/978-3-642-25324-9_40
22. Michel, O., Rohrer, F., Heiniger, N., et al.: Cyberbotics' Robot Curriculum. Wikibooks (2010). Edited from 18th January
23. Brutschy, A., Garattoni, L., et al.: The TAM: abstracting complex tasks in swarm robotics research. Swarm Intell. **9**(1), 1–22 (2015). doi:10.1007/s11721-014-0102-6

An Open-Source Tele-Operated Mobile Manipulator: CHAP V1

Guido Bugmann[1(✉)], Dominic Cassidy[1], Paul Doyle[2],
and Khushdeep Singh Mann[1]

[1] Plymouth University, Plymouth PL4 8AA, UK
gbugmann@plymouth.ac.uk, dominic.cassidy93@gmail.com,
khushdeepvnit@gmail.com
[2] Hereward College, Coventry CV4 9SW, UK
Paul.Doyle@hereward.ac.uk

Abstract. Teleoperated mobile manipulators are of use for disabled people and for the wider public interested in acting at distance. The high price of existing devices is a barrier to their diffusion. The paper reports on the first design produced in the Cheap Arm Project (CHAP). It costs less than £2000, uses easily available parts and can be assembled by anybody with basic technical skills. The manipulator can reach objects from floor-level up to shelves at a height of 170 cm using a new low-cost arm design. Teleoperation is be done using a tablet, smartphone or browser. The cost could be further reduced by using different servo motors. The design and assembly instructions are made available on the open-source repository GitHub, with the hope that the community will build and improve the design. The first version has been tested in a college for disabled young people who provided initial recommendations for improvement.

Keywords: Teleoperation · Teleoperated · Disability · Assistive · Robot

1 Introduction

Teleoperated mobile manipulators are of use for disabled people and for the wider public interested in acting at distance. We conducted this study with the disabled user in mind. The high price of existing devices significantly makes them inaccessible to most users. The most common designs consist of a mobile robot platform onto which a robot manipulator is attached. Manipulators usually have a limited reach and therefore need to be mounted on some sort of lifting device to cover a useful vertical operation range. An early example of such devices is the EL_E built at Georgia Tech. [1]. A nice study of a number of combinations of mobile platforms and manipulators can be found in [2], where a new low-cost combination is described, costing around $4400 without a lifting mechanism. These design are mainly aimed at autonomy, where the user issues a high level command that is then executed using on-board planning and sensing. In this

© Springer International Publishing AG 2017
Y. Gao et al. (Eds.): TAROS 2017, LNAI 10454, pp. 199–210, 2017.
DOI: 10.1007/978-3-319-64107-2_16

paper we initially only consider teleoperation, giving the user full control of the device. The system supports this by providing a simple web interface with visual feedback. This approach is evaluated through initial user tests.

2   Design

2.1   Concepts

It was important to minimize the cost of parts. We noted that commercial robot manipulators all aim at precision and reproducibility. These devices are essentially designed to operate "blindly". This is a significant cause for costs, due to the need for precisely engineered parts able to generate precise displacements for whatever load and position within their operational envelope. In our approach, we decided that such precision was not needed, as the user was there to correct the observed positions. Placing the user in the control loop (a form of "shared autonomy") was a way to reduce costs.

Placing a conventional robot manipulator on top of a mobile base creates a highly redundant system, as both manipulator and base provide x-y positioning. To save the cost of redundant servomotors, we used an omni-directional base also controlling the x-y position of the gripper. All that was needed was to provide a mechanism to control the height of the gripper.

2.2   Arm and Lift

We aimed at a device able to lift common objects used in everyday life, of which the heaviest is probably a 2 L bottle of water or fizzy drinks. So, we set the target to lift a maximum weight of 3 Kg, to have some margin. We aimed at a similar reach to the human arm, i.e. around 75 cm (including gripper length). The arm needed to reach the ground level to pick up objects on the floor, as well as reaching the height of head-height shelves. In order to eliminate an expensive elbow joint, we thought of a simple lever with axis appropriately placed to offer the whole range of heights (Fig. 1A). In order to reduce the length of the lever protruding at the back of the robot, we introduced the concept of a "virtual rotation point". In this approach, two points of the lever are actuated to cause the gripper to execute the desired trajectory. It turns out that, with an arm length of 50 cm (without gripper) and a protruding length of 25 cm, the back lever moves by 1/2 of the displacement of the lifting point. Hence both movements could be achieved with a double pulley activated by the same servomotor (Fig. 1B). Both pulleys have opposed actions: while the larger diameter one reels the cable in to lift the arm, the smaller one reels the cable out at 1/2 of the speed to let the back lever raise too. With this arrangement, the back lever actually reduces the torque required from the servomotor. The lifting force was further halved by using a pulley on both cables (see next section). Low stretch 2 mm Dyneema ropes were used. For more details, see the instruction notes on the Github site: https://mobile-chap.github.io/Web/.

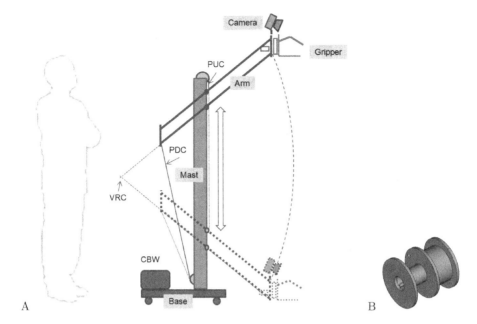

Fig. 1. A. Basic elements of the CHAP robot: VRC: Virtual Rotation Centre; PUC: Pull-Up Cable; PDC: Pull-Down Cable; CBW: Counter Balancing Weight. B. Lifting double pulley at the base of the mast.

The arm is designed as a four-bar parallelogram gliding in rails on each side of the mast. The design was a parallelogram to ensure that the end plate on which the gripper is attached is always vertical. Therefore, for instance, a cup picked up off the floor would automatically stay level during the lifting process.

The mast was built out of wood and plywood with a U-profile for rigidity. It was attached using four cables linking it to the base, similar to shrouds on a sailing boat. This ensured maximal strength for a very small weight. Without shrouds, the base of the mast would have had to be attached to the mobile platform using a very strong and rigid fixation.

Overall, the robot weighs 11 Kg and can easily be transported. If needed, the mast can be detached from the base by releasing the four shroud cables (using wing nuts).

2.3   Counterweight and Torques

We show hereafter how to estimate the mass of the counterweight and the torque required from the lifting servo motor at the bottom of the mast.

Counterweight. Le us consider the arm in a horizontal configuration, with the gripper holding the heaviest object it is designed for: A 3 L bottle of water. The gripper itself weighs approximately 1 kg and we will ignore the small difference between arm weight in front and behind the mast. The center of the bottle held

202 G. Bugmann et al.

by the gripper is located 60 cm away from the front of the mast (where the lifting cable is attached to the arm and where the guiding rails for the arm are located). The front wheels are 10 cm in front of the mast. So, the effective reach for calculating the tipping torque is 60 cm − 10 cm = 50 cm. The tipping torque is therefore $0.5 \, \text{m} \cdot 4 \, \text{kg} \cdot 9.81 \, \text{m/s}^2 \approx 20 \, \text{Nm}$[1]. The mast, the base and the battery weighing a total of around 9 Kg also contribute a counterbalancing torque of $0.1 \, \text{m} \cdot 9 \, \text{kg} \cdot 9.81 \approx 9 \, \text{Nm}$. The counterweight mass M_{CW} is placed 35 cm behind the front wheels. It needs to weigh $M_{CW} = (20 − 9)/(0.35 \cdot 9.81) \approx 3 \, \text{kg}$. This provided by a partially filled 5 L water tank that can be emptied during transport of the manipulator.

Lifting torque. The lifting cable lifts the arm (approx 1 kg), the gripper (approx 1 kg) and the load (at most 3 kg). For simplification, we will assume that all these masses are located 60 cm in front of the front of the mast. Let us consider that the back of the arm is held in place by the PDC cable (Fig. 1A) and is the rotation point for a lever. This is situated 25 cm behind the front of the mast. The torque τ_L generated by the arm, gripper and load is $\tau_L = (0.25+0.6) \cdot (1+1+3) \cdot 9.81 \approx 42 \, \text{Nm}$. This torque has to be compensated for by the lifting cable that is placed only 25 cm in front of the rotation point. The lifting force thus is: $42 \, \text{Nm}/0.25 \approx 168 \, \text{N}$, corresponding to 16 kg being lifted by the lifting cable.

In our design, this force is halved to 84 N by a cable pulley mechanism placed inside the mast.

At the bottom of the mast, there is a 3D-printed ABS double pulley (Fig. 1B). The larger pulley has a radius of 13 mm and is used to pull down the lifting cable. The torque τ_{PU} required for pulling down the lifting cable is $\tau_{PU} = 0.013 \, \text{m} \cdot 84 \, \text{N} = 1.1 \, \text{Nm}$.

The second pulley has a smaller radius of 6.5 mm and is used to pull down the back of the arm. To calculate the required force, we now consider the front of the mast to be the rotation point of a lever with a weight of 5 kg placed 60 cm in front of the mast, compensated by the pull-down force F_{PD} applied at a distance of 25 cm at the back. We find that F_{PD} is $5 \cdot 9.81 \cdot 0.6/0.25 \approx 120 \, \text{N}$. This also halved by a cable pulley, exerting a torque on the smaller pulley of $\tau_{PD} = 60 \cdot 0.0065 = 0.39 \, \text{Nm}$. In our design, when the arm is lifted, the PUC is wound in and the PDC is wound out. Thus the two torques τ_{PU} and τ_{PD} oppose each other and the servo needs to generate no more than $\tau_{SERVO} = 1.1 \, \text{Nm} − 0.39 \, \text{Nm} = 0.71 \, \text{Nm}$.

A Dynamixel RX-64 servo was used that has a stall torque of around 4.2 Nm and a no-load speed of around 35 RPM at 11.1 V, providing plenty of speed and torque to lift the arm.

2.4 Base

The base is an omni-directional platform with 3 motor units (Fig. 2). Each motor unit is 3D-printed to hold an omniwheel between two ball-bearings and a

---

[1] We approximate g = 9.81 with 10.

Dynamixel MX-28 servomotor. These servos are addressed using a serial protocol and can be daisy-chained. They can be controlled in position mode or in speed control mode. They allow for a precise and smooth positioning of the base. The plate is made of 25 mm thick plywood that can be laser-cut. The heart-shape enables it to approach furniture parts more closely. The front wheels are placed 10 cm ahead of the front of the mast. A counterweight is placed at the back. The counterweight is a flexible water container that can be filled up to 5 L when in use, and emptied when the robot is transported. The base can move in any direction and the calculation of the speed commands for each wheel is very simple (see e.g. documentation on our github site).

Fig. 2. Underside of the base showing three motor units. Parts of the arm can be seen in the background on the front side.

2.5 Gripper

The gripper had a design as simple as possible to support tasks of every day life, such as lifting a bottle, poring, lifting small objects from the floor, carrying small food trays, e.g. for microwave cooking. Although the initial impulse was to design a multi-fingered human-like hand, the aim here was to produce a gripper as simple as possible, using laser-cut parts, to enable initial testing and the collection of data for the real specification of the gripper. Nguyen et al. (2008) [3] noted that indoor objects are usually found on flat surfaces, and our gripper design is probably adequate for the task of collecting such objects.

The gripper is essentially a fixed 3 mm aluminium plate that can be rotated into a vertical or horizontal position. Then, a V-shaped knuckle presses the object against the plate and hold it in place for lifting. The edge of the plate is filed down to a thickness of 1 mm to help collect small objects and plates. Both plate and knuckle are covered with rubber to increase grip. We measured how much force was needed to press a 3 Kg bottle against the plate to stop it from slipping (15 Kg), and designed the gripping mechanism to provide that force. It uses a cable pulling the knuckle and a spring opening the hand. When the

A   B   C

Fig. 3. (A) Gripper lifting a 3 L bottle of water, (B, C) grabbing a bowl and a LiPo battery.

plate is horizontal, the small "finger" at the end of claw can be used to drag the object onto the plate. This finger is also useful for holding food containers, e.g. a bowl (Fig. 3). The gripper uses three dynamixel servos, 2 × AX-12 for the single finger and the wrist rotation and one MX-28 for the closing mechanism.

2.6 Software and User Interface

The developed control system was centered around a Raspberry Pi and direct Dynamixel communication through two USB2Dynamixels. Three independent sub-systems ran on the Raspberry Pi in parallel allowing full teleoperation of the robot by a user on the same Wi-Fi connection using any touch or non-touch device. The sub-systems were as follows:

- Web Server: Hosted HTML/CSS/JavaScript client teleoperation web page.
- Control Listener: Listened using a web-socket for client commands and passed these to the correct Dynamixels. Multiple conditional arguments were used in order to check the name of the incoming command and correctly process it.
- Stream Server: Hosted a live image stream (captured by OpenCV) from the camera mounted on the robot gripper.

The sub-systems were all built on the Python (2.7) programming language, with JavaScript used by the client for detecting user input and communicating these to the control listener.

This simple system enabled high concurrence with limited bottle necks between systems. Each sub system was capable of running fully independently and simply waited for either passive usage (web and stream server), or direct inputs (control listener).

Multiple Python modules were used to enable this behaviour cleanly. Specifically, Flask was used for hosting the web server, while Autobahn enabled the control listener to directly connect to the client using a web socket. Finally, Pypot enabled direct communication with the used Dynamixels individually and as groups. The live web stream was accessed by the client-loaded web-page and presented on the user interface background.

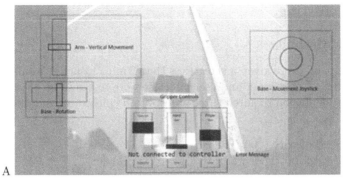

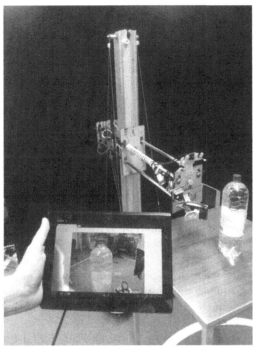

Fig. 4. A. User interface concept. The left controls act on the rotation of the base and the lift. The right control acts as a joystick to control the X-Y motion of the base. The three central controls act on the gripper. B. View of the interface in action.

To use the system, the user first connects with a smartphone or tablet to the wifi hotspot run on the Raspberry Pi. Then the user opens a browser to open the webpage (a default page at a dedicated IP number).

Figure 4 shows the placement of the controls that appear transparently on top of the video from the on-board camera when used (touching the screen will make the controls appear).

3   User Testing

3.1   Basic Usability

Four participants were given a short (less than 2 min) visual introduction to the control system. The gripper and user interface were tested in an object handling task. Experimentation required three objects to be picked up and moved a short distance.

- Task 1: Roll of wire (200 g)
- Task 2: 500 ml bottle of water (600 g)
- Task 3: Book (400 g)

The three items used were of very different shapes. The complexity of the objects required effective use of the robot's 4 degrees of freedom and, as found during the experiments, all 4° were used in response. The participants were placed in a seated position perpendicular to the work area 1 m from a table and the robot (see Fig. 5A). Objects were placed on the table prior to each experiment, with the user moving them from the right side of the table to the left (with the robot starting position being perpendicular to the object). The enforced seated position was to increase reliance on the image stream, and remove advantages of improved visibility that could not be replicated between users. During a prior pilot study, the gripper failed multiple times due to overload errors in the knuckle, and occasionally the finger. As a result, the main experiments required the researcher to be ready to power cycle the specific motors upon failure (a software-only procedure has been devised since).

Timed tasks showed mixed results. With $\frac{3}{4}$ of participants failing to pick-up the book; which was a deliberately slippery surface and reflected certain weaknesses in the gripper. One participant managed to pick up the bottle within 40 s compared to the other three participants who had an average time of 3 min 12 s. This result was due to superior technique (combined knuckle and finger use), and reflected the extent to which human participation may lower the effectiveness of the robot due to improper technique.

During each of these experiments no issues were found with the base or tower systems. The control system was reliable and worked as expected. The robot was capable of carrying all weights attempted, ranging from 100 g to 2 kg (during the pilot), and lifted these over 1.5 m from ground level. Controller usage showed that all degrees of freedom were used throughout the experiments.

No issues where found with the control system UI, although some confusion was seen in differentiating the right and left hand side controls. Controls were otherwise exact and highly responsive. The extent to which all controls were used is important as it shows that each degree of freedom was needed for object manipulation and therefore required constant access within the interface.

Some participants commented on the placement of the camera (view sometime hidden by the gripper), too many degrees of freedom to control (auto-alignment with the object was suggested), or found the gripper "crude" (shape not matching some objects) (Fig. 6).

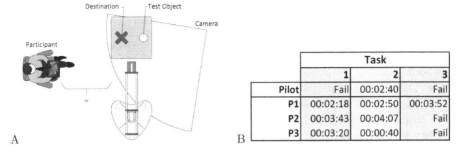

	Task		
	1	**2**	**3**
Pilot	Fail	00:02:40	Fail
P1	00:02:18	00:02:50	00:03:52
P2	00:03:43	00:04:07	Fail
P3	00:03:20	00:00:40	Fail

Fig. 5. A. Setup and B. Task execution time during basic usability tests. The indicated camera was used to record the tests. P1, P2 and P3 refer to the three subjects tested. "Pilot" refers to the subject used in the pilot study. Times larger than 5 min were deemed "Fail".

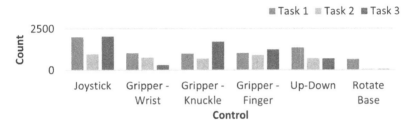

Fig. 6. Behaviour during the basic usability test, showing the total number of uses of the indicated controls.

3.2 Feedback from Disabled Users

For half a day, 7 disabled students at Hereward College were given the robot to try in various conditions, first in a meeting room, and then in their own rooms. Note that the camera had been moved to a more off-centre position with a view not obstructed by the gripper. After experimenting with the robot, the students were asked to answer following questions:

1. Would you like to have such a robot to own/use?
2. When/where/for what tasks would you use it?
3. What would you change to the prototype you have seen?
4. How would you source such a robot:
   (a) Build you own from provided designs/after modifying the design and source your own parts?
   (b) Build from a kit of pre-cut parts/3d Printed parts + source all the rest (servo + electronics), e.g. online shopping?
   (c) Build from a full kit?
   (d) Buy a fully assembled robot?
   (e) Rent a robot?
   (f) Use a robot owned by college?

Their answers can be summarized as follows. The number of replies in indicated by the number of 1's in brackets.

- They all wanted to have a robot.
- About sourcing the robot,
  - They were not prepared to build it themselves.
  - They would buy it assembled for themselves (111) or would be happy to use a robot provided by the school (1111).
- They would use it
  - in their rooms(111), in the kitchen (11), outdoors (1) and indoors (11), on the college site (11).
  - To pick up things (1111111), pick up rubbish (1), getting things that are high up (111), to cover the student up (1), turning light off (1), reaching things (111).
- What would they change?
  - Make it smaller (1111) (with the same height (111) and narrower (1), so that it is less of a hassle (1)).
  - Add a camera to help navigation (1).
  - Make the controls smoother (1). Left-right controls are confusing (1).
  - Make a coloured robot (1).
  - Have a different gripper (1) (We forgot to ask what should be different..), maybe a different gripper for different jobs (1).
  - Would be good to be able to use your own phone (1) (this student had a problem with the browser on his phone).
  - Make it faster (1) (the wheelchairs move really fast in corridors - In the common room, some commented that it was fast).

4   Discussion

Regarding the cost of the robot, a large contribution comes from the use of Dynamixel servomotors. One reason for using them was that we had a stock of them, but they are actually very convenient to control, almost directly from the USB port of a PC. Another important point is that they have a very good torque vs speed curve that no cheaper digital servo can match. As the servos are a big contributor to the total cost, it is worth looking for alternative, but at present, the only route seems to be the design of new servos from scratch. We estimate that this would save at least £600 on the cost of parts.

Many design decision ensured that the primary design and components of the robot were of materials and parts that can be accessed easily, and fabricated without expensive machinery. The reliance on 3D printing ensured effective and repeatable prototyping, however the limitations of this technique were also discovered, with specific difficulty caused by failures in accuracy and resolution. This was especially critical where parts were designed to fit into each others, such a those in the motor unit. While the continuous prototyping allowed by

3D printing solved or can solve these issues, this does cause concern in sharing computer-aided design documents as designs were adjusted with the specific peculiarities of the 3D printer used in mind.

Basic usability tests showed a good controllability of the x, y, z positioning and motion. Grasping some objects was slow and cumbersome.

Testing with disabled users showed a definite interest in using such a robot. The concept of an interface running on any smart phone or tablet was much appreciated. However, the controls were too responsive for some students leading to a frustrating jerky motion. Many student were using wheelchairs and would have liked the robot capable of the same displacement velocity as their wheelchairs. In short, CHAP is desirable with a smaller footprint, more speed, easier gripper controls and probably a redesign of the gripper. The latter is actually easy to replace on the prototype, without even using a screwdriver.

No wheelchair user suggested mounting the manipulator on the wheelchair itself (see e.g. the design in [4]), possibly due to the added advantage of remote action offered by a separate mobile device.

5   Conclusion

Overall the design proved to be highly effective considering the overall cost of under £2000 (over £1400 worth of which were motors). The Cheap Arm Project resulted in a mobile robot arm system capable of tasks usually reserved for robot systems 10-times the cost. This system is an important step towards developing a high-powered robot arm system that can be easily accessed by education institutions, developers, researchers, and those in need.

User interface design faced the usual issues of compatibility and latency, with design and functionality having to be shaped carefully around these issues. Nonetheless, a widely supported control system was implemented, allowing for simplified control of a high number of robot axis. For a robot arm lacking automation, some complexity existed in the degree of manual controls needed, and difficulty in adding these in an intuitive way while ensuring minimal clutter and complexity. This task was achieved, with all test participants capable of manipulating items with no prior experience.

Nevertheless, controlling the gripper was generally slow and some thoughts need to be given to a more intuitive approach, possibly relying on some in-built intelligence simplifying the user's task while preserving a sense of control. The mechanical design of the gripper is also open for improvements.

It appears that offering an open-source design is not sufficient to make the device available to potential users. Most users do not have the technical skills and tools (even simple ones) to build their own robot. Someone needs to build it for them.

We feel that a second design cycle is needed before manufacturing can be considered. This cycle does not need to take long and any help from the open source community will be welcome.

Acknowledgment. We gratefully acknowledge the contribution of Parag Khanna to the design of the gripper and that of Arunaganesan Swaminathan to the design of the base and its control.

References

1. Jain, A., Kemp, C.C.: EL-E: an assistive mobile manipulator that autonomously fetches objects from flat surfaces. Auton. Robots **28**(1), 45–64 (2010)
2. Eaton, E., Mucchiani, C., Mohan, M., Isele D. Luna, J.M., Clingerman, C.: Design of a low-cost platform for autonomous mobile service robots. In: Proceedings of IJCAI 2016 Workshop on Autonomous Mobile Service Robots (2016)
3. Nguyen, H., Anderson, C., Trevor, A., Jain, A., Xu, Z., Kemp, C.C.: El-E: an assistive robot that fetches objects from flat surfaces. In: Proceedings of HRI 2008 Workshop on Robotic Helpers: User Interaction Interfaces and Companions in Assistive and Therapy Robots, pp. 79–86 (2008)
4. Hillman, M., Hagan, K., Hagan, S., Jepson, J., Orpwood, R.: The weston wheelchair mounted assistive robot-the design story. Robotica **20**(2), 125–132 (2002)
5. Project source files: https://mobile-chap.github.io/Web/

Local Real-Time Motion Planning Using Evolutionary Optimization

Steffen Müller$^{(\boxtimes)}$, Thanh Q. Trinh, and Horst-Michael Gross

Technische Universität Ilmenau, 98693 Ilmenau, Germany
steffen.mueller@tu-ilmenau.de
http://www.tu-ilmenau.de/neurob

Abstract. In order to allow for flexible realization of diverse navigation tasks of mobile robots, objective-based motion planner proved to be very successful. The quality of a selected control command for a certain time step is inherently connected to the considered diversity of future trajectories. Therefore, we propose an evolutionary motion planning (EMP) method to solve this high-dimensional search problem without restricting the search space. The algorithm optimizes sequences of acceleration commands with respect to objective functions for evaluating the resulting movement trajectories. The method has been successfully deployed on two robots with differential drive, and experiments showed that it outperforms the Dynamic Window Approach [1] with its restricted discretized search space. Furthermore, car-like and holonomic robots could be controlled successfully in simulations.

Keywords: Motion planning · Motion control · Evolutionary optimization

1 Introduction

For a general purpose service robot, navigation skills in a populated and sometimes constricted environment are essential. The projects of our lab involving navigation in home environments [2] and also public buildings [3] showed that a simple target-directed, obstacle avoiding motion behavior often is not sufficient. For example, in a public environment social aspects have to be considered in order to perform a navigation behavior that is accepted by the people indirectly involved in the robot's activities. Soft constraints, like respecting people's personal space or driving on the right side of an aisle, have to be considered in the motion planning algorithm in addition to the hard criteria of collision avoidance and target directed motion. In a home environment, socially assistive robot companions additionally may want to communicate their internal emotional state by means of different movement styles while performing navigation tasks. As part

---

This work has received funding from the German Federal Ministry of Education and Research (BMBF) to the project SYMPARTNER (grant agreement no. 16SV7218).

Y. Gao et al. (Eds.): TAROS 2017, LNAI 10454, pp. 211–221, 2017.
DOI: 10.1007/978-3-319-64107-2_17

of the SYMPARTNER[1] project, we currently work on an objective function for rating movement trajectories of a robot according to emotional expressivity.

In order to realize diverse navigation behaviors, in our lab the Dynamic Window Approach (DWA), an objective-based motion planner introduced by Fox et al. [1], has been further developed and successfully applied for several real-world scenarios ranging from large public shopping centers and hospitals, to small and constricted senior apartments. Nevertheless, for generating very specific motion patterns, in our case the DWA reached its limits due to the very restricted types of hypothetical movement trajectories used for evaluation. The assumption of constant future velocity only generates arc-like trajectories. Especially, complex objective functions, like those for consideration of personal space and emotional expressivity, need more complex unrolled candidate trajectories than the arc-like ones of the DWA. Therefore, we propose a new method for generating trajectories with a high degree of freedom, which then are optimized in order to satisfy the various objectives mentioned before.

The remainder of this paper is organized as follows: First, a brief discussion of alternative motion planning methods is given followed by a description of the objective-based navigation framework used in our lab. After that, our evolutionary optimization approach will be introduced, followed by some experimental results.

2   Related Work

In the robotics field, decoupling the motion planning into global and local planner is a well established paradigm. The global planner operates on a coarser world representation and generates a route to the goal, whereas the local planner has to find optimal control commands to follow the global plan respecting the robot's dynamic constraints and the dynamics of the sensed environment.

One of the first local planner, which was able to operate a robot with non-holonomic dynamics, more specifically a synchro-drive robot, was the DWA [1]. The DWA directly searches in the velocity space adhering to the robot's dynamics. To keep the search computationally feasible, the velocity space is discretized, and a constant velocity is assumed for the whole planning horizon. However, this assumptions results in very restricted trajectories.

More flexible trajectories can be considered with a lattice-based discretization of the state space using motion primitives [4,5]. As result, the state space is represented as a graph with nodes standing for states, and edges connecting nodes which are reachable using the motion primitives. Then search algorithms are used on the graph to generate feasible trajectories. The trajectories' flexibility is determined by the amount of motion primitives. This must be chosen carefully as a greater number of motion primitives can result in a computational burden, but too few primitives generate inflexible trajectories as well. The Rapidly Exploring Random Tree (RRT) approach [6,7] is not subject to this restriction,

---

[1] SYMbiosis of PAul and RoboT companion for Emotion sensitive caRe (www.sympartner.de).

since it builds a representation by sampling the state space. Beginning with the robot's position as initial tree node, in each iteration a new state is sampled, and the tree is expanded towards that sample at the closest existing tree node. Although, RRTs can generate a feasible solution even for higher dimensional state spaces, the resulting trajectories for common mobile platforms are jerky, and additional smoothing is needed. Furthermore, the definition of a distance metric required to find the closest node is not always trivial (e.g. for car-like vehicles).

So, we propose to use an evolutionary algorithm [8] for solving the optimization problem. Similar to the DWA, our approach conducts the search in the space of possible control commands to satisfy the robot's dynamic constraints. Unlike other approaches, no constant velocity is assumed over the planning horizon, nor a discretization of the command space or predefined motion primitives are required. Overall, this is leading to more flexible candidate trajectories enabling a more accurate estimation of a control commands outcome in the future (see Fig. 1).

Fig. 1. Trajectories evaluated by the DWA (left) and our proposed approach (right), color codes for the costs (red high, blue low), the target is behind the lower border in direction of the red star. (Color figure online)

3 Objective-Based Motion Planning

The main requirement for a motion planner is the ability to satisfy different combinations of constraints on the movement in various scenarios. The objective-based approach introduced with the DWA [1] can realize this by decomposing the resulting navigation behavior into a set of objective functions, each of them responsible for a certain aspect. By means of an interface where the higher level application only specifies a navigation task, the objectives are activated or deactivated individually depending on the current needs (see [3] for further details on the architecture of our navigation stack). Each of the objectives is able to evaluate costs for a given hypothetic movement trajectory of the robot. These costs are real-valued numbers or even a hard deny which prohibits a trajectory if it led to a collision, for example. The motion planner then has to combine the costs of all active objectives by means of a weighted sum, in order to find a global rating for a given trajectory.

For our experiments, a basic set of objective functions has been applied, which comprises

1. a **path and heading objective** responsible for approaching the minimum in a globally planned navigation function (using E* planner [9]) and turning towards a given goal orientation in proximity to the goal position,
2. a **distance objective** for avoiding collisions with static and dynamic obstacles,
3. a **direction objective** preferring forward motion of the robot to account for the limited sensor capabilities in the rear,
4. a **personal space objective** to keep distance to people in the close proximity of the robot by predicting their movements with a linear model.

For all the objectives, the costs are computed for all the points along the trajectory. By averaging along the trajectories, future outcome as well as immediate costs are considered equally, which helps to find command sequences that contain the useful actions already in the beginning rather than in the far future parts, as it could be the case if only the trajectories' endpoints would be evaluated.

With these objectives, the aim of the motion planner is to generate potential movement trajectories which are associated with the next velocity command for the current planning cycle (250 ms in our case) and find the most suitable with respect to the rating yielded by the objectives. This means that a compromise of all active objectives has to be found. After that, the corresponding velocity command will be executed and the planning cycle starts again.

Since the selection of the next motor command has to be real-time capable, this optimization is only done for a local trajectory of a few seconds maximum. An appropriate time horizon has to be selected carefully. On the one hand, the minimum time frame considered is determined by the given physical properties of the robot. Maximum velocity and deceleration define a stopping time, which is the minimum planning horizon to include safe stopping trajectories in optimization. On the other hand, a small time horizon may lead to suboptimal solutions and potential oscillations. Therefore, the size of the predicted local trajectories should be as long as possible given the real-time restrictions. A robot then for example may be far-sighted enough to turn in front of a narrow passage in order to reach a target orientation at the end which may be unreachable if the robot could not turn inside the narrow gap. Also for avoiding moving obstacles (like walking people), a longer planning horizon with flexible trajectories allows to react on the changing situation more appropriate (see Sect. 5).

4   Evolutionary Optimization Algorithm

For a given time horizon (e.g. 3.5 s in our case), the set of possible movement trajectories is enormous. For each time step, a real-valued tuple of translational v_x, v_y ($v_y = 0$ in case of differential drive) and rotational velocity v_ϕ is possible which define the actual trajectory over time if applied to the robot's motor controllers. So, the motion planner has to solve a difficult search problem.

Contrary to the DWA, which exhaustively searches the whole discretized velocity space and to be computationally tractable assumes a constant velocity for the whole planning horizon, our approach's trajectories are far more flexible (see Fig. 1) by permitting individual velocities at each time step of the planning horizon. In order to search in this high dimensional trajectory space, an evolutionary algorithm is applied.

That means, we hold a population $P = \{A_i | i = 1, \ldots, M\}$ of possible acceleration sequences as individuals. These individuals $A_i = (\mathbf{a}^t | t = 0, \ldots, T)$ consist of an acceleration vector $\mathbf{a}^t = (a_x^t, a_y^t, a_\phi^t)$ for each time step t of the planning horizon. See Fig. 2 for a visualization of the encoding scheme. Most evolutionary algorithms consist of the following main steps, which can be found in our motion planner as well: (1) proper initialization of the population, (2) evaluation of each individual's fitness, (3) selection of the best individuals, and (4) producing a new generation by applying mutation and crossover operations on the best selected individuals. These steps are repeated for several generations to bring the population closer to an optimum.

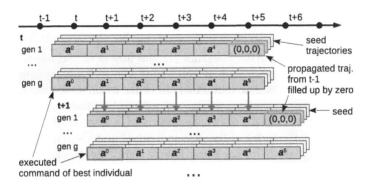

Fig. 2. Encoding of individuals as sequences of acceleration vectors which are optimized for g generations in each planner cycle, propagation of the final population of one planner cycle to the next helps reusing the optimization effort from past cycles and reduces number of generations needed in each planner cycle, which enables real time operation. (Color figure online)

For application in the motion planning domain, due to real time restrictions, only a small number g of generations ($g = 5$ in our case) can be evaluated in the available time slots, but we can benefit from the fact, that trajectories of the subsequent time step are not independent of the last population. A trajectory found for one situation is also valid for immediately succeeding situations, except that the robot has simply traveled along that trajectory for a small step.

Propagating Individuals. Therefore, we apply a propagation operation to the final population P of the last planning time step in order to initialize a new population P', which is going to be used as the start for the new planning cycle (see Fig. 2). The new population is built up from the best individuals of the last generation in the last planning cycle, which are shifted by one element in time. That means the acceleration vectors of $t = 0$ (which have been executed currently) are cut off, and a new vector $(0, 0, 0)$ will be appended at the end to fill up the sequence. The remaining individuals of the population will be generated deterministically in order to ensure that the population at least contains a minimum number of individuals encoding a safe stopping trajectory. Since a randomized search algorithm is used for finding an optimal trajectory, otherwise it can not be guaranteed, that a collision free trajectory is included in the population. This means the green seed individuals of Fig. 2 consist of deceleration trajectories which try to reach zero velocity at different rotational and translational speeds.

Fitness Evaluation. Having an initial population, we enter a loop of g generations for optimization. The first step in that loop is the evaluation of the fitness, for each individual in the population. Therefore, the acceleration sequence of each individual is transformed into a movement trajectory in space by means of a forward model of the robot. All these trajectories are then evaluated by the active objectives of our current motion task.

Selection of the Best. After determining the fitness of the individuals, the next generation will be generated by combining two individuals from the last generation as parent for a new individual. In order to prefer better rated individuals for reproduction, the individuals are ordered by fitness and two random indices in that sorted list are drawn by means of a normal distribution with mean 0 representing the index of the best individual and a given variance specifying the selection pressure for the evolutionary algorithm. Over all generations, the best rated individual is stored for execution at the end of the planning cycle (this ensures that safe stop trajectories can be executed if non of the recombined individuals satisfy the constraints of the objectives).

Mutation and Crossover. Once two parent individuals were drawn, the recombination of a new individual takes place by copying the acceleration vectors for each time step either from the first or from the second parent. With a probability of p ($p = 30\%$ in our case) the actual parent is switched after each time step. After, a new individual has been created, a mutation operation is applied, which operates in two modes. First, to each acceleration vector a normal distributed random acceleration is added and truncated to the physical limits. Second, a kind of symmetric mutation is executed. Therefore, two positions in the sequence are selected. Then a normal distributed random value is added to the acceleration at the first position and subtracted from the second position. This mutation is repeated for several iterations. Unlike the first mutation which results in curves and elongations of the resulting trajectories, small lateral translations are produced by the symmetric mutation.

Using only these operations on our robots, it showed that the resulting acceleration profiles are very noisy, and sometimes consecutive values compensate each other. Although, the evolution process would be able to find smooth trajectories if smoothness would be added as an objective, we decided to bias mutation towards smooth trajectories in order to reduce the search complexity. This has been achieved by randomly selecting segments of the acceleration sequence and applying a low pass filter on that part. As result, the trajectories are much smoother but still can take on arbitrary shapes.

The computational effort in our tests was selected to be equal to the DWA approach. Since the main time is consumed by the costs evaluation in the objective functions, we used 5 generations with 60 individuals each resulting in 300 trajectory evaluations per time step (250 ms), which is the same amount as for a DWA with 15×20 bins in the velocity space. On our on board Core-i5 processor, the motion planner needs only 50% of one CPU core, which leaves enough power for perception skills and other parts of the service application.

The presented approach is not limited to tuples of acceleration. Individuals could be built up from arbitrary control commands, as long as a forward model for predicting the movement trajectories exists (e.g. steering angle and acceleration for car like robots). Therefore, also non-holonomic robots can be controlled using the proposed method. Errors in the prediction model are of minor relevance, since only the first command of an individual is really executed. For a high fitness, it is sufficient to know that there exists a possible control sequence producing a suitable trajectory starting with that first command. Deviations in the real behavior of the robot will be compensated in subsequent optimization cycles, since in each time step the true robot state is taken as the starting point for rendering the candidate trajectories.

5   Experimental Results

The expected benefit of our evolutionary approach over the classical DWA is that it is more farsighted. The longer time horizon of locally planned trajectories can find solutions for the motion path, which can contain local cost peaks on a shorter scale. Therefore, the resulting movement behavior is much smoother and more natural than the one of the DWA, which has to slow down in narrow environments each time a fast bow trajectory would collide with an obstacle. Especially motion paths requiring many changes in the curvature can be driven much faster.

Experiments with two of our SCITOS-G3 robots Max and Ringo confirmed that hypothesis. Max [2], constructed for applications in narrow home environments, has a maximum velocity of 0.6 m/s in forward direction and 0.3 m/s in backward direction. Rotational velocity was limited to 180°/s. Ringo [3], intended for public environments, is also a differential drive robot but has a maximum velocity of 0.9 m/s. Figure 3 shows some exemplary trajectories in one of our test apartments. The color coding the velocity shows significantly smoother behavior of the evolutionary motion planner (right) compared to the DWA (left) using the same objectives for voting trajectories.

Even though the used objectives were identical, the behavior close to the goal is significantly different for the two planers. When in free space, the evolutionary

 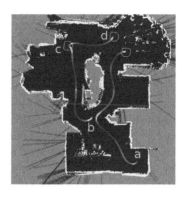

Fig. 3. Exemplary motion trajectories of the robot in one of the test apartments, (left) dynamic window approach, (right) evolutionary motion planner; the robot started at point (a) facing south for a first run and ended at the end pose depicted in yellow, the second run started at point (b), had an intermediate goal at (c) and ended at (d); color coded for velocity (red fast, blue slow). (Color figure online)

planner approaches the goal in a wide bow tangentially to the target orientation, while the DWA first approaches the goal region and finally turns in place. This allows for a much faster approaching using the EMP and causes a significant improvement in the task execution time. For 500 random target approaches in the home-like environment of our living lab, the DWA took 3:52 h compared to 2:51 h required by the evolutionary planning algorithm. Figure 4 shows some comparative histograms of the velocities reached by the DWA and the evolutionary motion planner during the autonomous navigation in our experiments. From the obstacle distance histogram and the velocity histogram one can see, that in narrow environments, like our living lab, the evolutionary planner more often reached higher velocities (max. 0.6 m/s for Robot Max), which explains the enormous speedup compared to the DWA. In the free space environment of our office building the difference is not as large as in the narrow setting. Since

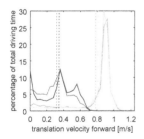 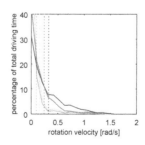 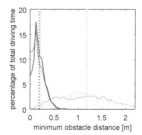

Fig. 4. Histograms of velocity and minimum obstacle distance during real-world random target navigation with our robots, Max in living lab (blue, red) and Ringo in office hallways (magenta, cyan); red and magenta: DWA; blue and cyan: EMP; dotted lines give the mean value of the histograms (Color figure online)

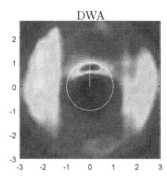
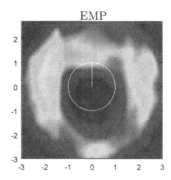

Fig. 5. Heat map of the robot's position relatively to all simulated persons. The white circle indicates the personal space of 1 m and the heading direction.

most of the navigation path is straight ahead, the DWA is also able to find the best command in these situations. Only in the goal region or when passing doors, the DWA shows little more slow movements. Besides the basic target oriented navigation, also the more complex objective functions for respecting the personal space (PS) were tested in comparison of DWA and evolutionary motion planning. Simulations were conducted to evaluate the planner's ability to avoid the PS of people in the robot's vicinity. To this end, a 20 m × 6 m sized room was constructed with eight moving pedestrians. The robot had to navigate across the room and had full knowledge of the surrounding persons' current positions and velocities within a radius of 5 m. To evaluate the performance, the relative positions of the robot to all the pedestrians were recorded. From this data, a heat map of the robot's positions and distances to the pedestrians (in the center) was extracted. Figure 5 proves that the evolutionary motion planning did not significantly violate the personal space of the pedestrians, whereas the DWA driven robot entered the personal spaces more often by driving in front of the people. Often it simply stops in front of an approaching person unable to plan a suitable evasion maneuver (visible as a cumulation at the border of the PS in front of the person), while the evolutionary planner quickly finds an avoiding movement.

In addition to the experiments with differential drive robots, we did simulations with a holonomic robot model (v_y not fixed to zero) as well. The planner could successfully control this kind of robot too. The basic idea of the EMP approach also seems to be applicable to control a car-like robot. Figure 6 shows an experimental simulation run of a car parking setup. Remarkable is the ability to plan a two phase movement with change of direction in order to reach the goal. For that experiment, the planning horizon and mutation rate was set very high in order to find satisfying trajectories within real-time constraints. Therefore, the resulting behavior is still relatively unstable. For such complex applications, further improvements to the algorithm are necessary.

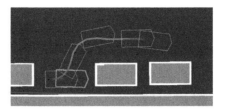

Fig. 6. Parallel parking of a vehicle with Ackermann steering geometry. The end position is marked in green. EMP was able to find the typical parking maneuver instead of using the shortest path to the parking spot. (Color figure online)

6   Conclusion

We could show that the search problem for local motion control of a wide range of robots could be successfully solved within real-time restrictions without giving up flexible trajectories with a high degree of freedom. A key benefit of the proposed evolutionary motion planning algorithm is the reusability of the population from past time steps in order to focus the search on future promising control sequences. Experiments showed that the resulting navigation behavior of an objective-based motion planner is not only defined by the cost functions, but mainly depends on the diversity of the set of sampled future trajectories.

Preliminary results in simulations give indication that the presented approach is also able to control holonomic and car-like vehicles, which we intent to study in our future work.

References

1. Fox, D., Burgard, W., Thrun, S.: The dynamic window approach to collision avoidance. IEEE Robot. Autom. Mag. **4**(1), 23–33 (1997)
2. Gross, H.M., Müller, S., Schröter, C., Volkhardt, M., Scheidig, A., Debes, K., Richter, K., Döring, N.: Robot companion for domestic health assistance: implementation, test and case study under everyday conditions in private apartments. In: IEEE/RSJ International Conference on IROS, 2015, pp. 5992–5999 (September 2015)
3. Gross, H.M., Debes, K., Einhorn, E., Müller, S., Scheidig, A., Weinrich, C., Bley, A., Martin, C.: Mobile robotic rehabilitation assistant for walking and orientation training of stroke patients: a report on work in progress. In: 2014 IEEE SMC, pp. 1880–1887, October 2014
4. Likhachev, M., Ferguson, D.: Planning long dynamically feasible maneuvers for autonomous vehicles. Int. J. Robot. Res. **28**(8), 933–945 (2009)
5. McNaughton, M., Urmson, C., Dolan, J.M., Lee, J.W.: Motion planning for autonomous driving with a conformal spatiotemporal lattice. In: IEEE ICRA 2011, pp. 4889–4895, May 2011
6. LaValle, S.M., Kuffner Jr., J.J.: Rapidly-exploring random trees: progress and prospects. In: Algorithmic and Computational Robotics: New Directions, vol. 5, pp. 293–308 (2007)

7. Karaman, S., Frazzoli, E.: Sampling-based algorithms for optimal motion planning. Int. J. Robot. Res. **30**(7), 846–894 (2011)
8. Back, T.: Evolutionary Algorithms in Theory and Practice: Evolution Strategies, Evolutionary Programming, Genetic Algorithms. Oxford University Press, New York (1996)
9. Philippsen, R., Siegwart, R.: An interpolated dynamic navigation function. In: Proceedings of the 2005 IEEE International Conference on Robotics and Automation, pp. 3782–3789, April 2005

Towards Automated Strawberry Harvesting: Identifying the Picking Point

Zhuoling Huang[1], Sam Wane[2], and Simon Parsons[1(✉)]

[1] Department of Informatics, King's College London, London, UK
{zhuoling.huang,simon.parsons}@kcl.ac.uk
[2] Harper Adams University, Newport, UK
swane@harper-adams.ac.uk

Abstract. With the decline of rural populations across the globe, much hope is vested in the use of robots in agriculture as a means to sustain food production. This is particularly relevant for high-value crops, such as strawberries, where harvesting is currently very labour-intensive. As part of a larger project to build a robot that is capable of harvesting strawberries, we have studied the identification of the picking point of strawberries—the point that a robot hand should grasp the strawberry— from images of strawberries. We present a novel approach to identify the picking point and evaluate this approach.

Keywords: Agricultural automation · Harvesting · Computer vision

1 Introduction

Strawberries are an important cash crop, and are grown all over the world. China, which is the largest producer and exporter of strawberries [3] produced 33.13 million tonnes of strawberries in 2014 [9]. However, strawberry production is quite labour intensive. According to research from Japan [2], the labour cost of harvesting strawberries alone can reach 900 hours per hectare, and this is only about 45% of the whole labour cost. This high labour cost makes the idea of using robots in strawberry production, and in particular strawberry harvesting, an attractive option. This is not a new idea, and the first patent concerning a strawberry harvesting robot was published in 1996 [1]. In recent years, more and more research has been done in this area. According to the data provided by the State Intellectual Property Office of China in November 2016 [14], Japan has the largest number of patents concerning strawberry harvesting robots, while in the past three years China has seen the largest increase in the number of such patents, followed by the US.

This increase in the number of patents for strawberry harvesting robots reflects the growing interest in using robots in agriculture. This in itself is part of a wider, and longer standing, trend towards greater automation in agriculture, and planting and harvesting of crops at a larger scale. This trend is increasingly

© Springer International Publishing AG 2017
Y. Gao et al. (Eds.): TAROS 2017, LNAI 10454, pp. 222–236, 2017.
DOI: 10.1007/978-3-319-64107-2_18

driven by the fertility decline and consequent aging population in many developed countries, which is projected to lead to labour shortages in agriculture. (Indeed, in many developed countries, including the UK, agriculture already relies heavily on migrant labour for harvesting.) Agricultural robots are seen by many as a necessary solution to all these problems. As a result, many kinds of robot have been invented to harvest vegetables and fruits, such as apples, oranges, and so on [5], making it possible to automate the harvest of many high-value fruit and vegetables[1]. However, berries, including strawberries and other soft fruit are much harder to harvest using robots. This is for several reasons. First, many berries are not spherical, making them harder to identify than fruit like apples and oranges. Second, the berries need to be harvested ripe, when they are soft, and this means that they need careful manipulation—squeezing them can cause them to become rotten quickly. This not only ruins individual berries, but, because the rot spreads, can cause widespread damage to a crop. As a result, strawberries and other soft fruit present challenges that mean that existing methods for fruit harvesting will not work.

As part of ongoing work towards the development of a strawberry harvesting robot, we are currently working on image processing to detect ripe strawberries. Detecting strawberries to pick, of course, is a necessary precursor to actually picking them. In this paper we describe a method for detecting ripe strawberries, and a new approach to identifying the *picking point*, the place on the stem of the strawberry where a harvester should aim to detach the strawberry from its parent plant. Compared with previous approaches, we dealt with images that included more "noise" in the background in the form of unripe strawberries, stems, and leaves. Our method uses the OHTA colour space to detect a target strawberry, and then calculates the slope of the stem of this strawberry based on the lowest point of the fruit and the centroid of the fruit. Then a candidate picking point is selected by finding a strawberry stem that has this slope.

The rest of this paper is structured as follows. Section 2 describes related work on image processing to detect fruit. Section 3 then describes our approach. Section 4 describes experiments that we carried out to test our method, and Sect. 5 gives the results of those experiments. Section 6 then concludes.

2   Related Work

According to the literature, the process of harvesting can be divided into three steps: mature fruit detection, fruit position location and fruit picking. We describe the most relevant work on these steps.

For fruit picking, there are three main methods to achieve the goal. One method is to separate the fruit and the branch by dragging the fruit or bending the branch by holding the fruit. For example [15] describes harvesting pineapples in this way. However doing this may easily damage strawberries, since the fruit is generally softer than pineapple. Another method for picking fruit is for

---

[1] Of course, the harvesting of crops such as grain has been heavily automated for a long time.

a robot hand, or a special cup, to hold the fruit, as described in [18]. In [18] a stationary robotic strawberry harvester was introduced, with the aim of dealing with strawberry plants which grow on a table-top or a shelf. In this work, a camera detected the maturity of the fruit from the side of the bench, while another camera located the position of strawberry from below. Viewing the strawberry from below is advantageous since from below the shape of strawberry is circular and so the fruit could be detected more easily than from the side. Nozzles, both horizontal and vertical, were used to blow adjoining strawberries away from the target strawberry. The harvesting success rate for this method was 67.1%. The final method for picking is to detect a suitable picking point for the fruit, a point that is typically on the stem that joins the fruit to the plant—the *peduncle* rather than on the fruit itself. This point can then be grabbed with a manipulator without damaging the fruit. This is the preferred method of harvesting many soft fruits as well as some other crops such as peppers [12].

[11] introduced the basic idea for detecting the picking point when harvesting tea shoots. [17] described a way to identify the picking point of oranges. When the orange reaches its lowest position during the pendulum movement, the picking point should be right above it. Thus, combined with the Circular Hough Transform (for detecting the orange itself), the picking point can be detected. [8] talked about finding the picking point of grapes. Grapes and branches were distinguished by colour difference, and then the Hough Transform was applied to the images of branches to find straight lines. The distance from the barycentre of the fruit to each straight line was calculated, and among them the midpoint of the line with minimal distance would be regarded as the picking point of the bunch of grapes. The accuracy of this method was shown to be higher than 85% when detection was performed during the day time. [16] introduced the design of a litchi picking manipulator, which included consideration of detecting the picking point. The litchi peduncle and the fruit were detected by colour, then the point in the image of the peduncle with maximal distance from the fruit cluster's centroid could be regard as the picking point. The accuracy of detecting the suitable picking point reached 94.2%. [7] introduced a method to find the picking point of tomato clusters. The minimal enclosing rectangle of a tomato cluster's boundary and the centroid were used to find the picking point, which was defined as the intersection point of a vertical line crossing the centroid and the upper edge of the rectangle.

Despite all this research, and the economic importance of strawberries, there has, as yet, been little work on detecting the picking point of strawberries. For strawberries, the picking point is on the stem, a centimetre or two above the calyx, so detecting the stem of the strawberry is important. T. Zhang [20] studied finding the picking point of a strawberry 2005, and, to our knowledge, and this is the first publication studying strawberry stem detection. According to [20], the picking point should be in on the projection a line between the peak of the strawberry and the centre of gravity of the strawberry. Since the strawberry is roughly conical, the peak of the fruit could be defined as the furthest point from the centre of mass. We found that this method worked best when the strawberry was of uniform density. No results on the performance of the method were reported in [20].

A few years later, Guo [4] used the principal axis of inertia of the strawberry to describe the position and the posture of the strawberry stem in order to detect the picking point. [4] reports a success rate for stem detection of 93% when working on images of strawberries with a pure colour background in a laboratory environment. This represents a relatively simple environment in which to perform stem detection, and later work by [6], who used a combination of images taken in the field, and images of strawberries taken from a Google image search, found the approach to be less effective—[6] reports a 26.9% success rate. More recently, [19] introduced a strawberry picking robot which uses the centroid of the strawberry and the axis of symmetry through the centroid to detect the picking point. This paper does not determine the accuracy of selecting the picking point, but does report that experiments gave an accuracy rate of 88% for picking mature strawberries, suggesting that the rate of selecting the picking point is no less than 88%. [19] used a somewhat more realistic environment than [4] for testing While [4] used strawberry branches cut from the plant, and placed on a pure colour background, [19] used strawberry plants in the green house, but hid extra strawberries and stems, covering the shelves used to grow the strawberries with a plastic film[2]. Note that the main difference between [4] and [19] is the move from laboratory to greenhouse and the use of a picking robot in the latter paper—the vision problem in both cases is very similar, with the task being simplified so that the images are easy to segment and the stem is easy to locate. In addition, both [4] and [19] used *Akihime* strawberries for their experiments. Akihime is a variety of strawberry which produces particularly long heart-shaped strawberries with low rate of producing ill-shaped fruit.

The latest work on this topic is [6], already mentioned above in the context of their critique of [4]. [6] investigates a method which is based on the Blum medial skeleton of the strawberry boundary. From the skeleton, three extreme points can be detected as key medial points to generate a triangle. The triangle is then used to describe the shape of the strawberry, and the stem can be identified from elements that are perpendicular to the base of the triangle. This method has a reported accuracy rate of 71%, which is much higher than the method using the principal axis of inertia (26.9%) on the images tested in [6]. However, this method only pointed out the possible area of stem selection—it outputs a bounding box around what is identified as the stem—and it does not identify the specific stem that was attached to the target strawberry from the others that may be in the background.

3   Method

Our method can be divided into three parts: image preprocessing, strawberry detection and picking point detection. The whole method is shown in Fig. 1.

---

[2] This setup can be seen in the images in [19].

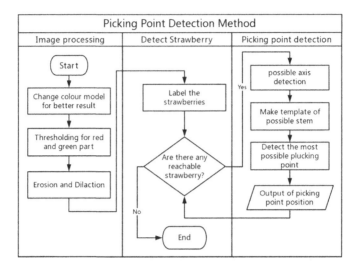

Fig. 1. The method we used for picking point detection.

3.1   Image Preprocessing

We start with standard RGB images, but quickly found that it is hard to detect strawberries and stems directly using the RGB colour model. As a result, we adopted the OHTA colour model, proposed by Ohta et al. [10]. This is a linear transform of the RGB colour model:

$$I_1 = \frac{R + G + B}{3}$$

$$I_2 = R - B$$

$$I_3 = \frac{2G - R - B}{2}$$

where R, G and B refer to the usual red, green and blue colour values respectively, in the range of $[0, 255]$.

Having applied this transform, we followed [13] in using a colour histogram to help identify suitable thresholds to segment strawberries and stems from images. We then used these thresholds to carry out a simple colour segmentation of ripe strawberries and stems. Sample results of this segmentation can be seen in Fig. 2. (The original image is shown in Fig. 5(d).) Figure 2(a) shows the result of the segmentation of an image containing a ripe strawberry, where pixels that have passed the threshold for a ripe strawberry are shown in white. Figure 2(b) gives some context to the previous image by showing these pixels as they appear in the original image. Figure 2(c) shows the same image, but after segmentation using the colour threshold for the strawberry stem, again with all the pixels that have passed the threshold shown in white, and Fig. 2(d) shows the same, but replacing the white pixels with the corresponding pixels from the original image. Looking at these four images together shows that while colour segmentation does a good

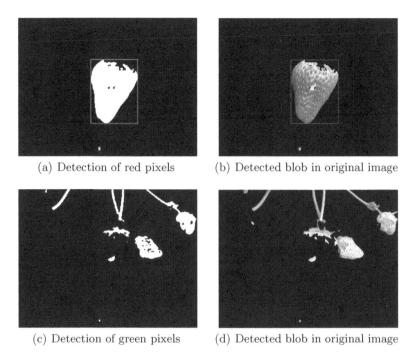

(a) Detection of red pixels   (b) Detected blob in original image

(c) Detection of green pixels   (d) Detected blob in original image

Fig. 2. Examples of colour segmentation of red (ripe strawberry) and green (stem and unripe strawberry) areas of an image. The original image is Fig. 5(d). (Color figure online)

job of identifying ripe strawberries, detecting stems (and hence the picking point) is more complex. There are multiple stems in the image, so deciding which one corresponds to the ripe strawberry is non-trivial, and the image also contains green, unripe, strawberries, which can segment with the stems.

Now, Fig. 2 also shows us that although the thresholds have been chosen carefully, there are still some small pieces of background that have been segmented with the ripe strawberry and the stems, while some parts of those objects have not been detected. To refine the results of the segmentation, we therefore apply both erosion and dilation to mitigate these problems. Erosion deletes small segmented areas that are not connected with other segmented regions, and dilation helps to fill in small gaps in segmented regions.

A further issue, and one that is still apparent after applying erosion and dilation, arises when a ripe strawberry in the original image is behind a stem. In such a case, the segmented ripe strawberry appears cut into a number of smaller pieces. To fix this, the gaps between pieces caused by stems should be filled. To ensure that we do not "complete" spurious gaps, we first test that the width of the gaps are within the range of the width of stems that we find in the image, and we also check that any pixels which are resegmented as a result have been segmented as stems. The result of this process can be seen in Fig. 3. Figure 3(a)

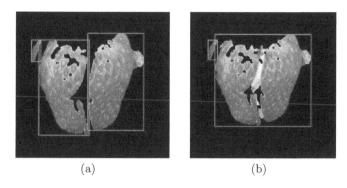

(a)   (b)

Fig. 3. Merging pieces of the same strawberry. (a) shows a ripe strawberry, that is crossed by a stem, after segmentation. (b) shows the same strawberry after the segmented image is "filled in" by the stem.

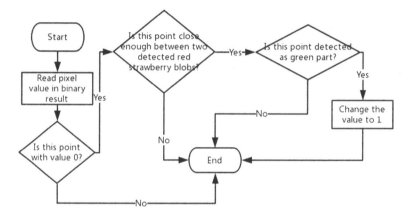

Fig. 4. The re-segmentation process for ripe strawberries.

shows a large ripe strawberry that has been bisected by a stem. Figure 3(b) shows the pixels that are resegmented to complete the strawberry. In the completed image, the stem pixels are shown in their original green. The process we follow is presented as a flowchart in Fig. 4.

3.2 Strawberry Detection

Following the pre-processing stage, the image has been segmented into regions that correspond to ripe strawberries ("red" regions) and regions that correspond to stems or unripe strawberries ("green" regions). Here we briefly describe how the red regions are processed to identify ripe strawberries. There are two issues. First, we have to ensure that regions that were segmented separately but represent a single strawberry whose image is crossed by a stem (as above) are handled as a combined region. Second, we have to ensure that we distinguish between strawberries that are near enough to pick, from those that are further away. This latter problem is particularly acute because in many commercial settings, such as that pictured in [19], strawberries are grown in raised beds so that the strawberries hang down for easy picking. These beds are often raised on pillars, and that means that an image can contain ripe strawberries from both the near side of the bed, strawberries that are accessible, and ripe strawberries from the far side of the bed, strawberries that are not accessible.

The first of these issues is a simple matter of book-keeping. After the initial segmentation, separate red segments are labelled uniquely. When we detect that two segments, as in Fig. 3(a), are part of the same strawberry (as described above), we have to relabel them as belonging to the same segment. The second issue is also easily handled. We assume that the size of ripe strawberries will be similar, and the images of the smallest strawberry will be no smaller than λ percent of size of the largest one. where size is determined by the count of pixels in the red segment. Then red segments smaller than this size will be regarded as strawberries on the other side of the bed and therefore unreachable. In our experiments, λ was set to 50%.

3.3 Picking Point Detection

As a strawberry stem is a herbaceous stem, and thus uses turgor pressure to hold the fruit, it is not strong enough to support a strawberry fruit from the bottom. Instead, strawberries are usually pendulous, with the stems bending downward. Hence, when harvesting strawberry, the picking point—the point at which to hold the fruit and sever the stem—is on the stem a centimetre or so above the calyx. A natural way to model the position of the stem as an oblique line—if we can identify this line, then it is easy to position the picking point on it. To identify the line, we first need to identify two fixed points on that line.

We use the lowest point in the fruit and the centroid of the fruit as the two fixed points which define the gradient of the line. From the segmented image, both the lowest point and the centroid are easy to find. The centroid can be found from:

$$\overline{x} = \frac{\sum\sum x \cdot f\left(x, y\right)}{\sum\sum f\left(x, y\right)}$$

$$\overline{y} = \frac{\sum\sum y \cdot f\left(x, y\right)}{\sum\sum f\left(x, y\right)}$$

where $f(x, y)$ returns 1 if the pixel at (x, y) is in the red segment and 0 if it is not. Once we have the gradient, we use template matching to find the picking point, searching the part of the green segment just above the highest point of the strawberry. We look for elements of the image that match the template, a small segment of line with the width of a typical strawberry stem and the same gradient as the line from the lowest point to the centroid.

The template matching part of our method is illustrated in Fig. 5. The initial image is shown in Fig. 5(d). (This is the same image was we saw being segmented in Fig. 2.) After segmenting the image (as in Fig. 2) and identifying the

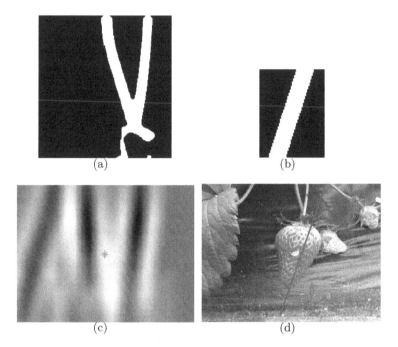

Fig. 5. Picking point detection: (a) shows the search area above the strawberry; (b) shows a stem template oriented as the line from lowest point to centroid; (c) shows the likelihood of points to be selected as the picking point, plus, in green, the most likely point; and (d) shows the original image with the selected picking point in red, and the line from the lowest point through the centroid is also drawn in red. (Color figure online)

strawberry, the area in which we search for the picking point is shown (somewhat magnified) in Fig. 5(a). This area is chosen to limit the picking point to be within a suitable distance of the calyx. The stem template for this image is shown in Fig. 5(b). This has been rotated to match the gradient of the line between centroid and the lowest point of the fruit. The result of template matching is shown in Fig. 5(c). This takes into account both the degree of matching with the template, and the distance of a given point from the calyx. Brighter areas are areas which, as a combination of degree of matching and proximity to the calyx, are more likely to be a good picking point. Figure 5(c) shows the most likely picking point as a green dot, and this is shown as a red dot in the original image in Fig. 5(d). The dot is on the stem above the ripe strawberry.

The reason for combining template matching and gradient is to enable our method to pick the most likely stem from a number of stems in an image. It is this aspect that makes our approach quite different from Zhang's [20] and Guo's [4] work. In both these papers, the authors only used images of single strawberries placed in front of a pure colour background, so only one possible stem ever appeared in the images, and hence there could be no confusion over which stem was connected to the target strawberry.

4 Experiments

In order to test how this method works, we took 185 pictures of Benihoppe strawberries in a commercial growing field in Jinhua, China. All of these pictures included at least one ripe strawberry that could be detected, and 7 images included two strawberries. Thus, overall we tested on 192 strawberries. Since there is no existing effective method for separating overlapping ripe strawberries, no such images were included. However, images with ill-shaped strawberries and ripe strawberries slightly covered by other unripe ones or leaves were included. We consider that 15 strawberries out of the total of 192 are ill-shaped[3], and 45 of the strawberries are partially obscured by leaves or unripe strawberries. The colour segmentation that we described above clearly identified every strawberry, so our results for picking point selection were obtained on all 192 strawberries.

As mentioned previously, both [4] and [20] used oblique lines to detect possible position of the strawberry picking point, and they are thus similar to the part of our method which detects the possible slope of the strawberry stem. We therefore also tested these two methods. As a result, for each image in our test set, we used three methods for identifying the gradient of the stem:

1. The gradient of a line crossing the lowest point of the strawberry blob and its centroid. This is the approach we developed. We call it the *nadir-centroid* (NC) method, because it uses the lowest point (nadir) of the fruit and the centroid to detect the stem.
2. The gradient of a line crossing the peak of the strawberry and the centroid of the blob. This is the method suggested by [20]. We call it the *peak-centroid* (PC) method because it uses the peak of the strawberry and the centroid.
3. The principle axis of inertia of the strawberry. This is the method suggested by [4]. We call it the *principle axis* of inertia (PA) method.

Each of these gradients was then used, as described above, with template matching to detect the most likely picking point. The three methods are illustrated in Fig. 6. For each method, a dotted line and a star is placed on the image. The line is line that the method uses to set the gradient of the stem that it is searching for, and the star is the picking point that the method selects. The line and star for the NC method is shown in yellow, those for the PC method are in blue, and those for the PA method are in red.

Note that the PC and PA methods are not exactly the methods suggested by [20] and [4]. Neither of those approaches used the template matching approach to locate the picking point. Rather both used simpler methods—in [20] an absolute offset from the calyx and in [4] the intersection of the axis of inertia and a line through the centres of mass of the green segments—that did not work in the more complex environment that we were using. As a result, we are comparing the ability of the methods to suggest a stem angle and thus to select a template.

---

[3] This is a subjective estimate since the concept of "ill-shaped" is itself ill-defined.

Fig. 6. The output of the three different methods on a sample image. NC is in yellow, PC is in blue, and PA is in red. (Color figure online)

5   Results

For each image, we predicted the position of the picking point using the methods described above. We then projected the point back onto the original image (just as in Fig. 5(d)). As shown in Fig. 7, the different methods give rather different results on some images. In Fig. 7, just as in Fig. 6, the picking point selected by NC is shown by a yellow star, the picking point selected by PC is shown by a blue star, and the picking point selected by PA is shown by a red star. When the star appears exactly on the stem of target strawberry, we consider that the picking point has been successfully selected. When the star appears on another stem, on the background or anywhere on the strawberry itself, including the calyx, we consider that the picking point has not been successfully selected. For example, in Fig. 7(a), the red and yellow stars are on the target stem and so are counted as successful selections, while the blue star on the mulching film will not be regarded as a successful selection[4]. Similarly, in Fig. 7(b), only the yellow star represents a successful picking point selection, while in 7(c), none of the methods have detected a suitable picking point since none of the stars fall on the stem of the ripe strawberry.

The accuracy of the three methods on our 192 strawberries is shown in Table 1. These results suggest that the NC method, which uses the lowest point of the strawberry and the centroid is the most accurate method of the three for

Table 1. Accuracy of detecting picking point

Points used to compute gradient	Accuracy
Lowest point and centroid (NC)	84.38%
Strawberry peak and centroid (PC) [20]	60.42%
Principle axis of inertia (PA) [4]	53.65%

---

[4] Though arguably it is close enough that a robot hand grabbing at this point might well connect with the stem.

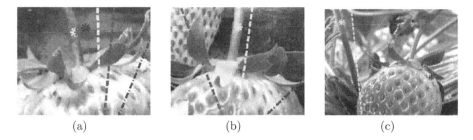

(a)   (b)   (c)

Fig. 7. Three examples of the three methods. In each picture the yellow star is the picking point selected by the NC method, the blue star shows the picking point selected by the PC method, and the red star shows the picking point detected by the PA method. In (a), PA and NC correctly detect the picking point, and PC does not; in (b) only NC correctly selects the picking point; in (c) none of the methods correctly selects the right picking point. (Color figure online)

selecting the picking point. Of course, in our experiments, the NC approach does not match the accuracies reported in [4] and implied in [19][5]. We believe that this is because, unlike the images used for testing by [4] and [19], our test images were taken in the field in its natural state. As a result, the background in our images is more complex, including mulch film, soil, dropped petals, leaves and other strawberries and stems. In addition, the strawberries in our images include many more ill-shaped strawberries—ones that diverge from the classical heart shape—making it harder to describe their shape and to identify both strawberry and picking point. This hypothesis is supported by the fact that when we used he NC method on images of strawberries which, like those in [4], were placed on a pure colour background, we obtained an accuracy of over 98%.

We believe that the extra complexity of the environment also accounts for the fact that the accuracy we obtained for the PA method is not as high as that reported in [4], where it was introduced (though we do obtain much better results for our version of the PA approach than [6] did) Tests on images of strawberries against a pure colour background, where we obtained 92% accuracy for PA, support this hypothesis. Since [20] did not report results, we cannot compare our results for the PC approach to previous results.

A more complex background is one reason for the poor performance of PA and PC. Other factors that we believe contribute are as follows. As shown in Fig. 6 the deviation of the strawberry from the classic shape means that the method [20] used to find the peak of the strawberry (defined as the furthest point from the centroid of the strawberry blob) is not that effective for ill-shaped strawberries. For similar reasons, the principle axis of inertia also lost its power to find the possible slope of stem in such cases. However so long as the strawberries are suspended and so are subject to gravity, the lowest point of the strawberry can still be used to find the probable slope of the target stem with reasonable

---

[5] Recall that [19] did not report accuracy of picking point, but a harvesting rate of 88% implies that picking point selection was at least 88% accurate.

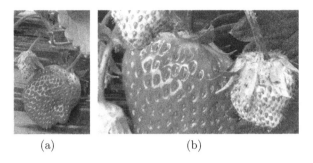

(a)   (b)

Fig. 8. Strawberries that are hard to detect. (a) is a typical ill-shaped strawberry; (b) is a ripe strawberry that is obscured by unripe strawberries.

precision, and this explains why the NC method performs with higher accuracy than the other two. The NC approach also outperforms the reported accuracy of [6], which also used more realistic images of strawberries than previous work, though we did not replicate their approach to determining the position of the stem so have no direct comparison on our image set.

Finally, we should discuss the cases in which the NC approach did not successfully select the picking point. There are three main reasons for the NC method to fail on our test images. First, the shape of the ripe strawberry is sometimes too strange even to use the lowest point to predict the slope of the stem. Such a case is shown in Fig. 8(a). Secondly, some strawberries and stems are too obscured, by mud or by other parts of the strawberry plant, to get an accurate estimate of the lowest point or of the centroid. Such a case is an shown in Fig. 8(b). Thirdly, a stem in the background might be sufficiently similar in angle to the target one that the NC approach has no way of knowing which stem is the right one. In such a case the approach can easily pick the wrong stem.

The number of each kind of failure is shown in Table 2. This shows that the main reason for failure is that either the stem or part of the strawberry fruit is obscured, and dealing with this issue is an area of ongoing work. (It is an area where we think machine learning could help). However, note that the method does not fail on every ill-shaped or partially obscured strawberry—there were 15 ill-shaped strawberries and 45 strawberries were partially obscured—and so is already somewhat robust.

Table 2. Reasons for failure when detecting picking point

Reasons for failure	Number of instances
Ill-shaped strawberry	4
Too much of the strawberry is obscured	14
Similar stem detected	2

6   Conclusions

We have introduced a novel approach to detecting the picking point of strawberries and evaluated its effectiveness on a large number of images taken in the field. Our approach was found to be accurate, correctly identifying the picking point of strawberries 84% of the time, despite the complexity of the images, which exceeded that of methods introduced in two landmark papers on strawberry stem detection [4, 20] when these were tested on our image set. Indeed, using the core stem identification methods of [4, 20], augmented with some new elements to deal with the more complex images, on our set of images, produced much lower accuracies than reported in papers such as [19, 20], and much lower accuracies than were achieved with our method.

There are several areas in which our approach can be improved. For now, our approach, like all existing approaches that we know of, cannot handle cases in which two ripe strawberries overlap. These are seen as a single strawberry, and any calculation of picking point is hopelessly inaccurate. Similarly, if there are many stems in the image that are close to the stem of the target strawberry, our approach can get fooled into detecting the wrong stem. These are cases where our method sees too much strawberry or too much stem. Another situation in which our approach does not perform well is where strawberries are heavily obscured, by other pieces of plant, or by mud. In such cases, our approach does not see enough strawberry to correctly locate the lowest point and/or the centroid. Similarly, detection of the stem is sensitive to the stem being obscured by mud or other material that is not the right colour. All of these problems are examples of common problems for techniques, like ours, that rely on simple colour segmentation. While colour is a good guide, in some situations we will need more. Our current thought is that supervised machine learning, along the lines described in [12], is one way to try and improve our approach.

Acknowledgments. Thanks to Mathew Butler at Harper Adams University for supplying images that helped in the development of the ideas described here.

References

1. Arima, S., Kondo, N.: Japan Patent No. JP3493801B2. Japan Patent Office, Tokyo (1996)
2. Chen, L.: Study on picking system for strawberry harvesting robot. Ph.D. thesis, China Agricultural University (2005)
3. Food and Agriculture Organization Corporate Statistical Database: Food and Agricultural Organization of the United Nations Statistics Division (November 2016). http://www.fao.org/faostat/en/#data/QC
4. Guo, F., Cao, Q., Masateru, N.: Fruit detachment and classification method for strawberry harvesting robot. Int. J. Adv. Rob. Syst. **5**, 41–48 (2008)
5. Jimenez, A.R., Ceres, R., Pons, J.: A survey of computer vision methods for locating fruit on trees. Trans. ASAE **43**, 1911–1920 (2000)

6. Leonard, K., Strawbridge, R., Lindsay, D., Barata, R., Dawson, M., Averion, L.: Minimal geometric representation and strawberry stem detection. In: 13th International Conference on Computational Science and Its Applications (2013)
7. Liang, X., Zhang, Y.: Recognition method of picking point for tomato cluster. J. Chin. Agric. Mech. **37**, 131–134, 149 (2016)
8. Luo, L., Zou, X., Xiong, J., Zhang, Y., Peng, H., Lin, G.: Automatic positioning for picking point of grape picking robot in natural environment. Trans. Chin. Soc. Agric. Eng. **31**, 14–21 (2014)
9. National Bureau of Statistics of China Statistical Database: National Bureau of Statistics of China (November 2016). http://data.stats.gov.cn/easyquery.htm?cn=C01&zb=A0D0L&sj=2014
10. Ohta, Y.I., Kanade, T., Sakai, T.: Color information for region segmentation. Comput. Graph. Image Process. **13**, 222–241 (1980)
11. Pei, W., Wang, X.: The two-dimension coordinates extraction of tea shoots picking based on image information. Acta Agriculturae Zhejiangensis **28**, 522–527 (2016)
12. Sa, I., Lehnert, C., English, A., McCool, C., Dayoub, F., Upcroft, B., Perez, T.: Peduncle detection of sweet pepper for autonomous crop harvesting: combined colour and 3D information. Report (2017). arXiv:1701.08608
13. Sezgin, M., Sankur, B.: Survey over image thresholding techniques and quantitative performance evaluation. J. Electron. Imaging **13**, 146–165 (2004)
14. Patent search and analysis: State Intellectual Property Office of the PRC (November 2016). http://www.pss-system.gov.cn/sipopublicsearch/patentsearch/searchHomeIndex-searchHomeIndex.shtml
15. Wu, P., Hua, J.: The practical design of pineapple-picking robots. J. Lanzhou Inst. Technol. **23**, 58–61 (2016)
16. Xiong, J., Zou, X., Peng, H.: Design of visual position system for litchi picking manipulator. Trans. Chin. Soc. Agric. Eng. **43**, 250–255 (2012)
17. Xiong, J., Zou, X., Peng, H.: Real-time identification and picking point localization of disturbance citrus picking. Trans. Chin. Soc. Agric. Eng. **45**, 38–43 (2014)
18. Yamamoto, S., Hayashi, S., Yoshida, H., Kobayashi, K.: Development of a stationary robotic strawberry harvester with a picking mechanism that approaches the target fruit from below. Jpn. Agric. Res. Q. **48**, 261–269 (2014)
19. Zhang, K., Yang, L., Wang, L., Zhang, T.: Design and experiment of elevated substrate culture strawberry picking robot. Trans. Chin. Soc. Agric. Eng. **43**, 156–172 (2012)
20. Zhang, T., Chen, L., Song, J.: Study on strawberry harvesting robot: II. Images based identifications of strawberry barycenter and plucking position. J. China Agric. Univ. **10**, 48–51 (2005)

Evaluating the Capabilities of a Flight-Style Swarm AUV to Perform Emergent and Adaptive Behaviours

Thomas S. Lowndes[1,2]([⊠]), Alexander B. Phillips[2], Catherine A. Harris[2],
Eric Rogers[1], Bing Chu[1], and Ekaterina Popova[2]

[1] University of Southampton, Southampton SO17 1BJ, UK
t.lowndes@soton.ac.uk, {etar,b.chu}@ecs.soton.ac.uk
[2] National Oceanography Centre, Southampton SO14 3ZH, UK
{abp,catherine.harris,e.popova}@noc.ac.uk

Abstract. Through simulation, this paper evaluates the capabilities of the EcoSUBμ, a small, low cost Autonomous Underwater Vehicle (AUV), to perform emergent and adaptive behaviours for environmental monitoring. It is assumed in realistic environments the vehicles cannot communicate simultaneously, leading to the development of a communication overhead. The limitations of an optical modem are found to be too extensive to conduct a flocking behaviour while an acoustic modem of increased range allows the EcoSUBμ to perform the flocking behaviour and locate a maxima, simulating tracking a chemical plume. The performance of large swarms degrades due to the communication overhead, whereas the performance of smaller swarms is comparable to an individual vehicle. The results highlight the heavy reliance of an emergent behaviour on communication and how the limitations of underwater communication mean this behaviour is unlikely to be suitable for the control of an AUV swarm in realistic ocean environments.

Keywords: Swarm robotics · Autonomous underwater vehicles · Optimisation

1 Introduction

With the advancement of technology, the cost and size of Autonomous Underwater Vehicles (Unmanned submarines) are constantly decreasing. Consequently, novel multi-vehicle approaches are increasingly being used to address challenges faced in traditional AUV operations, including localisation (Tan et al. 2016), power management (Amory et al. 2014) and rapid exploration (Read et al. 2014). Implementing a swarm of AUVs with the ability to communicate provides the means to perform adaptive behaviours utilising spatially distributed data. One of the major obstacles to networking multiple AUVs is communication due to the high attenuation of electromagnetic signals in water. Acoustic communication is the predominant technology in this area, but suffers from high latency,

© Springer International Publishing AG 2017
Y. Gao et al. (Eds.): TAROS 2017, LNAI 10454, pp. 237–246, 2017.
DOI: 10.1007/978-3-319-64107-2_19

low bandwidth and severe packet loss (Walls and Eustice 2014). This paper will examine the effect of a communication overhead and limited communication range on the ability of a homogeneous AUV swarm to perform emergent and adaptive behaviours through simulation in two dimensions. The AUVs will be modelled on the small, low cost EcoSUBμ (Planet Ocean Ltd. 2017), designed to perform marine science in an ocean environment. This work will contribute to research on the control of an AUV swarm to monitor ocean features such as oil spills and harmful algae blooms, aiming to improve knowledge and response times to minimise environmental impact.

2   Background

Dorigo and Şahin (2004) present a concise definition of what constitutes a robotic swarm. Firstly, the swarm should be scalable and not restricted to a maximum number. The swarm should be almost entirely homogeneous due to the high redundancy required and the implementation of a swarm should improve performance. Finally, each robot should only have local sensing and communication to allow scalability.

There have been several projects aimed at creating an AUV swarm. The Serafina project focussed on developing the prerequisites for AUV swarms, highlighting scalable communication (Schill and Zimmer 2012) and cooperative relative localisation (Kottege and Zimmer 2010) as two key factors to a successful swarm.

The MONSUN II (Osterloh et al. 2012) is a swarm AUV designed for environmental monitoring. A follow up paper by Amory et al. (2014) focusses on the simulation of five vehicles, flying in formation with three surface vehicles providing triangulation for two submerged vehicles. Communication amongst the swarm is provided by an acoustic modem capable of communication up to 50 m with a bandwidth of 1000 bits/s. The separation of the swarm between the surface and subsurface allows the swarm to employ energy load balancing, rotating vehicles through low power surface roles, extending missions up to 32%.

The CoCoRo project focusses on proof-of-concept, utilising simple vehicles in a small, controlled environment. Read et al. (2014) presents simulated swarm behaviours as a part of the CoCoRo project. The paper profiles shoaling of 11 vehicles against six metrics over a range of communication and sensing approaches, assuming communication is instantaneous and lossless. These assumptions would be unrealistic in the real world due to the detrimental effect of water turbidity and particulate matter on optical communications. The presented results indicate communication between members is vital for a well coordinated flock. Given communication can be achieved, the limited localisation capability of the AUV is not a hindrance to flocking performance. Furthermore, omni-directional communication to all vehicles within range shows a reduction in lost AUVs and the number of distinct shoals, benefits which are lost when the vehicle can only communicate with its closest neighbour.

3   Problem Definition

3.1   The Platform: EcoSUBμ

The EcoSUBμ platform is part of a new generation of small, low cost AUVs with basic sensor capabilities suitable for marine science.[1] The platform is currently in development by Planet Ocean Ltd. in collaboration with the National Oceanography Centre, Southampton, UK. Preliminary characteristics are given in Table 1.

Table 1. General characteristics of the EcoSUBμ

EcoSUBμ	
Length overall	0.912 m
Mass	4.1 kg
Max speed	1.0 m/s
Max Yaw Rate	15.0°/s

The EcoSUBμ is a flight-style AUV requiring continual forward motion to maintain depth and to make changes in heading. The EcoSUBμ is currently only equipped with WiFi and IRIDIUM communication capabilities. For the purposes of these experiments, communication payloads suitable for potential future integration are considered, these are detailed in Sect. 3.2.

3.2   Communication Assumptions

Underwater communication is one of the main challenges associated with AUV operation. This paper introduces the range and time constraints of optical and acoustic modems to a flocking behaviour. The Hydromea LUMA 250LP (Hydromea 2017) is used as an example of a suitable optical modem and the specification for the acoustic modem is taken from Amory et al. (2014). The ranges of the optical and acoustic modems are 5 and 50 m respectively and the communication is assumed lossless but not instantaneous. Each AUV is sequentially allocated a 0.5 s timeslot to broadcast their state to local neighbours. One-way acoustic broadcasting is implemented and increases the scalability of the algorithm, however the allocation of sequential time slots is still a limiting factor.

---

[1] The EcoSUBμ development is funded by the Innovate UK project 'Launch & Recovery of Multiple AUVs from an USV', Innovate UK Project Ref 102302 http://gtr.rcuk.ac.uk/projects?ref=102302 aiming to reduce the dependency of marine science on expensive research ships.

3.3   Scenario 1 - Flocking

In order for multiple vehicles to collaborate on a task and share data they need to remain within communication range while underway. In order to do this a control algorithm is required to maintain an aggregated swarm and avoid collisions between vehicles. These both become easier when the vehicles have low relative velocities.

3.4   Scenario 2 - Location of a Maxima

This paper focusses on the application of an AUV swarm to the environmental monitoring of potentially hazardous ocean features including oil spills and harmful algae blooms. In this study a radial Gaussian distribution is used to imitate a two dimensional chemical concentration gradient. The function dissipates to zero at 850 m from the maxima and the vehicles are released within acoustic communication range of each other at a random location, between 750 m and 800 m from the maxima.

4   Flocking Algorithm

Reynolds (1987) presents a distributed behavioural model aiming to create animations of flocking behaviours seen in nature. Each vehicle evaluates three rules based on its own state and the states of its local neighbours, local defined as within communication range. The three rules are depicted in Fig. 1 and are as follows: separation to avoid crowding local flockmates, cohesion to move towards the flock centre and alignment to match the velocities of local flockmates. These rules give three acceleration vectors which are then subjected to a weighted average to determine the heading and speed of the flock member, with pitch remaining constant to constrain simulation to the xy plane. In this application of the algorithm, a maximum and minimum separation are defined, beyond the maximum the vehicle acts according to the cohesion rule and within the minimum the vehicle acts according to the separation rule. The cohesion rule weights each vehicle's position by the number of vehicles in it's local neighbourhood to

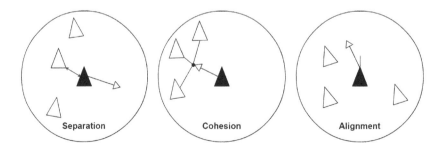

Fig. 1. The three rules of Reynolds' flocking

draw the vehicle towards the primary flock. The weights for the average are set to 150, 150 and 300 for separation, cohesion and alignment respectively. Alignment is set to a larger value as it dampens the response of the behaviour, inducing more gradual changes in heading.

4.1   Hill Climb Implementation

A hill climbing algorithm is implemented alongside Reynolds' flocking as one method of following a chemical concentration to identify the source. Included in a vehicles broadcast is its current concentration measurement. By evaluating the direction and gradient of the concentration across its local swarm, a vehicle can move towards a local maxima. Implementing this into the flocking behaviour introduces a fourth acceleration vector in the direction of the chemical concentration. This vector is included in the weighted average with a weighting of 1500, significantly higher than the weights associated with the flocking rules. It is important to find the balance between the flocking and hill climb behaviours by adjusting this weighting, to ensure neither is detrimental to the other.

5   Results

5.1   Scenario 1 - Flocking Performance

Table 2 details the five communication and flocking configurations, allowing varying flocking distances to be evaluated.

Table 2. Five communication and flocking configurations

Case	Modem	Range/m	Min separation/m	Max separation/m
(1)	Optical	5.0	3.0	4.0
(2)	Acoustic	50.0	5.0	15.0
(3)	Acoustic	50.0	10.0	20.0
(4)	Acoustic	50.0	15.0	25.0
(5)	Acoustic	50.0	20.0	30.0

It is difficult to quantify the performance of a flocking behaviour as there is no defined optimum configuration for the vehicles. Read et al. (2014) uses several metrics for assessing a flocking behaviour including polarisation, a measure of alignment of the vehicles, angular velocity about the flocks centre and the number of vehicles separated from the flock.

Figure 2 presents the first two metrics of flocking performance, polarisation and angular velocity, calculated as described by Couzin et al. (2002). Flocking performance is currently evaluated for the flocking behaviour alone as once an

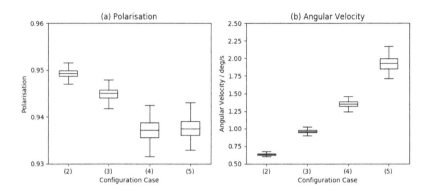

Fig. 2. Mean (a) polarisation and (b) angular velocity of a five vehicle swarm for the four acoustic configuration cases over 100 repeat experiments. The bounds of the box represent the upper and lower quartiles, highlighting the median value within the box. The whiskers represent the extents of the data set.

additional acceleration vector is introduced to induce a hill climb these metrics may change.

Figure 3 presents two further metrics of flocking performance, the number of lost AUVs through separation from the flock and the number of collisions in each of the five configuration cases, identified by the number in brackets. The number of collisions was not one of the six metrics presented by Read et al. (2014) however damage to the nose or tail fairings of the EcoSUBμ could result in loss of communication or actuation. One or two collisions are considered negligible as the vehicles most likely collided at the start due to the random starting positions.

The optical case is excluded from Fig. 2 due to attaining a mean angular velocity of approximately 1500°/s about the flocks centre and a polarisation ranging from 0 to 1, indicating the random starting heading has more of an influence on polarisation than the behaviour. After further investigation the high angular velocity is due to the separation between vehicles being very high and hence communication for alignment cannot be achieved yielding poor polarisation. These results demonstrate the EcoSUBμ, as a flight-style AUV, is not able to perform the flocking behaviour within the tight constraints imposed by the Hydromea optical modem (Case (1)). Figure 3 reinforces this result as all vehicles are lost regardless of flock size. This result highlights the limited actuation of the EcoSUBμ as a hindrance to performing close proximity flocking behaviours, especially with a communication overhead. Other swarm AUVs such as the MONSUN II and the Vertex are fully or over-actuated vehicles reinforcing the need for high manoeuvrability to perform close proximity behaviours. Examining Figs. 2 and 3 shows the increase in flocking separation in cases (2) through (5) due to the range of the acoustic modem improves the flocking performance considerably. Figure 2 displays high polarisation and low angular velocity indicating a well organised flock and the effect of increasing the target separation is minimal. Increasing the target separation reduces the number of collisions as

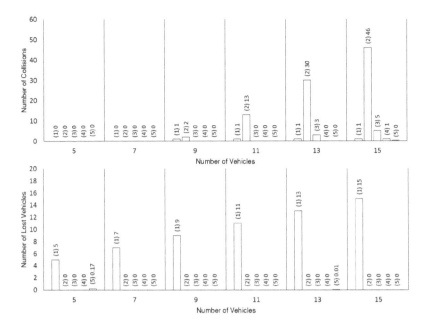

Fig. 3. The mean number of collisions (top) and lost AUVs (bottom) over 100 repeat experiments for the five configuration cases and increasing flock size. The number in brackets identifies the case while the other value indicates the magnitude.

expected with negligible loss of vehicles, as seen in Fig. 3. However increasing the number of vehicles without increasing separation results in increased collisions, partly due to the large communication overhead leading to vehicles acting upon data with increasing uncertainty.

5.2   Scenario 2 - Location of a Maxima

Figure 4 uses the time taken to identify a global maxima using a hill climb algorithm to evaluate the performance of swarms of increasing size. The variation in time for each swarm size is due to the random generation of starting positions, as the flocking algorithm is otherwise deterministic. The results represent 100 repeat experiments at swarm sizes 1 to 10 and 10 for sizes 11 to 15. The time taken is based off the number of time steps simulated before the completion condition was met.

The performance of a swarm consisting of 2 vehicles is extremely slow, this is due to the poor directional perception of the chemical concentration. A swarm size between four and eight vehicles gives an average performance comparable to an individual vehicle. A swarm size in this range gives a sample size large enough for improved perception of the direction to the maxima and small enough to experience minimal negative impact from the communication overhead. While the mean performance is comparable to an individual vehicle,

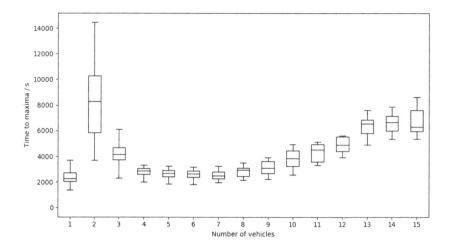

Fig. 4. Time taken to identify the maxima for increasing numbers of vehicles given configuration case (3). The bounds of the box represent the upper and lower quartiles, highlighting the median value within the box, while the whiskers represent the extents of the data set.

the performance in general is more consistent, achieving a lower variance in the time taken to determine the maxima, a property which is important for predictability of the behaviour. Returning to Fig. 3, this range also demonstrates good flocking performance with minimal collisions and no lost vehicles regardless of target separation.

When comparing individual and multi-vehicle scenarios it is important to consider the EcoSUBμ's limited localisation capabilities could be detrimental to an individual vehicle's performance. While an individual vehicle must surface regularly, the swarm is able to employ a localisation algorithm, such as the SUAVE algorithm presented by Liu et al. (2014) to maintain a consistent submerged, monitoring presence.

As shown for flocking performance, as the size of the swarm increases beyond 8 vehicles the performance of the hill climb algorithm degrades. Due to the communication overhead, the swarm data received by each vehicle is updated less frequently as swarm size increases and hence has a larger uncertainty causing vehicles to make poorly informed decisions.

6   Conclusion and Future Research

Examples of unrealistic communication assumptions including instantaneous, simultaneous and lossless communication in simulation of AUV swarms can be found in Amory et al. (2014) and Read et al. (2014). Due to the extensive limitations of underwater communication, this paper subjects swarm behaviours to more realistic communication assumptions, introducing a communication overhead. The swarm is unable to perform Reynolds' flocking utilising the optical modem due to the communication overhead coupled with the limited actuation of the EcoSUBμ. Using the acoustic modem improves the performance of flocking considerably, resulting in a well organised swarm with minimal collisions and vehicle losses at smaller swarm sizes.

Commenting on the use of an emergent behaviour, due to the stochastic nature of the algorithm there is no guarantee of performance. However scenario 2 demonstrates that through the use of multiple vehicles the variance in performance can be reduced. Furthermore, Reynolds' flocking is intended to be a scalable behaviour, however when implemented for AUVs the limitations of current communication approaches limit the scalability, shown through the evaluation of increasing swarm sizes. Considering the applications of an AUV swarm, as the size of the domain grows, more vehicles or a greater separation would be beneficial to increase coverage, however these both lead to an increased communication overhead. Reducing the assumptions made in this paper to introduce packet loss, a frequent problem in underwater communication, would only increase the overhead further. Finally the dynamic ocean environment will cause large errors in localisation, possibly increasing the reliance on communication through the need for cooperative localisation approaches such as SUAVE (Liu et al. 2014).

The findings in this paper indicate that communication intensive behaviours such as close proximity emergent flocking are unlikely to be suitable control methods for a swarm of flight-style AUVs.

References

Amory, A., Tosik, T., Maehle, E.: A load balancing behaviour for underwater robot swarms to increase mission time and fault tolerance. In: IEEE 28th International Parallel and Distributed Processing Symposium Workshops (2014)

Couzin, I., et al.: Collective memory and spatial sorting in animal groups. J. Theor. Biol. **218**, 1–11 (2002)

Dorigo, M., Şahin, E.: Swarm robotics - a special issue editorial. Auton. Robot. **17**(2–3), 111–113 (2004)

Kottege, N., Zimmer, U.R.: Underwater acoustic localization for small submersibles. J. Field Robot. **28**(1), 40–69 (2010)

Liu, J., Zhaohui, W., Peng, Z., Cui, J., Fiondella, L.: Suave: swarm underwater autonomous vehicle localisation. In: Proceedings of IEEE, INFOCOM, 2014 (2014)

Osterloh, C., Meyer, B., Amory, A., Pionteck, T., Maehle, E.: MONSUN II - towards autonomous underwater swarms for environmental monitoring. In: IROS 2012 - Workshop on Robotics for Environmental Monitoring (2012)

Read, M., Möslinger, C., Dipper, T., Kengyel, D., Hilder, J., Thenius, R., Tyrrell, A., Timmis, J., Schmickl, T.: Profiling underwater swarm robotic shoaling performance using simulation. In: Natraj, A., Cameron, S., Melhuish, C., Witkowski, M. (eds.) TAROS 2013. LNCS (LNAI), vol. 8069, pp. 404–416. Springer, Heidelberg (2014). doi:10.1007/978-3-662-43645-5_42

Reynolds, C.: Flocks, herds and schools: a distributed behavioral model. In: ACM SIGGRAPH Computer Graphics (1987)

Schill, F., Zimmer, U.R.: A scalable electro-magnetic communication system for underwater swarms. In: IFAC Proceedings of Manoeuvring and Control of Marine Craft (2012)

Schill, F., Bahr, A., Martinoli, A.: Vertex: a new distributed underwater robotics platform for environmental monitoring. In: Proceedings of the 13th International Symposium on Distributed Autonomous Robotic Systems (2016)

Tan, Y., Chitre, M., Hover, F.: Cooperative Bathymetry-based localization using low-cost autonomous underwater vehicles. Auton. Robot. **40**(7), 1187–1205 (2016)

Walls, J.M., Eustice, R.M.: An origin state method for communication constrained cooperative localization with robustness to packet loss. Int. J. Robot. Res. **33**(9), 1191–1208 (2014)

Hydromea: LUMA 250LP data sheet. http://hydromea.com/datasheets/Hydromea/LUMA/250/datasheet.pdf. Accessed 30 Jan 2017

Planet Ocean Ltd.: New Micro Autonomous Vehicles Launched by Planet Ocean. http://planet-ocean.co.uk/PDF/ecoSUB.pdf. Accessed 12 Feb 2017

Reactive Virtual Forces for Heterogeneous and Homogeneous Swarm Exploration and Mapping

Thomas Bridgwater[1,2]([✉]), Alan Winfield[1,2], and Tony Pipe[1,2]

[1] Bristol Robotics Laboratory, University of Bristol, Bristol, England
tom_bridgwater@msn.com
[2] Bristol Robotics Laboratory, University of the West of England (UWE),
Bristol, England

Abstract. Exploration and mapping of unknown environments is a vibrant topic of research in the robotics community. Virtual potential fields have been used in prior research largely for spatial distribution, path planning and pattern formation. These fields involve the use of functions, often grounded in physics, to generate virtual potential fields that may be used to guide robots. It is the contention of this paper that a similar 'virtual reactive forces' method may be used for exploration and mapping, in combination with the already established occupancy grid method. This process involves the use of multiple virtual forces, based on the fundamental forces of nature, to guide robots in collision avoidance, exploration, and mapping. This paper compares the effectiveness of this method on heterogeneous and homogeneous swarms.

Keywords: Swarm · Mapping · Reactive virtual forces · Heterogeneous · Homogeneous · Exploration · Virtual potential fields

1 Introduction

Potential fields have been used within the robotics community largely for spatial distribution, pattern formation and path planning, as will be evidenced in the subsequent section. The aforementioned applications are not dissimilar to the field of exploration: robots must move to specific areas of an environment whilst avoiding collision. A question follows from this - if these behaviours may be dictated by potential fields, then is it possible for the same method to be employed for exploration? Answering this question for the case of a heterogeneous vs homogeneous swarm is the aim of this paper. The hope is to utilise this method in a complex environment, and so heterogeneous locomotive and sensory capabilities may be required.

In past research, known environments have had potential fields overlaid upon them to aid with path planning. These potentials are then converted to forces which in turn are translated into appropriate motor velocities. In an unknown environment, this a priori knowledge is not available and so a reactive method

© Springer International Publishing AG 2017
Y. Gao et al. (Eds.): TAROS 2017, LNAI 10454, pp. 247–261, 2017.
DOI: 10.1007/978-3-319-64107-2_20

is required. This paper puts forward the method of reactive virtual forces as a solution to this problem.

The behaviours that guide robot exploration are largely collision avoidance, and attraction to a goal. In nature, there already exist laws that dictate these behaviours in particles; the four fundamental forces. These are the electromagnetic force, the gravitational force, the strong nuclear force and the weak nuclear force. The electrostatic force both attracts and repels charged particles, and hence may be harnessed for collision avoidance. The gravitational force attracts objects with mass from large distances, and so could be used to attract robots to distant goals. The strong nuclear force offers strong attraction in close proximity, and hence may be used to attract a robot to a near goal. Finally the weak nuclear force is responsible for radioactive decay, and though no analogue is drawn in this paper, its utility could lie in distributing a swarm at a given rate, among other potential uses.

These interacting forces account for the complex constructs that form the natural world. Utilising these forces in a virtual manner for robotic control should thus allow complex behaviours to emerge from few fundamental rules. In this case, these behaviours are guided toward robot exploration and mapping. As well as achieving complex behaviour from simple fundamental laws, the reactive virtual forces approach allows heterogeneity to be defined intrinsically in the system. This is achieved through assigning different virtual properties such as charge and mass. Assigning these different properties allows the method to be utilised for either heterogeneous or homogeneous swarms, with little or no alteration.

It is the authors' belief that this approach has three cardinal points of novelty. The first is that, to the best of the authors knowledge, potential fields have not been used previously for exploration and mapping. The second point is that multiple virtual physical forces have not been used to control the behaviour of a heterogeneous robotic swarm. Finally, the approach is applicable to unknown and complex environments, whereas most previous work has investigated known environments.

The remainder of this paper is organised as follows, first a chronological account of previous potential fields' research will be given. An explanation of the reactive virtual forces approach will then be provided. Next the experimental method will be outlined. Subsequently, the experimental results will be presented with a discussion of their relevance. Finally, conclusions will be drawn with suggestions for future work.

2   Background

In this section a history of potential fields research is given, although there is only space for a representative account, as opposed to one that is exhaustive. This starts with the first use of potential fields in robotics by Khatib [4]. This involved the use of 'artificial potential fields' to allow manipulators to avoid obstacles. This did not use potentials that were grounded in physics, but instead used an attractive force for the goal and a repulsive force from obstacles, whose function was designed by Khatib.

The first use of the term 'social potentials' was in 1999, in work by Reif et al. [7]. In this work inverse square laws were utilised as potential fields, to guide social behaviour in a group of robots.

In 2004 Spears et al. introduced the concept of 'physicomimetics' [8]. This concept uses physical forces, such as the Newtonian law for gravity, to allow pattern formation. In this work Spears et al. generate a hexagonal and a square lattice by leveraging the physical properties of mass and spin. They extended this work to a group of homogeneous robots forming a hexagonal lattice and moving towards a light source.

Zhou et al. utilised the physical traits of crystal lattices, combined with potential fields to create formations of robots [10]. This work focuses on the use of 'attraction sites', such as those found about a carbon atom when creating covalent bonds. These attachment sites become potential wells that other robots are attracted to. By varying the number and distribution of these attachment sites, different patterns were created.

In 2007 Barnes et al. furthered the use of potential fields with real robots [1]. A group of unmanned ground vehicles were used to maintain a pattern under the influence of potential fields. In this work, it was postulated that potential fields could be extended to heterogeneous groups of robots.

Further work exploring heterogeneity was compiled by McCook and Esposito [5]. In this work a convoy of simulated military vehicles are being harrassed by an attacker. The robots are classed as 'defender units' and 'supply units' and react differently. Supply units feel a force that drives them away from the attacker, whereas defenders feel an attractive force to stop the supply units being harassed. This is an interesting exploration of heterogeneity using potential fields, however physical forces are not implemented and knowledge of the entire workspace is assumed.

Finally, work by Wiegand et al. examines how potential fields could be used within a heterogeneous swarm [9]. This study states that for heterogeneity to be included each particle being used must have its mass and coefficient of friction defined. Following this an engineer must define any special relationships between interacting particles to create the appropriate behaviour with the potential fields. This is similar to the idea of utilising different virtual physical properties to leverage heterogeneity with virtual reactive forces.

Overall, it is clear there has been prior investigation into the use of potential fields for the distribution of robots in an environment. Despite this there has been little work examining potential fields for exploration. In addition, the use of heterogeneous swarms is still underdeveloped. To the best of the authors knowledge, there have been no studies using a heterogeneous swarm, under the influence of virtual reactive forces, for exploration. On top of this, there has been no use of physical forces outside of the gravitational force and electrostatic force. Thus, utilising the gravitational force, electrostatic force, and strong nuclear force in the same exploration control architecture appears to be novel, and their utility will be outlined in subsequent sections.

3   Reactive Virtual Forces

In this section the virtual reactive forces method shall be outlined. In its most basic sense the technique uses virtual physical forces to guide robots in collision avoidance and exploration, treating them as though they were particles. In addition, it is used to find areas that cannot be entered by some robots and then attempts to assign other robots to traverse these areas.

In this section, first the mapping technique will be detailed. Following this, the forces and their uses in the control architecture will be explored. Next, the motor actuation will be described. Finally, the method used to determine if areas are unreachable shall be explained.

3.1   Occupancy Grid for Mapping

The method used for mapping in this work is the occupancy grid. An occupancy grid splits an environment into discrete sub-spaces and stores the likelihood of occupation of each of them, based on sensor data [2]. In this implementation, the occupancy grid is split into squares, and the program requires only the dimensions of the area being mapped. Each square is stored as an element in a matrix, whose values are increased or decreased based on a robot's sensor data. The elements of the matrix are searched through recursively and then updated on each time step. If an obstacle is detected within a grid square, then the corresponding value in the matrix is increased by 3; if no obstacle is detected within the grid square then the value is decreased by 1. The gain is 3 as the end point of a sensor is more accurate than its middle points. Thus, detection of an obstacle is more definite than detection of no obstacles, and this is reflected in the update of the map. Finally, if the robot lies within the grid square, then the value of that square is decreased by 5, as it is more likely to contain no obstacles. The maximum likelihood of occupancy is 100, and the minimum is 0. The values of 1, 3 and 5 were chosen as they allowed the map to tend towards an accurate representation at an acceptable rate.

This process leads to three classifications of cells. The first is that a cell is known, that is its value is above 60 or below 40, and thus it is likely for it to be occupied by, or devoid of, an obstacle respectively. The second is unknown, this is when a cell has not been observed enough to be outside the range 40–60 and so its occupancy is unknown. The values of 40 and 60 were chosen as they meant that a cell must have had repeat observations before being classified as known or unknown. The final classification is frontier. These are unknown cells that are next to known cells and are hence on the frontier of the exploration effort.

Robots communicate their individual occupancy grids to one another when they are in sensor range. Maps are compared cell by cell. If it is found that one robot has a more definite determination of occupancy, the average between the communicating robots' cell values are found and these replace both robots' cell values. Though this may cause one robot to lose certainty, it also allows mistakes to be corrected. For example, if a robot observes another robot in a cell it may determine that cell to be occupied. When sharing maps, it will reveal that this cell is in fact vacant, as the observed robot knows more definitely that cell is unoccupied (having visited it). Over multiple map shares, between multiple robots, this will tend towards zero occupancy. In addition to correcting false observations, map sharing allows the mapping process to be expedited, as not all robots need visit the entire area. This is useful in a complex terrain with a heterogeneous swarm, as not all robots may be capable of reaching all areas.

3.2   Forces

Electrostatic. In physics the electrostatic force determines how two charged particles will interact. This will either be repulsive or attractive, depending on the comparative charges. In the virtual reactive forces architecture, this force is harnessed for collision avoidance. In nature, the range of this force is infinite, however in this control scheme it is limited to sensor range. As well as using the electrostatic force, a viscous friction coupling term was added to prevent infinite acceleration. The equation used to calculate the virtual electrostatic force is given in Eq. 1.

$$F = \frac{Qqk_e}{r^n} - \mu v \tag{1}$$

Where k_e is 8.99×10^9, q is the robot charge, Q is the obstacle charge and was determined through trial and error to be 2.5×10^{-7}, μ is the coefficient of friction, r is the distance to the obstacle, v is the velocity of the robot, and n is the order to which r is raised to (in the case of the electrostatic force in physics this is 2). These parameters were determined experimentally, this is detailed in the subsequent section. As the viscous friction term depends on the individual wheel velocities, the force is calculated separately for each wheel. The direction of the force is found by taking the current robot's trajectory and adding 45° to it, in the direction away from the detected obstacle. The value of 45° was chosen through trial and error, and was determined to give the best collision avoidance response.

Gravitational. In the virtual reactive forces approach the gravitational force is used to attract robots to distant goals. In this case, the goal is the centre of mass (CoM) of the unexplored cells. Or in the case where the CoM is explored, the nearest unexplored cell to the CoM. In nature the gravitational force is only attractive, this property is kept in its virtual analogue, as is the infinite range of the force. The equation used to calculate the gravitational force is given in Eq. 2.

$$F = \frac{GMm}{r^2} \tag{2}$$

Where M is the mass of the goal, m is the mass of the robot, G is the gravitational constant and r is the distance to the goal. Goal mass was determined experimentally and is a fixed value, this is detailed in the subsequent section. The direction of the force is found by finding the angle between the robot's position and the CoM of the unexplored grid cells in the occupancy grid.

Strong Nuclear Force. The strong nuclear force is used to attract robots to observed frontier cells. This force is intended to be short ranged, and only provides a goal when a frontier cell is in range of sensors. This is in keeping with the physical analogy, as the strong nuclear force only acts over short distances. In the case where a frontier cell is in range, the closest is found and becomes the goal. Otherwise, the goal remains the CoM with the gravitational force dictating motion. This means that the robot is often moving towards frontier cells and thus areas that are yet to be explored. However, when it is in an entirely explored area gravity takes over and attracts the robot to a further unexplored area. Due to this the robot is nearly always gathering new data. There is no analytical method for calculating the strong nuclear force due to its relativistic nature, instead its relative strength is used. The strong nuclear force has been found to be 137 times larger than the electrostatic force. Thus, if a frontier cell is in sensor range the electrostatic force is scaled by 137 and used to quickly move towards this goal.

3.3   Actuation

For the robots to move through the environment the virtual forces that are felt must be converted to motor velocities, and the direction of the forces must be acted upon. To do this, firstly the forces that are influencing the robot are summed; this is either a combination of electrostatic and gravitational, or electrostatic and strong nuclear, depending whether frontier cells are in range. This total force is then converted to motor velocities via Eq. 3.

$$\Delta v = \frac{F \Delta t}{m} \tag{3}$$

Once these velocities are calculated, the direction that the robot needs to turn is determined. The robot finds the smallest angle between its current heading and the desired heading. This then decides whether the robot should turn clockwise or anti-clockwise. The wheels are then actuated as follows:

- Clockwise turn: Δv is subtracted from the right wheel and added to the left wheel.
- Anti-clockwise turn: Δv is added to the right wheel and subtracted from the left wheel.

The robot continues turning until the desired angle is reached, within an acceptable error of $10°$.

3.4   Determining Unreachable Zones

The final aspect of the virtual reactive forces structure is its ability to determine if zones are unreachable for the swarm. This accounts for the complexities of the rough terrain and attempts to use the heterogeneity of the robots to overcome them.

If a robot is in the same vicinity for more than 10 s (or some time limit) it changes its goal and drops a virtual goal that may be passed to other robots. The goal should only ever be undertaken by one robot at a time, thus the robots should pass the goal only once each. To ensure this is adhered to a 'goal counter' is implemented, to keep track of how many times a goal has been passed. If the 'goal counter' reaches the number of robots that exist, then the area is assumed to be unreachable and can be marked as such. On top of this, goals could be placed in areas of interest that require further investigation. This simple method allows robots to determine if an area is unreachable without complex analysis, and is easily implemented via a finite state machine with the following states:

1. **Unknown** - the robot has not encountered the goal or another robot carrying it, robots are initialised in this state.
2. **Visiting** - The robot has received the goal from another robot and is currently making its way towards that goal.
3. **Carrying** - The robot has visited the goal and is currently waiting to encounter another robot that has not visited the goal, so that it may pass this robot the goal.
4. **Visited** - The robot has visited the goal and is currently continuing with mapping.

4 Experimental Methodology

4.1 Simulation

In order to test the virtual reactive forces method for exploration and mapping, a simulation was designed using the Matlab software. In the simulations, the aim was to emulate E-Puck robots [6]. This is so that later the tests undertaken in simulation could be replicated in real robots to validate any findings. In addition it is possible to imbue the E-Pucks with a false sensor limit and belief of their size, thus instantiating heterogeneity.

In addition to adhering to the E-Puck specifications, some assumptions were necessary to make the simulation possible. The first assumption was that the robot is capable of sensing proximity in a 40 cm circle with itself as the centre. This seemed a fair assumption, as the E-Puck has 8 infrared sensors about its circumference, used for proximity measures. The next assumption was that the robot can attain its own position, with the hope that later a localisation method would be implemented. The penultimate assumption is that the robot can control its differential wheel drive with no noise. Finally, it is assumed that the robot can measure its current bearing.

Having defined the parameters of the simulated robots, the Runge-Kutta method was employed to update the states of the robots. This involves utilising 4 estimations of a slope at different points which are then combined via a weighted sum to give a final estimate of the solution. The differential equations to be solved in this case are those relating to a differential wheel drive, these are Eqs. 4 and 5:

$$\dot{\Theta} = \frac{v_r - v_l}{d} \qquad (4)$$

$$v = \frac{v_r + v_l}{2} \tag{5}$$

Where v_l and v_r are the left and right linear wheel velocities, v is the total linear velocity of the robot, $\dot{\Theta}$ is the angular velocity and d is the diameter of the robot (distance between the two wheels).

Finally, the test arena needed to be created. This was a 1.5 × 1.5 m grid, filled with obstacles. The same arena was used for all tests, an example of the arena can be seen in Fig. 1.

4.2   Force Parameter Selection

Both force equations that are implemented in the reactive virtual forces approach have parameters that needed to be carefully selected. In the case of the electrostatic force these were q, n and μ, as defined in Eq. 1. For the gravitational force this is M, as defined in Eq. 2. Ideal values for these parameters were decided through experimentation, as will be outlined subsequently.

Electrostatic Force. Each parameter was varied 5 times leading to 125 combinations, these were run for 350 s of simulation time and 10 trials each. Observations were made to decide whether the path was acceptable for collision avoidance. A path was deemed poor if it looped back on itself, or did not successfully complete a turn.

Having completed the 350 s simulations, the best paths were continued for a second 1000 s simulation, to observe how they changed. After the 1000 s simulations were complete the effect each parameter had on the path of the robot became clear. μ changes the rate at which the robot levels out after a turn, a larger mu means the robot is less likely to loop back on itself and the turn has less angle. Charge changes the magnitude of the force causing the robot's acceleration to increase and making turns tighter. Finally, the distance order allows the robot to respond more severely to a closing distance between itself and an obstacle. After this was completed the parameters were chosen to be: $\mu = 0.04$, $q = 4 \times 10^8$ and n = 2.

Gravitational Force. As the gravitational force requires that the goal have a mass it was necessary to perform tests to find the optimum value of this mass. In addition to this, it was observed that often the robot can exhibit poor paths due to having too high a maximum speed, so it was decided at this point that the maximum speed would be reduced to 0.07 m/s. To test the effect of different masses first an order of magnitude that gives a gravitational force on the same scale as the electrostatic force was chosen, this was $\times 10^8$, other orders of magnitude were tested but it was found that best results were between 1×10^8 and 1×10^9. Thus, the parameter was varied from 1×10^8 to 1×10^9 to find the best choice of mass. For the test the robot was initialised in a random position, with the goal located at (1.3, 1.3). The time for 10 runs of the simulation was recorded for each of the masses and an average found. In addition, the minimum time that could have been recorded if the robot travelled straight to the goal at maximum speed was calculated for each run, to be compared against. After running these 10 trials it was found that the fastest time coupled with the minimum variation from the comparison time was given by a mass of 4×10^8.

4.3 Testing

Four experiments were conducted in the simulated environment. The first was conducted on a single robot, and was used to compare the reactive virtual forces method with and without the strong nuclear force. The second was to test and compare the algorithm on a homogeneous and a heterogeneous swarm. Next, individual heterogeneous parameters were investigated. Finally, the method for passing a goal that marks an unexplorable area was verified. The results of these experiments are outlined in the next section.

Verifying Strong Nuclear Force. To test the concepts of CoM and strong nuclear force two tests were run. The first was without the nuclear force, only using the CoM goal system, the second was implementing the frontier cell and CoM system with strong nuclear and gravitational forces. Trials were repeated 30 times, in keeping with the NIST statement that 30 trials give an 80% reliability [3]. From these trials an average was found for the time taken to attain 80% coverage of the arena, with the robot being initialised in a random position outside of the obstacles. In addition, the number of collisions each run was recorded.

Heterogeneous vs. Homogeneous. The next test to be carried out was a comparison between a heterogeneous swarm and a homogeneous swarm. Firstly, 30 trials were conducted with a homogeneous swarm of 4. These 4 robots used the initial values of the single E-Puck (diameter 0.07 m, mass 0.2 kg, maximum speed 0.07 m/s, sensor range 0.4 m and charge 4×10^8), and were initialised in random positions 20 cm from any obstacle. The test ended when three of the four robots had achieved 80% coverage. The same test was run for 4 heterogeneous robots (two robots with values the same as above, one with all values halved, and one with all values doubled), these parameters were chosen to give the same average values as the homogeneous swarm, for comparative purposes. The experimental set up can be seen in Fig. 1.

Individual Parameter Investigation. Following the experiments with an entirely heterogeneous swarm, it was decided that individual properties of the robots should be made heterogeneous to investigate their impact on exploration time. To this end, 5 more tests were run. In these tests, each of the five factors determining heterogeneity were changed individually. i.e. one factor out of sensor range, maximum speed, charge, diameter and mass was changed whilst keeping the other factors homogeneous. As with the previous tests, 30 trials were

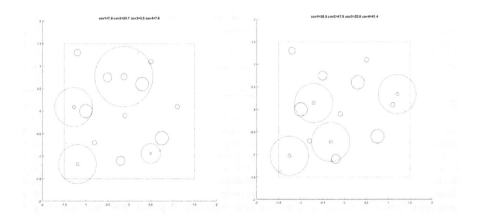

Fig. 1. Demonstrates the experimental set up for the comparison between heterogeneous and homogeneous robots. On the left is the heterogeneous experiment, and on the right the homogeneous.

conducted and an average for time taken to achieve 80% coverage was found. The heterogeneous conditions were kept the same as in the previous test (i.e. one robot with double values, two with standard and one with half, when compared to the E-Puck parameters).

Unreachable Areas. The goal of this test was to determine the time taken for the goal to be passed through all the robots. For the purposes of the test the robots are initialised in random locations with the goal location being (1.3, 1.3). One robot is assigned state 2 in the state machine described previously, and makes its way to the goal. The other robots continue mapping, if they reach 80% coverage they are given random goal locations in the map so that they are continuously moving. The goal is passed from robot to robot and the test ends when all robots have reached state 4 of the state machine. The test was first conducted on a homogeneous swarm, and then again on the heterogeneous swarm, with the parameters the same as in the heterogeneous vs. homogeneous test.

5 Results

5.1 Verifying Strong Nuclear Force

This simulation was used to verify the effectiveness of the strong nuclear force in the exploration algorithm. The comparison was made by the average time taken to reach 80% coverage both without and with the strong nuclear force. Without the strong nuclear force the average time was found to be 708 s with a standard deviation of 146 s. With the introduction of the strong nuclear force this time improved to 330 s with a standard deviation of 52 s. In addition to the times, the average number of collisions in each scenario was recorded. In the case where only the gravitational force was used the average number of collisions was found to be 3.7 per run, however when introducing the strong nuclear force this was decreased to 0.8 per run.

This result was expected, as when using only the gravitational force the robot spends much of its time revisiting cells that are already known. In the case of the strong nuclear force, the robot pushes the frontier of the exploration constantly, until it reaches an edge or some area it has already explored. At this point it moves to the centre of mass of the unexplored cells and continues exploring unknown regions. This result reinforces the utility of the strong nuclear force in this architecture.

5.2   Heterogeneous vs. Homogeneous

This test compared the effectiveness of a heterogeneous and a homogeneous swarm, both utilising the reactive virtual forces method. The metric for comparison was the average time for 3 robots to reach 80% coverage. The average time for the homogeneous swarm was found to be 231 s with a standard deviation of 36 s, whereas the time for the heterogeneous swarm was found to be 181 s with a standard deviation of 41 s. As the robots had the same average value it was assumed that a similar time would be recorded.

This is an interesting result, the significance of which is discussed in the 'T-testing' section. The average values of the homogeneous swarm parameters matched that of the heterogeneous swarm values, so why should they be faster? This question warranted the investigation of individual parameters, the results of which are described in the next section.

5.3   Individual Parameter Investigation

After finding that the heterogeneous swarm was faster than the homogeneous swarm, it was decided that individual variations of the heterogeneous characteristics should be made to see what the determining factor was. It was assumed that having a robot with double the sensor range would greatly increase the search time. The results of the experiment are given in Table 1.

Table 1. Shows the results of making individual parameters heterogeneous.

Swarm composition	Time (seconds)	Standard deviation
Homogeneous	231	36
Heterogeneous sensing	222	43
Heterogeneous speed	223	34
Heterogeneous charge	221	34
Heterogeneous diameter	232	50
Heterogeneous mass	242	38

It should be noted that in all cases the average parameter values were the same, so that the comparison can be made fairly. The results show that introducing heterogeneity to single parameters only very slightly affects the result.

If the means are examined, it seems that the sensor range, speed and charge all decrease the exploration time; the diameter of the robot makes little difference and the mass increases the exploration time. As before, a discussion of the significance of these results is reserved for the 'T-testing' section. The results for speed and sensor range make sense, as one robot can explore more of the map more quickly and transmit these results to the other robots. However, the sum of the difference between the individual parameters and the homogeneous group is 15 s. This is vastly different to the 50 s difference between the entirely heterogeneous swarm and the homogeneous swarm. This suggests that the combination of the heterogeneous characteristics makes the swarm more efficient than any one heterogeneous parameter.

5.4   T-Testing

To discern whether the improved result of the heterogeneous swarm was statistically significant, T-tests were conducted to compare the results. Such a test postulates a null hypothesis, which is then rejected if the calculated T-value is larger than a comparative value. The first null hypothesis was: 'the mean time for exploration for the heterogeneous swarms should be the same as that of the homogeneous swarm'. For 30 trials the T-value required to reject this hypothesis, and lend credence to the significance of the results, was 2.5. This gives a certainty of 98%. In addition, a second null hypothesis was examined: 'the mean time of exploration for the entirely heterogeneous swarm should be the same as that of the individual changed parameters for heterogeneity'. The T-test results are shown in Table 2.

Table 2. Shows the results of the T-testing.

Swarm composition	T-value under hypothesis 1	T-value under hypothesis 2
Homogeneous	N/A	5.04
Heterogeneous	5.04	N/A
Heterogeneous sensing	0.85	3.84
Heterogeneous speed	0.94	4.25
Heterogeneous charge	1.15	4.08
Heterogeneous diameter	0.05	4.28
Heterogeneous mass	1.12	5.96

An interesting result comes from hypothesis 1; only in the entirely heterogeneous case can we reject the null hypothesis. This shows that in the case where all parameters are heterogeneous, a significant difference is made to the exploration time. However, in the case of individual heterogeneity no significant difference is recorded.

The second hypothesis compares the results to the entirely heterogeneous case. From the T-values we see that making all parameters heterogeneous has a considerably more significant effect on the results than changing any one parameter.

5.5   Further Investigation

After observing that the heterogeneous swarm out performed its homogeneous counterpart, and having no explanation given by the individual parameter investigation, a further experiment was undertaken. This test compared the behaviour exhibited by both swarms when starting from the same initial positions; one robot in each corner of the map. This experiment had the same finishing conditions as the previous experiments.

After completion of this experiment it was observed that the symmetry of the homogeneous swarm appeared to be its limiting factor, whereas the asymmetry of the heterogeneous swarm aided exploration. This was due to the movement of the robots before and after sharing maps. Each robot in the homogeneous swarm tended to explore its initial corner, before heading to the middle. As all robots reached the centre at approximately the same time, they then shared their maps and continued exploring in similar areas. In fact, there appeared to be a tendency for the robots to pair off and explore similar areas together due to constant map exchange.

The heterogeneous swarm behaved differently. Each robot would again explore their own corner first, however due to different sensors profiles these corners would be investigated at different rates. Due to these differing rates of exploration, robots would arrive at the centre at different times. The fastest robot, with the largest sensor range, arrives first and then heads to another corner. This means that it transmits its map to the robot in that corner, so that robot moves towards the middle. This continues to happen until all the robots have exchanged maps. The heterogeneity, and imposed asymmetrical movement, causes the communication aspect of the behaviour to occur more often. This then speeds up the mapping process. A further interesting observation is that at the end of the heterogeneous simulation, the two robots with the same profiles ended up in the same place. This is not dissimilar to the pairing phenomenon observed in the homogeneous case.

5.6   Unreachable Areas

This simulation was a preliminary test into the feasibility of the goal passing strategy for determining if an area was unreachable. Robots assumed they were not able to reach an area and stored this goal, this goal was then passed from robot to robot until every robot had visited the goal. The average time for all robots to visit the goal was compared between the heterogeneous and homogeneous swarms. The average time to pass between all the robots in the homogeneous case was 561 s with standard deviation of 202 s, whereas in the heterogeneous case this reduced to 518 s with a standard deviation of 129 s.

This result suggests that the two swarm variations take comparable times to complete the goal passing exercise. This result was not expected. In this case, it was anticipated that the heterogeneous swarm would perform worse, due to the robot with half the sensor range. This was because the robots can only pass goals to other robots who are within range, and it was expected that the robot with restricted sensor range would cause a bottleneck. It is possible that the robot with enhanced sensor range made up for this bottleneck.

The results show that it is possible for the robots to pass a goal between themselves. This goal could represent an area that a robot could not traverse, or an area that requires further investigation due to its importance. The active use of this function was to mark areas that could not be explored due to all the robots not being able to reach it. This experiment captured the essence of this, but in future it is hoped that real robots can be used to verify this in a real mapping task.

6   Conclusion

This paper presented the method of virtual reactive forces for exploration and mapping, with the intent being to utilise this in a complex and unknown environment. The method involves the use of three of the four fundamental forces of physics to instigate collision avoidance and exploration.

Results were presented that show that utilising a combination of the gravitational force for distant goals, and the strong nuclear force for close frontier cells, yields a more efficient result for exploration than the gravitational force alone. In both instances, the electrostatic force is used to avoid collision.

The control scheme was tested on both a heterogeneous and homogeneous group. It was found that the heterogeneous swarm completed the exploration effort more efficiently than the homogeneous swarm. To investigate the cause of this result, the individual parameters defining the robot's characteristics were changed in isolation. From this experiment, it was found that making all characteristics heterogeneous had a much more significant impact than any one parameter. From observation, this difference in exploration time is likely caused by the asymmetry of the heterogeneous swarm, but more investigation is required to confirm this.

Finally, the utility of the method for assigning areas as unreachable was explored. It was found that both homogeneous and heterogeneous swarms performed similarly. This experiment investigated whether it was possible for all robots to pass the goal simply by random encounter, and proved that it is.

In future, it is hoped that this control method could be implemented on a real swarm of E-Puck robots, imbued with a virtual sense of heterogeneity. It is anticipated that the largest obstacle in moving the framework to real robots will be the communication. As the robots will be operating in an environment that may interfere with communication, one way of tackling this is to use UDP in order to broadcast each robot's map. The robots will be tested within a specific example: the nuclear cave, a complex area within a nuclear facility that is typically largely unknown. A further possibility for future work is the utilisation of an evolutionary algorithm to find the optimum value for parameters in the force equations.

In conclusion, this work has presented evidence that the reactive virtual forces method is a plausible solution to the exploration and mapping problem. Further, it extends the work on potential fields to the mapping domain, with the express purpose of mapping in a complex and unknown environment, utilising a heterogeneous swarm.

References

1. Barnes, L., Fields, M., Valavanis, K.: Unmanned ground vehicle swarm formation control using potential fields. In: Mediterranean Conference on Control and Automation, MED 2007, pp. 1–8. IEEE (2007)
2. Elfes, A.: Using occupancy grids for mobile robot perception and navigation. Computer $22(6)$, 46–57 (1989)
3. Jacoff, A.: Guide for evaluating, purchasing, and training with response robots using DHS-NIST-ASTM international standard test methods, March 2009
4. Khatib, O.: Real-time obstacle avoidance for manipulators and mobile robots. Int. J. Robot. Res. $5(1)$, 90–98 (1986)
5. McCook, C.J., Esposito, J.M.: Flocking for heterogeneous robot swarms: a military convoy scenario. In: 2007 Thirty-Ninth Southeastern Symposium on System Theory, pp. 26–31. IEEE (2007)
6. Mondada, F., Bonani, M., Raemy, X., Pugh, J., Cianci, C., Klaptocz, A., Magnenat, S., Zufferey, J.C., Floreano, D., Martinoli, A.: The e-puck, a robot designed for education in engineering. In: Proceedings of the 9th Conference on Autonomous Robot Systems and Competitions, vol. 1, pp. 59–65. IPCB: Instituto Politécnico de Castelo Branco (2009)
7. Reif, J.H., Wang, H.: Social potential fields: a distributed behavioral control for autonomous robots. Robot. Auton. Syst. $27(3)$, 171–194 (1999)
8. Spears, W.M., Spears, D.F., Hamann, J.C., Heil, R.: Distributed, physics-based control of swarms of vehicles. Auton. Robots $17(2$–$3)$, 137–162 (2004)
9. Wiegand, R.P., Potter, M.A., Sofge, D.A., Spears, W.M.: A generalized graph-based method for engineering swarm solutions to multiagent problems. In: Runarsson, T.P., Beyer, H.-G., Burke, E., Merelo-Guervós, J.J., Whitley, L.D., Yao, X. (eds.) PPSN 2006. LNCS, vol. 4193, pp. 741–750. Springer, Heidelberg (2006). doi:10.1007/11844297_75
10. Zhou, X.S., Roumeliotis, S.I.: Multi-robot slam with unknown initial correspondence: the robot rendezvous case. In: 2006 IEEE/RSJ International Conference on Intelligent Robots and Systems, pp. 1785–1792. IEEE (2006)

The Case for an Ethical Black Box

Alan F.T. Winfield[1(✉)] and Marina Jirotka[2]

[1] Bristol Robotics Lab, University of the West of England, Bristol, England
alan.winfield@uwe.ac.uk
[2] Department of Computer Science, University of Oxford, Oxford, England

Abstract. This paper proposes that robots and autonomous systems should be equipped with the equivalent of a Flight Data Recorder to continuously record sensor and relevant internal status data. We call this an ethical black box. We argue that an ethical black box will be critical to the process of discovering why and how a robot caused an accident, and thus an essential part of establishing accountability and responsibility. We also argue that without the transparency afforded by an ethical black box, robots and autonomous systems are unlikely to win public trust.

Keywords: Robot ethics · Ethical governance · Traceability · Transparency · Responsible robotics · Trust

1 Introduction

Driverless car accidents are headline news. The fatal Tesla accident of May 2016 [25] resulted in considerable press and media speculation on the causes of the accident. But there is a worrying perception that transparency is lacking in how these events are disclosed. System developers speak reassuringly but we may suspect they have a vested interest in giving events a positive gloss. This raises the crucial question of how the transparency of robot control systems can be guaranteed so as to avoid publics becoming fearful and to ensure that robots gain high levels of trust and acceptance in society [10]. Whilst our existing concepts of accountability and liability are being stretched by semi-autonomous machines, new heights of machine autonomy are likely to shatter them completely [31], giving urgency to the search for suitable revisions.

In this paper we propose that robots and autonomous systems should be equipped with the equivalent of an aircraft Flight Data Recorder to continuously record sensor and relevant internal status data. We call this an ethical black box. We argue that an ethical black box will play a key role in the processes of discovering why and how a robot caused an accident, and thus an essential part of establishing accountability and responsibility. We also argue that without the transparency afforded by an ethical black box, robots and autonomous systems are unlikely to win public trust.

This paper is structured as follows. In Sect. 2 we outline the development and practice of flight data recorders. Then in Sect. 3 we make the link between

© Springer International Publishing AG 2017
Y. Gao et al. (Eds.): TAROS 2017, LNAI 10454, pp. 262–273, 2017.
DOI: 10.1007/978-3-319-64107-2_21

ethical governance, transparency and trust. Section 4 discusses concerns over transparency in safety-critical artificial intelligence (AI) to propose an ethical black box, then suggests a generic specification. In Sect. 5 we consider the human processes of robot accident investigation.

2   Black Box Flight Data Recorders

Black box or flight data recorders were introduced in 1958, for larger aircraft, and since then have vastly expanded in scope in what flight data they record. Initially flight data recorders included time navigation data about the position of surfaces and the pilots' movement of controls; latterly sensor data on the internal and external environment as well as the functioning of components and systems are also recorded, alongside intentional autopilot settings such as selected headings, speeds, altitudes and so on [17]. The first black boxes recorded 5 flight parameters; data recorders on modern aircraft record more than 1000 parameters [7]. A significant innovation was the introduction of the Cockpit Voice Recorder (CVR) to capture the conversation of the pilots to aid interpretation of flight data. Although initially resisted [17], conversations captured by the CVR have proven to be an invaluable tool in reconstructing the circumstances of an accident by providing an intentional context from which to interpret flight data. Air accident investigations help to rule out systematic failure modes, help to preserve trust in aviation, provide accountability and produce lessons that contribute to overall levels of safety.

Factors that typically contribute to air accidents have parallels to incidents that may in the future arise through our increased dependence on robots. Air accidents are typically the result of unpredicted interactions between the intentions and actions of the aircrew, the integrity and behaviour of the aircraft systems, and the environmental circumstances of the flight. Somewhat analogously we anticipate future robots to be subject to a similar mix of factors. As we expect robots to do more for us, they will necessarily become more sophisticated, operate more autonomously, and do so within open, unconstrained settings. These greater freedoms come with the increased risk of unanticipated combinations of unforeseen factors leading to hazardous situations or actually resulting in harm. This is not to make a judgement about how frequently such events might occur, as with air disasters, significant harm may be rare. But we need to acknowledge hazardous events will inevitability take place. So our very ambition for robots to contribute to human activities in new ways implies giving robots new capabilities and freedoms, which in turn creates the potential for robots to be implicated in significant hazard and injury. This may prompt an overall assessment of the benefits versus the harms of expanding our dependency on robots, but our view is that more than this is needed and that a further analogy with aviation is also relevant. We suggest that acceptance of air travel, despite its catastrophes, is in part bound up with aviation governance, which has cultural and symbolic importance as well as practical outcomes. A crucial aspect of the former is rendering the tragedy of disaster comprehensible through the process of investigation and reconstruction.

The transfer of the black box concept into settings other than aviation is not novel. It has been mooted for software [9] and micro-controllers [8]. The largest deployment of black box technology outside aviation is within the automobile and road haulage industries for data logging [21, 28, 36], and perhaps the most relevant to this paper is work to develop an in-vehicle data recorder to study driver behaviour and hence better understand the reasons for common car accidents [23].

3   Ethical Governance and Trust

Ethics, standards and regulation are connected. Standards formalise ethical principles (i.e. [4]) into a structure which could be used either to evaluate the level of compliance or, more usefully perhaps for ethical standards, to provide guidelines for designers on how to conduct an ethical risk assessment for a given robot and mitigate the risks so identified [6]. Ethics therefore underpin standards. But standards also sometimes need teeth, i.e. regulation which mandates that systems are certified as compliant with standards, or parts of standards. Thus ethics (or ethical principles) are linked to standards and regulation.

Although much existing law applies to robots and autonomous systems [26], there is little doubt that rapidly emerging and highly disruptive technologies such as drones, driverless cars and assistive robotics require – if not new law – regulation and regulatory bodies at the very least.

Ethics and Standards both fit within a wider framework of Responsible Research and Innovation (RRI) [27]. RRI provides a scaffold for ethics and standards, as shown in Fig. 1. Responsible Innovation typically requires that research is conducted ethically, so ethical governance connects RRI with ethics. RRI also connects directly with ethics through principles of, for instance, public engagement, open science and inclusivity. Another key principle of RRI is the ability to systematically and transparently measure and compare system capabilities, typically with standardised tests or benchmarks [14].

In general technology is trusted if it brings benefits while also being safe, well regulated and – when accidents happen – subject to robust investigation. One of the reasons we trust airliners, for example, is that we know they are part of a highly regulated industry with an excellent safety record. The reason commercial aircraft are so safe is not just good design, it is also the tough safety certification processes and, when things do go wrong, robust and publicly visible processes of air accident investigation.

Regulation requires regulatory bodies, linked with public engagement [32] to provide transparency and confidence in the robustness of regulatory processes. All of which supports the process of building public trust, as shown in Fig. 1. Trust does not, however, always follow from (suggested) regulation. A recent survey of decision making in driverless cars reveals ambivalent attitudes to both preferences and regulation in driverless cars [5] "... participants approved of utilitarian Autonomous Vehicles (AVs) (that is, AVs that sacrifice their passengers for the greater good) and would like others to buy them, but they would themselves prefer to ride in AVs that protect their passengers at all costs. The study

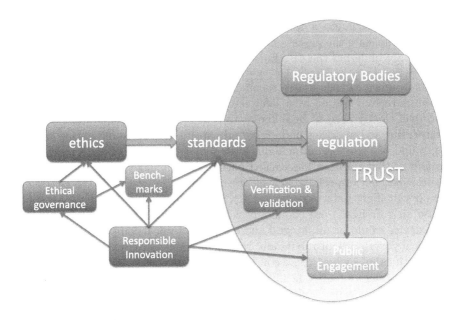

Fig. 1. A framework of ethical governance building public trust, from [35]

participants disapprove of enforcing utilitarian regulations for AVs and would be less willing to buy such an AV".

4   Safety Critical Artificial Intelligence and Transparency

All machines, including robots, have the potential to cause harm. Responsibly designed present day robots are designed to be safe and to avoid unintended harms, either accidentally or from deliberate misuse, see i.e. [19] for personal care robots.

The primary focus of this paper is robotics and autonomous systems, and not software artificial intelligence. However, a reasonable definition of a modern robot is 'an embodied AI' [33], thus in considering the safety of robots we must also concern ourselves with the AI controlling the robot. Three important classes of robot are drones, driverless cars and assistive robots (including care or workplace assistant robots); all will be controlled by an embedded AI of some appropriate degree of sophistication. Yet these are all *safety critical* systems, the safety of which is fundamentally dependent on those embedded AIs – AIs which make decisions that have real consequences to human safety or well being. Let us consider the issue of transparency, in particular two questions:

1. How can we trust the decisions made by AI systems and, more generally, how can the public have confidence in the use of AI systems in decision making? In [35] we argue that ethical governance is a necessary, but (probably) not sufficient, element of building public trust.

2. If an AI system makes a decision that turns out to be disastrously wrong, how do we investigate the process by which the decision was made? This question essentially underlies the case for an ethical black box.

Transparency will necessarily mean different things to different stakeholders – the transparency required by a safety certification agency or an accident investigator will clearly need to be different to that required by the system's user or operator. But an important underlying principle is that it should always be possible to find out why an autonomous systems made a particular decision (most especially if that decision has caused harm). A technology that would provide such transparency, especially to accident investigators, would be the equivalent of an aircraft flight data recorder (FDR). We call this an *ethical black box*, both because aircraft FDRs are commonly referred to as black boxes, and because such a device would be an integral and essential physical component supporting the ethical governance of robots and robotic systems. Like its aviation counterpart the ethical black box would continuously record sensor and relevant internal status data so as to greatly facilitate (although not guarantee) the discovery of why a robot made a particular decision or series of decisions – especially those leading up to an accident. Ethical black boxes would need to be designed and certified according to standard industry-wide specifications, although it is most likely that each class of robot would have a different standard; one type for driverless vehicles, one type for drones and so on.

4.1   An Outline Specification for an Ethical Black Box

All robots collect sense data, then – on the basis of that sense data and some internal decision making process (AI) – send commands to actuators. This is of course a simplification of what in practice will be a complex set of connected systems and processes but, at an abstract level, all intelligent robots will have the three major subsystems shown in blue, in Fig. 2. If we consider a driverless car, its sensors typically consist of a Light Detection and Ranging sensor (LIDAR), camera, and a number of short range collision sensors together with GPS, environmental sensors for rain, ambient temperature etc., and internal system sensors for fuel level, engine temperature, etc. The actuators include the car's steering, accelerator and braking systems.

The Ethical Black Box (EBB) and its data flows, shown in red in Fig. 2 will need to collect and store data from all three robot subsystems. From the sensors the EBB will need to collect either sampled or compressed raw data, alongside data on features that have been extracted by the sensor subsystem's post-processing (i.e. 'vehicle ahead, estimated distance 100 m'). From the AI system the EBB will need as a minimum high level 'state' data, such as 'braking', 'steering left', 'parking' etc. and, ideally, also high level goals such as 'turning left at junction ...' and alerts such as 'cyclist detected front left - taking avoiding action'. From the actuator system the EBB will need to collect actuator demands (i.e. 'steer left 10°') as well as the resulting effects (i.e. steering angles). All of these data will need to be date and time stamped, alongside location data from the GPS.

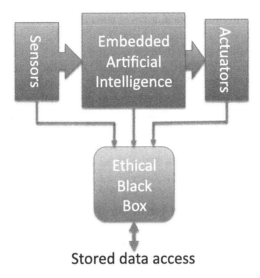

Stored data access

Fig. 2. Robot sub-systems with an Ethical Black Box and key dataflows. (Color figure online)

How much data could be stored in the EBB? Some reports have suggested that Google's driverless car generates 1 GB of raw data per second[1]. If we (reasonably) assume that we can sample and/or compress this to say 100MByte per second, then an EBB equipped with a 1 TB solid-state drive would allow it to continuously log data for about 3 h of operation. The EBB would, like an aircraft flight data recorder, continuously overwrite the oldest data logs, so that at any one time the EBB stores the most recent 3 h. This would seem to be sufficient given the need to record only the events leading up to an accident.

It is beyond the scope of this paper to specify exactly which data will need to be recorded in the EBB. We can however be clear about what those data are for: the key principle is that, from the data recorded in the EBB, it must be possible to *reconstruct* the timeline leading up to and during an accident; a timeline annotated with the key sensory inputs, actuator demands, and the high-level goals, alerts and decisions that drove those actuator demands. A full EBB specification will need to set out which data is to be recorded and, equally important, the specification of the interface(s) between the robot subsystems and the EBB. The interface specification must include the hardware (connectors), signaling and protocols. Note that the dataflows between robot subsystems and the EBB are one way only – the EBB must, as far as the robot is concerned, be an entirely passive subsystem.

The EBB specification must also cover the physical and data interface which allows an accident investigator to access data logged by the EBB (shown at the bottom of Fig. 2). There are many other aspects of the EBB that will need to be

---

[1] http://www.kurzweilai.net/googles-self-driving-car-gathers-nearly-1-gbsec.

specified. These include the physical form of the EBB noting that, like its aviation counterpart, it will need to be rugged enough to survive a very serious accident. Some would argue that the EBB does not have to be a physical component at all (see, for instance [20]) and that instead all data should be streamed to secure cloud storage. We would however counter that the high volumes of data (especially in an environment with a large number of, for instance, driverless cars) could overwhelm the local wireless infrastructure. The EBB will of course also need to be rugged, secure and tamper-proof.

As suggested here the EBB does not record the internal low-level decision making processes of the embedded AI (just as an aircraft FDR does not record the low-level processes within the vehicle's autopilot). The reason for this is that different robot AIs are likely to have very different internal architectures: some may be algorithmic, others based on artificial neural networks (ANNs). We should however note that in the case of robots which learn or adapt then any control parameters that change during the robot's operation (such as connection weights in an ANN) will need to be periodically saved in the EBB, thus enabling a deep investigation of accidents in which the robot's learning systems are implicated. Finding a common specification for capturing the low-level decision making processes for all embedded AIs is therefore likely to be impossible. Instead the transparency argued for in this paper is not achieved by the EBB alone but through the processes of accident investigation, as outlined in Sect. 5 below.

To what extent is an EBB based on the outline specification above a practical proposition? We have suggested that recording the most recent 3 h of data from a robot's sensing, AI and actuation sub-systems is achievable with current solid-state disk (SSD) technology. The most computationally intensive process in the EBB is likely to be data compression which – given that real-time video compression is commonplace in smart phones [29] – suggests that similar computing resources would be adequate for an EBB. The overall power consumption of an EBB is however likely to be significantly less than a smart phone given that the most power-hungry sub-system of a mobile phone is its wireless interface [12]. The size and mass of an EBB will be determined primarily by its strong tamper-proof enclosure and connectors. A unit size comparable to that of a ruggedised external HDD (approx. $15 \times 10 \times 5$ cm) seems both achievable and appropriate for mounting in either a driverless car or mobile service robot. An EBB for a lightweight flying robot will clearly be more challenging to engineer, but given that flying robots require wireless interfaces, either a wirelessly connected external EBB, or a cloud-based ('glass') EBB [20] might prove a more practical solution.

It is most unlikely that there could be one standard EBB for all robots, or indeed one standard specification for all EBBs. The most successful data transfer standards are either based on a common core specification which has sufficient flexibility that it can be extended to allow for manufacturer or device-specific data, or a foundational standard which can then be extended with a family of related standards. An example of the former is the Musical Instrument Digital

Interface (MIDI) with its manufacturer specified System Exclusive (SysEx) messages [22]. The latter is best illustrated by the IEEE 802 family of local area network standards, of which IEEE 802.11 (WiFi) is undoubtedly the most notable [16]. The extent to which a common core specification for an EBB interface is possible is an open question, although we would argue that for the class of mobile robots there is sufficient commonality of function that such a core specification is possible. We are unaware of efforts to develop such a specification, although one current standards effort that is aiming to define testable levels of transparency in autonomous systems is IEEE Standards Working Group P7001[2].

4.2   Ethical Black Boxes for Moral Machines

This paper makes the case that all safety critical robots should be equipped with an ethical black box. Consider now robots that are explicit moral agents. It is clear that some near future autonomous systems, most notably driverless cars are *by default* moral agents. Both driverless cars and assistive (i.e. care) robots make decisions with ethical consequences, even if those robots have not been designed to explicitly embed ethical values and moderate their choices according to those values. Arguably all autonomous systems implicitly reflect the values of their designers or, even more worryingly, training data sets (as dramatically shown in AI systems that demonstrate human biases [11]).

There is a growing consensus that near future robots will, as a minimum, need to be designed to explicitly reflect the ethical and cultural norms of their users and societies [6,18]. Beyond reflecting values in their design a logical (but difficult) next step is to provide robots with an *ethical governor*. That is, a process which allows a robot to evaluate the consequences of its (or others') actions and modify its own actions according to a set of ethical rules. Developing practical ethical governors remains the subject of basic research and presents two high level challenges: (1) the philosophical problem of the formalisation of ethics in a format that lends itself to machine implementation and (2) the engineering problem of the implementation of moral reasoning in autonomous systems [15]. There are two approaches to addressing the second of these challenges [1]:

1. a constraint-based approach – explicitly constraining the actions of an AI system in accordance with moral norms; and
2. a training approach – training the AI system to recognise and correctly respond to morally challenging situations.

The training approach is developed for an assistive robot in [2], while examples of constraint-based approaches are explored in [3,34]. One advantage of the constraint-based approach is that it lends itself to verification [13].

Extending the EBB outlined in this paper for a robot equipped with an ethical governor would in principle be straightforward: the EBB would need to additionally log the decisions made by the ethical governor so that an accident investigator could take those into account in building a picture of the processes that led to the accident.

---

[2] https://standards.ieee.org/develop/project/7001.html.

5   The Processes of Robot Accident Investigation

In aviation it is the investigation, not the black box data per se, which concludes why an air accident occurred. We anticipate this will also be true for accidents involving robots, where an investigation will draw upon EBB data amongst other information to determine the reason for an accident. So alongside the technical parameters of what to record within the EBB, we have also to consider how the interpretation of those data fits into the process of an investigation. Air accident investigations are social processes of reconstruction that need to be perceived as impartial and robust, and which (we argue) serve as a form of closure so that aviation does not acquire an enduring taint in the public's consciousness. We anticipate very similar roles for investigations into robot accidents.

Taking the example of driverless cars, an accident investigation would bring together data and evidence from a variety of sources. The extant local context will undoubtedly play a part in tracing the causes of the accident. While the EBB is witness to events that often would otherwise remain unwitnessed, the activities of driverless cars are likely to take place in populated spaces where there may be many witnesses, some of whom will record, share and publish details of the event via mobile phones and other devices, creating multiple perspectives on what may have happened. Thus, there may be bystanders, pedestrians, passengers or other drivers who will have particular views on the event and may have captured the accident as it unfolds in a variety of ways. Traditional police forensics will investigate the scene in the conventional way examining evidence such as, skid marks in the road or the impact of the crash on other objects (walls, cars) or people (for an example of the analysis of crash data see [36]). This raises the question of how the interpretation of EBB data sits alongside the interpretation of evidence from other witnesses, and brings to the fore consideration of the epistemological status of different types of witnessing.

As a further key part of the interdependent network of responsibilities in this case, the car's manufacturer and possibly also maintainer are likely to be called to provide input. This will be particularly important if initial investigation points to some incorrect internal low-level decision making process in the car's AI as the likely cause of the accident. Indeed companies may be required to release the data sets used to train the algorithms that are driving these systems when accidents occur; a requirement that may conflict with a corporation's desire to gain competitive advantage from such data.

An obvious concern is how conclusions might be reached where the data from these different types of witnessing is in conflict. It is clear that a specialist team with deep expertise in driverless car technology, perhaps within the umbrella of the road traffic investigation agency, will be needed to carefully weigh these data and reach conclusions about why the driverless car behaved the way it did, and make recommendations. But without doubt the data provided by the EBB sits at the very centre of the process of accident investigation, providing the crucial and objective timeline against which all other witness accounts can be superposed.

6   Concluding Discussion

The recent Tesla crash report [24] blames human error, often cited as a primary cause or contributing factor in disasters and accidents as diverse as nuclear power, space exploration and medicine. But in this case, we echo Jack Stilgoe's statement in the Guardian [30] that this conclusion and the process through which it was reached is a missed opportunity both to learn from such incidents about the systemic properties of such autonomous systems in the wild, and also to initiate a more transparent and accountable process for accident investigation. As reported, after the US National Highways and Transport Safety Agency (NHTSA) published their report, much of the media coverage concentrated upon the fact that no products were recalled thereby prioritising the business value for Tesla. But as Stilgoe recounts, "As new technologies emerge into the world, it is vital for governments to open them up, look at their moving parts and decide how to realise their potential while guarding against their risks". Human error is a common refrain and yet, "To blame individual users of technology is to overlook the systemic issues that, with aeroplanes, have forced huge safety improvements. When an aeroplane crashes, regulators' priority must be to gather data and learn from it. User error should be seen as a function of poorly-designed systems rather than human idiocy."

Responsibility within RRI is framed as a collective accomplishment which seems well matched to the interdependent systemic properties in the design, development and use of robots and autonomous systems. Whilst the EBB we propose in this paper seems to focus on determining accountability once an accident has happened, it is actually an outcome of reflections on applying anticipatory governance to these robot technologies. Accidents will be inevitable. Within that governance, it is vital to consider what bodies, processes and stakeholders need to be in place to determine a just account of the reasons for the accident, drawing upon the EBB record as one piece of evidence amongst others. Whilst the process itself may seem simple, it will be complicated by local contexts and the nature of the accident, political climates, legal actions, international differences and corporate concerns.

Acknowledgments. This work has, in part, been supported by EPSRC grant ref EP/L024861/1. We are also grateful to the anonymous reviewers for their insightful comments.

References

1. Allen, C., Smit, I., Wallach, W.: Artificial morality: top-down, bottom-up, and hybrid approaches. Ethics Inf. Technol. **7**, 149–155 (2005)
2. Anderson, M., Anderson, S.L.: GenEth: a general ethical dilemma analyzer. In: Proceedings of Twenty-Eighth AAAI Conference on Artificial Intelligence, pp. 253–261 (2014)
3. Arkin, R.C., Ulam, P., Wagner, A.R.: Moral decision making in autonomous systems: enforcement, moral emotions, dignity, trust, and deception. Proc. IEEE **100**(3), 571–589 (2012)

4. Boden, M., Bryson, J., Caldwell, D., Dautenhahn, K., Edwards, L., Kember, S., Newman, P., Parry, V., Pegman, G., Rodden, T., Sorrell, T., Wallis, M., Whitby, B., Winfield, A.F.: Principles of robotics. Connection Sci. **29**(2), 124–129 (2017)

5. Bonnefon, J.-F., Shariff, A., Rahwam, I.: The social dilemma of autonomous vehicles. Sci. **352**(6293), 1573–1576 (2016)

6. British Standards Institute: BS8611: 2016 Robots and robotic devices: guide to the ethical design and application of robots and robotic systems, BSI London (2016). ISBN 9780580895302

7. Campbell, N.: The evolution of flight data analysis. In: Proceedings of Australian Society of Air Safety Investigators (2007). http://asasi.org/papers/2007/The_Evolution_of_Flight_Data_Analysis_Neil_Campbell.pdf

8. Choudhuri, S., Givargis, T.: FlashBox: a system for logging non-deterministic events in deployed embedded systems. In: Proceedings of 2009 ACM Symposium on Applied Computing (SAC 2009), pp. 1676–1682 (2009)

9. Elbaum, S., Munson, J.C.: Software black box: an alternative mechanism for failure analysis. In: Proceedings of 11th International Symposium on Software Reliability Engineering, ISSRE 2000, pp. 365–376 (2000)

10. Hibbard, B.: Ethical artificial intelligence, arXiv:1411.1373v9 (2014)

11. Caliskan-Islam, A., Bryson, J., Narayanan, A.: Semantics derived automatically from language corpora necessarily contain human biases, arXiv:1608.07187v2 (2016)

12. Carroll, A., Heiser, G.: An analysis of power consumption in a smartphone. In: Proceedings of 2010 USENIX Annual Technical Conference, Boston, June 2010

13. Dennis, L.A., Fisher, M., Slavkovik, M., Webster, M.: Formal verification of ethical choices in autonomous systems. Robot. Auton. Syst. **77**, 1–14 (2016)

14. Dillmann, R.: Benchmarks for robotics research, EURON, April 2004. http://www.cas.kth.se/euron/euron-deliverables/ka1-10-benchmarking.pdf

15. Fisher, M., List, C., Slavkovik, M., Winfield, A.F.: Engineering moral machines. In: Informatik-Spektrum. Springer, Berlin (2016)

16. Gibson, R.W.: IEEE 802 standards efforts. Comput. Netw. ISDN Syst. **19**(2), 95–104 (1990)

17. Grossi, D.R.: Aviation recorder overview, National Transportation Safety Board [NTSB]. J. Accid. Investig. **2**(1), 31–42 (2006)

18. IEEE: Global initiative on Ethical Considerations in the Design of Artificial Intelligence and Autonomous Systems (2016). http://standards.ieee.org/develop/indconn/ec/autonomous_systems.html

19. ISO 13482:2014 Robots and robotic devices Safety requirements for personal care robots (2014). http://www.iso.org/iso/catalogue_detail.htm?csnumber=53820

20. Kavi, K.M.: Beyond the Black Box, IEEE Spectrum, Posted 30. http://spectrum.ieee.org/aerospace/aviation/beyond-the-black-box

21. Menig, P., Coverdill, C.: Transportation recorders on commercial vehicles. In: Proceedings of 1999 International Symposium on Transportation Recorders (1999)

22. Moog, R.A.: MIDI: Musical Instrument Digital Interface. J. Audio Eng. Soc. **34**(5), 394–404 (1986)

23. Perez, A., Garca, M.I., Nieto, M., Pedraza, J.L., Rodrguez, S., Zamorano, J.: Argos: an advanced in-vehicle data recorder on a massively sensorized vehicle for car driver behavior experimentation. IEEE Trans. Intell. Transp. Syst. **11**(2), 463–473 (2010)

24. National Highway Traffic Safety Administration: Investigation Report PE 16–007 (2017). https://static.nhtsa.gov/odi/inv/2016/INCLA-PE16007-7876.PDF

25. Vlasic, B., Boudette, N.E.: Self-Driving Tesla Was Involved in Fatal Crash, U.S. Says, New York Times, 30 June 2016

26. Palmerini, E., Azzarri, F., Battaglia, A., Bertolini, A., Carnevale, A., Carpaneto, J., Cavallo, F., Di Carlo, A., Cempini, M., Controzzi, M., Koops, B.J., Lucivero, F., Mukerji, N., Nocco, L., Pirni, A., Shah, H., Salvini, P., Schellekens, M., Warwick, K.: D6.2 Guidelines on regulating robotics, Robolaw project (2014). http://www.robolaw.eu/RoboLaw_files/documents/robolaw_d6.2_guidelinesregula-tingrobotics_20140922.pdf

27. The Rome Declaration on Responsible Research and Innovation (2014). http://www.science-and-you.com/en/sis-rri-conference-recommendations-rome-declaration-responsible-research-and-innovation

28. Thom, P.R., MacCarley, C.A.: A spy under the hood: controlling risk and automotive EDR. Risk Manag. Mag. **55**(2), 22–26 (2008)

29. Sharabayko, M.P., Markov, N.G.: H.264/AVC video compression on smartphones. J. Phys. Conf. Seri. **803**(1) (2017). Aricle No. 012141

30. Stilgoe, J.: Tesla crash report blames human error - this is a missed opportunity, The Guardian, 21 January 2017. https://www.theguardian.com/science/political-science/2017/jan/21/tesla-crash-report-blames-human-error-this-is-a-missed-opportunity

31. Vladeck, D.C.: Machines without principals: liability rules and artificial intelligence. Wash. L. Rev. **89**(117), 117–150 (2014)

32. Wilsdon, J., Willis, R.: See-through science: why public engagement needs to move upstream, DEMOS (2014)

33. Winfield, A.F.: Robotics: A Very Short Introduction, Oxford University Press, Oxford (2012)

34. Winfield, A.F.T., Blum, C., Liu, W.: Towards an ethical robot: internal models, consequences and ethical action selection. In: Mistry, M., Leonardis, A., Witkowski, M., Melhuish, C. (eds.) TAROS 2014. LNCS, vol. 8717, pp. 85–96. Springer, Cham (2014). doi:10.1007/978-3-319-10401-0_8

35. Winfield, A.F: Written evidence submitted to the UK Parliamentary Select Committee on Science and Technology Inquiry on Robotics and Artificial Intelligence, Discussion Paper, Science and Technology Committee (Commons) (2016)

36. Worrell, M: Analysis of Bruntingthorpe crash test data, impact. J. Inst. Traffic Accid. Investigators **21**(1), 4–10 (2016)

Robot Transparency: Improving Understanding of Intelligent Behaviour for Designers and Users

Robert H. Wortham$^{(\boxtimes)}$, Andreas Theodorou, and Joanna J. Bryson

University of Bath, Bath BA2 7AY, UK
{r.h.wortham,a.theodorou,j.j.bryson}@bath.ac.uk
http://www.robwortham.com
http://www.recklesscoding.com
http://www.cs.bath.ac.uk/~jjb/

Abstract. Autonomous robots can be difficult to design and understand. Designers have difficulty decoding the behaviour of their own robots simply by observing them. Naive users of robots similarly have difficulty deciphering robot behaviour simply through observation. In this paper we review relevant robot systems architecture, design, and transparency literature, and report on a programme of research to investigate practical approaches to improve robot transparency. We report on the investigation of real-time graphical and vocalised outputs as a means for both designers and end users to gain a better mental model of the internal state and decision making processes taking place within a robot. This approach, combined with a graphical approach to behaviour design, offers improved transparency for robot designers. We also report on studies of users' understanding, where significant improvement has been achieved using both graphical and vocalisation transparency approaches.

Keywords: Robot transparency · Reactive planning · Behaviour oriented design · Instinct planner · ABOD3 · Arduino · POSH

1 Introduction

Autonomous robots can be difficult to design. Robot designers often report that they have difficulty decoding the behaviour of their own robots simply by observing them. This may be because the robot behaviour provides too little information to enable the designer to envisage the internal processing within the robot giving rise to its behaviour, or it may be because the designer cannot store or recall all the program details necessary to create an adequate mental model against which the behaviour can be evaluated. As robot complexity increases, measured in terms of the range of possible behaviours, robot designers find it increasingly hard to debug their robots. This may lead to long periods of forensic offline debugging, reducing designer productivity and possibly leading to project abandonment or downsizing.

Those who encounter and interact with a robot without knowledge of the design and operation of its internal processing face an even greater challenge to

© Springer International Publishing AG 2017
Y. Gao et al. (Eds.): TAROS 2017, LNAI 10454, pp. 274–289, 2017.
DOI: 10.1007/978-3-319-64107-2_22

create a good model of the robot simply by observing its behaviour. *Transparency* is the term used to describe the extent to which the robot's ability, intent, and situational constraints are understood by users [3,18]. Humans have a natural if limited ability to understand others. However this ability has evolved and developed in the environment of human and other animal agency, which may make assumptions to which artificial intelligence does not conform. Therefore it is the responsibility of the designers of intelligent systems to make their products transparent to us [24,27].

We believe that transparency is a key consideration for the ethical design and use of Artificial Intelligence. We are working on a research programme to provide the knowledge and software tools to create a layer of transparency. This helps with debugging and with public understanding of intelligent agents. In this paper we review findings from user studies, using purpose-made tools, to back our original hypothesis regarding the usefulness of transparency.

2   Autonomous Agent Architectures and Transparency

Early work to build software architectures for real world robots soon recognised the problem that robots operate in dynamic and uncertain environments, and need to react quickly as their environment changes [13]. Brooks reinforced the point that a 'Sense-Model-Plan-Act' (SMPA) architecture is inadequate for practical robot applications [7]. Brooks' subsumption architecture is a design pattern for intelligent embodied systems that have no internal representation of their environment, and minimal internal state.

Modularity, hierarchically organised action selection, and parallel environment monitoring are recognised as important elements of autonomous agent architectures [8]. Modularity is important to simplify design. Hierarchical action selection focusses attention and provides prioritisation in the event that modules conflict. Parallel environment monitoring is essential to produce a system that is responsive to environmental stimuli and able to allow the focus of attention to shift. These ideas of modularity and hierarchy are essentially similar to some writers' modular and hierarchical models of human minds [15,19]. Bryson argues that both modularity and hierarchical structures are necessary for intelligent behaviour [9]. Subsequent work established the idea of reactive planning operating together with deliberative control, for example the Honda ASIMO robot [21] and the IDEA architecture used by NASA for the Gromit exploration rover [14].

2.1   Planning, Methodology, and Architecture

Bryson [10] extended Brooks' ideas, embracing agile and object oriented design [2], to create the Behaviour Oriented Design (BOD) development methodology. BOD requires some form of hierarchical dynamic planning system, and Bryson introduced the Parallel Ordered Slip-stack Hierarchical (POSH) planner for this purpose. The BOD architecture is used widely for both research and game AI [16,17]. POSH is straightforward to understand for beginners, allowing them to program their first agents quickly and easily [6]. Wortham has also recently re-implemented, extended, and optimised POSH for embedded microcontrollers [25].

Today, development frameworks for autonomous robots vary but are typically based on a behaviour based model, with reactive planning controlling the immediate behaviour of the robot, and a higher deliberative level serving to interact with the reactive layer to achieve longer term goals. Other design patterns also exist for specific application areas, for example in social robotics [20]. These patterns can be layered on top of the underlying reactive behaviour based model, as they specify behaviour at a high level of abstraction. These development frameworks, design patterns and architectures are valuable because they reduce the number of degrees of freedom that the robot designer has to develop their system. This may seem counter-intuitive, but as Boden shows in her seminal work on computational creativity [4], useful creativity is only achievable within some pre-existing framework to limit the search space within which individuals can search for novel solutions.

The Japanese Poka-yoke approach is used effectively within manufacturing, to guide employees in their work and reduce human error [22]. The purpose of Poka-yoke is to eliminate product defects by preventing, correcting, or drawing attention to human errors as they occur, and this is generally achieved by using templates, jigs or other devices to reduce the number of degrees of freedom available to operators within a manufacturing environment. A parallel can be drawn here with robot development frameworks, which similarly guide robot designers, helping them to achieve their desired robot functionality in a well structured, productive, and transparent environment. In this context transparency is taken both to mean the extent to which the framework is well known to the designer and to other designers, and the extent to which the framework itself provides timely and useful feedback to the designer during development.

The essential problem faced by a robot designer when observing a robot can be summed up as "why is the robot doing {X BEHAVIOUR}?" which for the developer really means "what code within the robot is executing to drive this behaviour?" Observers and users of a robot may ask the same question, but in this case what is meant is "What is the robot trying to achieve by doing {X BEHAVIOUR}? What is the purpose of this behaviour?" Fortunately, the action selection mechanisms within robots are typically arranged such that both the developer's question, and the observer or users' question may be answered in the same way, by identifying the names of the particular action modules being employed. More than one module may be active at any given time, however robot actions are typically hierarchically structured, and designers and users may be interested in receiving information from different levels within this hierarchy. In addition, during the robot behaviour design process, the designer needs rapid access to the structure of the robot's hierarchical control mechanism. This requirement favours a graphical approach to the problem of behaviour design, and has been addressed by various systems AI tools, such as the graphical Advanced BOD Environment (ABODE) [5,11].

2.2   Designing Systems for Traceability and Transparency

Consider the situation where a self-driving car does not detect a pedestrian and runs over them. Who is responsible? The robot for being unreliable? The human passenger, who placed their trust in the robot? The robot designer or manufacturer? Given that the damage done is irreversible, accountability needs to be about more than the apportionment of blame—you cannot punish a robot. These questions are matter of ethics, and beyond the scope of this paper [27]. However, what is clear is that when errors occur in autonomous systems they must be addressed, in order that they do not re-occur. Traceability of autonomous agent behaviour is essential to determine the causes of these errors. Transparency in an architecture can facilitate traceability, as data used by the decision making mechanism becomes accessible and thus recordable. This allows developers to recreate incidents in controlled environments and fix issues.

Transparency can help us trace incidents of misbehaviour even as they occur, as we can have a clear, real-time understanding of the goals and actions of the agent. However, errors are prone to be made, and when they do they must be addressed. In some cases errors in coding must be redressed, and in all cases these reports should be used to reduce the probability of future mishaps. Implementing transparency requires capture of both sensor data and the internal state of the robot. If these are retrievable, the cause of misbehaviour becomes more likely traceable. Adding traceability to the action selection mechanism allows us to record and understand the sequence of events the lead to an incident, similar to the purpose of an aeroplane's black box flight recorder. This can allow not only the apportionment of accountability for the incident, but also help robot designers to make appropriate adjustments in future versions of the robot.

In order to explore these problems of transparency further, and to develop simple software tools that can assist designers in the creation of robots, the authors have embarked upon a programme of research in robot transparency. As part of this work, we have developed a small maker robot, new graphical design tools and a graphical real-time debugger. We have also explored vocalisation of transparency information as an audible alternative to visual communication. Further details of the robot are provided in the next section. We have also conducted transparency experiments with subjects having no prior knowledge of the robot or its purpose. Section 4 reviews this work to date. We demonstrate that abstracted and unexplained real-time visualisation of a robot's priorities can substantially improve human understanding of machine intelligence, even for naive users. We further demonstrate that based on the same data feed, a vocalised output from the robot can also be used to improve understanding. Section 4.5 reports the efficacy of our visual design and debugging tools for robot developers. Section 5 describes our conclusions so far from this work, and also planned future activities.

3   The R5 Robot

As first presented by Wortham et al. [25], R5 is a low cost maker robot[1], based on the ARDUINO micro-controller [1], see Fig. 1. The R5 robot has active infra-red distance sensors at each corner and proprioceptive sensors for odometry and drive motor current. It has a head with two degrees of freedom, designed for scanning the environment. Mounted on the head is a passive infra-red (PIR) sensor to assist in the detection of humans, and an ultrasonic range finder with a range of five metres. It also has a multicoloured LED "headlight" that may be used for signalling to humans around it. The robot is equipped with a speech

Fig. 1. The R5 Robot. This photograph shows the head assembly with PIR and ultra-sonic range-finder attached. The loudspeaker and bluetooth audio adapter are also visible. The Four red LEDs are powered from the audio output, and serve as a visual indication of the vocalisation [25, 28]. (Color figure online)

---

[1] Design details and software for the R5 Robot: http://www.robwortham.com/r5-robot/.

synthesis module and loudspeaker, enabling it to vocalise textual sentences generated as the robot operates. In noisy environments, a blue-tooth audio module allows wireless headphones or other remote audio devices to receive the vocalisation output. The audio output is also directed to a block of four red LEDs, that pulse synchronously with the sound output. It also has a real-time clock (RTC) allowing the robot to maintain accurate date and time, a wifi module for communication and an electronically erasable programmable read only memory (EEPROM) to store the robot's configuration parameters. The robot software is written as a set of C++ libraries. The following section outlines the methodology and tools used to write its program.

3.1   BOD and Reactive Planning

Development of the software for the robot follows Bryson's BOD methodology [10]. We use the *Instinct* reactive planner [25] as the core action selection mechanism for the R5 robot. The Instinct Planner is based on a POSH Planner [10]. The Instinct reactive plan is produced using the Instinct Visual Design Language (iVDL) graphical authoring tool [25]; an example plan for the R5 robot is shown in Fig. 3. The development process follows this simple algorithm:

1. Develop low level behaviours and senses based on robot physical capabilities.
2. Develop more complex behaviours and sensor fusions (compound sensor models) as necessary, based on an analysis of the likely scenarios that the robot will face.
3. Produce a reactive plan using iVDL, again based on the functional requirements for the robot, and an analysis of the likely scenarios that the robot will face.
4. Test and iterate both the behaviour design, sensor model and reactive plan design until the robot behaviour is as required in the anticipated range of operational environments. During this iterative process, use the Instinct transparency feed both at runtime and offline to understand the interaction of subsystems and explain the resultant behaviour of the robot.

The Instinct Planner[2] includes significant capabilities to facilitate plan design and runtime debugging. It reports the execution and status of every plan element in real time, allowing us to implicitly capture the reasoning process within the robot that gives rise to its behaviour. The planner has the ability to report its activity as it runs, by means of callback functions to a monitor class. There are six separate callbacks monitoring the Execution, Success, Failure, Error and In-Progress status events, and the Sense activity of each plan element. In the R5 robot, the callbacks write textual data to a TCP/IP stream over a wireless (WiFi) link. A JAVA based Instinct Server receives this information and logs the data to disk. This communication channel also allows for commands to be sent to the robot while it is running. Figure 2 shows the overall architecture of

---

[2] The Instinct Planner and iVDL are available on an open source basis, see: http://www.robwortham.com/instinct-planner/.

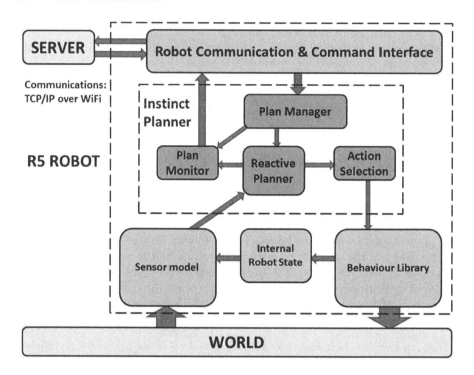

Fig. 2. R5 Robot Software Architecture showing the main architecture components and their structure. Note that the robot establishes a remote connection to the Server, from which it can optionally download an Instinct plan, download plan element names, receive user initiated commands and publish its transparency data feed [25].

the planner within the R5 robot, communicating via WiFi to either the logging server, or the ABOD3 tool, described in Sect. 4.1. The robot typically operates with a plan cycle rate of 8 Hz, yielding a transparency data rate of approximately 100 report lines per second (depending on the depth of the plan hierarchy), or 3,800 bytes of data per second.

4   Evaluation of Methods and Results

For all our experiments to date, the robot has operated with the same plan, see Fig. 3. The robot's overall function is to search a space looking for humans. Typical real world applications would be search and rescue after a building collapse, or monitoring of commercial cold stores or similar premises. As first presented by Wortham et al. [28], the robot reactive plan has six Drives. These are (in order of highest priority first):

– Sleep: this Drive has a ramping priority. Initially the priority is very low but it increases linearly over time until the Drive is released and completes successfully. The Drive is only released when the robot is close to an obstacle

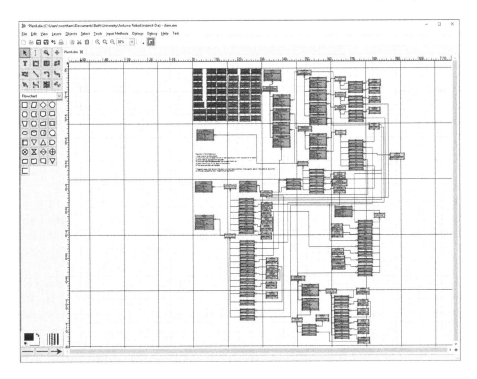

Fig. 3. An Instinct Reactive Plan for the R5 Robot, produced using iVDL within the Dia open source drawing tool. The plan labels are not visible at this resolution, but this screen shot gives an indication of the complexity of the reactive plan, and also shows how the plan was produced graphically [25].

and is inhibited whilst the robot confirms the presence of a human. The sleep behaviour simply shuts down the robot for a fixed interval to conserve battery power.

– Protect Motors: released when the drive motor current reaches a threshold.
– Moving So Look: enforces that if the robot is moving it scans for obstacles.
– Detect Human: released when the robot has moved a certain distance from its last confirmed detection of a human, is within a certain distance of an obstacle ahead, and its PIR sensor detects heat that could be from a human. This Drive initiates a fairly complex behaviour of movement and coloured lights, designed to encourage a human to move around in front of the robot. This continues to activate the PIR sensor, confirming the presence of a human (or animal). It is, of course, not a particularly accurate method of human detection.
– Emergency Avoid: released when the robot's corner sensors detect a nearby obstacle. This invokes a behaviour that reverses the robot a short distance and turns left or right by 90°.

– Roam: released whenever the robot is not sleeping. It uses the scanning ultrasonic detector to determine when there may be obstacles ahead and turns appropriately to avoid them.

We investigate two quite distinct methods for communicating the real-time transparency feed to both the robot designers and users. The first method uses a graphical approach, the second uses an audible approach. These are described in more detail below.

4.1   Graphical Presentation of Transparency Data

ABODE [5] is an editor and visualisation tool for BOD agents, featuring a visual design approach to the underlying lisp-like plan language, POSH. This platform-agnostic plan editor provides flexibility by allowing the development of POSH plans for usage in a selection of planners, such as JyPOSH [12] and POSHsharp [17].

Currently, we are working towards the development of a new integrated agent development editor, ABOD3 [23,24]. Rather than an incremental update to the existing ABODE, the new editor is a complete rebuild, with special consideration being given to producing expandable and maintainable code. It is developed

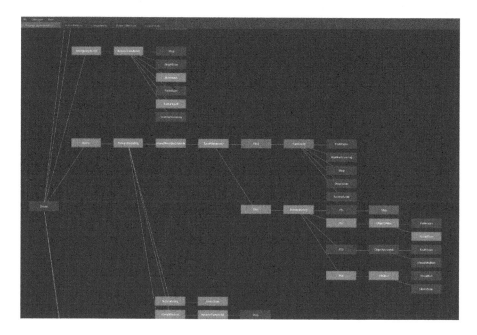

Fig. 4. The ABOD3 Graphical Transparency Tool displaying the Instinct plan [28, Fig. 3] in debugging mode. The highlighted elements are the ones recently called by the planner. The intensity of the glow indicates the number of recent calls [23,24].

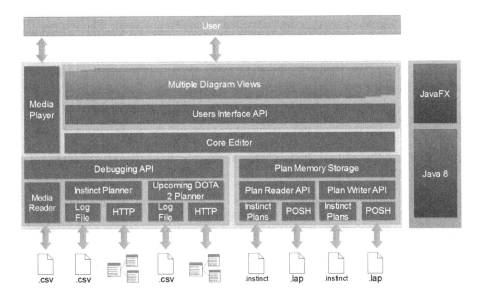

Fig. 5. System Architecture Diagram of ABOD3, showing its modular design. All of ABOD3 was written in Java for cross-platform compatibility. APIs allow the expansion of the software to support additional BOD planners for real-time debugging, BOD based plans, and User Interfaces. The editor can be tailored for roboticists, games AI developers, and even end users [23].

in Java and uses the JavaFX GUI-framework[3] to ensure cross-platform compatibility. A public Application Programming Interface (API) allows adding support for additional BOD derivatives, other than those already supported.

ABOD3 allows the graphical visualisation of BOD-based plans, including its two major derivatives: POSH and Instinct. The new editor is designed to allow not only the development of reactive plans, but also to debug such plans in real-time, to reduce the time required to develop an agent. This allows the development and testing of plans from the same application, facilitating rapid prototyping. Finally, the tool is domain-agnostic, as plans can be used in a variety of different planners, within differing execution environments including robots, agent based models and game AI. ABOD3 provides an API that allows the editor to connect with planners, presenting debugging information in real time. For example, it can connect to the R5 and the Instinct planner by using a built-in TCP/IP server, supporting the simple Instinct textual transparency feed, see Fig. 5. Plan elements flash as they are called by the planner and glow based on the number of recent invocations of that element, see Fig. 4. Plan elements without any recent invocations start dimming down, over a user-defined interval, until they return to their initial state. This offers abstracted backtracking of the calls. Sense information and progress towards a goal are displayed. Finally, ABOD3 provides integration with videos of the agent in action, synchronised

---

[3] See: http://docs.oracle.com/javafx/.

by the time signature within the recorded transparency feed. The simple UI and customisation provided by ABOD3 allow it to be employed not only as a tool for developers, but also to present transparency information to the end user. Establishing the most appropriate level of complexity with which users may interact with the transparency-related information is crucial. Hiding and rearranging subtrees allows developers using ABOD3 to tune what and how much information they will expose to end users.

4.2 Testing Graphical Robot Transparency for Observers with ABOD3

As first presented by Wortham et al. [29], our experiment with ABOD3 took place over three days at the At-Bristol Science Learning Centre, Bristol, UK. The robot operated within an enclosed pen as a special interactive exhibit within the main exhibition area, see Fig. 6.

Fig. 6. The arrangement of the R5 Robot experiment using ABOD3 at the At-Bristol Science Centre. Obstacles visible include a yellow rubber duck, a blue bucket and a potted plant. The position and orientation of the transparency display is shown [29, Fig. 6]. (Color figure online)

Visitors, both adults and children, were invited to sit and observe the robot in operation for several minutes whilst the robot moved around the pen and interacted with the researchers. Subjects were expected to watch the robot for at least three minutes before being handed a paper questionnaire. The questions sought to investigate the understanding of the robot by the participants, in terms of both its intelligence and cognitive capacity, and its objectives and means of achieving them. Half of the participants had access to the ABOD3 real-time display, whilst the other half did not (the monitor was simply switched off). Full details are available in Wortham et al. [29].

4.3 Plan Execution Vocalisation - iPEV

The R5 robot's transparency feed contains a single line of output each time an Instinct plan element is executed. It also contains another line to indicate whether the plan element execution was successful, failed, still pending or resulted in an error. Since plans are hierarchical, the execution notification is received on the way down the hierarchy, and the other notifications are received on the way up. A stack structure is used to track this tree traversal, and thus it is known whether this is the first, or subsequent invocation of the element. This information is then used, together with the element type and name, to form a candidate sentence about the processing of the element. These sentences are generated far too quickly to all be vocalised, and so a filtering mechanism is used based on the following factors

1. The plan element type: Drive, Competence, Action Pattern, Action, Competence Element, Action pattern Element.
2. The event type: Execution, Success, Failure, In-progress, Error.
3. The elapsed time since the sentence was generated. If a sentence waits too long before being vocalised then it is discarded.
4. Whether the sentence is being repeated within a given time interval.

These factors can be set using the robot command line interface and are stored within the robot EEPROM. Following extensive usage testing by the designers, including feedback from user testing with students, the default parameters give priority to sentences relating to Drive execution (the highest level in the hierarchy) and the success or failure of Competences, Action Patterns and Actions. These parameters were then used for the formal experiments to test the Instinct Plan Execution Vocalisation (iPEV) at the AtBristol Science Centre, see Fig. 7.

4.4 Testing Audible Robot Transparency for Observers with iPEV

These experiments were similarly conducted to those using ABOD3, and a very similar questionnaire was used, differing only in that it attempted to collect more data about the reported emotional response of participants to the robot. However in this experiment the robot operated on a large round tabletop rather than on the floor. This enabled participants to hear the robot more clearly, and interact with it at arms reach whilst standing, see Fig. 7. We now consider the benefits of transparency for both robot designers and naive observers of the robot.

4.5 Transparency for Designers

During development of the R5 robot, we can report anecdotal experience of the value of offline analysis of textual transparency data, and the use of ABOD3

Fig. 7. A frame from a video of experiments with the R5 Robot at the AtBristol Science Centre, Bristol, UK. Due the high background noise level, participants are wearing headphones connected to the iPEV audio output of R5 via blue-tooth. This enabled them to clearly hear the robot's audio output. The robot is shown successfully detecting a human, to the delight of participants [26].

in its recorded mode. These tools enabled us to quickly diagnose and correct problems with the reactive plan that were unforeseen during initial plan creation. These problems were not so much 'bugs' as unforeseen interactions between the robot's various Drives and Competences, and the interaction of the robot with its environment. As such these unforeseen interactions would have been extremely hard to predict. This reinforces our assertion that iterative behaviour oriented design (BOD) is an effective and appropriate method to achieve a robust final design. The BOD development methodology, combined with the R5 Robot hardware and the Instinct Planner has proved to be a very effective combination. The R5 Robot is robust and reliable, proven over weeks of sustained use during both field experiments and demonstrations. The iterative approach of BOD was productive and successful, and the robot designers report increased productivity resulting from use of the Instinct transparency feed and the ABOD3 tool.

4.6 Transparency for Observers

The experiment using R5 with ABOD3 investigates whether seeing a real-time graphical representation of the robot's internal state and action selection processes helps naive observers to form a more useful mental model of the robot. By 'useful' we mean a model that is more closely aligned with the robot's actual capabilities, intentions, goals and limitations. Full details of this experiment and the results obtained can be found in Wortham et al. [29]. However, to summarise, subjects show a significant improvement in the accuracy of their mental model of the robot if they also see the accompanying ABOD3 display. ABOD3 visualisation of the robot's intelligence makes the machine nature of the robot more transparent.

The experiment using R5 with iPEV (vocalisation) investigates whether hearing a real-time audible representation of the robot's internal state and action selection processes similarly helps observers to form a more useful mental model of the robot. Our preliminary analysis of results indicate that this is indeed the case, and that a significant improvement in the observers mental model of the robot was achieved ($N = 68$, $t(66) = 2.86$, $p = 0.0057$). The addition of vocalisation made no significant difference the users report of their emotional responses, nor to their report of perceived robot intelligence or capacity of the robot to 'think'. Interestingly it also made no significant difference to the users self report of their ability to understand the purpose of the robot's behaviour.

5 Conclusions and Further Work

Development frameworks for autonomous robots are an important contribution to assist robot designers in their work. Today these frameworks are typically based on a behaviour based model, with reactive planning controlling the immediate behaviour of the robot, and a higher, deliberative level serving to interact with the reactive layer to achieve longer term goals. These action selection mechanisms within robots are therefore amenable to the addition of various transparency measures by simply displaying or otherwise communicating the real time control state. Our programme of research indicates that by making transparency an important design consideration for a development framework, it becomes straightforward to productively design and deliver a reliable, useful robot. The R5 robot exhibits robust behaviour over prolonged time periods in varying environments. We are also developing a body of evidence to indicate that robot designers should consider transparency as a fundamental and important trait of a robot. Taking steps to improve robot transparency significantly improves understanding of a robot in naive observers.

We plan to develop ABOD3, adding features such as "fast-forward" debug functions in pre-recorded log files, the ability to set conditional breakpoints and additional views of the reactive plan hierarchy. A fuller analysis of the results of data obtained during the robot vocalisation experiments is being prepared for subsequent publication [26]. We also intend to run workshops for robot designers, where we will further evaluate the Instinct Planner, iVDL plan authoring, the ABOD3 debugger and iPEV plan execution vocalisation.

References

1. Arduino: Arduino Website (2016). https://www.arduino.cc/
2. Beck, K.: Extreme Programming Explained: Embrace Change. Addison-Wesley, Reading (2000)

3. Boden, M., Bryson, J., Caldwell, D., Dautenhahn, K., Edwards, L., Kember, S., Newman, P., Parry, V., Pegman, G., Rodden, T., Sorell, T., Wallis, M., Whitby, B., Winfield, A.: Principles of robotics. The United Kingdom's Engineering and Physical Sciences Research Council (EPSRC), April 2011. Web publication

4. Boden, M.A.: Creativity and artificial intelligence. Artif. Intell. **103**(1–2), 347–356 (1998)

5. Brom, C., Gemrot, J., Bída, M., Burkert, O., Partington, S.J., Bryson, J.J.: POSH tools for game agent development by students and non-programmers. In: Mehdi, Q., Mtenzi, F., Duggan, B., McAtamney, H. (eds.) The Ninth International Computer Games Conference: AI, Mobile, Educational and Serious Games, pp. 126–133. University of Wolverhampton, November 2006

6. Brom, C., Gemrot, J., Michal, B., Ondrej, B., Partington, S.J., Bryson, J.J.: Posh tools for game agent development by students and non-programmers. In: The Nineth International Computer Games Conference: AI, Mobile, Educational and Serious Games, pp. 1–8 (2006)

7. Brooks, R.A.: Intelligence without representation. Artif. Intell. **47**(1), 139–159 (1991)

8. Bryson, J.: Cross-paradigm analysis of autonomous agent architecture. J. Exp. Theoret. Artif. Intell. **12**(2), 165–189 (2000). http://www.tandfonline.com/doi/abs/10.1080/095281300409829

9. Bryson, J.J.: The study of sequential and hierarchical organisation of behaviour via artificial mechanisms of action selection. M. Phil., University of Edinburgh (2000). https://www.cs.bath.ac.uk/~jjb/ftp/mphil.pdf

10. Bryson, J.J.: Intelligence by design: principles of modularity and coordination for engineering complex adaptive agents. Ph.D. thesis, MIT, Department of EECS, Cambridge, MA, AI Technical report 2001–2003, June 2001

11. Bryson, J.J.: Advanced Behavior Oriented Design Environment (ABODE) (2013). http://www.cs.bath.ac.uk/~jjb/web/BOD/abode.html

12. Bryson, J.J., Gaudl, S.: jyPOSH (2013). https://sourceforge.net/projects/jyposh/

13. David, E.W., Karen, L.M., John, D.L., Wesley, L.P.: Planning and reacting in uncertain and dynamic environments. J. Exp. Theoret. Artif. Intell. **7**(1), 121–152 (1995). http://dx.doi.org/10.1080/09528139508953802

14. Finzi, A., Ingrand, F., Muscettola, N.: Model-based executive control through reactive planning for autonomous rovers. In: 2004 IEEE/RSJ International Conference on Intelligent Robots and Systems (IROS) (IEEE Cat. No. 04CH37566), vol. 1, pp. 879–884 (2004). http://ieeexplore.ieee.org/lpdocs/epic03/wrapper.htm?arnumber=1389463

15. Fodor, J.A.: The Modularity of Mind: An Essay on Faculty Psychology. A Bradford book. MIT Press, Cambridge, Mass (1983). http://books.google.co.uk/books?id=e7nrSeibJZYC

16. Gaudl, S., Bryson, J.J.: The extended ramp goal module: low-cost behaviour arbitration for real-time controllers based on biological models of dopamine cells. In: Computational Intelligence in Games 2014 (2014). http://opus.bath.ac.uk/40056/

17. Gaudl, S., Davies, S., Bryson, J.: Behaviour oriented design for real-time-strategy games: an approach on iterative development for STARCRAFT AI. In: Foundations of Digital Games Conference, pp. 198–205 (2013)

18. Lyons, J.B.: Being Transparent about transparency: a model for human-robot interaction. Trust and Autonomous Systems: Papers from the 2013 AAAI Spring Symposium, pp. 48–53 (2013)

19. Minsky, M.: The Society of Mind. Simon and Schuster Inc., New York (1985)

20. Ruckert, J.H., Kahn, P.H., Kanda, T., Ishiguro, H., Shen, S., Gary, H.E.: Designing for sociality in HRI by means of multiple personas in robots. In: ACM/IEEE International Conference on Human-Robot Interaction, pp. 217–218 (2013)
21. Sakagami, Y., Watanabe, R., Aoyama, C., Matsunaga, S., Higaki, N., Fujimura, K.: The intelligent ASIMO: system overview and integration. IEEE/RSJ Int. Conf. Intell. Robots Syst. **3**(October), 2478–2483 (2002)
22. Shingo, S., Dillon, A.P.: A Study of the Toyota Production System: From an Industrial Engineering Viewpoint. Produce What Is Needed, When It's Needed. Taylor & Francis, New York (1989). https://books.google.co.uk/books?id=RKWU7WElJ7oC
23. Theodorou, A.: ABOD3: a graphical visualization and real-time debugging tool for bod agents. In: EUCognition 2016, Vienna, Austria, December 2016. http://opus.bath.ac.uk/53506/
24. Theodorou, A., Wortham, R., Bryson, J.J.: Designing and implementing transparency for real time inspection of autonomous robots. Connection Sci. **29** (2017). http://opus.bath.ac.uk/55250/
25. Wortham, R.H., Gaudl, S.E., Bryson, J.J.: Instinct: a biologically inspired reactive planner for embedded environments. In: Proceedings of ICAPS 2016 PlanRob Workshop, London, UK (2016). http://icaps16.icaps-conference.org/proceedings/planrob16.pdf
26. Wortham, R.H., Rogers, V.E.: The Muttering Robot: Improving Robot Transparency Though Vocalisation of Reactive Plan Execution (2017, in prep)
27. Wortham, R.H., Theodorou, A.: Robot transparency, trust and utility. Connection Sci. **29**(3), 242–248 (2017)
28. Wortham, R.H., Theodorou, A., Bryson, J.J.: What does the robot think? Transparency as a fundamental design requirement for intelligent systems. In: IJCAI-2016 Ethics for Artificial Intelligence Workshop, New York, USA (2016). http://opus.bath.ac.uk/50294/1/WorthamTheodorouBryson_EFAI16.pdf
29. Wortham, R.H., Theodorou, A., Bryson, J.J.: Improving robot transparency: real-time visualisation of robot AI substantially improves understanding in naive observers. In: IEEE RO-MAN 2017, Lisbon, Portugal (2017)

Children's Age Influences Their Use of Biological and Mechanical Questions Towards a Humanoid

David Cameron[1($\boxtimes$)], Samuel Fernando[1], Emily Cowles-Naja[2], Abigail Perkins[2], Emily Collins[1], Abigail Millings[2], Michael Szollosy[1], Roger Moore[1], Amanda Sharkey[1], and Tony Prescott[1]

[1] Sheffield Robotics, University of Sheffield, Sheffield, UK
{d.s.cameron,s.fernando,e.c.collins,m.szollosy,r.k.moore,
a.sharkey,t.j.prescott}@sheffield.ac.uk
[2] Department of Psychology, University of Sheffield, Sheffield, UK
{ecowles-naja1,aperkins3,a.millings}@sheffield.ac.uk
http://easel.upf.edu/project

Abstract. Complex autonomous interactions, biomimetic appearances, and responsive behaviours are increasingly seen in social robots. These features, by design or otherwise, may substantially influence young children's beliefs of a robot's animacy. Young children are believed to hold naive theories of animacy, and can miscategorise objects as living agents with intentions; however, this develops with age to a biological understanding. Prior research indicates that children frequently categorise a responsive humanoid as being a hybrid of person and machine; although, with age, children tend towards classifying the humanoid as being more machine-like. Our current research explores this phenomenon, using an unobtrusive method: recording childrens conversational interaction with the humanoid and classifying indications of animacy beliefs in childrens questions asked. Our results indicate that established findings are not an artefact of prior research methods: young children tend to converse with the humanoid as if it is more animate than older children do.

Keywords: Human-robot interaction · Humanoid · Animacy · Psychology

1 Introduction

With the increase in social robots developed for children as users in human-robot interaction (HRI), understanding how children perceive and evaluate robots is critical for effective HRI progress. A theoretical understanding of childrens perceptions of social robots can both promote greater user-centered design, and address key psychological questions in child development (e.g., [1]). Given recent advances in autonomy and interaction capabilities, there is potential for social robots to span boundaries between object and agent in a child's perspective [2].

Children hold their own naive theories of animacy in early development. They can attribute objects substantially simpler than modern robotics as possessing

© Springer International Publishing AG 2017
Y. Gao et al. (Eds.): TAROS 2017, LNAI 10454, pp. 290–299, 2017.
DOI: 10.1007/978-3-319-64107-2_23

life [3] and invent conclusions of the objects having *intentions*. These naive beliefs are supplanted by an understanding of biology in later childhood [1,4]. However, even among adults with a biological understanding of animacy, their wider perceptions and interaction behaviors with robots are shaped by beliefs of a robot's animacy [5]. Children's early, naive understandings of animacy may have a significant impact on how they understand and interact with robots.

1.1 Children's Understanding Animacy in HRI

Current HRI research exploring animacy offers mixed indications concerning the development of children's perceptions of robots as (in)animate (see [6] for an overview). Studies point towards aspects of Carey's model of conceptual change [4] but others offer contrasting outcomes (e.g., young children have shown both consistent [7] and inconsistent [8] animacy beliefs about a robot dog).

The mixed picture that research findings offer has lead to development of a new approach in understanding children's perceptions of robots as beings that can exist 'between' animate and inanimate [9,10]. With this in mind, we explore children's beliefs of animacy concerning a responsive, autonomous, humanoid. Prior work suggests a continuum from animate to inanimate in children's beliefs [11], although this may be an artefact of the testing procedure (see Sect. 1.3); in this paper, we undertake a new method to examine children's beliefs of animacy.

1.2 Perceived Animacy of a Humanoid

Cameron and colleagues observed a significant difference between older and younger children in their ratings of a humanoid robot (Robokind Zeno R25 [12], Fig. 1): younger children (age five and six) considered the robot to be more 'like a person' than older children (age seven or eight) did [11]. On average, both groups of children rated the robot as having some elements of animacy, as a hybrid of machine and person. In that study, children took part in an interactive scenario with an autonomous, responsive, expressive robot; the authors suggest that the richness of the interaction, congruent with a humanoid morphology, may contribute to the mixed ratings.

Two subsequent studies show similar findings to [11], even with a substantially simpler interaction scenario [13,14]. In these studies, children played a simple guessing game about the robot's actions; the robot neither communicated with the children nor responded to their behaviour. Results indicate that, on average, children report the humanoid to be a hybrid of person and machine, albeit somewhat more machine-like than the ratings in [11]. Again, younger children are more likely to rate the robot as being more like a person, than older children do.

1.3 Measuring Animacy Beliefs

In developmental research, it can be a challenge to maintain children's attention for extended or repeated questions. Cameron and colleagues suggest that a key

Fig. 1. The Robokind Zeno R25 platform (humanoid figure approximately 60 cm tall)

advantage of the above studies is the single-item measure used for animacy [14], which keeps post-HRI questionnaires brief and preserves children's engagement. Moreover, results gathered from using 100 point thermometer scale [11] and Likert scale variants [13] of the measure offer theoretically consistent findings [4].

However, the brief measure does currently present a limitation. While the measures addresses the emerging idea that robots can exist as between animate and inanimate (e.g., [10]), specific findings using the measure may be an artefact of the question's design. In essence, children may describe the humanoid as a machine-person hybrid simply because the option is presented as a continuum and they feel obliged to. Given these limitations, it remains to be seen if children's beliefs of a robots animacy are well represented as a continuum.

The current study seeks to examine two key matters from earlier studies [11,13], namely (1) Are children's reports of a humanoid as being a person-machine hybrid artefacts of the measure used? (2) Do children show variation with age in their beliefs about animacy in HRI?

To address this, we use an alternative method of open-ended interviews, which have previously explored children's beliefs about robotic agents with promising results [15]. In contrast to prior work in which researchers may guide children to the towards the topic of animacy, We offer children the opportunity to ask self-generated questions towards the robot after HRI scenarios. We anticipate that the opportunity to converse with a robot on their own terms could promote children to explore topics of genuine interest to them. We anticipate:

(1a) Children will self-generate questions exploring a robot's animacy. (1b) Children will ask questions that reflect the perceived machine-person hybrid nature of the humanoid[1]. (2a) Younger children will, on average, ask more person-themed questions than older children. (2b) Older children will, on average, ask more mechanical-themed questions than younger children.

---

[1] This may be reflected within a single question, or reflected through status incongruency across multiple questions.

2   Method

2.1   Design

We employed a between subjects design, with an independent variable of age. The content of children's questions asked towards the Zeno R25 robot were used as the dependent variable.

2.2   Participants

Participants were drawn from two local primary schools. Both schools invited research staff to demonstrate current robotics. In total, 91 children took part, divided across three year-groups; twenty-seven children were from Primary school A, ages ranged from five to seven. Sixty-four children took part from primary school B, ages ranged from nine to ten. Consent was obtained prior to children's participant from teachers at both schools and, where applicable, parents.

2.3   Procedure

Participants' questions for the robot were recorded at the end of one of two HRI scenarios (see below). Children were invited to ask Zeno as many questions as they liked. Pre-scripted answers were provided for the anticipated likely questions; if there was no suitable answer for the question asked, a variety of stock phrases were used, such as 'What a great question!'. Zeno's responses were initiated by the lead computer scientist covertly selecting appropriate answers.

HRI Scenarios. Two interactive scenarios, developed to explore HRI in an educational context (Expressive agents for Symbiotic Education and Learning, EASEL [16,17]) were used for data collection. Both scenarios had been pre-tested for suitability as a social and educational interaction for the age groups in this study.

Younger children took part in a game of 'Simon-Says' with Zeno. The procedure for the interaction is described in detail in [18] and summarised here. Children completed ten rounds of the game Simon-Says, with Zeno verbally stating instructions and feedback on children's performance. The interaction was delivered autonomously and the robot was responsive to children's movements. Children completed this interaction alone. After the game, Zeno asked children questions about their exercise and asked if they had any questions to ask it.

Older children completed a 'Healthy-Living Tutoring' scenario. The procedure for the interaction is described in detail in [9] and summarised here. Children followed the verbal instructions from Zeno to engage in light, moderate, and intense physical activity. Zeno gave autonomous feedback on the energy used with each activity. Children completed the interaction in front of peers. After completing the physical activity, Zeno gave children a series of questions about physical activity and invited children to share questions they had.

Data Collection. The question recording differed across HRI scenarios as a result of the testing environment available.

The Simon-Says scenario was conducted in a lab-like environment. Children spoke their questions into a headset microphone as part of a corpus-development exercise used for training an automatic speech recognition program [19].

The healthy living scenario was conducted in a classroom environment. Children took turns in interacting with Zeno, while classmates observed. While waiting to take part, children completed a written task that included writing a description of the interaction and, critically, any questions that they would have for Zeno. Children were informed that, at the end of the whole classes interaction, randomly selected children would read out their questions for Zeno.

Text Analysis. Questions asked by children were transcribed and coded by two researchers, naive to conditions and hypotheses for the study. The pool of questions were divided equally between researchers. A random sample comprising 10% of transcriptions from each researcher were checked for accuracy by their counterpart; no content errors were detected.

A card-sort procedure was used to classify the questions asked. Each researcher was given the unique 263 questions children asked[2] and instructed to sort the questions into as many or as few mutually exclusive categories as they felt necessary to best reflected their own perceptions of the similarities and differences. After all questions were categorised, researchers were asked to name or describe each category that they had created to help identify commonalities between the questions within each group.

Researchers discussed their categories created to identify overlap in emergent themes. Themes agreed to be sufficiently similar were merged and questions redistributed amongst the categories as appropriate.

3   Results

There were no significant difference between the two groups in the number of questions asked $t(89) = .60$, $p = .55$. On average, older children asked 3.81 (S.D. $= 2.44$) questions, while younger children asked 3.48 (S.D. $= 2.28$) questions.

3.1   Classification of Questions

Researchers identified that, of the 263 unique questions asked, 40 are directed towards the research team *about* Zeno rather than being directed *towards* Zeno. Examples of such questions included 'Can he dance?' and 'How does Zeno talk?'. For each of the 40 questions asked to researchers, there were also examples of other children directing the same question to Zeno.

---

[2] 398 questions were asked in total, if duplicates are counted. Common duplicates included questions on Zeno's age, family, and abilities.

In general, there was strong agreement between researchers: Researcher A created eleven distinct categories, while Researcher B created seven. After discussion, researchers agreed on a total of seven over-arching categories, based on researcher B's classification, with two of those each containing two sub-categories, based on Researcher A's classification (see Table 1). Two categories suggested by Researcher A (Exercise and Routine Tasks) were agreed to be sufficiently similar to the Robot Capabilities category, so the questions were reallocated.

Table 1. Category development of questions children ask towards Zeno

Agreed categories	Example questions	Unique Q. count
Biological functions	What do you eat? When do you sleep?	27
Social relationships	Do you have a sister? Do you have friends?	17
Robot capabilities	What is 12 × 12? Can you Whip and Nae?	82
Favourites	What is your favourite animal [sport, colour]?	15
Robot feelings	Do you feel? What are you most afraid of?	34
Origin		
Manufacture	How were you programmed? Who made you?	17
Biological	When is your birthday? How old are you?	6
Identity		
As robot	Are you a robot? What do you think you are?	17
As gender	Are you a boy? Would you rather be a girl?	8

3.2   Question Frequency

Researchers identified multiple categories of questions exploring a robot's life-like nature: Biological Functions, Biological Origin, and Gender Identity. Researchers further identified cases where children asked conceptually inconsistent questions (or series of questions), suggesting issues for some children in establishing Zeno's animacy. Examples include: 'Do you go to the doctors to get your wires checked?' and 'When is your birthday?... How were you made?'.

A series of nine chi squares are run, with appropriate bonferroni correction, to examine differences between age groups in the frequency for each type of question asked[3]. If children asked multiple questions *across* categories, each were included in analysis; multiple questions *within* categories were counted as a single entry.

Younger children ask proportionally more questions than older children do concerning Zeno's Biological Functions $\chi^2(2, 91) = 9.37$, $p = .002$ and Zeno's Biological Age $\chi^2(2, 91) = 10.63$, $p = .001$.

---

[3] Given the nine tests run we consider a significant result to occur at p = .006.

In contrast, older children ask proportionally more questions concerning Zeno's Robot Capabilities $\chi^2(2, 91) = 7.89$, p $= .005$; Zeno's capacity for, or experience of, Robot Feelings $\chi^2(2, 91) = 7.76$, $p = .005$; Zeno's Gender Identity $\chi^2(2, 91) = 8.82$, $p = .003$; and at threshold for Zeno's Identity as a Robot $\chi^2(2, 91) = 7.48$, $p = .006$.

There are no observed differences between age groups for Zeno's Social Relationships $\chi^2(2, 91) = 1.71$, $p = .181$; Zeno's Favourites $\chi^2(2, 91) = .86$, $p = .355$; or Zeno's Mechanical origin $\chi^2(2, 91) = 3.27$, $p = .070$.

4   Discussion

The format of children asking open-ended questions towards a robot yields a substantial number that explore a robot's animacy and identity. It appears that these are of immediate personal interest to children during HRI, supporting hypothesis (1a). Results further indicate significant differences in the types of questions younger and older children tend to ask the humanoid robot, immediately following HRI. Younger children are more likely to ask questions concerning the humanoid's age and its biology, whereas older children tend to ask questions concerning the humanoid's identity and its capacity for behaviours and affect.

Prior research identifies that children tend to describe the humanoid Zeno as a hybrid of person and machine [11,13] and that younger children view the robot as being more person-like than older children do. The current study, using an unstructured and open-conversation format for children to ask questions of Zeno, offers early support to both claims in the prior work.

First, children ask questions that can blur the boundaries of animacy. They may also switch between questions of an animate and inanimate nature in the same conversation with the robot. However, these were infrequent in the data set collected and, as yet, not suited to statistical analysis, offering some support for hypothesis (1b). Further research on children's mixed beliefs about humanoids may be more fruitful with using greater-depth interviews, such as those used in developmental research [4] and in HRI with the biommimetic Aibo [20].

Second, younger children are more likely to address the robot as if it was animate than older children do, supporting hypothesis (2a). Younger children's questions primarily concern life supporting functions and the robot's age (in terms of Zeno having a birthday rather than date of manufacture). Older children's questions tended to show a mixed picture, suggesting an understanding that Zeno is a machine (as reflected in their interest in its mechanical capabilities), albeit an emotionally expressive [12] and cognizant one (particularly one that self-identifies as a robot), offering some support for hypothesis (2b). Responsive, autonomous, and expressive robots may blur the boundaries between object and agent even for older children [2].

Older children were substantially more likely than younger children to ask questions regarding Zeno's gender identity. Given the relative low frequency of older children asking other questions regarding Zeno's 'biology', we interpret this as a social question towards the robot. Young children are argued to understand their own and others' gender identities; however, in later childhood, children observe and learn that gender is used as a cue to shape the social expectancies and interactions of themselves and others [21]. In essence, the older children's questions of Zeno's gender may exist as an implied, 'Once I know your gender, I know how to treat you'. Issues of gender have been raised in prior work with the Zeno humanoid [13,18] and further work in this area may offer both insights into child development and more effective social robotics.

It should be noted that the children's questions came after interaction with a responsive and autonomous humanoid and, as such, are perhaps reflective of the children's cognitions *in the context of the HRI experience*. In addition to the robot's morphology, its behaviours in HRI, and a user's prior beliefs or experiences with robots, the *context* in which the HRI scenario takes place, may substantially shape the user's interaction experience [22]. In this context, children were instructed to direct questions towards the robot, which could prime beliefs of agency and animacy. In alternative contexts, children may generate different questions (e.g., writing a pen-pal style letter to a humanoid that a child has not yet met). A deeper understanding of children's beliefs concerning robot animacy can best come from an array of studies exploring aspects such as: morphology, autonomy, and responsiveness across a range of HRI contexts [14].

Further work to better develop an understanding of children's beliefs of animacy in robots could include expanding the corpus of questions, possibly thorough inclusion of children from different backgrounds and ages. Following this, the development of a more complete classification of questions, using a wider range of individuals to generate question categories. As it stands, the current research is an early starting point, offering insights into children's personal interests in understanding robotic agents. The format of open-ended questions is an unobtrusive means of exploring children's beliefs of animacy in robots and results suggest authentic beliefs of mixed or partial animacy in a humanoid. The current research offers support to use of measures [11,13] and research frameworks exploring mixed animacy [10] and findings consistent with theoretical understandings [4] of children's development in beliefs of animacy.

Acknowledgments. This work was supported by European Union Seventh Framework Programme (FP7-ICT-2013-10) under grant agreement no. 611971 Emily Cowles-Naja and Abigail Perkins were funded through the University of Sheffield SURE scheme.

References

1. Opfer, J.E., Gelman, S.A.: Development of the animate-inanimate distinction. In: The Wiley-Blackwell Handbook of Childhood Cognitive Development, pp. 213–238 (2010)
2. Sharkey, A., Sharkey, N.: Children, the elderly, and interactive robots. IEEE Robot. Autom. Mag. **18**, 32–38 (2011)
3. Piaget, J.: The Child's Conception of the World. Rowman & Littlefield, Lanham (1951)

4. Carey, S.: Conceptual Change in Childhood. The MIT Press, Cambridge (1985)
5. Bartneck, C., Kanda, T., Mubin, O., Al Mahmud, A.: Does the design of a robot influence its animacy and perceived intelligence? Int. J. Soc. Robot **1**, 195–204 (2009)
6. Somanader, M.C., Saylor, M.M., Levin, D.T.: Remote control and childrens understanding of robots. J. Exp. Child Psychol. **109**, 239–247 (2011)
7. Kahn Jr., P.H., Friedman, B., Perez-Granados, D.R., Freier, N.G.: Robotic pets in the lives of preschool children. Interact. Stud. **7**(3), 405–436 (2006)
8. Okita, S.Y., Schwartz, D.L.: Young children's understanding of animacy and entertainment robots. Int. J. Humanoid Robot **3**, 393–412 (2006)
9. Cameron, D., Fernando, S., Millings, A., Szollosy, M., Collins, E., Moore, R., Sharkey, A., Prescott, T.: Designing robot personalities for human-robot symbiotic interaction in an educational context. In: Lepora, N.F.F., Mura, A., Mangan, M., Verschure, P.F.M.J., Desmulliez, M., Prescott, T.J.J. (eds.) Living Machines 2016. LNCS, vol. 9793, pp. 413–417. Springer, Cham (2016). doi:10.1007/978-3-319-42417-0_39
10. Kahn, P., Reichert, A., Gary, H., Kanda, T., Ishiguro, H., Shen, S., Ruckert, J.H., Gill, B.: The new ontological category hypothesis in human-robot interaction. In: 6th ACM/IEEE International Conference on Human-Robot Interaction (HRI), pp. 159–160. IEEE (2011)
11. Cameron, D., Fernando, S., Millings, A., Moore, R., Sharkey, A., Prescott, T.: Children's age influences their perceptions of a humanoid robot as being like a person or machine. In: Wilson, S.P., Verschure, P.F.M.J., Mura, A., Prescott, T.J. (eds.) Living Machines 2015. LNCS, vol. 9222, pp. 348–353. Springer, Cham (2015). doi:10.1007/978-3-319-22979-9_34
12. Hanson, D., Baurmann, S., Riccio, T., Margolin, R., Dockins, T., Tavares, M., Carpenter, K.: Zeno: a cognitive character. AI Magazine, pp. 9–11 (2009)
13. Cameron, D., Fernando, S., Millings, A., Szollosy, M., Collins, E.C., Moore, R., Sharkey, A., Prescott, T.: Congratulations, its a boy! Bench-marking childrens perceptions of the Robokind Zeno-R25. In: 17th Proceedings of Towards Autonomous Robotic Systems, pp. 33–39 (2016). doi:10.1007/978-3-319-40379-3_4
14. Cameron, D., Fernando, S., Collins, E.C., Szollosy, M., Millings, A., Moore, R., Sharkey, A., Prescott, T.: You made him be alive: children's perceptions of animacy in a humanoid robot. In: Mangan, M., Cutkosky, M., Mura, A., Verschure, P.F.M.J., Prescott, T., Lepora, N. (eds.) Living Machines 2017. LNAI, vol. 10384 Springer, Cham (2017). doi:10.1007/978-3-319-63537-8_7
15. Kahn Jr., P.H., Kanda, T., Ishiguro, H., Freier, N.G., Severson, R.L., Gill, B.T., Ruckert, J.H., Shen, S.: Robovie, you'll have to go into the closet now: children's social and moral relationships with a humanoid robot. Dev. Psychol. **48**, 303 (2012)
16. Reidsma, D., et al.: The EASEL project: towards educational human-robot symbiotic interaction. In: Lepora, N.F.F., Mura, A., Mangan, M., Verschure, P.F.M.J., Desmulliez, M., Prescott, T.J.J. (eds.) Living Machines 2016. LNCS, vol. 9793, pp. 297–306. Springer, Cham (2016). doi:10.1007/978-3-319-42417-0_27
17. Vouloutsi, V., et al.: Towards a synthetic tutor assistant: The EASEL Project and its architecture. In: Lepora, N.F.F., Mura, A., Mangan, M., Verschure, P.F.M.J., Desmulliez, M., Prescott, T.J.J. (eds.) Living Machines 2016. LNCS, vol. 9793, pp. 353–364. Springer, Cham (2016). doi:10.1007/978-3-319-42417-0_32
18. Cameron, D., Fernando, S., Collins, E.C., Millings, A., Moore, R.K., Sharkey, A., Evers, V., Prescott, T.: Presence of life-like robot expressions influences children's enjoyment of human-robot interactions in the field. In: 4th International Symposium on New Frontiers in Human-Robot Interaction, pp. 36–41 (2015)

19. Fernando, S., Moore, R.K., Cameron, D., Collins, E.C., Millings, A., Sharkey, A.J., Prescott, T.J.: Automatic recognition of child speech for robotic applications in noisy environments. arXiv preprint arXiv:1611.02695 (2016)
20. Kahn Jr, P.H., Friedman, B., Perez-Granados, D.R., Freier, N.G.: Robotic pets in the lives of preschool children. Interact. Stud. **7**, 405–436 (2006)
21. Collins, W.A., Nurius, P.S.: Self-understanding and self-regulation in middle childhood. In: Collins, W.A. (ed.) Development During Middle Childhood: The Years From Six to Twelve. National Research Council (1984)
22. Cameron, D., Aitken, J., Collins, E., Boorman, L., Fernando, S., McAree, O., Martinez-Hernandez, U., Law, J.: Framing factors: the importance of context and the individual in understanding trust in human-robot interaction. In: 2015 IEEE/RSJ International Conference on Intelligent Robots and Systems (IROS) (2015)

aMussels: Diving and Anchoring in a New Bio-inspired Under-Actuated Robot Class for Long-Term Environmental Exploration and Monitoring

Elisa Donati[1]([✉]), Godfried J. van Vuuren[1], Katsuaki Tanaka[2],
Donato Romano[1], Thomas Schmickl[3], and Cesare Stefanini[1]

[1] The BioRobotics Institute, Scuola Superiore SantAnna (SSSA),
Viale Rinaldo Piaggio 34, 56025 Pontedera, Pisa, Italy
{e.donati,godfried.jansenvanvuuren,donato.romano,
c.stefanini}@santannapisa.it
[2] Graduate School of Science and Engineering, Waseda University,
3C201, 2-2 Wakamatsu-cho, Shinjuku-ku, Tokyo 162-8480, Japan
waseda-tanaka@toki.waseda.jp
[3] Artificial Life Lab., Department for Zoology, Karl-Franzens University Graz,
Universitätsplatz 2, 8010 Graz, Austria
thomas.schmickl@uni-graz.at

Abstract. In the last decade, the growing interest in underwater vehicles allowed significant progress in underwater robotic missions. Despite of this, underwater habitats remain one of the most challenging environments on earth due to their extreme and unpredictable conditions. The development of underwater platforms for environmental monitoring raises several challenges in terms of mobility. To monitor the huge extension of underwater habitats, vertical navigation, is needed in underwater robots. In this paper, several solutions for diving systems in a novel type of underwater robot called aMussel (artificial mussel) are investigated. These systems are: pump-based hydraulic, anchoring, a piston-type and a rolling diaphragm-based and they were compared in order to find the best trade-off between the aMussel's requirements: low-power work regime, resistance at high pressure (2.5 bar) and geometrical constraints. The solution that best meets all the requirements is the rolling diaphragm-based system, ensuring high performance and high reliability, with low maintenance and environmental impact and an acceptable low power consumption, suggesting this to be the best way to build such under-actuated and long-term running underwater robots.

Keywords: Underwater robotics · Swarm robotics · Autonomous robots

Electronic supplementary material The online version of this chapter (doi:10.1007/978-3-319-64107-2_24) contains supplementary material, which is available to authorized users.

Y. Gao et al. (Eds.): TAROS 2017, LNAI 10454, pp. 300–314, 2017.
DOI: 10.1007/978-3-319-64107-2_24

1   Introduction

Underwater habitats are among the most challenging places on the Earth due
to their unpredictable conditions. At the same time they are very interesting
for our society thanks to their richness of resources, their climate and ecological
equilibrium. Currently, oceanic missions involve 'Remotely Operated Vehicles'
(ROVs) and 'Autonomous Underwater Vehicles' (AUVs) equipped with multiple
long-range sensors and communication systems. A ROV is a tethered underwater mobile device and it is linked to a host ship by a series of cables. AUVs are
untethered mobile platforms which have actuators, sensors, and on-board intelligence to successfully complete underwater tasks. An AUV is free to explore
large spaces of the environment without supervision and constraints related to
the distance with the ship. One of the key aspects of these vehicles is their
autonomous mobility. For 2D navigation, the most common form of propulsion
are propellers. For depth movements both propellers and a variable buoyancy can
be used. Vertical displacement in underwater vehicles can be categorized in the
following configurations [1]: (i) piston type ballast tank, (ii) hydraulic pump,
(iii) diaphragm-based system, and (iv) direct thrust systems. The first three
methods are static diving systems, while the last concept is a dynamic configuration. In the static method, the robots change their density by ingesting/ejecting
water. The piston ballast tank is one of the most used systems. It consists of
a piston that moves in a cylinder, with one end in contact with water. When
retreating, the piston draws water into the ballast tank causing the immersion.
When advancing, the piston pushes water out of the tank, emptying it and causing the AUV to surface. An example of robot with piston system is the Guanay
II [2]. This method was chosen because Guanay is an AUV developed for measuring oceanographic variables, in fact, thanks to piston system it can measure
without generating perturbations in the environment. Other examples of piston
tank systems are also used in [3,4]. A hydraulic pump system is similar to the
piston one, except for a built-in water reservoir inside of the shell. Pump control
allows the pumping of water in/out of the reservoir [5], changing the density
of the AUV. In the previously mentioned two systems the diving principle is to
change the mass of the device to change its average density. An opposite method
is represented by the diaphragm-based system where the robot changes its volume in order to affect its average density. This working principle is inspired by
the swim bladder of fish where a fish can quickly adjust its average density relative to the density of its surrounding water body by changing the volume of the
swim bladder. [6] is one of the most successful buoyancy system and two other
implementations of this diving system can be found in the ANGELS robots [7]
and the Jeff robots [8], developed within the CoCoRo project [9]. These systems
are composed of an actuation system connected to the rolling diaphragm which,
when moves, produces the displacement of the diaphragm, thus modifying the
volume of the robot. Propeller-based systems are also widely used in underwater
vehicles, by using multiple propeller thrust can be provided in both directions
and good maneuverability can be achieved. The AUV type 'Serafina' [10] is an
AUV robot which moves horizontally and vertically by means of such propellers.

Another example is the 'AMOUR' [11], which has a buoyancy system that is composed of propellers in combination with a buoyancy control module. Finally, the 'Monsun II' system [12] is a team of AUVs aimed for environmental monitoring. The robots have four propellers mounted in each of the four fins for vertical displacement.

Recently, some researchers tried to emulate diving system inspired by whales [13]. This method eliminates the presence of a ballast by using paraffin wax, instead of spermaceti oil as in the animal. By heating and cooling the wax it is possible to change the volume, and therefore, the average density of the robot.

In this article we present a novel type of AUV for underwater long-term in-place monitoring of underwater environments that aims for application of large swarms of such units. This AUV type is an artificial mussel (called 'aMussel'): It has limited actuation and a strong but reversible anchoring device. It sits most of the time on the ground (like a mussel) and it surfaces only to re-charge and to perform long-range communication via radio signals to human operators or other autonomous surface devices. The aim of this article is to study which is the best solution for a diving system needed on such devices by investigating several methods presented in literature on this specific novel platform and type of application. Four different static diving systems will be presented and compared in order to find the best trade-off solution among the aMussels' requirements.

The 'aMussel' is one robotic species developed in the subCULTron project, which aims to control a distributed information-processing and actuation system consisting of up to 150 autonomous robots for weeks in the channels of Venice. There will be three classes of bio-inspired robotic agents which interact and monitor the Venetian water (and underwater) habitats: artificial mussels, 'aMussels', artificial fish, 'aFish', and artificial lilypads, 'aPads' (Fig. 1).

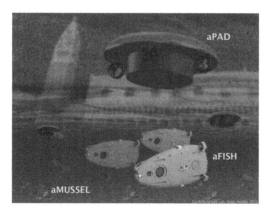

Fig. 1. aMussels form subcultures and adapt by evolutionary adaptation to the local habitat. aFish carry behavioural traits between those subcultures. aPads provide global information used for local fitness evaluation of the whole swarm.

One key concept that we follow in the subCULTron project is the new strategy of 'vegarization', which is that actively maneuvering robots aFish will move into new habitats and conquer those by trigger aPads to distribute many cheap autonomous devices (aMussels) on the seabed which then support them in coping with the new habitat and which help them by enhancing their efficiency. These aMussels are interacting by localized underwater communication and act, besides being a sensor-network, as beacons, and as a shared collective memory for the aFish. This form of a 'collective memory' allows asynchronous information exchange between several aFish and can hold specific localized fractions of a map that is built up and updated collectively over time. With such a supporting infrastructure, the actively moving aFish robots can, for example, lay down a virtual "pheromone trail" on the seabed without doing any ecological harm and behave like a group of ants in foraging and exploration trips. As the mission progresses, the network of aMussels has to reconfigure and to adapt, e.g. by selective drifting in times of favorable water currents [14]. At the end of the mission, in order to protect the environment, all these devices have to remove themselves from the habitat, e.g. by going back to the surface for being collected there. Repeated surfacing also allows for recharging via autonomous surface platforms or solar panels in order to allow long-term operation of this underwater 'smart infrastructure'.

In this work at hand we focus on the aMussel robot type and its diving and surfacing technology. The variability of depth ranges from 15 m to less than 1 m in a small area. The paper is organized as follows: Sect. 2 starts with an overview of the robotic platform and its tasks. The different diving mechanism are presented and compared in Sect. 3. Section 4 describes the final optimized prototype and, finally, Sect. 5 concludes with some proposals for future works.

2 The aMussels

The aMussel design is a novel concept of autonomous and cooperative underwater sensor/cognitive robotic platform. The swarm of aMussels is composed of 100–120 elements, that can dive up to 15 m. They sit mostly on the ground, thus they have limited actuation and strong but reversible anchoring devices. The aMussel has a binary location in the sea: it is more than 99% of the time either on the surface or on the bottom of the seabed, with only a short, but important, transitional diving phase in between. On the seabed the aMussels are distributed in the habitat in way they collect data for a long period of time and communicate each others. In order to work on the seabed for long time without charging, the aMussels are able to harvest energy by converting chemical energy in electric energy by means of fuel cells. This keeps them running for a long time. Their function is a passive and energy-free one, in order to minimize the units power requirements.

An aMussel has a cylindrical shape, manufactured from Poly-methyl methacrylate (PMMA). The cylindrical shape was chosen because it resists to the outside pressure deformation, performs well in water currents and is not prone to be accidentally caught in underwater obstacles (e.g., seagras or debris). Additionally, the bio-inspired electric sense system which is implemented on those robots for local underwater sensing and communication works best when it is implemented in such symmetrical geometric shapes. The used material was also chosen for its physical and ecological properties: It is durable in salt water, it resists well to fouling and it is transparent. Transparency is important because aMussels are equipped with a camera inside the body and blue-light LEDs for near-range communication.

As mentioned above, each unit is provided with short- and medium-range underwater communication plus a long-range surface communication system. A short-range underwater communication system that operates well in murky and loud underwater habitats is provided to the robots by the 'electric sense' system, following a bio-inspired approach [15]. This system can be used for robot-to-robot communication as well as for obstacle sensing. The range of this sense is about one body length in navigation and three times this range during communication. As a backup solution in non-murky waters, blue-light LEDs and receptors are included for the case of electric sense failure [16] and as a simpler means of communication wherever it is possible. The aMussel AUVs have a rich set of environmental monitoring sensors onboard: electric sense, pressure, temperature, turbidity, light, LEDs for monitoring the internal state of the robot, plus a simple camera. In addition, long range communication is also present and it is composed by a GPS, GSM and bluetooth technologies, however those only are operational when the aMussel is surfaced. In order to use those long-range communication and orientation systems aMussels can actively dive and surface, what allows them also to recharge autonomously. The docking and charging unit is produced in medium-density polyethylene (MDPE) and consists of three charging coils. The charging method is wireless and the current of recharging is around 300 mA/h per coil. The battery consists of a single Li-Po battery at 3.7 V@5000 mA/h. Another Li-Po battery of 3.7 V@850 mA/h is present in the robots for emergency purposes. Li-Po batteries are a subclass of the Lithium batteries with the additional advantage that they provide the highest specific energy and energy density in a thin form factory, which is of particular interest in mobile applications. The electronic part is composed of a custom low-power board for controlling motors and sensors that is produced by Cybertronica UG (Stuttgart, Germany) and a rasberyPi for monitoring and computer vision.

3   Diving Systems

In this section four different solutions for the vertical motion of aMussels will be investigated and compared, in order to identify the one that best meets the AUV requirements. In all proposed solutions the aMussel preserves the same sensors and communication skills and the same general shape, whereas the height, weight and arrangement of internal components changes among them.

The aMussel is designed in order to respect four main requirements: working depth, low-power regime, geometrical constraints and affordable cost. In more detail:

- The aMussels are designed to work in the Venice lagoon where the maximum depth is 15 m with an external pressure of 2.5 bar.
- They are mostly under a low-energy consumption regime and optimized sleep modes to maximize their lifetime, allowing them to survive for days or even weeks in the water. Long-lasting experimental sessions are ensured by custom high efficiency solutions for diving system and docking capability. During the period the robot stays at the seabed the most power-consuming components are for monitoring the surrounding, especially the camera. Generally, the robots are most of the time in sleeping mode and wake up either by a signal of other robots or after a pre-defined interval. The average power requirement in normal mode is around 100 mA compared to 100 μA in sleep mode. The amount of power required for the diving system is not a-priori defined but it should be as small as possible. The diving component is active only twice between two charging phases: after charging to immerse the robot and before charging when the robot go back to the surface.
- The mechanism should be compact to limit the robot dimensions, with a diameter of the shell of 120 mm and maximum height (of the whole robot) of approx. 600 mm. To avoid the robot from loosing the equilibrium and for creating momentum, the heavy parts of the diving system should be designed in the bottom part of the body. An additional weight can be also included to ensure the robot's stability.
- The design should aim for affordable costs, what is essential to allow experiments with a large swarm of AUVs (100–120 robots). Thus, the cost for the diving system was ceiled at ∼500€.

3.1 Pump-Based Hydraulic System

The first method which we explored was the pump-based design, one of the most common used methods for this task described in literature. The designed hydraulic pumping system (Fig. 2) uses an internal reservoir of hydraulic fluid (a), two pumps for displacing water (b) and two solenoid actuated valves (c). Control of the valves and the pump for the hydraulic fluid allows the fluid to flow in and out of the water chamber, so that the surrounding water can be pumped in and out. The neutral position is with the top of the robot outside the water. The robot moves vertically because the weight changes as the water enters, increasing therefore its density.

The solenoid actuated valves are mono-directional, and this required to use two valves and two connected pumps. They are active in alternate phase, one is for the immersion and one for the surfacing, that means, when one is open the other one is closed. During the immersion, one pump opens and the water is pumped into the chamber. The valve closes when the pressure inside the chamber reaches at the same value as the outside pressure. This control is performed

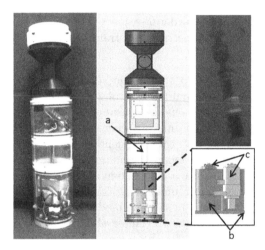

Fig. 2. CAD and picture of an aMussel with a hydraulic system. On the CAD the chamber (a) is shown while the box highlights the arrangement of the pumps (b) and valves (c).

by using two pressure sensors, one inside of the chamber and one outside of the shell. In order to surface, the pressure needed is greater than 2.5 bar. Commercial pumps that can provide such pressure, required a power supply of 12 V in our analysis. The nominal voltage of the aMussel is maximum 4.2 V, therefore, it is necessary to have an additional boost board. Adding an additional board in each robot increases the price and this has to be avoided. In fact, this placed this method outside of our window of acceptance, as it is given by our requirements. Tests in water showed an average speed of diving (considering the entire cycle immersion+surfacing) around 1 m/s. The robot takes 30 s for the entire cycle with this diving mechanism, consuming an average current of approx. 1.3 A.

3.2   Anchoring System

This method is performed using a pinch valve with an anchor. Compared to the previous system, here only one valve is required. The system can be considered to be a "passive method", where the water goes in and out for the different outside pressure. Therefore, the price can be considerably reduced. Figure 3 depicts this diving system: It is composed of a water chamber (a) for the variable diving system, an actuation system (b), the external anchor (c) and a pinch valve (inside d). The water chamber has diameter of 120 mm and height of 90 mm, allowing to collect and eject around 0.850 g of water. The water chamber (a) has an internal compartment to connect the sensor wires from the top (e) to the electronic boards. The system of releasing and recovering is actuated by a DC gear motor (Fig. 3 framed picture a), gear ratio 290:1 b, rated load 200 mNm, rated load speed 15 rpm (Precision Microdrives, 225-204) and a reel d with a nylon wire of 15 m of length, attached to the external lead weight (1.1 kg). The reel, located in the wet chamber, is actuated by means of a magnetic coupling. The magnetic coupling allows transmitting torque from the motor to the reel without any mechanical connection ensuring complete waterproofing [8]. Each half of the magnetic coupling consists of eight cylindrical N50 neodymium magnets with height and diameter of 5 mm and axial magnetization e. The magnets are arranged in a circular path (diameter of 16 mm) with alternating magnetization. When the dry part of the magnetic coupling rotates axially with respect to the reel a torque is generated.

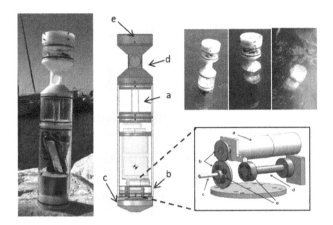

Fig. 3. The aMussel with anchoring system: (a) water chamber, (b) valve-anchoring actuation system, (c) lead weight, (d) docking system, and (e) top with sensors. In the right down box an exploded view of the main mechanics components of magnetic coupling system is shown: a. motor, b. gearbox, c. support gear, d. reel, e. internal and external magnets.

The motor has a torque of 200 mNm and, in an ideal situation, without losses due to friction, the reel can produce a force of 66.68 N. In the worst case, when a 15 m length of wire is wound around the reel, it produces a wire diameter of 18 mm, with a resulting force of around 29.63 N. Calculating in a 50% loss of force the remaining force equates to 1.51 kg. Therefore, the weight of the anchor is within the working range of the system.

Experimental tests have been performed to understand the real force transmitted by the magnetic coupling by using a ±10 kN load cell connected to a 4464 Instron machine. Figure 4 shows the result with increasing the reel diameter. To avoid the detachment of magnetic coupling, the experiment shows that a force less than 10.6 N must be applied. The power consumption is not high, the actuation required maximum 0.25 A with 4.2 V, but considering the losses in friction and in the magnetic coupling the performances are poor. The average velocity of releasing and recovering of the weight corresponds to the time of the robot of surfacing and diving. This value was measured to be around 1 m/s.

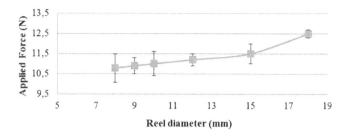

Fig. 4. The graph shows the average force required to disconnect the magnetic coupling, versus the diameter of the reel. The error bar is the standard deviation.

3.3 Piston-Based System

The piston ballast tank is one of the most common diving methods applied in submarines. Figure 5 shows the components for the one designed for the aMussel: cylinder and a movable piston (a), that works as a large syringe pump, a motor (Precision Microdrives^{TM} 225-204) (b) and a support (c) where the piston moves through. The system uses a telescopic mechanism that required large space for passing through a long lead screw. The piston is implemented from a syringe. The inner part is reinforced with white polyoxymethylene (POM) to sustain the pressure. The external part of the syringe is embedded inside a block of POM, which provides the function of weight to ensure stability against water current. The syringe is connected with a nut which is fixed to the lead screw, connected

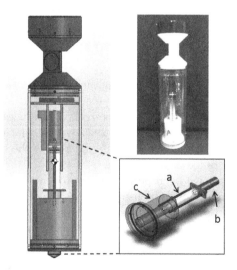

Fig. 5. aMussel with a piston-based system, CAD drawing and photo of a prototype. In the right lower box (a) the syringe, (b) the motor and (c) the support are highlighted.

to the motor. One side of the syringe is connected to the surrounding water, and its movement sucks water in or pushes it out. The robot is normally neutrally buoyant and when the syringe moves inside, the water fills the gap, negative buoyancy is achieved, therefore, the AUV starts to descend. Conversely, when the tank is emptied, the AUV is positively buoyant, so it ascends. The length of the lead screw depends on the amount of water needed to become negative buoyant, given the diameter of the syringe. This value is equivalent to 55 ml of water (d = 26.5 mm and h = 100 mm). The motor provides a sufficient torque to the syringe, in order to win the external pressure of the water at 15 m deep, that is, 2.5 bar. Given the dimension of the syringe, and the area in contact with water, the force to escape is around 165 N. Using the maximum continuous torque the transmitted force to the syringe is: $F = \frac{T2\pi\eta}{p}$ where T is the torque of the motor, η the is the efficiency and p the spindle lead (pitch). The force transmitted by the motor to the screw is around 217 N, thus, it is enough for the scope. The speed of rotation is $v = \frac{np}{60}$ where n is the speed of the motor and the resulting speed is around 22.5 mm/min. Therefore, to complete the travel of the screw, it requires 4.5 min. We measured the same time period during in-water experiments for the AUV to move a vertical distance of 15 m. The power consumption of the system is around 1 A at 4.2 V.

The performance of the piston-based system has been experimentally measured in static conditions. During those tests, voltages from 3.3 V to 5 V with 0.2 V steps were applied to the DC motors. Current was recorded as well as the force of the syringe (measured with a ±10 kN load cell connected to a 4464 Instron machine). The force generated by the syringe as a function of the overall electrical power consumption is shown in Fig. 6.

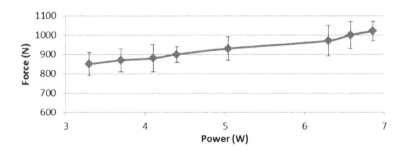

Fig. 6. Average force generated by the syringe, versus the electric power consumption. The error bars indicate standard deviations.

3.4 Rolling Diaphragm-Based System

This type of buoyancy system apparatus includes a rolling diaphragm and a linear driving mechanism. The rolling diaphragm, attached to the bottom of the platform, is pushed and pulled by actuating the linear driving mechanism. This behaviour increases/decreases the volume and density of the platform, thus changing its depth under water. The volume that can be changed within the platform is such as to push the head above the water surface when floating, allowing for communication. A lead screw is used as a linear mechanism since its design can produce large force to overcome the high pressures at depth. Indeed, when the robot is 15 m under the sea, the mechanism requires 0.75 kN to push against the water and surface. In order to operate the mechanism within a low powered electrical system, multiple motors (i.e. 3) are used, as a novel method, to rotate a driving nut. The powerful motor that can be operated at the low voltage was selected for the main actuator of the buoyancy system. Metal gear motor that was produced by Pololu is one of the most high-powered motor. This type of design produces a very high torque and reduces the actuation time of the driving mechanism. This gear motor consists of a high-power, 6 V brushed DC motor combined with a 34:1 metal spur gearbox with 280 rpm and 550 mA (max) free-run. A geared module was designed for stabilizing the leadscrew. The nut connector couples the two outer nuts with the central spur gear. The lower nut and the central spur gear are directly fastened to the nut connector whereas the upper nut is connected via the shaft collar. The driving mechanism, especially the lead screw, becomes more stable by using two nuts instead of one. The performance of the rolling diaphragm-based system has been experimentally measured in static conditions. During the test, the voltage was fixed at 4.2 V, to simulate the battery voltage, and the limited current ranged from 0.5 A to 3 A. The force of the system was measured with a ± 10 kN load cell connected to a 4464 Instron machine. The force generated by the system as a function of the current is shown in Fig. 7. Experiments similar to the one of Fig. 6 were performed, and they showed the system reached 1 kN for each value of power.

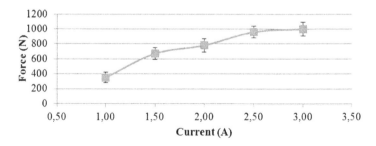

Fig. 7. Average force generated by the rolling diaphragm-based system, versus the current. The error bars indicate standard deviations.

Figure 8 depicts the cross-sectional view of the buoyancy system. The central spur gear is rotated by three spur gears connected to the motors. The module moves the screw up and down pushing the lead screw. Table 1 summarized the experimental results on the four diving mechanisms. Both for the average speed and average diving time it was considered the average of the diving and surfacing phases.

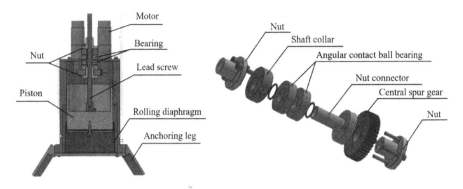

Fig. 8. Overview of buoyancy system and components of the geared module.

Table 1. Performances comparison

	Average speed	Average diving time	Power consumption
Pump	1 m/s	30 s	12 V@1.3 A
Anchoring	1 m/s	30 s	4.2 V@0.25 A
Piston	0.06 m/s	540 s	4.2 V@1 A
RD	0.35 m/s	43 s	4.2 V@1.4 A

4   Final Optimized Prototype

Table 2 shows the main features take in consideration during the design of the diving system. Environmental Impact is a definition related to amount of noise and perturation produced by the robot in water during diving. Noise and water perturances can disturb and/or scare the animals in the environment or modify the environmental conditions, making not trustworthy the measurements performed. Reliability is the probability of mechanical failure performances over a specified task, under specified environmental conditions. Maintenance is the activities required to conserve as nearly as possible the original condition. Performance/Energy budget takes in consideration the speed of the diving and the depth considering the amount of power required by the system. Each of these parameters are quantified in stars *, from low, one * to high three ***. Pump-based system has a really low environmental impact, the noise produced is low and the water pumped in and out does not produce water perturbances. To the contrary, the anchoring system can modify the animals behaviour because of the anchor wire, they can be scared and they can move away. The piston-based system produces a little noise and a small water perturbance while the Rolling diaphragm system is silent and without creating water interferences. The reliability is quite high for all the systems, except for the anchoring system, in fact the wire can get stuck somewhere and it can detach the magnetic coupling. Finally, all the systems with water chamber require maintenance.

Table 2. Parameters of selection of the diving system.

	Pump	Anchoring	Piston	RD
Environmental impact	*	***	**	*
Reliability	**	*	**	***
Maintenance	**	**	**	*
Performance/Energy budget	*	*	*	**
Cost	**	*	**	***

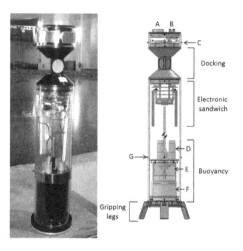

Fig. 9. aMussel CAD: A = Acoustics, B = Turbidity sensor, C = E-sense receivers, D = Motors, E = Piston, F = Rolling diaphragm, G = E-sense emitters.

Considering that all the system proposed are able designed to reach 15 m in depth the decision of the final solution was based on the other parameters of Table 2. Table 1 shows the performances of the four system: piston and anchoring based systems are faster than the others two. The best trade-off between all the required features is the diaphragm-based system, see Fig. 9. Even if it is expensive, the expected maintenance is minimal. It is extremely reliable and there is no environmental impact expected. Additionally, the system is silent, there are no internal parts in contact with water and the overall performance is very high, considering the power consumption. In the anchoring system the cost of production is low but the system is not reliable and the wire for the anchoring can disturb the surrounding environment and prevent swarm applications as wires might interact and might intertwine, just like the cables of ROVs would likely do in a swarm application. The hydraulic system requires an additional board and finally, the piston approach was rejected because its performance and reliability is lower and the environmental impact is higher than with the diaphragm approach, requiring, at the same time, more maintenance. The final optimized prototype is shown in Fig. 9, the robot has an overall diameter of

120 mm, and an overall height of 630 mm. The bottom part of the platform has three gripping legs/anchoring legs that work simultaneously with the buoyancy system. The anchoring legs are capable of grasping different substrates when the platform reaches the sea floor. An additional vibrating motor will also be added to assists the anchoring legs in the initial process of piercing various substrates.

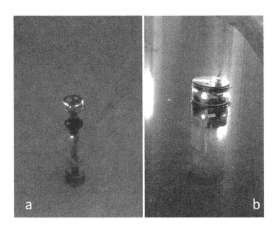

Fig. 10. Pictures from experiments. (a) shows an aMussel on the seabed and (b) an aMussel at the surface.

Several tests (Fig. 10) were performed with this final prototype of the aMussel to measure its performance and with other robot types of the subCULTron project. Tests of the rolling diaphragm-based system showed that the robot is able to dive and surface, with the an average speed of 0.35 m/s.

5   Conclusion

This paper has investigated different methods for diving systems of aMussels, a miniature AUV that has been conceived to perform swarm experiments open underwater environments. Four diving mechanisms were considered and our conclusion was that the rolling diaphragm-based system was the best option considering performance, power consumption, environmental impact, reliability, cost and suitability for multi-robot swarm systems. Indeed, this method is extremely reliable and there is no environmental impact, maintenance is almost not required, and the performance metrics are very high considering the power consumption. Moreover, compared to conventional sealing solutions, it has the advantage to be almost frictionless and watertight.

Future work mainly involves the implementation of cognition- and awareness-generating algorithms in order to perform swarm experiments in applications of many such AUVs in an heterogeneous swarm setting.

Acknowledgment. This work was supported by the European Union, by funding the Project: EU H2020 FET-Proactive project 'subCULTron', no. 640967.

References

1. Watson, S.A., Green, P.N.: Propulsion systems for micro-autonomous underwater vehicles (AUVs). In: 2010 IEEE Conference on Robotics Automation and Mechatronics (RAM), pp. 435–440 (2010)
2. Masmitj, I., Gonzlez, J., Gomriz, S.: Buoyancy model for Guanay II AUV. In: OCEANS 2014, Taipei, pp. 1–7 (2014)
3. Sumantr, B., Karsiti, M.N., Agustiawan, H.: Development of variable ballast mechanism for depth positioning of spherical URV. In: International Symposium on Information Technology, ITSim 2008, vol. 4, pp. 1–6 (2008)
4. Minh-Thuan, L., Truong-Thinh, N., Ngoc-Phuong, N.: Study of artificial fish bladder system for robot fish. In: 2011 IEEE International Conference on Robotics and Biomimetics (ROBIO), pp. 2126–2130 (2011)
5. Makrodimitris, M., Aliprantis, I., Papadopoulos, E.: Design and implementation of a low cost, pump-based, depth control of a small robotic fish. In: 2014 IEEE/RSJ International Conference on Intelligent Robots and Systems (IROS 2014), pp. 1127–1132 (2014)
6. http://www.argo.net/
7. Mintchev, S., Stefanini, C., Girin, A., Marrazza, S., Orofino, S., Lebastard, V., Manfredi, L., Dario, P., Boyer, F.: An underwater reconfigurable robot with bioinspired electric sense. In: 2012 IEEE International Conference on Robotics and Automation (ICRA), pp. 1149–1154 (2012)
8. Mintchev, S., Donati, E., Marrazza, S., Stefanini, C.: Mechatronic design of a miniature underwater robot for swarm operations. In: 2014 IEEE International Conference on Robotics and Automation (ICRA), pp. 2938–2943 (2014)
9. Schmickl, T., Thenius, R., Möslinger, C., Timmis, J., Tyrrell, A., Read, M., et al.: CoCoRo-the self-aware underwater swarm. In: 2011 Fifth IEEE Conference on Self-Adaptive and Self-Organizing Systems Workshops (SASOW), pp. 120–126 (2011)
10. Kalantar, S., Zimmer, U.R.: Contour shaped formation control for autonomous underwater vehicles using canonical shape descriptors and deformable models. In: MTTS/IEEE TECHNO-OCEANS 2004, vol. 1, pp. 296–307 (2004)
11. Vasilescu, I., Detweiler, C., Doniec, M., Gurdan, D., Sosnowski, S., Stumpf, J., Rus, D.: Amour V: a hovering energy efficient underwater robot capable of dynamic payloads. Int. J. Robot. Res. **29**(5), 547–570 (2010)
12. Osterloh, C., Pionteck, T., Maehle, E.: MONSUN II: a small and inexpensive AUV for underwater swarms. In: 7th German Conference on Robotics; Proceedings of ROBOTIK 2012, pp. 1–6 (2012)
13. Inoue, T., Shibuya, K., Nagano, A.: Underwater robot with a buoyancy control system based on the spermaceti oil hypothesis development of the depth control system. In: 2010 IEEE/RSJ International Conference on Intelligent Robots and Systems (IROS), pp. 1102–1107 (2010)
14. Varughese, J.C., Thenius, R., Wotawa, F., Schmickl, T.: FSTaxis algorithm: bioinspired emergent gradient taxis. In: Proceedings of the Fifteenth International Conference on the Synthesis and Simulation of Living Systems. MIT Press (2016). http://dx.doi.org/10.7551/978-0-262-33936-0-ch055. ISBN:9780262339360
15. Boyer, F., Lebastard, V., Chevallereau, C., Servagent, N.: Underwater reflex navigation in confined environment based on electric sense. IEEE Trans. Robot. **29**(4), 945–956 (2013)
16. Schill, F., Zimmer, U.R., Trumpf, J.: Visible spectrum optical communication and distance sensing for underwater applications. In: Proceedings of ACRA, pp. 1–8 (2004)

Autonomous Vehicle Decision-Making: Should We Be Bio-inspired?

Christopher M. Harris[✉]

School of Psychology, Centre for Robotics and Neural Systems,
Plymouth University, Plymouth, Devon PL4 8AA, UK
cmharris@plymouth.ac.uk

Abstract. On our crowded roads, drivers must compete for space but cooperate to avoid occupying the same space at the same time. Decision-making is strategic and requires mutual understanding of other's choices. Fully autonomous vehicles (AVs) will need risk management software to make these types strategic decisions without human arbitration. Accidents will occur, and what constitutes rational and 'safe' decisions will be scrutinized by the legal system. It is far from clear how AV-Human and AV-AV interactions should be managed. Game Theory provides a framework for analyzing mutual 'games' with 2 or more players. It assumes that players mutually optimize their outcomes according to Nash equilibria (NE), but do humans follow Nash equilibria in Human-Human interactions? We implemented simple two-player competitive games to see whether people played rationally according to Nash equilibria. On each of 100 trials, each player was instructed to maximise their reward by pressing one of three buttons labelled "4", "6", and "12", without knowing the other players choice. If players pressed different buttons, they received a reward of 4, 6, or 12 points accordingly. If players pressed the same button, the reward was reduced depending on the game type. Results showed that players did not follow NE, but played a probabilistic game that included the "4" button, even though pressing this button is always suboptimal. We suggest that this may be an evolutionary strategy, but it clearly shows that people do not follow the 'rational' Nash strategy. It seems that AV-human interactions will be probabilistic. In AV-AV interactions, software may be playing itself, and may also require probabilistic optimal evolutionary-type strategies. We doubt that the full implications of autonomous decision-making have been fully worked out. Whether probabilistic decisions will tolerated legally and actuarially is doubtful. One way to avoid them would be to allow regulated AV-AV communications, and force software decisions to be deterministic according to some protocol. However, AV-Human interactions seem likely to remain problematic.

Keywords: Rationality · Decision making · Nash equilibrium · Reward · Matching law · Autonomous agents · Evolutionary game theory

© Springer International Publishing AG 2017
Y. Gao et al. (Eds.): TAROS 2017, LNAI 10454, pp. 315–324, 2017.
DOI: 10.1007/978-3-319-64107-2_25

1   Introduction

We are on the cusp of a brave new world of fully autonomous robots including drones, missiles, ships, cars, and software robots. The future is difficult to predict, but driverless cars appear to be imminent and very much in the public eye. Hardly a month goes by without a car manufacturer or a software enterprise announcing their intention to develop an autonomous vehicle (cars) (AV). Initially, AVs will be semi-autonomous, but as technical and legislative issues are sorted out, AVs will become fully autonomous probably in 2020s. The commercial market is enormous with billions of AVs at stake, and competition among manufacturers will be fierce.

At the heart of a fully autonomous agent is the necessity to make decisions autonomously without direct arbitration by a human controller. Decision will be in real-time and have real life consequences, not only economically (cost, energy consumption, time, etc.) but also in terms of human injury. There are two broad categories of decisions: *non-strategic* and *strategic* games. In non-strategic games (sometimes called 'games against nature'), the agent makes a decision based on expected probabilities of outcomes. Any other agents are assumed to act independently. The traditional approach is to 'rationally' choose deterministically the alternative that optimises some decision criterion, such as maximising expected utility or payoff, or minimising maximum loss, etc. Non-strategic decision-making is dominant in low-density traffic where encounters with other vehicles are infrequent. The goal is to navigate the road, avoid obstacles, stop at traffic lights, and generally obey the rules of driving. There is a trade-off between journey time, safety, and risks from violating rules.

In strategic games, a decision needs to take into account the decisions of other agents (human or robot) who simultaneously make decisions based on the agent's expected decision. Such decisions are dominant in high-density traffic where there is contention for road space (slots in a moving queue). Such competition must be tempered with some degree of cooperation amongst drivers to avoid having (or causing) and 'accident'. Competition is most fierce when joining a queue at roundabouts, junctions, slip roads, and lane changes. Competition for road space lead to other frequency effects. A particular route may be the fastest and optimal, but if all drivers select the same route, it may become the slowest and suboptimal. Waiting at re-fuelling (re-charging) stations increases with the number of vehicles. Traditionally, analysis of strategic games comes under the rubric of "Game Theory", where agents are assumed to be rational and fully informed. The optimal decisions attempt to maximise individual gains in a stable way by finding Nash Equilibria (NE), which are the choices for which all agents cannot improve their outcomes (but not necessarily Pareto optimal). Solutions to strategic games may be deterministic, but may also be probabilistic ('mixed strategies'). Probabilistic plays are particularly relevant and intriguing. Should an AV manufacturer program random plays, and if so, how will the legal courts interpret liability in the event of an unlucky outcome?

How to program risk management in an AV is far from clear. Initially, most interactions will be between AVs and human drivers (AV-H interactions). The problem for the AV manufacturer is to be able predict the decisions of human decision-makers contingent on the AV decision options. Do humans follow Nash equilibria? Evidence, based mostly on the prisoner's dilemma game and the ultimatum game, is mixed. Sone humans tend to be cooperative and do not follow NE, others are more individual and do follow NE. There is also considerable complication in interpreting results from games that are played more than once against the same 'opponent' (iterative games), as opposed to one-shot games. AV-H interactions are one-shot, although similar scenarios may arise with different opponents.

As AVs proliferate, interactions will become increasingly between AVs (AV-AV interactions). AVs with the same manufacturer (model) and software will presumably inherit the same decision making strategy leading to the strange situation where a decision strategy will effectively play itself – reminiscent of evolutionary game theory, where members of a species inherit the same strategy [1].

Nature has been making strategic decisions for eons via natural selection, and one wonders whether we could learn from her. An example is foraging where the gain from competition for resources decreases with number of competitors due to sharing or fighting. This is a simple frequency dependent game. When there are alternative food sources, animals distribute themselves probabilistically across the sources rather than all competing for the same source – called the matching law (ML) [2]. Thus, Nature seems to prefer a probabilistic solution. Some have argued that the ML is an evolutionary stable equilibrium strategy [3–6]. We are not aware of any game-theoretic studies on how humans compete for limited resources. We therefore set up a simple experiment to see how pairs of humans make Game Theoretic decisions in a simulated competition. Of course driving is much more complicated, but such games are simple and directly address the question of whether humans compete or cooperate and make deterministic or probabilistic decisions?

2   Implementation of Foraging Games

We implemented the foraging games in the following way. Two computers were synchronized via Ethernet. On each computer monitor, three buttons were displayed labelled "4", "6", and "12". On each trial, each player was instructed to choose a button to press (via a mouse). If players pressed different buttons they received the corresponding reward of, 4, 6, or 12 points. If both players pressed the same button (a clash), the reward was reduced depending on the type of game, which we call 'SPLIT' and 'ZERO'. Once both players had made a choice, the trial ended, and each player's running total of points was incremented and displayed to the player. Each player could only see their own display and their own total points – not the other player's points. The game was iterated over 100 trials. Eighty psychology undergraduate students were recruited, and randomly allocated to 40 pairs. Each pair played only once, either the SPLIT or ZERO game. The game type was randomly determined at the beginning of the game resulting in 21 SPLIT games and 19 ZERO games.

In the SPLIT game, when players clashed their reward was reduced by a half, receiving 2, 3, or 6 points depending on which button was pressed. Thus a clash is moderately expensive (e.g. sharing food, reduced journey time when same route is chosen). The payoff bimatrix is shown in Table 1. As can be seen for Player A, the maximum gain is maximised by choosing button 12 for any strategy by Player B.

Table 1. Top: Bimatrices of games. Bottom: Nash equilibria.

SPLIT		Player B		
		12	6	4
Player A	12	**(6, 6)**	(12,6)	(12,4)
	6	(6,12)	(3, 3)	(6, 4)
	4	(4,12)	(4, 6)	(2, 2)

ZERO		Player B		
		12	6	4
Player A	12	(0,0)	**(12,6)**	(12,4)
	6	**(6,12)**	(0,0)	(6,4)
	4	(4,12)	(4,6)	(0,0)

Player A				Player B			
4	6	12	PO	4	6	12	PO
0	0	1	12	0	1	0	6
0	1	0	6	0	0	1	12
0	0	1	6	0	0	1	6

Player A				Player B			
4	6	12	PO	4	6	12	PO
0	0	1	12	0	1	0	6
0	1	0	6	0	0	1	12
0	1/3	2/3	6	1/2	0	1/2	4
1/2	0	1/2	4	0	1/3	2/3	6
0	1/3	2/3	4	0	1/3	2/3	4

Similarly, for Player B, the maximum is also to choose 12 (the game is symmetric). Thus, the NE is [12, 12] with payoff (6, 6), which is also Pareto efficient. There are, however, two addition NE: when player A plays 6 and player B plays 12 [6, 12]; and vice versa: Player A plays 12 and player B plays 6 [12, 6]. Clearly, if player B never wavers from the 12 play, player A could also play 6 with same result. If player B does waver from the 12 play, then player A should not play 6, but only 12. It is also obvious that Nash players should never press the 4 button.

In the ZERO game, players received no reward when they pressed the same button. Thus, a clash is very expensive (e.g. fighting and being disabled, choosing the same traffic slot and crashing). In this case there is no dominant strategy but two pure NE at [6, 12] and [12, 6], which are contentious. Both playing 12 at [12, 12] is no longer optimal. There are also 3 additional mixed strategies (probabilistic) that are NE.

3   Results

In both game types (SPLIT and ZERO), the sequential pattern of button presses were highly variable across games (Fig. 1). Within a game, some players were highly variable and seemed to press all three buttons in a haphazard way (Fig. 1a), but others were much more consistent (Fig. 1b) with some pressing the "12" button on almost every trial. Across all games, a player's button press was significantly dependent on the players previous button press and also dependent on the other player's previous button press (χ^2, p→0). Thus, players' responses were contingent on the other players'.

We next computed the frequency of button presses for each button for each player and plotted them on triangle plots for comparison with the NE (Fig. 2). The majority of players did not align with an expected NE.

Plotting each player's strategy revealed some distinct patterns: (a) some played "12" mostly, "6" occasionally, and "4" rarely; (b) few played "6" more than "4" or "12"; (c) few played "4" more than "6" or "12"; (d) most played "4", "6" and "12" in

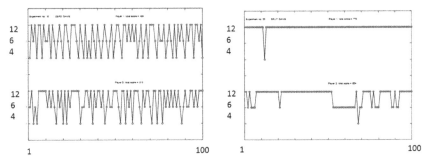

Fig. 1. Two examples of games played. Left: a typical game involving variable play. Note "4" button is frequently pressed. Right: a game with consistent play by one player, and intermediate variability by the other.

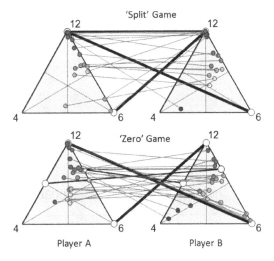

Fig. 2. Triangle plots of proportion of responses for each player A and B in the two game types. Black lines and white circles show Nash equilibria (NE). NE joining vertices are pure (deterministic) strategies; NE from edges are mixed (probabilistic) strategies. Small circles show each player's proportion of button presses for the "4", "6", and "12" buttons; thin lines join players in the same game. Note that most players do not align with NE.

increasing bands (Fig. 2). Patterns a and b were consistent with NE. Pattern c was clearly not consistent with NE. However, Pattern d seemed to approximate the ML with an increase in probability with button value.

3.1   Matching Law

Herrnstein's original matching law relates rate of behaviour to obtained reinforcement. We therefore plotted the proportion of button presses against the actual points awarded per button press (i.e. taking clashes into consideration) (Fig. 4a). There was a clear linear trend consistent with the ML.

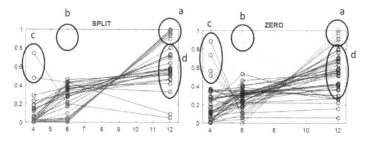

Fig. 3. Categorization of clusters of individual player strategies (see text).

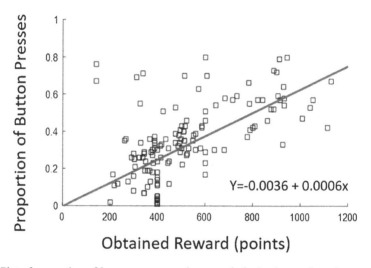

Fig. 4. Plot of proportion of button presses against actual obtained reward per button press for all pattern d responses across both game types (see Fig. 3). Plot is collapsed across the three buttons. Note approximate linear trend as expected from the matching law. Line is linear robust regression.

3.2   Evolutionary Game Theory Equilibria

An important insight can be gleaned from evolutionary game theory (EGT). The basic assumption is that strategies are inherited, and that successful strategies will dominate the gene pool through natural selection (presumably AVs will also inherit from their manufacturers). A consequence is that players will tend to adopt the same strategy. There may actually be a small set of stable strategies, but for the sake of argument, let us assume that players A and B share the same genes and always have the same strategy (Fig. 5). What is their optimal strategy? First consider the SPLIT game (Fig. 6a).

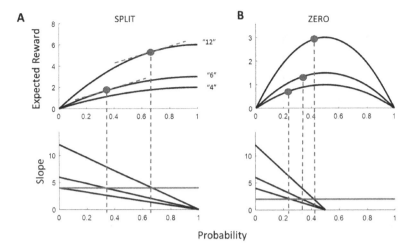

Fig. 5. Schematic to show how an equilibrium can be reached when players adopt the same strategy. At equilibrium, the slope of expected reward (dashed lines) become equal so that switching to a new button offers no advantage. The optimum strategy is then determined since the sum of probabilities (vertical dashed lines) add to unity.

If a player presses the "12" button with increasing probability, the expected payoff will increase as a compressive function such that the slope (rate of increase in reward with probability) decreases. This is because the other player is also pressing "12" with increasing probability. As the probability of playing "12" increases, there comes a point where the players are better off switching to the "6" button because the slope on the "6" button is greater than the "12" button. (This is equivalent to switching habitats in EGT). The slope of the "6" button will also decrease and eventually it will pay to switch to the "4" button. The process will stabilise when the slopes of buttons become the same, since then there is nothing to be gained by switching. Because the sum of probabilities must always add to unity, the final equilibrium point is given by the horizontal line in Fig. 6a. For the SPLIT game, the equilibrium strategy is (0, 0.33, 0.67) (for both players). Thus, it still does not pay to press "4", but the equilibrium point is very close to zero and any fluctuations would involve the "4" button.

For the ZERO game, the equilibrium is different and is (0.25, 0.33, 10/24) (Fig. 6b), and does require "4" presses. These equilibria are optimal but not at a NE. In Fig. 6, these optimal strategies are plotted on dual triangles and compared to observed strategies (pattern d in Fig. 3). They are mixed strategies and similar to, but not precisely the same as, the ideal ML (4/22, 6/22, 12/22). There is some agreement, but it is not perfect especially for the ZERO game. However, there is considerable variability in observed data, and clearly the optimal strategy would depend on how well players could determine their expected payoffs.

This is based on the EGT assumption of identical strategies, which is open to question for human behaviour. However, it demonstrates the key point that when expected reward for each choice is a compressive function (decreasing slope) of probability/frequency of play (Fig. 6), it may pay to switch to a less rewarding choices

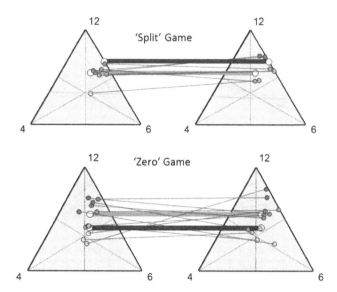

Fig. 6. Optimal strategy when players have same strategy (dark blue line) and the ideal matching law (light blue line) compared to observed players' strategies (for pattern d). (Color figure online)

(depending on their slopes). This will lead to non-NE mixed strategies. It must be emphasised, though, that players do not simply play a fixed mixed strategy independent of the other player, but their choices do depend on the opponent's choices. Thus, a player's expected reward would need to depend on the other player's choices. At present we do not know how players derive expected reward, but if it is based on past experience, then it is plausible that stable compressive functions similar to that in Fig. 3 could emerge. This is a complex problem that we have not yet explored.

4   Discussion

It is clear from this simple experiment that humans do not as a rule adopt NEs. For either the SPLIT or ZERO games, players did not adopt the same strategy, and most pairs of players did not converge on any Nash equilibrium. In the SPLIT game, 5 pairs approximately played the optimum [12, 12] strategy, and 2 pairs approximated the [12, 6] or [6, 12] NE, but 10 pairs appeared to choose a mixed strategy with no NE alignment (Fig. 2) (there are no mixed NE in this game). For the ZERO game, there are two pure NE, [6, 12] and [12, 6], which were approximated by 4 pairs. The remaining pairs, however, chose a mixed strategy. In this game, there are mixed NE (see Table 1); two involved playing the "4", but no pairs adopted these. The other required a mixture of 6 and 12, and it is possible that some pairs approximated this strategy, but we are doubtful as players also approximated this strategy in the SPLIT game which is not a NE. Thus, we conclude that some but most do not adhere to NE.

It could be argued that one-shot NEs are not applicable to iterative games (many trials with the same players), but this is not the case for our games. It is easy to see that for the SPLIT game, playing "12" is always the optimal strategy regardless of the other player's strategy. Playing "6" is risky as the reward could drop to 3 points if the other player also plays "6", and playing "4" is always suboptimal. We also thought that this optimal strategy would be obvious to any player, but evidently this was not the case. In the ZERO game, the optimal strategy is less obvious and requires negotiation between playing "6" and "12": if one player chooses "12", the other should choose "6" and vice versa. So it possible that a player could learn the other's preference and adapt to it or interfere with it. Playing "4" is always suboptimal (for two players).

A few players chose "4" with the highest probability. It is possible that it was strategic if the player assumed that the other player would play "6" or "12" and believed that "4" was the safest option. This would fail, of course, if the other player adopted the same strategy.

In both game types, most players clustered around a mixed strategy with increasing frequency with "4", "6", and "12", although some chose "6" more often than "12". This pattern is reminiscent of the Matching Law, and there is clear trend of a button being pressed increases with the amount of actual reward obtained (Fig. 4a). The ML has long been a contentious issue, and often considered as irrational, or at least a non-maximising strategy.

4.1   Implications for AVs

We need to consider AV-H and AV-AV interactions separately. Based on the results of this experiment with human-human interactions, we cannot assume that a human will act deterministically or even follow a mixed Nash equilibria. Instead, humans appear to adopt probabilistic decision-making at is, an alternative with low expected pay-off is sometimes chosen, but there are individual differences. It seems that Nature prefers probabilistic plays. Should we, therefore, be bioinspired and incorporate such a strategy in decision-making software? There are two problems.

First, we do not know why humans (and animals) are probabilistic. It may be an evolutionary stable strategy, but we cannot be sure. If we assume that it is nevertheless an optimal strategy, there is no guarantee that it would optimal for a man-made AV machine. That is, is it optimal for any decision-making machine or is it peculiar to biological organisms (see Harris [7]). Given that unlucky outcomes are likely to have serious health and financial outcomes, perhaps the gamble of bio-inspiration is a step too far. This brings us to the second problem. A probabilistic strategy will inevitably have unlucky outcomes. Will it be acceptable by the legal system and insurance companies that an 'accident' is perceived to have occurred because of a random number generated in AV software? It is doubtful. The problem for AV risk management software is predicting what a human will do. It will need to make some legally defensible assessment of human behaviour and arrive at a defensible deterministic decision. An AV's speed of processing and response to external events will be much faster than a human's. This may provide some advantage for an AV evading a collision, but it may influence the ongoing human decision-making process and possibly cause unexpected human behaviour.

A different scenario occurs in AV-AV interactions, which will become increasingly common in the next 20 years. AVs will have the same (or similar) technology and decision-making strategies (presumably depending on the AV brand). Their interactions will inevitably be different from AV-human interactions. Presumably, AVs will need to broadcast their autonomous status so that other AVs can make decisions accordingly. Vehicles that do not broadcast will be assumed to have human drivers. A potential problem arises when AVs make the same decision in a conflict scenario, so that the decision-making software plays against itself, as in evolutionary game theory. It is not possible to predict the outcome at present, but deterministic decisions could be uneconomic as all AVs could make the same error. One way to avoid this scenario would be for AVs to communicate with each other in order to resolve competitive/conflict situations. However, this would need enforcement via some a regulatory body, as seen in air traffic control.

AV-H and AV-AV interactions will be inevitable in the near future. Although currently challenging, it seems likely that autonomous non-strategic driving will become at least as safe as human driving. On the other hand, how autonomous strategic decision-making in high density traffic will evolve remains unclear and could remain persistently problematic until the game - theoretic implications are better understood.

References

1. Maynard Smith, J.: Evolution and the Theory of Games. Cambridge University Press, Cambridge (1982)
2. Herrnstein, R.J.: Relative and absolute strength of responses as a function of frequency of reinforcement. J. Exp. Anal. Behav. **4**, 267–272 (1961)
3. Mailath, G.J.: Do people play Nash equilibrium? Lessons from evolutionary game theory. J. Econom. Lit. **36**, 1347–1374 (1998)
4. Seth, A.K.: The ecology of action selection: insights from artificial life. Philos. T. Roy. Soc. B. **362**, 1545–1558 (2007)
5. Houston, A.I., McNamara, J.M., Steer, M.D.: Do we expect natural selection to produce rational behaviour? Phil. Trans. R. Soc. B **362**, 1531–1543 (2007)
6. Fretwell, S.D., Lucas Jr., H.L.: On territorial behavior and other factors influencing habitat distribution in birds. I. Theoretical development. Acta Biotheor. **19**, 16–36 (1970)
7. Harris, C.M.: Biomimetics of human movement: functional or aesthetic? Bioinspiration Biomimetics **4**, 33001 (2009)

Homeostatic Robot Control Using Simple Neuromodulatory Techniques

James C. Finnis[✉]

Computer Science, Aberystwyth University, Penglais, Aberystwyth SY23 3DB, UK
jcf1@aber.ac.uk

Abstract. The UESMANN (Uniform Excitatory Switching Multifunction Artificial Neural Network) architecture has been shown to produce interesting transitions between multiple behaviours using an extremely simple neuromodulatory regime. Previous work has concentrated on discrete classification tasks. In this work, three different simple neuromodulatory architectures including UESMANN are used to control a robot in a homeostatic task.

The experiments show that UESMANN produces interesting and useful transitional behaviour in an embodied system, learning the two tasks in the same number of parameters (i.e. network weights) as networks which learned each individual task.

Keywords: Neuromodulation · Neural network · Backpropagation · Robotics · Long-term autonomy · Homeostasis

1 Introduction

This work compares three methods of modulating the behaviour of a neural network with a single parameter to perform some "blend" between two learned behaviours. Smooth transitions between behaviours may be useful in situations where a system's behaviour should change with environmental conditions, perhaps to achieve homeostasis. In such systems, a small change in the environment (or time) should induce a similarly small change in the behaviour. However, often it can help if this transition is not completely smooth – some complexity in the transition can help by introducing variety into the output, as our experiments on a physical robot show.

The three methods compared are neuromodulatory techniques based on feedforward artificial neural networks. They are: linear interpolation between the outputs of two networks (output blending), using an additional input to carry the modulator value (h-as-input), and the UESMANN architecture. The latter, introduced in [1], is interesting because it is extremely simple and requires no extra parameters beyond the weights and biases: it is based on multiplying all the weights by a function of the modulator. It may be possible to train more than two functions in a UESMANN network, although this may not converge if the functions are too dissimilar. The work referenced above has examined the network in pattern recognition problems.

© Springer International Publishing AG 2017
Y. Gao et al. (Eds.): TAROS 2017, LNAI 10454, pp. 325–339, 2017.
DOI: 10.1007/978-3-319-64107-2_26

The present work involves generating homeostatic behaviour in a robot using two behaviours learned offline: sonar-based wall-avoidant wandering, and phototropic (simulated) charging. Such homeostatic systems, striking a balance between task performance and exploitation of resources, are useful in long-term autonomous settings [11]. While this is a well understood action selection task, using a real robot with noisy sensors and actuators to perform a neuromodulatory task may bring out important differences in the three methods.

2   UESMANN

In biological systems, the behaviour of a group of neurons may be modulated by neuromodulatory chemicals, typically by acting on the synapses between them [4]. Much work has been done on artificial neuromodulatory systems such as GasNets [3,6,13] and Artificial Endocrine Systems [7,8,11]. Because CTRNNs can realize any dynamical system [2], CTRNNs may also encompass a neuromodulatory model. CTRNNs and GasNets are typically generated by evolutionary algorithms [5].

UESMANN networks, in contrast, are trained using a variant of backpropagation of errors [10]. They are much simpler, consisting of a single modulator with a single, uniform action across all the weights – thus forming an artificial analogue of a group of neurons acted on by a single modulator.

The UESMANN architecture is a feed-forward network with one or more hidden layers, with a global modulation parameter h. Each unit has the form

$$a_i^l = \sigma \left(b_i^l + (h+1) \sum_j w_{ij}^l a_j^{l-1} \right) \tag{1}$$

and will perform one function at $h = 0$ where the weights take their nominal values, and one at $h = 1$ where the weights are doubled. As such, they are close to the simplest possible form of neuromodulatory ANN. Training the network is currently done by UESMANN-BP, a stochastic hill-climbing technique. This involves presenting alternate examples from each function, with h set to the appropriate value, and backpropagating the errors. Full details are in [1].

3   Methodology

Our aim is to compare the behaviours of different multi-function network architectures in a problem domain with continuous outputs and noisy inputs, in contrast with the discrete classification tasks studied in [1]. Robot control is a difficult problem which often requires switching or blending different behaviours in order to balance various objectives, such as data collection and power management. Robot sensors are also noisy, and actuators often do not respond in an ideal manner.

The target robot is a Pioneer 2DX with eight sonars and an omnidirectional camera as light sensor, and our aim is to produce wandering behaviour with the simulated charge high, and phototaxis with the charge low (i.e. the light is simulating a power source beacon).

Neural network training is not guaranteed to converge to a solution, particularly where one network is required to learn two functions. The initial weights and the training data provided may result in a poor local minimum being found. Therefore a number of networks are trained for each architecture and tested using a simple simulator with perfect differential steering and sensors. Using the simulator allows us to run at a suitably high speed to both generate sufficient training data (different for each network instance) and evaluate the networks over a number of runs. 10 networks were generated for each type, and evaluations done on each network.

The best networks are carried forward into the robot experiments, where they are evaluated at two different levels of charging efficiency and two different initial directions. Five runs for each combination are performed and analysed to determine differences in learning ability and transition behaviour.

4   Simulator Experiments

Our very simple simulator runs two rule-based controllers to generate training data. One controller will wander and avoid using sonars, the other will head towards the light and stop at a particular intensity: this is a simple model of an "exploration/exploitation" problem. When generating training data, there is no charge model, just a small probability of the robot switching from one controller to the other (0.001 per tick). The log of inputs, outputs and controller ID comprise the training input for the networks. A new set of training data is generated for each network instance, to avoid any irregularities in an individual training set skewing the result. Each training set consists of 200000 training log entries (recorded every 0.01 s of simulated time), and the robot's maximum speed is $1 \, \text{ms}^{-1}$. The training environment is an enclosed $12 \times 12 \, \text{m}$ box, with 2 walls extending from the sides interrupting the space. During training, the robot is occasionally randomly turned and repositioned to avoid loops and ensure as many situations are represented in the data as possible. Note that the *light* controller will also stop when the light is bright, to add some complexity to the behaviour and hopefully cause stopping at the light when charge is low. The IDs stored in the log for the controllers are 0 for *sonar* and 1 for *light*. During evaluation, setting the modulator h to 0 should produce *sonar* behaviour, and 1 should produce *light*.

Training the networks is done offline after the data-generating run is complete. Each network is presented with the randomly shuffled examples, with 3×10^7 presentations in total (i.e. each example is presented 150 times). In the case of output blending, the appropriate network is presented with the example; for UESMANN and h-as-input the network is trained with the controller ID as the parameter h.

All networks had 8 sonar inputs, 8 light inputs and 2 motor outputs, with a single hidden layer of 16 nodes. The learning rate $\eta = 0.1$.

4.1 Simulator Evaluation

Each trained network is evaluated, this time on a simpler arena without the internal walls: during actual experiments, the arena must be obstacle-free since the *light* controller cannot pathfind (we ignore this during the initial training data generation). 10 runs are performed for each network, each starting at a random position and orientation. The runs end at a simulated 1000 s or when the system runs out of charge.

The charge and modulator model used is very simple. The virtual battery has a charge in the range [0, 1]. The motor uses power linearly with speed, on top of a base power usage. Thus, if the commanded speeds are s_l and s_r (which are in the range [0, 1]), the power input is p, the time step is Δ_t, the base usage is k_{base} and the motor power factor is k_m, then the charge C_t and modulator h_t are given by

$$C_t = \text{clamp}\left(C_{t-1} + \Delta_t\left(k_{power}p - (k_{base} + k_m(s_l + s_r))\right)\right) \qquad (2)$$

where $\text{clamp}(x) = \max\left(0, \min(1, x)\right)$

$$h_t = 1 - C_t \qquad (3)$$

The power input p is obtained from the sum of the pixel inputs, multiplied by the charging efficiency constant k_{power}: one of the variables modified in the robot experiments. The values used were $k_m = 0.01, k_{base} = 0.005, k_{power} = 0.0025$. Once 10 runs have been obtained for each of the 10 networks generated by the 3 methods, they are evaluated according to three metrics, which are combined together by $\sum_i \log_2\left(\frac{m_i}{r_i}\right)^2$, where m_i is the obtained value for each measure and r_i is a reference value. This provides a useful measure whereby $+1$ is "twice as good" and -1 is "half as good" [9,12]. The three measures are: the mean of the standard deviation across time windows of the data (to provide a measure of variability across the whole time to avoid artificially high values when the robot only moves in one section of the run), the distance travelled multiplied by the distance from the origin (the light is at the origin, this shows exploration), and the total time survived before the charge dropped to zero. This metric requires three reference values – the obvious value for r_t is the maximum run time, the others were determined from the best runs.

$$m_d = \frac{\sum\limits_{i=1}^{N} \sigma\left(d_{(i-1)s<t<is}\right)}{N}, \quad s = t_{max}/N, d_i = \sqrt{(x_i{}^2 + y_i{}^2)} \qquad (4)$$

(time-windowed standard deviation of distance)

$$m_t = \max\ t \qquad (5)$$

(time survived)

$$m_T = \sum_{j}^{n-1} \left(\sqrt{(x_j - x_{j+1})^2 + (y_j - y_{j+1})^2} \sqrt{x_j^2 + y_j^2} \right) \tag{6}$$

(distance travelled biased for edge, for exploration)

$$S = \frac{1}{3} \left(\log_2 \left(\frac{m_d}{r_d} \right)^2 + \log_2 \left(\frac{m_t}{r_t} \right)^2 + \log_2 \left(\frac{m_T}{r_T} \right)^2 \right) \tag{7}$$

where N is the number of segments for windowing the SD and was set to 10 for these experiments, m_* indicates individual metrics, r_* indicates the reference values: $r_d = 2.45, r_t = 1000\,\mathrm{s}, r_T = 2183$. The values for r_d and r_T are just over the maxima achieved across all the runs.

4.2   Simulator Results

The metric and sub-metric results of all the simulator runs are shown in Fig. 1. According to the (somewhat arbitrary) combined metric, UESMANN and h-as-input perform better than output blending, but there is little difference between the mean performance of the former two. In the individual metrics, h-as-input has much more variation in performance, with several networks performing consistently very well while others often fail. UESMANN also shows variation, with fewer failing runs but fewer extremely good performers. Output blending is very consistent and always survives the full time, but doesn't appear to travel far.

Typical runs of the best performing networks for all three methods are shown in Fig. 3. Clearly the best performing network is h-as-input, and this can be seen in Fig. 1: the best network performs much better than UESMANN, but other poor networks pull the overall performance down. All networks rapidly converge to a limit cycle, as shown in the distance/charge phase plots. With output blending, this is a very tight figure-8 around the origin. This is because output blending is always performing some combination of phototaxis and wandering, and at anything but a very high charge phototaxis will always draw it back to the light. Both h-as-input and UESMANN appear to have a narrower transition region (as shown in previous experiments in [1]), and so show distinctive phase changes: when the charge drops below a certain point, the behaviour will change to light-seeking; and when the charge is high enough, the robot will wander again. The triangular shape in phase space is a consequence of this: the left-hand side of the triangle is phototaxis, the base is recharging stopped at the light, and the right-hand side is exploration. The double peak in h-as-input, and the initial irregularity, is due to the robot wandering far enough to "bounce" off the walls of the arena. UESMANN appears to show a much more "chaotic" limit cycle than h-as-input, which gives the positional plot a more "random" appearance: whereas h-as-input follows a fixed course, UESMANN varies more.

While UESMANN does not perform as well, it is considerably more conservative than h-as-input: in the latter, the transition to phototaxis occurs at

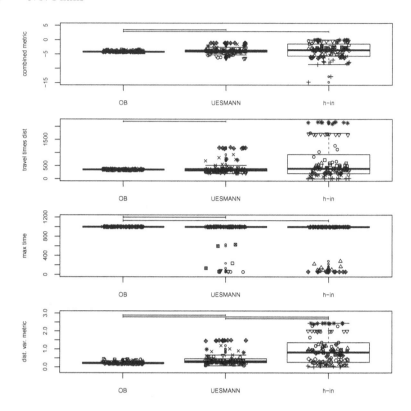

Fig. 1. Box plots of all runs of all networks, showing the combined and submetrics. The point shape indicates the network from which the run comes. Significant differences are indicated by brackets (Mann-Whitney U-test, $p < 0.05$).

$C \approx 0.3$ in h-as-input, leaving it at $C \approx 0.14$ at the return. In a larger arena h-as-input may run out of charge – here it has been helped by the "bounce" off the far wall. UESMANN transitions to phototaxis at $C \approx 0.55$, leaving it with $C \approx 0.4$ at the return.

One interesting feature in the UESMANN run is the "blip" in the base of the triangle in the phase plot, which manifests in the position plot as a tiny inner loop: at a certain point in the recharge phase, the robot performs a "microexcursion", and then returns to recharge. This appears to be a consequence of the interesting dynamics of the UESMANN architecture, and was present in all runs of this particular network.

In order to examine the transitional behaviour, the three best networks by combined metric were each run for 100 s, for 100 different fixed modulator values 0 to 1. This was repeated 50 times, and the mean distance-from-light of the all the runs at each modulator level plotted. No charge model was used. If the network is predominantly wandering at that modulator level, the mean distance should be high; if performing phototaxis, the mean distance should be low.

The results are shown in Fig. 2. Output blending shows the expected gradual shift from long distances to short, while h-as-input shows a transition of width around 0.2. UESMANN is interesting: while it follows the trend of output blending (the "ideal" blend between two networks), it shows a very complex transitional behaviour with the robot changing priorities between phototaxis and wandering in distinct stages, a pattern we came to call "dithering". This pattern proved useful in the real robot by supplying a source of complexity allowing the robot to follow different courses in different runs and by helping with a steering problem, as the next section will show.

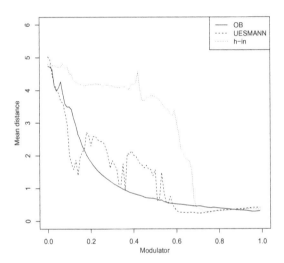

Fig. 2. Mean distance at different hormone (i.e. modulator) levels for 50 runs of the simulated robot.

5   Robot Experiments

The best networks (according to the combined metric) for the three network types were taken forward into the robot experiments. The robot used was a Pioneer 2DX: a differential-drive robot as in the simulator, with 2 large driven wheels and a caster wheel at the back. It was fitted with an omnidirectional camera to act as a light sensor, and carried its own sonar sensors of which the front 8 were used, which were oriented the same way as in the simulator. The network software was run on a host laptop, communicating over TCP to the robot, which appeared as a ROS node on the laptop.

The light source was a 60 W incandescent bulb in an opaque hood, suspended ∼1.5 m above the floor, shining a diffuse circle on the floor. The on-board omnidirectional camera image was gaussian blurred and summed across 32 radii, giving 32 pixels around the robot. This was downsampled to 8 pixels on the laptop.

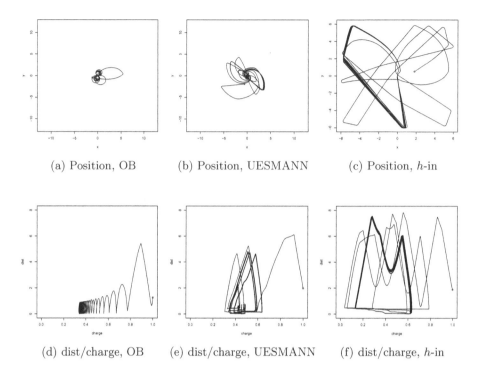

(a) Position, OB   (b) Position, UESMANN   (c) Position, h-in

(d) dist/charge, OB   (e) dist/charge, UESMANN   (f) dist/charge, h-in

Fig. 3. Typical runs of best seeds in simulation, position and distance from light/charge

Figure 4 shows a picture of the robot with the light source and two on-board camera views, one for far and one for near light.

Positional tracking was done by mounting a diffused red LED on the robot (above the centre of rotation) and using a commodity webcam, filtering for red

(a) Robot and light source   (b) Camera image, blurred, far light   (c) Camera image, blurred, near light

Fig. 4. Robot and light source, and two omnidirectional camera views showing dots for the 32 summed radii.

blobs, finding the centroid of the largest blob and transforming from screen space to a plane in 3D space by perspective transform. The accuracy of the tracking was from ~0.01 m close to the camera, to ~0.2 m at the far distance. The tracking data was captured at a frequency of roughly 1 Hz, and sent over ROS to the main program for logging purposes. Some parts of the arena were not visible to tracking – notably a long section in which the LED was obscured by the light source hood. In the logs, points for which no tracking data were received have the same position as the last logged point.

The arena was bounded by a (nearly) sonar-opaque mesh, and was of an irregular, roughly triangular shape providing the largest possible area. The light source was suspended (due to environmental constraints) over the narrow end, and is indicated by a circle in the figures below. Thus, the experiments often involve cycling around the "safe" narrow area with occasional excursions into the wide, dark area.

12 experiments were done, with five repetitions each. The factors were: network type (OB/UESMANN/h-as-input), initial direction ("south" into the narrow end or "north" into the dark area) and two values of k_{power}: the constant used to determine how efficiently the simulated battery charges. The values chosen were 0.0025 and 0.003. Otherwise the same power model was used. One major difference is that the speeds were scaled down: $1\,\mathrm{ms}^{-1}$ is not a viable speed for a Pioneer. The outputs of the network s_l, s_r were multiplied by 0.05. Naturally this makes it difficult to compare the results with the simulator, any comparisons made must be qualitative.

5.1   Results

During the runs for h-as-input it was found that the best network in simulation performed extremely badly, colliding frequently with the mesh and putting the robot and environment in danger. Only eight runs (two for each k_{power} and direction) were performed before the network was abandoned. Three of these runs, showing typical behaviour, are shown in Fig. 5. Note that the arena boundary is approximate: in all these runs, the robot became entangled in the mesh. It seems that this particular network responded very late to sonar, which allowed it to traverse very far in simulation but caused problems with the very noisy sonar on the robot (see below). Therefore the second-best network was used for all remaining experiments, which was rather more conservative.

Below we present a largely descriptive analysis of the behaviours of the different networks. The survival times for all runs are shown in Table 1, and the performance metric used in the simulation experiments (with new reference values obtained from the raw results) is shown in Table 2. Both tables are sorted by the means. Note that the ordering is nearly the same: h-as-input is penalised by the metric because it does not travel far. The other sub-metrics show very similar ordering. The mean metrics for all runs are shown in Table 3.

Looking at the metrics can be deceptive, because survival and coverage is often dependent on serendipitous sonar bounces and the modulator level at

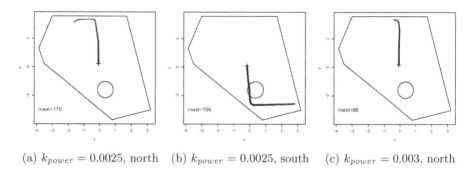

(a) $k_{power} = 0.0025$, north   (b) $k_{power} = 0.0025$, south   (c) $k_{power} = 0.003$, north

Fig. 5. h-as-input runs from the best simulator network. The arena walls are shown as lines in the position plot, and the light source by a grey circle. Charge is indicated by shading (the paler, the lower). The maximum achieved time is also shown.

Table 1. Survival times for all runs, sorted by mean. The number in the row name refers to k_{power}.

Name	r1	r2	r3	r4	r5	Mean
h-in south 0.0025	1000	1000	1000	1000	1000	1000.00
OB north 0.003	946	1000	1000	1000	1000	989.28
UESMANN south 0.0025	1000	1000	636	1000	1000	927.16
UESMANN south 0.003	1000	1000	1000	955	521	895.30
OB south 0.0025	649	1000	596	639	619	700.64
OB south 0.003	167	383	392	1000	780	544.30
h-in south 0.003	361	364	398	399	884	481.16
UESMANN north 0.003	1000	176	183	169	170	339.62
h-in north 0.003	147	167	150	157	149	153.82
OB north 0.0025	126	122	122	125	120	123.10
UESMANN north 0.0025	117	118	115	116	118	116.78
h-in north 0.0025	110	113	114	112	110	111.74

which transitions occur, which can easily be changed by modifying the modulator in some way. We are more interested in the nature of the transition between behaviours and how it helps or hinders in this application.

However, there are some general observations to be made. Overall, output blending fares only slightly better than UESMANN while h-as-input is worst. This is surprising, given that UESMANN is using a single network with the same number of weights as each of the two networks used in OB, and has fewer weights than the h-as-input network (although we are using the second-best h-in network).

No network does well starting into the dark ("north") with low power: they all turn too late to return in time to recharge, but the nature of these turns is

Table 2. Combined performance metric for all runs, sorted by mean.

Name	r1	r2	r3	r4	r5	Mean
OB north 0.003	−0.15	−0.21	−0.45	−0.40	−0.34	−0.31
h-in south 0.0025	−0.72	−0.66	−0.23	−0.48	−0.35	−0.49
UESMANN south 0.0025	−0.39	−0.48	−1.77	−0.60	−0.65	−0.78
UESMANN south 0.003	−0.31	−0.52	−1.13	−1.16	−2.47	−1.12
OB south 0.0025	−1.69	−0.67	−1.64	−2.04	−1.67	−1.54
OB south 0.003	−5.77	−2.73	−2.68	−0.46	−1.05	−2.53
h-in south 0.003	−2.86	−3.16	−3.02	−3.08	−1.30	−2.68
UESMANN north 0.003	−0.28	−4.92	−5.11	−5.11	−5.12	−4.11
h-in north 0.003	−4.31	−5.53	−5.84	−5.86	−5.91	−5.49
OB north 0.0025	−5.85	−6.15	−5.86	−5.87	−6.01	−5.95
UESMANN north 0.0025	−5.85	−5.90	−5.86	−5.99	−6.27	−5.97
h-in north 0.0025	−6.70	−6.69	−6.64	−6.57	−6.66	−6.65

Table 3. Means of all metrics for all runs.

	Survival time	Windowed SD	Edge-biased travel	Combined metric
OB	589.33	0.42	79.97	−2.58
UESMANN	569.71	0.36	73.03	−2.99
h-as-input	436.68	0.29	57.03	−3.83

quite different. UESMANN does well facing initially into the light, while output blending does not. Facing into the dark, the position is reversed: output blending has a tendency to always follow the same track, which leads it into trouble facing south: it finds a path into the dark area and cannot return. UESMANN follows a variety of paths and is more conservative.

All networks occasionally touch the mesh, but turn out of it fairly quickly (unlike the original h-as-input network). Tests show that this may be due to the nature of the mesh and the walls behind it, which are strongly sonar-reflective: the sonars sometimes get echoes from the wall instead of the mesh.

Output Blending. Figure 6 shows the position and phase plots for typical output blending network runs. We are no longer seeing the tight cycling which this network performed in simulation: this is because the differential steering is not perfect in the robot. Tests show that the robot will continue to drive straight while one motor's requested speed is reduced, until the speeds differ by around 0.3 (if the other is at 1). Thus, the robot can make straight runs even when it is being commanded (partially) towards the light. The environment here is imposing a narrower transition between the behaviours than is being produced by the network outputs.

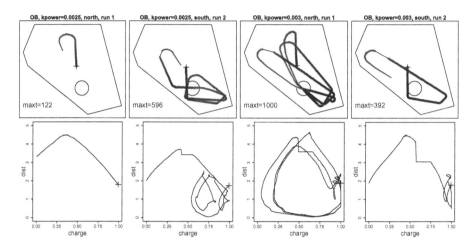

Fig. 6. Typical runs for output blending, position and phase plots. See Fig. 5 for an explanation.

In general, the runs are very similar within each experiment, although one run south at $k_{power} = 0.003$ succeeds where the others fail by fortuitously being turned towards the light slightly earlier by sonar reflection.

UESMANN. Figure 7 shows the results for UESMANN runs. The turns are tighter here – inspection of the variable data shows that the motor responses are varying more during transitions, showing the "dithering" behaviour described

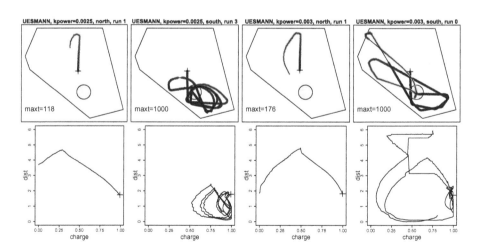

Fig. 7. Typical runs for UESMANN, position and phase plots. The arena walls are shown as lines in the position plot, and the light source by a grey circle. Charge is indicated by shading (the paler, the lower). The maximum achieved time is also shown.

earlier in simulation. These slight oscillations between the two behaviours through the transition seem to counteract the steering lag which affects output blending by providing higher rotational accelerations in the motor. UESMANN's run also appear more "chaotic" (in the informal sense), with the robot following different routes in each run by turning at slightly different points and angles. This is also likely to be due to the complex transition behaviour – small differences in the modulator can lead to larger changes in behaviour than in the other networks, although the overall transition is still gradual.

This is particularly notable in south-facing runs with $k_{power} = 0.003$, a particularly interesting instance of which is shown. Here, the robot made its way to the far corner, stopped to recharge (there is enough light to do so if the motors are not turning), and then returned. Stopping in darkness seems to be an emergent property of the network (note that the robot did not actually hit the mesh in this instance – the left-top corner of the arena is slightly further to the left in reality).

h-as-input. Figure 8 shows the results for this network. This is a conservative network, as can be seen from the low power 0.0025 plots. All the runs are very similar within each experiment. At high power, some problems can be seen. The nature of the turn running north is unusual, with a partial sonar turn followed by a turn towards the light. The slight drop in power may potentiate the network towards taking action on a sonar signal here. Many of the south-facing high power runs resulted in running into the mesh, as shown here. This is odd, because both behaviours should drive it to turn in the same direction at this point. It should be borne in mind, however, that this is the second-best

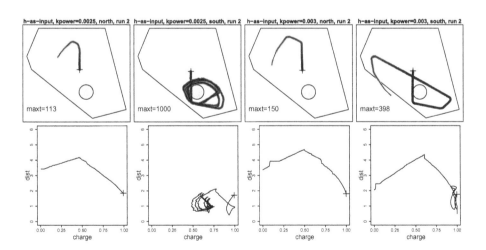

Fig. 8. Typical runs for UESMANN, position and phase plots. The arena walls are shown as lines in the position plot, and the light source by a grey circle. Charge is indicated by shading (the paler, the lower). The maximum achieved time is also shown.

h-as-input network – although the first also had difficulties with turning (see the opening of this section).

Analysis of Motor Differential. To investigate the behaviour of the motors, a histogram of $|s_l - s_r|$ was plotted for all runs: see Fig. 9. Output blending shows large variation in the differential, with many intermediate values used as the subnetworks blend their outputs, but heavily weighted towards smaller values. UESMANN shows a similar effect, but the distribution is much more even across the range (apart from 0 and 1). The h-as-input network shows a tendency to go either straight ahead (0) or turn (1). UESMANN's higher use of the entire range of motor differentials may reflect increased complexity in its behaviour.

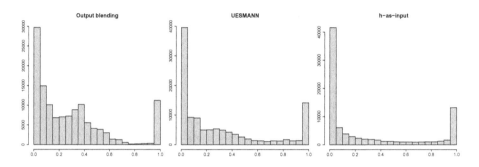

Fig. 9. Histogram of motor differential across all runs

6   Conclusion

It is often useful to move smoothly from one behaviour to another, particularly in embodied systems. While it is generally true that a small change in environment should lead to a small response in behaviour, it is also true that some complexity in the transition between behaviours can be useful. It may allow the system to find fortuitous escapes from difficult situations, or new ways of exploring and exploiting its environment.

Whereas naïve output blending produces a smooth, "ideal" transition, and using the modulator as just another input gives a fairly sharp transition (and sometimes does not learn well) the UESMANN architecture seems to provide such a complex transition, while maintaining the essential nature of the blend between the behaviours.

It is remarkable that UESMANN is able to learn two complex functions fairly well using the same number of weights as a network which performs one of those functions only a little better, and with such a simple modulatory and learning technique. Currently work is being done on analysing the behaviour of single UESMANN nodes to gain insights into how this is achieved, starting at first principles with 2-2-1 networks blending boolean operators. The study of such a simple system's capacity to learn multiple behaviours may yield important results for more complex systems. Future work should include testing the current application with lower hidden node counts, before moving onto dynamical systems analysis of the UESMANN training process and the resulting networks, consideration of other learning methods (such as artificial evolution) and incorporating UESMANN-like layers into deep learning networks to perform multiple functions.

References

1. Finnis, J.C., Neal, M.: UESMANN: a feed-forward network capable of learning multiple functions. In: Tuci, E., Giagkos, A., Wilson, M., Hallam, J. (eds.) SAB 2016. LNCS, vol. 9825, pp. 101–112. Springer, Cham (2016). doi:10.1007/978-3-319-43488-9_10
2. Funahashi, K., Nakamura, Y.: Approximation of dynamical systems by continuous time recurrent neural networks. Neural Netw. **6**(6), 801–806 (1993)
3. Husbands, P., Philippides, A., Smith, T., O'Shea, M.: Volume signalling in real and robot nervous systems. Theory Biosci. **120**(3–4), 253–269 (2001)
4. Kaczmarek, L.K., Levitan, I.B.: Neuromodulation: The Biochemical Control of Neuronal Excitability. Oxford University Press, New York (1987)
5. Magg, S., Philippides, A.: GasNets and CTRNNs – a comparison in terms of evolvability. In: Nolfi, S., Baldassarre, G., Calabretta, R., Hallam, J.C.T., Marocco, D., Meyer, J.-A., Miglino, O., Parisi, D. (eds.) SAB 2006. LNCS, vol. 4095, pp. 461–472. Springer, Heidelberg (2006). doi:10.1007/11840541_38
6. Moioli, R.C., Vargas, P.A., Von Zuben, F.J., Husbands, P.: Towards the evolution of an artificial homeostatic system. In: IEEE Congress on Evolutionary Computation, pp. 4023–4030. IEEE (2008)
7. Neal, M.: Once more unto the breach: towards artificial homeostasis. In: De Castro, L.N., Von Zuben, F.J. (eds.) Recent Developments in Biologically Inspired Computing, pp. 340–365. Idea Group (2005)
8. Neal, M., Timmis, J.: Timidity: a useful emotional mechanism for robot control? Informatica (Slovenia) **27**(2), 197–204 (2003)
9. Rodriguez, G., Weisbin, C.R.: A new method to evaluate human-robot system performance. Auton. Robots **14**(2–3), 165–178 (2003)
10. Rumelhart, D.E., Hinton, G.E., Williams, R.J.: Learning representations by back-propagating errors. Nature **323**(6088), 533–536 (1986)
11. Sauze, C., Neal, M.: Artificial endocrine controller for power management in robotic systems. IEEE Trans. Neural Netw. Learn. Syst. **24**(12), 1973–1985 (2013)
12. Tunstel, E.: Operational performance metrics for Mars exploration rovers. J. Field Robot. **24**(8–9), 651–670 (2007)
13. Vargas, P.A., Paolo, E.A., Husbands, P.: Preliminary investigations on the evolvability of a non spatial GasNet model. In: Almeida e Costa, F., Rocha, L.M., Costa, E., Harvey, I., Coutinho, A. (eds.) ECAL 2007. LNCS, vol. 4648, pp. 966–975. Springer, Heidelberg (2007). doi:10.1007/978-3-540-74913-4_97

Probabilistic Combination of Noisy Points and Planes for RGB-D Odometry

Pedro F. Proença$^{(\boxtimes)}$ and Yang Gao

Faculty of Engineering and Physical Sciences, Surrey Space Centre,
University of Surrey, Guildford, UK
{p.proenca,yang.gao}@surrey.ac.uk

Abstract. This work proposes a visual odometry method that combines points and plane primitives, extracted from a noisy depth camera. Depth measurement uncertainty is modelled and propagated through the extraction of geometric primitives to the frame-to-frame motion estimation, where pose is optimized by weighting the residuals of 3D point and planes matches, according to their uncertainties. Results on an RGB-D dataset show that the combination of points and planes, through the proposed method, is able to perform well in poorly textured environments, where point-based odometry is bound to fail.

Keywords: Visual odometry · Depth cameras · Uncertainty propagation · Probabilistic plane fitting

1 Introduction

Historically, the problem of visual odometry and SLAM [8] has been mostly addressed by using image feature points. However, low-textured environments pose a problem to such approaches, as interest points can be insufficient to estimate precisely the camera motion and map the environment. Thus, other primitives (e.g. planes and lines) become more relevant, particularly in indoor environments, where planar surfaces are predominant.

The geometry of indoor environments can be unambiguously captured by active depth cameras, which are capable of capturing dense depth maps, at 30 fps, regardless of the image textures. Therefore, the combination of such depth maps with RGB images, known as RGB-D data, has led to the emergence of several robust visual odometry methods. Likewise, in this work, we propose a visual odometry method that uses both points and planes, extracted from RGB-D. While Iterative Closest Point (ICP) has been the standard approach [12] to exploit dense 3D information, plane primitives are an attractive alternative, as they can be handled more efficiently during pose estimation [14] and be used for mapping to yield highly compact representations [12]. In the context of the former, we introduce a novel plane-to-plane distance, as an alternative to the typical point-to-plane distances.

© Springer International Publishing AG 2017
Y. Gao et al. (Eds.): TAROS 2017, LNAI 10454, pp. 340–350, 2017.
DOI: 10.1007/978-3-319-64107-2_27

Due to the systematic noise of these depth sensors, our method models the uncertainty of the 3D points and planes in order to estimate optimally the camera pose. This is done by propagating the depth ucertainty to the pose optimization, so that pose is estimated by minimizing the distances between feature matches, that are scaled according to the 3D feature geometry uncertainties. The intuition behind this probabilistic framework is that points and planes that are far from the camera should have less impact on the pose estimation than closer ones and the weights of estimated plane equations should depend on the number and distribution of point measurements on the planes.

Results on a public RGB-D dataset show the benefit of modelling uncertainty, for a structured-light camera, and show more robustness, in low-textured scenes, by combining points and planes rather than just using points.

2   Related Work

Several works have recently addressed RGB-D SLAM by using plane primitives. Trevor et al. [15] proposed a planar SLAM that used data from 2D laser scans and depth cameras as they complement each other in terms of field of view and maximum range. Renato et al. [12] proposed mapping the environment using bounded planes and surfels to represent both planar and non-planar regions. Taguchi et al. [14] avoided the geometric degeneracy of planes by proposing the combination of 3D points and planes through both a closed-form solution and bundle adjustment. Kaess [6] proposed a minimal plane parameterization more suitable for least-squares solvers than the frequently used Hessian normal form. Ma et al. [10] proposed combining a global plane model with direct SLAM to reduce drift.

The combination of 3D lines and points has also shown to be advantageous for RGB-D odometry, by Lu and Song [9], who proposed taking into account the depth uncertainty of a structured-light camera, by modelling the uncertainty of 3D line and point extraction and optimizing simultaneously the camera pose and the 3D coordinates of the primitives through maximum likelihood estimation. Moreover, the uncertainty of plane extraction has been analyzed by Pathak et al. [11], who compared several direct and iterative plane fitting methods, in terms of accuracy and speed.

3   System Overview

The proposed system, outlined in Fig. 1, starts by detecting points and planes from an RGB-D frame. Samples from the noisy depth map are used to obtain 3D points, through back-projection, and the 3D points corresponding to detected planes are used in turn to estimate the plane parameters through a weighted least squares framework, which takes into account the depth measurement uncertainties. Once, point and plane matches are found between two adjacent frames, pose is estimated in iteratively reweighted least squares by minimizing both the point and plane residuals, according to their uncertainties. For this purpose, uncertainty is propagated throughout this process. The modules of the system and the derivation of uncertainty are described in further detail below.

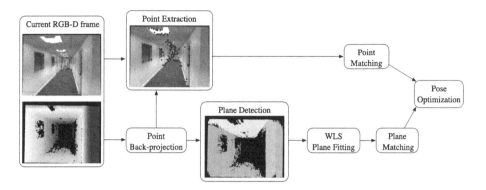

Fig. 1. System overview

4   Point Extraction and Back-Projection

Image points are detected by relying on SURF features [1]. Given a calibrated RGB and depth image pair, the 3D coordinates: $P = [X, Y, Z]^\top$ of a detected image point $p = \{u, v\}$ can be directly obtained by back-projecting the respective depth pixel value Z:

$$P = Z \begin{bmatrix} (u - c_x)/f_x \\ (v - c_y)/f_y \\ 1 \end{bmatrix} \qquad (1)$$

where $\{f_x, f_y\}$ and $\{c_x, c_y\}$ are respectively the focal length and principal point of the RGB camera. As shown by [9], the uncertainty of the 3D point coordinates: Σ_P can be obtained by the first order error propagation of (1):

$$\Sigma_P = J_P \begin{bmatrix} \sigma_p^2 & 0 & 0 \\ 0 & \sigma_p^2 & 0 \\ 0 & 0 & \sigma_Z^2 \end{bmatrix} J_P^\top \qquad (2)$$

where J_P is the Jacobian of (1) with respect to p and Z, σ_p^2 is the pixel uncertainty and σ_Z^2 is the uncertainty of the depth value. While it is generally accepted that a $\sigma_p = 1/2$ approximates the pixel quantization error, the depth measurement uncertainty depends on the type of sensor used. Since structured-light cameras (e.g. Kinect V1) were used in our experiments, we adopt the theoretical model of [7]: $\sigma_Z = 1.425 \times 10^{-6} Z^2$ [mm], which addresses the depth quantization of this type of sensors.

5   Plane Extraction

Planes are first detected by using the method of [3], which processes efficiently organized point clouds in real-time, yielding a segmentation output, as the one shown in Fig. 1. However, the detected planes may contain outliers, thus RANSAC is used additionally to filter each detected plane. Although, plane fitting is already performed by this RANSAC process, we use the method proposed below to obtain the plane parameters and derive their uncertainty.

5.1   Plane Fitting Through Weighted Least Squares

It is useful to express planes as infinite planes in the hessian normal form: $\theta = \{N_x, N_y, N_z, d\}$. However, such a representation is overparameterized, thus the estimation of these parameters by unconstrained linear least squares is degenerate. This issue has been solved in [11] by using constrained optimization and in [16] by using a minimal plane parameterization. Similarly to [16], we use a minimal plane representation: $\theta_m = \left[N_x, N_y, N_z\right]/d$, as an intermediate parameterization. Since, a plane with $d = 0$ implies detecting a plane that passes through the camera center (i.e. projected as a line), it is safe to use this parameterization. The new parameters are then estimated by minimizing the point-to-plane distances through the following weighted least-squares problem:

$$E = \sum_{i=1}^{N} \frac{w_i(\theta_m P_i + 1)^2}{2} \tag{3}$$

where the scaling weights were chosen to be the inverse of the point depth uncertainties: $w_i = \sigma_Z^{-2}$, although other choices are also found in literature [11]. By setting the derivative of (3), with respect to θ_m, to zero, we arrive at the solution of the form: $\theta_m^\top = A^{-1}b$, where:

$$A = \begin{bmatrix} \sum_{i=1}^{N} w_i X_i^2 & \sum_{i=1}^{N} w_i X_i Y_i & \sum_{i=1}^{N} w_i X_i Z_i \\ \sum_{i=1}^{N} w_i X_i Y_i & \sum_{i=1}^{N} w_i Y_i^2 & \sum_{i=1}^{N} w_i Y_i Z_i \\ \sum_{i=1}^{N} w_i X_i Z_i & \sum_{i=1}^{N} w_i Y_i Z_i & \sum_{i=1}^{N} w_i Z_i^2 \end{bmatrix} \tag{4}$$

$$b = - \begin{bmatrix} \sum_{i=1}^{N} w_i X_i \\ \sum_{i=1}^{N} w_i Y_i \\ \sum_{i=1}^{N} w_i Z_i \end{bmatrix} \tag{5}$$

and the covariance of θ_m is given by the inverse Hessian matrix, i.e., $\Sigma_{\theta_m} = H^{-1}$ where H is simply A. The Hessian normal form can then be recovered by:

$$\theta = \frac{\left[\theta_m \ 1\right]}{\|\theta_m\|} \tag{6}$$

and the respective uncertainty is obtained via first order error propagation: $\Sigma_\theta = J_\theta \Sigma_{\theta_m} J_\theta^\top$, where J_θ is the Jacobian of (6).

6   Point and Plane Matching

Both point and plane feature matching capitalize on small frame-to-frame motion. Point correspondences are estabilished between consecutive frames by matching the feature descriptors through a k-NN descriptor search. Given a set of putative matches k to point p, we select the closest match, whose point coordinates lie in a circular region defining the neighbourhood of p.

For matching planes, we first obtain 1-to-N candidate matches by enforcing the following constraints:

- Projection overlap: The projections of two planes, defined as the image segments covered by the inliers of the planes, must have an overlap of at least 50% the number of plane inliers of the smallest plane. This can be checked efficiently by using bitmask operations.
- Geometric constraint: Given the Hessian plane equations of two planes: $\{N, d\}$ and $\{N', d'\}$, the angle between the plane normals: $\arccos(N \cdot N')$ must be less than $10°$ and the distance: $|d - d'|$ must be less than $10\,\mathrm{cm}$.

To select the best plane match between the plane candidates, we introduce here the concept of plane-to-plane distance, so that the plane candidate with the minimum plane-to-plane distance is selected. Let $\{N', d'\}$ and $\{N, d\}$ be the equations of two planes then the distance between the two planes is expressed by:

$$\|C - C'\| = \|d'N' - dN\| \tag{7}$$

where C and C' represent points on the planes, as shown in Fig. 2.

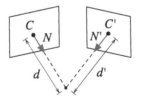

Fig. 2. Geometry of two planes and their representation as points: $\{C, C'\}$

7   Pose Estimation

To estimate the rigid body transformation $\{R, t\}$ between frames, we minimize simultaneously the distance residuals of points and plane matches in a nonlinear least squares problem. Given two 3D point matches: $\{P, P'\}$ we express their residual in the vector form as:

$$\tilde{P} = P' - (RP + t) \tag{8}$$

whereas for two plane matches: $\{N, d\}$ and $\{N', d'\}$ we make use of the plane-to-plane distance, introduced in (7), such that, the residual can be derived, in the vector form, as:

$$\widetilde{C} = (N'R(N't + d') - dN)^\top \tag{9}$$

These residuals are then weighted, stacked together and minimized by using Levenberg-Marquart algorithm. More formally, we minimize the following joint cost function:

$$E = \sum_{i=1}^{N} w(\widetilde{P}_i)\widetilde{P}_i^2 + \alpha \sum_{j=1}^{M} w(\widetilde{C}_j)\widetilde{C}_j^2 \tag{10}$$

by iteratively recomputing the weights $w()$ based on the residual uncertainties, since these depend on the pose parameters. The residual uncertainties are computed using the first order error propagation of (8) and (9), given the pose estimate and the uncertainties of the point Σ_P and plane extraction Σ_θ. Let Σ_r represent the obtained uncertainty of the residual r where $\{\sigma_1^2, \sigma_2^2, \sigma_3^2\}$ is the diagonal of Σ_r then $w(r) = \begin{bmatrix} \sigma_1^{-2} & \sigma_2^{-2} & \sigma_3^{-2} \end{bmatrix}$. Unlike the Mahalanobis distance, this weighting function neglects the covariances of Σ_r. Although, this is sub-optimal, in practice it is more efficient than using the Mahalanobis distance since it does not require inverting the 3×3 residual uncertainties and it allows maintaining the residuals as vectors in the least squares problem, which we have found to improve convergence.

Since the plane uncertainties depend on the weighting choice of the WLS plane fitting and planes are generally fewer than points, we introduce the scaling factor α in (10) to increase the impact of the planes on the optimization. Furthermore, an M-estimator with Tukey weights is used to further reweight the point residuals in order to down-weight the impact of outliers, whereas plane matching outliers are already addressed by the plane matching method (see Sect. 6) and plane matches are too few to rely on statistics.

To avoid degenerate feature configurations, if the total number of point and plane matches is less than 3, pose optimization is avoided and instead a decaying velocity model [8] is applied. Additionally, after the optimization, the uncertainty of the pose parameters Σ_ξ can be calculated since the Hessian evaluated at the solution is: $H = \Sigma_\xi^{-1}$. In this work, we use the Gauss-Newton approximation to the Hessian: $H \approx J_r^\top J_r$, where J_r is the combined Jacobian matrix of the residuals with respect to the pose parameters, and then validate the estimated parameters by checking the largest eigenvalue of the obtained Σ_ξ. If it is larger than a given threshold, we ignore the optimized pose and use the decaying velocity model instead.

8   Experiments and Results

To validate the proposed visual odometry using plane primitives, we collected an RGB-D sequence with a Kinect sensor pointing towards a room corner, as shown in Fig. 3, for a corner is formed by three planes in a non-degenerate configuration. The camera was moved randomly in all 6 DoF, as shown in Fig. 3,

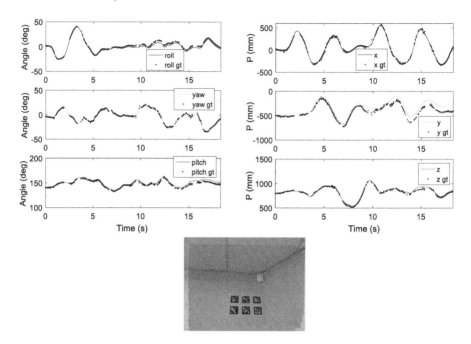

Fig. 3. Top: Estimated pose for plane-based odometry on the corner sequence with ground-truth (gt) measured by using the markerboard. Bottom: Example from the corner sequence with detected planes overlayed on the color image.

during approximately 18 s. The final error of the position estimated by the plane odometry was around 114 mm.

Moreover, the proposed method was evaluated on the TUM RGB-D dataset [13], which contains several RGB-D sequences along with the pose ground-truth, provided by a motion capture system. The sequences that were evaluated, in this work, are shown in Fig. 5. To assess the performance of the visual odometry, pose drift was measured as the relative pose error per second, as suggested by [13].

First, as can be observed in Table 1, the visual odometry based on 3D-to-3D point matches is significantly improved by incorporating uncertainty in the pose estimation instead of relying simply on the Euclidean distance. Figure 4 shows

Table 1. RMSE of relative pose per second for point-based odometry on TUM dataset. The probabilistic version corresponds to the proposed point odometry with uncertainty weighting, whereas the deterministic version uses unweighted residuals.

Sequence	Point odometry	
	Deterministic	Probabilistic
fr1/desk	43 mm / 2.3°	38 mm / 2.2°
fr1/360	109 mm / 3.7°	86 mm / 3.5°

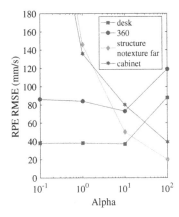

Fig. 4. Alpha tuning. The higher the alpha, the more impact planes have on the pose estimation

the impact of changing α, i.e., the scale factor of the plane residuals, in the point and plane odometry, for each capture. Although, the performance on the 'desk' sequence does not seem to benefit from the introduction of planes, in the low textured sequences, using planes proves to be advantageous. Furthermore, even though planes are not suited to be used alone, due to degeneracy, the curves of the low textured sequences indicate low error for high alpha. The contrary is observed for the other sequences, which suggests that better overall performance could be achieved by adjusting α dynamically based on the number of point matches.

Nevertheless, the results for point and plane odometry, with the best overall tradeoff: $\alpha = 10$, are reported in Table 2. Although the sequences 'desk' and '360' were captured in the same space, the sequence '360' was captured under more sudden rotations, which blurred the images, consequently yielding fewer good feature points, therefore using planes improved significantly the performance on that sequence.

Table 2. RMSE of relative pose per second for visual odometry with only points and with combination of points and planes. We also report, to the best of our knowledge, the best published relative translational error obtained by other frame-to-frame odometry methods that use neither loop closure detection nor map optimization. Since the method [17] uses only a monocular camera, scale post-estimation was performed to best fit the groundtruth trajectory.

Sequence	Features		State-of-the-art
	Points	Points & Planes	
fr1/desk	38 mm / 2.2°	37 mm / 2.1°	26 mm [4]
fr1/360	86 mm / 3.5°	73 mm / 2.9°	84 mm [9]
fr3/structure_notexture_far	Fail	50 mm / 1.5°	43 mm [17]
fr3/cabinet	Fail	80 mm / 4.0°	133 mm [17]

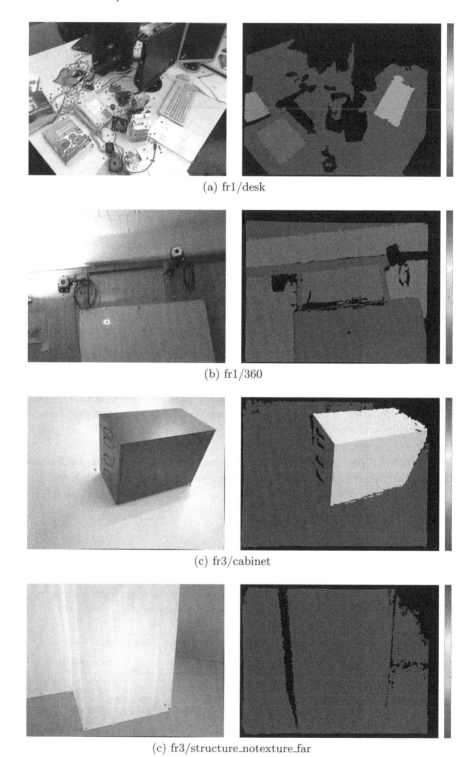

(a) fr1/desk

(b) fr1/360

(c) fr3/cabinet

(c) fr3/structure_notexture_far

Fig. 5. Examples of frames from the evaluated dataset sequences. Left: Detected image points. Right: Detected planes colored by the normalized uncertainty of their estimated distance to the origin

9   Conclusion and Future Work

This paper presents a visual odometry method that combines points and planes based on their measurement uncertainties. Our results demonstrate that this feature combination is beneficial, when few image feature points are detected either due to non-textured planar surfaces or blur caused by sudden motion.

Furthermore, results of point-based odometry show that the systematic noise of a structured-light camera affects significantly the pose estimation based on 3D-to-3D alignment, since our weighing method leads to superior results. Therefore working on the Euclidean space [14] should be avoided when using such sensors. Alternatively, using the reprojection error has also been advocated [5], as it is less susceptible to depth errors, however the intent of this work was to demonstrate the effect of modelling depth uncertainty in the worst case.

As future work, we plan to extend the framework to line features and investigate more comprehensive uncertainty models, such as [2], which addresses depth discontinuities, unlike the model used in this work.

Acknowledgments. This work was supported by Sellafield Ltd.

References

1. Bay, H., Tuytelaars, T., Gool, L.: SURF: speeded up robust features. In: Leonardis, A., Bischof, H., Pinz, A. (eds.) ECCV 2006. LNCS, vol. 3951, pp. 404–417. Springer, Heidelberg (2006). doi:10.1007/11744023_32
2. Dryanovski, I., Valenti, R.G., Xiao, J.: Fast visual odometry and mapping from RGB-D data. In: IEEE International Conference on Robotics and Automation (ICRA), pp. 2305–2310 (2013)
3. Feng, C., Taguchi, Y., Kamat, V.R.: Fast plane extraction in organized point clouds using agglomerative hierarchical clustering. In: IEEE International Conference on Robotics and Automation (ICRA), pp. 6218–6225 (2014)
4. Gutierrez-Gomez, D., Mayol-Cuevas, W., Guerrero, J.J.: Dense RGB-D visual odometry using inverse depth. Robot. Auton. Syst. **75**, 571–583 (2016)
5. Henry, P., Krainin, M., Herbst, E., Ren, X., Fox, D.: Rgb-D mapping: using kinect-style depth cameras for dense 3D modeling of indoor environments. Int. J. Robot. Res. **31**(5), 647–663 (2012)
6. Kaess, M.: Simultaneous localization and mapping with infinite planes. In: IEEE International Conference on Robotics and Automation (ICRA), pp. 4605–4611 (2015)
7. Khoshelham, K., Elberink, S.O.: Accuracy and resolution of kinect depth data for indoor mapping applications. Sensors **12**(2), 1437–1454 (2012)
8. Klein, G., Murray, D.: Parallel tracking and mapping for small AR workspaces. In: IEEE and ACM International Symposium on Mixed and Augmented Reality (ISMAR), pp. 225–234 (2007)
9. Lu, Y., Song, D.: Robust RGB-D odometry using point and line features. In: IEEE International Conference on Computer Vision (ICCV) (2015)
10. Ma, L., Kerl, C., Stückler, J., Cremers, D.: CPA-SLAM: consistent plane-model alignment for direct RGB-D SLAM. In: IEEE International Conference on Robotics and Automation (ICRA), pp. 1285–1291 (2016)

11. Pathak, K., Vaskevicius, N., Birk, A.: Uncertainty analysis for optimum plane extraction from noisy 3D range-sensor point-clouds. Intell. Serv. Robot. **3**(1), 37–48 (2010)
12. Salas-Moreno, R.F., Glocken, B., Kelly, P.H., Davison, A.J.: Dense planar SLAM. In: IEEE International Symposium on Mixed and Augmented Reality (ISMAR), pp. 157–164 (2014)
13. Sturm, J., Engelhard, N., Endres, F., Burgard, W., Cremers, D.: A benchmark for the evaluation of RGB-D SLAM systems. In: International Conference on Intelligent Robots and Systems (IROS) (2012)
14. Taguchi, Y., Jian, Y.D., Ramalingam, S., Feng, C.: Point-plane SLAM for hand-held 3D sensors. In: IEEE International Conference on Robotics and Automation (ICRA), pp. 5182–5189 (2013)
15. Trevor, A.J., Rogers, J.G., Christensen, H.I.: Planar surface SLAM with 3D and 2D sensors. In: IEEE International Conference on Robotics and Automation (ICRA), pp. 3041–3048 (2012)
16. Weingarten, J.W., Gruener, G., Siegwart, R.: Probabilistic plane fitting in 3D and an application to robotic mapping. In: IEEE International Conference on Robotics and Automation (ICRA), vol. 1, pp. 927–932 (2004)
17. Yang, S., Scherer, S.: Direct monocular odometry using points and lines. arXiv preprint arxiv:1703.06380 (2017)

Low-Power and Low-Cost Stiffness-Variable Oesophageal Tissue Phantom

Alexander Thorn[1], Dorukhan Afacan[1], Emily Ingham[2], Can Kavak[1,3], Shuhei Miyashita[4], and Dana D. Damian[1(✉)]

[1] Department of Automatic Control and System Engineering,
Centre of Assistive Technology and Connected Healthcare, University of Sheffield,
Portobello Ln, Sheffield S1 3JD, UK
d.damian@sheffield.ac.uk
[2] Department of Bioengineering, University of Sheffield, Sheffield, UK
[3] Department of Mechanical Engineering,
Izmir Institute of Technology, Izmir, Turkey
[4] Department of Electronic Engineering, University of York, York, UK

Abstract. Biological tissues are complex structures with changing mechanical properties depending on physiological or pathological factors. Thus they are extendible under normal conditions or stiff if they are subject to an inflammatory reaction. We design and fabricate a low-power and low-cost stiffness-variable tissue phantom (SVTP) that can extend up to 250% and contract up to 5.4% at 5 V (1.4 W), mimicking properties of biological tissues. We investigated the mechanical characteristics of SVTP in simulation and experiment. We also demonstrate its potential by building an oesophagus phantom for testing appropriate force controls in a robotic implant that is meant to manipulate biological oesophageal tissues with changing stiffness in vivo. The entire platform permits efficient testing of robotic implants in the context of anomalies such as long gap esophageal atresia, and could potentially serve as a replacement for live animal tissues.

1 Introduction

We are interested in developing an actuatable phantom oesophagus that will compose a part of our robotic implant system presented in [9]. The robotic implant aims to lengthen oesophageal tissue in vivo for a duration of weeks in order to reconstruct missing oesophageal tissue in the treatment of long-gap oesophageal atresia (LGEA) [10,11]. During the in vivo performance, the oesophageal tissue experiences not only a change in length as a result of physiological factors, e.g., growth, peristaltic motion [13], but also a change in stiffness, as a consequence of inflammatory responses that are expected in any surgical intervention or implantation over time [6,7]. It is desired to have an oesophageal phantom capable of mimicking these responses realistically, as a benchtop testing platform for the robotic implant before in vivo evaluation.

A. Thorn and D. Afacan—Contributed equally.

© Springer International Publishing AG 2017
Y. Gao et al. (Eds.): TAROS 2017, LNAI 10454, pp. 351–362, 2017.
DOI: 10.1007/978-3-319-64107-2_28

In this work, we show the progress in the development of an entirely soft, low-power, low-cost and easy to assemble elastomeric actuator, inspired by [14] where a coiled heat-reactive nylon is introduced, that can be used as a replacement (phantom) for a biological oesophageal tissue (Fig. 1).

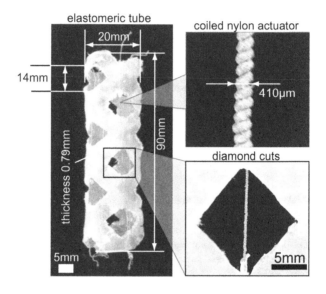

Fig. 1. Elastomeric-embedded coiled actuators as a tubular tissue phantom. Details show the coiled nylon actuator, and a portion of the elastomer with a diamond cut where the a coiled nylon actuator is exposed.

Biological tissues are complex structures with changing mechanical properties depending on physiological or pathological factors. For example, they are soft under normal conditions and stiff if they experience scarring as a result of an inflammatory reaction; or voluntarily alternate states to perform programmed functions, e.g., peristalsis for the oesophagus. As medical robots are playing an increasing role in diagnosis and treatment [3,18,23,24,30,31], realistically simulating biological tissues will contribute significantly to the development of efficient medical robots, and replacement or reduction of animal use for in vivo testing.

Although much progress has been achieved in mimicking the physiology of tissue and organs using microchip manufacturing methods [4,15], contributions to realistic simulation of mechanically-functional biological tissues are limited. Most of the simulation tissues are passive having been used to characterize palpation [8,22] or for estimating parameters of viscoelastic interactive models of biological tissues during intervention of surgical robots [23,26].

Soft actuators are most appropriate for building functional structures and robots that mimic the behavior of biological tissues. Challenges in mimicking biological tissues include: (1) extensibility at a large degree; (2) thinness and smoothness; (3) changes in stiffness that do not dramatically change the elastic modulus of the tissue but still maintain its softness; (4) low-cost and low-profile, from the perspective of engineered fabrication.

Muscle-like motion has been achieved most popularly based on pneumatic motion, which is mostly desired for power assisting devices [5,17,21,25,27]. Shape Memory Alloys (SMA) are also commonly used actuators for controlling stiffness, shape, or vibratory motions, but they would not render it an entirely soft structure [2,19,29]. Similar features have also been engineered into polymers [20]. Dielectric elastomer actuators that extend in planar directions provide necessary softness as needed for mimicking biological tissue, though they require considerably high voltage for the attached compliant electrodes [16]. Others soft actuators that can change stiffness are fabricated using a conductive propylene-based elastomer [28] or are driven by an electro-magnetic principle [12]. These technologies all provide advances in compliant actuators, though they are in contradiction to at least one of the properties desirable for building soft tissue phantoms, e.g., require large structures, external pump attachments, or high power consumption.

In this paper, having considered that a challenge resides in realising a medically congruent artificial tissue for in vivo use, we aim to develop a low-power and low-cost stiffness-varying tissue phantom that can support the advancement of in vivo robotic implants. The contributions of this paper are:

1. the concept, design, and fabrication of an active composite material combining thermo-active thread embedded in an elastomer,
2. development of an stiffness variable oesophagus phantom capable of elongation and exhibiting different levels of stiffness,
3. implementation of a varying target force to the closed loop controller depending on the intrinsic properties of the phantom,
4. verification of the proposed model in experiments tested with the robotic implant.

2   Stiffness-Variable Tissue Phantom (SVTP)

2.1   Design

The SVTP is created by embedding coiled nylon actuators [14] in an elastomeric sheet based on a diamond cut stencil (Fig. 1). Given these compounds, this design is entirely soft, exhibiting high stretchability, as well as thermo-electrical contraction, which is similar to how biological tissues function. The fabrication of the SVTP can be low-cost, and easy to fabricate. A reasonable extent of contraction of the SVTP is achieved at the application of low-power, approx 1.4 W for voltages of up to 7 V, making it practical for portable medical device platforms. The diamond-cut stencil embedding the coiled nylon actuator typically reduces the contraction capability as compared with a bare coiled nylon actuator. Nonetheless, this design of the stencil fastens the coil which otherwise would easily curl up around itself rendering it unusable. The cuts where the coil is exposed ensure that the ability of the coil to contract is optimally maintained. Further details of the design on the SVTP are presented in the following sections.

2.2   Coiled Nylon Actuators

The coiled nylon actuators contained within the body of the device contract through its lengthwise axis upon the application of heat [14]. These actuators are made of a Shieldex 117/17 dtex 2-ply HC+B wire (Statex Produktions+Vertriebs GmbH) which is a nylon multi-filament yarn coated in silver. Contraction can also be obtained using a coil of bare nylon wire. The actuator is fabricated by hanging the wire from the shaft of a motor with a weight of 68.3 g attached to the other end, keeping the yarn taut. The weight is restricted from rotation and the motor is powered to induce twists into the fibre eventually resulting in a coil forming around itself into a spring-like shape. It was found that the Shieldex yarn had a coiling ratio of 4:1 whereby the original wire becomes its length once fully coiled. These coils are to be tested using a heat gun to prove that they can contract lengthwise under heat. This process also requires the untwisting of the coils under a weight of 16 g until they lift this weight by a minimum of 1 cm. This process of coil fabrication is easily carried out and requires minimal equipment.

2.3   Fabrication of SVTP

The process of fabrication is illustrated in Fig. 2. The SVTP is fabricated by moulding Ecoflex 00-10 (Smooth On) embedded with coiled nylon actuators, according to a checkerboard stencil with a diamond orientation. This stencil is fabricated from sheets of plain paper and double-sided acrylic adhesive sheets in an alternating order. The checkerboard design is either hand-cut or laser-cut (LS6840 Laser Engraving Machine, Laserscript). The latter version provides a neater finish to the checkerboard stencil. This layout features squares of $1 \times 1 \, cm^2$ separated by bridges of $0.2 \times 1 \, cm^2$. Four alternative sheets of paper and adhesive stencils are placed in a container ($11.8 \times 20.5 \, cm^2$ (length×width)). The first layer of adhesive sheet ensures that the template is well held in the container. Pre-prepared coiled nylon actuators (length 10.5 cm, diameter 0.41 mm) are placed in a taut configuration along each column of diamonds over this template. Subsequently, a top template consisting of a layer of adhesive sheet and a layer of paper is placed on top. This layer of adhesive ensures that the coiled nylon actuators are kept in place above the lower template. The checkerboard stencil design has the purpose of exposing the coiled nylon actuators in diamond-shape cuts. The two templates (bottom and top) that sandwich the actuators ensure that they are well embedded in the target elastomeric structure. Once the template and the coil actuators are firmly in place, the bridges between the squares are manually removed from the container. Finally, an even layer of Ecoflex 00-10 is poured in the gaps with a thickness equal to that of the overall template (0.79 mm) and takes approximately 4 h to set. Once fully set, the contents of the tray are removed and the paper is manually extracted from the elastomeric sheet

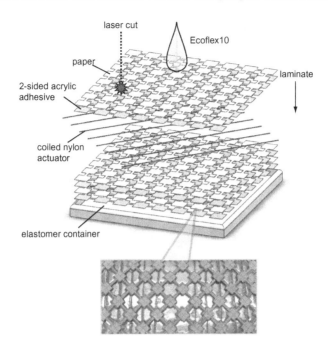

Fig. 2. Fabrication process of SVTP. Laminated layers of paper and double-sided acrylic adhesive sheets sandwich coiled nylon actuators. A checkerboard stencil with a diamond orientation is used to control the exposure of the coiled nylon actuators outside of an elastomeric substrate that is poured into the stencil structure.

to produce the SVTP. The resulting sheet is folded into a cylinder by connecting the two edges parallel to the coils using Ecoflex 00-10 or silk surgical sutures.

2.4   Finite Element Analysis of SVTP Contraction

We have analyzed the deformation of the SVTP by a given force input from a single coiled nylon actuator using finite element method (FEM) analysis. The simulated structure was a model of a single section of the SVTP containing one diamond cut spanning $20 \times 20 \times 1.4 \, \text{mm}^3$.

Fixed support was added to the top and the bottom faces of the section, and an experimentally obtained value of the initial shear modulus of elastomer, $G = 920.6 \, \text{Pa}$, was used. Forces were applied to the top and the bottom corner of the cut at magnitude of 0.08 N toward the bottom and 0.08 N toward the top, along the vertical axis, respectively. Commercially available software (Ansys) was used for analysis.

Figure 3(a) shows the result of the analysis. The maximum deformation of 3.85 mm was yielded under these circumstances.

Figure 3(b and c) shows before and after the contraction of SVTP comprising 4 columns of diamond cuts and thus 4 coiled nylon actuators involved to produce force. A value of 16.33 g was experimentally applied (0.082 N at each end of the diamond) which is comparable to the condition in Fig. 3(a). The observed contraction was about 3 mm which is 72% of the value predicted in FEM analysis.

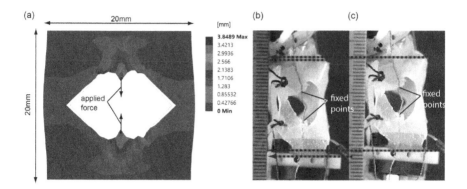

Fig. 3. Contraction of the SVTP. FEM analysis of the contraction of one section of SVTP induced by a coiled nylon actuator (a), experimental result of contraction with four coiled nylon actuator before force is applied (b) and after force is applied (c).

2.5   Robotic Implant

The SVTP assembled as an oesophagus phantom is a reliable platform to test the adaptive force control of a robotic implant, before it is used in vivo on biological tissue. The implant is a 1-DOF linear actuator Fig. 4. Prototype design is taken from [9] targeting 2-year-old patients of (LGEA), for which treatment of tissue reconstruction requiring the application of mechanical stimulation to the tissue. The device uses two suspender rings to attach to the oesophagus phantom, and applies traction to the tissue by gap adjustment between the suspender rings using a DC motor connected to a worm gear. It is equipped with two sensors: (1) Force sensor (FS Series, Honeywell) whose signal is amplified by a non-inverting differential amplifier (MCP6004, Microchip). (2) K-type thermocouple whose signal is amplified by Adafruit MAX31855 amplifier and transmitted via SPI communication protocol. An Atmega 328 microcontroller (Baby Orangutan, Pololu) is used to receive force sensor and thermocouple feedback.

2.6   Robot Implant's Control

Direct force control is implemented to manipulate the traction force applied on the oesophageal phantom by actuating the suspender ring. The robotic implant and the oesophageal phantom are holistically brought together and regarded as a single plant since there is no non-contact to contact transition. The unpredictable tissue mechanics induce uncertainty to the plant structure, and as a result the

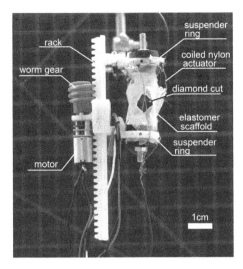

Fig. 4. The robotic implant setup with a 4-coil tubular SVTP.

controller design relies on identification of the plant model. Model identification adaptive control previously yielded that the holistic approach is plausible as the tissue mechanics affect the implant behaviour with the reaction force as the elastomeric structure elongates [1]. After system identification trials under a step input, which approximated the plant as a first order system, a PI force controller is implemented on the plant by adjusting the force controller gains for the desired over damped behaviour. The tissue adaptive capability of the implant was furthered by stiffness based adjustment of target force being provided to the tuned controller.

3 Experimental Results

3.1 Experimental Procedure for Measuring SVTP Stiffness

In order to extract the characteristics of the SVTP an experimental setup and procedure for testing the compression were established. The oesophagus phantom was thermo-electrically actuated through Joule heating from a power source in which the voltage was gradually increased in steps of 1 V. At each step, the heat was distributed uniformly along the actuator with maximum differences of 2 °C. As the coil acts as a resistor the increase in voltage increases the current and results in a higher heat and a lengthwise contraction of the coil. The SVTP was then extended by adding weights until the coil returned to its original length showing the force of the contraction. This process of heating was limited to an experimentally found maximum, as higher voltages resulted in an increased chance of structural damage in the coiled nylon actuator. The contraction of the tubular structure is reflected in a temperature change which is acquired by the thermocouple.

3.2   One-Coil SVTP Comparative Stiffness

Figure 5 shows the comparative differences in stiffness performance of a bare coiled nylon actuator as shown in [14], a coiled nylon actuator embedded in plain elastomeric sheet, and a one-coil SVTP. In this experiment coiled nylon actuators of length 10–10.5 cm were used. The elastomer sheets had an average length of 9.45 cm, width of 2.3 cm and thickness of 0.98 cm. The SVTP had 57% of its coil exposed outside the elastomer. When the maximum voltage of 6 V is applied to each end of the coil (a maximum of 5 V for the coiled nylon actuator embedded in a plain elastomeric sheet), the average maximum contraction ranges up to 10–11 mm and a temperature maximum ranges within 50–60 °C. The resistance of each individual coil varied with average values of 69.1 Ω, 50.75 Ω and 71.4 Ω, for the bare coiled nylon actuator, the actuator embedded in plain elastomeric sheet and the SVTP samples.

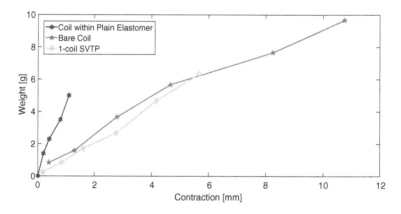

Fig. 5. The results of averaging 3 trials of compression for three separate individual coiled nylon actuators within either no elastomer (red), a plain elastomer sheet coating (blue) or an SVTP coating (green). (Color figure online)

It can be seen that placing a coil within a flat plain sheet of elastomer resulted in a large degradation in performance whereas the diamond cut structure performs in proportion to the bare coil with regards to the amount of exposed coil length. It showed 52.7% of the average maximum contraction and held 65.5% of the maximum weight compared to the exposed coil. The deviations from the proportionality can be explained by taking into account errors relating to humans in experimentation and manufacturing errors during coiling.

3.3   Oesophagus Phantom Stiffness

In Fig. 6 the compression outcome resulting from experiments as described in Sect. 3.1 are shown for the SVTP prototype. This SVTP contains within it

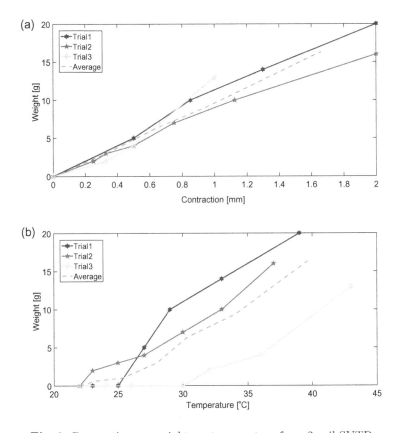

Fig. 6. Contraction vs. weight vs. temperature for a 3-coil SVTP.

3 coils of 8 cm average total length whereas 5.5 cm of it (68.8% ratio) is the average length exposed outside. They had an average total resistance of 39.4 Ω and had a maximum 7 V applied across them. It can be seen that the average maximum contraction is 2.1% of its total length. This takes the coils to a maximum temperature range 37–46 °C.

3.4   Force Control of Oesophageal Phantom

During oesophageal lengthening treatment, tissue length and stiffness are subject to change and thus uncertain. As the tissue gets stiffer or as it contracts with peristaltic motion, it will apply a higher reaction force on the implant ring, elongating it. Thus lowering the target force can induce a compliant behaviour in the presence of such unpredictable occurrences. As a result, the target force is set depending on the stiffness of the oesophageal phantom. A 4-coil SVTP is incorporated to robotic implant platform seen in Fig. 4. The information about the reaction force is obtained from the temperature change of the coiled nylon actuators in the oesophageal phantom as current passes through them. As the temperature increases while the coiled nylon actuators contract, the increase in the force applied by the oesophagus phantom (F_e) is accounted as the reaction force induced by the increasing stiffness. Computed F_e is used to define a new target force based on an inversely proportional affine relationship in each iteration of the controller with the function

$$F_{target} = 0.6 - 25\,F_e, \tag{1}$$

where the target force is bounded by $0.6\,\text{N}$ to avoid damage to SVTP and the coils. The response of the robotic implant to the varying stiffness of the esophagus phantom is shown in Fig. 7.

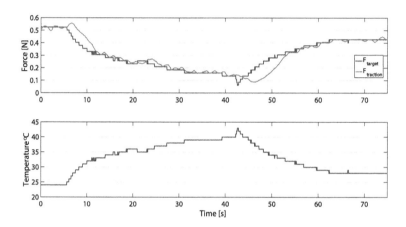

Fig. 7. Elastomer scaffold contracts increasing the overall stiffness. This induces a reaction force and an increase in the temperature of the coiled nylon actuators. Target force changes with respect to the temperature. Traction force response follows the target force with overdamped convergence.

4   Discussion and Conclusion

This work presents an energy efficient, low-profile tissue phantom whose stiffness or length can be varied. The developed phantom, SVTP, jointly with the robotic implant poses a desirable aid for the bench top synthesis of a tissue stiffness adaptive force controller of the implant for oesophageal atresia treatment.

The elastomer structure forms a casing around the coiled nylon actuators, sheltering them from damage and also encouraging their elongation. It also does this with proportional stroke length and force to the amount of coil exposed. The implemented controller has been enhanced to produce a desired target force that will also contribute to avoiding tissue damage during elongation.

The method of electrical actuation of SVTP using low power consumption to achieve reasonable contractions is suitable to develop portable applications for in vivo medicine. These contractions were yielded at body temperatures which make the SVTP a candidate for in vivo tissue manipulation.

The current limitation of the proposed oesophageal phantom is that while it can change the stiffness and the length, both features cannot be altered at the same time. The capability of changing these properties simultaneously is a desired feature in order to simulate both induced tissue growth and stiffness changes.

Another constraint is the magnitude of achievable contraction with the given power. While this is sufficient for the purpose of designing force controls with a qualitative value, the actuators should allow a broader range of contraction in order to more accurately mimic specific properties of biological tissues.

In this respect, future work includes increasing the stroke length that could be undertaken by following [14] further to create coils with a larger Spring Index (the ratio between the coil and fibre diameter). We also plan to embed soft sensors in the tissue phantoms in order to build a complete robotic structure, and to advance the soft robot to full biocompatibility such that it can also function as an implant in vivo.

Acknowledgment. We thank Emily Southern for her help with the paper revision. This work was supported by the University of Sheffield.

References

1. Afacan, D.: Stiffness-adaptive control of tissue manipulation using a robotic implant. Master's thesis, University of Sheffield, Sheffield, UK (2016)
2. Balapgol, B.S., Kulkarni, S.A., Bajoria, K.M.: A review on shape memory alloy structures. Int. J. Acoust. Vibr. **9**(2), 61–68 (2004)
3. Bergeles, C., Guang-Zhong, Y.: From passive tool holders to microsurgeons: safer, smaller, smarter surgical robots. IEEE Trans. Biomed. Eng. **61**(5), 1565–1576 (2014)
4. Bhatia, S.N., Ingber, D.E.: Microfluidic organs-on-chips. Nat. Biotech. **32**, 760–772 (2014)
5. Caldwell, D.G., Medrano-Cerda, G., Goodwin, M.: Control of pneumatic muscle actuators. IEEE Control Syst. Mag. **15**(1), 40–48 (1995)
6. Cartabuke, R.H., Lopez, R., Thota, P.N.: Long-term esophageal and respiratory outcomes in children with esophageal atresia and tracheoesophageal fistula. Oxford J. Med. Health Gastroenterol. Rep., 1–5 (2015)
7. Corr, D.T., Hart, D.A.: Biomechanics of scar tissue and uninjured skin. Adv. Wound Care (New Rochelle) **2**(2), 37–43 (2013)
8. Costa, I.F.: A novel deformation method for fast simulation of biological tissue formed by fibers and fluid. Med. Image Anal. **16**(5), 1038–1046 (2012)
9. Damian, D.D., et al.: Robotic implant to apply tissue traction forces in the treatment of esophageal atresia. In: IEEE International Conference on Robotics and Automation (ICRA), pp. 786–792 (2014)
10. Foker, J.E., et al.: Development of a true primary repair for the full spectrum of esophageal atresia. Ann. Surg. **226**(4), 533–543 (1997)
11. Foker, J.E., et al.: Long-gap esophageal atresia treated by growth induction: the biological potential and early follow-up results. Semin. Pediatr. Surg. **18**, 23–29 (2009)
12. Fries, F., et al.: Electromagnetically driven elastic actuator. In: International Conference on Robotics and Biomimetics, pp. 309–314 (2014)

13. Goyal, R.K., Chaudhury, A.: Physiology of normal esophageal motility. J. Clin. Gastroenterol. **42**(5), 610–619 (2008)
14. Haines, C., et al.: Artificial muscles from fishing line and sewing thread. Science **343**, 868–872 (2014)
15. Huh, D., Hamilton, G.A., Ingber, D.E.: From three-dimensional cell culture to organs-on-chips. Trends Cell Biol. **21**(12), 745–754 (2011)
16. Jung, K., Kim, K.J., Choi, H.R.: Self-sensing of dielectric elastomer actuator. Sens. Actuators A Phys. **143**, 343–351 (2008)
17. Klute, G.K., Czerniecki, J.M., Hannaford, B.: Mckibben artificial muscles: pneumatic actuators with biomechanical intelligence. In: IEEE/ASME International Conference on Advanced Intelligent Mechatronics, pp. 221–226 (1999)
18. Kummer, M.P., et al.: OctoMag: an electromagnetic system for 5-DOF wireless micromanipulation. In: IEEE International Conference on Robotics and Automation (ICRA), pp. 1006–1017 (2010)
19. Laschi, C., et al.: Soft robot arm inspired by the octopus. Adv. Robot. **26**(7), 709–727 (2012)
20. Lendlein, A., Kelch, S.: Shape-memory polymers. Angew. Chem. Int. Ed. **41**, 2034–2057 (2002)
21. Martinez, R.V., et al.: Elastomeric origami: programmable paper-elastomer composites as pneumatic actuators. Adv. Funct. Mater. **22**, 1376–1384 (2012)
22. Misra, S., Ramesh, K., Okamura, A.M.: Modeling of nonlinear elastic tissues for surgical simulation. Comput. Meth. Biomech. Biomed. Eng. **13**(6), 811–818 (2010)
23. Miyashita, S., et al.: Ingestible, controllable, and degradable origami robot for patching stomach wounds. In: IEEE International Conference on Robotics and Automation (ICRA) (2016)
24. Nelson, B.J., Kaliakatsos, I.K., Abbott, J.J.: Microrobots for minimally invasive medicine. Annu. Rev. Biomed. Eng. **12**, 55–85 (2010)
25. Ogawa, K., Narioka, K., Hosoda, K.: Development of whole-body humanoid "pneumat-BS" with pneumatic musculoskeletal system. In: IEEE/RSJ International Conference on Intelligent Robots and Systems, pp. 4838–4843 (2011)
26. Palacio-Torralba, J., et al.: Quantitative diagnostics of soft tissue through viscoelastic characterization using time-based instrumented palpation. J. Mech. Behav. Biomed. Mater. **41**, 149–160 (2015)
27. Roche, E.T., et al.: A bioinspired soft actuated material. Adv. Mater. **26**(8), 1200–1206 (2014)
28. Shan, W., et al.: Rigidity-tuning conductive elastomer. Smart Mater. Struct. **24**(6), 343–351 (2015)
29. Umedachi, T., Vikas, V., Trimmer, B.A.: Softworms: the design and control of non-pneumatic, 3D-printed, deformable robots. Bioinspiration Biomimetics **11**, 025001 (2016)
30. Valdastri, P., Simi, M., Webster III, R.J.: Advanced technologies for gastrointestinal endoscopy. Annu. Rev. Biomed. Eng. **14**, 397–429 (2012)
31. Yim, S., Goyal, K., Sitti, M.: Magnetically actuated soft capsule with the multimodal drug relase function. IEEE/ASME Trans. Mechatron. **18**(4), 1413–1418 (2013)

Soft Robotic Snake with Variable Stiffness Actuation

Ryan Draper[1], Jane Sheard[1(✉)], Matt Troughton[1],
and Martin F. Stoelen[2]

[1] School of Computing, Electronics and Mathematics,
Plymouth University, Plymouth, UK
{ryan.draper,jane.sheard,
matt.troughton}@students.plymouth.ac.uk
[2] Fieldwork Robotics Ltd, Plymouth, UK
martin.stoelen@plymouth.ac.uk

Abstract. In this paper, we present a prototype of a 3D printed snake-like robot for search and rescue applications, inspired by biological snake anatomy and locomotion. Unlike traditional robotics, this design takes advantage of soft materials to create a robot that is resilient to shock impacts, such as from falling debris or unsound flooring, and that can very its stiffness. The robot uses a flexible spine to connect multiple sections, allowing controlled actuation while providing a sturdy structure. Variable stiffness actuation is implemented through the use of elastic materials to act as tendons for the body, in an agonist-antagonist setup. Actuation occurs through the use of Robotis Dynamixel AX-12A servos, controlled by a Trossen Robotics Arbotix-M Robocontroller. The design features a head, containing a Raspberry Pi 3 and a Pi Camera Module. This added embedded computation can connect to a remote PC via wireless communication, allowing an operator to control the robot. This paper discusses the design and early stage testing for the prototype, and shows that robots based on soft 3D printed materials and mechanisms are viable, and effective.

Keywords: Soft robotics · Bio-inspired robotics · Locomotion · Variable stiffness

1 Introduction

Limbless creatures have evolved to use methods of locomotion that differ quite radically from methods seen in limbed creatures. However, these methods are just as effective when manoeuvring over uneven terrain or through small areas, which makes them an interesting and useful study for facilitation in search and rescue robotics (Fig. 1).

R. Draper—MEng(hons) Robotics students, Plymouth University

Y. Gao et al. (Eds.): TAROS 2017, LNAI 10454, pp. 363–377, 2017.
DOI: 10.1007/978-3-319-64107-2_29

a) 3D rendering of the snake robot design.　　　**b)** Basic working prototype of the snake robot.

Fig. 1. The prototype variable-stiffness snake robot design

Snake locomotion consists of various techniques, typically of a wave-like motion, where lateral movement and bending propagates from head to tail to propel the body. The methods of snake motion are serpentine, concertina, sidewinder, and rectilinear motion [1]. Of these locomotion methods, the side winding motion involves the snake moving itself laterally in an S-shape. This is typically used in areas where there are few resistance points for the snake to push its body forwards. The concertina motion involves folding the body into a compressed shape to move itself forwards in sections. This works well for tree climbing, as the snake can use its scales to grip the surface, bunch its body, and spring its head forwards to find a new grip surface. Rectilinear uses vertical contraction and extension of the body to create a ripple effect, which causes a slower method of motion. And lastly the serpentine motion, which is the creation of side to side contractions, and the most common method of locomotion seen in sea and land snakes. The snake's scales are used to push against resistance points, thrusting its body forwards [2].

Using soft materials, the robot can be designed to withstand impacts, as well as provide a flexible structure to the body. This allows the anatomy of a snake body to be recreated, creating a main spine to support the body, as well as providing the flexibility to bend. Ribs can be replicated to add protection to its internal assembly, and add impact resistance to the design by using a material with high toughness and resistance to deformation. Combining these, a prototype and early stage design for a soft robotic snake is created, tested and examined for search and rescue methods.

Implementing an agonist-antagonist muscle pair structure, with a flexible tendon material, variable stiffness actuation can be employed to control the robots stiffness and movement. This muscle pair works by contracting one muscle, while the other relaxes, to move a structure along a specific plane. By contracting both muscles at the same time, the joint can be held at a stable position. The design is currently only fully controlled in the horizontal plane, but could easily be expanded to be fully actuated. A fully actuated robot would function as a continuum-type design.

2　Design Process

2.1　Mechanical Design

One of the design goals was to use as few moving or fragile components as possible, creating a design as robust as possible in unsafe environments. To achieve this, a structure composed of a flexible spine supported by rigid ribs was designed. As the snake is only fully controlled in the horizontal plane, the spine is flexible in the horizontal direction and stiff along the vertical. The ribs are designed to act as a body, allowing the actuation of the spine to push against objects and generate motion. The ribs are also able to cushion sensitive components against impacts by partially flexing. The 3D model of the spine and rib structure can be seen in Fig. 2.

The body is intended to be moved using a form of soft agonist-antagonist actuation, rather than a structure based on wheeled motion [3]. An extensible fibre is used to transfer the servo actuation to the body. The servos are all of type Dynamixal AX-12 (Robotis, Korea). The tendons are made from a length of FilaFlex (Recreus, Spain) 3D printable filament, wrapped with nylon fishing wire. These filaments have close to quadratic response between load and extension, similar to biological tendons [4]. The tendon design was inspired by that used on the GummiArm variable-stiffness robot manipulator [5]. Each tendon is attached to a pulley, connected to one horizontal actuation servos, and to the rear of the next section[1]. Each section then has a tendon pulling in both horizontal directions, allowing control over the stiffness of the structure. Most current snake robots use mechanical joints or hinges rigidly connected to servo-motors to create movement. This is susceptible to damage that can render the joint immobile: either by direct deformation of a linkage, or by damage to the gears or motor due to the high effective inertia of the rigid joint. By using a flexible spine structure and elastic connections to the servos, the risk of damage that can reduce the robot mobility is greatly lessened.

Fig. 2. 3D model of the body structure, showing the structure of the robot's ribs and the flexible spine

2.2 Electrical Design

The electrical system is designed to be resistant to damage and allow an easy addition of multiple sections. Every section is identical, except the main section immediately following the head. A single section can contain three servos, and a small 12 V 1100 mAh Lithium-Polymer battery. The section following the head also holds an Arbotix-M micro-controller (Trossen Robotics, Downers Grove, Illinois, USA). The Arbotix-M is

---

[1] Repository for the GummiArm robot project: https://github.com/mstoelen/GummiArm.

connected to each servo through a daisy chained TTL and power wire, allowing it to control the motion of every section. This is a software emulation of the central pattern generators found in Vertebrates, similar to a Central Pattern Generator found in vertebrates [6].

The batteries in each section are wired in parallel, and connect to an adjacent section. This design prevents the sections from individually running out of power. It also allows the possibility of partial retained functionality in the case of a section being severed; if an additional wireless radio is mounted on each section, and an Arbotix-M is present in both sides of the severance, each portion can remain in contact and operational. The radio would then provide a method of wireless communication with this section, allowing an operator to control it.

The maximum current for each servo is 900 mA, and the Arbotix-M can draw up to 500 mA, therefore the minimum possible battery life is around 20 min, extended slightly with any added sections. This is shown in Eq. 1.

$$\text{Lifetime (minutes)} = \text{Sections} * 1/(\text{Sections} * 0.9 * 3) + 500 \qquad (1)$$

It is likely that the servos will draw on average about one third maximum current, depending on stiffness settings. This leads to an average battery life of around 60 min, again increasing slightly with the number of sections. This is also shown in Eq. 2.

$$\text{Lifetime (minutes)} = \text{Sections} * 1/(\text{Sections} * 0.3 * 3) + 500 \qquad (2)$$

Section position is monitored through the spine angle, measured with strain gauges (Spectra Symbol, Salt Lake City, Utah, USA) connected to the ribs and running along the top of the spine. The resistance of the gauges is measured by the Arbotix-M through the use of a potential divider. The Arbotix-M uses this data in a PI control algorithm to control the spine curvature [7].

2.3   Control Unit Design

The snake robot's head has been designed to include a Raspberry Pi 3 microcomputer to act as the robot main control centre, to interface with a camera, the servo controller, and to pass messages between the robot and the user. The robot can either use the Pi Camera Module v2 or the Pi NoIR Camera v2, depending on requirements. Both camera modules have a Sony IMX219 8 MP sensor, which gives a 1080 p image at 30 fps, but the NoIR Camera doesn't contain an infrared filter, so it allows night vision when used with infrared lighting or LED's.

For search and rescue applications, the robot will either be equipped with the Pi Camera and the option of regular LED's for lighting up dark areas, or the NoIR Camera with infrared lighting. For testing of the robot, the head has been designed using the Pi Camera without any LED's, as it will only be tested in well-lit conditions.

The Raspberry Pi 3 requires 5 V at 2.5 A for full power, so a method of internal power has been evaluated for use without main power. As the Raspberry Pi is only communicating with the camera module, the Arbotix-M via TTL, and currently no other peripherals, its current usage is estimated at about 750–1000 mA. A 10 Ah USB power pack was chosen, as it offers 5 V at 2.1 A, which will satisfy this current usage.

Power usage of the Raspberry Pi:

$$5\,V * 1\,A = 5\,W \tag{3}$$

Power supply capacity from battery pack:

$$5\,V * 10\,Ah = 50\,Wh \tag{4}$$

Run time for powering Raspberry Pi:

$$\frac{50\,Wh}{5\,W} = 10\,h \tag{5}$$

Therefore, using this internal battery pack, the head system will be expected to run continuously for 10 h between charges. Doubling the current usage of the Raspberry Pi to 2 A, the head can still be supported by the battery pack, and provide power for 5 h.

3 Implementation

3.1 Snake Body

The snake body was designed using Autodesk Fusion360's parametric modelling system, which allowed quick creation and modification of the design as it progressed. By utilising Fused Filament Fabrication (FFF) 3D printing technology, it was possible to rapidly develop, test, and improve the designs.

The snake robot is built from multiple sections, consisting of servo mounts and spine structures. There is no limit to the amount of sections that can be implemented, but a head and the movement control section must be at the front of the robot.

Multiple variations of spine and printing methods were tested. It was found that for ease of 3D printing, and horizontal-only flexibility, the best shape for the spine was an ellipse. There are 1 mm thick ridges, separated by 78 mm, along the structure. The ridges are for the placement of the ribs, and are designed to fit into the groove in the centre of the ribs.

Throughout the design, different spines were trialled with both 3 and 4 ribs, and tested using various materials and infill percentages. The results of these tests can be seen in Sect. 4.1. The ideal spine in this experiment holds 3 ribs and would be printed at a low infill using NinjaFlex (NinjaTek, Manheim, PA, USA), however, in practice low infill spines have a strong tendency to buckle, causing non uniform bending and severely hampering both the strain sensors and PI control. For this reason, the most appropriate makeup of a spine is high infill NinjaFlex.

The ribs were similarly tested through tensile and compressive testing, as seen in Sects. 4.3 and 4.4. The rib material found to be most suitable was high infill SemiFlex (NinjaTek, Manheim, PA, USA) ribs, as it provided a good resistance to deformation, whilst not breaking at high strain. This allows the ribs to absorb the forces from an impact.

The servos providing horizontal movement are mounted between two boards that connect the two adjacent section spines, as seen in Fig. 3. The servos control the spine for the section in front of them, and wind the tendons upon actuation. The tendon materials were also evaluated for tensile strength, as seen in Sect. 4.3. The non-linear behaviour of the tendon allows for variable stiffness control of each section, accompanied with the use of the servos as an agonist-antagonist muscle pair [8].

An additional servo can be mounted on the underside of the servo mounting board. This servo can control a brake that provides additional grip, or a flexible connection to other servo mounts, allowing for some slight control in the vertical direction by curling the snake. In addition to this, a rough surface plate made of NinjaFlex can be mounted on the bottom of the servo mount. This plate grants additional friction, making movement more efficient.

Fig. 3. 3D model of the servo mount section, displaying ribs either side, which attaches to the spine, servo mounting boards, servos, and underside servo brake and plate

3.2   Movement Control

The calculations for section position are handled by the Arbotix-M, which uses data from 2 variable resistance strain sensors attached to a spine. These sensors have a linear response in one direction, and a mostly-linear response in the other. The sensors are powered by 5 V from the Arbotix-M, and their voltage read by the Arbotix-M through a 20 K Ohm resistor, connected to Ground. The relationship between voltage and spine position must be determined for each spine section individually.

The Arbotix-M uses the determined position value as the control unit for the PI algorithm, which drives the servos to pull the spine to its required position. The PI outputs a desired torque and direction for each servo. The servos are configured in wheel mode, rather than position mode, as positional only allowed 270° of movement. This was unpractical for the design, because the pulley diameter required to drive large movements with only 270° of rotation would be quite large. As the spine itself acts as a third spring in the system, always pulling towards the centre, the torque required for greater angles does not increase linearly.

As the servos are torque controlled, the servo that is unspooling runs at a third of the rate of the spooling servo. This prevents the servo from unspooling too fast, and winding the tendon in the wrong direction. When the robot is within a few degrees of the target position, both motors will begin to tighten the tendons by winding them in. This allows the snake to resist being pushed off target, and ensures the tendons are always spooled correctly.

The robot is being designed to have four methods of locomotion, based on the real snake movement patterns studied [9]. The method of locomotion that the robot will attempt is determined by the user input from the control PC, and relayed to the Arbotix-M. The possible locomotion methods recreate the 4 methods of snake motion: Serpentine, Concertina, Sidewinder, and Rectilinear motion. Serpentine motion is emulated through each section moving through a sinusoidal pattern, out of phase by 90°. As true serpentine motion is not possible without axial and oblique actuation, this is only an approximation [10]. Concertina motion makes use of the 3rd servo mounted underneath to control a brake. The brakes are placed down to generate additional friction with the floor, while either curling sections up or using them to push the body. Sidewinder motion also makes use of the brakes, by holding the snake in place while pushing the centre section to one side, before anchoring the centre and moving the front and rear sections in line. Rectilinear motion can be created by using a flexible connection between the bottom servos. Moving the servos in alternating directions causes the segments to curl alternately, creating a caterpillar like motion.

3.3   Communication

The Raspberry Pi in the snake head receives the images from the Pi Camera, and sends them to the operator PC, to be viewed by the user. The user can then control the robot with the keyboard buttons, which send commands back to the Raspberry Pi as a message, and further sends them to the Arbotix-M for servo control.

To implement this, the Raspberry Pi uses the Ubuntu operating system to allow the use of Robot Operating System (ROS) for sending messages. ROS provides a network, or communication, infrastructure, to send data between nodes, running multiple different processes in parallel. These nodes can be within the same computer, or across different computers, transferring data via Ethernet or Wi-Fi. Thus, messages can be sent from the Raspberry Pi to the PC, and vice versa, simultaneously. Figure 4 outlines the overall communications throughout the robot.

The image messaging system was implemented to provide the user with a form of feedback from the movement mechanisms. After testing, the frame rate of communication between both computers was found to be approximately 5 s between each image, in comparison with 0.3 s between each frame when simply communicating with the Raspberry Pi itself. Other methods of streaming the camera images were evaluated, deciding on the use of the MJPG streamer module, which takes a live sequence of images and streams them to a web browser via HTTP.

The system for sending movement commands to the robot was tested using different methods. The first method involved sending character messages from the keyboard using ASCII keys. This method didn't work simultaneously upon key pressing events, and instead required the user to send each character as a separate command. However, this method allowed a wider range of functionality when controlling the robot, as more buttons (and hence commands) are available. This was chosen to allow more flexibility of motion control, by allowing a choice of type of motion, individual section control, and total body control.

The other method of control evaluated required the use of the ROS package key_teleop, which reads the PC arrow keys and maps them to a linear and angular

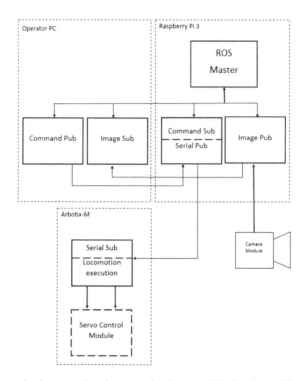

Fig. 4. Communication overview between the Operator PC, Raspberry Pi and Arbotix-M

velocity command, where up and down correspond to 0.8 and −0.5 linear motion respectively, and left and right correspond to 1.0 and −1.0 angular rotation respectively. This method provided less overall control of the robot, as it only allowed basic forwards, backwards, left and right commands; but it was the simplest method for user friendliness, as well as working simultaneously with each button press, and could be used for total motion control of the robot.

The commands, from either method, are then published via ROS to a topic from the operator PC. The Raspberry Pi subscribes to the same topic, and receives these commands – either as velocity or string messages. The Raspberry Pi then communicates with the Arbotix-M via serial, sending corresponding messages to call the required locomotion function to control the body.

Figure 5 shows the data flow using ROS, indicating the 2 separate processes running in parallel. The first sending messages from the Raspberry Pi to the PC, and the second sending commands back to the Raspberry Pi. This shows how the 2 systems run without interfering with each other, with improves the functionality of the system, allowing continuous processing rather than running sequentially. The project code is published open source on GitHub[2].

---

[2] Project on GitHub for full code development: https://github.com/JaneSheard/roco504 See also channel on YouTube for videos of testing and first attempts at locomotion: https://www.youtube.com/channel/UC-NMGpYUNjFGybRwE0-Zjaw.

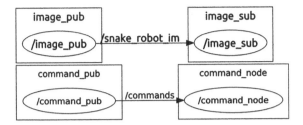

Fig. 5. RQT graph showing the ROS system in terms of nodes, topics and data flow

4   Experiments

4.1   Stiffness Testing

Stiffness tests were conducted on various spine structures at different values of motor torque. The snake section was placed on the edge of a surface, and a 1 kg mass hung from the end. Deflection from 90° was measured at different levels of servo torque. Both servos were set to wind in, to stiffen the snake body.

Figure 6 shows that the SemiFlex spine is the most resistant to bending, as its deflection is typically lowest, but also has the smallest change in deflection with torque, suggesting it is too stiff. The low infill NinjaFlex spine is the least stiff, as it deflects the most, with the greatest sensitivity to change from little motor torque input. High infill NinjaFlex has the most linear response and also a good range of stiffness.

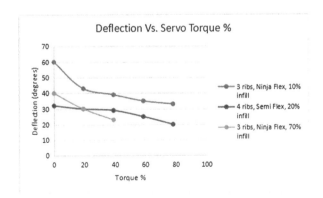

Fig. 6. Stiffness analysis of spines fabricated from different materials, evaluating spine deflection at various motor torques

From these results, the ideal spine appears to be low infill NinjaFlex, due to the low power required to move it and its large range of deflection available. However, a low infill material will be prone to buckling, therefore the high infill NinjaFlex was used for the robot spine structure due to its stiffness and deflection range.

4.2   Finite Element Analysis (FEA) Testing

FEA analysis was carried out on the 3D modelled rib structure, as these components receive the greatest load bearing. This analysis was carried out with three different possible materials: acrylonitrile butadiene styrene (ABS) plastic, polylactic acid (PLA), and Nylon. This analysis was done in Autodesk Fusion360's simulate workspace. These materials were selected for virtual testing as options for 3D printing, whilst flexible materials such as SemiFlex and NinjaFlex were tested practically in other methods, as discussed in Sects. 4.3 and 4.4.

The ribs were constrained at the contact point with the floor, and a force of 10 N was placed on the servo board mounting points. The results of the test can be seen Fig. 7. It is noticeable that ABS has deformed the most, followed by Nylon and finally PLA.

The results from this analysis show that PLA would be the most appropriate material to use, however this test may not be accurate. The model has deformed by a significant percentage, which may have cause inaccuracies. Additionally, the simulation does not take into account the anisotropic properties of 3D printed materials, likely leading to over-estimated strength.

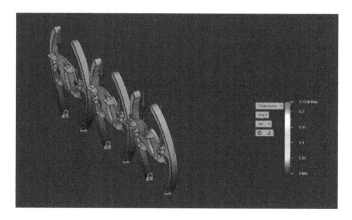

Fig. 7. FEA analysis of the 3 rib materials: PLA, Nylon and ABS, respectively

4.3   Tensile Testing

Tensile testing was performed on 3 ribs of different materials: PLA, 70% infill SemiFlex and 80% infill NinjaFlex. The ribs were tested at 10 mm/min, held lengthways and constrained just below the arcs.

Figure 8 shows the results from tensile testing 3 types of rib, displaying PLA, SemiFlex and NinjaFlex.

PLA extended only 9 mm before failure, with a steep gradient in the elastic region before reaching its elastic limit, which shows it has a high stiffness. SemiFlex extended 317 mm before breaking, with a larger elastic region, high Ultimate Tensile Strength (UTS), and greater flexibility than PLA. NinjaFlex failed in completing the test, as the material was too flexible to be pulled, falling out of the machine grips. It remained in its elastic region throughout its testing, displaying a low Young's Modulus.

This test shows that high infill SemiFlex is the most appropriate rib material, due to its large elasticity and high toughness. The yield strength is very high, at over 1100 N, equivalent to a 110 kg weight. This is larger than any tensile weight likely to occur, providing a large safety factor.

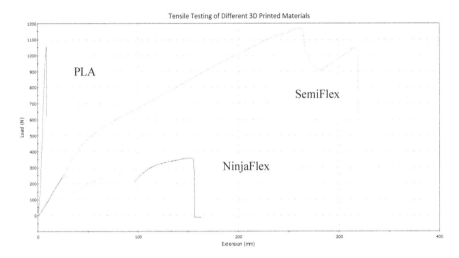

Fig. 8. Tensile testing different 3D printed materials for the rib structure: PLA, SemiFlex and NinjaFlex, respectively

Two tendons were also tested for tensile strength, as seen in Fig. 9. The tendons were identical except for the pitch of the coiled nylon thread. The tendons were tested at a rate of 100 mm/min and were pre-loaded with 1 N.

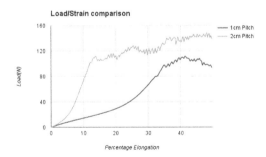

Fig. 9. Tensile testing tendon structures, evaluating different nylon thread pitch

Each tendon eventually failed as the wound nylon detached from the FilaFlex. It can be seen that the 1 cm pitch tendon extended much further than the 2 cm pitch before failing, with less load. This shows that smaller pitch leads to a more extensible tendon.

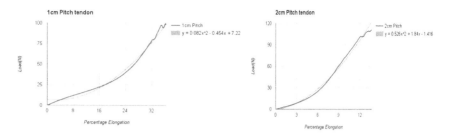

Fig. 10. Analysis of load-strain relationship of tendons with different nylon thread pitch

It can also be seen in Fig. 10, that the 1 cm pitch tendon has a load-strain relationship much closer to a quadratic. This would make the 1 cm pitch tendon more suitable for a variable stiffness system, by making exclusive control of stiffness and position more easily possible.

4.4   Compressive Testing

Compressive testing was also performed on the ribs to analyse their impact potential. Three rib terminators were used, PLA, 20% infill NinjaFlex, and 80% infill NinjaFlex. These samples were compressed at 50 mm/min, and were preloaded with 1 N. The NinjaFlex ribs were tested 3 times to ensure correct results. The PLA rib failed in its first test.

It can be seen in Figs. 11 and 12, that the 80% NinjaFlex rib is much tougher than the 20%. It also maintained its structure far better and distributed load more evenly. The PLA rib, in Fig. 13, required a large amount of force to fail, but failed in a brittle fashion, with very little compression.

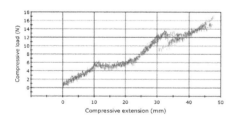

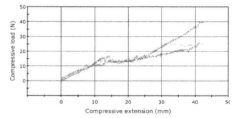

Fig. 11. Compressive testing 20% infill NinjaFlex

Fig. 12. Compressive testing 80% infill NinjaFlex

From these tests, it is clear that either a high infill SemiFlex or NinjaFlex material would be suitable for the rib structure, with a high infill SemiFlex being chosen due to its high toughness and flexibility, whilst maintaining its structural integrity.

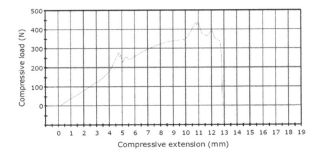

Fig. 13. Compressive testing 20% infill PLA

5 Discussion

Extensions to this project focus on increasing its functionality for search and rescue missions. The addition of artificial intelligence approaches would give the robot more autonomous functionality for search and rescue. This could be implemented by developing camera processing, to understand its environment, and including a thermal imaging camera for locating humans in rubble.

Extra hardware would be beneficial to the system, such as microphones to detect any possible noise, and to transmit these readings to the robot user. A method of navigation would aid the system, by adding a GPS and a 3D simulated model of the path taken during search missions. This would create a simple method for the snake to follow its own path, and for easy localisation of the robot by the user.

Current-controlled DC motors would likely be a more efficient actuation method, as they do not require as much space and would allow for more degrees of control, and a smaller total size. It may be that an alternative actuation system to motors altogether would be preferable.

The locomotion of this prototype is very slow. A majority of the energy expenditure by the robot is wasted as it cannot maintain grip on most surfaces. Using the serpentine method, the sections tended to slip horizontally rather than provide thrust. Average travel speed was around 1 cm per minute. Concertina and Sidewinder both suffered a similar problem, and averaged a travel speed of near 2 cm per minute. Rectilinear was the most effective form of movement, due to a portion of the robot weight being lifted from the floor and all motion occurring in the plane of the desired forward direction.

To ensure reliable and efficient propulsion of the robot, extra degrees of control need to be added. Particularly important is the addition of oblique actuation, allowing the snake to twist and push against the ground more efficiently, similarly to a biological snake. Adding a flexible skin, with external pressure sensing, to the robot body would create a smoother surface when moving through rubble, provide a surface of friction to aid thrust, and allow the robot to react to tight spaces and collisions on its body [11]. Further to this, the lower the centre of gravity of the body, the better it will perform for snake-like locomotion, so a lower placement of the control servos would be recommended in a future design [12].

6   Conclusion

In this paper, a first prototype of a snake with flexible, and variable-stiffness, joints have been presented. Such joints have several advantages over traditional rigid joints: they are more resilient to damage from sudden impacts, and can conform to the environment. Full control over the stiffness is possible through implementation of an agonist-antagonist system, with actuation through custom-made soft tendons driven by servos. The implementation of a spine structure can also be expanded to an omni-directional joint, or with many in series could be used to develop a continuum structure.

This paper also shows that 3D printing methods can be used to rapidly prototype a soft robot design. The tests show that soft 3D printed materials can perform remarkably well already, and they will inevitably improve. With improvements in 3D printing technology, the quality and complexity of components will also increase. It can also be used to rapidly create replacements for any field robot.

The snake robot is still somewhat inefficient in locomotion, but we believe that including more degrees of freedom and improved actuation is possible. This could result in a soft snake robot with interesting properties for real-world tasks, like search and rescue.

References

1. Gray, J.: The mechanism of locomotion in snakes. J. Exp. Biol. **23,** 101–120 (1946)
2. Hu, D.L.: The mechanics of slithering locomotion. In: Proceedings of the National Academy of Sciences of the United States of America, vol. 106, no. 25, pp. 10081–10085. doi:10.1073/pnas.0812533106
3. Ohashi, T., Yamada, H., Hirose, S.: Loop forming snake-like robot ACM_R7 and its serpenoid oval control. In: International Conference on Intelligent Robots and Systems (IROS), pp 413–418 (2010). doi:10.1109/IROS.2010.5651467
4. Massoud, E.I.E.: Healing of subcutaneous tendons: influence of the mechanical environment at the suture line on the healing process. World J. Orthop. **4**(4), 229–240 (2013). doi:10.5312/WJO.v4.i4.229
5. Stoelen, M.F., Bonsignorio, F., Cangelosi, A.: Co-exploring actuator antagonism and bio-inspired control in a printable robot arm. In: 14th International Conference on the Simulation of Adaptive Behaviour (SAB2016), Aberystwyth, UK, August 2016, pp. 244–255
6. Hooper, S.L.: Central Pattern Generators. Encyclopaedia of Life Sciences. Wiley, New York (1999–2010)
7. Tesch, M.: Parameterized and scripted gaits for modular snake robots. Adv. Robot. **23,** 1131–1158 (2012). doi:10.1163/156855309X452566
8. Rollinson, D.: Design and architecture of a series elastic snake robot. In: IEEE International Conference on Intelligent Robots and Systems, pp. 4630–4636 (2014). doi:10.1109/IROS.2014.6943219
9. Jafari, A.: Actuators. Coupling between output force and stiffness in different variable stiffness actuators. MDPI **3**(3), 270–284 (2014). doi:10.3390/act3030270

10. Shi, P., Shao, Q., Liang, D.: Design and improved serpentine curve locomotion control of a planar modular snake. In: International Conference on Information and Automation (ICIA), pp. 1398–1402 (2016). doi:10.1109/ICInfA.2016.7832038
11. Wright, C.: Design of a modular snake robot. In: International Conference on Intelligent Robot Systems, pp. 2609–2614 (2007). doi:10.1109/IROS.2007.4399617
12. Luo, M., Tao, W., Chen, F., Khuu, T.K., Ozel, S., Onal, C.D.: Design improvements and dynamic characterization on fluid elastomer actuators for a soft robotic snake. In: International Conference on Technologies for Practical Robot Applications (TePRA), pp. 1–6 (2014). doi:10.1109/TePRA.2014.6869154

Model Identification of a 3 Finger Adaptive Robot Gripper by Using MATLAB SIT

Amirul Syafiq Sadun and Jamaludin Jalani[✉]

Faculty of Engineering Technology, Universiti Tun Hussein Onn Malaysia,
Parit Raja, Johor, Malaysia
{amirul,jamalj}@uthm.edu.my

Abstract. This paper presents the method of finding the estimated plant transfer function of the 3 Finger Adaptive Robot Gripper by using the MATLAB System Identification Toolbox (SIT). The robot gripper consists of 3 under actuated fingers, where the active joint is driven by a DC motor and the passive joint is driven by the underactuated mechanism (elastic tendons). To simplify the study, the model identification only considers the single angular joint of each finger. The approach of fast variable step input (i.e. stairs input) and slow variable step input (i.e. slope input) was introduced while the output of the robot gripper is referring to the motor encoder position of each finger. The best estimated modelling of the gripper is obtained by selecting the transfer function that has the most similar performance (in term of position control) compared to the actual system. Moreover, the result shows that the transfer function obtained by using fast variable step input is sufficient to represent the 3 Finger Adaptive Robot Gripper. Additionally, the PID position control was employed and the result shows that the gripping performance is satisfactorily achieved in simulation and experiment.

Keywords: Model identification · SIT · Robotic hand · Gripper · PID control

1 Introduction

Nowadays, many types of robot gripper are produced and the recent development has shown various improvements in term of designs and performances. The robot performance can be analysed not only via the actual system but also by using the simulation approach. To simulate the robot gripper, it is important to have a model that accurately represents the robot system. This is to ensure, any optimization and parameter variable that is used in the simulation will have a significant result of the actual system. To optimize the performance of a robot gripper, a suitable approach of system identification can be used such as MATLAB System Identification Toolbox (SIT). According to [1], by performing the system identification, a high performance control can be observed in simple models if some basic structure is accurately captured. Commonly, a robot gripper is equipped with a DC motor system, including gearing system and position feedback. Thus, the fundamental concept of attaining the system identification of a robot gripper is similar to the DC motor system. However, the parameter variables are different (i.e. the gearing ratio and the finger load) [2]. General

© Springer International Publishing AG 2017
Y. Gao et al. (Eds.): TAROS 2017, LNAI 10454, pp. 378–392, 2017.
DOI: 10.1007/978-3-319-64107-2_30

methods of system identification for a DC motor has been demonstrated by [3] whereas the transfer function of the DC motor can be represented in the z-domain (discrete) or s-domain (continuous) depending on the complexity of the modelling. Recently, a 3 Finger Adaptive Robot Gripper has been developed by the ROBOTIQ. In brief, the robot gripper consists of 3 under actuated fingers, where the active joint is driven by a DC motor and the passive joint is driven by the underactuated mechanism (elastic tendons). The robot can be conveniently communicating with robot controllers such as Ethernet/IP, TCP/IP, and Modbus RTU. In addition, the MATLAB/Simulink can also be used to develop the control algorithm by using the available communication platform. Figure 1 illustrates the 3 Finger Adaptive Robot Gripper.

Fig. 1. The 3 Finger Adaptive Robot Gripper

This paper presents the method of finding the estimated plant transfer function of the 3 Finger Adaptive Robot Gripper by using the MATLAB System Identification Toolbox (SIT). The best estimated modelling of the gripper is obtained by selecting the transfer function that produces the closest performance (in term of position control) compared to the actual system. Additionally, the PID position control was employed to observe the gripping performance of the modelling and actual system.

2 Experimental Setup

2.1 Communication Setup

In this experiment, the robot is controlled by using Modbus RTU protocol via MATLAB Simulink Instrument Control Toolbox. The protocol involves serial communication between MATLAB Simulink and the robot gripper. The command and response to the robot gripper are "real time" with the accuracy of 1 ms. Moreover, the interface is fast and reliable where all the input and output data recording process is run via Matlab Simulink software. Figure 2 shows the communication platform used in this study.

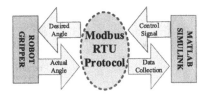

Fig. 2. Communication platform

2.2   The Open Loop System

As mentioned earlier, the model identification approach used in the study is based on the MATLAB SIT. The technique is simple and reliable to perform the model identification process. Essentially, an open loop setup is employed to measure the robot gripper's input and output data. Similar setup approach can be found in [4–6]. Figure 3 shows the hardware setup for the model identification process.

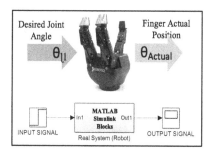

Fig. 3. Hardware setup

The setup is straight forward where the input and output data is recorded via MATLAB Simulink. Additionally, the data need to be saved into the MATLAB workspace before it can be imported into the SIT GUI [2]. It is worth noting that the input and output unit should be the same to ensure the accuracy of the model identification by using MATLAB SIT.

2.3   Gear Mechanism

The 3 Finger Adaptive Robot Gripper came with 3 identical fingers design where each joint is equipped a "worm gear" mechanism as shown in Fig. 4. The DC motor that located inside the robot palm are equipped with encoders for the position feedback during the operation. The DC motor drive gear is also identical for each finger, whereas the fingers are capable of generating the same amount of gripping force. Similar design concept can be seen for the robot used in [7]. Figure 4 shows that one of the advantages of the "worm gear" mechanism is it enable the robot gripper to achieve a high torque for the grasping in low gear ratio.

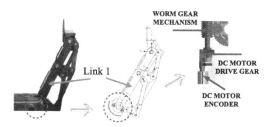

Fig. 4. The 3 Finger Adaptive Robot Gripper with a "worm gear"

2.4   Joint Angular Position

For the simplicity of the study, only one joint is considered for each robot finger, which involved the angular position of link 1 (l_1). The angle is referring to the distance between link 1 (l_1) and palm axis (θ_{l1}). Based on the preliminary test, it is known that the joint angular position for link 1 (θ_{l1}) is between 65° (minimum) to 125° (maximum). Thus, the desired input for the experiment was set between these angular ranges. The link 1 (l_1) is shown in Fig. 5.

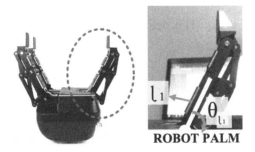

Fig. 5. Joint angular position for link 1, (l_1)

Meanwhile, it is also known that the encoder position feedback produces values ranged between 0 to 255 (depending on the robot finger position). The relationship between the encoder value and the physical position of the finger must be computed to allow a proper grasping control. Thus, a program is executed in order to find the correlation of the joint angular position from 65° (ungrip) to 125° (grip) with respect to the encoder turn.

3   Single Joint Equations

Theoretically, the DC motor for each robot finger consists of an armature circuit, rotor, and fixed field. The rotor is connected to the gearing mechanism with "n" ratio depending on the hardware requirement. By referring to [8], the equivalent circuit for each robot finger is shown in Fig. 6.

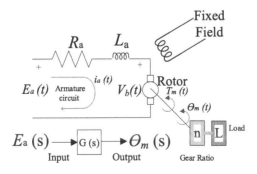

Fig. 6. Equivalent circuit for each finger

Figure 6 shows the armature voltage, $E_a(t)$, to control a DC motor. The motor has a resistance R_a, inductance L_a and back electromotive force constant, K_b. The back emf voltage, $V_b(t)$ is induced by the rotation of the armature windings in the fixed magnetic field. The counter *emf* is proportional to the speed of the motor with the field strength fixed.

The *back emf* voltage, $V_b(t)$ is written as

$$V_b(t) = K_b \frac{d\Theta}{dt} \tag{1}$$

Laplace transform of Eq. (1) is derived as

$$V_b(s) = s.K_b\theta(s) \tag{2}$$

Based on Fig. 6, circuit equation for electrical motor is shown as

$$E_a(s) = R_a I_a(s) + L_a s\, I_a(s) + V_b(s) \tag{3}$$

Equation (3) can be rearranged as:

$$I_a s = \frac{E_a(s) - K_b S\Theta(s)}{L_{as} + R_a} \tag{4}$$

Equation for torque that produced by motor is written as

$$T_m(s) = K_t I_a(s) \tag{5}$$

where, K_t is the torque constant.

Moreover, the equation connecting torque and shaft angle is computed as follows:

$$T(t) = J\frac{d^2\theta_m}{dt^2} + D\frac{d\theta_m}{dt} \tag{6}$$

where:
θ_m the motor shaft angle position.
J   all inertia connected to the motor shaft.
D   all friction (air friction, bearing friction, etc.) connected to the motor shaft.

Furthermore, the laplace transform for Eq. (6) is

$$T_m(s) = J_s^2\theta_m(s) + D_s\theta_m(s) \tag{7}$$

Then, the shaft angle is

$$\theta_m(s) = \frac{T_m}{J_s^2 + D_s} \tag{8}$$

Assumed that gear train mechanisms connect the motor and load, rotation angle on the load is differ from motor shaft. This angle difference depends on the gear ratio relationship which can be represented in (9):

$$S = R_m\theta_m = R_L\Theta_L \tag{9}$$

Assumed that R_m and R_L have N_m and N_L gear teeth, Eq. (9) can be expressed as follows:

$$N_L\Theta_L = N_m\Theta_m \tag{10}$$

or

$$\frac{\theta_m}{\theta_L} = \frac{N_m}{N_l} = n \tag{11}$$

The equations derived above can also be represented in a control system block diagram as shown in Fig. 7.

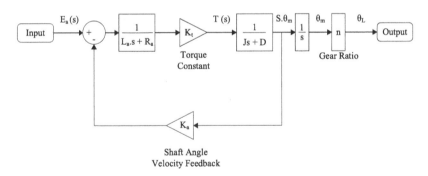

Fig. 7. Control system block diagram

By simplifying the block diagram in Fig. 7, the armature-controlled motor transfer function is:

$$Gs = \frac{\theta_L(s)}{E_s} = \frac{K_t n}{s[(J_s + D)(L_{as} + R_a) + K_b K_t]} \tag{12}$$

4 Model Identification

MATLAB has the capability in analyzing and calculating a complex data specifically in linear and nonlinear environments. System Identification Toolbox (SIT) from MATLAB where the modelling of the plant transfer function was achieved and used throughout this study. The SIT GUI can be started by typing "ident" at the MATLAB command window where the input and output data from the Matlab *workspace* can be imported. The GUI has the capability to analyze up to eight sets of data in a single session. Furthermore, the transfer function of the imported data can be estimated. The plant model identification by using the MATLAB SIT GUI is shown in Fig. 8.

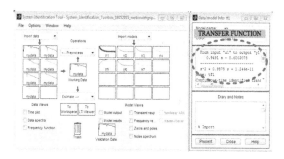

Fig. 8. Model identification by using MATLAB SIT

The SIT requires a set of equally sampled data from the input and output of the robot gripper. As mentioned earlier, the output data from the plant was obtained precisely by setting the robot gripper hardware to be at an open-loop operation. The GUI for the SIT can be run through the MATLAB window as soon as the data is gathered. Two sets of the input signal; a fast response step input (i.e. multiple step variable) and a slow response step input (i.e. slope) were tested. Figure 9 shows the type of response used for the model identification test in this study (for each finger).

As recommended by [2], the model identification should achieve the best fit more than 90%. The higher best fit values indicate that the input and output signal are significantly closed [9]. However, in some cases (i.e. non-linear system), the best fit value may not represent the accuracy of the estimated transfer function [2]. Table 1 summarized different response of step input test.

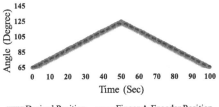

(a) Slope Δt=100 Second (Grip and Un-grip)

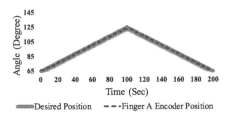

(b) Slope Δt=200 Second (Grip and Un-grip)

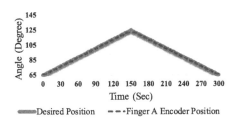

(c) Slope Δt=300 Second (Grip and Un-grip)

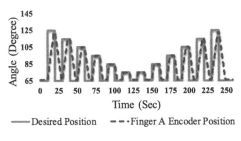

(d) Multiple Step Variable (Grip and Un-grip)

Fig. 9. Type of response for model identification

Table 1. Different response of step input test.

Test	Input	Output
Test 1	Slope Δt = 100 s (grip and un-grip)	Link 1 Encoder Position (each finger)
Test 2	Slope Δt = 200 s (grip and un-grip)	Link 1 Encoder Position (each finger)
Test 3	Slope Δt = 300 s (grip and un-grip)	Link 1 Encoder Position (each finger)
Test 4	Multiple step response (grip and un-grip)	Link 1 Encoder Position (each finger)

Table 1 exhibits the desired angle (input) and the actual angle (output) measured by using MATLAB Simulink Scope. The data from the Scope was saved in the MATLAB *workspace*, which can be imported into the SIT GUI. The MATLAB Simulink blocks used for all tests showed in Fig. 10.

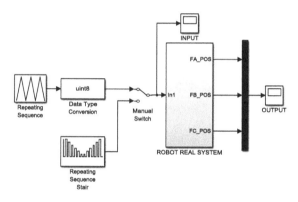

Fig. 10. Simulink block for model identification

By using the Simulink programming setup as shown in Fig. 10, the results of model identification for Finger A, Finger B, and Finger C were obtained and recorded as seen in Tables 2, 3 and 4 respectively. Next, these transfer functions were validated.

Table 2. Model identification for Finger A

Data	Plant transfer function	Best fit (%)
Test 1	$\frac{11.27\,S + 13.91}{S^2 + 12.9\,S + 13.93}$	99.33%
Test 2	$\frac{23.88\,S + 22.92}{S^2 + 24.82\,S + 22.95}$	99.33%
Test 3	$\frac{8.98\,S + 3.557}{S^2 + 9.389\,S + 3.562}$	97.65%
Test 4	$\frac{0.1303\,S + 0.2759}{S^2 + 0.9497\,S + 0.2737}$	72.2%

Table 3. Model identification for Finger B

Data	Plant transfer function	Best fit (%)
Test 1	$\dfrac{248.6\,S + 85.05}{S^2 + 248.6\,S + 85.19}$	99.26%
Test 2	$\dfrac{12.29\,S + 6.677}{S^2 + 13.41\,S + 6.689}$	99.26%
Test 3	$\dfrac{5.238\,S + 1.993}{S^2 + 5.622\,S + 1.996}$	97.5%
Test 4	$\dfrac{0.131\,S + 0.2794}{S^2 + 0.9601\,S + 0.2773}$	72.36%

Table 4. Model identification for Finger C

Data	Plant transfer function	Best fit (%)
Test 1	$\dfrac{-120.2\,S + 69.33}{S^2 + 120.8\,S + 69.47}$	99.26%
Test 2	$\dfrac{-32.28\,S + 280.2}{S^2 + 69.05\,S + 280.7}$	99.26%
Test 3	$\dfrac{240.8\,S + 39.73}{S^2 + 250.5\,S + 39.8}$	97.29%
Test 4	$\dfrac{0.1311\,S + 0.2807}{S^2 + 0.9626\,S + 0.2787}$	72.38%

5   Model Validation

This section discusses the validation of the plant transfer function obtained through experiment. The validation approach was performed by comparing the transfer function with the actual robot gripper position response in an open loop hardware setup. This validation process is carried out to determine which transfer functions (from test 1 until test 4) are best to represent the actual 3 Finger Adaptive Robot Gripper in term of position control. The Simulink setup for the validation is shown in Fig. 11.

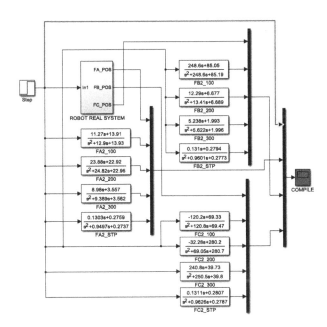

Fig. 11. Simulink block for model validation (Finger A, Finger B and Finger C)

Figure 12 demonstrates the captured data for Finger A, Finger B and Finger C at a similar span of time. Here, the results from the model validation are shown and discussed.

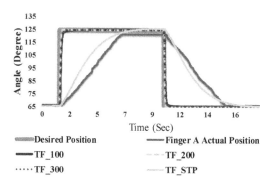

(a) Finger A Validation Results

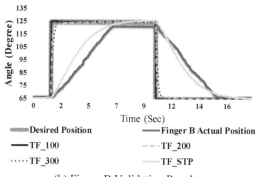

(b) Finger B Validation Results

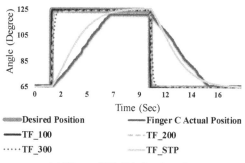

(c) Finger C Validation Results

Fig. 12. The model validation results (Color figure online)

Figure 12(a), (b) and (c) show that the transfer function for Test 4 (yellow colour) produced the most accurate response compared to the robot actual finger position (red colour). To further analyse the results, a measurement of standard deviation for the data was carried out as shown in Table 5, to identify which of the estimated responses are most similar to the actual response of the plant. The standard deviation for the actual robot gripper response is $SD_{Actual} = 22.05$.

Table 5. Standard deviation of Finger A

Data	Standard deviation (SD)	$SD_{Actual} - SD_{Test}$
Test 1	29.57	7.52
Test 2	29.81	7.76
Test 3	29.65	7.6
Test 4	23.87	1.82

Table 6. Standard deviation of Finger B

Data	Standard deviation (SD)	$SD_{Actual} - SD_{Test}$
Test 1	29.93	7.88
Test 2	29.32	7.27
Test 3	29.47	7.42
Test 4	23.85	1.8

Table 7. Standard deviation of Finger C

Data	Standard deviation (SD)	$SD_{Actual} - SD_{Test}$
Test 1	30.2	8.15
Test 2	29.57	7.52
Test 3	28.98	6.93
Test 4	23.86	1.81

Despite the best fit value of Test 4 is less than 90%, the standard deviation analysis results as in Tables 5, 6 and 7 can also be used to confirm the accuracy of plant transfer functions. The value of $SD_{Actual} - SD_{Test}$ for Test 4 shows the smallest difference as compared to the other 3 tests. This indicates that Test 4 model identification produces the highest similarities of the input and output data. Hence, the estimated plant transfer function from Test 4 was selected and further validated by implementing closed loop PID position control. Figure 13 shows the Simulink block setup for the implementation.

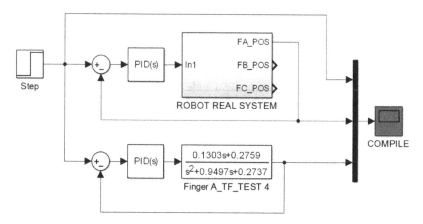

Fig. 13. Simulink blocks for PID position control (Finger A)

Figure 13 illustrates the Simulink programming block for Finger A. The setup is carried out individually for each finger. However, for the simplicity of this study, only the implementation of closed loop PID position control for Finger A is considered. Similar results can be expected for Finger B and C due to the same motor used for all fingers (mentioned in Sect. 2.3). Figure 14 shows the results for the actual Finger A position versus the estimated plan transfers functions (obtained via Test 4) before the PID tuning optimization. Meanwhile, Fig. 15 shows the results after the PID tuning optimization.

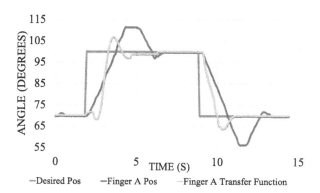

Fig. 14. Before PID tuning optimization

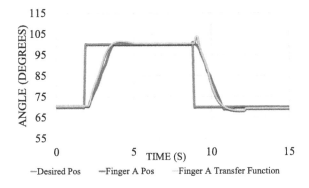

Fig. 15. After PID tuning optimization

Based on Figs. 14 and 15, it can be observed that the transient response improved with the reduction of overshoot for the robot actual finger and the estimated transfer function of Finger A. Table 8 summarizes the results before and after tuning. Meanwhile, Table 9 summarizes the tuning parameter before and after the PID optimization.

Table 8. Improvement comparison (before and after PID optimization)

Data	Overshoots (%) (Actual|Estimated TF)		Settling time (s) (Actual|Estimated TF)	
Before optimization	30%	15%	4 s	3 s
After optimization	<5%	<5%	3 s	3 s

Table 9. PID tuning parameter

Parameter	Un-tuned		Tuned	
	Actual	$TF_{Finger\ A}$	Actual	$TF_{Finger\ A}$
P	−0.3	22.4	−0.5	43.5
I	−1.5	7	−1.6	1.83
D	3.5	−0.045	−0.186	−0.25

6   Conclusions

This paper provides a detailed description of the method in finding the estimated plant transfer function of the 3 Finger Adaptive Robot Gripper by using the MATLAB System Identification Toolbox (SIT). The fast and slow responses of the step input were introduced to investigate the best fit transfer function of the actual robot system. The results showed that it is possible to obtain the best transfer function by using the fast response (multiple step response) despite the obtained best fits data were less than

90% for all fingers (in this case 72%). On the other hand, the study also successfully compares the performances of the estimated transfer function and the actual robot finger by using closed loop PID position control. The results show that the selected estimated transfer function are tunable and can be used in the closed loop environment. The obtained transfer function is certainly beneficial for future analysis particularly to run the simulation of the robot gripper in a more complex control system.

References

1. Gevers, M.: A personal view of the development of system identification. Historical Perspectives, pp. 93–105 (2006)
2. Sadun, A.S., Jalani, J., Sukor, J.A.: Model identification of a low-cost robot gripper by using matlab system identification toolbox (SIT). ARPN J. Eng. Appl. Sci. 11(14), 8965–8971 (2016)
3. Unbehauen, H., Rao, G.P.: A review of identification in continuous-time systems. Ann. Rev. Control 22, 145–171 (1998)
4. Liarokapis, M.V., Calli, B., Spiers, A.J., Dollar, A.M.: Unplanned, model-free, single grasp object classification with underactuated hands and force sensors. IEEE Int. Conf. Intell. Robot Syst. 2015, 5073–5080 (2015)
5. Odhner, L.U., Ma, R.R., Dollar, A.M.: Precision grasping and manipulation of small objects from flat surfaces using underactuated fingers. In: Proceedings of IEEE International Conference on Robotics and Automation, pp. 2830–2835 (2012)
6. Odhner, L.U., Ma, R.R., Dollar, A.M.: Open-loop precision grasping with underactuated hands inspired by a human manipulation strategy. IEEE Trans. Autom. Sci. Eng. 10(3), 625–633 (2013)
7. Hasan, M.R., Vepa, R., Shaheed, H., Huijberts, H.: Modelling and control of the Barrett hand for grasping. In: Proceedings - UKSim 15th International Conference on Computer Modelling and Simulation, UKSim 2013, pp. 230–235, April 2013
8. Ramesh, S.: Modelling of geared DC motor and position control using sliding mode controller and fuzzy sliding mode controller. In: International Conference on Innovations in Intelligent Instrumentation, Optimization and Signal Processing, vol. 13, pp. 16–23 (2013)
9. Tajjudin, M., Ishak, N., Ismail, H., Rahiman, M.H.F., Adnan, R.: Optimized PID control using Nelder-Mead method for electro-hydraulic actuator systems. In: 2011 IEEE Control and System Graduate Research Colloquium, ICSGRC 2011, no. 1, pp. 90–93 (2011)

Towards Fault Diagnosis in Robot Swarms: An Online Behaviour Characterisation Approach

James O'Keeffe[1(✉)], Danesh Tarapore[2], Alan G. Millard[1], and Jon Timmis[1]

[1] Department of Electronic Engineering, University of York, York, UK
jhok500@york.ac.uk
[2] School of Electronics and Computer Science, University of Southampton,
Southampton, UK

Abstract. Although robustness has been cited as an inherent advantage of swarm robotics systems, it has been shown that this is not always the case. Fault diagnosis will be critical for future swarm robotics systems if they are to retain their advantages (robustness, flexibility and scalability). In this paper, existing work on fault detection is used as a foundation to propose a novel approach for fault diagnosis in swarms based on a behavioural feature vector approach. Initial results show that behavioural feature vectors can be used to reliably diagnose common electro-mechanical fault types in most cases tested.

Keywords: Fault diagnosis · Feature vector · Behaviour characterisation · Swarm robotics

1 Introduction

For many years, robustness – the ability of a system to tolerate the presence of faults or failures – was considered to be an inherent property of swarm robotics systems [15]. However, investigations by Winfield and Nembrini [18] revealed that swarm robustness cannot be taken for granted in all scenarios, particularly those in which partial faults or failures are present.

A further study, conducted by Bjerknes and Winfield [3], demonstrated that the scalability of a swarm system may also suffer in scenarios where the system is not robust to the presence of faults. In light of these two supposed advantages of swarm robotics being lost or severely hindered in the presence of partial failures, the authors [3] advocate for an active approach to improving the fault tolerance of swarm systems – specifically Artificial Immune Systems (AIS), which are defined by De Castro and Timmis [9] as:

"adaptive systems, inspired by theoretical immunology and observed immune functions, principle and models, which are applied to problem solving."

Timmis et al. [17] argue that an AIS can be considered a type of swarm intelligent system. In the context of the natural immune system, Cohen [8] defines

© Springer International Publishing AG 2017
Y. Gao et al. (Eds.): TAROS 2017, LNAI 10454, pp. 393–407, 2017.
DOI: 10.1007/978-3-319-64107-2_31

maintenance as the ability of the immune system to maintain its host despite the unpredictable blows that it will undoubtedly encounter over the course of its life. The idea of maintenance in biological systems is comparable to that of fault tolerance in engineered systems – both pertain to systems that continue to operate under unusual or unexpected circumstances. Cohen [8] argues that maintenance comprises three stages:

1. Recognition – distinguishing what is normal from what is abnormal
2. Cognition – making decisions based on available information
3. Action – doing something as a result of any decisions made

Recognition, cognition and action (RCA), taken alone as a three part programme, do not do justice to the complexity of the natural immune system. However, it could be argued that some of the more complex elements of the natural immune system, such as its ability to seemingly learn and remember, exist largely to enhance the process of RCA. Therefore, it is proposed that RCA be considered the core process of an immune response – and that establishing RCA in swarm robotics systems is a step toward solving the problems outlined in [3]. Cohen's definitions of recognition, cognition and action [8] map nicely to the control engineering subfield of fault detection, diagnosis and recovery (FDDR). If RCA is considered to be the core process in the natural immune response then, by extension, FDDR may be considered as the foundation of an artificial immune response in swarm robotics systems.

The first part of any active FDDR approach is fault detection. There are a number of examples where fault detection in swarm systems, by various methods, has been successful in simulation (see the work by Millard et al. [11], Khadidos et al. [10] and Tarapore et al. [16]), and in hardware (see the work by Christensen et al. [7]). In contrast, there has been limited research on fault diagnosis in robots, examples include the immune-inspired work by Bi [1] and Bi et al. [2]. However, these works only consider single-robot systems. To the best of our knowledge, very little research has been conducted with regard to fault diagnosis in swarm robotics systems, as defined by Şahin [15].

Some of the previous work on fault detection in swarms (such as [7,10]) opts to omit an attempt at fault diagnosis, and, instead, removes or shuts down any robot which is detected as faulty. Although such approaches have shown themselves to be effective in the controlled scenarios in which they are tested, this is an expensive approach, and one which may not always be justifiable - particularly in cases where the cost of replacing a faulty part of an individual robot is significantly less than replacing the whole unit.

It is not unreasonable to assume that, as the field of swarm robotics continues to expand and develop, so too will the complexity of the tasks they are assigned to, as well as the complexity of their constituent robots. If this is the case, omitting fault diagnosis and partial recovery options will become an increasingly inefficient approach – inhibiting a swarm robotics system's scalability and their capability to operate in challenging environments. Furthermore, some emergent behaviours typically require a minimum number of functional robots in a swarm, so approaches that simply remove faulty individuals from the collective may jeopardise long-term autonomy [3].

For the reasons outlined above, the problem addressed in this paper is that of fault diagnosis in swarm robotics systems. Although fault diagnosis is the focus of this paper, a complete artificial immune response will include fully-integrated FDDR. Therefore, when developing a means of fault diagnosis, there should be some consideration as to how this might bridge the gap between fault detection (which is a prerequisite to any integrated autonomous diagnosis mechanism) and fault recovery.

Winfield and Nembrini [18] show that different fault types will cause a robot to exhibit behaviour that deviates from its expected behaviour in different ways. The hypothesis of this work is that, if individual robot behaviours can be appropriately characterised as a series of features, different fault types will produce unique patterns of these features – thereby making them classifiable. This paper therefore proposes a fault diagnosis approach based on behavioural feature vectors (BFV), which encode a robot's behaviour as a series of binary features. Such feature vectors have been previously used successfully by Tarapore et al. [16] for the purpose of fault detection in swarm robotics systems and, as is shown in this paper, can similarly be used to perform fault diagnosis via the characterisation of robot behaviour.

The contribution of this paper is to propose a novel approach to combine proprioceptively sensed and externally sensed features to diagnose fault types. This is in line with the fault tolerant and swarm robotics perspectives proposed by Winfield and Nembrini [18] and Şahin [15], respectively.

2   Behaviour Characterisation

The problem now is in defining a BFV that will allow for the reliable classification of fault types. Given that a swarm robotics system may exhibit a number of different normal behaviours, this must be taken into account when defining the BFV and selecting an appropriate classification method.

There are a variety of ways to design a feature vector for an individual robot. For example, assuming access to the relevant hardware/software documentation, it should be possible to systematically reduce every possible functionality to a series of base behaviours. For example, for ground based vehicles, individual features could relate to whether or not its wheels are turning and, if so, which wheels and how fast? To do this exhaustively, however, may prove to be a time consuming process and, in the context of fault classification, may not be necessary as it may not exclusively produce *discriminating features*. Discriminating features, which are actively sought, are features that allow a system to distinguish different fault types based on their presence, absence, or in more complex systems, their intensity. By way of example, a complete sensor failure and power failure would both result in an individual robot becoming unresponsive to its neighbours. However, a sensor failure would not necessarily prevent the robot from moving, whereas a power failure would. Hence, a feature describing the motion of the robot could be considered discriminatory in this case.

It may be possible for a system to develop, and even evolve in real-time, its own discriminatory BFV using search-based optimisation techniques. However, the focus in this paper will be on predefined and unchanging BFVs. It is necessary, if it is to be discriminatory, that a BFV for an individual robot be designed in sympathy with the behaviour(s) that the robot will exhibit. It is therefore also necessary for the swarm robotics system to exhibit static user-defined, or at least user-selected, behaviour(s). It should then be possible for the user to systematically atomise these behaviours into sub-behaviours. For example, obstacle/neighbour proximity sensing and linear and angular motion could be considered sub-behaviours of general obstacle avoidance behaviour. If the user atomises a known finite number of behaviours into sub-behaviours of an appropriate granularity (some of which will be common to multiple behaviours) and assigns a feature to each of these, the resultant repertoire of BFVs should then be representative of every behaviour the system can exhibit.

Although this makes a number of assumptions regarding swarm systems and their applications, it is anticipated that, in a vast majority of cases, a swarm system will have been designed or selected for use with a specific application, or applications, in mind. It is therefore reasonable to say that, assuming the systems behaviours are non-evolving, the chosen system will exhibit a finite number of pre-determined behaviours when performing its task(s).

There has been previous mention of work by several researchers toward fault detection in swarm robotics systems [7,10,12,16]. In each piece of work, the fundamental mechanism that enables a fault to be detected can be essentially reduced to the comparison of an individual's observed behaviour to that which the swarm or observer expects it to exhibit. We also acknowledge that the problems associated with endogenous fault detection (fault detection performed proprioceptively), such as a robot suffering controller software hang being unable to communicate this to the swarm [6], also applies to fault diagnosis – using the same example, the faulty robot would report a BFV that did not reflect its true behaviour, potentially leading to misclassification. Interestingly, the same could also be said of exogenous approaches (fault detection performed using external observations) when applied to fault diagnosis; it would be very difficult for an independent observer to distinguish a robot suffering an onboard software hang that renders it unresponsive to its neighbours from a common sensor failure, as both could potentially have the same net effect on robot's behaviour.

It is proposed that one way in which this problem could be solved is by combining proprioceptively and externally estimated BFVs, producing what can be thought of as a behavioural feature quasi-matrix. To do this, the proprioceptive BFV is designed such that it reflects what an individual robot *believes* its state is, and the externally estimated BFV such that it reflects what its neighbours ascertain its state to *actually* be. It is anticipated that multiple methods of feature estimation will not only improve the reliability of reported behaviour, but also represent a useful starting point for a classification process, as some faults will create discrepancies in features directly relating to the ways in which they manifest. For example, motor failure will a cause discrepancy in features relating to motion where one feature reflects the inclination of the robot's controller and the other reflects the robot's true movement.

2.1 Deriving Behavioural Features from Robot Behaviours

For fault diagnosis to be a useful technique in swarm robotics systems, it is important that any fault classification technique is compatible with the swarm's requirement to be flexible, and should therefore be applicable to any range of behaviours one might expect a given swarm system to exhibit. This paper chooses to use flocking, aggregation, and dispersion behaviours as a case study (see Algorithms 1, 2, and 3) based on their widespread use in swarm robotics research. These three behaviours can each be considered similar at an individual level, sharing simple and identical functionalities, yet produce significantly different collective behaviours – satisfying the behavioural conditions for swarm robotics systems described in [15]. This is therefore a simple, yet representative, starting point for work towards a fault diagnosis mechanism for swarm systems.

The flocking threshold, k, in Algorithm 1 is a user-defined threshold that indicates the point at which a robot's desire to be close to the swarm is over-ridden by its desire to be travelling in the same direction as the swarm (approximately 8 cm from the average neighbour position, after noise). The close-proximity threshold, C, which appears in Algorithm 1, Algorithms 2 and 3 dictates the distance at which a robot will avert its course to avoid collision (approximately 3 cm, after noise). The precise values of k and C were decided upon with consideration to the scales of the particular robots and arena used for this work. The values for both are liable to vary in proportion to the system under consideration.

This work considers every instance in which a robot executes an action, and then assigns one feature to that action and one feature in sympathy with the conditions that necessitate it. Following this process leads to the following BFV that is proposed to be sufficiently representative of the aforementioned behaviours. Following Tarapore et al. [16], the BFV described here is a concatenation of five individual binary features, where a returned value of 1 or 0 indicates the presence or absence of the feature, respectively:

$$F_1 = 1 \text{ if } N_R > 0, \text{ otherwise } F_1 = 0 \tag{1}$$

where N_R is the total number of neighbours in sensing range of the robot.

$$F_2 = 1 \text{ if } N_C > 0, \text{ otherwise } F_2 = 0 \tag{2}$$

where N_C is the total number of neighbours at a distance less than the close proximity threshold, C, to the robot.

$$F_3 = 1 \text{ if } |v| > \frac{4}{5}|v_{max}|, \text{ otherwise } F_3 = 0 \tag{3}$$

where $|v|$ is the magnitude of linear velocity.

$$F_4 = 1 \text{ if } |v| > \frac{1}{5}|v_{max}|, \text{ otherwise } F_4 = 0 \tag{4}$$

Algorithm 1. Flocking

1: **while** Running **do**
2:     **if** Distance to object < close-proximity threshold (C) **then** avoid object
3:     **if** Average neighbour distance < flocking threshold (k) **then** calculate target heading from the average bearings of all neighbours in range
4:     **else** Calculate target heading from the average positions of all neighbours in range
5:     **if** Robot heading **not in range** target heading ± 15 ° **then** turn toward target heading
6:     **else** Move forward

Algorithm 2. Aggregation

1: **while** Running **do**
2:     **if** Distance to object < close-proximity threshold (C) **then** avoid object
3:     Calculate target heading from the average positions of all neighbours in range
4:     **if** Robot heading **not in range** target heading ± 15 ° **then** turn toward target heading
5:     **else** Move forward

Algorithm 3. Dispersion

1: **while** Running **do**
2:     **if** Distance to object < close-proximity threshold (C) **then** avoid object
3:     **else** Move forward

$$F_5 = 1 \text{ if } |\omega| > \frac{2}{5}|\omega_{max}|, \text{ otherwise } F_5 = 0 \tag{5}$$

where $|\omega|$ is the magnitude of the robots angular velocity.

Each feature is updated once per control-cycle (10ms). Because of the nature of the externally sensed features, this means that F_3, F_4 and F_5 are measured over a very small window. Exactly how long a period these features should be measured over is itself an optimisation problem. Measuring them over a longer period will reduce the effects of noise. However, each time these features change there will be some resultant discrepancy. This is because proprioceptively sensed features will update in real-time, whereas the externally sensed features are only able to update, at best, one tick subsequently. Therefore, increasing the window over which these features are measured necessarily increases the amount of time proprioceptive and externally sensed features will be discrepant - possibly producing undesirable results. This is a problem that may have to be revisited in the future, however, for the purposes of this work in simulation, updating features at each control-cycle produced adequate results.

The proprioceptive BFV is estimated via an individual robot's sensors (for features relating to object/neighbour proximity) or its controller (for features relating to a robot's movement). The externally estimated BFV uses a simulated overhead sensor to obtain coordinate information for each robot at every time-step. It is acknowledged that the use of an overhead sensor cannot be considered traditionally 'swarm-like', nor realistic for multi-robot system in various scenarios, and it is not proposed as a long term solution. Rather, it should be thought of as a virtual sensor, in so far as it provides data that could be obtained locally but, for ease of experimentation, has been obtained via an overhead sensor with consideration given to a decentralised system i.e. robots will not be provided with neighbour information if that neighbour is not in range of a local sensor. Furthermore, the main objective of this work is not to provide a fully integrable fault diagnosis mechanism for swarm systems, but to provide evidence that a feature vector approach has merit in the context of fault diagnosis, and is something that is worth developing towards a more complete system. Therefore this work meets the criteria for swarm robotics systems, as described by Şahin [15].

Feature Thresholds. The combination of features F_3, F_4 and F_5 allow for a distinction to be made between a robot that has completely stopped, one that is turning and one that is moving in a straight line. The thresholds for these features were chosen with consideration to robot behaviours and system noise.

Given that a normally behaving robots wheels can only be in one of two states (moving at maximum speed or not moving), a normally behaving robot is either moving in a straight line at maximum speed, turning (which is approximate to moving at half speed, albeit not in a straight line), or stationary. It is desirable that each of these states be distinct from one another.

The threshold for F_3 is defined to be 80% of v_{max}. In a noiseless system it could have been set to v_{max}, however, even with noise, there is no scenario in which a normally behaving robot would ever reach this velocity if it were not moving in a straight line. Therefore the presence of F_3 is the sole indicator for that particular behavioural state.

The threshold for F_4 is defined to be 20% of v_{max}. Similarly to F_3, this could have been set to 0 in a noiseless system. The purpose of this feature is to distinguish a robot which has completely stopped. Although a robot with $0 < v < v_{max}$ is obviously not stationary in absolute terms, for this experiment there is no scenario where a normally behaving robot should ever have a velocity in this range once its behaviour has stabilised. Therefore, if a robots velocity does lie in this range, it can be attributed to overhead sensor noise about a stationary robot. Consequently, the absence of F_4 is the sole indicator that a robot has stopped moving.

The purpose of F_5 is to distinguish a robot that is turning. Given that a normally behaving robot is either turning with maximum angular velocity or not turning, this threshold could lie anywhere between 0 and ω_{max} in a noiseless system. In this work the threshold was set to be as low as possible whilst retaining a reliable reading.

This is by no means an exhaustive list of discriminatory features for the given behaviours and, similarly to the use of an overhead sensor, should only be viewed as a provisional BFV that can provide an adequate proof-of-principle. Notably, there is not a feature to reflect the presence of a non-neighbour object. The reason for this is that every feature must be reliably measured internally by an individual, as well as externally by an observing neighbour. It is not immediately clear how this feature could be measured by an observing neighbour in a distributed manner, and so it has been omitted from this particular BFV.

2.2   Fault Types

If a fault or failure occurs in a system that does not cause the system to exhibit a behaviour that deviates from what could be considered normal, then the system can be said to be tolerant to the failure and thus no further action is required. Therefore, research into swarm FDDR need only consider faults or failures that cause disruption to the swarm's collective behaviour. Exactly what these faults are will vary from system to system and depend largely on the behaviour that particular system is exhibiting at a particular time. More important at this stage is obtaining a proof-of-concept that different fault types are indeed distinguishable from one another via the BFVs they produce. Defined below are a number of representative fault types for a simulated marXbot robot [4], based on a cross-section of the literature that informs this work.

Motor failure: The study by Winfield and Nembrini [18], in which they reject the notion of inherent swarm robustness, is among the most significant in motivating this work. In their study, motor failure is, by far, the most damaging to collective behaviour. It is therefore an obvious choice for inclusion in this study. Motor failure is split into two parts for this experiment. The first being a complete failure of an individual's left motor, the second being a partial failure of the same motor. For a complete failure the motor will stop and henceforth become unresponsive to its controller. For a partial failure the motor will remain responsive, however will only cause its associated wheel to turn at half speed.

Sensor failure: Sensor failure is another recurring example used in fault tolerant swarm research [5,18]. The exact details of a sensor failure will vary from robot to robot, depending on their hardware. In this case, it is once again split into complete sensor failure and partial sensor failure. For a complete sensor failure an individual's range and bearing (RAB) sensor, as well its infra-red (IR) proximity sensor, will completely fail and return 0. That is, the robot will be totally unable to detect the presence of its neighbours or the walls of the arena. For a partial sensor failure, similar to the definition used in [11], a robot will only be able to detect the presence of neighbours within ±45° of its current heading (but still able to detect the arena walls).

Power failure: Again, a recurring example in work on fault tolerance [5,18]. A robot that suffers a power failure will completely stop moving and remain unresponsive to its surroundings. However, other robots in the swarm will still be able to detect its presence. This assumes that, in a physical system, each robot will be able to detect the presence of its neighbours independently of whether or not that neighbour is responsive. This may not be the case for all systems, however, in cases where robots are unable to communicate their presence for one reason or another, they will go unacknowledged by the swarm and essentially become nothing more than objects in an arena. Such cases have been shown to have little to no detriment to collective swarm behaviour [18], so are therefore not a priority for FDDR.

Software hang: Software hang is given as an example of a fault that necessitates exogenous, or at least partly exogenous, approaches to fault detection [6]. For this work, software hang will cause a robot to get stuck performing whatever action it was performing at the last moment it was normally functioning. It is worth noting that the robot is allowed to continue broadcasting its own BFV to the swarm (although this BFV will also be stuck and unresponsive to changes in the robot's behaviour from external factors e.g. encountering a wall). This, again, works on the assumption that robots can sense their neighbours independently, the justification for which is outlined in the previous discussion on power failure.

3   Experimental Setup

To design and test this initial method for a BFV-based approach to fault classification, Autonomous Robots Go Swarming (ARGoS) [13] – a widely-employed robot swarm simulator – is used. The use of a simulator is only a short-term

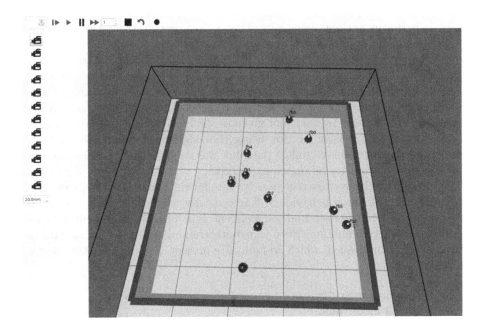

Fig. 1. ARGoS simulation of 10 marXbot robots performing a dispersion behaviour. Lines connecting pairs of robots represent mutual neighbour acknowledgement via RAB sensor. Lines protruding from each robot represent IR sensor range.

solution, and it is used only with the intention of trialling any fault diagnosis mechanism in a hardware system at the first reasonable opportunity. Given that the work presented in this paper is primarily concerned with developing an approach to fault classification and diagnosis, it is proposed that simulation is sufficient for this proof-of-principle.

A swarm of 10 marXbots [4] are simulated. These robots collectively perform one of the three behaviours described previously in an otherwise empty enclosed arena, representing approximately $16\,\mathrm{m}^2$ (see Fig. 1). Simulated Gaussian noise is added to each robot's sensor ($\mu = 0$, $\sigma = 1°$), as well the overhead sensor ($\mu = 0$, $\sigma = 2\%\ d_{max}$) – where d_{max} is the maximum distance that a robot can travel in one tick. The noise on the overhead sensor is applied to the co-ordinate values for each robot. Therefore 95% of the estimated linear velocity values of each robot will be within a window equal to 4% of the robots maximum velocity around it's true velocity. The BFV of each robot is recorded over five minutes of simulated time for all behaviour–fault combinations for 10 separate and independent runs. In each run, swarm behaviour stabilised after 50 s. This was therefore chosen as the point after which one of the six fault types would be injected into a single robot.

4   Results and Discussion

To ascertain how useful BFVs are for classifying fault types a set of data is obtained, consisting of an individual robot's BFV for each of the 6 fault types whilst it performs flocking behaviour. This is then used to train a decision tree [14], after which one can observe how well this tree can classify the same fault types for different behaviours. The advantage of using a decision tree for this process over, for example, a neural network, is that a decision tree allows a user to easily ascertain whether or not a feature is discriminatory. Flocking is used as the normal behaviour for training data because it is the most complex of the behaviours. Consideration is not given to the behaviour of non-faulty robots in the swarm. The reason for this being that significant differences in robot behaviour were not observed unless the robot was itself faulty. It is acknowledged that this may not always be the case, as in [18].

Table 1 shows the average true positive rate for the trained decision tree when it is applied to all three behaviours. These results were obtained by taking an average over all 10 separate and independent runs of this experiment for each behaviour–fault combination. Note that both training and test sets of data do not include the first 50 s in which no faults are present. Fault types are indicated in Table 1 as follows:

- H_1 – Complete motor failure
- H_2 – Partial motor failure
- H_3 – Complete sensor failure
- H_4 – Partial sensor failure
- H_5 – Power failure
- H_6 – Software Hang

Table 1. Average true positive rate ± std.dev. (σ) % for a trained decision tree over 10 replicates.

Fault type	Flocking	Aggregation	Dispersion
H_1	79.5 ± 20.4%	85 ± 14.7%	27.9 ± 13.8%
H_2	98.3 ± 2.9%	88.8 ± 31.3%	80.6 ± 11.3%
H_3	100%	91.8 ± 12.3%	92.1 ± 9%
H_4	86 ± 5.8%	89.3 ± 8%	94 ± 3.6%
H_5	100%	100%	100%
H_6	43.1 ± 39%	8.1 ± 25.6%	40.4 ± 42.6%

The results show that, bar a few notable exceptions, a decision tree is able to correctly classify fault types with a high average reliability based on their proprioceptive and externally estimated BFVs. Visualising the trained decision tree confirmed that all 10 features were used in the classification process, and were therefore discriminatory (See Fig. 2). The bounds used for each decision, as seen in Fig. 2, are all set to 0.5 ($\forall b = 0.5$). This is a result of optimisation, as 0.5 represents the midpoint between 0 and 1. However, as each feature can only take on a value of 0 or 1, the decision tree would give an identical output for $0 < \forall b < 1$.

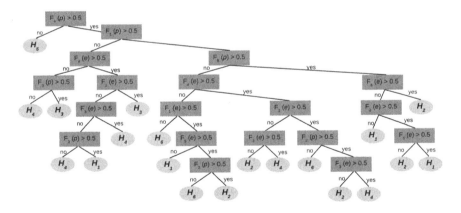

Fig. 2. Visual representation of the trained decision tree where p and e indicate proprioceptively and externally estimated features, respectively.

As the decision tree was trained on a swarm exhibiting flocking behaviour, the best performance is observed when it is applied to a swarm exhibiting flocking behaviour. Although the performance of the decision tree is generally good when applied to swarms exhibiting aggregation or dispersion behaviours, it is expected that the performance observed for each would be even better if the decision tree used were trained on either of these behaviours, respectively.

There is a notably high rate of correct classification across all behaviours for a robot exhibiting power failure. The reason for this is that a robot exhibiting power failure will produce a feature vector that is not only distinct from that of any of the other fault types, but also one that will remain largely constant. The only features that will change once a robot experiences a power failure will be externally sensed neighbour features. All other features will return 0 for the entire duration of the failure. It can be observed in Fig. 2 that a robot will be classified with a power failure (denoted as 'PF') immediately and exclusively when feature 7 (corresponding to proprioceptively estimated linear velocity) returns 0. This is a characteristic unique to a power failure fault, as for all other faults the robot controller will still attempt to keep the robot moving, making it immediately recognisable.

Interestingly, there is a high rate of misclassification when a complete motor failure is present in a swarm performing dispersion, despite the opposite being true for other behaviours. In these instances, the fault is misclassified as being a partial motor failure (see Table 2). This occurs because complete motor failure in flocking behaviour, on which the decision tree is trained, produces generally different behaviour (robot is static for large periods of time) compared to complete motor failure in dispersion - which far more closely resembles the effects of partial motor failure in flocking (robot spends large periods of time in circular motion). Although this is not ideal, for all practical intents and purposes, this does not pose a significant problem for two reasons:

Table 2. Mean classification accuracy for 10 replicates of complete motor failure in dispersing robotic swarms.

H_1	H_2	H_3	H_4	H_5	H_6
$27.9 \pm 13.8\%$	$61.7 \pm 34.6\%$	0%	$10.2 \pm 21.8\%$	0%	$0.2 \pm 0.4\%$

- Firstly, feature thresholds could be altered in order to distinguish between partial and complete motor failures more effectively. For example, complete motor failure would produce circular motion with a smaller diameter than partial motor failure, essentially making this a calibration problem.
- Secondly, complete and partial motor failures will likely have very similar, if not identical, associated recovery actions. Therefore discriminating between the two from a practical perspective may be redundant in many scenarios.

Additionally, there is a persistently high rate of misclassification of software hang across all behaviours. The reason for this is that software hang can produce entirely different behaviours depending on what the robot was doing at the point of fault injection. The training data used an example where software hang was injected whilst the robot was moving in a straight line. However, for many subsequent examples, particularly where the swarm behaviour was aggregation, the robot was turning at the point of fault injection - leading to a classification of partial or complete motor failure. Furthermore, even when the robot was moving in a straight line, if the robot had no neighbours in sensing range at the point of fault injection, the subsequent behaviour was indistinguishable from complete sensor failure (see Table 3).

Table 3. Mean classification accuracy for 10 replicates of software hang failure in aggregating and dispersing robotic swarms.

	H_1	H_2	H_3	H_4	H_5	H_6
Aggregation	$1 \pm 2.8\%$	$79.9 \pm 42.1\%$	$8 \pm 25.3\%$	$3 \pm 6.6\%$	0%	$8.1 \pm 25.6\%$
Dispersion	$3.8 \pm 8.3\%$	$32.1 \pm 47.1\%$	$17 \pm 36.1\%$	$6.7 \pm 6.8\%$	0%	$40.4 \pm 42.6\%$

How an individual fault might produce several different behaviours, dependent on external factors, is a consideration that was absent from the work described. However it is one that may be very important, if not essential, to a reliable fault diagnosis mechanism. Another absent consideration from this work, and one that could have decreased misclassification, is how different fault types may produce distinct time-dependent BFV patterns. Observing software hang over a period of time would make the fault easily identifiable, as a static proprioceptive BFV would be observed for a changing externally estimated BFV.

5 Conclusion

In this work it has been shown that by characterising robot behaviour as a BFV one is able to diagnose fault types occurring in individuals with a generally high reliability. Having said that, it is acknowledged that the work, described here, towards fault diagnosis in swarms is by no means complete. There are still a number of issues to address, such as how a system can reliably diagnose fault types which can manifest in different ways, or consideration of how one can diagnose faults in real-time.

In future work the feature vector approach will be carried forward and developed, for instance by considering time-based patterns, however there will also be a move towards an online and largely unsupervised approach to fault diagnosis. Furthermore, the work will move from simulation to a hardware system. It is acknowledged that working with the sensor noise observed in a hardware system will not be the same as working in simulation with controlled noise, and that the feature vectors described in this paper may not be appropriate for such a system. It is expected that a reduction in performance will be observed when making that transition. However, as each feature has an associated user-defined threshold to determine it's value, these thresholds (along with other parameters) should be modifiable for compatibility with a hardware system.

Although decision tree algorithms can be useful for identifying discriminating features, they are not envisaged as being a long term solution to a classification problem on account of their inflexibility. Rather, this work will move towards a more complex system whereby a previously unseen fault can be associated with a recovery option via a series of diagnostic tests and a process of trial and error, after which the BFVs of subsequent faults can be tested for similarities to known faults. It is proposed that, based on the results previously described, not only would such a system be possible, but that it could also be built to satisfy the conditions for swarm robustness, flexibility, and scalability.

References

1. Bi, R.: Immune-inspired fault diagnosis for a robotic system. Ph.D. thesis, University of York (2012)
2. Bi, R., Timmis, J., Tyrrell, A.: The diagnostic dendritic cell algorithm for robotic systems. In: 2010 IEEE Congress on Evolutionary Computation (CEC), pp. 1–8. IEEE (2010)
3. Bjerknes, J.D., Winfield, A.F.T.: On fault tolerance and scalability of swarm robotic systems. In: Martinoli, A., Mondada, F., Correll, N., Mermoud, G., Egerstedt, M., Hsieh, M.A., Parker, L.E., Støy, K. (eds.) Distributed Autonomous Robotic Systems. Springer Tracts in Advanced Robotics, vol. 83, pp. 431–444. Springer, Heidelberg (2013). doi:10.1007/978-3-642-32723-0_31
4. Bonani, M., Longchamp, V., Magnenat, S., Rétornaz, P., Burnier, D., Roulet, G., Vaussard, F., Bleuler, H., Mondada, F.: The marXbot, a miniature mobile robot opening new perspectives for the collective-robotic research. In: IEEE/RSJ International Conference on Intelligent Robots and Systems (IROS), pp. 4187–4193. IEEE (2010)
5. Carlson, J.: Analysis of how mobile robots fail in the field. Ph.D. thesis, University of South Florida (2004)
6. Christensen, A.L., O'Grady, R., Birattari, M., Dorigo, M.: Fault detection in autonomous robots based on fault injection and learning. Autonom. Robots 24(1), 49–67 (2008)
7. O'Grady, R., Dorigo, M.: From fireflies to fault-tolerant swarms of robots. IEEE Trans. Evol. Comput. 13(4), 754–766 (2009)
8. Cohen, I.R.: Tending Adam's Garden: Evolving the Cognitive Immune Self. Academic Press, London (2000)
9. De Castro, L.N., Timmis, J.: Artificial Immune Systems: A New Computational Intelligence Approach. Springer, London (2002)
10. Khadidos, A., Crowder, R.M., Chappell, P.H.: Exogenous fault detection and recovery for swarm robotics. IFAC-PapersOnLine 48(3), 2405–2410 (2015)
11. Millard, A.G.: Exogenous fault detection in swarm robotic systems. Ph.D. thesis, University of York (2016)
12. Millard, A.G., Timmis, J., Winfield, A.F.T.: Run-time detection of faults in autonomous mobile robots based on the comparison of simulated and real robot behaviour. In: IEEE/RSJ International Conference on Intelligent Robots and Systems, pp. 3720–3725. IEEE (2014)
13. Pinciroli, C., Trianni, V., O'Grady, R., Pini, G., Brutschy, A., Brambilla, M., Mathews, N., Ferrante, E., Di Caro, G., Ducatelle, F., Stirling, T., Gutiérrez, A., Gambardella, L.M., Dorigo, M.: ARGoS: a modular, multi-engine simulator for heterogeneous swarm robotics. In: 2011 IEEE/RSJ International Conference on Intelligent Robots and Systems (IROS), pp. 5027–5034. IEEE (2011)

14. Quinlan, R.J.: Induction of decision trees. Mach. Learn. **1**(1), 81–106 (1986)
15. Şahin, E.: Swarm robotics: from sources of inspiration to domains of application. In: Şahin, E., Spears, W.M. (eds.) SR 2004. LNCS, vol. 3342, pp. 10–20. Springer, Heidelberg (2005). doi:10.1007/978-3-540-30552-1_2
16. Tarapore, D., Lima, P.U., Carneiro, J., Christensen, A.L.: To err is robotic, to tolerate immunological: fault detection in multirobot systems. Bioinspiration Biomim. **10**(1), 16014 (2015)
17. Timmis, J., Andrews, P., Hart, E.: On artificial immune systems and swarm intelligence. Swarm Intell. **4**(4), 247–273 (2010)
18. Winfield, A.F.T., Nembrini, J.: Safety in numbers: fault-tolerance in robot swarms. Int. J. Model. Ident. Control **1**(1), 30–37 (2006)

Measuring the Effects of Communication Quality on Multi-robot Team Performance

Tsvetan Zhivkov[1]([✉]), Eric Schneider[1,2], and Elizabeth I. Sklar[1]

[1] Department of Informatics, King's College London, London, UK
{tsvetan.zhivkov,eric.schneider,elizabeth.sklar}@kcl.ac.uk
[2] Department of Computer Science, University of Liverpool, Liverpool, UK

Abstract. Maintaining network connectivity is crucial for multi-robot and human-robot teams. If robots lose their network connection, they cannot receive commands or share sensor data with teammates. Most research in the multi-robot systems and human-robot interaction communities assumes 100% network connectivity, 100% of the time; but this is unrealistic for real-world domains. Indeed, this assumption could be associated with significant risk, depending on the robots' task domain. This paper presents preliminary results for measuring the impact of communication loss on multi-robot team performance. A series of controlled experiments were conducted, with physical and simulated robots, where the probability of packet loss is gradually increased from 0% to 75%. The experiments show that the multi-robot team exhibits a non-linear decrease in performance with respect to an increase in percentage of packets dropped.

Keywords: Multi-robot team · Communication · Empirical results

1 Introduction

Consideration of *communication network quality* is a real and significant issue in multi-robot and human-robot teams. An unreliable network connection can mean that messages get dropped and robots lose their ability to receive commands, transmit sensor data and generally interact with either human or robot teammates. In real-world settings, mobile phones drop calls and bandwidth degrades when signal strength declines, even with high-speed 4G networks. As autonomous mobile robots transition from research laboratories into operational environments such as factories, hospitals, schools and homes, it becomes imperative that they are able to communicate reliably with those around them, whether human or robot. Humans in close proximity rely on non-digital forms of communication, such as speech and gestures; and there is much attention paid, in human-robot interaction and artificial intelligence, to the investigation of methods for robots to communicate in similar ways, using speech recognition, natural language generation and gesturing. In addition, robots will frequently be deployed in task domains where they are not co-located with humans, such as search-and-rescue, humanitarian de-mining or nuclear plant monitoring. It is these types of non-proximal relationships that are of concern in our work.

© Springer International Publishing AG 2017
Y. Gao et al. (Eds.): TAROS 2017, LNAI 10454, pp. 408–420, 2017.
DOI: 10.1007/978-3-319-64107-2_32

The study presented here examines the impact of degrading communication quality in a multi-robot team. The long term goal of this line of work is to quantify the effects and assess the risks associated with poor communication quality on multi-robot and human-robot teams in a physical environment. In the study described in this paper, we conducted a series of experiments in which the success of message transmission in a multi-robot team is not guaranteed. Our working hypothesis is that poor-quality communication will hinder the execution of tasks which require interaction amongst robots or between robots and local server(s), for example, where mission-critical information is stored, such as a detailed map of the robot's environment. To evaluate this hypothesis, a simple method of random packet loss was implemented and applied to infect communication functions, to measure how a robot team copes with poor communication. Our overarching objective is to demonstrate how changes in communication quality impact task performance, using a number of metrics and experimental conditions. Experiments were conducted in simulation and with physical robots. The experiments show that the multi-robot team exhibits a decrease in performance with respect to an increase in percentage of packets dropped. This result is not unexpected, but the contribution of this work is that now we have a framework and results that allow us to quantify the impact of communication loss on specific performance metrics.

The remainder of this paper is organised as follows. Section 2 presents our approach and describes details of our methodology. Section 3 outlines our experimental setup, including the software and hardware environment developed for empirical studies. Section 4 presents the results and statistical analysis of our experiments. Section 5 briefly highlights related work in multi-robot and human-robot systems. Finally, Sect. 6 summarises our results and mentions our immediate next steps and future directions with this line of research.

2   Methodology

In order to experiment with the notion of packet loss in a multi-robot team, we implemented a probabilistic function that is interjected into our system's messaging server (detailed in the next section). This function will fail to send messages, at a rate no greater than a value passed to the function. In other words, in order to simulate 25% packet loss, this function is called with a value of 0.25; and inside the function, messages are only transmitted 75% of the time. During an experimental run, the chosen packet-loss value remains static until the end of that experiment.

An experimental schema F is defined as a tuple: $F = \langle N, T, S, P \rangle$ where N is the size of the robot team (number of robots); S is a specific experimental *scenario*; T is a set of tasks; and P is a simulated loss in communication quality. The values used for the experiments described here are:

- $N = 2$
- $T = 6$

- $S = \{S_1, S_2\}$
- $P = \{0\%, 25\%, 50\%, 75\%\}$

Each scenario, S, is defined as having a map M, a team of robots with starting locations $\{(x_1, y_1)...(x_N, y_N)\}$ and a set of task locations $\{(x_1, y_1)...(x_T, y_T)\}$. Following other related work [4,7,12,13], the tasks and locations can be classified as: single-robot (SR) vs multi-robot (MR) tasks; clustered start (CS) vs distributed start (DS) locations; independent (IT) vs constrained (CT) tasks; static (SA) vs dynamic (DA) arrival of tasks; instantaneous (ID) vs extended (ED) task duration. In the work presented here, we restrict the scenarios to $\langle SR, CS, IT, SA, ID \rangle$; although future work will explore the full range of types of tasks.

3 Experiments

Our experiments were conducted using the *MRTeAm* framework [12], which integrates ROS [9] controllers for individual robot navigation with the RabbitMQ[1] messaging system for handling inter-robot communication. The ROS navigation stack provides communication, localisation and path-planning capabilities. A key feature of ROS is that the same robot controllers can be used in a simulated environment as well as with physical platforms. We used the Stage [3] environment for simulation experiments, which includes an emulator for our physical platform: the Turtlebot2[2]. This robot has a differential drive base and an RGB-depth camera (the Asus Xtion[3], which is a clone of the Microsoft Kinect [10]), and an on-board laptop (the Acer Travelmate B117[4] running Ubuntu). The robots communicate with each other by sending and receiving messages via WiFi. Our RabbitMQ service runs on a local server.

The operating environment for our robots is an office setting with rooms opening off of a circular corridor (illustrated in Figs. 4 and 5). The corridor has multiple sets of fire doors, which typically stay closed. Thus our physical experiments were restricted to that portion of the corridor which could be reached without needing to open the fire doors. We use the campus WiFi for our robots, which is a local instantiation of *eduroam*[5] that supports IEEE 802.11b and 802.11 g standards.

For our experiments, we had our robot team execute missions consisting of exploration tasks in which the robots went to particular locations, ostensibly to perform surveillance tasks, though the experiments described here only involved the robots travelling to their assigned locations. At the beginning of a mission, robots received from the server a set of tasks—locations to visit. While robots moved to each of their assigned task location(s), messages[6] passed between the

---

[1] https://www.rabbitmq.com/.

[2] http://www.turtlebot.com/.

[3] https://www.asus.com/3D-Sensor/Xtion_PRO_LIVE/.

[4] https://www.acer.com/ac/en/GB/content/professional-series/travelmateb.

[5] https://www.eduroam.org/.

[6] Specifically, the messages that were passed were ROS `amcl_pose_msg` messages.

robots, via our server (running RabbitMQ), facilitating the robots' sharing their locations ("pose" information). This helps the team members know where each other are in the environment during a mission.

During an experiment, data are obtained by using a particular schema F_i with a given scenario and packet-loss value. In total eight different schema configurations are identified ($N \times T \times S \times P$ with $|N| = 1, |T| = 1, |S| = 2, |P| = 4$). Two scenarios, S_1 and S_2 (illustrated in Figs. 4 and 5) were defined for running experiments in simulation and with physical robots, respectively. The packet loss parameter P has four allocated values, $\{0\%, 25\%, 50\%, 75\%\}$ (also denoted as PL-0, PL-25, PL-50 and PL-75, respectively). For each configuration, a total of 25 simulations and 20 physical runs were obtained.

3.1   Performance Metrics Rationale

The MRTeAm framework collects thirty-two performance metrics in all, recorded after each experimental run. Only the parameters relevant to the research question considered here are reported in this paper, namely: **execution time**, **total movement time**, **total distance travelled**, **near collisions**, **delay time** and **idle time**. These are described, in turn, below.

The **execution time** is the total time taken for the robot team to complete all the tasks allocated to them. As can be seen in Fig. 1a, for the simulation runs, the execution time increases with each increase in parameter P. For the physical runs, shown in Fig. 1b, the trend is similar but with greater variance in results. The increase in variance is as expected, and it is a result of the noisy physical environment.

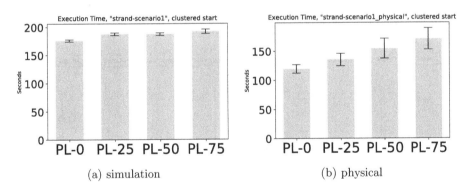

(a) simulation   (b) physical

Fig. 1. Results for *execution time*, with increasing P

The **total movement time** metric (Fig. 2) shows the time spent moving during a mission by all the robot team members combined. For both the simulated and physical runs, a pattern similar to that exhibited by execution time is noticed, which shows that the robots spend more time moving with increasing P. However, as noted in the previous metric, the variance for the physical runs is much greater than that of the simulated runs.

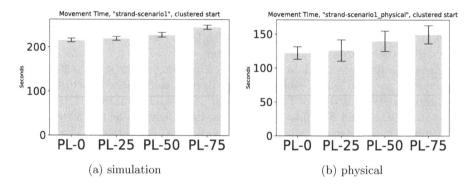

Fig. 2. Results for *total movement time*, with increasing P

The **total distance travelled** metric is the total distance travelled by all the robot team members combined. The trend is identical to execution time and total movement time.

The **total collisions** metric counts the number of times that the robots either collided or came close to each other and had to execute a collision avoidance behaviour. This metric exhibits unexpected results, as shown in Fig. 3. The results have identical patterns for both simulated and physical runs (discussed further in Sect. 4). The increase between PL-0 and PL-25 is expected, though it is unexpected for collisions to decrease for P greater than PL-25. This outcome has been identified to result from the high amount of messages being dropped by the function in the code which updates the pose of consequent robot-team members. Note that, for purposes of these experiments, the robot controller does not record collisions detected by the robot's bump sensors.

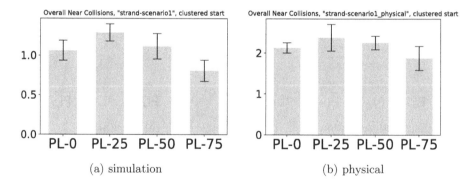

Fig. 3. Results for number of *near collisions*, with increasing P

The performance metrics **total delay time** and **total idle time** are not as relevant for testing communication quality directly, but still reflect aspects of team performance. Delay time is related to the total "near collisions". The

MRTeAm framework employs a simplistic collision avoidance behaviour: when two robots come within a pre-defined ϵ of each other, they both stop; the robot that is closest to its next task location is given right-of-way, and the other robot waits until the first robot has cleared its path. The amount of time that a robot stops in order to let another robot pass is called "delay time". The second metric, idle time, is related to the efficiency with which the team collectively completes all the tasks assigned to the them. When a robot finishes executing its assigned tasks, it waits until all the other robots on the team have finished executing their assigned tasks. That amount of waiting time is called "idle time".

4 Analysis of Results

In this section, we describe our statistical analysis of the experimental results obtained and presented in the previous section. Our aim is to show that there are statistically significant differences between the different levels of packet loss. First we test the distribution of the raw data for normality, to determine whether our data sets are parametric or non-parametric. Then we run t-tests to evaluate for statistical significance.

4.1 Shapiro-Wilk Test

The Shapiro-Wilk test is used to show that the data samples obtained from the experiment are more likely to have a normal distribution. The algorithm used for the Shapiro-Wilk test is from *scipy.stats.shapiro* [1].

Shapiro-Wilk test is highly recommended for sample sizes less than 50. For a sample size of ≤ 25, the Shapiro-Wilk value (W) needs to be in the range 0.918–0.989 [14], and for a sample size of ≤ 20, the W value needs to be in the

Table 1. Shapiro-Wilk values for *execution time.*

(a) Simulation	
Parameter	Shapiro-Wilk (W)
PL-0	0.974
PL-25	0.979
PL-50	0.983
PL-75	0.956
(b) Physical	
Parameter	Shapiro-Wilk (W)
PL-0	0.606
PL-25	0.746
PL-50	0.718
PL-75	0.799

Table 2. Shapiro-Wilk values for *total movement time*.

(a) Simulation

Parameter	Shapiro-Wilk (W)
PL-0	0.892
PL-25	0.926
PL-50	0.876
PL-75	0.907

(b) Physical

Parameter	Shapiro-Wilk (W)
PL-0	0.868
PL-25	0.708
PL-50	0.836
PL-75	0.930

Table 3. Shapiro-Wilk values for *distance travelled*.

(a) Simulation

Parameter	Shapiro-Wilk (W)
PL-0	0.967
PL-25	0.557
PL-50	0.917
PL-75	0.974

(b) Physical

Parameter	Shapiro-Wilk (W)
PL-0	0.724
PL-25	0.634
PL-50	0.842
PL-75	0.833

range 0.905–0.988 [14]. However, since the test is very biased on sample size and is only hypothesised, we additionally examined quantile-quantile (Q-Q) plots to visually verify the normality of the distribution. Since the Q-Q plots are used as a visual aid we did not include these in the Analysis Section. The "near collisions" metric returns non-parametric data. Therefore, it needs to be interpreted in a different fashion compared to the other metrics. Moreover, the results actually show an increase in near collisions with P equal to PL-25, but a sudden decrease for P greater-than-equal to PL-50, which is an unexpected decrease due to the individual robots' navigation dropping localisation messages. Below, Tables 1, 2 and 3 show the performance metrics given a packet-loss parameter, which

are expected to be parametric. The simulation results for the W value indicate that the data is normally distributed, whereas the physical results initially show similar properties but with much higher variance in the data (primarily because there is noise in communication and localisation in the physical environment).

4.2   Paired t-test

The paired t-test is used to analyse the experimental data and test for the null hypothesis (H_0). The H_0 tests if, for a given metric, two different and independent packet-loss parameters return identical means. The method *scipy.stats.ttest_ind* [1] is used to perform a standard independent paired t-test calculation. In this experiment, the alternate hypothesis (H_A) is accepted if the significance level is 5% or less, which means that there is 95% probability that the results achieved did not occur by chance.

In the general case for the simulation runs, the alternative (H_A) hypothesis is accepted for the performance metrics for the highest subsidiary parameter (PL-75). This implies that, for the tested performance metrics, if P is greatly increased, it shows significant reduction in performance for the multi-robot team. This result is not observed across all the performance metrics tested in the physical runs. We believe that several factors contribute to this result: the scenario (S_2) is

Table 4. The table shows the t-test, p-value and the hypothesis decision for *execution time* for the simulation runs.

Primary parameter	Subsidiary parameter	T	p	Hypothesis (H_0/H_A)
PL-0	PL-25	−3.63	0.00	**H_A**
	PL-50	−3.86	0.00	**H_A**
	PL-75	−3.87	0.00	**H_A**
PL-25	PL-50	0.03	0.98	H_0
	PL-75	−1.18	0.27	H_0
PL-50	PL-75	−1.03	0.31	H_0

Table 5. The table shows the t-test, p-value and the hypothesis decision for *execution time* for the physical runs.

Primary parameter	Subsidiary parameter	T	p	Hypothesis (H_0/H_A)
PL-0	PL-25	−1.22	0.23	H_0
	PL-50	−1.83	0.07	H_0
	PL-75	−2.55	0.01	**H_A**
PL-25	PL-50	−0.94	0.36	H_0
	PL-75	−1.66	0.10	H_0
PL-50	PL-75	−0.67	0.51	H_0

Table 6. The table shows the t-test, p-value and the hypothesis decision for *total movement time* for the simulation runs.

Primary parameter	Subsidiary parameter	T	p	Hypothesis (H_0/H_A)
PL-0	PL-25	-0.63	0.53	H_0
	PL-50	-1.86	0.07	H_0
	PL-75	-4.79	0.00	**H_A**
PL-25	PL-50	-1.19	0.24	H_0
	PL-75	-3.97	0.00	**H_A**
PL-50	PL-75	-2.50	0.02	**H_A**

Table 7. The table shows the t-test, p-value and the hypothesis decision for *total movement time* for the physical runs.

Primary parameter	Subsidiary parameter	T	p	Hypothesis (H_0/H_A)
PL-0	PL-25	-0.21	0.83	H_0
	PL-50	-0.99	0.33	H_0
	PL-75	-1.67	0.10	H_0
PL-25	PL-50	-0.63	0.53	H_0
	PL-75	-1.14	0.26	H_0
PL-50	PL-75	-0.48	0.63	H_0

Table 8. The table shows the t-test, p-value and the hypothesis decision for *total distance* for the simulation runs.

Primary parameter	Subsidiary parameter	T	p	Hypothesis (H_0/H_A)
PL-0	PL-25	-0.33	0.75	H_0
	PL-50	1.07	0.23	H_0
	PL-75	2.03	0.05	**H_A**
PL-25	PL-50	0.98	0.33	H_0
	PL-75	1.59	0.12	H_0
PL-50	PL-75	0.75	0.46	H_0

much simpler to navigate than scenario S_1 and there is noise in the localisation for the physical robots (but not in the simulation). Similar to Sect. 3.1, two separate tables are used to show the hypothesis decision for each particular performance metric for the simulation and physical runs (Tables 4, 5, 6, 7, 8 and 9).

Table 9. The table shows the t-test, p-value and the hypothesis decision for *total distance* for the physical runs.

Primary parameter	Subsidiary parameter	T	p	Hypothesis (H_0/H_A)
PL-0	PL-25	-0.54	0.59	H_0
	PL-50	-1.90	0.06	H_0
	PL-75	-2.48	0.02	$\mathbf{H_A}$
PL-25	PL-50	-1.10	0.28	H_0
	PL-75	-1.72	0.09	H_0
PL-50	PL-75	-0.75	0.50	H_0

4.3 Trajectories

The results of the trajectory representations are analysed to identify change in performance with change in P. Trajectory Fig. 4 represents a simulated run, showing scenario S_1, and trajectory Fig. 5 represents a physical run, showing scenario S_2. With the trajectory representations, it can clearly be seen why there are differences between the simulated and physical run results.

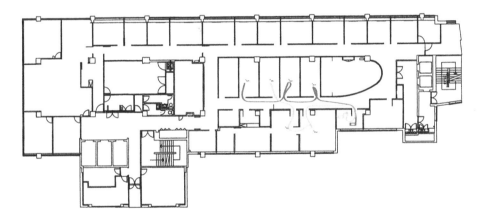

Fig. 4. Simulation run showing robot team trajectory in an office setting, with PL-0, and 2 robots (robot 1 shown in red and robot 2 shown in green). (Color figure online)

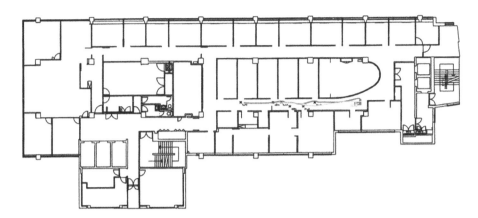

Fig. 5. Physical run showing robot team trajectory in an office setting, with PL-0, and 2 robots (robot 1 shown in red and robot 2 shown in green). (Color figure online)

5   Related Work

The primary motivation for this line of research was due to past experiences with multi-robot teams where there had been a variety of network connectivity problems. Multi-robot team communication is an important and complex issue when it comes to performing heterogeneous tasks (e.g. two or more robots working together to move heavy objects out of the way to reach a goal). However, communications have limitations and infrastructure may break down.

In works by Zadorozhny and Lewis [18] and Murphy *et al.* [8] the authors investigate different communication methods in the human-robot communication domain. An extra constraint exists on the human-robot system, which is that robots need to be equipped with specific sensors to communicate/transmit information to a human controller, as highlighted by Murphy *et al.* [8]. [8,18] mention the constraints experienced by communication limitations, but none of the aforementioned works focus on solving or quantifying this issue.

By widening our research, we found similar issues in the human-human communication domain. The researched works [2,15,17] all had the common goal of establishing a communication network in a disaster area, where a network would be fragmented or non-existent. The purpose of this was to then allow a "tethered" link between the general public and first responders (police/ambulance). In [2] the authors investigate ways to improve message passing and to create effective ad-hoc networks.

In [16], the authors examine possible formation strategies in simulations to assist and maintain communications, while multi-robot teams perform exploration and victim-locating tasks. Moreover, although [16] does not focus on reducing communication failure, they concentrate on providing improved communication for multi-robot teams. The research by Jensen *et al.* [6] employs their own *Sweep Exploration Algorithm (SEA)* for the coverage of unknown environments. The algorithm allows a multi-robot team to expand their exploration in a tree-like structure. A constraint is placed on the multi-robot team to always maintain communication between members. The method used by Jensen *et al.* [6] introduces some weaknesses prone to failure, particularly in physical environments. Another work by Gunn and Anderson [5] describes a framework for multi-robot teams that allocates roles and allows robots to dynamically change roles depending on mission requirements or environmental conditions (e.g. to compensate for a lost team member or to complete a victim-locating task). The primary goal for the framework is to assist in team maintenance and task management, but the authors note that for large percentages of communication loss, the performance of all methodologies was poor. This was mainly due to a very high message failure rate, which resulted in failure to allocate tasks, and made team coherence impossible to maintain over time.

These findings are the source of our long-term motivation with respect to the eventual deployment of multi-robot teams to help first responders.

6   Conclusions and Future Work

We have presented results of a preliminary set of experiments that attempt to quantify the impact of packet loss on a multi-robot team. Two different scenarios were evaluated, one with a team of simulated robots and the other with a team of physical robots. The two scenarios (S_1 and S_2) are very different and thus limit the accuracy of the results for the simulation and physical runs. However, when examining the results of the simulation and physical runs, similar trends emerge specifically in the "execution time", "total movement time", "total distance travelled" and the "near collisions" metrics. The results obtained give a starting baseline for how communication quality affects multi-robot teams. However, the experiments do not give conclusive insight on how degradation of communication quality affects the performance metrics that are tested. Unfortunately, it is difficult to run S_1 with the physical robots because the locations of the tasks in scenario S_1 are inside people's offices, and we don't necessarily have access to all those points. Instead, our immediate next step is to develop a third scenario S_3 that adds complexity to the mission and can be evaluated both in simulation and with physical robots.

In future work, we will use an *ad-hoc* network (similarly to those described in [2,8,11]) to facilitate communication amongst robots and between the robots and the server. This will allow the robots to measure real signal strength and adapt their behaviour accordingly, so that they do not lose connectivity. We will investigate further the strategies proposed by Takahashi *et al.* [16] in a physical environment, and additionally employ certain aspects of the SEA algorithm by Jensen *et al.* [6].

References

1. Python: Scipy stats library (2008–2016). https://docs.scipy.org/doc/scipy-0.15.1/reference/stats.html
2. Al-Akkad, A., Raffelsberger, C., Boden, A., Ramirez, L., Zimmermann, A.: Tweeting when online is off? opportunistically creating mobile ad-hoc networks in response to disrupted infrastructure. In: 11th International ISCRAM Conference Proceedings, Pennsylvania, May 2014

3. Gerkey, B., Vaughan, R.T., Howard, A.: The player/stage project: tools for multi-robot and distributed sensor systems. In: Proceedings of the 11th International Conference on Advanced Robotics (2003)
4. Gerkey, B.P., Mataríc, M.J.: A formal analysis and taxonomy of task allocation in multi-robot systems. Int. J. Robot. Res. **23**(9), 939–954 (2004)
5. Gunn, T., Anderson, J.: Dynamic heterogeneous team formation for robotic urban search and rescue. J. Comput. Syst. Sci. **81**(3), 553–567 (2015)
6. Jensen, E.A., Nunes, E., Gini, M.: Communication-restricted exploration for robot teams. In: Proceedings of the 28th AAAI Conference on Artificial Intelligence (2014)
7. Landén, D., Heintz, F., Doherty, P.: Complex task allocation in mixed-initiative delegation: a UAV case study. In: Desai, N., Liu, A., Winikoff, M. (eds.) PRIMA 2010. LNCS, vol. 7057, pp. 288–303. Springer, Heidelberg (2012). doi:10.1007/978-3-642-25920-3_20
8. Murphy, R.R., Srinivasan, V., Henkel, Z., Suarez, J., Minson, M., Straus, J., Hempstead, S., Valdez, T., Egawa, S.: Interacting with trapped victims using robots. In: IEEE International Conference on Technologies for Homeland Security (HST), Waltham, Massachusetts, November 2016
9. Quigley, M., Conley, K., Gerkey, B.P., Faust, J., Foote, T., Leibs, J., Wheeler, R., Ng, A.Y.: ROS: an open-source robot operating system. In: ICRA Workshop on Open Source Software (2009)
10. Rowan, D.: Kinect for Xbox 360: The inside story of Microsoft's secret 'Project Natal'. Wired, 29 October 2010
11. Ruiz-Zafra, A., Nez, A.G., Penads, M.C., H.Cans, J., Borges, M.R.: SUCRE: supporting users, controllers and responders in emergencies. In: 11th International ISCRAM Conference Proceedings, Pennsylvania, May 2014
12. Schneider, E., Sklar, E.I., Parsons, S.: Evaluating multi-robot teamwork in varied environments. In: Proceedings of the 17th Towards Autonomous Robotic Systems (TAROS), awarded Best Student Paper Prize (2016)
13. Schneider, E., Sklar, E.I., Parsons, S., Özgelen, A.T.: Auction-based task allocation for multi-robot teams in dynamic environments. In: Dixon, C., Tuyls, K. (eds.) TAROS 2015. LNCS, vol. 9287, pp. 246–257. Springer, Cham (2015). doi:10.1007/978-3-319-22416-9_29
14. Shapiro, S.S., Wilk, M.B.: An analysis of variance test for normality. Biometrika **44**(3/4), 591–611 (1995)
15. Sutton, J., Spiro, E., Fitzhugh, S., Johnson, B., Gibson, B., Butts, C.T.: Online message amplification in the boston bombing response. In: 11th International ISCRAM Conference Proceedings, Pennsylvania, May 2014
16. Takahashi, T., Kitamura, Y., Miwa, H.: Organizing rescue agents using ad-hoc networks. In: Pérez, J., et al. (eds.) Highlights on Practical Applications of Agents and Multi-Agent Systems. AISC, vol. 156, pp. 139–146. Springer, Heidelberg (2012). doi:10.1007/978-3-642-28762-6_17
17. Tapia, A.H., LaLone, N., Kim, H.W.: Run Amok: group crowd participation in identifying the bomb and bomber from the boston marathon bombing. In: 11th International ISCRAM Conference Proceedings, Pennsylvania, May 2014
18. Zadorozhny, V., Lewis, M.: Information fusion for USAR operations based on crowdsourcing. In: 16th International Conference on Information Fusion (FUSION), Istanbul, Turkey, July 2013

Mechanism Selection for Multi-Robot Task Allocation

Eric Schneider[1,2(✉)], Elizabeth I. Sklar[1], and Simon Parsons[1]

[1] Department of Informatics, King's College London, London, UK
{eric.schneider,elizabeth.sklar,simon.parsons}@kcl.ac.uk
[2] Department of Computer Science, University of Liverpool, Liverpool, UK

Abstract. The work presented here investigates how environmental features can be used to help select a task allocation mechanism from a portfolio in a multi-robot exploration scenario. In particular, we look at clusters of task locations and the positions of team members in relation to cluster centres. In a data-driven approach, we conduct experiments that use two different task allocation mechanisms on the same set of scenarios, providing comparative performance data. We then train a classifier on this data, giving us a method for choosing the best mechanism for a given scenario. We show that selecting a mechanism via this method, compared to using a single state-of-the-art mechanism only, can improve team performance in certain environments, according to our metrics.

Keywords: Multi-robot team · Auction mechanism · Task allocation

1 Introduction

We are studying task allocation in multi-robot teams, known as the *multi-robot task allocation* (MRTA) problem. This is an issue of critical importance in the deployment of such teams, and an issue that must be addressed if the future potential of autonomous robots is going to be fullfilled. A popular approach to the problem is to apply market-based methods, such as auctions [3]. In this approach, tasks are offered to the team members and team members bid against each other for the tasks. A typical bidding strategy has bids derived from the distance of the robot from the site at which the task needs to be carried out. Allocating tasks to the robot making the lowest bid can then ensure an allocation which reduces the total distance travelled by the team.

Many market-based mechanisms have been suggested for the task allocation problem. These mechanisms vary considerably in the trade-offs that they make between computation time and space, and the quality of solutions that they deliver, measured by metrics such as the total distance covered by the team while completing a set of tasks. In addition, the performance of mechanisms seems to be greatly affected by the environments in which they are deployed. In some environments, a simple, greedy mechanism which might not be expected to perform well in the general case may, in fact, perform competitively with more

© Springer International Publishing AG 2017
Y. Gao et al. (Eds.): TAROS 2017, LNAI 10454, pp. 421–435, 2017.
DOI: 10.1007/978-3-319-64107-2_33

sophisticated mechanisms, with the advantage of scaling better. Prior work has shown evidence that this is the case in both simulated and physical experiments [22–24].

In particular, in our earlier work, we showed [23,24] that while the sequential single-item auction [12] performs better than the parallel single-item auction [12] when the allocation is carried out with robots clustered together geographically, this advantage diminishes as robots are distributed over space and tasks are distributed over space and time. Based on this observation, in this paper we propose a portfolio-based approach to the MRTA problem. Given a set of task allocation mechanisms and a set of environmental features that we can measure, we would like to be able to classify a previously unseen environment in order to choose a task allocation mechanism that performs well in it.

By "environments", we refer here to the spatial arrangements and distributions of robots and tasks. It seems appropriate to apply the tools and techniques of cluster analysis to these environments. We need to consider environmental obstacles like walls, so it seems natural to model environments as graphs, where nodes may be robots and/or task locations, and edges are paths computed by a path planner (e.g., A* [8]) between these nodes, around obstacles. The graphs we can construct in this way resemble something like road networks, and that suggests an approach to characterising different environments.

The distribution of sites over road-network-like graphs is a well-studied research area in Geographic Information Systems (GIS). One particular class of problem from GIS that is useful to apply here is *location-allocation* or *facility location*, which seeks to determine the ideal locations for "facilities" and allocates "demand points" to them in a way that minimises some measure of overall cost or maximises some overall utility. Examples of facilities and demand points might be warehouses and customers, or police stations and potential crime scenes, respectively. In the family of facility location problems [19], the p-median problem seems most suitable here, with p representing the number of facilities one wishes to locate.

In our case we can think of robot team members as facilities and task locations as demand points. If we can solve such a facility location problem for one of our scenarios, where the number of facilities is equal to the number of team members, we might find an ideal set of team starting locations for a simple, greedy mechanism like the parallel single-item auction. Our hypothesis is that if actual robot start locations are close to ideal facility locations, then the parallel single-item auction will lead to competitive performance. Conversely, if actual robot start locations are far away from ideal facility locations, then a more sophisticated mechanism like the sequential single-item auction is a better choice. Furthermore, it will be possible to select the best mechanism for specific sets of start and facility locations based only on knowledge about those locations. This paper provides an empirical test of this hypothesis and finds that, at least for some sets of locations, we can use machine learning to identify the best mechanism to use. We show that this approach can produce significant improvements in team performance.

The rest of this paper is structured as follows. Section 2 reviews the related literature. Section 3 then introduces our methodology, and Sect. 4 describes the experiments that we carried out to test our hypothesis. Section 5 presents our results; Sect. 6 discusses our results, arguing that they support our hypothesis, at least for some sets of robot start locations and some performance metrics; and Sect. 7 concludes.

2   Related Work

The use of market mechanisms in distributed computing can be considered to start with Smith's *contract net* protocol [25]. A strength of market-based approaches is their reliance only on local information and/or the self-interest of agents to arrive at efficient solutions to large-scale, complex problems that are otherwise intractable [3]. The most common instantiations of market mechanisms in multi-robot systems are auctions. Auctions are commonly used for distribution tasks, where resources or roles are treated as goods and auctioned to agents. Existing work analyses the effects of different auction mechanisms on overall solution quality [1,3,13,30]. A body of work has grown up around the *sequential single-item auction* (SSI) [12], which has been proven to create close to optimal allocations, exploiting synergies of related tasks while not suffering from the complexity issues of combinatorial auctions.

Location theory sits at the intersection of Geographic Information Systems (GIS) and economics. The *p-median* problem is one class of *location-allocation* or *facility location* problem that seeks to find optimal locations among existing sets of points that either maximize some measure of distribution utility or minimize some measure of cost [19]. Hakimi developed such problems on a graph to locate optimal switching centres for communication networks or police stations in a highway system [7]. Kariv and Hakimi showed that finding solutions to *p*-median problems is NP-hard on a general graph [11], but heuristics have been developed to make this more efficient [2,26].

Clustering or bundling of tasks has been investigated in the design of task allocation mechanisms. Sandholm extended Smith's Contract Net Protocol with *C-contracts* (cluster contracts), which award bundles of tasks, rather than single tasks, to agents [21]. Dias and Stentz proposed a mechanism that clusters geographically close tasks into a forest of minimum spanning trees, which may then be auctioned and potentially swapped [4]. Heap proposed sequential-single-cluster (SSC) auctions, an extension to SSI that uses an agglomerative clustering algorithm to create task bundles, which are then auctioned as in SSI [9]. Liu and Shell [16] develop a hybrid distributed-centralised approach to MRTA. The task set is first partitioned into subsets that are then solved in parallel using a centralised assignment algorithm [14].

The problem of algorithm selection and criteria for selecting an algorithm were proposed at least as early as Rice [20]. Computational or algorithm portfolios that use domain knowledge to define features of problem instances in order to select an appropriate algorithm have been investigated by Huberman et al. [10],

Gomes and Bart [6], and Leyton-Brown et al. [15]. Portfolio-based SAT solvers like SATzilla [29] and Hydra [28] have had success in selecting appropriate heuristics to solve NP-hard problems. As far as we are aware, a portfolio-based approach to market-based mechanism selection for MRTA problems, as we propose here, is novel.

3   Methodology

Here we define terms and notation and describe the software architecture used to conduct our experiments before detailing the proposed method for mechanism selection.

3.1   Definitions and System Architecture

As discussed above, our work focuses on task allocation in multi-robot teams. As in prior work [23], we consider that a set of n robots $R = \{r_0, \ldots, r_{n-1}\}$ comprises a *team* and a *mission* is a set of m tasks $T = \{t_0, \ldots, t_{m-1}\}$. A *task scenario* defines a map and the locations of tasks in T. Finally, a *parameterised environment* defines a task scenario, the starting locations of the team, and properties of tasks such as precedence ordering or arrival time. In the work presented here, all parameterised environments are, in the classification of [24], *SR-IT-SA*, that is, they comprise single-robot, independently ordered, statically allocated tasks.

Also as discussed above, this work makes use of the concept of the median of a graph. In particular, we consider the **p-median problem**:

> Given a graph or a network $G = (V, E)$, find $V_p \subseteq V$ such that $|V_p| = p$ and the sum of the shortest distances from the vertices in $\{V \setminus Vp\}$ to their nearest vertex in V_p is minimized [19].

We use the p-medians of a graph that spans robot start locations and task locations to determine which task allocation mechanism to employ in a given scenario.

Our work makes use of MRTeAm, a software framework for conducting multi-robot coordination experiments [23,24]. It is written on top of ROS [18] and its main components are a central *auctioneer* agent and multiple *robot controller* agents. The auctioneer is responsible for loading a task scenario and conducting auctions according to the rules of one of several types of auction mechanisms. That is, it announces tasks to, receives and aggregates bids from, and finally awards tasks to the robot controller agents. The robot controllers are responsible for computing and submitting bids using an A* path planner [8] and executing tasks once they have all been awarded.

3.2   Task Allocation Mechanisms

The portfolio method proposed here considers two auction mechanisms that we have investigated in previous work. In a sequential single-item auction (SSI) [12], unallocated tasks are advertised to all robots at once. Each robot bids on the task with the lowest path cost and each task is allocated to the robot that made the lowest bid for that task. The winning task is removed from the set of tasks to be advertised in the next round and the process is repeated until all tasks have been allocated. In a parallel single-item auction (PSI) [12], allocation starts like SSI but all robots bid on all points from their current locations. All the tasks are allocated in one round, with each task going to the lowest bidding robot that bid on it. In later sections we also refer to SEL, which represents our portfolio selection method.

3.3   Classification of Mechanism Selection Methods

The method we propose works as follows. On a map (shown in Figs. 1 and 2), we generate a large number of parameterised environments in which task and robot starting locations are randomly chosen over a uniform distribution with some buffer distance from walls (and robots from each other). For each environment, we conduct an experimental run with both PSI and SSI mechanisms. This generates a pair of results with the same starting conditions but different performance outcomes. From these results, we create a training instance for each environment by recording properties of that environment as training features (Table 1) and the winning mechanism, for some performance metric we wish to optimise, as a label. Finally, after balancing the training set and selecting features, we train a (binary) classifier to predict a winning mechanism.

We can now, in previously unseen environments (i.e., arrangements of task and robot starting locations), query our classifier at runtime to select the mechanism that is predicted to perform best in that environment.

3.4   Features and Training

The features used to build our training sets are defined in Table 1. For a given parameterised environment, there are three main steps to produce a training instance:

1. *Building the graph*: ROS's global planner[1] is invoked to construct a path between each pair of task locations. The result is a complete graph whose nodes are task locations and whose edges are paths planned between them. The graph is complete for the sake of simplifying the calculation in step 2, but completeness comes at a price: the path planner is invoked $O(m^2)$ times. This cost is important to consider, as the graph ultimately needs to be constructed at runtime.

---

[1] http://wiki.ros.org/global_planner.

Table 1. Environmental properties recorded as training features

Feature	Description
total distance to assigned medians	Sum of all robots' distances to their (SSI-) assigned medians
total distance to all medians	Sum of all robots' distances to all medians
maximum distance to assigned median	Maximum distance of any robot to its (SSI-)assigned median
maximum distance to any median	Maximum distance of any robot to any median
minimum distance to assigned median	Minimum distance of any robot to its (SSI-)assigned median
minimum distance to any median	Minimum distance of any robot to any median
assigned median distance spread	*maximum distance to assigned median* minus *minimum distance to assigned median*
total median distance spread	*maximum distance to any median* minus *minimum distance to any median*
greedy median count spread	Max. number of p-medians greedily (PSI-)assigned to any one robot minus min. number of the same
team diameter	Longest distance between any two team members

2. *Finding the medians*: The task graph is represented as a weighted adjacency matrix as input for a p-median solver. We use the Teitz-Bart method [26] from Xiao [27]. The result is a list of $p = n$ nodes, coincident with task locations, which we hypothesise to be ideal start locations for the robot team members when using PSI.

3. *Assigning medians to robots*: Deciding which median should be assigned to which robot is a task allocation problem in itself. Here we use both the PSI and SSI mechanisms to compute possible assignments. With all data in the memory of a single process (the auctioneer), no messages need be communicated among separate agents. Once an assignment of medians to robots has been computed, we can calculate the distance of each robot's start location to its assigned median(s). Examples of assignments are shown in Figs. 1 and 3. Assignments in Fig. 3 are shown as straight line paths for clarity of illustration. It should be mentioned that different robot-to-median assignments will produce different distance measurements (Table 1).

4   Experiments

Our main hypothesis is that if robot start locations are close to medians (i.e., ideal "facility" locations), then PSI will perform at least as well as SSI, if not

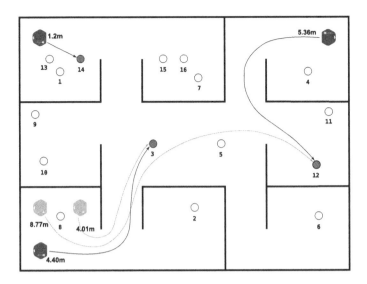

Fig. 1. The path distance of each robot to its assigned median for *clustered* (faint) and *distributed* (dark) start configurations with the same set of task locations.

better. We ran experiments to investigate if this hypothesis could be supported over a range of environments. One shortcoming of our prior work was that task and robot start locations were somewhat ad hoc, being chosen manually. To address this, in the experiments reported here, locations were randomised as described in Sect. 3.3.

4.1 Environments

To test our mechanism selection method, two types of randomised environments were investigated:

1. In *fixed start, random task location* environments, robot start locations were fixed in the *clustered* and *distributed* arrangements shown in Figs. 1 and 2b[2] and task locations were chosen randomly.
2. In *random start, random task location* environments, both robot start locations and task locations were chosen randomly.

In all environments that we investigated, the size of the robot team ($n = 3$) and number of tasks ($m = 16$) were fixed. All experiments were conducted using the Stage simulator [5]. For *fixed start, random task location* environments, 150 environments were generated to test mechanism selection, for a total of 150 × {*clustered*|*distributed*} starts × {PSI|SSI|SEL} mechanisms = 900 experimental runs for each performance objective. For *random start, random task location* environments, 300 environments were generated for a total of 300 × {PSI|SSI|SEL} mechanisms = 900 experimental runs for each performance objective.

---

[2] These are the same arrangements as used in [23,24].

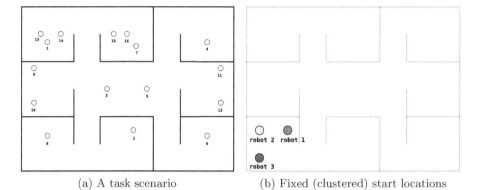

(a) A task scenario   (b) Fixed (clustered) start locations

Fig. 2. Examples of task and start locations discussed in Sect. 4.1. (a) shows an example task scenario with randomly chosen task locations. (b) shows one of the fixed (*clustered*) sets of robot starting locations.

4.2   Performance Metrics

While there are a number of ways to measure performance, we generally measure the travel distance and the time it takes for the team to reach all of the task locations. Specifically, we define four performance metrics.

Total distance travelled (meters) is the sum of the lengths of the paths travelled by team members over the course of an experiment. This is a measure of the use of resources (e.g. battery power or fuel) by the team as a whole. *Maximum robot distance* (meters) is the maximum distance travelled by any one robot. It also measures resource usage, but gives an indication of how balanced the load of a mission is across the team for a given allocation. *Execution phase time* (seconds) measures how long it takes the team, after an allocation has been computed, to travel to all task locations. *Total run time* (seconds) measures the time it takes for a mechanism to compute and conduct an allocation, plus execution phase time. Smaller values are preferred. Ideally, a task allocation mechanism will seek to perform well by minimising all of these metrics.

5   Results

We present results from three stages of our experiments. First we show some properties of the initial set of experiments that served as training data for classifiers. Second, we show classifier accuracy on held-out portions of the training data. Finally, we show the ultimate results of using these classifiers to select mechanisms from our portfolio.

5.1   Training Data

Properties of the initial set of experiments that served as training data are shown in Tables 2, 3 and Fig. 3. In general, PSI was better, in all environments tested,

Table 2. Fixed start, random task locations

Metric	PSI wins	%	SSI wins	%
Team distance	**403**	**90.97**	40	9.03
Maximum robot distance	135	30.47	**308**	**69.53**
Total run time	148	33.41	**295**	**66.59**
Execution phase time	117	26.41	**326**	**73.59**

Table 3. Random start, random task locations

Metric	PSI wins	%	SSI wins	%
Team distance	**744**	**81.2**	172	18.8
Maximum robot distance	85	9.28	**831**	**90.72**
Total run time	230	25.11	**686**	**74.89**
Execution phase time	118	12.88	**798**	**87.12**

at producing allocations that led to shorter *team distances* than SSI. SSI was better, in all environments, at producing shorter *maximum robot distances*. In the *random start, random task locations* environments (Table 3), SSI greatly outperformaned PSI on the *maximum robot distance, total run time*, and *execution phase time* objectives. In the *fixed start, random task locations* environments (Table 2), SSI was somewhat less dominant. These results show that, while SSI performs better overall, PSI allocations do sometimes result in performance that is competitive with SSI allocations, as we have seen in previous work [23,24].

5.2   Classifier Performance

Initially, the training sets had a severe class imbalance. In the training set for the *maximum robot distance* objective, for example, SSI was the winning mechanism in 1139 cases compared to PSI's count of 220 (Tables 2 and 3). We balanced the training sets using a random undersampling method,[3] although other methods are also possible.

Table 4. Accuracy of several classifiers trained for different performance objectives.

Classifier type	Objective	Accuracy	Std. Dev.
Random forest	Execution phase time	75.22%	0.91%
SVM	Execution phase time	74.55%	1.00%
Random forest	Maximum robot distance	80.88%	1.26%
SVM	Maximum robot distance	76.80%	1.20%

---

[3] https://github.com/scikit-learn-contrib/imbalanced-learn.

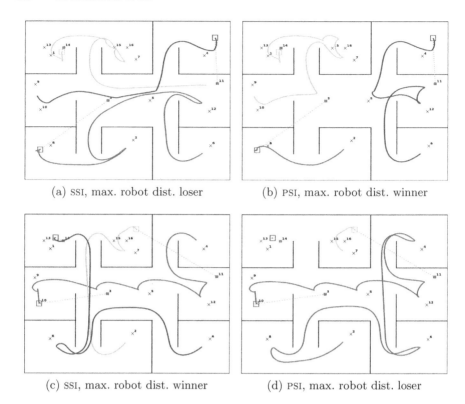

(a) SSI, max. robot dist. loser   (b) PSI, max. robot dist. winner

(c) SSI, max. robot dist. winner   (d) PSI, max. robot dist. loser

Fig. 3. Trajectories and p-median assignments for two sets of *random start, random task location* environments. Robot start locations are shown as large open coloured squares, task locations are shown as × marks, and medians are shown as small closed coloured squares. (a) and (b) show an environment where the PSI allocation led to a smaller maximum robot distance. (c) and (d) show an environment in which an SSI allocation led to a smaller maximum robot distance.

We used the scikit-learn [17] library to select features and train classifiers. Various types of classifier were investigated, including decision trees, k-nearest neighbours, random forests and support vector machines. Table 4 shows the average accuracy of some of these classifiers on held-out data over 10-fold cross validation.

As a result of these experiments, we selected the random forest classifier for the remainder of the work presented here. The features selected for the random forest classifier trained to optimise the *execution phase time* objective discussed in the next section were: {*maximum distance to assigned median, assigned median distance spread, team diameter,* and *greedy median count spread*}. Features selected for the random forest classifier trained to optimise the *maximum robot distance* objective were: {*total distance to all medians, maximum distance to any median, team diameter,* and *greedy median count spread*}. Hyper-parameters of the classifiers were tuned using a grid search.[4]

5.3   Mechanism Selection Results

Having trained a classifier, we then used it in experiments to see if a method which uses initial locations to pick an allocation mechanism using this classifier, a method we called SEL, can outperform either SSI or PSI. Some of the ultimate results of these experiments are shown in Figs. 4, 5, 6 and 7. Each figure shows the average value measured for a particular metric and mechanism with 95% confidence intervals. Figures 4, 5 and 6 show results for *fixed start, random task locations* environments. Figure 7 shows results for *random start, random task locations* environments. We trained classifiers for both the *maximum robot distance* and *execution phase time* performance objectives, but only the results for the *execution phase time* objective are shown here.

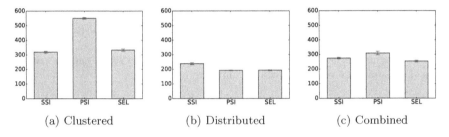

Fig. 4. Execution phase time for clustered starts (a), distributed starts (b), and the combination of clustered and distributed starts (c). Units are seconds.

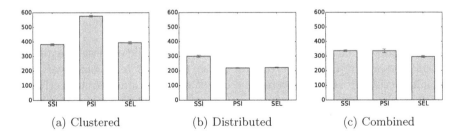

Fig. 5. Total run time for clustered starts (a), distributed starts (b), and the combination of clustered and distributed starts (c). Units are seconds.

---

[4] http://scikit-learn.org/stable/modules/grid_search.html.

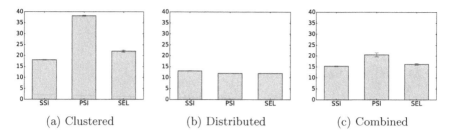

(a) Clustered   (b) Distributed   (c) Combined

Fig. 6. Maximum robot distance for clustered starts (a), distributed starts (b), and the combination of clustered and distributed starts (c). Units are meters.

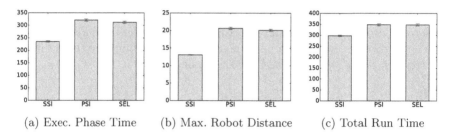

(a) Exec. Phase Time   (b) Max. Robot Distance   (c) Total Run Time

Fig. 7. Mechanism selection results for *random start, random task locations* environments. Time units are seconds. Distance units are meters.

6   Discussion

Examining the full range of environments we investigated, the performance improvements of our mechanism selection method are mixed.

In *random start, random task location* environments, the classifier we trained to predict which of the two mechanisms would minimise the *execution phase time* objective did not perform better, on average, than SSI. It led to execution phase times and total run times that were only slightly lower than PSI (Fig. 7a and c). It also did not lead to significantly shorter maximum robot distances (Fig. 7b), but then it was not trained to do so.

In *fixed start, random task location* environments, we did observe a significant performance improvement in *execution phase time* and *total run time* when combining results from the *clustered* and *distributed* fixed start locations (Fig. 4c and 5c). SSI led to an average execution phase time of 274.95 ± 10.04 s while SEL reduced that to 252.10 ± 11.23 s. (Both figures are 95% confidence intervals; an independent t-test yields a t-statistic of 2.99 at $p = 0.0029$.)

These early results are encouraging, but the current SEL method has room for improvement. In addition to reducing execution phase time for randomised task locations with fixed start locations, we would like it to do so for randomised robot starting locations as well. We can make two general kinds of improvements.

First, to improve classifier accuracy we might devise more descriptive environmental features than those listed in Table 1. We might also develop better methods of producing or preparing the training data, train different kinds of classifiers, or learn weights that reward the contributions of these (or other) features. Secondly, we can improve the time it takes to perform the selection method itself. As described in Sect. 3.4, the current method requires the construction of a complete graph with a number of edges that scales quadratically with the size of the mission. A simply connected, rather than complete, graph may suffice, so that building the graph scales linearly with the size of the mission.

7 Summary

We have developed a method of selecting an auction-based task allocation mechanism from a portfolio of mechanisms to address the multi-robot task allocation (MRTA) problem. We have shown that, in some environments, this method can provide an allocation that leads a robot team to execute its mission in significantly less time than that of a single, state-of-the-art mechanism. While these early results are encouraging, the method can be improved in several ways. We are working to improve its performance for more general cases of a known environment, in particular for randomised robot start locations. We are also working to generalise the approach to consider more mechanisms and richer environments—combining it with our previous work on multi-robot, precedence-ordered, and dynamically appearing tasks [23, 24]—and on other maps.

References

1. Berhault, M., Huang, H., Keskinocak, P., Koenig, S., Elmaghraby, W., Griffin, P.M., Kleywegt, A.: Robot exploration with combinatorial auctions. In: Proceedings of the International Conference on Intelligent Robotics and Systems (IROS) (2003)
2. Densham, P.J., Rushton, G.: A more efficient heuristic for solving large p-median problems. Pap. Reg. Sci. **71**(3), 307–329 (1992)
3. Dias, M.B., Zlot, R., Kalra, N., Stentz, A.: Market-based multirobot coordination: a survey and analysis. Proc. IEEE **94**(7), 1257–1270 (2006)
4. Dias, M.B., Stentz, A.: Opportunistic optimization for market-based multirobot control. In: Proceedings of the International Conference on Intelligent Robots and Systems (IROS), vol. 3, pp. 2714–2720 (2002)
5. Gerkey, B., Vaughan, R.T., Howard, A.: The player/stage project: tools for multi-robot and distributed sensor systems. In: Proceedings of the 11th International Conference on Advanced Robotics (2003)
6. Gomes, C.P., Selman, B.: Algorithm portfolios. Artif. Intell. **126**(1–2), 43–62 (2001)
7. Hakimi, S.L.: Optimum locations of switching centers and the absolute centers and medians of a graph. Oper. Res. **12**(3), 450–459 (1964)

8. Hart, P., Nilsson, N., Raphael, B.: A formal basis for the heuristic determination of minimal cost paths. IEEE Trans. Syst. Sci. Cybern. **4**(2), 100–107 (1968)
9. Heap, B.: Sequential single-cluster auctions for multi-robot task allocation. Ph.D. thesis, The University of New South Wales, November 2013
10. Huberman, B.A., Lukose, R.M., Hogg, T.: An economics approach to hard computational problems. Science **275**(5296), 51–54 (1997)
11. Kariv, O., Hakimi, S.L.: An algorithmic approach to network location problems. ii: the p-medians. SIAM J. Appl. Math. **37**(3), 539–560 (1979)
12. Koenig, S., Tovey, C., Lagoudakis, M., Kempe, D., Keskinocak, P., Kleywegt, A., Meyerson, A., Jain, S.: The power of sequential single-item auctions for agent coordination. In: Proceedings of National Conference on Artificial Intelligence (2006)
13. Kraus, S.: Automated negotiation and decision making in multiagent environments. In: Luck, M., Mařík, V., Štěpánková, O., Trappl, R. (eds.) ACAI 2001. LNCS, vol. 2086, pp. 150–172. Springer, Heidelberg (2001). doi:10.1007/3-540-47745-4_7
14. Kuhn, H.W.: The Hungarian method for the assignment problem. Naval Res. Logistics Q. **2**(1–2), 83–97 (1955)
15. Leyton-Brown, K., Nudelman, E., Andrew, G., McFadden, J., Shoham, Y.: A portfolio approach to algorithm selection. In: International Joint Conference on Artificial Intelligence (IJCAI), vol. 1543, pp. 1542–1543 (2003)
16. Liu, L., Shell, D.A.: Large-scale multi-robot task allocation via dynamic partitioning and distribution. Auton. Robots **33**(3), 291–307 (2012)
17. Pedregosa, F., Varoquaux, G., Gramfort, A., Michel, V., Thirion, B., Grisel, O., Blondel, M., Prettenhofer, P., Weiss, R., Dubourg, V., Vanderplas, J., Passos, A., Cournapeau, D., Brucher, M., Perrot, M., Duchesnay, E.: Scikit-learn: machine learning in Python. J. Mach. Learn. Res. **12**, 2825–2830 (2011)
18. Quigley, M., Conley, K., Gerkey, B.P., Faust, J., Foote, T., Leibs, J., Wheeler, R., Ng, A.Y.: ROS: an open-source robot operating system. In: ICRA Workshop on Open Source Software (2009)
19. Reese, J.: Solution methods for the p-median problem: an annotated bibliography. Networks **48**(3), 125–142 (2006)
20. Rice, J.R.: The algorithm selection problem. Adv. Comput. **15**, 65–118 (1976)
21. Sandholm, T.: Contract types for satisficing task allocation: I theoretical results. In: Proceedings of the AAAI Spring Symposium: Satisficing Models, pp. 68–75 (1998)
22. Schneider, E., Balas, O., Özgelen, A.T., Sklar, E.I., Parsons, S.: Evaluating auction-based task allocation in multi-robot teams. In: Workshop on Autonomous Robots and Multirobot Systems (ARMS) at Autonomous Agents and MultiAgent Systems (AAMAS), Paris, France, May 2014
23. Schneider, E., Sklar, E.I., Parsons, S.: Evaluating multi-robot teamwork in parameterised environments. In: Alboul, L., Damian, D., Aitken, J.M.M. (eds.) TAROS 2016. LNCS (LNAI), vol. 9716, pp. 301–313. Springer, Cham (2016). doi:10.1007/978-3-319-40379-3_32
24. Schneider, E., Sklar, E.I., Parsons, S., Özgelen, A.T.: Auction-based task allocation for multi-robot teams in dynamic environments. In: Dixon, C., Tuyls, K. (eds.) TAROS 2015. LNCS, vol. 9287, pp. 246–257. Springer, Cham (2015). doi:10.1007/978-3-319-22416-9_29
25. Smith, R.G.: The contract net protocol: high-level communication and control in a distributed problem solver. In: Bond, A.H., Gasser, L. (eds.) Distributed Artificial Intelligence. Morgan Kaufmann Publishers Inc. (1988)
26. Teitz, M.B., Bart, P.: Heuristic methods for estimating the generalized vertex median of a weighted graph. Oper. Res. **16**(5), 955–961 (1968)

27. Xiao, N.: GIS Algorithms. SAGE Publications, Thousand Oaks (2015)
28. Xu, L., Hoos, H.H., Leyton-Brown, K.: Hydra: automatically configuring algorithms for portfolio-based selection. In: Proceedings of the Twenty-Fourth AAAI Conference on Artificial Intelligence, pp. 210–216. AAAI Press (2010)
29. Xu, L., Hutter, F., Hoos, H.H., Leyton-Brown, K.: Satzilla: portfolio-based algorithm selection for sat. J. Artif. Intell. Res. **32**, 565–606 (2008)
30. Zlot, R., Stentz, A., Dias, M.B., Thayer, S.: Multi-robot exploration controlled by a market economy. In: Proceedings of the IEEE Conference on Robotics and Automation (2002)

The Power of GMMs: Unsupervised Dirt Spot Detection for Industrial Floor Cleaning Robots

Andreas Grünauer, Georg Halmetschlager-Funek[✉], Johann Prankl, and Markus Vincze

Vision for Robotics Laboratory, Automation and Control Institute, TU Wien, 1040 Vienna, Austria
{ag,gh,jp,mv}@acin.tuwien.ac.at
http://www.acin.tuwien.ac.at/

Abstract. Small autonomous florr cleaning robots are the first robots to have entered our homes. These automatic vacuum cleaners have only used ver low-level dirt detection sensors and the vision systems have been constrained to plain-colored and simple-textured floors. However, for industrial applications, where efficiency and the quality of work are paramount, explicit high-level dirt detection is essential. To extend the usability of floor cleaning robots to theses real-world applications, we introduce a more general approach that detects dirt spots on single-colored as well as regularly-textured floors. Dirt detection is approached as a single-class classification problem, using unsupervised online learning of a Gaussian Mixture Model representing the floor pattern. An extensive evaluation shows that our method detects dirt spots on different floor types and that it outperforms state-of-the-art approaches especially for complex floor textures.

Keywords: Visual floor inspection · RGBD · GMM · Unsupervised learning · Industrial cleaning robots

1 Introduction

During the last decade the first robots made their way into our homes. Among the first robots have been automated floor cleaning (or vacuuming) systems. The task of floor cleaning (vacuuming) provided many preconditions that paved the way for early robot-based automation. Flat surfaces, a well defined work space, and a simple task made it possible to narrow down the robot's functional requirements to the essentials: wander around with an activated cleaning system and drive back to the docking station as soon as the energy drops below a predefined level. These types of tasks are sufficiently handled with low-level sensors and behavior-based control algorithms.

This work is supported by the European Commission through the Horizon 2020 Programme (H2020-ICT-2014-1, Grant agreement no: 645376).

Y. Gao et al. (Eds.): TAROS 2017, LNAI 10454, pp. 436–449, 2017.
DOI: 10.1007/978-3-319-64107-2_34

However, as suitable those small devices are for our homes they become inappropriate when they have to deal with large-scale industrial floor cleaning. Different to domestic vacuum cleaning, industrial cleaning deals with large-scale areas, daily and intra-daily cleaning missions, various pollution patterns, and challenging environments as factory buildings, hospitals, supermarkets, train stations, and airports. Due to the omnipresent limitation of a robot's resources and the growing awareness for the need of more efficient and ecological machines, the system demands sophisticated optimization strategies to meet the derived requirements and to make them suitable for an industrial and profitable application.

To this end, we aim to make our industrial cleaning robot[1] more efficient and to extend its operational radius. We add a vision algorithm that enables the robot to recognize heavily polluted areas, so that it can adapt the amount of used cleaning products and energy to achieve a more efficient cleaning procedure.

The underlying core task simplifies to the classification of clean and polluted areas (cf. Fig. 1). The detection of pollution has hardly been tackled so far in robotics. An exception is the method proposed in [1,2], which assumes different image frequencies of the background and the polluted areas. This assumption limits applications to floors of single color or texture patterns much larger than the particle that are to be detected.

We propose a new, and more general solution that is an unsupervised novelty detection algorithm and does not have to learn the clean target appearance of the floor a-priori. We model the appearance of the floor with a mixture of a finite number of Gaussian distributions (GMMs [3]). Our algorithm learns a GMM background model of the floor and identifies dirt spots for each image. For the evaluation of our algorithms we extract 850 ground truth annotated images from the framework provided by [1,2], add 240 challenging real life images with new floor patterns, develop a new evaluation framework that is compatible but independent of the Robot Operation System (ROS), and evaluated our method against the algorithm published in [1].

Fig. 1. Summary of the main concept: learning of the floor structure and determination of dirt probabilities. Left: original image. Right: extracted probabilities.

In summary, our contributions are (i) a novel dirt detection algorithm that takes advantage of an unsupervised online learning algorithm and uses GMMs to

---

[1] www.flobot.eu.

distinguish between the floor and dirt spots, (ii) an evaluation of our algorithm against an existing algorithm [1], and reevaluation of the existing algorithm against a firmer dataset, containing difficult dirt detection scenarios, and provide (iii) an extended database, containing 1090 annotated ground truth images that can be utilized by the community for further research. The full dataset can either be found on the Vision 4 Robotics lab homepage that can be accessed via www. acin.tuwien.ac.at/ or directly via https://goo.gl/6UCBpR.

The paper is structured as follows. After reviewing the related work in Sect. 2, we present our method in Sect. 3, and proceed with the description of the dirt databases used for our experiments in Sect. 4. Then we discuss the experiments and the results in Sect. 5, followed by our conclusion and outlook in Sect. 6.

2 Related Work

Visual dirt detection for autonomous cleaning devices is a recent research field. Various manufacturers released commercial robotic vacuum cleaners such as the iRobot Roomba[2] or the Dyson 360 Eye[3]. These devices are designed to clean the entire floor several times a week. Typically optical and piezo-electronic sensors inside the vacuum bin inform the robot about the degree of pollution for the adaption of the cleaning process. However, these sensors are incapable of detecting certain kinds of dirt, e.g. stains on a carpet. Another drawback is that each location needs to be treated at least once to detect its cleanliness. In industry, the first cleaning robots introduced were the robots from Intellibot[4] or Cyberdyne[5]. However, they were designed to clean a certain type of area rather than check cleanliness and to adapt depending on the feedback.

Visual detection of dirt spots on floors closely relates to the problem of identifying and removing film defects such as dirt particles and scratches in digital movie restoration. Work in this field [4,5] incorporate spatial-temporal segmentation methods that are based on the appearing of noise in only a single or few consecutive frames. Nevertheless, these temporal filtering methods are not directly applicable to the visual floor inspection task because dirt spots do not appear and disappear from the floor in consecutive camera frames.

Another approach is to train an object detection system either on all possible appearances of dirt, or the appearance of clean floors, similar to the approach of learning a background model in static scenes [6]. While the first is in feasible due to the various different appearances of dirt, the latter has the disadvantage that the model needs to be learned a-prior for each new individual floor pattern.

A naïve approach to detect dirt is to interpret dirt as objects that stick out of an estimated ground plane, which would not work for extremely flat objects such as paper or liquids. 3D saliency methods [7,8] detect objects based on color, depth and curvature to segment objects. These approaches involve

---

[2] www.irobot.com.
[3] www.dyson360eye.com.
[4] www.intellibotrobotics.com.
[5] www.cyberdyne.jp.

analysis of point cloud data and are therefore not applicable on our problem, as the dimensions of small dirt particles are smaller than the spatial resolution of current RGB-D sensors.

[1,2] introduce a learning-free 2D saliency method that identifies dirt as the salient parts in the scene using the algorithm of Hou et al. [9]. Hou et al. found that most images roughly share the shape of their logarithmic amplitude spectra. Assuming that this common shape corresponds to the background in the images, the difference of the original and the smoothed logarithmic amplitude spectrum represents the prominent parts of the image. Bormann et al. calibrate the saliency filter response against the response of a modified scene image containing artificially added standard pollution. The regions of the calibrated filter response which are above a empirically depicted threshold are subsequently considered as dirt. In successive work [10] the algorithm was enhanced to reduce the high false-positive rate by matching potential false-positive image patches against a database of known false-positive floor templates (e.g. power plugs in the floor).

Another possible solution is the application of novelty detection, which is the task of identifying data that differ from the vast majority of available training data. An overview of the state-of-the-art novelty detection approaches is given in [11]. In [12] novelty detection based on GMMs is used for face detection. Inspired by this work, our contribution is a patch-wise color gradient feature that transforms this initially supervised classification problem into a novelty detection task, which enables an unsupervised solution of the dirt detection task using GMMs and pure RGB data. The selected feature and the robust unsupervised learning method uses geometric information and makes sufficient camera calibration obsolete. I.e. the presented method does not need any warping of the camera image into the bird's eye perspective as in [1].

3   Unsupervised Dirt Detection

The presented dirt detection algorithm is based on the extraction of a patch-wise texture feature vector followed by a novelty detection using GMMs. An overview of the processing pipeline is depicted in Fig. 2. The individual steps are explained in detail in the following subsections.

3.1   Color Gradient Feature

Novelty detection requires the extraction of a set of feature vectors to obtain a model that has the power to discriminate between *one* class (the clean floor) and all other possibilities (dirt). Therefore, we introduce a color gradient feature. RGB images of real world scenarios often exhibit unbalanced lighting conditions, which introduces a high variation in color appearance of the same floor texture appearing in different parts of an image. Classification of feature vectors based on this color space would therefore not generalize well in such conditions. Consequently, we first decompose the RGB input image into the lightness channel L^*,

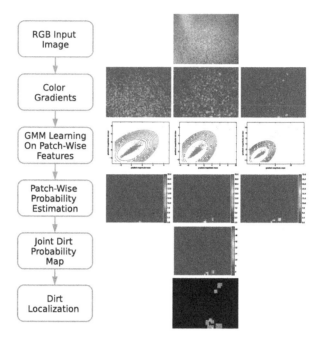

Fig. 2. Pipeline of the dirt detection system.

the color channel along the red-green axis a^*, and the color channel along the yellow-to-blue axis b^* of the CIE $L^*a^*b^*$ color space [13], which allows for the color information to be separated from the illumination in a scene. For each color channel, we extract feature vectors in the following way: We compute the gradient magnitude image and split the image into patches using a sliding window with fixed dimensions and step sizes as depicted in Fig. 3.

For each patch we compute a 2D feature vector holding mean and standard deviation of its gradient magnitude values. More formally, we define $X^{(c)}$ to be a feature representation of patch $\mathcal{P}$ computed on channel $c \in \{L^*, a^*, b^*\}$. Each image $\mathcal{I}$ is therefore described by the mean and standard deviation of its gradient magnitudes for each color channel.

3.2   Novelty Detection Using GMMs

The proposed dirt detection reformulated as novelty detection problem assumes that the vast majority of samples represent clean floor, and polluted regions will appear as outliers. The previous calculation of the texture feature yields a sample in two dimensions for each patch in the color channels that represents the polluted floor. We separately train three GMMs (one per color channel) with K mixture components. We denote the set of all estimated parameters of a GMM by $\theta^{(c)}$. Therefore, the likelihood of a sample X under the floor model is calculated as

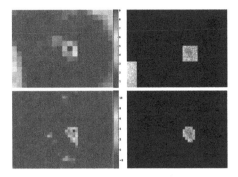

Fig. 3. Influence of two different patch sizes $\mathbf{p_n} = [p_x, p_y]^T$ and step widths $\mathbf{w_n} = [w_x, w_y]^T$ on the joint dirt probability map (left) and the masked output image (right). Starting from top: $\mathbf{p_0} = [64, 64]$, $\mathbf{w_0} = [32, 32]$ and $\mathbf{p_1} = [32, 32]$, $\mathbf{w_1} = [16, 16]$.

$$p(X|\theta) = \prod_{c \in \{a,b,L\}} p(X^{(c)}|\theta^{(c)})$$

where statistical independence between the channels is assumed. The probability of a patch considered as dirt is consequently defined as $1 - p(X|\theta)$. A patch is labeled as dirt if its dirt probability is above a fixed dirt probability threshold T_p.

4 Dirt Database

The following section gives a short overview of the evaluation database, that combines the reference data from Bormann et al. [1] (IPA Dirt Database) and adds data recordings inspired by the targeted industrial cleaning task.

4.1 IPA Dataset

In order to evaluate the dirt detection method described in Sect. 3 we adapted the office dirt database published in [1], which contains various dirt scenarios recorded on three different surfaces (*carpet, tiles, linoleum*) at five different locations. The original evaluation framework makes use of a transformation step that projects the detected dirt into an occupancy grid to enable spatial filtering over several frames. In addition, ground truth (GT) annotation is provided in the 3D space. The projection and the annotation makes the framework dependent on odometry and RGB-D data and makes it difficult to add new data. Since we aim to open up the data for a broad community, we extended the framework with interface classes, extracted the original bird's-eye RGB image of the floor, projected the GT annotation to the image frame, stored the 2D GT image, and saved the unthresholded result of the framework's core detection algorithm of each image for later evaluation. Due to the error prone nature of odometry, the original annotation is only sufficiently precise for the first few frames of the recorded sequences. Hence, we manually interrupted the extraction of the images as soon as the projection of the annotation showed a misalignment between the RGB and the GT image. With this, we were able to extract 850 precisely annotated image sets, each consisting of the masked floor image, the GT image, and the saliency image generated with the algorithm described in [1] (ref. Fig. 4).

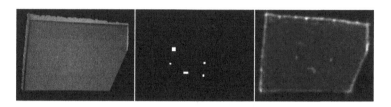

Fig. 4. Image set extracted from [1] (from left to right): bird's-eye RGB image, GT image, saliency image.

4.2 ACIN Dataset

We recorded an additional dataset with the goal of extending the dataset presented in [1]. It is focused on imbalanced lighting conditions, high-frequent floor textures, and motion blur to cover more realistic and challenging industrial cleaning scenarios.

For our recording setup we used the Pioneer P3-DX mobile robot platform, with a Asus Xtion Pro Live RGB-D camera mounted 1.10 m above the ground and tilted 40° downwards. The platform was steered remotely by an operator at a speed of 0.5–1.0 m/s, imitating an industrial cleaning robot during operation.

Fig. 5. Types of dirt used in the database (from left to right): cardboard, cigarettes and spilled liquid.

We have recorded two types of floor: single-colored *linoleum* as found in laboratories and hospitals, and a *hallway* with granular texture. For each of the floor types we used three different kinds of dirt: *cardboard* snippets, *cigarette* ends and spilled *liquid* stains, as shown in Fig. 5. For the experiments the dirt was uniformly distributed along the path of the robot at distances of 0.20–0.50 m. Instead of annotating the GT of the dirt locations in a reconstructed 3D scene, we labeled the dirt pixel-wise in 40 consecutive color images. This was performed for each scene, resulting in a total of 240 images of GT data. The advantage of this time-consuming annotation is that the precision of the GT is independent from the accuracy of the 3D localization and mapping system. Together with the data we publish an evaluation script which other developers can easily adapt to execute their algorithms on each data set. The script also saves the evaluation scores and generates the scoring plots as shown in Sect. 5.

5   Evaluation

We compare our unsupervised dirt detection algorithm with optimized parameter configurations with the state-of-the-art algorithm published in [1]. As performance measure we use the Receiver Operating Characteristic (ROC) curve, which shows the performance of a binary classifier under variation of its cut-off threshold. The ROC curve is created by plotting the fraction of true positives out of positives (true-positive rate) versus the number of false positives out of the negatives (false-positive rate), in which the positive class represents dirt. In the presented approach the parameter under variation is the dirt probability threshold T_p as defined in Sect. 3.2. For the evaluation of the method of [1] the parameter under variation is the threshold T_d applied on the rescaled filter response image.

As the quality of the floor model strongly depends on the pureness of the training set, a filter (mask) may be crucial to avoid the model fitting to structures that do not belong to the floor (cf. Sect. 5). This is realized i.e. by using a method similar to [1] where a mask is generated using RGB-D data and ground plane detection.

The three different parameters (number of mixture components K, patch size and step width) have been assessed using grid search. Table 1 shows the selection of four parameter configurations that demonstrate the performance of the presented algorithm under variation of the parameters. For a comparison with the state of the art, the method of [1] was evaluated both *with* and *without* line removal, denoted as (Spectral-WL) and (Spectral-NL).

Table 1. Overview of the evaluated parameter sets.

Param. set	Patch size [px]	Step width [px]	K (GMM)
GMM1-32	(32, 32)	(16, 16)	1
GMM3-32	(32, 32)	(16, 16)	3
GMM1-16	(16, 16)	(8, 8)	1
GMM3-16	(16, 16)	(8, 8)	3

In our first experiment we evaluate these six methods on the ACIN dataset as reported in Sect. 4 to assess their performance under realistic conditions that an industrial cleaning robot would encounter in the field. The ROC curves in Fig. 6 show that the proposed method outperforms the state-of-the-art. In Fig. 8 each boxplot summarizes the distribution of area under the ROC curves (AUC) over all frames belonging to the same floor type, computed for each method. The largest performance gains are achieved for hallway floor scenes. The AUC scores grouped by type of dirt in Fig. 7 demonstrate that our method delivers more stable results with less variation and works exceptionally well for liquids.

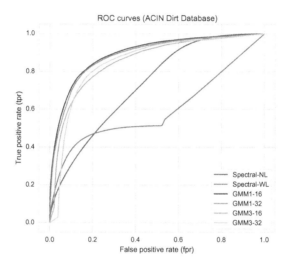

Fig. 6. ROC curves of the assessed methods evaluated for the ACIN dataset.

Figure 9 shows the masked RGB input image of the ground plane, the scaled filter response by the state-of-the-art method [1], the dirt probability map of the proposed method, and the labeled GT image with dirt represented by white color. The examples show coffee stains both on linoleum and hallway (columns 1 and 2) as well as cigarette ends on hallway (column 3). The dirt probability maps computed by our method yield high values at the location of the liquid stain and the cigarettes, whereas the spectral filter response of Spectral-WL exhibits high responses at the heterogeneous, fine grained floor pattern, but not at the dirt locations. This is due to the fact that the state-of-the-art method is based on spectral image saliency from [9], which assumes that foreground objects are represented by high frequencies and background objects are represented by low frequencies in the frequency domain. For heterogeneous, highly textured floor types as in the given example, this assumption does not hold, hence the state-of-the-art method cannot distinguish dirt from floor in these types of scenarios.

In a second experiment the same six methods have been evaluated on the adapted office dataset as described in Sect. 4. The resulting ROC curves in Fig. 10

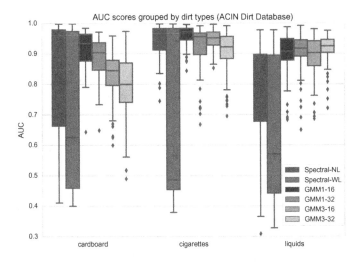

Fig. 7. Box plots showing the variation of frame-wise AUC scores evaluated on the ACIN dataset, grouped by dirt type.

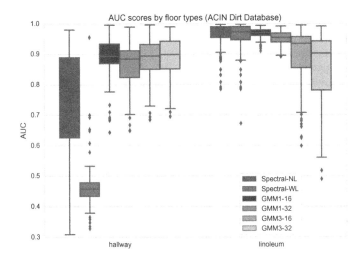

Fig. 8. Box plots showing the variation of frame-wise AUC scores evaluated on the ACIN dataset, grouped by floor type.

show that the presented method yields comparable results to the method of [1]. The AUC scores grouped by floor type in Fig. 11 show some limitations of our proposed method in detecting dirt in the kitchen scenes. An example of a kitchen scene is shown in Fig. 9 (column 5), where the dirt probability map exhibits high dirt probabilities for visible parts, but low probabilities for the actual dirt regions in the image. The limited performance in this particular scene can be derived from tainted input data that include parts of the wall surface that are

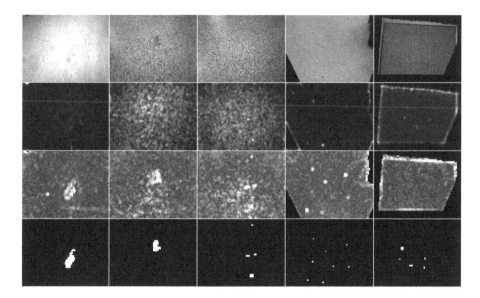

Fig. 9. Examples of input and output images computed on various scenes of the dataset. The *rows* show (from top to bottom): (1) the masked RGB input image of the ground plane, (2) the scaled filter response by the state-of-the-art method of Bormann et al. [1] with no line removal (SPECTRAL-NL), (3) the dirt probability map of our method using a patch size of 16 × 16 pixel (GMM1-16) and (4) the labeled ground truth image. The *columns* show the following combinations of floors and dirt type (from left to right): (1) linoleum & liquid, (2) hallway & liquid and (3) hallway & cigarettes, (4) linoleum & paper, and (5) kitchen & fuzz. The first two scenes are taken from the office dataset of [1] and the second three scenes have been recorded as described in Sect. 4.2.

detected by our algorithm but not marked as dirt spots in the GT data. These wall patches are – from the novelty detection point of view – correctly detected as outliers, as their features differ clearly from the floor. At the same time the GMM adapts to these isolated points in the feature space. Compared to these outliers, the features of true dirt are much more similar to the features of the floor and therefore yield a low dirt probability. As mentioned in Sect. 3.2 a sufficient pre-filtering of the input data could guarantee pureness of the input data.

Another interesting finding is the performance loss of the state-of-the-art method with line removal (Spectral-WL) on the corridor from the office and hallway in the ACIN dataset, as depicted in Figs. 8 and 11. The removal of high responses along the straight joints between the tiles in the corridor scene wrongly suppresses valid dirt responses close to the corners and edges. For the hallway case, the high responses of the coarse floor texture leads to a high number of randomly detected lines, which mask out the spectral filter response almost completely, including dirt peaks.

Figure 6 demonstrates that the configuration of a GMM of one component in combination with a patch size of 16 × 16 pixels and a step size of 8 × 8 pixels achieves the best results on the ACIN data. A visual comparison of the influence of different patch sizes on the probability map and dirt mask is presented in Fig. 3. The same figure shows that the presented algorithm is capable of detecting dirty regions that spread over several adjoining patches, as they differ more greatly from patches of clean floor on which the floor model was trained on. The similarity of the ROC curves in Fig. 6 indicates that the proposed algorithm is robust against the change of patch size and number of GMM components. This shows that the descriptiveness power of the introduced color gradient feature in Sect. 3.1 allows for the application of simple, well-generalizing models. Additionally the dirt probability maps computed by our method demonstrate that the presented approach works on unwarped (Fig. 9, row 3, columns 1–3) and warped (Fig. 9, row 3, columns 4–5) images. This confirms that our approach is independent of any preprocessing step that includes a transformation of the data into the bird's eye view.

The implementation of the proposed algorithm runs in average at a frame rate of 5.5 Hz on a single core of an i7 CPU with 2.7 GHz and 4 GB RAM.

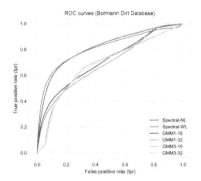
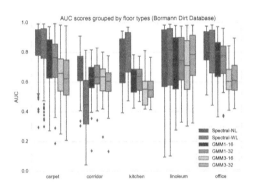

Fig. 10. ROC curves of the assessed methods evaluated for the ACIN dataset.

Fig. 11. Box plots showing the variation of frame-wise AUC scores evaluated on the office dataset, grouped by floor type.

6   Conclusion

In this paper we presented an unsupervised learning approach based on GMMs to learn floor patterns and to detect dirt for the purpose of targeted robotic floor cleaning. The algorithm overcomes the challenge of unknown floor types and does not need a separate step of learning the clean target appearance. With these characteristics the method sets out to solve industrial cleaning tasks in large areas such as supermarkets and airports where the type of floor may change and initial learning may hinder deployment.

Our proposed method reveals its strength on data that offer low image quality (e.g. motion blur), inhomogeneous floor structures, or high-frequent floor texture. The evaluation confirmed that the existing approach offers good performance within strict boundaries, especially on floors with low-frequent patterns, while our approach achieves competitive results for such scenarios. Nevertheless, the combination of both approaches appears as a promising way to detect dirt independently from the regularity or frequency of the floor pattern.

The database that has been created is public available to initiate further improvements for this industrial use case. The database contains 1090 image sets, including the input images showing clear and polluted areas, ground truth annotated images, saliency images that have been extracted with the baseline algorithm of [1], and an image showing dirt probabilities generated with our GMM approach. In addition, we provide an easy to use evaluation script that will allow other researches to validate their algorithms with our database and compare their results to the baseline of [1] and to our approach.

Although the evaluation showed significant improvements over previous methods, there is clear scope for further work. For example, the system could be developed into a multi-frame system by re-using the generated GMM model as a prior for consecutive frames. This would directly result in lower computational cost and could achieve a higher frame rate and real-time capability. However, this approach demands for an intelligent algorithm that is capable of maintaining or updating the prior GMM.

References

1. Bormann, R., Weisshardt, F., Arbeiter, G., Fischer, J.: Autonomous dirt detection for cleaning in office environments. In: Proceedings of IEEE International Conference on Robotics and Automation, pp. 1260–1267 (2013)
2. Bormann, R., Fischer, J., Arbeiter, G., Weisshardt, F., Verl, A.: A visual dirt detection system for mobile service robots. In: 7th German Conference on Robotics, Proceedings of ROBOTIK 2012, pp. 1–6 (2012)
3. Duda, R.O., Hart, P.E., Stork, D.G., et al.: Pattern Classification, vol. 2. Wiley, New York (1973)
4. Ren, J., Vlachos, T.: Detection and recovery of film dirt for archive restoration applications. In: 2007 IEEE International Conference on Image Processing, vol. 4, p. 21. IEEE (2007)
5. Wechtitsch, S., Schallauer, P.: Robust detection of single-frame defects in archived film. In: International Conference on Pattern Recognition (ICPR), pp. 2647–2650 (2012)
6. Bischof, H., Grabner, H., Rot, P.M., Grabner, M.: Autonomous learning of a robust background model for change detection. In: Ferryman, J.M. (ed.) IEEE International Workshop on Performance Evaluation of Tracking and Surveillance (PETS 2006), pp. 39–46. IEEE (2006)
7. Potapova, E., Zillich, M., Vincze, M.: Attention-driven segmentation of cluttered 3D scenes. In: 2012 21st International Conference on Pattern Recognition (ICPR), pp. 3610–3613 (2012)
8. Potapova, E., Zillich, M., Vincze, M.: Local 3D symmetry for visual saliency in 2.5D point clouds. In: Asian Conference on Computer Vision, pp. 434–445 (2013)

9. Hou, X., Zhang, L.: Saliency detection: a spectral residual approach. In: Proceedings of the IEEE Computer Society Conference on Computer Vision and Pattern Recognition, pp. 1–8 (2007)
10. Bormann, R., Hampp, J., Hägele, M.: New brooms sweep clean - an autonomous robotic cleaning assistant for professional office cleaning. In: 2015 IEEE International Conference on Robotics and Automation (ICRA), pp. 4470–4477 (2015)
11. Pimentel, M.A.F., Clifton, D.A., Clifton, L., Tarassenko, L.: A review of novelty detection. Sig. Process. **99**, 215–249 (2014)
12. Drews, P., Núñez, P., Rocha, R.P., Campos, M., Dias, J.: Novelty detection and segmentation based on Gaussian mixture models: a case study in 3D robotic laser mapping. Robot. Auton. Syst. **61**, 1696–1709 (2013)
13. Jain, A.K.: Fundamentals of Digital Image Processing. Prentice-Hall, Inc., Englewood Cliffs (1989)

Autonomous Object Handover
Using Wrist Tactile Information

Jelizaveta Konstantinova[1(✉)], Senka Krivic[2], Agostino Stilli[3],
Justus Piater[2], and Kaspar Althoefer[1]

[1] School of Engineering and Material Science,
Queen Mary University of London, London, UK
j.konstantinova@qmul.ac.uk
[2] Department of Computer Science, University of Innsbruck, Innsbruck, Austria
[3] Department of Informatics, King's College London, London, UK

Abstract. Grasping in an uncertain environment is a topic of great
interest in robotics. In this paper we focus on the challenge of object
handover capable of coping with a wide range of different and unspecified
objects. Handover is the action of object passing an object from one agent
to another. In this work handover is performed from human to robot. We
present a robust method that relies only on the force information from
the wrist and does not use any vision and tactile information from the
fingers. By analyzing readings from a wrist force sensor, models of tactile
response for receiving and releasing an object were identified and tested
during validation experiments.

1 Introduction

Fully autonomous grasping and manipulation of objects is a topic of great importance in robotics. One of the main challenges is stable grasping of an undefined
object in uncertain environments [1]. To successfully grasp an object, the robot is
required to appropriately time the motion of the fingers. Enveloping the fingers
around the object too early or too late might lead to a weak grip or a complete
miss [2]. Often, the capability of grasping an object fully autonomously is not
required as the robot is collaborating with a human when performing a task.
Robotic systems are becoming safer and are entering the living or work space
of people [3]. This is important for scenarios such as household assistance and
elderly care, hospital nursing or assistance during rehabilitation or disabilities.
In such contexts close interaction between the human and the robot is essential.
Safety is an issue, as the robot might inadvertently endanger or harm the human;
hence, the timing of object grasping and releasing actions is an important aspect
in this context.

Handover of an object from human to robot is one of the most common
tasks where human-robot interaction is required. Handover simplifies grasp planning and implementation [4] as the object is given to the hand directly. However, it requires an accurate detection mechanism to discriminate stable grasps.

© Springer International Publishing AG 2017
Y. Gao et al. (Eds.): TAROS 2017, LNAI 10454, pp. 450–463, 2017.
DOI: 10.1007/978-3-319-64107-2_35

The following studies addressed the problem of robotic object handover. Generally, handover is performed based on human motion patterns that are studied and implemented on the robot [5], or they are used as input to a learning-by-demonstration system [6]. Whether the human action is learned or used as a reference, the existing approaches are computationally complex, require online robotic learning or a large data set of demonstrations.

A common problem between fully autonomous grasping and collaborative grasping is the ability to understand whether an object is safely grasped or not. It is possible to formally discriminate whether an object is successfully gripped. For example, Nagata et al. [7] presented a grasping system based on force and torque feedback that senses when the human has a stable grasp on the object, after which the robot can release the object. Such techniques are computationally intensive or require too detailed information regarding the placement of the fingers on the object. It is possible to detect a good grasp by relying on a tactile sensor or a multi-modal sensory system. In [8] authors use the wrist's current to discriminate a stable grasp. This is a simplistic approach, and does not scale well to objects with different geometries, friction and material properties. Work in [9] presented a robotic grasping controller inspired by human trials to grasp an object with minimal normal forces while ensuring the object does not slip. Such approach, however, requires a good estimate or prior knowledge of the friction of the objects to be successful. Multi-modal sensory systems increase the information available to the robot to take decisions such as detecting the contacts with the object [10]. However, such systems require additional computational complexity to perform sensor fusion in real time.

We describe a simple controller that is able to cope with different objects of different mechanical properties. It was tested on a multifingered hand and is targeted at human-robot interaction. This paper presents work addressing the problem of object handover using an algorithm which relies on wrist force and torque feedback only. Both actions of handing over the object to the human and taking it back from the user are studied. This work is performed as part of the EU project SQUIRREL. The control algorithm is implemented on the SQUIRREL robot platform, which is intended to be used in domestic environments such as a nursery for children.

Section 2 describes the design of the methodology of our studies, including the design of the robotic system and the handover problem. In Sect. 2.3 we present the experimental studies that were conducted for data collection. Then, in Sect. 3 the modeling of tactile data for object reception and release is presented. Section 4 presents validation studies that were performed to evaluate the performance of the algorithm. Conclusions are drawn out in Sect. 5.

2   Methodology

2.1   SQUIRREL Robot

The work presented here uses a robotic platform developed for the EU-FP7 project SQUIRREL (Fig. 1). It consists of a mobile base (FESTO Robotino),

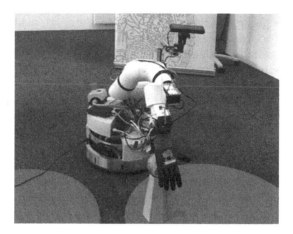

Fig. 1. SQUIRREL robot with the SoftHand as an end effector.

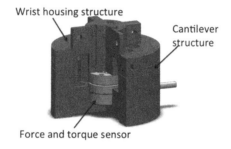

Fig. 2. Wrist sensor and wrist housing structure.

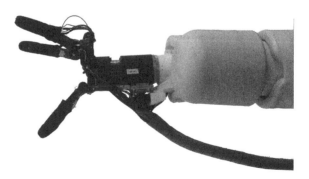

Fig. 3. KCL metamorphic hand with reconfigurable palm mounted on the SQUIRREL robot.

a custom-made 5 degree-of-freedom lightweight robotic arm (FESTO) and the end effector. In this version of the robot system the Pisa/IIT SoftHand [11] is used. It is an underactuated multifingered robotic hand with a single actuated degree of freedom. The hand pose is not predetermined; it adapts depending on the physical interaction of its body with the environment. Therefore, this brings more challenges for the design of the handover detection algorithm, as the pose of the hand cannot be taken into account. The second version of the SQUIRREL robot is equipped with a KCL metamorphic hand [12] (Fig. 3). This hand has a reconfigurable palm and is able to adopt a wide range of different grasping postures. Therefore, this paper focuses on methods to detect handover independently of the end effector, and uses force information obtained at the wrist.

The wrist of the robotic hand is equipped with a 6-axis force/torque sensor (FT17 from IIT). Apart from the detection of contact during handover, the purpose of this sensor is (1) to act as a safety switch in case of unexpected collision, (2) to detect forces applied during kinesthetic teaching, and (3) to detect the weight of an object during grasping.

The structure of the wrist, shown in Fig. 2, is designed to fulfill the following requirements. First, it creates a mechanical limitation on the maximum deflection of the wrist to protect the sensor from overloading and to prevent damage of the structure. In addition, it expands the force range where the sensor can operate safely before saturation, acting as a spring with a large elastic constant (in comparison to the sensor alone) in parallel with the sensor itself. In order to produce a spring-like behavior using a rigid material (ABS 3D printing material), a flexible cantilever structure was integrated directly with the walls of the structure.

2.2   Object Handover

A handover action is a structured action that is composed of different intermediate steps. For instance, human-to-human handovers [13] are composed of three main stages: reaching the receiving agent, signaling the intention to do a handover, and passing the object to the receiver. In this work, we study handovers of objects between a human and a robot (object reception) and vice-versa (object releasing).

The action of handover is part of more a complex robot behavior, where the robot acts as a companion and assistant to a human. In the general system, handover is triggered by a high-level planner which defines the type of handover. The handover type is determined by the final hand pose and orientation while performing the transfer of the object. There are different types that depend on the class of the object and the subsequent robot task.

Different types of handovers are discriminated by the hand posture used to hold or receive the object, i.e., which edge of the object is grasped, whether an object has a handle or a specific grasping area such as a knife, etc. Detecting the most suitable type of handover is outside the scope of this paper. Nevertheless, in this work, the robot is required to identify the contact with an object to be

Fig. 4. Handover of an object to a human.

grasped or a request to release an object for different postures of an end-effector. An example of a handover is shown in Fig. 4.

Our definition of handover between a human and a robot is as follows. To receive an object from a human subject, the robot is required to approach the human, to open the end effector, and to signal to the human the intention of receiving the object. Then, the robot is required to ensure that the object is in contact with the end effector in order to perform a successful grasp and to restrain the object in the robotic hand (Fig. 5a). Handing over an object to a human requires approaching the subject while carrying the object in the end effector, ensuring that the object is safely restrained by the human, and releasing the object (Fig. 5b). Force sensing is used to confirm that the object is in contact with the robotic hand before receiving it, then to confirm that the object is grasped successfully, and, finally, that it can be safely given to a human for a release stage.

2.3   Experimental Studies

Experimental studies were conducted, recording tactile data from the wrist for analysis and design of a handover detection algorithm. The case study presented in this work and the associated project is a kindergarten scenario, where the robot interacts with children and helps them sort and clean up toys. Such a complex scenario contains a variety of objects of different shapes, sizes and textures. The set of objects used for the handover is shown in Fig. 6. Six objects, different in weight, dimension and stiffness, were selected from toy objects typically found in nurseries.

During this stage of experiments, the decision to grasp or release an object was made based on human visual observation. In all experiments for the

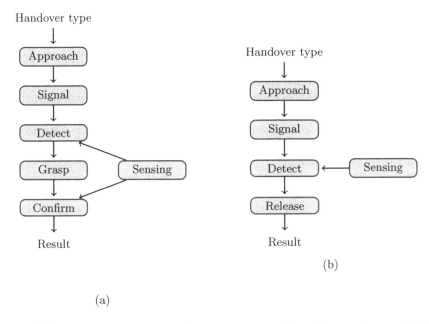

(a)

(b)

Fig. 5. (a) The handover sequence for reception an object from a human; (b) the handover sequence for releasing an object to a human.

algorithm design, the hand pose of the robot was fixed, while during validation studies (Sect. 4) new handover types (with different hand poses) were tested.

3   Modeling of Tactile Information

3.1   Object Reception

Algorithm. Giving an object to the robot is the first stage of the handover. The orientation of the robotic hand before receiving an object is not predefined, as it depends on the previous task and can be different for each trial. However, the wrist remains at the same position during handover. Three-dimensional forces

Fig. 6. Set of objects used in the experiments, containing six objects of various properties.

acting on the sensor by the mounted robotic hand alone change according to its orientation. To compensate for the effect of the orientation of the end effector, the magnitude F of the force vector is considered in this analysis.

The forces encountered while pushing the object into the robotic hand depend on the weight of the specific object and the strength of the subject. When the object is pushed into the robotic hand by a person, dynamic changes in the force magnitude appear. In order to understand those changes, the time derivative or rate of change of force is analyzed. Assuming constant mass, the derivative of force is the derivative of acceleration, or jerk. This value indicates how slowly or how fast the force is changing.

The final step of the algorithm is to assign a threshold or a classification algorithm that triggers a handover action. In order to detect those changes, an empirical approach was used. A threshold is derived from the experimental data set using the standard deviation of the derivative of force. It is described in the next section and is tested during validation studies as described in Sect. 4.

Analysis of Experimental Data Set. This section presents the analysis of tactile data recorded during the experimental studies. The target subjects of the scenario are children of pre-school age. Therefore, the push of a child cannot be compared with the same action performed by an adult. For instance, our data show that the standard deviation of the force encountered for different subjects and trials varies from 0.24 N to 3.14 N. As a handover is characterized by a change of force, the effect of mean magnitude should be removed. The resulting, non-dimensional representation of standard deviation is the coefficient of variation, or relative standard deviation, that shows the variability of trials irrespective of the mean magnitude. It is expressed as the ratio of standard deviation over the mean. The mean value of relative standard deviation for force magnitude is just 0.03, while the same value for the derivative of force (jerk) is 17.6. This means that the use of jerk can provide a better estimate of the time instant when the contact occurs.

Figure 7 displays the derivative of force for four randomly-selected trials. It can be seen that the force exhibits sudden changes that might correspond to the instant when the object is pushed into the robotic hand.

The next step of the empirical approach is to establish a threshold to detect those changes. The grasp threshold is derived from the standard deviation across all trials. If the jerk of the force is beyond the threshold then initiating a grasp would lead to a safe grip. The threshold that identifies the contact with an object can be calculated in several ways. Figure 8 shows the distribution of standard deviation values across the experimental data set. The minimum value is $0.22 \, \text{m/s}^3$ and the maximum value is $1.44 \, \text{m/s}^3$. Thus, the variance of the distribution of standard deviation is $1.22 \, \text{m/s}^3$. Further on, in Sect. 4 ten different thresholds from minimum to maximum vale with a step of 0.12 were evaluated.

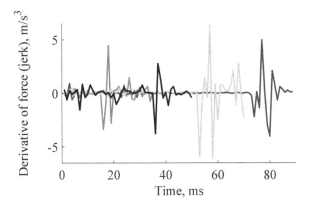

Fig. 7. Derivative of force (jerk) for four randomly-selected trials. Peaks indicate the instant of contact.

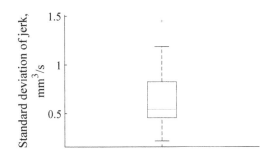

Fig. 8. Distribution of standard deviation for jerk for object reception across the validation data set.

3.2 Object Releasing

Algorithm. Release of the grasped object to the human is the last stage of a handover action. During object release the robot is required to open the hand. A release is triggered when the human securely holds or pulls an object. A release request is identified by observing the force sensor at the wrist only, as it is already done for the reception stage of an object. Based on the analysis of force magnitude, it was found that the release action consists of two different force patterns. Therefore, it requires a different approach compared to the action of object reception.

For this reason, a second ad-hoc algorithm was developed and evaluated. The pseudocode of the algorithm is presented in Algorithm 1. The algorithm requires as input the force magnitude calculated from the forces of the wrist. The force magnitude was detrended by removing the mean. A release action is triggered after N consecutive samples of sign opposite to the reference are detected. In other words, detection of a steady change of the direction of force magnitude is required. The value of N was empirically set to five. In addition, the empirical

```
Input: F: force magnitude
Output: true if and only if release is confirmed
m ← mean(F[0], F[1], ..., F[K]);
refSign ← sign(F[K] − m);
n ← 0;
/* When countStarted is true the algorithm counts the number of
   samples with opposite sign                                      */
countStarted ← false;
for i = 1; n < N; i++ do
    detectSign ← sign(F[K + i] − m);
    if detectSign != refSign then
        countStarted ← true;
        n++;
    end
    else if countStarted then
        n ← 0;
        // Swap the sign: positive to negative and vice-versa
        refSign ← invert(refSign);
        countStarted ← false;
    end
end
return true /* The loop terminates if N samples in a row with
   opposite sign to the reference are detected                     */
```

Algorithm 1. Detection algorithm for releasing an object. The mean is calculated from an arbitrary number K of samples.

algorithm based on standard deviation of force derivative as used for object reception was tested.

Analysis of Experimental Data. The release-request motion patterns can be divided in two main categories as shown in Fig. 9. The first strategy, shown as a red dotted line, corresponds to sharp, sudden peaks, and is more similar to the strategy that is observed for object reception. The second strategy, shown as a blue solid line, represents the scenario when the object is grasped and then pulled with a steady force. The change of force magnitude corresponds to a ramp in the recorded data.

Similarly to the stage of object reception, the empirical approach uses the distribution of standard deviation of jerk that is shown in Fig. 10. The minimum value of jerk distribution is $0.26 \, \mathrm{m/s^3}$, and the maximum is $1.20 \, \mathrm{m/s^3}$. Therefore, the evaluation of optimal threshold for the empirical approach was performed from the minimum to the maximum value with a step of $0.09 \, \mathrm{m/s^3}$.

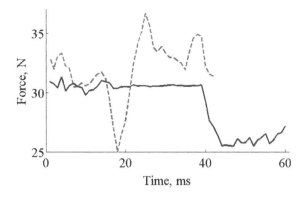

Fig. 9. Two types of strategies detected during the handover action of object release. Trials are randomly selected from two types of patterns.

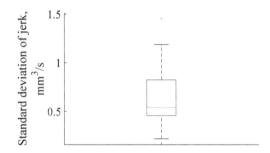

Fig. 10. Distribution of standard deviation for jerk for object releasing across experimental data set.

4 Validation Studies

This section describes the validation studies that were carried out in order to test and to determine the best performance of the proposed handover detection methods. Five new subjects and a set of different objects was used in this section. The objects are shown in Fig. 11, and each subject arbitrarily selected six objects. The subject was standing in the reachability space of the object.

To assess and compare the performance of the proposed algorithms, experimental studies were carried out on the real robot. The grasping and releasing scenarios were tested separately, and for both actions the proposed approaches were tested and compared. The success rate of the each approach was evaluated. In other words, it was studied how often a certain algorithm is able to detect a grasp or a release request correctly, as well as to estimate the number of false positives.

Fig. 11. Objects used for validation studies.

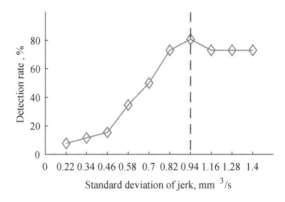

Fig. 12. Detection rate in percentages for different thresholds derived from the distribution of jerk for object reception.

4.1 Validation of Object Reception

The validation of the empirical approach for object reception is performed. The optimal threshold is calculated based on the performance of the evaluation data set to discriminate the moment of contact for approaching. Figure 12 shows the performance of the empirical algorithm for different thresholds. It can be observed that the performance of the algorithm is improving until it reaches a peak $(0.94\,mm^3/s)$ and after reaching it, stays at the same level. Therefore, the thresholds that corresponds to the highest detection rate is chosen for this algorithm.

4.2 Validation of Object Releasing

Two approaches were tested for the validation of the object releasing action of handover. The empirical method used for the grasping algorithm shows poor performance with the maximum detection rate of 46%. The performance for the empirical method is shown in Fig. 13. The ad-hoc algorithm developed for

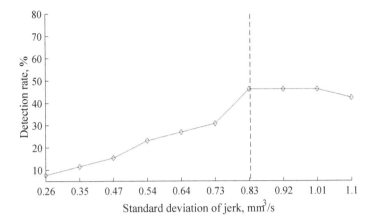

Fig. 13. Detection rate in percentages for different thresholds derived from the distribution of jerk for object releasing.

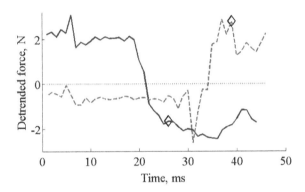

Fig. 14. The performance of the ad-hoc algorithm for both strategies, shown in different lines, of release the action; markers indicate the moment of the hand release.

release detection, instead, had a good performance with 89% correct classification. Figure 14 shows the example cases of classification for the ad-hoc algorithm. The black dot indicates the time instant of successful release detection. It can be seen that the algorithm performs well for both release strategies. The ad-hoc algorithm is also simple to implement and fast to execute.

5 Conclusions

In this paper we present an approach of handover detection using only the information from the wrist force/torque sensor. The algorithms for object reception and release were developed based on experimentally collected data, and were validated via a separate set of experimental studies. The proposed algorithm was developed for a wide range of toy objects that is typical of objects commonly found in household environments.

In future work, it is planned to develop a learning algorithm for the ad-hoc approach. Additionally, a recurrent neural network can be tested to take into account the influence of the previous force readings when deciding whether to take an action or stay idle.

Acknowledgment. The research leading to these results has received funding from the European Community's Seventh Framework Programme under grant agreement no. 610532, SQUIRREL, and from the European Unions Horizon 2020 research and innovation programme under grant agreement no. 287728, FourByThree.

References

1. Katz, D., Pyuro, Y., Brock, O.: Learning to manipulate articulated objects in unstructured environments using a grounded relational representation. In: Proceedings of Robotics: Science and Systems IV, Zurich, Switzerland, pp. 254–261, June 2008
2. Cotugno, G., Mohan, V., Althoefer, K., Nanayakkara, T.: Simplifying grasping complexity through generalization of kinaesthetically learned synergies. In 2014 IEEE International Conference on Robotics and Automation (ICRA), pp. 5345–5351, May 2014
3. Maurtua, I., Pedrocchi, N., Orlandini, A., de Gea Fernández, J., Vogel, C., Geenen, A., Althoefer, K., Shafti, A.: Fourbythree: imagine humans and robots working hand in hand. In: 2016 IEEE 21st International Conference on Emerging Technologies and Factory Automation (ETFA), pp. 1–8, September 2016
4. Edsinger, A., Kemp, C.C.: Human-robot interaction for cooperative manipulation: handing objects to one another. In: The 16th IEEE International Symposium on Robot and Human interactive Communication, RO-MAN 2007, pp. 1167–1172. IEEE (2007)
5. Huang, C.-M., Cakmak, M., Mutlu, B.: Adaptive coordination strategies for human-robot handovers. In: Robotics Science and Systems (2015)
6. Kupcsik, A., Hsu, D., Lee, W.S.: Learning dynamic robot-to-human object handover from human feedback. arXiv preprint arXiv:1603.06390 (2016)
7. Nagata, K., Oosaki, Y., Kakikura, M., Tsukune, H.: Delivery by hand between human and robot based on fingertip force-torque information. In Proceedings of 1998 IEEE/RSJ International Conference on Intelligent Robots and Systems, Innovations in Theory, Practice and Applications (Cat. No.98CH36190), vol. 2, pp. 750–757, October 1998
8. Mellmann, H., Cotugno, G.: Dynamic motion control: Adaptive bimanual grasping for a humanoid robot. Fundamenta Informaticae **112**(1), 89–101 (2011)
9. Sadigh, M.J., Ahmadi, H.: Robust control algorithm for safe grasping based on force sensing. In: 2008 IEEE International Conference on Robotics and Biomimetics, pp. 1279–1284, February 2009
10. Felip, J., Morales, A., Asfour, T.: Multi-sensor and prediction fusion for contact detection and localization. In: 2014 14th IEEE-RAS International Conference on Humanoid Robots (Humanoids), pp. 601–607. IEEE (2014)

11. Manuel, G.C., Grioli, G., Serio, A., Farnioli, E., Piazza, C., Bicchi, A.: Adaptive synergies for a humanoid robot hand. In: 12th IEEE-RAS International Conference on Humanoid Robots (Humanoids 2012), Osaka, Japan, November 29–December 1, 2012, pp. 7–14 (2012)
12. Dai, J.S., Wang, D., Cui, L.: Orientation and workspace analysis of the multifingered metamorphic hand-metahand. IEEE Trans. Rob. **25**(4), 942–947 (2009)
13. Strabala, K., Lee, M.K., Dragan, A., Forlizzi, J., Srinivasa, S., Cakmak, M., Micelli, V.: Towards seamless human-robot handovers. J. Human-Robot Interact. (2013)

A Flexible Component-Based Robot Control Architecture for Hormonal Modulation of Behaviour and Affect

Luke Hickton[(✉)], Matthew Lewis, and Lola Cañamero

Embodied Emotion, Cognition and (Inter-) Action Lab, School of Computer Science, University of Hertfordshire, College Lane, Hatfield, Herts AL10 9AB, UK
{L.Hickton2,M.Lewis4,L.Canamero}@herts.ac.uk

Abstract. In this paper we present the foundations of an architecture that will support the wider context of our work, which is to explore the link between affect, perception and behaviour from an embodied perspective and assess their relevance to Human Robot Interaction (HRI). Our approach builds upon existing affect-based architectures by combining artificial hormones with discrete abstract components that are designed with the explicit consideration of influencing, and being receptive to, the wider affective state of the robot.

1 Introduction

The ability of embodied agents to integrate within a human-centric environment may depend upon their capacity to respond to affective and behavioural cues: attainment of their goals, and possibly even their survival, could be contingent on their capacity to interpret and convey emotion.

Affect-based systems can provide a practicable mechanism of managing internal resources and conflicting goals. They can also facilitate the expression of needs so as to elicit appropriate emotional responses and empathy from human observers, which is important in the context of Human Robot Interaction (HRI).

Research on affect has traditionally been focussed on one of two directions: works that explore emotional traits aimed at facilitating interaction with humans, versus those that focus on the adaptive mechanisms that are advantageous for survival. Some authors (e.g. [1–3]) suggest that the former approach tends to model 'shallow' or 'superficial' aspects of emotions unless combined with the latter. This view is consistent with the perspective that emotions should be grounded in the agent's architecture and internal value system, rather than modelled from the point of view of an observer [1,4]: a key tenet of the Animat approach [5].

Damasio suggests that emotion is a vestigial mechanism for maintaining homeostasis [6], hence modelling homeostatic variables and hormone production can provide a compelling approach to the grounding problem [7]. Brooks' summary of Kravitz's work on hormonal responses in lobsters [8], defines eight distinct principles in his computation model of hormones [9]. This paper focuses

© Springer International Publishing AG 2017
Y. Gao et al. (Eds.): TAROS 2017, LNAI 10454, pp. 464–474, 2017.
DOI: 10.1007/978-3-319-64107-2_36

on the fourth of these: effects of hormones on 'sensory elements...higher processing centers, and motor or hormonal output systems'.

Brooks' implementation [9] of Kravitz's work controlled sensory elements, higher processing centers, and motor output systems via behaviours, which are in turn influenced by hormones. Subsequent works [2,10,11] have tended to take a similar position, focusing on gross level systems like the Action Selection Mechanism (ASM) to determine behaviour, rather than allowing it to occur as a consequence of modulating finer-grained elements of sensory, cognitive or motor function. This is analogous to mechanisms like pupil dilation in mammals, occurring as part of the 'fight or flight' stress response triggered by the sympathetic branch of the nervous system. Pupil dilation has the benefit of facilitating predator detection, which is a prerequisite of any behaviour intended to increase the likelihood of evading capture. Hence hormone induces behaviour as result of altering the sensory experience, rather than by changing the response to it.

This distinction can be illustrated in terms of behaviour-based robotics by a scenario using stress hormones to modulate response to a predator. On the one hand, an approach that modulates perception at the gross level, such as the one adopted in [12], uses hormonal modulation of exteroception (i.e. perception of external stimuli) to intensify the predator's perceived proximity, and increase the likelihood that the ASM will select a behaviour consistent with predator evasion. A similar method uses hormonal modulation of interoception (i.e. hormonal modulation of internal stimuli) to amplify the internal perception of tissue damage, causing the ASM to select a behaviour tailored to the detection of potential threats in order to prevent further injury. In both cases, the behaviour of the robot changes, whilst the behaviour of the sensor remains the same.

This contrasts with models that create direct associations between hormone levels and the functional properties of individual sensory elements, such as their range or update frequency [13]. Following this other approach, the presence of stress in the above example could increase the energy employed by the sensors for the purposes of threat detection. Whilst this could be a useful adaptive mechanism in isolation, it becomes more powerful when several sensors are combined with 'higher processing centres' [8] to form simple sensory systems, as we seek to demonstrate later in this paper. These sensory systems can provide more properties that can be modulated by affect, and provide a degree of autonomy that more closely resembles the reflexive mechanisms found in biological systems, such as saccadic responses in the mammalian vision system. Furthermore, by modelling these characteristics, and grounding their operation more firmly in the affective context of the robot, we postulate that the resulting behaviour driven by these systems will appear more natural and expressive to human observers.

Whilst this discussion has focussed predominantly on sensory systems, other functional units that could benefit from being grounded to the robot's affective state include motor output systems [8]. Kinesic properties such as posture, quality of movement and motion dynamics are all good communicators of affect in mammals [14]. Anger, for example, is usually expressed by large, jerky movements coupled with an erect stance whilst sadness is often characterised by collapsed posture coupled with small slow movements [15]. This kinesic colouring can determine how a core behaviour is interpreted by an observer: avoidance behaviour combined with 'angry' kinesics could give the appearance of a creature that is seeking to avoid confrontation, but which is ultimately prepared to fight. Conversely avoidance combined with 'sadness' might convey resignation or exhaustion.

We have described the benefits of separating the coarse-grained elements that remain the domain of the primary ASM, the 'what', from the finer-grained nuances which are critical to the 'how'. The former relates to the satisfaction of motivations via appropriate action, whilst the later pertains to regulation of internal systems to maximise their relevance to the robot's present context. In this paper we propose how sensory systems, motor output and other 'higher processing centers' [8] could be modelled via a decentralised architecture consisting of loosely coupled components that use hormones to coordinate discrete aspects of their operation. In doing so we hope to describe the benefits from both an adaptive viability and an HRI perspective.

After briefly outlining our architecture, we will consider the key properties of hormones and how they can be represented using components and sockets. An example component, the Perceptual Memory Map, will be introduced followed by an illustration of how elements of its operation can be coordinated via sockets. We will then suggest how these elements could be integrated within a wider Motivational Action Control Architecture before concluding with a summary of the key benefits of this approach and an outline of future work.

2   Architecture

This section presents a robot architecture that has been designed to model some of the key properties of hormone interaction upon the wider system. Hormones have the ability to target multiple areas of the nervous system in different ways and for different durations. In addition to the level of hormone present, salient factors include the site's sensitivity to the hormone, presence of inhibitors and duration of exposure [12,16,17]. We have attempted to reproduce these features by combining functional units, representing areas of the nervous system, with interfaces that enable their properties to be connected to a hormone source via a weighted link. We have labelled the former constructs 'components' and the latter 'sockets'.

2.1   Components

Our first component is the Perceptual Memory Map (PMM), which provides a residual memory of captured sensory data, coupled with a confidence estimate of how reliable that data is, as explained in detail below. It is designed to model cognitive phenomena such as attention and surprise, and models the area in the immediate surroundings of the robot by dividing it into a variable number of segments. When a new sensor value is obtained, the segment closest to

its azimuth is updated, as shown by Fig. 1a below. Following movement of the
agent, the recorded sensor values and their corresponding angles are mapped
into two-dimensional space and transformed relative to the robot's new position, shown by Fig. 1b and c respectively. If two samples share the same angle,
the smallest is retained. A potential fields mechanism is used to calculate a
desired movement vector, which is then interpreted by the movement controller,
as illustrated by Fig. 1d. The model can also output a vector indicating the most
advantageous movement in terms of sensory data acquisition, which the action
selection mechanism can integrate with the movement vector, depending on the
holonomic constraints of the robot.

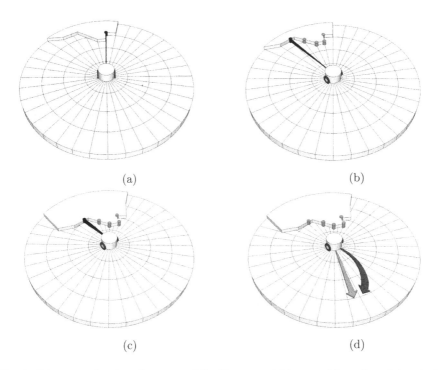

(a)

(b)

(c)

(d)

Fig. 1. Diagrams showing the state of the Perceptual Memory Map after: (a) a single
proximity sensor captures distance in real-time, (b) the robot rotates on the spot by
$30°$, (c) the robot has moved forward 10 mm and (d) the resultant movement vector is
calculated.

The transformation of sensory data is contingent on the orientation and position of the robot, which we obtain via differential drive forward kinematic equations, using live motor speeds sampled at 100 ms intervals. This open-loop approach fails to take account of acceleration or deceleration occurring between the
sample periods or external physical factors, such as loss of traction, but these
cumulative errors are of little concern since the captured sensor values decay over
time. This decay represents loss of confidence due to environmental changes that

could have occurred without the agent's knowledge, which O'Regan labels insubordinateness [18], and also limits to the robot's ability to accurately track its location over extended time periods. When a value is first captured by a sensor the recorded confidence is 100%, which decreases as the sensor is moved away. If the confidence level decays to zero, the value is removed. Similarly, it is also removed if the robot is more than a given distance from the mapped value. Later experiments will seek to control the decay, range and resolution of the model via hormonal control.

Our model was inspired by the findings of studies on spatial mapping in rats and path integration in cockroaches and other insects. Rats were found to have specialised cells in the parahippocampal cortex: head direction cells that fire when the animal faces a specific direction, grid cells that map distances and border cells which represent proximity to boundaries [19]. Path integration research on insects revealed how proprioceptive sensation is used to measure distance travelled and orientation relative to their environment [20,21] which is consistent with the approach we have taken. The PMM is flexible enough to be useful in a number of contexts. We have applied it to the whole agent, but it could equally be utilised at a more localised level, for example simulating saccadic movement in an ocular sensory system.

2.2   Sockets

Sockets are software constructs that enable weighted connections to be made between hormones and the discrete properties components make available for hormones modulation. There are two types of socket: input and output sockets. Input sockets enable many hormones to modulate a single property, whereas output sockets enable a single property to affect a number of hormones. Figure 2 illustrates the structure of the input socket. In common with a Perceptron [22] the input socket incorporates an activation function and an output function. An additional 'temporal filter' inhibits the output if it has been active for too long. Unlike a Perceptron, our activation function calculates the average of the weighted inputs, rather than the sum. The inputs are constrained to values between 0 and 100, hence the output from the activation function will also be within this range. Since we are currently using a linear output function, the value passed to the component's property will be the same as the socket's activation. The temporal function will be explored in future experiments, but is currently unused. Output sockets allow components to influence hormone levels within the system via a weighted link from the property to the hormone. The inbound connection to the hormone itself is made using an input socket.

Figure 3 provides an example which illustrates how a single hormone can simultaneously modulate both perception and motor function via socketed components. The two components considered are a PMM and a Motor Controller. The PMM has input sockets to set decay rate, resolution of the map, sensitivity to movement and update frequency. These are connected to weights 7, 8, 9 and 10 respectively. The Motor Controller's input sockets, connected to weights

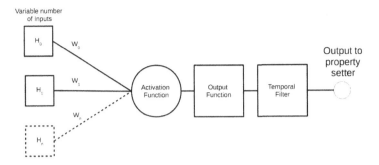

Fig. 2. Diagram showing the structure of an input socket, connected to a variable number of hormone sources by weighted links.

11 and 12, enable minimum and maximum speeds to be changed. Therefore specifying positive values for weights 7 to 11 would result in greater alertness coupled with faster movement speeds, simulating some of the aspects of hormones such as Epinephrine, which trigger physiological arousal. The PMM also has an output socket that connects the presence of movement to the hormone level via weight 6.

Providing positive values for this weight would increase the levels of hormone whenever movement was detected, simulating the roles of the endocrine system and hypothalamus in mammals. This example shows the grounded physiological consequences of affect in precipitating the allocation of internal resources in response to environmental challenges, and behaviour that an external observer can interpret as an emotional response, in this case anxiety. It also shows how the architecture facilitates the coordinated change of individual subsystems, which collectively result in a behavioural response relevant to the agent's affective state.

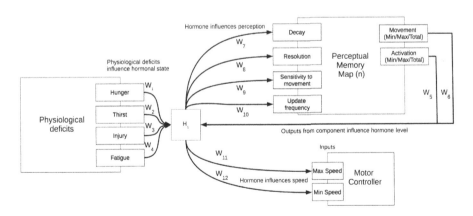

Fig. 3. Diagram showing a socketed architecture in which a single hormone modulates aspects of perception and motor control.

2.3   Integrating the Perceptual Memory Map as Part of a Motivational Action Selection Control Architecture

Figure 4 illustrates how the perceptual map component has been integrated into a motivational control system, based on our group's longstanding approach [12, 23, 24]. Our architecture has been designed to enable the agent to interact in the environment shown in Fig. 5.

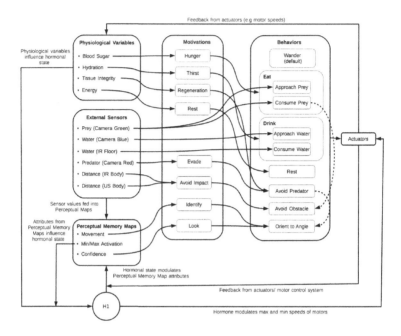

Fig. 4. Diagram showing the Perceptual Memory Map integrated in an Extended Motivational Action Control System.

Besides the robot, initially a Khepera 3, environmental features include large blocks and smaller pillar-like objects, designed to require careful detection for the robot to avoid them successfully. Predator and prey are represented by red and green robots which slowly move around the arena, attracted to and repelled by the agent respectively. A blue circle of 10 cm in diameter is affixed to the floor of the arena to represent a static source of hydration. Maintenance of homeostasis is dependent upon four physiological variables: blood sugar, hydration, tissue integrity and energy. Blood sugar is replenished by collision with a mobile prey robot; hydration is restored by moving over a blue circle in the arena; energy is depleted by movement and replenished by inactivity and tissue damage occurs as a result of collisions with static obstacles or mobile predators. Deficits in the homeostatic variables drive motivations to rectify the imbalance, which in turn weight the ASM towards appropriate behaviours. Behaviours will not be selected without appropriate motivations, but additional sensory stimuli may

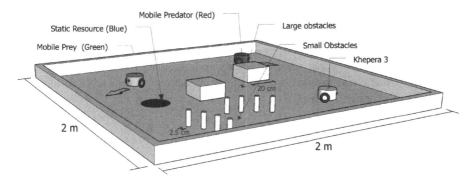

Fig. 5. Diagram showing the environment the agent was designed to occupy. (Color figure online)

also be required. For example, water will not be consumed unless there is a motivation to drink coupled with the presence of water, which is indicated by stimulation of the floor facing IR sensor. Actions that are dependent on both motivations and sensory cues are represented by shaded boxes on the diagram.

Predators, prey and water are detected via a front-facing camera which captures levels of red, green and blue in a 60° field of view. Obstacles are sensed via a ring of infra-red (IR) and ultrasound emitters and objects less than 20 mm away from the robot will generally cause damage unless the prey sensor is highly stimulated. In this case, damage is suppressed for forward-facing sensors and blood sugar is replenished instead. Water is consumed via stimulation of a floor facing IR sensor. The proximity sensors are also associated with the PMM, which are able to pass vectors and other contextual information into the ASM. Output properties of the PMM include movement detection, activation and confidence. Movement will trigger a motivation to identify the source with the main camera, whilst low confidence in the validity of its internal representation will trigger a motivation to look around. The total activation of the PMM is used to influence hormone levels within the system, in this case simulating fear of being trapped, and hormone level is also increased by physiological deficits.

The input sockets are not shown on the diagram for the sake of clarity, since they have been discussed in previous sections, but elevated levels of hormone increase motor speed, heighten sensitivity to movement and reduce overall confidence, creating behaviour that might equate to anxiety. Note that the implementation details of the ASM are not considered to be important, since the architecture is compatible with most action selection approaches, including winner-takes-all and voting-based methods. However, our implementation uses a winner-takes-all approach, and the inbound connections to each behaviour are assumed to be directly proportional to the probability of it being selected as the dominant activity.

Coupling the PMM tightly with the hormone facilitates the positioning of sensors with the aim of maximising their acuity and relevance to the agent's affective context, allowing it to actively drive behaviour that meets the current requirements of the sensory system. The ASM helps coordinate this behaviour with competing demands from other sensory systems. We believe this mechanism is scalable, and can support many other components that will collectively produce more behavioural properties that human observers will be able to identify with those of other creatures.

3 Discussion

This paper has described an architecture intended to facilitate subtle forms of expression and adaptive behaviour. It has also suggested how the properties of sensory perception, higher reasoning and motor control can be represented by loosely coupled components coordinated via hormones. We believe this granular approach provides the following benefits: a grounded link between affect and behaviour, an approach that can be implemented using a variety of paradigms, and an architecture that can be applied to different morphologies of robot with only minor adjustment.

In terms of grounding, we have endeavoured to ensure our model of affect directly influences aspects of perception, cognitive function and motor activity. This granular, component-driven focus reflects the findings of neuroscience research suggesting that different sensory aspects, such as colour and edge detection, are spatially separated in the brain, even within the same sensory systems [25]. Regarding flexibility of implementation, we represent components via programatic constructs but other paradigms, such as Artificial Neural Networks, could have been adopted instead [26,27]. A benefit of our design is that different approaches can also be used interchangeably within the same architecture, which enables broad components to be used as temporary proxies until they can be decomposed into smaller units of functionality. Finally, we contend that our architecture promotes flexibility, since it facilitates encapsulation of elements that are specific to the morphology of the platform, such as sensor input and motor output. If, for example, the architecture is migrated to a platform that has additional motor capabilities, these additional properties can easily be associated with the affect mechanism and coordinated via this secondary control system without making any fundamental changes to the behaviours or ASM.

We believe this model could help simple situated robots to respond to the affective and behavioural cues of humans and other actors and facilitate communication of their needs in a way that mirrors the familiar forms of non-verbal communication which are typical of many mammals. However, we are still in the preliminary stages of empirical testing and are currently carrying out experiments to assess the adaptive value of the PMM in different environments and with different sensory configurations.

Acknowledgements. Luke Hickton is supported by a PhD studentship of the University of Hertfordshire.

References

1. Cañamero, L.: Building emotional artifacts in social worlds: challenges and perspectives. In: Proceedings of 2001 AAAI Fall Symposium in Emotional and Intelligent II: The Tangled Knot of Social Cognition, pp. 22–30 (2001)
2. Cañamero, L.: Emotion understanding from the perspective of autonomous robots research. Neural Netw. 18(4), 445–455 (2005)
3. Herrera Perez, C., Sanchez Escribano, G., Sanz, R.: The morphofunctional approach to emotion modelling in robotics. Adapt. Behav. 20(5), 388–404 (2012)
4. Pfeifer, R.: Building "Fungus Eaters": design principles of autonomous agents. In: Proceedings of the Fourth International Conference on Simulation of Adaptive Behavior SAB 1996 (From Animals to Animats), pp. 3–12 (1996)
5. Wilson, S.: The Animat path to AI. In: From Animals to Animats: Proceedings of the First International Conference on the Simulation of Adaptive Behaviour, vol. 1, pp. 15–21. MIT Press, Cambridge (1991)
6. Damasio, A.R.: The Feeling of What Happens: Body and Emotion in the Making of Consciousness (1999)
7. Harnad, S.: The symbol grounding problem. Physica D 42, 335–346 (1990)
8. Kravitz, E.A.: Hormonal control of behavior: amines as gain-setting elements that bias behavioral output in lobsters. Integr. Comp. Biol. 30(3), 595–608 (1990)
9. Brooks, R.A.: Integrated systems based on behaviors. ACM SIGART Bull. 2(4), 46–50 (1991)
10. Krichmar, J.L.: A neurorobotic platform to test the influence of neuromodulatory signaling on anxious and curious behavior. Front. Neurorobot. 7, 1–17 (2013)
11. Lowe, R., Kiryazov, K.: Utilizing emotions in autonomous robots: an enactive approach. In: Bosse, T., Broekens, J., Dias, J., Zwaan, J. (eds.) Emotion Modeling. LNCS, vol. 8750, pp. 76–98. Springer, Cham (2014). doi:10.1007/978-3-319-12973-0_5
12. Cañamero, L., Avila-García, O.: A bottom-up investigation of emotional modulation in competitive scenarios. In: Paiva, A.C.R., Prada, R., Picard, R.W. (eds.) ACII 2007. LNCS, vol. 4738, pp. 398–409. Springer, Heidelberg (2007). doi:10.1007/978-3-540-74889-2_35
13. Lones, J., Lewis, M., Cañamero, L.: From sensorimotor experiences to cognitive development: investigating the influence of experiential diversity on the development of an epigenetic robot. Front. Robot. AI 3 (2016)
14. Lhommet, M., Marsella, S.: Expressing emotion through posture and gesture. In: The Oxford Handbook of Affective Computing (Gratiolet 1865), pp. 273–285 (2015)
15. Beck, A., Canamero, L., Bard, K.A.: Towards an affect space for robots to display emotional body language. In: 19th IEEE International Symposium on Robot and Human Interactive Communication Principe, pp. 464–469 (2010)
16. Gadanho, S.C., Hallam, J.: Robot learning driven by emotions. Adapt. Behav. 9(1), 42–64 (2001)
17. Levitan, I.B., Kaczmaret, L.K.: The Neuron: Cell and Molecular Biology, 3rd edn. Oxford University Press, Oxford (2002)
18. O'Regan, J.K., Noe, A.: What it is like to see: a sensorimotor theory of perceptual experience. Synthese 129(1), 79–103 (2001)
19. Derdikman, D., Moser, E.I.: A manifold of spatial maps in the brain. Space Time Number Brain 14(12), 41–57 (2011)
20. Durier, V., Rivault, C.: Path integration in cockroach larvae, Blattella germanica (L.)(insect: Dictyoptera): direction and distance estimation. Learn. Behav. 27(1), 108–118 (1999)

21. Dyer, F.C., Dickinson, J.A.: Sun-compass learning in insects: representation in a simple mind. Curr. Dir. Psychol. Sci. **5**(3), 67–72 (1996)
22. Rosenblatt, F.: The perceptron: a probabilistic model for information storage and organization in the brain. Psychol. Rev. **65**(6), 386–408 (1958)
23. Cañamero, L.: Modelling motivation and emotions as a basis for intelligent behavior. In: First International Conference on Autonomous Agents (AGENTS 1997), pp. 148–155. ACM, New York (1997)
24. Lewis, M., Canamero, L.: Hedonic quality or reward? A study of basic pleasure in homeostasis and decision making of a motivated autonomous robot. Adapt. Behav. **24**(5), 267–291 (2016)
25. Fellous, J.: The neuromodulatory basis of emotion. Neuroscientist **5**(3), 283–294 (1999)
26. French, R.L.B., Cañamero, L.: Introducing neuromodulation to a braitenberg vehicle. In: 2005 Proceedings of IEEE International Conference on Robotics and Automation, pp. 4188–4193, April 2005
27. Husbands, P.: Evolving robot behaviours with diffusing gas networks. In: Husbands, P., Meyer, J.-A. (eds.) EvoRobots 1998. LNCS, vol. 1468, pp. 71–86. Springer, Heidelberg (1998). doi:10.1007/3-540-64957-3_65

Drivers' Manoeuvre Classification for Safe HRI

Erwin Jose Lopez Pulgarin[1](✉)📷, Guido Herrmann[1]📷, and Ute Leonards[2]📷

[1] Mechanical Engineering, University of Bristol, Bristol, UK
{erwin.lopez,g.herrmann}@bristol.ac.uk
[2] Experimental Psychology, University of Bristol, Bristol, UK
ute.leonards@bristol.ac.uk

Abstract. Ever increasing autonomy of machines and the need to interact with them creates challenges to ensure safe operation. Recent technical and commercial interest in increasing autonomy of vehicles has led to the integration of more sensors and actuators inside the vehicle, making them more like robots. For interaction with semi-autonomous cars, the use of these sensors could help to create new safety mechanisms. This work explores the concept of using motion tracking (i.e. skeletal tracking) data gathered from the driver whilst driving to learn to classify the manoeuvre being performed. A kernel-based classifier is trained with empirically selected features based on data gathered from a Kinect V2 sensor in a controlled environment. This method shows that skeletal tracking data can be used in a driving scenario to classify manoeuvres and sets a background for further work.

Keywords: HRI · Semi-autonomous vehicles · Vehicles · Driver actions · Classification · Machine learning

1 Introduction

Recent trends in automotive driver assist systems point towards cars becoming more robot-like. Advanced sensing and actuating capabilities allow for increased autonomy in the form of advanced driver assistance systems (ADAS) (e.g. Lane Keeping Assistant, Cruise Control, etc.) and permit some basic autonomous navigation, while recent commercial efforts have pushed for fully autonomous operation of passenger vehicles [4].

An increasing trend when having an automated method dealing or interacting with users is to use physiological measurements (i.e. signals measured from a person related to mind and body state) in order to get insight into the user's inner states like stress levels [5], which could prove to be useful in different applications like semi-automatic driving [7]. Among these measurements, movement information or skeletal tracking data has become very popular due to low-cost sensors that enable to track human position and that permit its use in different indoor scenarios [8,17].

Recent advances in ADAS systems [13] and estimation techniques using advanced sensor input from vehicles [2,8,18] show the multiple possibilities of

© Springer International Publishing AG 2017
Y. Gao et al. (Eds.): TAROS 2017, LNAI 10454, pp. 475–483, 2017.
DOI: 10.1007/978-3-319-64107-2_37

implementing vision-based solutions for in-cabin operation to observe a driver's action like hand posture recognition [18], in-car movement [8] and general human pose estimation [2]. However, the use of skeletal tracking data has been fairly limited.

In this paper, a classification method for driver manoeuvres is developed using a data-driven approach with a Support Vector Machine (SVM) classifier, including skeletal tracking and driver input data. First, the main techniques are explained in Sect. 2. Section 3 explains the results and Sect. 4 talks about conclusions and future work.

2   Skeletal and In-Car Sensor Information

Limb position and movement are related to the final output of a decision making process, and provide information about complex, long repetitive movements or motion patterns that could be quickly identified.

Studies [10] have shown that, for a trained and controlled task such as driving, the muscles, i.e. the general movement of the arms, do not differ between test subjects with different driving experiences. This is a strong indication about movement repeatability whilst driving and it is thus possible to use body movement information as a measured quantity.

Sensors that acquire colour (RGB) data from the environment are usually called RGB cameras, and have enabled numerous developments by exploiting the 2D representation of the amount of light reflected in a 3D scene; RGB-D cameras provide information about the distance between sensor and the scene being recorded, which allows for the development of faster, more precise classification and recognition methods like human body detection and tracking [1,6,14,16].

Data acquired from a set of driving experiments is presented. Thus, a controlled simulated environment was selected, providing a trade-off between repeatability and ease in implementation. A driving simulation environment for a UK based car (left lane driving) is implemented, using a gaming-grade user input device (Logitech G27), a semi-professional racing simulator (Live for Speed) and a Kinect V2 sensor (see Fig. 1). The use of the Kinect V2 for body movement

Fig. 1. Experimental setup for data acquisition whilst driving. Driving simulator output (left), recording screen with skeletal tracking (right)

observation creates technical challenges whilst working in a car-like environment [8,17]. In our case, the Kinect V2 faces down, pointing towards the driver to achieve a better view (see Fig. 2), with a 70 cm distance in line of sight from the sensor to the steering wheel. The overall arrangement attempts to recreate a similar arrangement as in a road vehicle (although inner spacing is not ideal, as the shift stick is at the same level as the steering wheel's and the steering wheel vertical position is 10 cm higher than in normal vehicles).

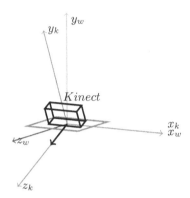

Fig. 2. Kinect Coordinate frame (x_k, y_k, z_k) related to World Coordinate frame (x_w, y_w, z_w) (rotated in x axes)

Data was acquired from six test subjects during two driving experiments using different driving styles (i.e. drive as fast as possible and driving carefully on the track) with 5 turns per side (i.e. left turn, right turn) during 2 min each in a racing track and a data sampling of 30 ms. Two different driving styles were used to roughly take into account the difference in arms movement whilst driving at different speeds. Duration of turns can be from 0.5 to 2 s, getting between 150 and 600 data points per turn. Hence, these data allow to model their behaviour during different manoeuvres.

After testing the geometrical and operational constraint of the sensor and the experimental setup, some empirically selected features based on limb angle position, combined with the driver's input, have been used as defined below:

- **azimuthEL:** Azimuth angle of the spherical projection of the angle between the left elbow and the left shoulder.
- **elevationEL:** Elevation angle of the spherical projection of the angle between the left elbow and the left shoulder.
- **azimuthER:** Azimuth angle of the spherical projection of the angle between the right elbow and the right shoulder.
- **elevationER:** Elevation angle of the spherical projection of the angle between the right elbow and the right shoulder.
- **BackLean:** Difference between torso and back position in z axes.

– **dCenterX:** Difference between left hand position and torso in x axes.
– **Steering Wheel Angle:** Turning angle recorded by the Logitech G27 device.

These features were selected from a set of 95 signals. They were a trade-off between numerical load of the machine learning approach and success rate in feature detection.

2.1   Data-Driven Techniques

Data-driven techniques have proven useful to classify data for vehicle manoeuvres and other related scenarios [9].

In the area of common classifiers used in data-driven techniques (e.g. SVM, neural networks, random trees), kernel-based methods such as Support Vector Machines (SVM) provide a high flexibility of generalizing linear and non-linear processes whilst maintaining small training and execution periods. Hence, SVM is used in this case. SVM theory was initially developed by V. Vapnik in the early 1980s and focused on binary classification problems, using the paradigm of statistical learning theory. The basic idea behind SVM is to find an optimal hyperplane that maximizes the separation margin between classes. Finding this hyperplane is equivalent to solving a constrained optimization problem whose solution is a linear combination of training examples that are located outside the region that lies between what is known as the support vectors [3].

In our specific scenario, a state-transition model (i.e. Markov chain) of the driving process is set up with a transition probability equal for all states. Three states are proposed, with "straight" being the initial state and "left turn" or "right turn" the possible next states, always having to go back to the initial state to transition between turning. The reduced set of states and the equal probability for transitions restriction simplify a possibly more complex state model, avoids coupling between manoeuvres and establishes an intuitive way of performing basic turning movements, that can lead to more complex manoeuvres (see Fig. 3).

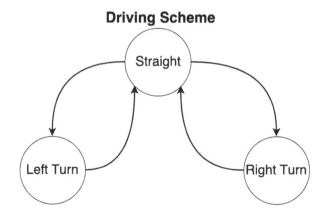

Fig. 3. Driving manoeuvres modelling with basic transitions.

Based on a data-driven approach to model the problem, and using the state transition explained in Fig. 3, a classification scheme using three classes is designed. The scheme estimates the current manoeuvre performed between 3 possible types of manoeuvre (turn left, turn right, straight movement), with a feature vector only using data from one time-step (i.e. data at time t) (see Fig. 4).

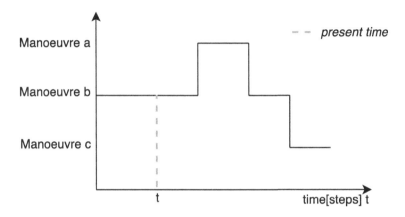

Fig. 4. Driving manoeuvres classification description in time.

Labels corresponding to the state transition model in Fig. 4 (i.e. left turn, right turn and straight) are given manually to segments of the recorded data, based on the position on the track and the steering wheel angle seen on the video recordings of the driver.

Classification results were evaluated with respect to metrics for binary classifiers, namely *Precision*, *Recall* and *F*1 score. These are based on the number of true-positives tp (i.e. predicted true, expected true), true-negatives tn (i.e. predicted false, expected false), false-positives fp (i.e. predicted true, expected false) and false-negatives fn (i.e. predicted false, expected true) (see [15] for a general definition).

$$Precision = \frac{tp}{tp + fp} \qquad Recall = \frac{tp}{tp + fn} \qquad F1 = 2\frac{Precision * Recall}{Precision + Recall}$$

$$(1)$$

Precision represents the repeatability of the prediction or how many predictions are relevant, recall represents how many relevant predictions are done and F1 is the harmonic mean between precision and recall to represent a balanced predictor.

As a general objective, a high precision (no prediction left undone), high recall (high probability of having a good prediction) and a close to 1 F1 Score is desired.

The model was trained and tested from the above explained experimental data with a stratified (i.e. separated by classes) cross-validated set of 25% testing data, 75% training data. This means that the dataset from the test trials is divided into the 3 available classes. Each class has about 60 intervals of data of different temporal lengths. The data from every class is randomly selected and divided into training and testing data.

The dataset is filtered with different combinations of common skeletal tracking and pre-processing filtering techniques [12]: raw data, data filtered by a Double Exponential Smoothing Filter, the same filtered data with normalization by dimensions mapping the min and max values of a given dimension to 0 and 1 (i.e. hard whitening) and the same previous filtered data with normalization by dimensions subtracting the mean of the values and divide by twice the standard deviation (i.e. soft whitening). The data used in this learning process are those 7 signals explained at the end of the previous section. An SVM classifier with a multiclass strategy of one-vs-one is used with standardized input, radial based kernel function and ISDA solver.

3   Results

Performance metrics averaged from the results of all 6 test subjects can be seen in Table 1, with "NoFilter" showing the results with non-filtered training data, "Filter" showing the results with double-exponential filter training data, "FilterHW" showing the results with filtered + hard-whitened training data and "FilterSW" showing the results with filtered + soft-whitened training data. The used feature vector, together with the selected classification algorithm, allow us to discriminate between various manoeuvres whilst generalizing throughout different drivers, successfully classify it.

Mean performance metrics are all above 85% without filtered training data and above 90% with filtered data, including the F1 metric which is above 90%

Table 1. Manoeuvre classification performance metrics

		NoFilter	Filter	FilterHW	FilterSW
Turn left	Precision	0.8617	0.9259	0.9247	0.7111
	Recall	0.9709	0.9841	0.9849	0.9418
	F1	0.9130	0.9541	0.9538	0.8104
Straight	Precision	0.9878	0.9901	0.9946	0.9764
	Recall	0.9266	0.9617	0.9570	0.8711
	F1	0.9562	0.9757	0.9754	0.9208
Turn right	Precision	0.9461	0.9747	0.9677	0.9141
	Recall	0.9663	0.9794	0.9828	0.9314
	F1	0.9561	0.9770	0.9752	0.9227

in all cases; the F1 metric shows a balanced performance between missed classifications and true classifications, as can be seen in Fig. 5, with low numbers of missed classifications throughout the tests whilst remaining sensible to changes.

The proposed method is able to learn to classify the 3 manoeuvres using a relatively small dataset per test subject, exploiting the repeatability of arm movement before and whilst performing a driving manoeuvre, being the main advantage compared to other methods that require big training sets to obtain performance over 85%.

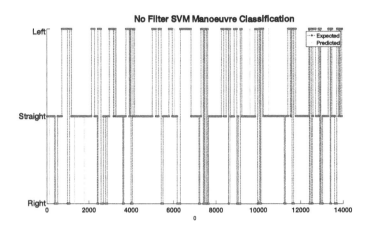

Fig. 5. Manoeuvres classification for all test subjects.

4   Conclusions

Current implementation shows that empirically selected features based on skeletal tracking information and driver input are sufficient to create models that classify the type of manoeuvre being performed by a driver, using both filtered and unfiltered training data. This scheme shows the ability of skeletal-tracking-based features to generalize a movement, being able to classify driving manoeuvres with relatively small datasets, compared to the usual big datasets required for classification tasks.

The generated scheme was general enough to classify new data from the test subjects, but not enough to classify data from people whose driving style is unknown (i.e. model sensitive to training data). More information could prove to be useful into creating richer models but consideration must be taken due to limitation of kernel-based approaches like the one used (e.g. the hyperplane or high dimension description could grow too big or too complex that it's infeasible to separate).

Future work will focus on using more sensors to acquire driver-related information and enrich our understanding of the driver's inner model. We will also look into creating richer driving scenarios that allow to simulate different mental workloads or distraction levels, in order to know how driver behaviour changes during manoeuvres when affected by different levels of distractions.

Data relevant to the research results is openly available at the time of publication [11].

References

1. Bo, L., Ren, X., Fox, D.: Unsupervised feature learning for RGB-D based object recognition. In: Desai, J.P., Dudek, G., Khatib, O., Kumar, V. (eds.) Experimental Robotics. Springer Tracts in Advanced Robotics, vol. 88, pp. 387–402. Springer International Publishing, Switzerland (2013). doi:10.1007/978-3-319-00065-7_27

2. Crabbe, B., Paiement, A., Hannuna, S., Mirmehdi, M.: Skeleton-free body pose estimation from depth images for movement analysis. In: The IEEE International Conference on Computer Vision (ICCV) Workshops, December 2015

3. Duda, R.O., Hart, P.E., et al.: Pattern Classification and Scene Analysis, vol. 3. Wiley, New York (1973)

4. Franke, U., Pfeiffer, D., Rabe, C., Knoeppel, C., Enzweiler, M., Stein, F., Herrtwich, R.: Making bertha see. In: 2013 IEEE International Conference on Computer Vision Workshops (ICCVW), pp. 214–221 (2013)

5. Healey, J.A., Picard, R.W.: Detecting stress during real-world driving tasks using physiological sensors. IEEE Trans. Intell. Transport. Syst. **6**(2), 156–166 (2005)

6. Henry, P., Krainin, M., Herbst, E., Ren, X., Fox, D.: RGB-D mapping: using Kinect-style depth cameras for dense 3D modeling of indoor environments. Int. J. Robot. Res. **31**(5), 647–663 (2012). http://dx.doi.org/10.1177/0278364911434148

7. Koenig, A., Caruso, A., Bolliger, M., Somaini, L., Omlin, X., Morari, M., Riener, R.: Model-based heart rate control during robot-assisted gait training. In: 2011 IEEE International Conference on Robotics and Automation (ICRA), pp. 4151–4156, May 2011

8. Kondyli, A., Sisiopiku, V., Barmpoutis, A.: A 3D experimental framework for exploring drivers' body activity using infrared depth sensors. In: 2013 International Conference on Connected Vehicles and Expo (ICCVE), pp. 574–579, December 2013

9. Kumar, P., Perrollaz, M., Lefvre, S., Laugier, C.: Learning-based approach for online lane change intention prediction. In: 2013 IEEE Intelligent Vehicles Symposium (IV), pp. 797–802, June 2013

10. Liu, Y., Ji, X., Ryouhei, H., Takahiro, M., Lou, L.: Function of shoulder muscles of driver in vehicle steering maneuver. Sci. China Technol. Sci. **55**(12), 3445–3454 (2012). http://link.springer.com/article/10.1007/s11431-012-5045-9

11. Lopez Pulgarin, E.J., Herrmann, G., Leonards, U.: Dataset for drivers' manoeuvre classification for safe HRI, August 2017. https://doi.org/10.5281/zenodo.556961

12. Nocedal, J., Wright, S.J.: Numerical Optimization, 2nd edn. Springer, New York (2006)

13. Perrett, T., Mirmehdi, M., Dias, E.: Cost-based feature transfer for vehicle occupant classification. arXiv:1512.07080, December 2015. http://arxiv.org/abs/1512.07080

14. Ren, X., Bo, L., Fox, D.: RGB-(D) scene labeling: features and algorithms. In: 2012 IEEE Conference on Computer Vision and Pattern Recognition, pp. 2759–2766, June 2012

15. Sokolova, M., Lapalme, G.: A systematic analysis of performance measures for classification tasks. Inf. Proces. Manage. **45**(4), 427–437 (2009). http://www.sciencedirect.com/science/article/pii/S0306457309000259

16. Spinello, L., Arras, K.O.: People detection in RGB-D data. In: 2011 IEEE/RSJ International Conference on Intelligent Robots and Systems, pp. 3838–3843, September 2011

17. Tran, C., Trivedi, M.: Towards a vision-based system exploring 3D driver posture dynamics for driver assistance: issues and possibilities. In: 2010 IEEE Intelligent Vehicles Symposium (IV). pp. 179–184, June 2010

18. Zhao, C., Zhang, B., He, J., Lian, J.: Recognition of driving postures by contourlet transform and random forests. IET Intell. Transp. Syst. **6**(2), 161–168 (2012)

From Vision to Grasping: Adapting Visual Networks

Rebecca Allday[✉], Simon Hadfield, and Richard Bowden

Centre for Vision, Speech and Signal Processing, University of Surrey, Guildford, UK
{R.Allday,S.Hadfield,R.Bowden}@surrey.ac.uk

Abstract. Grasping is one of the oldest problems in robotics and is still considered challenging, especially when grasping unknown objects with unknown 3D shape. We focus on exploiting recent advances in computer vision recognition systems. Object classification problems tend to have much larger datasets to train from and have far fewer practical constraints around the size of the model and speed to train. In this paper we will investigate how to adapt Convolutional Neural Networks (CNNs), traditionally used for image classification, for planar robotic grasping. We consider the differences in the problems and how a network can be adjusted to account for this. Positional information is far more important to robotics than generic image classification tasks, where max pooling layers are used to improve translation invariance. By using a more appropriate network structure we are able to obtain improved accuracy while simultaneously improving run times and reducing memory consumption by reducing model size by up to 69%.

Keywords: Robotic grasping · Machine learning · CNNs · SqueezeNet · AlexNet

1 Introduction

In the field of robotics, grasping is a fundamental yet challenging problem. It is considered even more challenging when attempting to generalise grasps to previously unseen objects using just sensor data rather than heuristics or 3D models. Robotic grasping requires solving several problems in the different stages of grasping. Initially, these could include object segmentation and object recognition, in order to find an object in a possibly cluttered environment and determine what the object is. Then we need a method for grasping the given object. In the simplest case, these grasps may be estimated from a 3D model, which itself is a challenging task. However, depending on the sensor modalities, the challenges are further exacerbated by the need to simultaneously reason about the object's shape and optimal grasping points. Finally there is the problem of motion planning and robust execution of the proposed grasp. In this paper we will be looking at a key aspect of this pipeline, specifically finding a planar grasp configuration in the challenging case where we do not know the shape of the object.

© Springer International Publishing AG 2017
Y. Gao et al. (Eds.): TAROS 2017, LNAI 10454, pp. 484–494, 2017.
DOI: 10.1007/978-3-319-64107-2_38

In recent years deep learning with CNNs has emerged within computer vision and related fields as the dominant approach to simultaneously learn feature representations and classifiers. This means that instead of engineering an explicit 3D representation for objects, we can learn an alternative intermediate representation. Networks such as AlexNet [7], GoogLeNet [14] and SqueezeNet [5] have shown how deep learning can be used to deliver excellent results for image classification on large object datasets such as ImageNet. However, whilst deep networks perform extremely well for tasks such as image classification, and have been successfully applied to robotics applications, we should consider the difference in application when designing and training them.

In order for robotic grasping to be useful we need to be able to make decisions about how to grasp objects quickly, so large deep neural networks which take a long time to process data are not practical. Furthermore, online learning where the robot iterates through stages of exploration and learning phases by definition require the learning phase to be fast. Unlike image classification we cannot farm data from the internet, grasping databases take a long time to collect because example grasps must be individually executed and recorded, whether that be via a simulator or a real robot. Avoiding large data collection phases would also be an advantage in robotics especially since data may need to be collected every time new hardware such as grippers are used. In addition to this, many robotics systems may have space constraints when it comes to storing models, sometimes requiring them to be on an embedded system, so smaller models would be required. The controllers for these systems may also not have the power that a desktop computer would. All of these problems mean we need to adapt CNNs used for general vision tasks to robotics.

In this paper we will look at how to adapt networks designed for visual recognition to the task of robotic grasping. In Sect. 2 we review the related work. Then in Sect. 3 we describe in more detail the problem of robotic grasping we address and how we intend to adapt our visual networks. Section 4 evaluates the proposed changes to the network architecture. Finally, we conclude in Sect. 5 and discuss the possibilities of future work.

2   Related Work

There are many different approaches to tackle robotic grasping, the survey by Bohg et al. [1] splits them into analytic and data-driven methods. Analytic methods tend to use geometric and dynamic criteria to form grasp maps to find force closure grasps. Alternatively data-driven methods rank sampled grasps from the grasp space based on some specified metrics. This is the area we will be focusing on, it can be divided into 3 subsections:

- Known objects: Requires use of object recognition and pose estimation to retrieve a suitable grasp from an experience database. Often these methods have access to geometric models of the objects.

- Familiar objects: Assumes any object encountered is similar to another object and uses a measure of similarity (shape, colour, texture) to find a possible grasp.
- Unknown objects: Does not assume any access to models or grasp experience. Translates features of an object directly to ranking grasp candidates.

Data-driven methods often use existing knowledge of grasps. This can be as a direct way of mapping grasps onto a known or familiar object. Alternatively existing knowledge can be used as training data for a machine learning method to learn general rules for mapping features of objects to grasps. We will be focusing on methods using machine learning in this paper.

Learning for grasping has been attempted with many different types of data including 2D images [13], 3D data [2,4] and multi-modal data combining both of these [8,12]. Both El-Khoury and Sahbani [2] and Pelossof [10] use superquadratics to approximate an object and then train an artificial neural network network (ANN) and Support Vector Machine (SVM) respectively. The drawback for both of these approaches is that they require access to accurate 3D models of the objects. More work has been done recently on learning grasp configurations from RGB images directly. Levine et al. [9] train CNNs to learn a mapping straight from raw images to torques at the robot's motors, however they only use a few hundred examples to train a deep network. Pinto et al. [11] focus on this problem collecting around 40,000 random trial and error grasp attempts to adapt a CNN based on AlexNet. Given an image patch, the output of their CNN predicts the likelihood of a successful planar grasp at the center of the patch in 18 discreet angles ($0°$, $10°$, ... $170°$), making it 18-way binary classification problem. Whilst the amount of data they have collected is an improvement on many previous grasping datasets, it is not a significant amount when compared to the number of parameters in the network which is pre-trained on over 1 million images.

Within the context of deep learning for computer vision, Inandola et al. [5] created SqueezeNet which is designed to have far fewer parameters in comparision to AlexNet whilst maintaining accuracy. Their motivation for this was to increase efficiency in training and decrease the size of deployed models. They achieved this by the use of Fire modules which are comprised of a squeeze convolution layer which feed into an expand convolution layer. Fire modules only have 1×1 and 3×3 filters in their convolution layers keeping the number of parameters to a minimum. This makes it a suitable architecture for embedded systems and problems where there is a reduced volume of training data, however it has as of yet not been applied to the problem of robotic grasping.

3   Approach

We define the problem as predicting a successful planar grasp configuration (x, y, θ), where (x, y) is the center point of the grasp and θ is the angle of the gripper, from an image of an object centred at (x, y). We use CNNs to predict whether a grasp configuration results in a successful grasp for a given image.

The input into our CNN will be an image patch centred on the center point of the grasp. Whilst learning for grasping is often treated as a continuous problem, aiming to find the optimal (x, y, θ), this is difficult because there are many possible successful grasp options for each object and CNNs tend to perform better at classification problems. Therefore similarly to Pinto et al. [11] we make our problem discrete by setting the output of our network to be N likelihoods. Each of which predicts if the object in the center of the patch is graspable at $\theta_n = \frac{(n-1)\pi}{N}$ rad, where $n \in \{1, ..., N\}$. Thus we can think of this as an N-way binary classification problem. A smaller N decreases the number of parameters in the network but leaves us with a much coarser angle selection which could impact the accuracy of the grasp.

We have N outputs to our CNN but for each image patch input, a robotics system can only trial one of the angles corresponding to a single output. This means our input image patch only has a single label, $l_n \in \{0, 1\}$, corresponding to attempted angle θ_n, whereas the network has N binary output layers. In order to integrate training with robot control our loss layers must be able to block different back propagation paths depending on the decision as to which angle the robot has tried. This is done using a softmax layer followed by an adapted multinomial logistic loss layer on each of the N outputs. Each adapted multinomial logistic loss layer only calculates a loss if the label for an image states that the angle corresponding to that output has been attempted.

Given a single $n \in \{1, ..., N\}$ the output from the softmax layer gives the probability of angle θ_n being successful as

$$p_n = \frac{e^{x_1^n}}{\sum\limits_{k \in \{0,1\}} e^{x_k^n}}, \tag{1}$$

where x_k^n are the outputs from the nth binary output layer. The loss for the nth output is then given as

$$L_n = \begin{cases} -l_n log(p_n) - (1 - l_n) log(1 - p_n) & \text{if } \exists\, l_n \\ 0 & \text{otherwise.} \end{cases} \tag{2}$$

Then the gradient of the loss being fed back to the output layer is

$$\frac{\partial L_n}{\partial p_n} = \begin{cases} -\frac{l_n}{p_n} + \frac{1 - l_n}{1 - p_n} & \text{if } \exists\, l_n \\ 0 & \text{otherwise.} \end{cases} \tag{3}$$

We can see that, as required, this blocks back propagation on the layers where a label, l_n, does not exist indicating the angle θ_n has not been attempted.

Based on the differences between robotic grasping and computer vision applications we train adapted visual CNNs, based upon both AlexNet and SqueezeNet architectures. Here we describe the adaptations we propose in further detail.

3.1   Network Adaptation

Translation Invariance. A key difference between the problem of object classification and grasping is that object classification only cares about what an object is, not its position in the image. For robotic grasping, the precise position of an object and its grasp points are important. In visual neural networks, max pooling layers are often used to improve the translation invariance when classifying objects. They are also used to reduce the size of the data going through the network to make it more manageable for training and testing. For robotic grasping it is likely that this damages the specificity of the grasps. Therefore it may be advantageous to avoid spatial accumulation in the later stages of visual networks to reduce the effect of translation invariance while keeping the early pooling layers to keep the network size manageable.

Reduced Feature Complexity. Another issue is that visual networks for classification tend to be used to classify hundreds if not thousands of different objects. Conversely, in this task we have simplified the problem down to N binary classifiers (one for each angle). The problem is far simpler than general classification in that it has fewer outputs. We also tend to have far less data available for grasping problems making it infeasible to train complex networks with many parameters. We can combat this partially by using pre-trained convolution layers on a dataset such as ImageNet, but the weights of these networks will still need to be adapted to the task at hand.

When a network is too complex for the given task information may be spread sparsely through the network, with some parts being unused. Here we give an example of this. When we convolve an input image I_{in} with the i_{th} convolution layer filter $conv_i$ we get $I_{out} = conv_i * I_{in}$. We can also apply a Rectified Linear Unit (ReLU) layer to an image with the function $I_{out} = max(I_{in}, 0)$. When we combine these functions across two convolution layers both followed by ReLU layers we get

$$I_{out} = max(conv_{i+1} * max(conv_i * I_{in}, 0), 0). \tag{4}$$

If the network is too complex for the given task it is possible for the network learn to give $conv_i * I_{in} > 0$ for all elements. In this case the first maximum function becomes redundant giving

$$I_{out} = max(conv_{i+1} * conv_i * I_{in}, 0). \tag{5}$$

Now due to the linear nature of the convolutions, $conv_{i+1} * conv_i$ can be combined into a single convolution $conv_i'$, meaning we can write

$$I_{out} = max(conv_i' * I_{in}, 0). \tag{6}$$

This shows that if the network is too complex then it is possible for two sets of ReLU and convolution combinations can give the same output as a single set.

Our suggestion is to create a simpler network with less convolution layers which may be better constrained by the problem, making it more accurate and more efficient. We do this by removing convolution layers from later in visual networks and randomly initialising the last remaining convolution layer whilst keeping the others pre-trained. This is because the penultimate convolution layer is specialised to feed into the final layer. Random re-initialisation of this penultimate layer ensures it encodes the penultimate and final stages for the task at hand.

4 Results

For our experiments we will be using the data set collected by Pinto et al. [11] for planar grasping. A Baxter robot by Rethink Robotics with a two fingered parallel gripper was used to collect random trial and error grasp attempts on a table of objects. For a single grasp attempt, a random point is selected 25 cm above the region of interest containing an object. This forms the grasp point and a random angle in the range $(0, \pi)$ is chosen as the gripper angle. For each trial, the grippers are instructed to close until the motors are stalled, this force on the motors tells us that the gripper has stopped before full closure so is grasping an object. The grasp configuration for each attempt is recorded along with whether the grasp was a success or a failure depending on the readings from the force sensors in the grippers. This data assumes that we split the angles between $(0, \pi)$ into 18 angle bins so choosing $N = 18$ from Sect. 3. Therefore our labels will consist of which angle was attempted and whether is was a success.

Deep learning requires vast quantities of data, especially if networks have more parameters than are truly necessary. To help artificially increase the amount of data the image patches are rotated by random θ_r and this is added to the angle label. Another problem with trial and error data sets in grasping is that there are overwhelmingly more failure examples than successful examples. This bias can cause problems when training neural networks since they can improve their accuracy by always predicting a failure. To avoid this in our experiments we use balanced numbers of successful and failed grasp attempts when training our networks by sub-sampling the failure cases. The bias can then be added back in later by using a higher threshold on the output probability of a successful grasp.

The networks which will be training are modified versions of CNNs normally used for image classification. The two networks we will use are AlexNet and SqueezeNet. AlexNet has 5 convolution layers with max pooling after convolution layers 1, 2 and 5. AlexNet then has two fully connected layers and a final fully connected layer for classification. For this application the final fully connected layer is removed and replaced with 18 binary fully connected layers, as shown in Fig. 1a. SqueezeNet is made up of Fire modules which consist of a *squeeze* convolution layer and an *expand* convolution. As you can see in Fig. 1b, SqueezeNet is comprised of a standalone convolution layer and then 8 fire modules (fire 2–9), and then another standalone convolution layer. Max pooling layers are included following the first convolution layer, fire4, and fire 8, whilst a global average pooling layer is used to convert the output from the final convolution layer to a suitable output. Unless otherwise stated when using these networks, we initialised the parameters of the convolution layers in AlexNet and the first convolution layer and the Fire modules in SqueezeNet with models pre-trained on ImageNet.

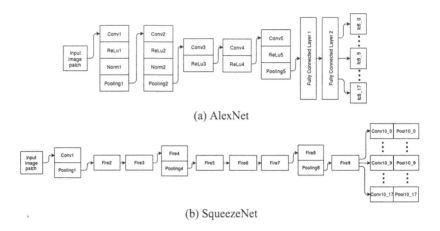

(a) AlexNet

(b) SqueezeNet

Fig. 1. Visual networks to be adapted for robotics

In order to decrease the time taken training CNNs we initially chose to take attempts from one of the 18 angle bins and train our network with a single binary output layer. This allows us to see any effect on learning before evaluating on the full dataset.

4.1   Evalutation of Translation Invariance

Evaluation of Removing Pooling Layers. The first experiment uses AlexNet with a single binary output trained on the data from angle 0 as the base and compares this to removing the final pooling layer in the network, Pooling5. These were both trained with an initial learning rate of 0.0001 for 30 epochs. The results of training two network configurations can be seen in Fig. 2. The original network achieved 75.72% accuracy on the validation set after 30 epochs of training. In comparison the network without the final pooling layer achieved 78.60%. This small change to our network increased our accuracy by 2.88%. As stated earlier, we believe this is because we do not lose position based information which is necessary to accurately determine successful grasp points on an object. We were unable to remove earlier pooling layers from AlexNet as this changes the data size, rendering the pre-trained network unusable.

Conversely, the fully convolutional structure of SqeezeNet allows us to attempt removing more pooling layers earlier in the network. As a base we trained SqueezeNet in the same way we trained the base AlexNet achieving

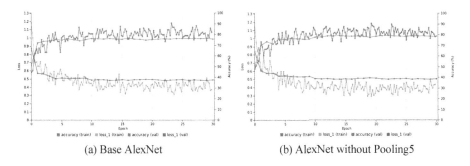

(a) Base AlexNet   (b) AlexNet without Pooling5

Fig. 2. Graphs to show training of AlexNet with and without the final max pooling layer.

75.48% final accuracy on the validation data. We can see in Table 1 that removing the later pooling layers for this network did not improve the accuracy, however removing the first pooling layer, Pooling1, did. However, this was at a large cost of the time taken to train the network since the data being passed through the network was much larger meaning this is not a practical solution especially if we wish to use this system for online training.

Table 1. Comparing the effect of removing max pooling layers from SqueezeNet

Pooling layer removed	Validation accuracy	Time taken for 30 epochs
-	75.48%	5 min 16 s
Pooling8	73.79%	5 min 57 s
Pooling4	71.95%	6 min 47 s
Pooling1	75.96%	42 min 24 s

Evaluation of Reduced Feature Complexity. To test the removal and random initialisation of later convolution layers we again used standard SqueezeNet with a single binary output training on angle 0 and all Fire modules pre-trained on ImageNet. We remove a single Fire module from the end of the network and reinitialise the final remaining Fire module. We repeat this until we have only 6 Fire modules remaining. We chose to use Xavier initialisation for stability in this set of results. We found it was difficult to avoid the exploding gradient problem using Gaussian initialisation when layers were removed. In Table 2 we see that without removing and layers we can improve accuracy by just randomly initialising Fire9, this probably helps the network learn more specifically for the task of grasping rather than object recognition. We can see that removing further layers in this network does not increase the accuracy. However, the file size for a single model does decrease by 69% whilst still having an accuracy of 71.63%. This is extremely beneficial in embedded systems and robotics where the space for large network models is often not available.

Table 2. Comparing the effect of removing Fire modules from SqueezeNet and randomly initialising the final remaining Fire module

Number of fire modules	Randomly initialised module	Validation accuracy	Size of model
9	-	74.03%	2.9 MB
9	Fire9	77.16%	2.9 MB
8	Fire8	73.79%	2.1 MB
7	Fire7	73.07%	1.4 MB
6	Fire6	71.63%	0.9 MB

We took a similar approach to evaluating this solution with AlexNet. First we randomly initialised conv5 without removing any other layers, then we removed conv5 and randomly initialised conv4, then removed conv4 and randomly initialised conv3 and finally removed conv3 and randomly initialised conv2. The results to these experiments can be seen in Table 3. We can see that all of the networks we trained with less than 5 convolution layers in this experiment achieve a higher accuracy on the validation set than the original AlexNet. The most impressive aspect of these results is that we can see that for this problem a much shallower network - for example one with only two convolution layers - is able to achieve accuracy higher than a deeper network. However, we find that removing layers in fact increases the size of the model. This is due to dimensions of the final convolution layer increasing when we remove layers meaning the number of weights to connect to the first fully connected layer increases. SqueezeNet avoided this problem due to it's fully convolutional nature.

Table 3. Comparing the effect of removing convolution layers from AlexNet and randomly initialising the final remaining layer.

Total convolution layers	Randomly initialised layer	Validation accuracy	Size of model
5	-	75.72%	0.2 GB
5	Conv5	75.24%	0.2 GB
4	Conv4	77.64%	1.1 GB
3	Conv3	76.92%	1.1 GB
2	Conv2	77.16%	0.7 GB

Cross-Learning Between Angles. The final set of experiments we ran used the full 18 binary layer outputs to see how our changes can affect the whole system. Firstly we trained our SqueezeNet base with all the angles, which gave an average of 86.39% accuracy on the validation data across all the angles. We see an improvement here compared to the single angle problem, with the accuracy of angle θ_0 being 74.03% on the single angle compared to 86.92% for θ_0 when trained with all the angles. This indicates that whilst the individual angles can be treated as separate problems, combining them with shared features leads to cross-training significantly improving the performance.

Next we ran the experiment on SqueezeNet with a randomly initialised final Fire module, this gave an average accuracy of 87.51% showing an improvement on our base network consistent with our single angle experiments. We also attempted removing the final layer and randomly initialising the penultimate Fire module giving an average of 85.01% accuracy but also reducing the model size by 24%. This shows that we can still maintain a high performing network with fewer parameters.

Finally, we trained our base AlexNet with the full set of output layers. This gave us an average accuracy of 80%. Despite the greatly improved results from removing a pooling layer on the single angle problem, removing the final pooling layer with the full network gave an average accuracy of 78.44%. Removing the final convolution layer and randomly initialising the penultimate layer gave an average accuracy of 78.93%. The reason for this discrepancy is likely to be that our methods excel with limited data. The full angle problem has 18 times more data than the single angle problem, but does not have 18 times more parameters. It is likely that in the 18 angle case our networks would out perform the base network in situations where less data is available such as for online learning robotics applications.

5 Conclusion

In this paper, we have proposed steps for adapting networks designed for computer vision tasks to robotic grasping. We have shown that due to the differences in these tasks it is vital for robotics researches to consider the network architectures to improve accuracy, obtain smaller models and improve training efficiency. The fact that the exact position of an object is far more important for accurate grasping means that decreasing translational invariance in our networks helped improve the accuracy by 2.88% when using AlexNet. We also saw that by reducing the number of parameters being trained we were able to achieve improved accuracy in this problem over the base SqueezeNet while also obtaining a 69% reduction in model size. These methods can be used to create space efficient networks with improved accuracy which can be used in robotic control systems.

Given smaller networks and faster training times we feel this could lend itself to online learning systems. It would be interesting to explore the results of using these methods with reinforcement learning in a full end to end system. In the future we want to further investigate other advanced architectures developed, such as Residual Networks (ResNets)[3], 3D convolution systems [15] and Recurrent Neural Networks [6], to not only adapt vision networks to the task of robotics but to find which provided the best base architecture for this problem.

Acknowledgements. This work was supported by the Marion Redfearn Trust, EPSRC and Tesco Labs, with particular thanks to Paul Wilkinson for his support.

References

1. Bohg, J., Morales, A., Asfour, T., Kragic, D.: Data-driven grasp synthesis - A survey. CoRR abs/1309.2660 (2013)
2. El-Khoury, S., Sahbani, A.: Handling objects by their handles. In: IROS Workshop on Grasp and Task Learning by Imitation (2008)
3. He, K., Zhang, X., Ren, S., Sun, J.: Deep residual learning for image recognition. CoRR abs/1512.03385 (2015)
4. Huebner, K., Kragic, D.: Selection of robot pre-grasps using box-based shape approximation. In: 2008 IEEE/RSJ International Conference on Intelligent Robots and Systems, pp. 1765–1770, September 2008
5. Iandola, F.N., Moskewicz, M.W., Ashraf, K., Han, S., Dally, W.J., Keutzer, K.: SqueezeNet: AlexNet-level accuracy with 50x fewer parameters and <1 MB model size (2016)
6. Jaeger, H.: Tutorial on training recurrent neural networks, covering BPPT, RTRL, EKF and the "echo state network" approach (2002)
7. Krizhevsky, A., Sutskever, I., Hinton, G.E.: Imagenet classification with deep convolutional neural networks. In: Advances in Neural Information Processing Systems (2012)
8. Lenz, I., Lee, H., Saxena, A.: Deep learning for detecting robotic grasps. Int. J. Robot. Res. **34**(4–5), 705–724 (2015)
9. Levine, S., Finn, C., Darrell, T., Abbeel, P.: End-to-end training of deep visuomotor policies. CoRR abs/1504.00702 (2015)
10. Pelossof, R., Miller, A., Allen, P., Jebara, T.: An SVM learning approach to robotic grasping. In: 2004 IEEE International Conference on Robotics and Automation, 2004, Proceedings, ICRA 2004, vol. 4, pp. 3512–3518, April 2004
11. Pinto, L., Gupta, A.: Supersizing self-supervision: Learning to grasp from 50k tries and 700 robot hours (2015). arXiv:1509.06825
12. Redmon, J., Angelova, A.: Real-time grasp detection using convolutional neural networks. CoRR abs/1412.3128 (2014)
13. Saxena, A., Driemeyer, J., Ng, A.Y.: Robotic grasping of novel objects using vision. Int. J. Robot. Res. **27**(2), 157–173 (2008)
14. Szegedy, C., Liu, W., Jia, Y., Sermanet, P., Reed, S.E., Anguelov, D., Erhan, D., Vanhoucke, V., Rabinovich, A.: Going deeper with convolutions. CoRR abs/1409.4842 (2014)
15. Tran, D., Bourdev, L.D., Fergus, R., Torresani, L., Paluri, M.: C3D: generic features for video analysis. CoRR abs/1412.0767 (2014)

Design and Implementation of a Low Cost Prosthetic Hand

Victorino Sepúlveda-Arróniz[1], Cesar Ivan Lamas-Aguilar[1],
Julio C. Salinas-Maldonado[1], Juan C. Tudon-Martinez[1],
Ricardo Ramirez-Mendoza[2], and Jorge de-J. Lozoya-Santos[1(✉)]

[1] Research Department, Universidad de Monterrey, Av. Morones Prieto 4500 Pte,
66238 San Pedro Garza García, NL, Mexico
{victorino.sepulveda,cesar.lamas,julio.salinas,juan.tudon,
jorge.lozoya}@udem.edu
[2] School of Engineering, Tecnologico de Monterrey,
Av. E. Garza Sada 2501, Monterrey, NL, Mexico
ricardo.ramirez@itesm.mx

Abstract. The development of a low cost transradial prosthesis based on existing models is done. The system is controlled by electromyography with adjustable socket for comfort and better adaptation. The goal is the performance of job duties and physiological needs for an amputee. A study of the state of the art allows to potentiate the functionality of the prototype. The methodology includes modification of 3D designs "open source" to expedite design stage, FEM analysis to prototype 3D display reference efforts and have critical points where it would have to modify the design. A main issue is the implementation of a mechanism to add degrees of freedom in the wrist. A mapping of the areas to have higher electric potential to the electrode location has been accomplished. The implementation of software to recognize patterns based on electrical signals to create an intelligent system and facilitate the movement as well as greater freedom of movement for the user has been achieved. The use of frequency response functions is key in the control strategy. The prototype has four different types of grip and connectivity to mobile devices.

Keywords: Prosthetic hand · Frequency response functions · Low cost device

1 Introduction

The need for prosthetics has been a problem since the beginning of time. Individuals have tried to compensate the loss of a limb by replacing it with a similar artifact. The hand, which is an extension of the human, is a complex system that is made up of 27 bones, more than 20 articulations and more than 30 muscles [1,2]. Because of this the representation of an exact model is a difficult task, but it is not impossible.

© Springer International Publishing AG 2017
Y. Gao et al. (Eds.): TAROS 2017, LNAI 10454, pp. 495–506, 2017.
DOI: 10.1007/978-3-319-64107-2_39

An amputation can be caused by different factors [3]:

- Vascular Diseases
- Accidents
- Infections
- Tumors
- Congenital Amputation

The development of prosthetics is not something new. In Egypt when someone lost a limb the Egyptians would replace it with fibers, just to fill the void but did not pay attention to functionality [4]. Years after, wars brought many wounded soldiers who needed help to get back to fighting. Across different ages, prosthetics were made of iron, wood and copper. Now men know how to design mechanisms similar to a real hand but the real problem was how it could be powered and created without using a large amount of resources and time. The transistor took the development of prosthetics to the next level. People already had hooks and mechanical prosthetics but these provided very limited mobility for its users.

Universities started researching and producing different models, mechanisms and patents that later established big companies. Electronic prosthetics are mainly powered by electromyography (EMG) [5], using voltage signals from the muscles the user can move articulations, fingers and have full control on prosthesis.

This kind of prosthetics usually represent a big investment, normally myoelectric prosthesis can cost more than $30,000.00 [6]. This last five years 3D printing [7] created another alternative for the development of this prosthetic. They may be not as durable and strong as the ones made with metals but they are still useful. The internet played a mayor role when sharing and creating 3D models that people could download and print in their own houses. Most of these models are mechanical hands that are easy to assemble, but they can only perform one movement and they can produce exhaustion when using it for a long time.

The next sections of this paper discuss the proposed design for the transradial prosthesis powered by EMG, capable of four different grips plus rotation, an adjustable socket, with a precise signal detection algorithm, which is low cost and customizable.

2   Methodology

- Requirements
- Design
- Implementation
- Unit and Integration Test
- System and Acceptance Test

Requirements. It's important to define the prosthesis user to establish limits. An open source model will be chosen depending on the mechanical design that meets the degrees of freedom and other requirements. The material in which it will be printed will be defined as well as the control system.

Design. After selecting an open source design it will be modified based on the selected degrees of freedom and control system. The control design will be divided in EMG design, electronic design and algorithm design. Finally the power supply will be chosen based in the electric design.

Implementation. After taking into consideration the requirements, new parts for the model will be designed using Autodesk Inventor as well for mechanism test. After selecting the components, EMG channels will be tested individually by using a wave generator to review if the amplifying works. Then the same test will be made using electrodes to visualize the EMG signal. After obtaining the EMG signals, they have to be converted from analog to digital to detect voltage peaks and maximums, by using the Arduino Micro and the Arduino IDE.

Unit and Integration Test. After finishing the 3D model, the prototype will be printed and assembled before adding the components. Once the final EMG circuit is working, the PCB will be developed and tested individually before integrating it to the microcontroller. After testing the actuators with the micro-controller and the power supply, the PCB can 'be developed and tested with the EMG signals. Different algorithms will be tested, evaluating how accurate they are regarding the desired inputs and desired outputs. Before assembling the servomotors inside the palm the limits need to be set, this defines the degrees of freedom of the prosthesis. The power supply will be tested for each section individually to determine if the voltage and current consumption is enough.

System and Acceptance Test. When the prototype is fully assembled, mechanical tests will be made to review the expected degrees of freedom before adding the electronic components. Using the different grips the prototype has, a test will be made to evaluate which kind of objects the prototype can carry. The power supply will be tested to evaluate the battery life before the next charge.

Similar to using a waterfall model, a V-Model was used in which it breaks down into discrete phases but including feedback when testing to validate the design to meet the requirements. Adapting the project to the model, it can be broken down to.

3   Development

Based in the methodology the prosthesis requirements will be established for development of the design. The design includes the mechanical, electrical and software design. For the implementation each section will be independently produced before the unit and system test.

3.1 Requirements

In order to perform job duties and other needs it is important to define the prosthesis degrees of freedom. The hand will perform four different grips:

- Precision grasp
- Hook grasp
- Planar grasp
- Cylindrical/Circular grasp

All these grasps can be combined with a 90° rotation when needed. The hand is designed to grab small objects otherwise the hand could break or damage the electronic components.

3.2 Design

Using the requirements as foundations and limitations the design was developed. The design emphasizes on mechanical, electrical and software design.

Open Source. To speed the development open source designs were revised and compared to choose the one that met the expectations.

Materials. The initial printing is going to be made using ABS, while the second printing will be made using PLA. Different materials were used to decrease the friction coefficient for moving parts.

Electronic Design. For the data processing a microcontroller with ATmega32U4 that runs at $5\,V/16\,MHz$ was used. This microcontroller will take the EMG analog inputs, run an algorithm and will move the desired Servo Motor. The power supply that will be used is a rechargeable lithium polymer battery ($11\,V$). This will power the microcontroller, the servo motors and the EMG circuit. The instrumentation amplifiers that are used for the EMG circuit need dual supply, to only use one battery a virtual dual supply was built using zener diodes.

EMG. Two instrumentation amplifiers (AD620) were used for the amplifying stage. The gain of both is 1400. After that a high pass filter ($fc = 1\,Hz$) was placed to remove the DC component experienced when obtaining the signals. More filters might be added in the future to remove frequencies that affect the EMG readings, still the circuit is in process to become the final design. In total five electrodes were used, two per instrumentation amplifier plus the ground electrode. For better results electrodes must be placed two centimeters apart from each other and in the center of the muscle. The two muscles that were evaluated are:

- Flexor Carpi Ulnaris
- Forearm Extensors

Table 1. EMG input

CH1	CH2	Movements	Output
Low	Low	Relaxed	No movement
Low	High	Extension	Thumb
High	Low	Flexion	Wrist rotation
High	High	Forearm contraction	Close hand

With this configuration there are four different inputs that can be achieved, each muscle working as a channel they can display low or high voltages that can be established and serve as an indicator as seen in Table 1. This channel outputs will be used for the algorithm test and will dictate the movement of the prosthesis.

Control Algorithms. For the processing of the signals, it is important to make tests with different algorithms to evaluate the performance Fig. 1. All algorithms follow the same conditions to take a decision: detect highs and lows from two channels, making four possible combinations. The three main algorithms are:

Peak Voltage. This algorithm instantly detects an analog input then compares conditions regarding the voltage level of each channel, after comparing both channels a movement is done if needed and a small delay between the movement and the next measure is present.

Mean Value. Each channel fills an array of values sampled at an established rate, after filling this array the average is calculated to later proceed on the conditions and produce the movement when both channels are at a high level, this method is popular because it is reliable and easy to implement.

FEB. Similar as the mean value algorithm an array of values is calculated, after that the arrays is derived to obtain an estimation the frequency in a certain interval by doing a numerical integration to compute the discrete rms values of both arrays [8].

3.3   Implementation

For the model selection the one that was the most complete and the most documented was the exiii HACKberry [9], this open source design was made in Japan and makes use of well thought out mechanisms and good spacing for the electronic components.

For the movement, it uses three servo motors that are located inside the hand. Primarily the hand has three degrees of freedom. The index and thumb are connected to a servo motor and can move separately while the other three fingers are connected to a joint that is connected to a servo motor. To control the movement an IR sensor is placed at the forearm to detect a contraction and this produces the open/close movement.

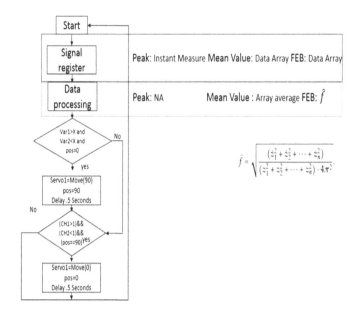

Fig. 1. Algorithms

Modifications. Taking the hand mechanism from Exiii, there were some modifications that were made. First another servo motor was added for the wrist rotation, the wrist, forearm and socket models were designed from scratch so the rotation could be achieved and for better slump integration. The exploded view of the full prototype can be seen in Fig. 2. For transradial amputees wrist rotation is needed, most prosthetics do not include this degree of freedom. An example would be the grasp of a water bottle, the orientation would change how the hand should be positioned. By giving the user this extra movement he would be able to rotate the wrist and hold objects with different orientations without trying to rotate the forearm. Just by adding this degree of freedom the prosthetic can now compete with commercial prosthetics based on movement.

FEM. The new pieces that were designed need validation before printing them, by using stress analysis functions available. Inside the modeling software simulated loads were applied to certain points. Even though the hand is not made to carry big loads this is helpful to establish limits, as seen in Fig. 3 a load of 50 lb was applied to the hole insertions that connect to the fore arm. One of the problems is that the printing method and resolution of the printer affects directly the resistance of the material, 3D printers that use fused deposition modeling (FDM)create cracks underneath each layer. The 3D parts that were printed were fragile so they need to be printed again with a better quality printer.

Data Register. After obtaining the desired EMG signals, data was registered from a small group of people to detect voltage peaks using only one channel at a time. After that two channels were used to detect what kind of movements

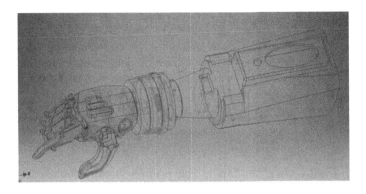

Fig. 2. First design

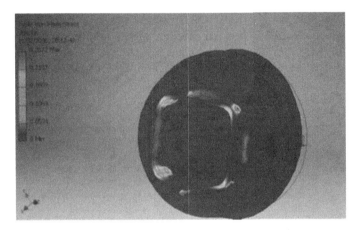

Fig. 3. Wrist FEM

were giving high voltage values and were natural for the user. Using an (A/D) converter was useful to create a data bank for later algorithm test. Signals were registered with a frequency of 50, 100 and 500 Hz. Power spectrum and spectral density were obtained from the signals to visualize the main frequencies that were present during each movement, this to evaluate if movement based from frequency detection was possible. Also by analyzing the range of frequencies in a signal, it can be useful when designing filters to remove noise from EMG readings.

Algorithms. Three different algorithms were developed, the mean and peak value were programmed using Arduino IDE. For the FEB it was developed using matlab.

3.4   Unit and Integration Test

Before finishing the protoype, each unit must be tested individually to detect any problem or design change that should be implemented before being used in the first prototype. Similar to the design, the divitions are the mechanical unit, electronic unit and the algorithm test.

Mechanical Unit. The 3D model was printed and assembled. After assembling the proposed degrees of freedom were tested before applying any electronic component to evaluate the movement.

Electronic Unit. After developing the printed circuits for each component they were tested. The EMG circuit was tested using electrodes on the forearm to detect the EMG signals. As seen in Fig. 4 the first graph is a signal reading that registers both channels, channel 1 is the white signal and channel 2 is the red signal. The first three graphs are movements that activate certain motors depending which channel is over an specific voltage amplitude. Last graph is a mixture of all three movements, this signal was the one used for testing because it involves all the movements and different combinations in one sequence.

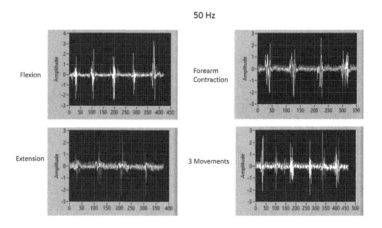

Fig. 4. EMG recorded signal using 2 channels

Algorithm Test. Three algorithms were tested to evaluate the signal received, the processing and the motor movement. To select a control system it necessary to plot a receiver operating characteristic (ROC) [10] curve, this method gives a relation between the true positive rate and the false positive rate. To plot the curve the system was tested 10 times using both system, (voltage peak and mean value) the true positive rate in each test is the vertical axis, and the horizontal axis is the false positive rate, the EMG signal were previously recorded, the same signal was used for all tests and the input noise was the same in all cases. Both system were plotted in the same graph to compare the better system, the mean value method is the better option due to the fact that the curve has a bigger area under it as Fig. 6 shows. For this ROC representation an EMG signal was produced that was made up of 6 different movements, in total with the 10 tests 60 movements were recorded and evaluated for each method. For each method tests were made changing the number of samples, delay per samples and delay after the servo motor movement. The FEB method was tested in Matlab software to later test it with the microcontroller, Fig. 5 shows five flexion moves represented by the voltage amplitude through time and in the image below shows the same signal but the muscular contractions are represented by the frequency. The current results show a high correlation between the frequency change and the muscular contraction, therefore this control system could be an accurate method to produce movement. The mean value method that had better results used a sample of 50, with a delay of .005 s per sample and a delay of .5 s after movement. The method takes approximately 1 s to sample and produce a movement.

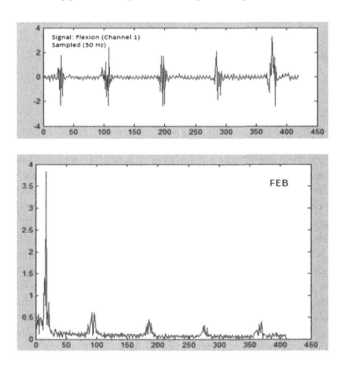

Fig. 5. Flexion FEB

3.5   System and Acceptance Test

After testing each unit separately now the prosthetic is ready to make tests as a system. By inserting the motors and electronic circuits as well as the power supply the prototype will be tested to evaluate the grasp performance and sensing precision.

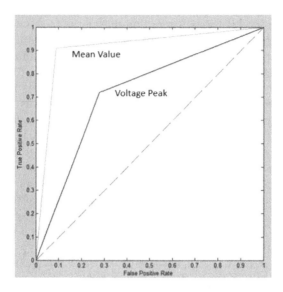

Fig. 6. ROC curve

4   Discussion

As seen in Fig. 7 the first prototype was assembled and ready for tests. The EMG PCB was bigger than expected so it became exposed at the top. The only wires are the EMG cables that connect straight to the electrodes and the power cable that it's connected to the battery. The socket has velcro to haver better fit as well for being comfortable, the weight of the whole hand is 500 g and the 44 cm of length. 3D printing can help in the manufacture and development but also can cause some problems that should be taken in consideration during the design stage. Some parts and holes can shrink, as well the printing orientation can affect on the mechanical properties of the piece. The printed circuits were home made, this can also have an effect on the amplifying characteristics of the design. When using amplifiers the distance of each component and welding hability could produce some noise and unwanted signals. Some design optimizations could be done in the future after finishing the prototype. The wrist size could be smaller using other kind of motor or a smaller one. Other materials could be implemented like metals to increase the strenght as well for the use of screws instead of tapping screws. The original design for the sensing uses cables that attach to the electrodes on the forearm using an external cable that uses a plug. To avoid noise and disconnections, the cable could be placed from inside the prosthetic.

Another aspect that still needs to be tested is the amputee comfort and socket validation. The velcro may not be the best system but for early design stages can be implemented and used for the prosthesis testing. The power supply also needs to be changed for other type of batteries, LiPo batteries can be dangerous and not as reliable as a lithium ion battery. After doing the tests for the first protype and having a fully working prosthetis some other degrees of freedom might be added, all this to develop a low cost prosthetic that can compete with commercial prosthetics but also to give more tools to the amputees.

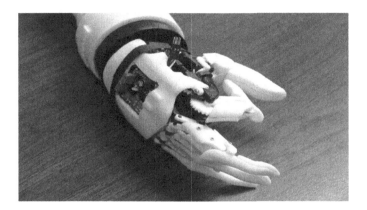

Fig. 7. First prototype

5   Conclusion

The paper presented the modified 3D design, electric design and algorithm proposal, mechanical tests are still pending. Three different algorithms were proposed, currently only two of them are working and tested while the last one (FEB) is still in development. The purpose of this article is the presentation of the current process of all the different components that integrate a functional prosthetic, starting with a versatile design that incorporates multiple degrees of freedom, the amplifying and filtering EMG stage, electronic components integration, microcontroller processing and finally the implementation on a subject. The prototype is fully assembled and each unit was tested individually, the systems tests are still pending. After finishing the first prototype the design will be shared to get input from the open source community.

References

1. Chao, E.Y.: Biomechanics of the Hand: A Basic Research Study. World Scientific (1989)
2. Duncan, S.F., Saracevic, C.E., Kakinoki, R.: Biomechanics of the hand. Hand Clin. **29**(4), 483–492 (2013)
3. Osorio, L.: Módulo de Amputados (2012). http://www.elportaldelasalud.com/index.php
4. Norton, K.: Un Breve Recorrido por la Historia de la Protésica. Motion Mag. **17**(7), 11–13 (2007)
5. Florez, S., Fernando, B.: Analisis de Seales Mioelectricas Orientadas a la Robotica, B.S. thesis (2010)

6. Loaiza, J.L., Arzola, N.: Evolution and trends in the development of hand prosthesis. DYNA **78**(169), 191–200 (2011)
7. Barnatt, C.: 3D Printing: The Next Industrial Revolution. ExplainingTheFuture.com (2013)
8. Lozoya-Santos, J.d.J., Morales-Menendez, R., Ramírez Mendoza, R.A.: Control of an automotive semi-active suspension. Math. Probl. Eng. **2012** (2012)
9. exiii Inc., Exiii HACKberry Open Source Community (2016). http://exiii-hackberry.com/
10. Lozoya-Santos, J., Morales-Menendez, R., Gutierrez, A.M., et al.: Fault Detection for an Automotive MR Damper. IFAC Proceedings Volumes, vol. 45(6), pp. 1023–1028 (2012)

The Virtual Bee Hive

Vince Gallo[1(✉)] and Mark Witkowski[2(✉)]

[1] Reigate Beekeepers Association, Dorking, UK
Vince.gallo@btinternet.com
[2] Department of Electrical and Electronic Engineering, Imperial College,
Exhibition Road, London SW7 2BT, UK
m.witkowski@imperial.ac.uk

Abstract. This short paper introduces the Virtual Bee Hive, a behavioural and graphic simulator for the major functions of a Honey bee (*Apis mellifera*) hive. Honey bees have a social structure apparently formed from actions of many individuals leading to the construction of specific physical structures (the hive) and the appearance of coordinated behaviours. The purpose of the Virtual Bee Hive is to explore how such "super-organism" behaviour can result from a large number of simple individual actions without any suggestion of an overall controlling agency. The starting assumption is that every bee within the hive has a limited repertoire of elementary activities, which are activated by prevailing circumstances (for example: the need to forage for food, maintain the honeycomb, nurture the pupae, or regulate hive temperature) and which taken as a whole maintain the hive and allow it to prosper.

We describe the support provided by the Virtual Bee Hive simulator for three key aspects of hive activity: maintaining the comb, foraging for nectar and pollen, and temperature regulation within the hive. The simulation offers a bee action selection behaviour model based on known parameters coupled to an extended graphical model of the hive and its immediate environs. In operation the model is instantiated with 1000s of individual bees and the operation of the hive - and of individual bees - can be observed and recorded. Success within the Virtual Bee Hive is indicated by the generation of realistic "emergent behaviours". Much is known about these individual aspects of hive behaviour. However, in formulating the simulation questions necessarily arise that encourage detailed consideration of the available research data and underlying assumptions.

1 Introduction

There have been centuries of practical beekeeping experience (Adam 1975; Hooper 1976 and Snelgrove Snelgrove 1935), but it was largely the work of ethologist Karl von Frisch (1886–1982) that established the scientific basis of our current understanding of bee behaviour. In particular his identification of the "round" and "waggle" dances as a way for individual bees to indicate the locality of food resources to hive mates (von Frish 1967). He also established the importance of the honey bee's "sense of smell" that is now considered central to pheromone and chemical regulation and control within the hive (von Frisch 1950).

© Springer International Publishing AG 2017
Y. Gao et al. (Eds.): TAROS 2017, LNAI 10454, pp. 507–515, 2017.
DOI: 10.1007/978-3-319-64107-2_40

A hive comprises one queen, some hundreds of male bees (drones) and tens of thousands of workers (infertile females) who undertake all of the work to support the colony[1]. Task distribution across the population of worker bees and during the lifespan of each of these individual bees (polyethism) is largely regulated by a number of hormone and pheromones and overall achieves a balance of tasks amongst a mixed age. The Virtual Beehive models every individual, including its response to various influences, throughout its life giving rise to the macroscopic organisation of a hive.

2 Related Work

Several insect families employ collective behaviours to form "super organisms", in which the cumulative effect of individual actions manifests itself in extensive physical construction and intricate social organisation. This is particularly the case for ant and termite species, but also of a significant number of wasp and bee populations. The ability of simple individual organisms to create complex and efficient social structures has given rise to many algorithms that attempt to exploit this phenomenon (e.g. Bonabeau et al. 1999).

For the economically important honeybee, Becher et al. (2014) report on BEE-HAVE, which models bee colony dynamics incorporating the impact of foraging and varroa destructor mite by dynamic modelling of a small number of population sub-sets such as foragers and nurse bees. Khoury et al. (2013) present a model of honey bee population growth and vulnerability using a set of differential equations. Using a similar approach, Schmickl and Crailsheim's (2007) HoPoMo (Honeybee Population Model) models intracolony population dynamics as a set of delayed feedback loops. de Vries and Biesmeijer (1998) developed a set of simple condition-action rules to model the collective foraging patterns of honey bees in a variable nectar supply task.

These models use dynamic modelling to describe total population development, and how internal and external factors impact population size and efficiency. The Virtual Beehive Model differs in that it models the lifecycle and behaviour of an individual bees, and so emulates the entire virtual hive by instantiation of some thousands of the individual virtual bees.

The Virtual Beehive Model only considers the behaviour of the bee colony whilst in its parent hive, however colony reproduction and the formation of new hives via the swarming mechanism has been extensively studied elsewhere (see Karaboga and Akay 2009, for a review).

3 The Bee Model

Our model of polyethism assumes a number of roles to be undertaken by individual bees. The tasks of interest are eating (maintain energy levels), housekeeping (waste and bee corpse disposal, cleaning cells), feeding (food prepared and fed to brood), queen

---

[1] Consequentially, references to worker bees will be "she" or "her".

rearing (queen cell production and feeding of selected grubs), cleansing (personal hygiene), foraging (gathering of foodstuff for the colony), storing (placing of forage in honeycomb), making honey (moving and drying nectar to create honey), heating (increasing hive and localised brood temperature), cooling (reduce hive temperature by ventilation and evaporation), ailing (ill health and death). Each task is encoded as a collection of software methods respectively: `eating`, `housekeeping`, `feeding`, `queenrearing`, `cleansing`, `foraging`, `storing`, `makingHoney`, `heating`, `cooling`, `ailing`. A worker not engaged in any of these tasks is deemed to be in an idle state and ready to adopt the task to which she is most inclined.

The completed Virtual Bee Hive will include the software necessary to encode each of the identified behaviours (Fig. 1) and potentially others such as hive defense and the actions of drones. Any particular bee may be observed to perform just one of these possible tasks at any particular time, however she will, over time, take on different tasks. The change from one task to another has been observed to comprise a shifting from one to another over a short time within a limited group, as well as a more elongated shift from one collection of tasks to another as she ages. The model that we have chosen for this behaviour is, we believe, key to the overall behavioural construct that will balance the short and long term distribution of tasks amongst the bee population.

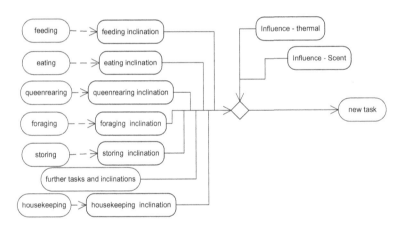

Fig. 1. The honey bee action selection model; tasks and task inclination

The model implements a map of inclinations for every one of the tasks. Each bee will also be subject to factors external to her, absolute temperature, thermal gradient, and the strength of each of the many different scents. Individual scents, or in combination with other scents and temperature, provide an influence directing all bees (those within the zone of influence) to switch to performing a particular task. The map of inclination for a particular bee will determine whether the influence is sufficient to cause that individual to undertake that task. Each bee will have a pattern of inclinations, initialised with random variation to simulate genetic variability, therefore those most inclined to that task will be the first to switch. When an environmental influence increases more bees will join that taskforce, similarly if the influence decreases so the less-inclined bees will drop out.

An example of a short term fluctuation of a bee's inclination map would be where she has become hungry, i.e. her energy reserves, implemented as a `FoodAndEnergy` object, have run low and so increased her inclination to feed. A longer term variation of her inclination map would be to model where, for example, when first hatched her Hypopharyngeal gland (for the production of brood-food) is under-developed but grows over the first two days, and then reduces significantly after two weeks. The value for her `Feeding` inclination would be changed to reflect this.

4   The Hive Model

The bee model interacts with the hive model (partial shown schematically in Fig. 2) which itself comprises a number of additional objects, each representing a real world physical entity (as visualised in Fig. 3) or some abstract property. The primary object within the hive that will be manipulated by worker bee activity is the honeycomb. The hive is constructed of many honeycomb frames, typically 11, each `Frame` object is associated with two `Honeycomb` objects (one each side). Each `Honeycomb` holds some thousands of `Cell` objects. Each `Cell` can store an instance of a `Brood` object or `Forage`. A `Brood` instance will migrate with time from egg to grub to pupae eventually hatching to create a new adult `Bee` object.

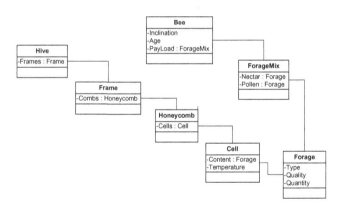

Fig. 2. Representation of key hive components; hive structure and bee population

In operation a `Brood` object creates (simulated) scents indicating its need for warmth or food. These simulated scents influences the behaviour of nearby worker bees to remedy the deficit and, as a consequence, reduce the influence. This negative feedback thus balances the number of workers performing `Feeding`. Research has shown that odours and pheromones can be distributed by being airborne as well as by trophallaxis, carried in food which workers habitually share (von Frisch 1950). The model includes a simulation of the distribution and dissipation of scents, to be reacted to by a workers in their idle state.

A balanced workforce depends on not just the environmental influences that push the population towards a task, but also that the successful execution of that action will produce an inhibiting influence or reduce a positive influence, and so reduce the need for further effort. An example of the balance by a negative influence would be the natural inclination to produce queens that is inhibited by Scent produced by a healthy Queen. When the Queen is lost or unwell this inclination will be uninhibited leading to the creation of a replacement.

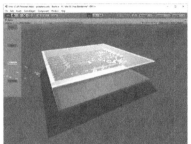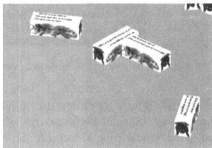

Fig. 3. Visualisation of the hive and individual worker bees (detail)

5   The Foraging and Storing Model

The Bee has been programmed with a number of elementary actions, which have been purposefully employed to implement some of the tasks discussed above. The elementary actions include such as walking around the inside of a hive, navigating obstacles such as walls and honeycomb, and flying outside the hive, visiting flowers and negotiating obstacles such as trees (Fig. 4). The process of collecting pollen and nectar and placing it into storage has been observed to comprise two distinct tasks; foragers bring the forage to the hive and then pass it to worker storage bees who then place it in honeycomb cells.

These tasks each break down to a series of actions, hence foraging is a sequence of SeekEntrace, DepartHive, SeekForage, GatherForage, SeekHive, EnterHive, SeekStorer, UnloadForage. Once a Forage sequence has been completed the Bee will switch to a new task, according to her inclination and the influence to which she is subjected, but if her inclination and the influence have not much changed then she will restart a new Forage task. Similarly the Storing task has been broken into the sequence of actions; SeekForager, UnloadForager, SeekStorageLocation, StoreForage and on completion she could switch task, but more likely will repeat the Storage task.

Foraging itself is a task which can be implemented in one of two fashions. Bees are known to explore, seeking new sources to harvest, and they will repeatedly exploit known sources. Woodgate et al. (2016) have attached devices to Bumble Bees (*Bombus terrestris audax*) and tracked their flights over their foraging lifetime using harmonic radar technology. We have used this data on the assumption that honey bee behaviour

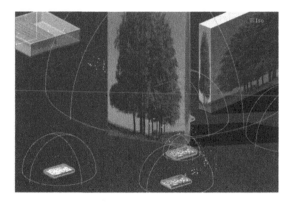

Fig. 4. The hive and its environs; hive, tree obstacles and flower clusters

is similar, but will incorporate new data as it becomes available. This research showed that bees follow different flight patterns when exploring and exploiting (as implemented in the Virtual Hive Model, Fig. 5).

Individual Bees are modelled so that memory of a quality source to be exploited will cause her to do so, otherwise she will explore. When exploiting she will fly directly to the known source (Fig. 5 left), although her flight path will avoid any obstacles (Fig. 5 right). This will continue until the source becomes exhausted, when she will seek new sources by exploration.

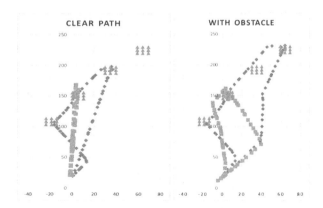

Fig. 5. Foraging, exploration (Blue) vs. exploitation (Orange) (Color figure online)

An exploration flight will proceed as a random walk, the parameters of which will be refined in the light of existing and future data. The exploration search model incorporates a response to the smell of a candidate patch of flowers. The smell detection zone is implemented as a `collider` shown as domes around the flower clusters (Fig. 4). The size of the zone is adjusted to be proportional to the number of flowers and the amount of forage available at a flower site. Forage collection on an Exploration flight is modelled as multiple samples to provide the means of choosing the best from several candidate sources of forage which will then be the target of future exploitation flights.

Interactions between worker bees, each performing a different task, are common and an example can been seen in our model where a `Forage:SeekStorer` having returned to the hive to unload the forage encounters a `Storer:SeekForager`. They change actions to `Forager:UnloadForage` and `Storer:AcceptForage` respectively and the model will then transfer some `Forage` from one `Bee` object to the other (see Fig. 3).

6 The Hive Thermal Model

Temperature is crucial to the rearing of healthy brood and workers will adopt the task of heating or ventilation as needed to maintain the correct local and general temperature. Individual bees will raise their body temperature to heat specific cells; alternatively bees will use their wings to drive air through the hive when cooling is required. Both of these behaviours are modelled. In order to achieve this it was necessary to construct a thermal model of the hive including thermal mass, conductivity and air movement. To enhance monitoring and use of the model we have implemented a virtual infrared view (Fig. 6 right) which shows clearly the outcome of the modelled behaviour.

Fig. 6. Hive Thermal Model (Visible left, Temperature representation right)

A number of worker bee actions, including brood cell preparation, brood rearing and placement of food stores reveal a spherical structure to the hive (sliced over the honeycomb). Brood mostly occupies the middle of the honeycomb, surrounded by cells holding pollen and then nectar/honey. This layout is also revealed in the hive thermal distribution.

The behavioural mechanism that underpins this distribution is as yet unclear, and may be an inherent sense of the hive geometry, but could be guided by the temperature distribution. We have initially constructed our model using a thermally driven scheme, but the flexibility of a software model allows alternatives to be tested and the outcomes compared.

7   Implementation and Performance

The graphical aspects of this model have been coded using the Unity3d development software[2] and the custom behaviour classes have been written in C#.

Unity3d is marketed as a games engine and hence provides support for 3D object manipulation, processing as well as rendering and multi-object process scheduling. Within the Unity framework we have used the facility whereby software, written in C#, can be added to the 3D objects. These class extensions and a number of support classes are where we have implemented the virtual hive model. We have used Microsoft Visual Studio Community Edition for editing and debugging.

Note that the visualised objects within the model (for example Fig. 3) have been rendered as cuboids for efficiency. This does not appear to detract from the usefulness of the behavioural model and objects can be rendered to any level of detail that is required. Using a mid-range laptop, more than 1000 bee objects can be modelled at more than 20 frames per second. Each frame involves updating every object within the model, including bees, honeycomb cells and flowers. We expect the model broadly to scale linearly with bee numbers and this will primarily effect simulation frame rate for any given processor capability.

8   Discussion and Future Work

This paper reports on preliminary work[3] which will continue towards a full scale graphical hive model. Work to date has focused on the construction of the framework necessary for more advanced activity modelling, and has used this to model the explore/exploit foraging behaviour as described by Becher et al. (2014). This can be extended immediately to include the transfer of knowledge described by Smolla et al. (2016) and von Frisch (1967). We shall continue to investigate how thermoregulation within the hive can constrain and influence the organisation of brood and stores.

Bees are an important - possibly essential - natural resource, not only for the products they create directly, such as honey, but specifically in the role they play in the pollination of commercially important crops. Recently there has been much concern over and research into the widespread occurrence of Colony Collapse Disorder (Becher et al. 2013; CCD 2017; Schmickl and Crailsheim 2007) in which whole hives die for unexplained reasons putting at risk some aspects of agriculture. The cause is yet to be established, but the parasitic varroa destructor mite is a candidate as are the effects of various pesticides. Although not fatal to the insect, it is known that small aberrant changes in behaviour can precipitate the catastrophic loss of a complete group or colony (e.g. Witkowski 2007).

---

[2] https://unity3d.com/.

[3] https://virtualbeehive.000webhostapp.com.

The Virtual Bee Hive model offers the potential to investigate such aberrant behaviour as well as increase our understanding of this important and fascinating species. The rigour necessary to encode each behaviour forces us to investigate and consider in detail the nature of the honey bees' activity.

References

Abou-Shaara, H.F.: The foraging behaviour of honey bees. Apis mellifera: a review. Veterinarni Medicina **59**(1), 1–10 (2014)

Becher, M.A., Grimm, V., Thorbeck, P., Horn, J., Kennedy, P.J., Osborne, J.L.: BEEHAVE: a systems model of honeybee colony dynamics and foraging to explore multifactorial causes of colony failure. J. Appl. Ecol. **51**(2), 470–482 (2014)

Becher, M.A., Osborne, J.L., Thorbek, P., Kennedy, P.J., Grimm, V.: Towards a systems approach for understanding honeybee decline: a stocktaking and synthesis of existing models. J. Appl. Ecol. **50**, 868–880 (2013)

Bonabeau, E., Dorigo, M., Theraulaz, G.: Swarm Intelligence: From Natural to Artificial Systems. Oxford University Press, New York (1999)

Adam, B.: Beekeeping at Buckfast Abbey. Northern Bee Books, Hebden Bridge (1975)

CCD. Colony Collapse Disorder (2017). www.epa.gov/pollinator-protection/colony-collapse-disorder. Accessed Feb 2017

de Vries, H., Biesmeijer, J.: Modelling collective foraging by means of individual behaviour rules in honey-bees. Behav. Ecol. Sociobiol. **44**(2), 109–124 (1998)

Karaboga, D., Akay, B.: A survey: algorithms simulating bee swarm intelligence. Artif. Intell. Rev. **31**, 61–85 (2009)

Khoury, D.S., Barron, A.B., Myerscough, M.R.: Modelling food and population dynamics in honey bee colonies. PLoS One **8**(5), 7 (2013)

Hooper, T.: Guide to Bees and Honey. Northern Bee Books, Hebden Bridge (1976)

Schmickl, T., Crailsheim, K.: HoPoMo: a model of Honeybee intracolonial population dynamics and resource management. Ecol. Model. **204**(1–2), 219–245 (2007)

Smolla, M., Alem, S., Chittka, L., Shultz, S.: Copy-when-uncertain: Bumblebees rely on social information when rewards are highly variable. R. Soc. Biol. Lett. **12**, 20160188 (2016)

Snelgrove, L.: Swarming, Its control and Prevention. Northern Bee Books, Hebden Bridge (1935)

Stabentheiner, A., Kovac, H., Brodschneider, R.: Honeybee colony thermoregulation - regulatory mechanisms and contribution of individuals in dependence on age, location and thermal stress. PLoS One **5**(1), 13 (2010)

von Frisch, K.: Bees: Their Vision, Chemical Senses, and Language. Cornell University Press, Ithaca (1950)

von Frisch, K.: The Dance Language and Orientation of Bees. Harvard University Press, Cambridge (1967)

Witkowski, M.: Energy sharing for swarms modelled on the common vampire bat. Adapt. Behav. **15**(3), 307–328 (2007)

Woodgate, J.L., Makinson, J.C., Lim, K.S., Reynolds, A.M., Chittka, L.: Life-long tracking of bumblebees. PLoS One **11**(8), 22 (2016)

Strategies for Selecting Best Approach Direction for a Sweet-Pepper Harvesting Robot

Ola Ringdahl[1], Polina Kurtser[2(✉)], and Yael Edan[2]

[1] Department of Computing Science,
Umeå University, 901 87 Umeå, Sweden
[2] Department of Industrial Engineering and Management,
Ben-Gurion University of the Negev, P.O.B. 653, 8410501 Beer Sheva, Israel
`kurtser@post.bgu.ac.il`

Abstract. An autonomous sweet pepper harvesting robot must perform several tasks to successfully harvest a fruit. Due to the highly unstructured environment in which the robot operates and the presence of occlusions, the current challenges are to improve the detection rate and lower the risk of losing sight of the fruit while approaching the fruit for harvest. Therefore, it is crucial to choose the best approach direction with least occlusion from obstacles.

The value of ideal information regarding the best approach direction was evaluated by comparing it to a method attempting several directions until successful harvesting is performed. A laboratory experiment was conducted on artificial sweet pepper plants using a system based on eye-in-hand configuration comprising a 6DOF robotic manipulator equipped with an RGB camera. The performance is evaluated in laboratorial conditions using both descriptive statistics of the average harvesting times and harvesting success as well as regression models. The results show roughly 40–45% increase in average harvest time when no a-priori information of the correct harvesting direction is available with a nearly linear increase in overall harvesting time for each failed harvesting attempt. The variability of the harvesting times grows with the number of approaches required, causing lower ability to predict them.

Tests show that occlusion of the front of the peppers significantly impacts the harvesting times. The major reason for this is the limited workspace of the robot often making the paths to positions to the side of the peppers significantly longer than to positions in front of the fruit which is more open.

1 Introduction

Due to the lack of skilled workforce and increasing labor costs, advanced automation is required for greenhouse production systems [1]. Despite intensive R&D on harvesting robots, there are no commercial harvesting robots for sweet peppers [2, 3]. Robotic harvesting of sweet peppers includes several tasks: detecting the fruit, approaching it, deciding whether the fruit is ripe, and finally detaching the fruit from the stem [4, 5]. The major limitation most commonly tackled today is the non-optimal detection rates; Bac et al. [3] reported state of the art being 85% in their 2014 review. Viewpoints analyses in harvesting robotics indicate that only 60% of the fruit can be detected from a single detection direction [6]. Therefore, current research focuses on detection

© Springer International Publishing AG 2017
Y. Gao et al. (Eds.): TAROS 2017, LNAI 10454, pp. 516–525, 2017.
DOI: 10.1007/978-3-319-64107-2_41

algorithm development [3, 6–8]. Another challenge often described in the literature is the task of how to grasp a fruit, due to the limitations of available robotic grippers and the inherent difficulties of grasp planning [9, 10]. Eizicovits and Berman [10] developed geometry-based grasp quality measures based on 3D point cloud to determine the best grasping pose of different objects, including sweet peppers. This kind of solution depends on detailed 3D sensor information of the object [11] which is very difficult to achieve in dense greenhouse environments. These environments have an unstructured and dynamic nature [12]: fruits have a high inherent variability in size, shape, texture, and location; in addition, occlusion and variable illumination conditions significantly influence the detection performance. Given the complexity of both detection and grasp planning tasks, approaching the correct fruit pose must be done dynamically, taking into account obstacles such as stems and leaves. The most common way to do this is visual servoing, i.e. using eye-in-hand sensing to guide the robot towards the fruit by always keeping it in the center of the image [13]. When using this method, it is crucial to choose the best approach direction with least occlusion from leaves and other obstacles to maximize the chance for the visual servoing to reach the desired grasping pose. This research focuses on measuring the value of ideal information regarding the best approach direction for successful visual servoing, compared to a method using a search pattern to find the best direction.

2   Methods

A 6DOF robotic manipulator Fanuc LR Mate 200iD equipped with an eye-in hand iDS Ui-5250RE RGB camera and a Sick DT20HI displacement measurement laser sensor was placed in-front of an artificial plastic pepper crop with yellow plastic fruits and green leaves (Fig. 1). The workflow of the robot was implemented using a generic software framework for development of agricultural and forestry robots [14]. The framework is constructed with a hybrid robot architecture, using a state machine implementing a flowchart as described by Ringdahl et al. [15].

Fig. 1. The experimental setup consisted of a robotic harvester in front of an artificial crop.

Fig. 2. An overview image taken from the robot's camera looking at a laboratorial scene with 5 peppers on two stems covered by leaves.

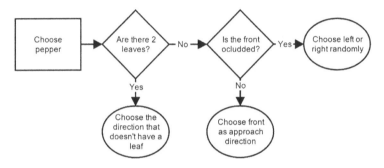

Fig. 3. Decision flowchart for manually selecting the optimal approach direction to a pepper.

A scene consisting of five plastic fruits placed at different locations on two artificial stems was setup before each experiment. The number of fruits were set to 5 to be similar to an actual sweet pepper plant, the right stem had three fruits, the left had two fruits. Each fruit had one or two leaves placed on different side (left/front/right) of it to create occlusion. An example of an overview image taken by the robot can be seen in Fig. 2. For each fruit the best fit harvesting approach, defined as the "optimal" harvesting approach direction, was set as the angle from either left ($-45°$), front ($0°$), or right ($45°$) where the target was least occluded, was noted manually. Figure 3 shows a flowchart describing the decision process for the manual selection.

2.1   Harvesting Scenarios

Two harvesting scenarios were tested. The first scenario, the _full a-priori knowledge scenario_, represents the ground-truth where both position $P_i(x_i, y_i, z_i)$ and approach direction θ_i^* are known for each fruit i. The harvesting cycle consists of approaching a pre-defined overview waypoint $W_0(x, y, z)$, and then selecting each target fruit in order from the list of positions and optimal approach directions of all fruits. The control unit then calculates the path of the robotic manipulator to a waypoint $W_i(x, y, z)$, positioned at a defined distance from fruit i with respect to the optimal harvesting approach direction and position $(x_i, y_i, z_i, \theta_i^*)$. After reaching the waypoint, a visual servo procedure based on color blob detection and distance measurements received from the laser guides the manipulator towards the target until the end-effector touches the fruit. If the manipulator reaches the target fruit, the harvest of that fruit is marked as successful and the path to the next waypoint is then calculated. In case the fruit was not found or was lost from view while in visual servo, the harvest of the fruit is marked as failed and the path to the next waypoint is calculated. The cycle ends when all fruits have been attempted to be approached. The left part of Fig. 4 shows a flowchart of this harvesting scenario.

The second scenario, the *auto approach direction search scenario*, is a variation of the ground-truth scenario in which the optimal approach direction θ_i^* is unknown, and therefore must be searched from a list of predefined possible approach directions $\theta_1..\theta_k$. For each target fruit i and possible approach direction θ_j the control unit calculates the path of the robotic manipulator to a waypoint $W_{ij}(x, y, z)$ positioned at a defined distance from the target fruit with respect to θ_j until the harvest of the fruit is marked as successful or sight of the fruit is lost. If successful, the path to the waypoint W_{ij} for fruit $i+1$ and θ_1 is calculated. If the fruit was lost during visual servoing, the next approach direction θ_{j+1} is selected. In case all approach directions $\theta_1..\theta_k$ were attempted without being able to reach the fruit, the harvest of the target fruit is marked as failed and the path to the waypoint W_{ij} for fruit $i+1$ and θ_1 is calculated. The right part of Fig. 4 shows a flowchart of this harvesting scenario.

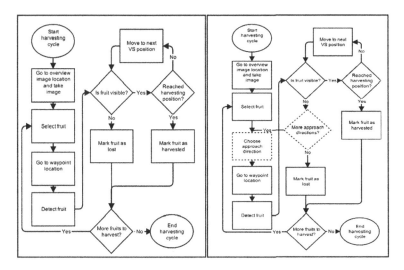

Fig. 4. Flowchart describing the two different harvesting scenarios. Left: auto approach direction search scenario. Right: full a-priori knowledge scenario (differences marked with dashed lines).

2.2 Experimental Protocol

Six laboratory scenes with different leaves and optimal approach directions were set up as defined in Table 1. The pose of each pepper was measured by manually moving the robotic arm in the desired approach direction into the position where the gripper touched the fruit, as seen in Fig. 5.

Table 1. Six scenes with different configurations for leaf (L = left, F = front, R = right) and approach direction (−45°, 0°, 45°).

Scene	Pepper 1			Pepper 2			Pepper 3			Pepper 4			Pepper 5		
	L	F	R	L	F	R	L	F	R	L	F	R	L	F	R
1	×	×	45	×		0	×		0	×		−45		×	0
2	×		0	×	×	−45		×	−45	×		0		×	0
3	×		0	×	×	−45	×		0		×	0	×		−45
4	×		0		×	0	×	×	0	×		−45	×	×	45
5		×	0	×		45	×	×	0	×		0	×	×	45
6	×		0		×	0	×	×	0	×		−45	×	×	45

Fig. 5. The pose of each pepper was measured by manually moving the robotic arm in the desired approach direction to the position where the gripper touched the fruit.

A harvesting cycle is performed for each of the defined scenes and scenarios according to the following configurations. Each one of the scenes defined is performed in three possible configurations:

- Full a-priori knowledge scenario selecting the optimal approach direction from the set {−45°, 0°, 45°}
- Auto approach direction search scenario with two different search patterns:
  - Side first: $\theta_j = [-45°, 0°, 45°]$ (left-center-right)
  - Center first: $\theta_j = [0°, -45°, 45°]$ (center-left-right)

Each configuration is performed at 50% and 100% of maximum speed respectively to enable sensitivity analysis in relation to the robot speed. At the end of each harvesting attempt cycle times and the result of the attempt (success/failure) are registered.

2.3   Measures and Statistical Analysis

To evaluate the performance, the following three measures are defined:

- *Pepper harvest time Th* is the time it takes from a fruit is selected from the list of fruit poses until the fruit has been successfully harvested (all fruits were harvested in the experiments).
- *Average logarithmic harvest time LTh* as shown in Eq. 1.

$$LTh = \frac{1}{n}\sum\nolimits_{i=1}^{n} \ln(Th_i) \tag{1}$$

Where n is the number of successfully harvested fruits.
- The *number of attempted approach directions* $N\theta_i$ for fruit i.

In addition to descriptive statistics of the aforementioned measures, the statistical significance of the differences in the value of the measures was measured. The pepper harvest time *Th* is analyzed in a form of a log transformed linear regression [16]:

$$\ln(Th_i) = \beta_0 + \beta_1 H_{c_i} + \beta_2 O_i + \beta_3 V_R + \beta_4 O_{F_i} + \beta_5 H_{c_i} * O_i + \epsilon_i \tag{2}$$

Where H_{c_i} is the harvesting scenario of pepper i, O_i is the number of occluding leaves, V_R is the robot speed, O_{F_i} is the front occlusion (1 if the front is occluded, 0 otherwise), and β_0, β_1, β_2, β_3, β_4, β_5 the corresponding weights of the regression to be estimated. Additionally, independence χ^2 test [17] is performed for analyzing the relation between the number of failed approach directions $N_{\theta F_i}$ and the harvesting scenario H_{c_i}.

3   Results

To determine the value of an optimal harvesting approach direction, a total of 180 fruit harvesting attempts were performed on 6 scenes with 5 artificial peppers each, in a set up according to Table 1, with different harvesting scenarios (full a-priori, center first search pattern, and side first search pattern) using two different robot velocities (50% and 100% of maximum). The total average harvest time $\overline{Th}$ for all combinations was 8.56 s (SD = 3.88). The distribution among the three harvesting scenarios is presented in Fig. 6. The results show roughly 40–45% increase in average harvest time when no a-priori information of the correct harvesting direction is available.

Homogeneous subsets Tukey-HSD test show a significant (p-value = 0.011) differences between *LTh* (Eq. 1) calculated from the full a-priori and the center first search pattern harvesting scenarios. The difference between *LTh* for full a-priori and side first search pattern harvesting scenarios was also significant (p-value = 0.006). The

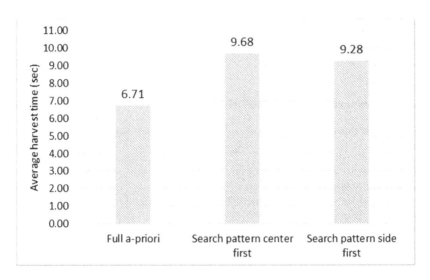

Fig. 6. Average harvesting time as function of the harvesting scenario

differences between *LTh* for the two search patterns were found to be statistically insignificant (p-value = 0.98).

Results of the logarithmic transformed *ln(Th)* regression model (Eq. 2) revealed significance for front occlusion (p-value < 0.001) and harvesting scenario (p-value = 0.02). The number of occluding leaves was not found significant (p-value = 0.774) on its own but was borderline significant in an interaction with the harvesting scenario (p-value = 0.098). A profile plot describing the interaction is presented in Fig. 7. It shows that both search patterns have shorter harvesting times for less occluded scenes. It seems that in the full a-priori information scenario it takes slightly less time to harvest in more complicated scenes with higher occlusion then for simpler scenes. However, this difference was found statistically insignificant (p-value = 0.16). The difference between the two robot velocities (50% or 100% of maximum) was found to be insignificant (p-value = 0.155). This can be explained by the visual servoing technique that limits step sizes between images causing the robot not to obtain the maximum speed during this phase. This is needed to provide sufficient time to process image data during visual servoing.

From the total of 180 harvesting attempts performed, all 60 approaches (100%) performed with full a-priori information were successful on the first attempt with an average harvesting time of 6.71 s (SD = 3.05). Out of the 120 cycles performed using a search pattern, 76 (63%) were successful on the first attempt with average harvesting time of 6.62 s (SD = 2.78). 30 cycles (25%) were successful on the second attempt with average time of 11.16 s (SD = 5.4) and the remaining 14 cycles (12%) were successful only on the third attempt with average time of 21.34 s (SD = 6.9). The number of highly occluded peppers and partially occluded peppers were roughly the same (46% and 54% respectively). While the average harvesting time increased as a nearly linear function of the number of attempts, the standard deviation also increased for more complex cases requiring more attempts until harvesting. The analysis of the

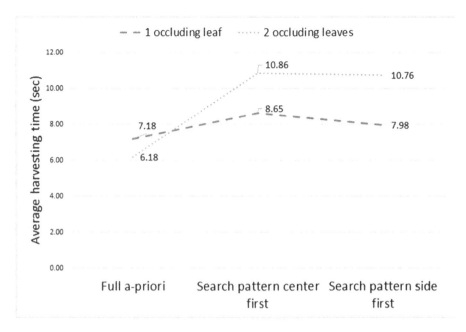

Fig. 7. Profiles plots for occlusion level and search method

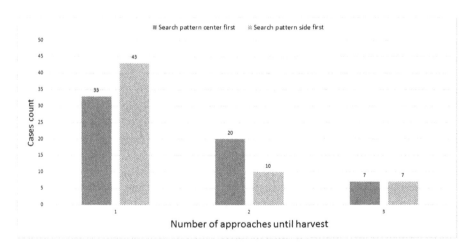

Fig. 8. Number of approaches until successful harvest as function of the search pattern method

number of approaches performed until successful harvest as function of search pattern method is presented in Fig. 8. It can be seen that about 30% more fruits were harvested at the first attempt using the side first search pattern than the center first pattern. An independence χ^2 test showed border line significant dependences between the search methods and the number of attempts (p-value 0.0978).

4   Conclusions

Results show significant increase in harvesting times for a search pattern compared to ideal initial information about the harvesting direction. The harvesting time grows near linearly with the number of approaches required until successful harvest. Furthermore, the variability of the harvesting time grows with the number of approaches required, causing lower ability to predict harvesting times. Therefore, it is clear that ideal information about the best harvesting approach direction is valuable for increasing the performance of a robot harvesting system.

The harvesting time does not significantly differ for the two different harvesting direction search patterns. This should be validated on a greater variation of search patterns and in greenhouse conditions where the occlusion is less likely to appear in a random manner as designed in the given experiment. To see how this depends on the kind of robot used, validating the results using a robot with different kinematic setup would also be beneficial. It has been shown that if there is an occlusion of the front of a fruit the harvesting times significantly increase compared to fruits that can be harvested from front, regardless of search method. The major reason for this is the limited workspace of the robot; the distance to the fruits is around 35–40 cm, with leaves often being even closer, and the gripper mounted on the end of the robot is 24 cm long. This makes it difficult to reach positions to the side of the peppers and the paths often become quite long due to the limited space and the joint limitations of the robot. Pruning techniques used for crops optimization might take this into consideration to facilitate robotic harvesting.

30% more fruits were harvested at the first attempt when using the side first search pattern than when using the center first pattern. Equal number of scene configurations had fruits blocked by leaves from left and center, therefore the number of approaches would have been expected to be equal for both search patterns. A probable explanation is that some fruits were detected during visual servoing even though they were (partly) blocked by leaves and therefore should not have been possible to harvest. This occurred in 26% of all attempts of harvest from the left and in 13% of all attempts from the front. However, this most likely did not affect the reported recall and precision since they are calculated in comparison to actual harvest approach success rates, i.e. that the robot actually reached the fruit.

The results of this research have shown significant factors affecting harvesting times and success rates in laboratorial conditions. Suggested validation of the results is to perform experiments in greenhouse conditions, which must be done during the growing season when ripe fruits are available.

Acknowledgments. This research was partially supported by the European Commission (SWEEPER GA no. 66313), by the Helmsley Charitable Trust through the Agricultural, Biological and Cognitive Robotics Center, and by the Rabbi W. Gunther Plaut Chair in Manufacturing Engineering, both at Ben-Gurion University of the Negev. The authors would like to acknowledge Peter Hohnloser at Computing Science department, Umeå University for his significant support and implementation of parts of the software system used in this research.

References

1. Comba, L., Gay, P., Piccarolo, P., Ricauda Aimonino, D.: Robotics and automation for crop management: trends and perspective. In: International Conference Ragusa SHWA 2010, pp. 471–478 (2010)
2. Bac, C.W.: Improving obstacle awareness for robotic harvesting of sweet-pepper (2015)
3. Bac, C.W., Henten, E.J., Hemming, J., Edan, Y.: Harvesting robots for high-value crops: state-of-the-art review and challenges ahead. J. F. Robot. **31**, 888–911 (2014)
4. Edan, Y., Flash, T., Peiper, U.M., Shmulevich, I., Sarig, Y.: Near-minimum-time task planning for fruit-picking robots. IEEE Trans. Robot. Autom. **7**, 48–56 (1991)
5. Harel, B., Kurtser, P., Van Herck, L., Parmet, Y., Edan, Y.: Sweet pepper maturity evaluation via multiple viewpoints color analyses. In: CIGR-AgEng Conference (2016)
6. Hemming, J., Ruizendaal, J., Hofstee, J.W., van Henten, E.J.: Fruit detectability analysis for different camera positions in sweet-pepper. Sensors **14**, 6032–6044 (2014)
7. Gongal, A., Amatya, S., Karkee, M., Zhang, Q., Lewis, K.: Sensors and systems for fruit detection and localization: a review. Comput. Electron. Agric. **116**, 8–19 (2015)
8. Vitzrabin, E., Edan, Y.: Adaptive thresholding with fusion using a RGBD sensor for red sweet-pepper detection. Biosyst. Eng. **146**, 45–56 (2016)
9. Rosenbaum, D.A., Cohen, R.G., Meulenbroek, R.G.J., Vaughan, J.: Plans for grasping objects. In: Motor Control and Learning, pp. 9–25. Kluwer Academic Publishers, Boston (2006)
10. Eizicovits, D., Berman, S.: Efficient sensory-grounded grasp pose quality mapping for gripper design and online grasp planning. Rob. Auton. Syst. **62**, 1208–1219 (2014). doi:10.1016/j.robot.2014.03.011
11. Eizicovits, D., van Tuijl, B., Berman, S., Edan, Y.: Integration of perception capabilities in gripper design using graspability maps. Biosyst. Eng. **146**, 98–113 (2016). doi:10.1016/j.biosystemseng.2015.12.016
12. Kapach, K., Barnea, E., Mairon, R., Edan, Y., Ben-Shahar, O.: Computer vision for fruit harvesting robots–state of the art and challenges ahead. Int. J. Comput. Vis. Robot. **3**, 4–34 (2012)
13. Barth, R., Hemming, J., van Henten, E.J.: Design of an eye-in-hand sensing and servo control framework for harvesting robotics in dense vegetation. Biosyst. Eng. **146**, 71–84 (2016). doi:10.1016/j.biosystemseng.2015.12.001
14. Hellström, T., Ringdahl, O.: A software framework for agricultural and forestry robots. Ind. Robot. Int. J. **40**, 20–26 (2013). doi:10.1108/01439911311294228
15. Ringdahl, O., Kurtser, P., Barth, R., Edan, Y.: Operational flow of an autonomous sweet pepper harvesting robot. In: The 5th Israeli Conference on Robotics 2016, Air Force Conference Center Hertzilya, Israel, 13–14 April 2016
16. Benoit, K.: Linear regression models with logarithmic transformations. London School of Economics, London (2011)
17. Greenwood, P.E., Nikulin, M.S.: A Guide to Chi-Squared Testing. John Wiley & Sons, New York (1996)

Algorithmic Approach to Planar Void Detection and Validation in Point Clouds

Thomas Wright[(✉)] and Barry Lennox

School of Electrical and Electronic Engineering, University of Manchester,
Sackville Street Building, Sackville Street, Manchester M1 3BB, England
thomas.wright-6@postgrad.manchester.ac.uk

Abstract. When using exploratory robotics for nuclear decommissioning, the generation of accurate and complete maps of the environment is critical. One format these maps can take is point clouds. However, when generating point clouds it is likely that voids, resulting from shadows created by features within the environment for example, will exist within them. Previous research studies have developed techniques which enable such voids to be interpolated. Unfortunately, for hazardous environments, this interpolation can be detrimental and have severe safety implications. This paper proposes a new algorithmic method for simplifying the detection of voids in point clouds. Once detected, the voids are validated, to make sure they exist within the scan-able part of the environment and if they do then they are marked for further investigation by the robot. This enables a more complete point cloud to be generated. To demonstrate the capabilities of the method, it was initially applied to a set of simplified scenes, where it was able to detect all the voids that were present, whilst also being compared to another algorithm. Following this the method was applied to a more realistic scenario. In this example, many, but not all of the voids were correctly identified. A discussion follows explaining why some voids were not detected and how future research aims to address this.

Keywords: Field robotics · Point clouds · Hazardous environments · Safety verification and validation · Mapping

1 Introduction

In many exploratory robotics projects, knowledge of the environment is key. This knowledge is usually in the form of a map or a representation of the environment, which can be used by the robot or user for navigation or assessment of the robot's environment. It is not always possible to investigate all areas of an environment due to constraints such as single passes through the environment or areas being obstructed. This leads to data being absent from the data set when reconstructed. Due to this, research has been undertaken into filling these voids by post-processing the point cloud (PC) to locate the voids and then using interpolation algorithms to fill them in. Approaches include:

© Springer International Publishing AG 2017
Y. Gao et al. (Eds.): TAROS 2017, LNAI 10454, pp. 526–539, 2017.
DOI: 10.1007/978-3-319-64107-2_42

1. Statistical estimation of the missing surface [1–3]. These algorithms use fitness functions such as least squares to identify a model that fills the void in the surface, such that it fits the existing points. [1] used a Kernel Conditional Density Estimation in conjunction with Total Variation estimators to influence a Gaussian-based likelihood estimator. This produces more realistic surfaces by taking into account local structures and neighbouring surfaces.
2. Volumetric diffusion of the known geometries within the PC [4]. The known data from the scanned scene is generated into surfaces. Where voids exist, the surrounding surfaces are expanded in all directions until two expanded surfaces intersect. A best fit model is then fitted to the points from the edges of each un-diffused surface and the point of intersection to fill the void.
3. Model fitting of common or known items to the PCs [5,6]. [5] uses predefined CAD models of items known to be in the environment to complete incomplete scans, fitting the models to the environments using a RANdom SAmple Consensus (RANSAC) algorithm to find any areas where the scan is found to fit well to the known model, filling in the missing data, with that from the CAD model. [6] uses generic models to complete PCs, using relationships in geometry of the generic model to interpolate the missing data in the subject PC.

The above algorithms result in voids being closed, at the cost of accuracy and without identification of void location. This is acceptable for many situation, however, in the nuclear sector completeness is vital. It would be unacceptable from a health and safety standpoint to interpolate large areas of missing data, potentially leading to objects within the environment going undetected. Some of the research currently undertaken into the area of void detection and PC processing requires evenly sampled dense PCs, such as [7] which uses a set of mathematical criteria to determine if a point is a boundary point of a void. This requires a consistent sampling of the scene to allow for changes in PC density to be detected. Robots in the nuclear sector are often non-recoverable leading to the use of low cost LiDAR scanners, with the robots potentially needing to operate in unlit environments making colour aided algorithms unusable. Furthermore, as a robot moves around the floor of an environment it is likely that more samples will exist close to the robot and hence the PC will not be evenly sampled. Due to these constraints the work presented in this paper has been designed to work with unevenly sampled PCs absent of colour data. The algorithm has been developed with low power online processing in mind for in-situ evaluation of the PC. Originally intended for exploratory robotics in nuclear environments, this algorithm could be applied to any environment where the failure to detect and locate voids may cause problems.

The algorithm presented has been inspired by the work presented in [8,9], where algorithms have been designed to reconstruct PCs using simple geometric models, planes in [8] and planes, spheres, cylinders and cones in [9]. These algorithms generate simplified versions of the environment, making them easier to process for tasks such as navigation. The approach is extended in this work by using these models to find voids within the simplified environments and validate any such void by assessing the surrounding geometries. This new approach allows voids to be found in the environment and determine whether it exists within the scan-able environment, requiring further investigated. An overview of the proposed algorithms steps are shown in Fig. 1 with explaination throughout the paper.

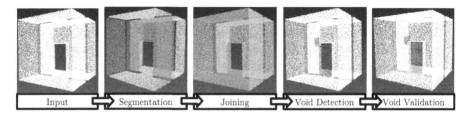

Fig. 1. Steps of the proposed algorithm when applied to a PC of a doorway (NB: regions with fewer than 5 points were omitted from the Segmentation PC)

1.1 Segmentation

The algorithm works by taking a PC of the environment in Cartesian form, passing it through a voxel filter to downsample the cloud and reduce the number of points [10]. The voxel filter used is from the point cloud library [11], which splits the PC (C) up into a number of user defined cubes, calculating the centroid (P) of the points within each cube, using these centroids as the downsampled PC.

The normal of each downsampled point is then calculated, based on a plane created by the point of interest and the closest surrounding points. A region growing algorithm is then used to find all of the surfaces within the PC (Function Region Growing). Region growing algorithms break up a PC (P) into a set of surfaces, by looking at the relationship each point has with its neighbours. For points to be deemed of the same region they must meet two criteria. They must be within a user defined distance D_{lim} of each other and the normals (N) calculated for each point must have an angle below a user specified limit θ_{lim} [12–14]. A point within the PC is selected and assigned to a region R. The algorithm then checks for any points which lie within a user defined radius D_{lim} of the point. Of those points, the angle θ_k between the normals are calculated. The angle is compared to a user defined maximum angle θ_{lim} which, if it is below, the point is added to the current region R_i. Once all possible points have been added to the region based on the current point, it is marked as checked. The process is repeated for all of the points assigned to the current region until all points are marked as checked and no more points can be added. The region number i is incremented and a new unassigned point is selected. This process continues until all points have been assigned to a region.

The impact of noise in the measurements can cause larger than expected differences in the angles between neighbouring normals, leading to more regions being created than would be expected when analysing the PC by eye. To deal with this, a region joining algorithm is used, which uses the normals of the entire region, reducing the impact of noise.

A RANSAC algorithm is used on each region R to find the equation of the plane M which best fits the points in the region. The process starts by randomly selecting a subset of the data points and producing a model which best fits the subset. All points are then tested against the model. If a point fits well, i.e. is within a user defined distance to the model it is made an inlier. The model is then deemed good or bad based on the number of inliers. The model is then re-estimated using all inliers, with the fitness of the estimation then being calculated based on the error between all of the inliers and the model. This process is then repeated using different randomly selected sets of data, a user defined number of times, comparing the fitness of each model to the previous best model, retaining the best fitting model. RANSAC requires a suitable model to be used for the data set, with unsuitable models returning ill fitting results. The normals of the plane models M generated by the RANSAC algorithm are then calculated ∇M. All combinations of pairs of planes are then processed to find the minimum distance D_{min} between two points; one from each region R_a and R_b and the angle θ between the two planes. If the angle θ and D_{min} between the two planes is found to be smaller than the user defined limits θ_{lim} and D_{lim}, a check is made to determine whether the planes are offset along the normal and overlapping $\pm$ a user defined margin of error e. This is done by first checking the angles between the planes, looking for very small angles, before rotating both PCs so that one sits on the plane $z = 0$. From this configurating a check on the average value of Z for each cloud, to find the average offset and whether if the concave hulls of the PCs XY coordinates intersect in made. If two planes are found in this configuration a smaller distance criteria is used to avoid joining two planes which should not be joined. Planes which meet these criteria are then combined into a new region and placed in R. This replacement allows for more than two regions sharing a plane to be combined. The first two planes found will be combined when being processed, with the resulting plane then being combined with the additional planes in subsiquent loops. D_{lim} is set to be larger than in the region growing algorithm but the angle criteria θ_{lim} remains unchanged. This allows for the joining of two partial planes which could be separated, due to the joining data being missing as a result of obstructions when scanned e.g. a pillar in the foreground blocks a section of the scene, which could cause the floor to be seen as two regions, one either side of the pillar. Due to the global nature of the normals being calculated from all of the points in a region, these checks allow for regions close together which share a common plane to be combined, which may have previously not been combined due to noise or missing data.

The final stage of segmentation is to find points in small regions R_s which are near points within a larger region R_l and fit the plane model that the larger region forms M_l, appending points from the small regions to the larger region if this criteria is met. If a point is found to fit models of multiple regions, then the closest region is retained for appending R_p (Function Append Small Clouds).

Algorithm 1. An algorithm for joining detected regions, which share common planes into a single region

1: **function** PSEUDO: JOIN REGIONS$(R, D_{lim}, \theta_{lim}, e)$
2:    **for** $a = 0; a < \text{size}(R); a + +$ **do**
3:       $M_1 = \text{GenBestModelUsingRANSAC}(R_a)$ ▷ Returned in form
         $Ax + By + Cz + D = 0$
4:       **for** $b = 0; b < \text{size}(R); b + +$ **do**
5:          **if** $a \neq b$ **then**   ▷ R_a can't be the same as R_b
6:             $M_2 = \text{GenBestModelUsingRANSAC}(R_b)$
7:             $\theta = \arccos(\frac{\nabla M_1 \cdot \nabla M_2}{\|\nabla M_1\| \|\nabla M_2\|})$
8:             **if** planes are offset along the normal and overlapping **then** Reduce
                D_{lim}
9:             **if** $\theta <= \theta_{lim}$ **then**
10:                **for** $c = 0; c < size(R_a); c + +$ **do**
11:                   **for** $d = 0; d < size(R_b); d + +$ **do**
12:                      $D_{min} = \|R_a[c] - R_b[d]\|$ ▷ Find the minimum distance
                         between the two regions
13:                      **if** $D_{min} < D_{lim}$ **then**
14:                         $R_j \leftarrow \text{JoinRegions}(R_a, R_b)$
15:                         Remove R_a and R_b from R and append R_j ▷
                            Replace the two original regions with the joined
                            region in the array of regions R
16:                         BREAK

Algorithm 2. An algorithm for reassigning points of rapidly changing normals to larger existing planar models

1: **function** PSEUDO: APPEND SMALL CLOUDS(R_j, D_{lim})
2:    $R_l \subset R_j$ ▷ R is split into large regions
3:    $R_s \subset R_j$ ▷ & small regions based on number of points
4:    $M_l = \text{GenBestModelUsingRANSAC}(R_l)$ ▷ Returned in form
      $Ax + By + Cz + D = 0$
5:    **for** all p in R_s **do**   ▷ p are the points in the form $[x_p, y_p, z_p]$
6:       $D_p = \infty$
7:       $A_t = N/A$
8:       **for** all M in M_l **do**   ▷ Compare to all models
9:          $D_q = \frac{Ax_p + By_p + Cz_p + D}{\sqrt{A^2 + B^2 + C^2}}$ ▷ Distance between the plane model and each
            point
10:         **if** $D_q < D_{lim}$ **then**
11:            $D_r = \min \|(p - R_l)\|$ Find the smallest distance between the region
               R_l and point p
12:            **if** $((D_r < D_p) \& (D_r < D_{lim}))$ **then** ▷ If the region is the closest to
               point p and within an acceptable distance.
13:               $D_p = D_r$ ▷ Retain the minimum distance
14:               $A_t = M$ ▷ Retain the best fitting model
15:      **if** $A_t \neq N/A$ **then**
16:         Append p to R_l which plane model M

This allows neighbouring points to be joined to the same region, even if the difference in their normals is large. This is often the case in areas of high noise or the crease between two adjoining surfaces, due the large change in the normals of point. This causes the points along the crease to be assigned to neither of the adjoining surfaces of the regions, but rather form their own region. The effects of Algorithms 1 and 2 can be seen in the differences between the input, segmentation and joining PCs in Fig. 1 respectively with more outputs presented in Sect. 3. Note that between the Segmentation PC and Joining PC, the nearest walls have been combined into a single plane and the small clouds which exist along the creases, have been combined into the larger wall/floor planes. By doing this regions can be made to extend all the way into the crease removing any small regions formed along it.

1.2   Void Detection

RANSAC is then used to find the equations of the remaining planes M (Fig. 2a). A grid of test points can then be generated which lie on the plane of these equations. The grid spacing should be related to the minimum spacing between points required not to be a void, which is a user defined variable. It is suggested that this variable in an ideal world, would be half the minimum point spacing to be a void. This would mean if a point cloud existed with a point spacing of this minimum size, then no voids would be detected.

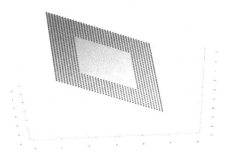

(a) Simple PC of a hole in a plane (blue markers) and the plane of best fit (green surface) from which the normals are calculated

(b) Void detection algorithm generating cylinders around the plane normal at each test point. Green cylinders contain points and red contain no points

Fig. 2. Basic void detection algorithm (Color figure online)

Cylinders are then generated around each of the test points T_p along the normal N to the plane model M, and the points of the region R are then tested to see if any point p lies within the volume of the cylinder. Ideally a cuboid would be used, as this is a grid based algorithm, however a cylinder is used as it is mathematically easier to define. Points are tested for their distance D_p to the centre line of the cylinder and that they exist within the planes which form the end caps (Appendix i). The length of the cylinder L_{cyl} is user defined and the radius of the cylinder r_{cyl} is based on the spacing of the test grid, with the radius being half of the diagonal distance between points. This radius means that all of the space in the test area is checked, with some redundant overlap. If the cylinders are found not to contain any test region points R, then the test point is marked as a potential void and added to the void marker list V (Fig. 2b).

After void detection is complete, a check can be made against each of the sets of void markers to find how many void markers are assigned to each void V. This allows the user to define a minimum number of grouped void markers required to be a void. Users could then decide if only a single void marker exists, its value could be interpolated, whereas a larger group would need investigating.

2   Void Validation

Once all of the potential voids V have been detected, each void is checked to ensure that it is valid. A further algorithm is then used to determine whether the void exists inside of a known object, or has the characteristics of existing outside of the scan-able environment (Appendix ii). This algorithm works by finding the point of intersect P_i between the models M_v of region in which the void exists R_v and all other pairs of region models M_a and M_b, highlighted as yellow dots in Fig. 3c. Checks are then made to find the points of intersect near to the void markers and if the void markers need splitting up, shown by the different coloured void markers in Fig. 3c. The void markers are split if it is found that any of the planes used to find the points of intersect bisect the markers, with the markers on each side of the plane forming a new void to be reprocessed through the void validation algorithm.

If the void is not split a check is made as to whether it is possible for all of the void markers to be encapsulated within the intersect points, Fig. 3d. If any markers are not encapsulated, it would suggest that some information is missing and the void is valid. If all void markers are contained within the points of intersection, then the perimeter points of the void markers are determined using the concave hull. The distance H_r between each of these perimeter points h and the points of the region, within which the void markers lie p or is intersected by are then calculated. If all perimeter point falls within two minimum void radii $2H_{min}$ of any of the region points p, then the void is deemed invalid, as it is likely that it is completely contained with other known features, shown by the green markers in Fig. 3d. Any points H_{remain} which are not within this distance are then checked to see if they exist outside of the scan. In this scenario it is likely that the void would not be singular, which can be exploited to check if the void is contained within a combination of known planes and planes formed by other voids. A search for other nearby sets of void markers V can then be made, calculating the shortest distance D_h between the two sets of void markers; one being the markers currently being processed H and the other being other known voids for the scan. As void markers do not extend all the way to the edge of the expected void a larger acceptable distance was used of four times the minimum void size H_{min}, which if D_h is less than, the markers are deemed close. If another set of void markers is found to be close, the model of the plane M_u of the markers is calculated and the distances between each of the leftover points H_{remain} and plane are compared to the value of two void radii. This can be seen in Fig. 3e, with the void points of intersect and lines of intersect being shown in yellow. Here it can be seen that the void in the floor of the cube is bounded by the two front faces of the cube and the two voids of the unscanned back faces. If all leftover points fall within this distance to the plane it is likely that these points exist outside of the scan and can be removed. If any point is found to be too far away then the void is deemed valid. This process is repeated until all of the regions have been processed, leaving only the valid voids Fig. 3f.

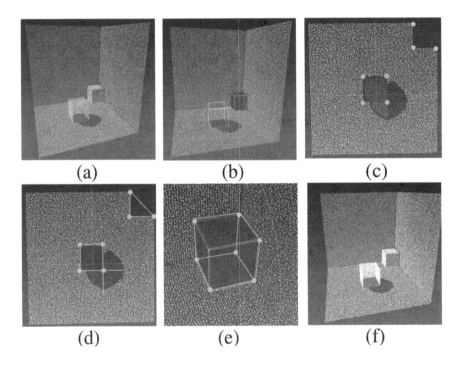

(a)   (b)   (c)

(d)   (e)   (f)

Fig. 3. Various stages of the validation process

An optional step is to join voids that are located close together, which were split during the validation process. Voids which are deemed valid are compared to the convex hull of the region they exist in, with only points existing inside the convex hull being displayed. This means that voids that extend beyond the scanned area will not be detected.

3   Results

A sample of outputs of the algorithms are shown in Figs. 4, 5, 6, 7 and 8, with sub-figure (a) of each figure showing the segmented point cloud, with each region in a different colour. The implemented segmentation algorithm allows for splitting of the surfaces as would be expected by eye, with surfaces running all the way into the crease between planes. Sub-figure (b) of each figure shows the output of the void detection and validation with coloured points being added to the point clouds. Red points show voids which have been found and determined to be valid, whereas green points have been determined to exist inside complete objects within the scan, or outside of the scanned area. The yellow points in the (b) sub-figures show the output from the algorithm described in [7], using equal weighting for the combination criteria. In each sub-figure (b) the sides of the boxes have been removed, to allow for ease of viewing of the voids detected. Figures 4, 5, 6, 7 and 8 show the algorithm applied to several different scenarios.

Figure 4 shows the output of a box on a plane, with data removed from the plane. When applied to this scenario the algorithm is able to successfully find the void, split the void up based on the nearby planes intersecting the markers and determine that the void under the box was not valid, highlighting the same area as the algorithm from [7].

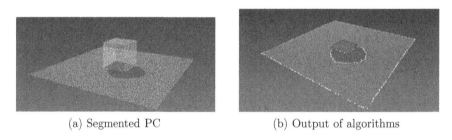

(a) Segmented PC   (b) Output of algorithms

Fig. 4. Box on a plane with missing floor data

Figure 5 shows the output when applied to a box with two of its sides removed. The algorithm is able to locate the void in the floor. This void is classified as a valid void because not all of the void markers were located inside the convex hull of the nearby points of intersect. The missing sides have not been marked as voids as the lack of data on these sides means no plane has been estimated. The yellow markers have highlighted the edges of the missing sides, highlighting the void in a different way, but also suggesting Bendel's algorithm may struggle with thin objects with little depth such as sheet metal [7].

Figure 6 shows a box which has blocked the rear side of itself and prevented part of the floor being scanned. The algorithm was able to determine that the void is valid due to it not being completely enclosed by surrounding geometries, which agrees with the algorithm from [7], highlighting the void is a different way.

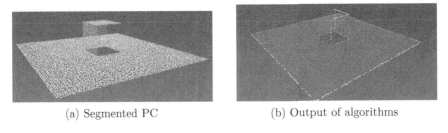

(a) Segmented PC   (b) Output of algorithms

Fig. 5. Box on a plane with two sides missing

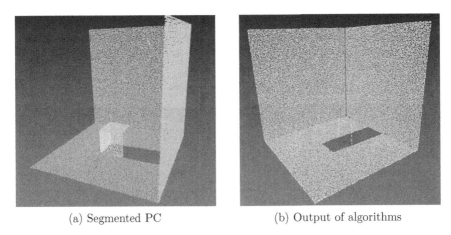

(a) Segmented PC   (b) Output of algorithms

Fig. 6. Box casting shadow onto the ground

When the back of the box is added to the data set then the void is split, with the part existing inside the box being determined as not valid.

Figures 7 and 8 show scenarios where the box has been pushed up against a surface, leading to sides of the box and parts of the walls being obscured. In these scenarios the algorithm determines that the voids are not valid due to them being outside of the scanned area which agrees with the output from the algorithm from [7]. This was deduced from all of the marks within each void being enclosed within a combination of known geometries i.e. the box sides and the planar models produced from the other voids as each void is non-singular, with each aiding to encapsulating the others.

Figure 9 shows the algorithm applied to scan of a real world scene. The algorithm has detected the large voids in the dominant planes, however some areas that would be associated as voids when inspected by eye have not been highlighted. This is due to points not contained within the convex hull of the region being removed so as not to extend outside of the scanned area. Likewise areas of no data have not been highlighted i.e. the tops of the crates. The output of the algorithm described in [7] has also been included for comparison, outlining

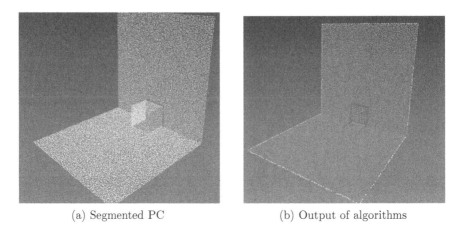

(a) Segmented PC   (b) Output of algorithms

Fig. 7. Box pushed up against a wall

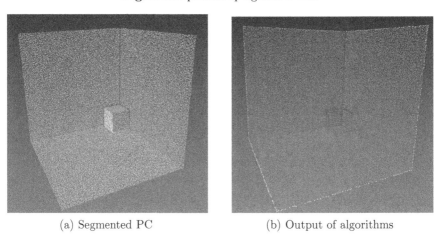

(a) Segmented PC   (b) Output of algorithms

Fig. 8. Box pushed into a corner

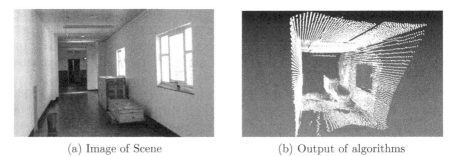

(a) Image of Scene   (b) Output of algorithms

Fig. 9. Algorithm applied to a real scene

many of the same areas, however, it should be noted that this algorithm has highlighted several points in the ceiling and walls, which are not voids, due to the algorithms susceptibility to noise.

4   Conclusion

The algorithm has been shown to successfully locate voids in point clouds of relatively simple scenarios, which were used to enable easy illustration of its capabilities. The algorithm has been applied to many real world scenes and compared to another algorithm, with results from one of these applications presented in this paper. This application has shown that although many of the voids within the scene were correctly identified, because only planar models were used, not all the voids could be faithfully reproduced, however it is less affected by noise than its comparator. Future work is focused on refining the techniques to ensure they are able to accurately detect more voids in realistic scenes and on optimising the algorithms so that all the processing can take place on a robot with limited computational power.

A   Appendices

Algorithm 3. An algorithm for finding planar voids in segmented regions

---

1: **function** APPENDIX I: PSEUDO CODE VOID DETECTION(R, L_{cyl}, r_{cyl})

2:     $M =$ GenBestModelUsingRANSAC(R)

3:     $\hat{N} = \nabla \hat{M}$ ▷ Calculate unit vector normals

4:     **for** Each Test Point T_p **do**   ▷ Each point on the test grid

5:         VoidTest $= 1$

6:         **for** All p in R **do**   ▷ Points in region point cloud

7:             $D_{cyl} = L_{cyl}\hat{N}$ ▷ Generate centre point of end cap

8:             $D_p = p - T_p$ ▷ Translate so T_p is at [0,0,0]

9:             $L_p = D_p \cdot D_{cyl}$ ▷ Calculate the component magnitude of vector
                between [0,0,0] and p along $\hat{N}$

10:            **if** $|L_p| < L_{cyl}$ **then**   ▷ If the magnitude is $>$ than the cylinder length
                it exists outside of the cylinder.

11:                $r = \frac{\|D_p \times (D_p - D_{cyl})\|}{\|D_{cyl}\|}$ ▷ Calculate point to centre line distance

12:                **if** $r < r_{cyl}$ **then** ▷ If this distance is smaller than the user defined
                    r_{cyl} it exists inside the cylinder

13:                    VoidTest $= 0$

14:        **if** VoidTest $= 1$ **then**

15:            $V \leftarrow T_p$ ▷ If no points were found inside the cylinder add the test
                point to the void list

Algorithm 4. An algorithm for validating if a void is valid and scan-able

---

1: **function** APPENDIX II: PSEUDO CODE VOID VALIDATION(R, V, H_{min})
2:    M =GenBestModelUsingRANSAC(R)
3:    **for** Each M_v **do**   ▷ M_v is the model of the region the current void H was found in
4:       $H = \subset V$ ▷ H is the currently being processed void subset
5:       **for** $a = 0; a < \text{size}(M); a + +$ **do**
6:          **for** $b = 0; b < \text{size}(M); b + +$ **do**
7:             **if** $(a \neq b)\&(M_v \neq M_a)\&(M_v \neq M_b)$ **then**   ▷ Make sure all of the planes are different
8:                $P_i \leftarrow$ FindPointOfInterSection(M_v, M_a, M_b)
9:    **if** size($P_i < 3$) **then** return True   ▷ 3 is the min number of points to form a hull
10:   **for** each p in P_i **do**   ▷ For each point of intersection
11:      $D_{min} = \|(H - p)\|$ ▷ Find distance between void markers and points of intersect
12:      **if** $D_{min} > 2 * H_{min}$ **then**
13:         Remove p from P_i ▷ Remove those deemed too far away
14:   **if** size($P_i < 3$) **then** return True
15:   S =SplitVoidCheck(H)   ▷ Check if any planes bisect the void markers
16:   **if** The void markers have been split **then** return Split ▷ Return and reprocess as two separate sets of markers
17:   C_p =GenConvexHull(P_i)   ▷ Check for encapsulation
18:   **if** Not all markers in H are contained within C_p **then** return True   ▷ Void valid if any points exist outside of the hull
19:   C_H =GenConcaveHull(H)
20:   **for** all h in current C_H **do**
21:      $H_{near} = 0$
22:      **for** all p in R which H belong to **do**   ▷ Points in the region the void was found in
23:         $H_r = \min \|(h - p)\|$ ▷ Calc distance between markers and region points
24:         **if** $H_r < 2H_{min}$ **then**   ▷ Check if it is within the defined distance
25:            $H_{near} = 1$
26:      **if** $H_{near} == 0$ **then**
27:         $H_{remain} \leftarrow h$ ▷ H_{remain} receives any markers not near a region point
28:   **if** size($H_{remain} == 0$ **then** return False   ▷ Void is invalid if all markers are near a region point
29:   **for** all h in H_{remain} **do**
30:      **for** all p in other V **do**
31:         $H_r = \min \|(h - p)\|$ ▷ Calculate min distance between the marker sets
32:         **if** $H_r < 4H_{min}$ **then**   ▷ Determine if the other void is nearby
33:            M_u =GenBestModelUsingRANSAC(H_{other})   ▷ Returned in form $Ax + By + Cz + D = 0$
34:            $D_h = \frac{Ax_h + By_h + Cz_h + D}{\sqrt{A^2 + B^2 + C^2}}$ ▷ Generate nearby planes model and check void markers distance to it
35:            **if** D_h for all V is $> 2H_{min}$ **then** return True ▷ If any point is not found close to any plane the void is valid
36:   return False   ▷ If all points are found close to a plane the void is invalid

---

References

1. Tanner, M., Pini, P., Mar, L., Newman, P., et al.: What lies behind: Recovering hidden shape in dense mapping. In: 2016 IEEE International Conference on Robotics and Automation (ICRA). IEEE, pp. 979–986 (2016)
2. Baker, T.J.: Interpolation from a cloud of points. In: IMR, pp. 55–63 (2003)
3. Wang, J., Oliveira, M.M.: A hole-filling strategy for reconstruction of smooth surfaces in range images. In: XVI Brazilian Symposium on Computer Graphics and Image Processing, SIBGRAPI 2003, pp. 11–18. IEEE (2003)
4. Davis, J., Marschner, S.R., Garr, M., Levoy, M.: Filling holes in complex surfaces using volumetric diffusion. In: Proceedings of First International Symposium on 3D Data Processing Visualization and Transmission, pp. 428–441. IEEE (2002)
5. Bey, A., Chaine, R., Marc, R., Thibault, G., Akkouche, S.: Reconstruction of consistent 3D CAD models from point cloud data using a priori CAD models. In: ISPRS Workshop on Laser Scanning, vol. 1 (2011)
6. Pauly, M., Mitra, N.J., Giesen, J., Gross, M.H., Guibas, L.J.: Example-based 3D scan completion. In: Symposium on Geometry Processing, No. EPFL-CONF-149337, pp. 23–32 (2005)
7. Bendels, G.H., Schnabel, R., Klein, R.: Detecting holes in point set surfaces (2006)
8. Sanchez, V., Zakhor, A.: Planar 3D modeling of building interiors from point cloud data. In: 2012 19th IEEE International Conference on Image Processing, pp. 1777–1780. IEEE (2012)
9. Schnabel, R., Wahl, R., Klein, R.: Efficient RANSAC for point-cloud shape detection. Comput. Graph. Forum **26**(2), 214–226 (2007). Wiley Online Library
10. He, T., Hong, L., Kaufman, A., Varshney, A., Wang, S.: Voxel based object simplification. In: Proceedings of the 6th Conference on Visualization 1995, ser. VIS 1995, Washington, DC, USA, pp. 296–303. IEEE Computer Society (1995). http://dl.acm.org/citation.cfm?id=832271.833850
11. Rusu, R.B., Cousins, S.: 3D is here: Point Cloud Library (PCL). In: 2011 IEEE International Conference on Robotics and Automation (ICRA), pp. 1–4. IEEE (2011)
12. Holz, D., Behnke, S.: Fast range image segmentation and smoothing using approximate surface reconstruction and region growing. In: Lee, S., Cho, H., Yoon, K.J., Lee, J. (eds.) Intelligent Autonomous Systems 12, pp. 61–73. Springer, Heidelberg (2013)
13. Woo, H., Kang, E., Wang, S., Lee, K.H.: A new segmentation method for point cloud data. Int. J. Mach. Tools Manufact. **42**(2), 167–178 (2002)
14. Hoffman, R., Jain, A.K.: Segmentation and classification of range images. IEEE Trans. Pattern Anal. Mach. Intell. **5**, 608–620 (1987)

Elastomeric Spring Actuator Using Nylon Wires

Emily Ingham[1], Shuhei Miyashita[2], and Dana Damian[3(✉)]

[1] Department of Bioengineering, University of Sheffield, Sheffield, England
[2] Department of Electronics, University of York, York, England
[3] Department of Automatic Control and Systems Engineering,
University of Sheffield, Sheffield, England
d.damian@sheffield.ac.uk

Abstract. Medical devices are designed for collaboration with the human body, which makes the steps to create them increasingly more complex if the device is to be implanted. Soft robots have the unique potential of meeting both the mechanical compliance with the interacting tissues and the controlled functionality needed for a repair or replacement. Soft devices that fulfill fundamental mechanical roles are needed as parts of soft robots in order to carry out desired tasks. As the medical devices become increasingly low-profile, soft devices must feature multi-functionality that is embedded in the structure. A device embedded with nylon actuators allows for the controlled collapsing of an elastomeric spring by compression alone or compression and twisting. In this paper we present the concept of a novel elastomeric spring, its fabrication and mechanical characterization.

1 Introduction

Soft devices that fulfill fundamental mechanical roles are becoming increasingly important in the design of soft robots. Especially for low-profile soft robots, it is important that their complex behavior is embedded in the design of the composite material thus reducing the integrated components and the complexity in control [1]. Applications of these low-profile soft robots can be found in human-machine interaction, and mostly in surgery and tissue engineering.

For example, there is a need of devices that approximate tissues together in the treatment of long-gap oesophageal atresia (LGOA). This is a congenital dysfunction affecting about 2000 babies in US and UK every year, in which babies are born with an incomplete oesophagus that is reconstructed by pulling together the two oesophageal stubs [2]. Also in tissue engineering, scaffolds may be proffered to exhibit mechanical capabilities that may lead to a better cell orientation and more functional tissue product. For these application, we need linear actuators that are soft, compressible and potentially scalable.

In terms of soft actuators, recent research by [3–5] introduces polymer fibres as linear actuators for the possible future use as artificial muscles. This would be approached by the combination of several of the actuators which, together would increase their strength and movement capabilities. Other actuators used

© Springer International Publishing AG 2017
Y. Gao et al. (Eds.): TAROS 2017, LNAI 10454, pp. 540–547, 2017.
DOI: 10.1007/978-3-319-64107-2_43

for soft robots include shape-memory polymers powered by heat [6,7], or polymer/carbon nanotube (CNT) composite fibres [8,9]. Pneumatic and hydraulic-based soft actuators have also been employed in many applications [10–13]. Electrically driven actuators such as in [14,15] have been shown to change rigidity, however, thermally driven actuators such as [16] proved to be some of the simplest and cheapest to power.

We present a soft device that is able to contract, like the basic mechanical spring, or twist, due to the full elasticity of its underlying structure and the configuration of its embedded soft coiled actuators.

The design outlined in the paper is linearly designed to contract and then relax uniaxially. However, other forms of linear actuators such as [13,17] contract and bend as a result. Compared to the actuators aforementioned, the presented actuators are both inexpensive and low power, and can be developed to be biocompatible and easily integrated in low-profile medical devices.

Ideally, a controlled form of collapsing would allow the elastomeric spring to fold neatly and apply traction to a tissue to which is being attached, much like other deployable but stiffer actuators, as detailed in [18,19], may perform.

In the following, we present the design concept of the elastomeric spring actuator, its fabrication and analyze its electro-mechanical properties.

2   Design of Elastomeric Spring Actuator (ESA)

2.1   Materials

The elastomeric substrate was a translucent rubber (TangoPlus) that is soft with a degree of pliability. The spring structure was designed using SolidWorks with two specifications of width, as shown in Fig. 1. This was 3D printed (Objet500 Connex3 3D Printer) to produce a collapsed string design, presented in Fig. 1, that can be assembled into a functional spring. This structure was designed so that it maintained its shape when fully contracted, with no increase in width.

Properties of elastomers do not typically allow for structured folding, however, by placing linear actuators within the structure a controlled compression

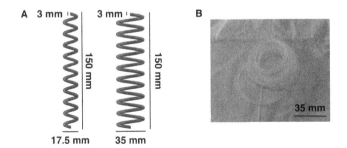

Fig. 1. (A) Design of springs with different dimensions; (B) Soft printed spring of dimensions 150 × 35 × 3 mm

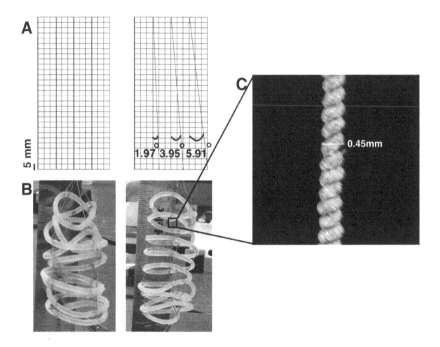

Fig. 2. (A) Parallel design vs. angled design; (B) Image of spring with parallel design vs. angled design

of the spring can be achieved. To complete the design of the collapsible spring, the spring was embedded with four nylon-coiled actuators, as shown in Fig. 2. These coiled actuators encompass nylon and silver wires that contract under the application of heat generated by electricity. The production of these actuators is outlined in [3].

2.2   Design of ESA with 17.5 mm Width

The first type of ESA weighed 4.8 g. Each coil actuator was manually sewn through the elastomeric spring, using a surgical needle that was similar to the coils diameter of 0.45 mm. The coils were sewn in a parallel configuration as depicted in Fig. 2A. Combining the coils and elastomer resulted in a smaller overall length of the elastomeric spring than that shown in Fig. 1A. At rest, the length was approximately 108 mm. Once the coils had been embedded in the elastomer, the resistance of each coil was measured. Once this had been established, the elastomeric spring actuators were placed in a circuit where a potential difference between 1 V and 12 V was applied at maximum 0.2 A and the contraction measured accordingly.

2.3   Design of ESA with 35 mm Width

The second type of ESA weighed 9.8 g. To examine the best arrangement of the coils to produce the ideal orientation for the contraction of the spring, two different designs were tested (Fig. 2). The designs in Fig. 2A show the outlines for the paths of the nylon actuators through the spring. The first one is the parallel design, characterized by coiled actuators sewn in parallel along the longitudinal axis of the spring. The second one is the angled design, in which coiled actuators were sewn at an increasing angle compared to the first actuator. The angle of the each of the paths is increasing gradually until the end the fourth path meets the end of the first. Ideally, this design should produce a rotational contraction, in addition to an axial contraction as in the case of the parallel design. Figure 2B shows the designs of the springs once completed. Figure 2C presents a detail of the coil actuator.

Both the parallel and angled designed elastomeric spring actuators were individually placed into the circuit as described in the previous section. The contractions were then visually assessed using a ruler placed behind the actuators.

3   Experimental Results

3.1   Results for Contraction of ESA with 17.5 mm Width

As the purpose of the small spring was to test the contraction, results in Fig. 3 show the style of contraction being close to linear and capable of bearing the 4.8 g weight of the spring. The largest contraction was 2.5 mm. The contraction of the actuators resulted in a minor rotational effect of around 5°, most likely attributed to human error while manually sewing the coils.

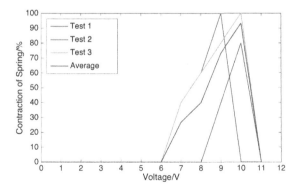

Fig. 3. Percentage contraction of the small spring

3.2   Results for Contraction of ESA with 35 mm Width

The second set of full size springs with the patterns set out in Fig. 2 were tested using the same method. Figure 4 shows the comparison between the elastomeric spring actuator with the angled design at zero contraction and at maximum contraction. The application of low current was significant enough to register a 4 mm contraction.

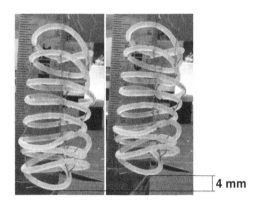

Fig. 4. No contraction vs. contraction

Before the current was applied to the elastomeric spring actuator with the parallel design, the resistances of the individual coils were measured (130, 174, 122 and 143 Ω) and used to calculate the overall resistance of the actuator (34.9 Ω). This reasonably low resistance meant the applied current could be as low as 0.2 A.

The results of the larger spring with the parallel design are shown in Fig. 5A. Upon the application of potential difference from 1 V until 8 V, the elastomeric spring actuator reached a maximum contraction of 11 mm at 8V. Two subsequent tests were undertaken after the first, however, one of the coil actuators had stopped conducting. As the graphs in Fig. 5 show, between 8 and 10 V, the elastomeric spring actuators begin to relax and revert to a state of zero contraction. We believe this is due to the inability to further conduct after the system short-circuits. A strong application of current can lead to a break in a coil actuator, resulting in an inability to contract. This occurred within the elastomeric spring actuator with the parallel design.

The elastomeric spring actuator with the angled design was subsequently tested after recording the resistances (116, 157, 141 and 198 Ω) and calculating the total resistance (36.9 Ω). This also resulted in the application of a potential difference from 1 V to 12 V and a current of around 0.2 A.

The results of the elastomeric spring actuator with the angled design are shown in Fig. 5B. The results in relation to maximum contraction are very similar to that of the parallel design and also result in breakage after 8 V. None of the

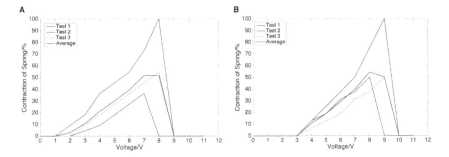

Fig. 5. (A) Results relating to the percentage contraction of the large spring with the parallel design; (B) Results relating to the percentage contraction of the large spring with the angled design

coil actuators in the angled design experienced a break to such an extent that all the nylon actuators were still fully functional after the tests had concluded.

3.3   Rotational Contraction Results for ESA

The rotation of the half-size elastomeric spring actuator with the parallel design was observed to be approximately 5°. This was a similar value to that of the elastomeric spring actuator with the angled design. The results are shown in Fig. 6. The results for the elastomeric spring actuator with the angled design were not considered as the rotation produced was influenced heavily by a loss of integrity of the elastomeric spring's structure.

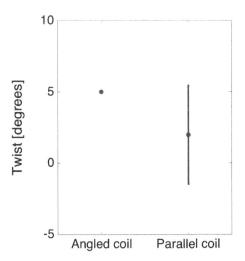

Fig. 6. Results comparing the rotational effects of the small parallel spring and the large angled spring, including possible errors

Figure 6 shows that there is a larger twist in the elastomeric spring with angled-coil design than in the one with parallel design. The latter one showed a rather large standard deviation prompting to further tests that need to be undertaken.

4 Discussion and Conclusion

Whilst the elastomeric spring actuators have sufficient strength to contract the spring of weight 9.8 g and dimensions $150 \times 35 \times 3$, their strength is currently insufficient to cause complete approximation of tissues for the treatment of LGOE. However, an improvement in the spring design, e.g., Archimedean spiral, and in the sewing pattern of the coiled actuator can be further achieved.

Future developments of this technology could include a design with more coil actuators within a thicker spring. These would overcome some of the limitations as an increased number of coils may allow for a greater or stronger contraction and the nylon coils would be less damaged as a thicker needle could be used to sew the coils through the spring. As this would produce less strain on the coils, it might also result in a design more efficient with use of power as a lower applied voltage could be used due to a lower resistance.

The integration of soft sensors such as [20,21] is also a future avenue of research for such soft actuators.

Acknowledgment. This work was supported by the University of Sheffield.

References

1. Pfeifer, R., Lungarella, M., Lida, F.: Self-organisation, embodiment and biologically inspired robotics. Science **318**(58530), 1088–1093 (2010)
2. Foker, J.E., Kendall Krosch, T.C., Catton, K., Munro, F., Khan, K.M.: Long-gap esophageal atresia treated by growth induction: the biological potential and early follow-up results. Semin. Pediatr. Surg. **18**, 23–29 (2009)
3. Haines, C., Lima, M., Li, N., Spinks, G., Foroughi, J., Madden, J., Kim, S., Fang, S., Andrade, M., Gktepe, F., Gktepe, S., Mirvakili, S., Naficy, X., Lepr, J., Oh, M., Kozlov, S., Kim, X., Xu, B., Swedlove, G., Wallace, R.: Baughman: artificial muscles from fishing-line and sewing thread. Science **343**, 868–872 (2014)
4. Mirvakili, S.M., Ravandi, A.R., Hunter, I.W., Haines, C.S., Li, N., Foroughi, J., Naficy, S., Spinks, G.M., Baughman, R.H., Madden, J.D.W.: Simple and strong: twisted silver painted nylon artificial muscle actuated by Joule heating. In: Proceedings of SPIE, vol. 9056 (2014)
5. Yip, M.C., Niemeyer, G.: High-performance robotic muscles from conductive nylon sewing thread. In: IEEE International Conference on Robotics and Automation (ICRA) (2015)
6. Leng, J., Lan, X., Liu, Y., Du, S.: Shape-memory polymers and their composites: stimulus methods and applications. Prog. Mater Sci. **56**, 1077–1135 (2011)
7. Miaudet, P., Derr, A., Maugey, M., Zakri, C., Piccione, P., Inoubli, R., Poulin, P.: Shape and temperature memory of nanocomposites with broadened glass transition. Science **318**, 1294–1296 (2007)

 8. Koerner, H., Price, G., Pearce, N., Alexander, M., Vaia, R.: Remotely actuated polymer nanocomposites - stress-recovery of carbon-nanotube-filled thermoplastic elastomers. Nat. Mater. **3**, 115–120 (2004)
 9. Baughman, R.H., Zakhidov, A.A., de Heer, W.A.: Carbon nanotubes - the route toward applications. Science **297**(5582), 787–792 (2002)
10. Connolly, F., Polygerinos, P., Walsh, C., Bertoldi, K.: Mechanical programming of soft actuators by varying fiber angle. Soft Robot. **2**(1), 26–32 (2015)
11. Wakimoto, S., Suzumori, K., Ogura, K.: Miniature pneumatic curling rubber actuator generating bidirectional motion with one air-supply tube. Adv. Robot. **25**, 1311–1330 (2011)
12. Stilli, A., Wurdemann, H.A., Althoefer, K.: Shrinkable, stiffness-controllable soft manipulator based on a bio-inspired antagonistic actuation principle. In: IEEE International Conference on Intelligent Robots and Systems (IROS) (2014)
13. Russo, S., Ranzani, T., Gafford, J., Walsh, C.J., Wood, R.J.: Soft pop-up mechanisms for micro surgical tools: design and characterisation of compliant millimeter-scale articulated structures. In: IEEE International Conference on Robotics and Automation (ICRA) (2016)
14. Shan, W., Diller, S., Tutcuoglu, A., Majidi, C.: Rigidity-tuning conductive elastomer. In: Smart Materials and Structures (2015)
15. Lima, M.D., Li, N., Andrade, M., Fang, S., Oh, J., Spinks, G., Kozlov, M., Haines, C., Suh, D., Foroughi, J., Kim, S., Chen, Y., Ware, T., Shin, M., Machado, L., Fonseca, A., Madden, J., Voit, W., Galvo, D., Baughman, R.: Electrically, chemically, and photonically powered torsional and tensile actuation of hybrid carbon nanotube yarn muscles. Science **338**, 928–932 (2012)
16. Balasubramanian, A., Standish, M., Bettinger, C.: Microfluidic thermally activated materials for rapid control of macroscopic compliance. Adv. Funct. Mater. **24**(30), 4860–4866 (2014)
17. Martinez, R.V., Fish, C.R., Chen, X., Whitesides, G.: Elastomeric origami: programmable paper-elastomer composites as pneumatic actuators. Adv. Funct. Mater. **22**, 1376–1384 (2012)
18. Miyashita, S., Guitron, S., Yoshida, K., Li, S., Damian, D., Rus, D.: Ingestible, controllable and degradable origami robot for patching stomach wounds. In: IEEE International Conference on Robotics and Automation (ICRA), pp. 909–916 (2016)
19. Kuribayashi, K., Tsuchiya, K., You, Z., Tomus, D., Umemoto, M., Ito, T., Sasaki, M.: Self-deployable origami stent-grafts as a biomedical application of Ni-rich TiNi shape memory alloy foil. Mater. Sci. Eng. **419**, 131–137 (2006)
20. Roberts, P., Damian, D., Shan, W., Lu, T., Majidi, C.: Soft-matter capacitive sensor for measuring shear and pressure deformation. In: IEEE International Conference on Robotics and Automation (ICRA), pp. 3514–3519 (2013)
21. Park, Y., Majidi, C., Kramer, R., Brard, P., Wood, R.J.: Hyperelastic pressure sensing with a liquid-embedded Elastomer. J. Micromech. Microeng. (2010)

Characterization of Kinetic and Kinematic Parameters for Wearable Robotics

Rodrigo D. Solis-Ortega$^{(\boxtimes)}$, Abbas A. Dehghani-Sanij,
and Uriel Martinez-Hernandez

University of Leeds, Leeds LS2 9JT, UK
{ell4rdso,a.a.dehghani-sanij,u.martinez}@leeds.ac.uk

Abstract. The design process of a wearable robotic device for human assistance requires the characterization of both kinetic and kinematic parameters (KKP) of the human joints. The first step in this process is to extract the KKP from different gait analyses studies. This work is based on the human lower limb considering the following activities of daily living (ADL): walking over ground, stairs ascending/descending, ramp ascending/descending and chair standing up. The usage of different gait analyses in the characterization process, causes the data to have great variations from one study to another. Therefore, the data is graphically represented using Matlab® and Excel® to facilitate its assessment. Finally, the characterization of the KKP performed was proved to be useful in assessing the data reliability by directly comparing all the studies between each other; providing guidelines for the selection of actuator capacities depending on the end application; and highlighting optimization opportunities such as the implementation of agonist-antagonist actuators for particular human joints.

Keywords: Wearable robotics · Gait analysis · Lower limb · Kinematics · Kinetics

1 Introduction

The characterization of kinetic and kinematic parameters (KKP), described as follows, is focused on wearable robotics applications for human assistance, such as exoskeletons, exosuits, soft orthoses, etc. The latter devices provide assistance by delivering rotational forces (torques) to the body joint of interest, using different types of actuators. The broad range of actuation technologies currently available has given birth to many functional prototypes capable of assisting human motions during several activities.

The design process of a wearable robotic device includes the characterization of both KKP for the human joints intended to be assisted which allows the device to be tailored to a particular application, whether assisting an elder adult or allowing a disable patient to walk. The effectiveness of each prototype is commonly assessed by measuring the metabolic cost reduction delivered to the user while performing an activity [1]. However, the latter requires specialized equipment. An alternative way is comparing the range of motion and torque delivered to the assisted joint with the values commonly found in humans during a certain activity. This type of data is available in gait analysis studies. In addition to the latter application, this data can be used as design

© Springer International Publishing AG 2017
Y. Gao et al. (Eds.): TAROS 2017, LNAI 10454, pp. 548–556, 2017.
DOI: 10.1007/978-3-319-64107-2_44

guidelines when developing a wearable robotic device, e.g. the torque information can be used to choose the proper actuation technology. Therefore, the gait analysis data is commonly used in the development of wearable robotic devices since it can provide design guidelines specific to the activity of interest and can be used to assess the degree of assistance provided by a prototype.

Gait analysis studies usually provide KKP. The kinematic parameters describe the human body motion, e.g. the joint angle, velocity, and acceleration; whereas the kinetic parameters describe the forces causing this motion, e.g. joint torque and power. The most commonly implemented method to extract these parameters is motion capture. However, other technologies such as soft strain sensors [2], electrogoniometers [3], and inertial measurement units (IMU) have also been used. Lastly, it is important to mention that these studies differ between one another in many aspects, apart from the choice of technology, such as subjects' gender, age, weight, etc., as well as the setup of the experiments.

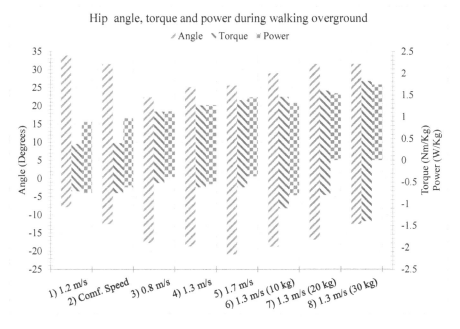

Fig. 1. Data compiled from several experiments for walking over ground activities. The weight next to the name of some activities dictates the load carried by the subjects during the experiment. The torque and power are presented in the same axis since their values share the same order of magnitude. The gait analysis studies are as follows: (1) [4], (2) [5], (3–8) [6].

This work is focused on describing the characterization process that, based on the extraction of the KKP from human lower limbs, can be used as guidelines in the design of wearable robotic devices. The gait analysis studies mentioned here were selected according to the activities of daily living (ADLs) of interest: walking, ascending/ descending stairs, ascending/descending ramps and chair standing up. The data for the hip, knee and ankle joints is extracted and compiled. Furthermore, the data is visually represented in charts of clustered stacked bars in order to allow for quick comparisons to be made between different gait analysis studies. Finally, 12 charts were produced from the compiled data using Excel®, one of them is presented in Fig. 1 which concentrates the data for a single joint during different activities, in this case, variations of walking over ground. The parameters of the joint angle, torque and power are included. Activities are named to provide insight to the main features of the experiment, i.e. the walking speed and load carried by the subjects. Finally, the compiled data is presented in two more chart styles, in the following sections, to highlight the benefits of this graphic representation.

2   Gait Analysis Data

Gait Analysis studies provide the description of the performed experiment, including: the number of subjects in the group, subjects' characteristics such as age, weight, height, gender and health condition; experiment characteristics such as walking speed, ramp inclination, stairs geometry, initial sitting position and special conditions, such as, whether subjects are carrying a load or not. The subjects' characteristics are always presented in mean (average) values of the whole group. In a similar way, the derived data (torque and power) is presented in mean values and is normalized using the subjects' height, in the case of the gait cycle speed; and the subjects' weight, in the case of the torque of each joint. The normalization is appreciated in the units for torque and power in Fig. 1, being Nm/kg and W/kg respectively. The data used in the normalization process is usually provided as mean values of the subjects' group's height and weight. However, in some studies like the one in [5], the gait cycle speed is not explicitly provided nor it can be calculated because the normalization process is done considering each subject's characteristics and not the mean values of the subjects group. Again, this is reflected in Fig. 1, where the walking speed for activity 2) is not included in the name.

From one study to another, the subjects group is expected to be different and diverse in several characteristics. This diversity causes segmentation of the whole group, e.g. in the study performed in [4], there is a segmentation of the group in two different range of ages. One group included subjects from 22 to 72 years old, meanwhile, the subjects from the other group have ages ranged from 6 to 17 years old. The latter presented evidence of age-related differences which disproved the conclusions on previous works where these difference are non-existent. Nevertheless, when no significant difference is appreciated in the data despite the subjects' age diversity, the data is compiled into a single cluster and no segmentation is performed, such as the case in [5].

The usage of motion capture allows the extraction of the kinematic parameters, such as the joint angle. Similarly, the kinetics of the human body are obtained using force plates which measure the ground reaction forces, a required parameter to calculate the joint torque and power. Therefore, the set of parameters usually found in gait analysis studies contains the joint angle, joint torque, and joint power. The activity gait cycle is usually presented in a chart accompanied with tables highlighting the maximum, minimum and mean values of the gait cycle.

For the characterization of the human KKP, the values for the maximum and minimum of each parameter are of interest, more specifically, the differences between them. Most studies present these values in the form of tables and charts [6, 7], some of them even provide the whole experiment dataset [8]. When a data table is available, the extraction of the values is straight forward. Nevertheless, cases such as [9–13] do not provide any table and the data have to be extracted visually, decreasing the data accuracy, hence its reliability. Likewise, it can be the case for some studies to focus on specific features of the gait cycle, such as maximum and minimum values of each parameter; or even worse, not provide one or more of the parameters of interest (angle, torque or power).

3 Characterization of Lower Limb Parameters

The variations of the data from one experiment to another can be reduced by focusing on the range obtained from the difference between the maximum and minimum values of each parameter. As illustrated in Fig. 1, despite the variations between the maximum and minimum values from one experiment to another, the actual range of each parameter is similar among all the experiments. The mean range of motion for the hip joint angle throughout all the experiments showed in Fig. 1 (walking over-ground) was found to be 44.63°. When comparing the latter mean range value with the range value of each experiment, the greatest variation between those is 18%. The previous calculation can be used to decide design parameters of the wearable robotic device to be developed, such as which range of motion should be covered by the device depending on which sector of the population is intended to be assisted; or if the mean range of motion value is used, the percentage of the focused population being covered. Nevertheless, the objective in representing the data visually, as in Fig. 1, is to allow quick comparisons with good accuracy, hence avoiding early calculations.

Table 1 contains the torque mean range of the hip joint during several ADLs. The data was extracted from a previously compiled table containing several clinical studies. The mentioned table is not presented in this work due to its large size. However, the obtained mean range values and the clinical studies used to extract the maximum and minimum values of the torque for each activity are provided in Table 1 which are sufficient enough to describe the benefits of visualizing the data graphically.

Table 1. Torque mean ranges for the hip joint during several ADLs. Each main activity is composed of several clinical studies with different parameters between one another.

Main activity	Hip Torque Mean Range (Nm/kg)	Clinical studies
Walking	−0.1875–1.5988	[4–6]
Stairs ascending	0–1.27	[9, 10]
Stairs descending	0–1.1275	
Ramp ascending	−0.15–1.033	[11]
Ramp descending	0–1.44	
Chair stand up	−0.4833–0.60	[12, 13]

The data presented in Table 1 is used to plot the chart illustrated in Fig. 2 using Matlab®, following a similar approach as the one presented in [14], where the range of motion of the knee joint is compiled into a chart for 11 different ADLs. The chart style used in Fig. 2 highlights two important design parameters: the actuators implemented in the wearable robotic device to be developed must be able to deliver torques in both clockwise and anti-clockwise directions, and the actual actuator torque capacity depending on the activities of interest.

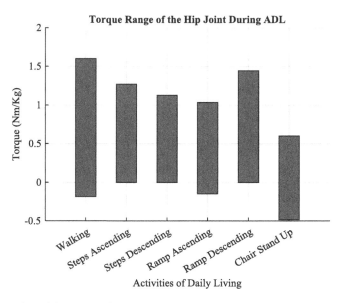

Fig. 2. Illustration of the range values of the torque during several activities. The values for the maximum and minimum torque are mean values obtained by averaging the data of all the different gait analysis experiments enclosed in one main activity. The data used to create this chart is presented in Table 1.

An alternative visual representation of the data available in gait analyses works to group the range of a specific parameter and comparing it with one of the subjects' physical characteristics, e.g. the age range. Figure 3 illustrates the dependency of the subjects' age with the knee range of motion. The colour code used in Fig. 3, the age ranges and knee ranges of motion are presented in Table 2.

The chart shown in Fig. 3 concentrates the data from three different gait analyses, in which six age groups are contained. The approach used in Fig. 3 is to overlap areas of different colours, each area represents the range of motion of the knee for a specific age range. The area in which several areas intersect can be appreciated due to the enabled transparency property. Nevertheless, the areas where three and two areas are intersected are manually highlighted by a surrounding solid line and dotted line respectively, to improve their visualization. This simple intersection of areas can provide information regarding the required range of motion to be delivered by the wearable robotic device, depending the sector of the population focused on.

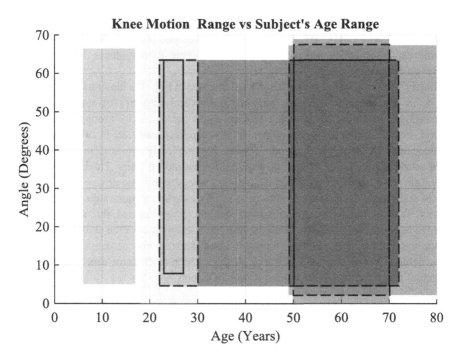

Fig. 3. Chart illustrating the comparison between subjects' age and the knee range of motion during walking over ground. The areas surrounded by solid lines and dotted lines represent the intersection between three and two areas, respectively. The overlapping squares highlight the great similarity among the range of motion despite subjects' age. The data used to create this chart is presented in Table 2. (Color figure online)

Table 2. Colour code used in Fig. 3 for each combination of age range and knee range of motion. The knee range of motion is provided in degrees. The clinical studies where the data was extracted from are also provided.

Colour code	Knee Range of Motion (°)	Age range (years)	Clinical study
Red	2.2–67.4	49–90	[14]
Green	5–66.5	6–17	[4]
Blue	4.5–63.5	22–72	
Yellow	0–69	18–30	[5]
Magenta	0–69	50–70	
Cyan	8–63.6	23–27	[6]

For example, if a wearable robotic device was aiming to assist the population sector aged from 50 to 70 years old, then a range of motion of the knee joint from 5 to 63 would be enough to cover the mentioned population. The later range of motion is taken from the triple intersection of areas illustrated in Fig. 3, which can provide a certain degree of confidence since three different clinical studies were compared. This approach can be used to compare other characteristics, e.g. subject's weight against torque. Summarizing, the areas overlapping approach can provide guidelines to avoid oversizing of the wearable robotic device to be developed by analysing the intersection of different areas which ultimately provides a degree of confidence when deciding design parameters.

Lastly, the same visual presentation implemented in Fig. 1 is illustrated as follows in Fig. 4, in this case for the knee joint during several activities of stairs ascending/descending. The important detected feature is not the similarity among the range of motion, but the mirrored values shown for the torque parameter. In other words, the torque values required for descending stairs is completely opposite in direction and twice as big in magnitude as the one required for ascending stairs. The latter illustrates an optimization opportunity. When designing a wearable robotic device for human for human assistance, the actuator is chosen to satisfy a certain torque range of a particular activity. Without the characterization of the parameters performed, the actuator is most likely to be oversized to comply with the most demanding part of the activity. However, a different approach could be proposed: agonist-antagonist actuators; a technique implemented in several wearable robotic devices which at the same time complies with the actual functionality of the human musculoskeletal system.

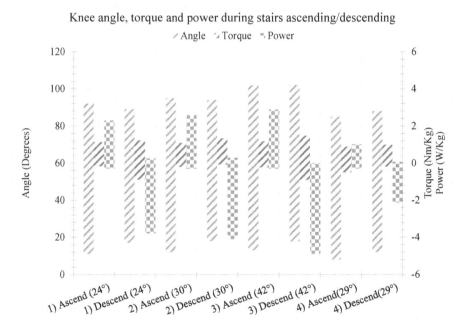

Fig. 4. Data compiled from several stairs ascending/descending experiments. The number enclosed in brackets represents the stairs slope. The parameters of torque and power are presented in the same axis since their values have the same order of magnitude. The gait analysis studies are as follows: (1) [10], (2–4) [15].

4   Conclusion

The work presented here described the process of characterizing the human lower limb kinematics and kinetics parameters during some ADLs. The relevant information provided in gait analysis experiments was described, as well as possible challenges when extracting it. Data compiled for the activities of walking, ascending/descending stairs, ascending/descending ramps and chair standing up were presented in the form of clustered stacked bar charts.

The usefulness of compiling a data table and visually representing it was mentioned. The clustered stacked bar chart allowed quick and easy detection of similarities/ differences between several clinical trials of the same activity. The similarity between the ranges of values of a specific parameter also dictates the reliability when implementing the data as design guidelines. The data feasibility can be corroborated by the chart style with subjects' age ranges against the knee ranges of motion by assessing the number of overlapping areas. In contrast, the spotted differences, as the ones for the knee torque values during ascending/descending stairs, are indicators for optimization opportunities where instead of using a single actuator to satisfy the torque range, an agonist-antagonist system could be more suitable. Moreover, the chart style with the ranges of motion versus activities facilitates the choice of the actuator type and dimension (depending on the activities of interest). Finally, the style used to represent the charts in this work was kept as simple as possible while providing useful information about the KKP. However, more complex plotting methods can be used, e.g. the patterned frames used in the chart of overlapping areas could be automatically created by the plotting software instead of being manually added, allowing a faster assessment of the feasibility of the data.

References

1. Panizzolo, F., Galiana, I., Asbeck, A.T., Siviy, C., Schmidt, K., Holt, K.G., Walsh, C.J.: A biologically-inspired multi-joint soft exosuit that can reduce the energy cost of loaded walking. J. Neuroeng. Rehabil. 1–13 (2016). doi:10.1186/s12984-016-0150-9
2. Menguc, Y., Park, Y.-L., Pei, H., Vogt, D., Aubin, P.M., Winchell, E., Fluke, L., Stirling, L., Wood, R.J., Walsh, C.J.: Wearable soft sensing suit for human gait measurement. Int. J. Rob. Res. 33, 1748–1764 (2014). doi:10.1177/0278364914543793
3. Wu, S.K., Waycaster, G., Shen, X.: Electromyography-based control of active above-knee prostheses. Control Eng. Pract. 19, 875–882 (2011). doi:10.1016/j.conengprac.2011.04.017
4. Bovi, G., Rabuffetti, M., Mazzoleni, P., Ferrarin, M.: A multiple-task gait analysis approach: kinematic, kinetic and EMG reference data for healthy young and adult subjects. Gait Posture 33, 6–13 (2011). doi:10.1016/j.gaitpost.2010.08.009
5. Lee, S.J., Hidler, J.: Biomechanics of overground vs. treadmill walking in healthy individuals. J. Appl. Physiol. 104, 747–755 (2008). doi:10.1152/japplphysiol.01380.2006
6. Han, Y., Wang, X.: The biomechanical study of lower limb during human walking. Sci. China Technol. Sci. 54, 983–991 (2011). doi:10.1007/s11431-011-4318-z

7. Yali, H., Xingsong, W.: Biomechanics study of human lower limb walking: implication for design of power-assisted robot. In: 2010 IEEE/RSJ International Conference on Intelligent Robots and Systems. pp. 3398–3403. IEEE, Taipei, Taiwan (2010). doi:10.1109/IROS.2010. 5650497

8. Moore, J.K., Hnat, S.K., van den Bogert, A.J.: An elaborate data set on human gait and the effect of mechanical perturbations. PeerJ **3**, e918 (2015). doi:10.7717/peerj.918

9. Protopapadaki, A., Drechsler, W.I., Cramp, M.C., Coutts, F.J., Scott, O.M.: Hip, knee, ankle kinematics and kinetics during stair ascent and descent in healthy young individuals. Clin. Biomech. **22**, 203–210 (2007). doi:10.1016/j.clinbiomech.2006.09.010

10. Riener, R., Rabuffetti, M., Frigo, C.: Stair ascent and descent at different inclinations. Gait Posture. **15**, 32–44 (2002). doi:10.1016/S0966-6362(01)00162-X

11. McIntosh, A.S., Beatty, K.T., Dwan, L.N., Vickers, D.R.: Gait dynamics on an inclined walkway. J. Biomech. **39**, 2491–2502 (2006). doi:10.1016/j.jbiomech.2005.07.025

12. Roebroeck, M.E., Doorenbosch, C.A.M., Harlaar, J., Jacobs, R., Lankhorst, G.J.: Biomechanics and muscular activity during sit-to-stand transfer. Clin. Biomech. **9**, 235–244 (1994). doi:10.1016/0268-0033(94)90004-3

13. Mak, M.K.Y., Levin, O., Mizrahi, J., Hui-Chan, C.W.Y.: Joint torques during sit-to-stand in healthy subjects and people with Parkinson's disease. Clin. Biomech. **18**, 197–206 (2003). doi:10.1016/S0268-0033(02)00191-2

14. Rowe, P.J., Myles, C.M., Walker, C., Nutton, R.: Knee joint kinematics in gait and other functional activities measured using flexible electrogoniometry: how much knee motion is sufficient for normal daily life? Gait Posture **12**, 143–155 (2000). doi:10.1016/S0966-6362 (00)00060-6

15. Reid, S.M., Lynn, S.K., Musselman, R.P., Costigan, P.A.: Knee biomechanics of alternate stair ambulation patterns. Med. Sci. Sport. Exerc. **39**, 2005–2011 (2007). doi:10.1249/mss. 0b013e31814538c8

A Material-Based Model for the Simulation and Control of Soft Robot Actuator

Constantina Lekakou[1(✉)], Seri M. Mustaza[2], Tom Crisp[1],
Yahya Elsayed[1], and C.M. Saaj[2]

[1] Department of Mechanical Engineering Sciences,
University of Surrey, GU2 7XH Guildford, Surrey, UK
C.Lekakou@surrey.ac.uk
[2] Department of Electrical and Electronic Engineering,
University of Surrey, GU2 7XH Guildford, Surrey, UK

Abstract. An innovative material-based model is described for a three-pneumatic channel, soft robot actuator and implemented in simulations and control. Two types of material models are investigated: a soft, hyperelastic material model and a novel visco-hyperelastic material model are presented and evaluated in simulations of one-channel operation. The advanced visco-hyperelastic model is further demonstrated in control under multi-channel actuation. Finally, a soft linear elastic material model was used in finite element analysis of the soft three-pneumatic channel actuator within SOFA, moving inside a pipe and interacting with its rigid wall or with a soft hemispherical object attached to that wall. A collision model was used for these interactions and the simulations yielded "virtual haptic" 3d-force profiles at monitored nodes at the free- and fixed-end of the actuator.

Keywords: Elastic material · Hyperelastic material · Visco-hyperelastic material · SOFA

1 Introduction

Soft robotics is being considered for use in many applications where work need be completed in confined environments. In particular a large amount of work has been focused on their use in non-invasive surgery. A flexible arm is able to alter its shape based on the space in which it is operating, something which is impossible with rigid tools which would require entry to the region from many different angles. Additional application investigated by our group includes the use of a soft robot arm in sampling operations at the internal wall of a pipe for pipe inspection or inspection of any enclosed spaces, oil or other mineral exploration, repairs in well casings and maintenance of tunnel boring machines. In many cases, it is important to provide a force or stress feedback either as an input variable to the control system to sense if and when the actuator tip reaches and touches the required location or a "haptic" feedback force to the user during robotic surgery. Hence, a material-based model is of great importance not only for the accurate simulation of the soft actuator deformation and motion but also to enable prediction of force or stress at interfaces of the soft robot and its environment.

© Springer International Publishing AG 2017
Y. Gao et al. (Eds.): TAROS 2017, LNAI 10454, pp. 557–569, 2017.
DOI: 10.1007/978-3-319-64107-2_45

Initial efforts in modelling soft robotic manipulators focused mainly on kinematic modelling [1–3] and such approach may be still useful in the case of a system of multiple, linked, soft actuators. The next step for such a system has been to consider a kinematic model of a multi-segment manipulator and a piece-wise constant curvature assumption for each soft bending segment [4]. Continuum dynamics, involving forces in addition to geometry, is a most significant step to better describe the motion and deformation of soft actuators and, in the current study, is envisaged to predict the interactions with the environment, which in addition to the previously cited applications could be considered in describing the grasping and gripping processes of a manipulator. Such continuum dynamics models may contain a stiffness matrix [5], a series of springs or a series of spring-and-dashpot models to also take into account the damping effects [6]. On the other hand, hyperelastic constitutive models are used to generally describe the behavior of rubber, Ecoflex® and other silicone-type materials used in soft robotics [7] that our team has fitted to experimental data for Ecoflex and used in finite element analysis (FEA) to investigate and minimize the ballooning effect in a soft, three-pneumatic channel actuator [8].

The present study employs a novel visco-hyperelastic constitutive model for the soft material which has been incorporated in a unique material-based continuum dynamics model for a soft, three-pneumatic channel actuator. Simulations of the actuator are presented on the basis of this novel model and are compared with the case where the viscous terms are omitted from the model. This is followed by the simulation of the soft actuator operating in a pipe in the SOFA software platform, and results of the interaction forces between the soft robot and the pipe walls are presented. Finally, the novel model is implemented in control and a case-study using the visco-hyperelastic material-based continuum dynamics model incorporated in control is presented.

2 Soft Actuator

Figure 1 presents the model of the soft, three-pneumatic channel actuator, where each channel is wrapped with a fiber [9] that eliminates the ballooning effect.

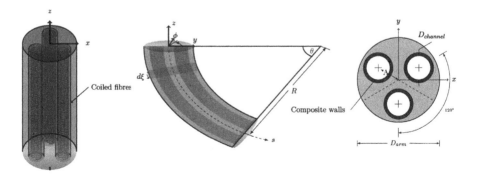

Fig. 1. Three-pneumatic channel, soft actuator (a) CAD model; (b) coordinate system used for the model; (c) cross-section of the actuator

Kinematics is used decomposed into two mappings [10] as follows:

- Robot dependent mapping - mapping between joint space $q = \{q_1, q_2, q_3\}^T$ and configuration space $\{\kappa, \varphi, L\}^T$
- Robot independent mapping - mapping between configuration space $\{\kappa, \varphi, L\}^T$ and task space $\{x, y, z\}^T$

where q_i describe the length change of each actuator which in the case of this paper are the length change of each pneumatic chamber and the arc parameters are curvature, plane angle containing the arc and the arc length, respectively.

The overall dynamical model of the system is obtained by employing Lagrangian analysis. The equation of motion can be obtained by applying the Euler-Lagrange equation [11]:

$$\mathbf{F} = \left(\frac{d}{dt} \frac{\partial L}{\partial \dot{\mathbf{q}}} \right) - \left(\frac{\partial L}{\partial \mathbf{q}} \right) \tag{1}$$

where L is the Lagrangian defined as

$$L = E_k - E_g - E_m \tag{2}$$

$\mathbf{F}$ in Eq. (1) is the generalized force and $\mathbf{q}$ is the joint space coordinate vector. In Eq. (2), E_k is the kinetic energy, E_g is the gravitational potential energy and E_m is the mechanical energy due to mechanical stresses (elastic and viscous stresses for a viscoelastic material).

The mechanical stress-related energy takes into account the axial strain energy due to extension or compression of a channel and the shear energy present during bending of the module:

$$E_m = E_{strain} + E_{shear} \tag{3}$$

$$E_{strain} = \frac{1}{2} \sum_{i=1}^{3} \sigma_i \varepsilon_i v_{si} \tag{4}$$

$$E_{shear} = \frac{1}{2} \tau \frac{\theta}{2} v_s \tag{5}$$

where σ_i is the chamber tensile stress, ε_i is the chamber axial strain and v_{si} is the chamber volume, for each of the three chambers to $i = 1$ to 3; τ is the module shear stress and v_s is the module volume. A constitutive model, to be described in the next section, links stress and strain.

3 Material Model

The visco-hyperelastic constitutive model proposed for the soft silicone in this study is described by a system of a non-Newtonian viscous dashpot and a hyperelastic spring in parallel which is equivalent to the simplified Kelvin-Voigt model so that the stress, σ, is given by:

$$\sigma = \sigma_{he} + \sigma_v \tag{6}$$

where σ_{he} and σ_v are the hyperelastic and viscous stress component respectively.

For this study, Yeoh's reduced polynomial hyperelastic model [12] has been chosen to describe the hyperelastic energy potential:

$$U_{he}(q) = \sum_{j=1}^{3} C_{j0}(I_1(q) - 3)^j \tag{7}$$

where I_1 is the first deviatoric strain invariant. The values of C_{i0} are obtained from fitting experimental mechanical test data of tensile and shear tests for the soft robot material.

The viscous part of the visco-hyperelastic material model is expressed by the following equation:

$$\sigma_v = \eta \frac{d\varepsilon(t)}{dt} \tag{8}$$

where η is the power law viscosity given by:

$$\eta(\varepsilon) = \eta_0 \left| \frac{d\varepsilon(t)}{dt} \right|^{n-1} \tag{9}$$

where η_0 is the consistency and n is the power law index of the soft material.

4 Simulation of Soft Actuator Under Single Channel Actuation

Open-loop numerical simulation and experimental testing were carried out for one-pneumatic channel actuation to evaluate the performance of the proposed model. The input pressure for the validation test was a step-on- step pressure command, as in Fig. 2, from 0.2 bar to 1 bar pressure with 0.2 bar increments. A low-level closed-loop control system was constructed to maintain the pressure at its desired level. The experimental result is compared against the model output in Fig. 2(b).

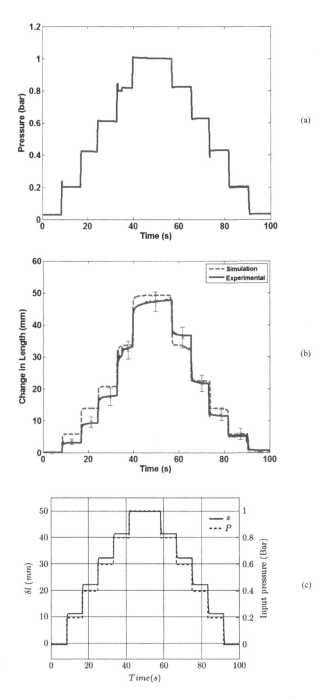

Fig. 2. Simulations of a single-pneumatic channel actuator under stepwise increase of pressure: (a) pressure profile; (b) chamber response-experimental and simulation data, the latter based on a visco-hyperelastic material model; (c) inputted pressure profile and simulation predictions based on a hyperelastic material model

The experimental data shows the average change in length as chamber 1, 2 and 3 were actuated independently. In the experiment three runs were conducted, where in each run the considerable deviation in the experimental data represents fabrication differences between the three pneumatic channels, local defects and random distortions during actuation of individual channel. From all these three runs, the error bars represent the standard deviation in changes in length between these three runs. As depicted in Fig. 2(b), the model emulates the behavior of the module quite well for pressure above 0.4 bar. The discrepancy at lower range is due to several factors such the initial gas filled-in phase where the air under low injected pressure takes some time to occupy the space within the pressure chamber. Most importantly, it can be seen in Fig. 2(b) that the novel dynamic visco-hyperelastic continuum model captures well the strain hysteresis at all steps of pressure reduction, as also evidenced by the experimental data.

Figure 2(c) displays simulation results based on a hyperelastic model only without any viscous terms. It can be seen that the simulated soft actuator elongation response is regular and symmetric as the model does not contain any viscous terms.

5   Control with Material-Based Dynamic Model

A model-based closed-loop control as in Fig. 3 was implemented to demonstrate the capability of the visco-hyperelastic model and also whether it can be used in real-time control or it is too slow to be able to follow the real process. An IntelR CoreTM i5 3230 M at 2.6 GHz processor was used for running the model-based control algorithm. An ellipse was set as the tested input trajectory, consisting of 36 equal time steps of trajectory for a total trajectory time of 50 s. The controller is driven by the error signal between the desired trajectory and the $\{L, \theta, \varphi\}$ values provided by the model. The output of the controller is fed back to the model block to update the current length of each chamber. Based on Fig. 4 it can be concluded that the proposed novel visco-hyperelastic material-based continuum mechanics dynamic model is reliable in tracking the desired trajectory.

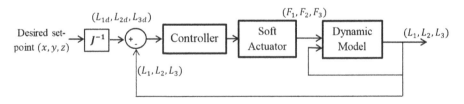

Fig. 3. Model based feedback control

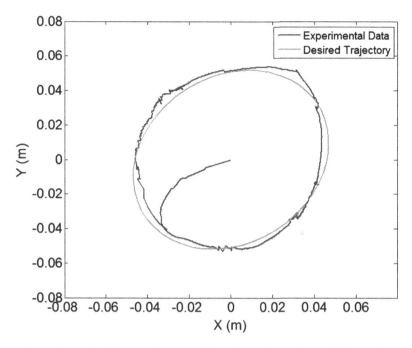

Fig. 4. Comparison of real-time trajectory tracking, where the experimental data are the result of model based feedback control using the visco-hyperelastic material-based dynamic model

6 FE Analysis of Interface Interactions Between an Actuated Flexible Robot Arm and Its Environment

SOFA - Simulation Open Framework Architecture- (version V15.12, installed on a Dell laptop pc running on windows 7 (64 bit)) was used as the software platform for these simulations. SOFA is an open source library written in C++ primarily for real-time simulations [13]. The software provides many features including finite element (FE) capabilities in a modular format. It is envisaged for the simulation within SOFA to provide "virtual" haptic feedback by virtually linking the simulation result of interaction forces to a haptic device via a spring.

A 70 mm length, soft, three-pneumatic channel actuator was simulated with the same cross-section and other dimensions as in the simulations in the previous sections. The FE analysis within SOFA was carried out for an elastic soft material of a modulus of 1 MPa to ensure real-time results and also for a hyperelastic model. Table 1 and Fig. 5 present the scenarios for which simulations have been conducted in SOFA. The CAD models were meshed in GMSH and imported into SOFA. A pressure load was applied to the surfaces at the end of the channel to simulate pneumatic actuation. The soft body attached at the wall was represented by a hemispherical object with a radius of 20 mm and linear elastic material properties of a modulus of 1 MPa. The external surface of the soft actuator was equipped with collision nodes from which five

Table 1. Simulation scenarios in SOFA

Scenario	Channel A	Channel B	Channel C	Rigid pipe	Soft body at pipe wall
	Actuator- Pneumatic channel pressure (bar)			Diameter (mm)	
I	1	0.5	0.5	50	None
II	1.5	0	0	100	None
III	1	0	0	100	Hemisphere

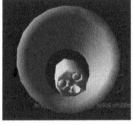   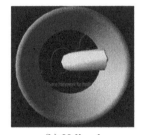   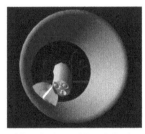

(a) 'Constrained' environment   (b) 90 °bend   (c) Collision with soft body

Fig. 5. The three scenarios simulated in SOFA, all including a soft, three-pneumatic channel actuator exploring within a rigid pipe, and for case (c) it encounters a soft hemisphere attached to the wall

nodes were defined at the free tip of the actuator at which the interaction forces were monitored: C at the center of the tip surface, E, W, N and S at the extreme east, west, north and south of the tip surface, respectively.

The simulations within SOFA predicted force (F_x, F_y, F_z) profiles at all the monitored nodes at both fixed- and free-end of the soft actuator (arm). Figures 6, 7 and 8 present the "virtual" force results for either F_x or F_y. It is clear that force peaks indicate a first contact or re-contact. For scenario I, it can be seen that at the free end of the arm, at which the collision occurs, a large spike in force is experienced which quickly reduces as the arm decelerates; however, at the fixed end of the arm the force response is much smoother and more oscillatory, with a non-zero steady state value. Further investigations need to be carried out to properly confirm the actual value of contact forces (not normalised) as it depends on the given value for contact stiffness. In scenario II the face of the free end of the arm made full contact with the outer walls therefore in this case, the collision force occurred at all of the monitored nodes. At the free end, the impact force is no longer a single spike as in scenario I, as following the initial collision the arm continues to rotate causing further variation in the force and increasing the time taken to reach steady state; in many of the nodes a secondary spike occurs as node 'S' makes contact. The instantaneous impact force is lower than in scenario I. In scenario III, the results obtained from the collision with a soft body show that this case was much more erratic than the previous cases. After the initial impact,

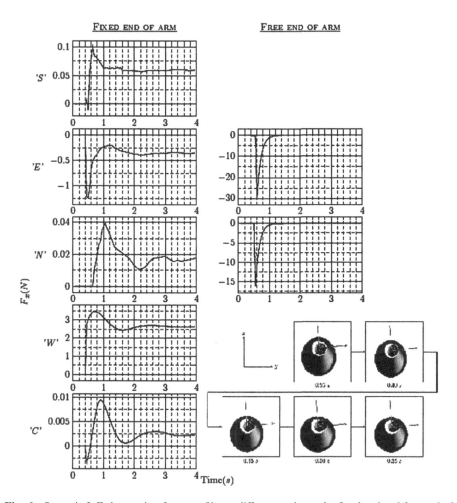

Fig. 6. Scenario I: F_x interaction force profiles at different nodes at the fixed end and free end of the soft actuator

the hemispherical shape of the soft body was included in the simulation which means that the arm began to slide after collision causing variations in the reaction forces. Moreover the body was able to readily deform making the response more complex and causing a more oscillatory response. The geometry and size of the soft body is therefore expected to have a large impact on the forces experienced by the actuator. As would be expected the peak collision force with a soft body was also lower than that in scenarios I and II, however the force was sustained for longer time. The increase in force following the initial collision is believed to be due to the squeezing of the soft body between the robotic arm and rigid environment, making the soft body stiffer and increasing the reaction force.

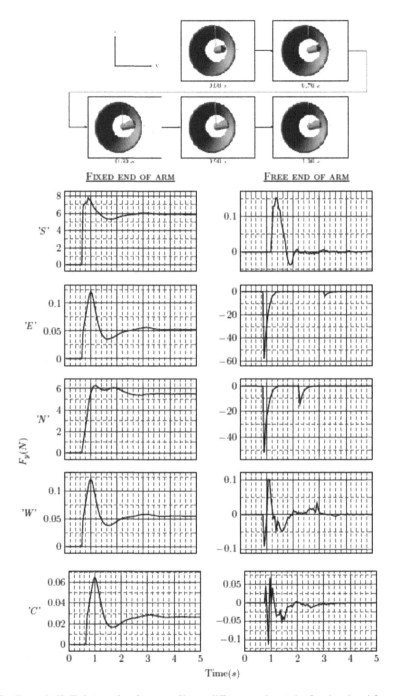

Fig. 7. Scenario II: F_y interaction force profiles at different nodes at the fixed end and free end of the soft actuator

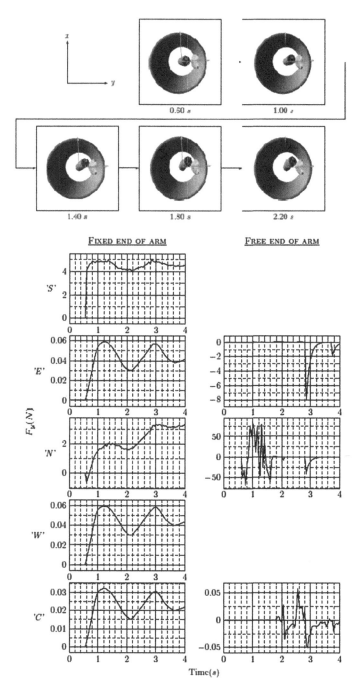

Fig. 8. Scenario III: F_y interaction force profiles at different nodes at the fixed end and free end of the soft actuator

7   Conclusions

The presented studies have proven the usefulness of the innovative material-based continuum dynamic model in the simulation and control of soft robotics. Henceforth, the selection of the most appropriate type of material-model is based on accuracy and run speed of the algorithm compared to the required speed for real-time operation required in control or haptic feedback. The visco-hyperelastic model proved the most accurate material model modelling the viscous hysteresis and non-linear elastic response of the soft actuator. It was also able to be used in real-time control where the combined simulation-control algorithm took less than 1.4 s to run, therefore being able to follow the full step for all 36 steps of the trajectory. However, neither the visco-hyperelastic nor the hyperelastic material models were able to follow in real-time the actuation operation of the soft arm in FE analysis coupled with a collision contact model in SOFA; in this case, a linear elastic model was used with low modulus (1 MPa) and the analysis undertaken was able to provide "virtual" 3d-force profiles describing the interaction between the soft actuator and its environment (rigid walls or another soft body).

References

1. Jones, B., Walker, I.: Kinematics for multisection continuum robots. IEEE Trans. Robot. **22**(1), 43–55 (2006)
2. Jones, B.A.: Practical kinematics for real-time implementation of continuum robots. IEEE Trans. Robot. **22**(6), 1087–1099 (2006)
3. Bailly, Y., Amirat, Y., Fried, G.: Modeling and control of a continuum style microrobot for endovascular surgery. IEEE Trans. Robot. **27**(5), 1024–1030 (2011)
4. Marchese, A.D., Rus, D.: Design, kinematics, and control of a soft spatial fluidic elastomer manipulator. Int. J. Robot. Res. **35**(7), 840–869 (2016)
5. Chirikjian, G.S.: Conformational modeling of continuum structures in robotics and structural biology: a review. Adv. Robot. **29**(13), 817–829 (2015)
6. Jung, J., Penning, R.S., Ferrier, N.J., Zinn, M.R.: A modeling approach for continuum robotic manipulators: effects of nonlinear internal device friction. In: Proceedings 2011 IEEE/RSJ International Conference Intelligent Robots and Systems, pp. 5139–5146. IEEE, San Francisco (2011)
7. Khajehsaeid, H., Arghavani, J., Naghdabadi, R.: A hyperelastic constitutive model for rubber-like materials. Eur. J. Mech. A. Solids **38**, 144–151 (2013)
8. Elsayed, Y., Vincensi, A., Lekakou, C., Geng, T., Saaj, C.M., Ranzani, T., Cianchetti, M., Menciassi, A.: Finite element analysis and design optimization of a pneumatically actuating silicone module for robotic surgery applications. Soft Robot. **1**(4), 255–262 (2014)
9. Fraś, J., Czarnowski, J., Maciaś, M., Główka, J., Cianchetti, M., Menciassi, A.: New stiff-flop module construction idea for improved actuation and sensing. In: 2015 IEEE International Conference on Proceedings Robotics and Automation (ICRA), pp. 2901–2906. IEEE, Seattle (2015)
10. Webster III, R.J., Jones, B.A.: Design and kinematic modelling of constant curvature continuum robots: a review. Int. J. Rob. Res. **29**(13), 1661–1683 (2010)

11. Siciliano, B., Khatib, O. (eds.): Springer Handbook of Robotics, 2nd edn. Springer, Switzerland (2008)
12. Martins, P.A.L.S.: Natal Jorge, R.M., Ferreira, A.J.M.: A comparative study of several material models for prediction of hyperelastic properties: application to silicone-rubber and soft tissues. Strain **42**(3), 135–147 (2006)
13. Faure, F., Duriez, C., Delingette, H., Allard, J., Gilles, B., Marchesseau, S., Talbot, H., Courtecuisse, H., Bousquet, G., Peterlik, I., Cotin. S.: SOFA: a multi-model framework for interactive physical simulation. In: Soft Tissue Biomechanical Modeling for Computer Assisted Surgery. Studies in Mechanobiology, Tissue Engineering and Biomaterials, vol. 11, pp. 283–321. Springer, Heidelberg (2012). doi:10.1007/8415_2012_125

A Robot Gripper with Sensor Skin

Alexander E. Watts and Constantina Lekakou$^{(\boxtimes)}$

Department of Mechanical Engineering Sciences,
University of Surrey, Guildford, Surrey GU2 7XH, UK
C.Lekakou@surrey.ac.uk

Abstract. Innovative capacitive-type distributed sensor skins are presented of very high sensitivity compared to other such sensors in the literature. The paper presents the first two parts of the present project: (a) the testing of these sensor skins in terms of measuring pressure-type normal force and in-plane force and (b) the design, fabrication and testing of a two-"finger" gripper to be used as a test bed for the sensor skins.

Keywords: Sensor grids · Tactile sensors · 3D-force/stress sensors

1 Introduction

Sensor skins for the gripper pads may cover different senses, including "seeing" distance from an approaching object, "touching", 3D-force including normal and slip force, feeling the extent of stretching, temperature, moisture and other. In this manner, they may be superior of the human skin but, on the other hand, they would have much fewer sensor nodes.

Humans see approaching objects using their eyes as discrete sensors. Typical graspers are two-rigid "finger" tools led by long-range sensors such as cameras or infra-red (IR) distance sensor. Hsiao et al. [1] found that approximately 65% of the grasp failures were because they used only long range sensors and lacked a reactive controller with sufficient local surface pose information. Gunji et al. [2] constructed center-of-pressure (CoP) tactile sensors by fitting a pressure-sensitive conductive rubber layer over the gripper finger and only four wires to measure the center position of distributed load. Later works recognized the importance of compliant pads on the gripper fingers and use more force sensors but still discrete (10×5 mm for each sensor [3]). Studying the human processes of grasping and manipulation has revealed [4] great use of tactile signals from several different types of mechanoreceptors in the glabrous (non-hairy) skin of the hand, with vision and proprioception providing information that is less essential. The human tactile and mechanical processes for grasping include: detect contact of the fingers with the object; increase the grasp force to the target level, using both pre-existing knowledge about the object and tactile information gathered during the interaction; the load phase ends when the target grasp force is reached with a stable hand posture. In fact, the human hand has 17,000 tactile sensors (about 2500 per cm^2 on the finger tip) consisting mainly of superficial, Type I slow adapting (SA) sensors (at 5 Hz response), about 100 per cm^2, with small, sharply defined areas, to provide spatial information about contact shape and pressure; deep,

© Springer International Publishing AG 2017
Y. Gao et al. (Eds.): TAROS 2017, LNAI 10454, pp. 570–575, 2017.
DOI: 10.1007/978-3-319-64107-2_46

Type II fast adapting (FA) sensors (at 5–50 Hz), about 140 per cm^2 on average in the skin, and very fast sensors (at 50–1000 Hz) with large receptive areas and poor defined boundaries that provide temporal information [5].

Current tactile sensors in grasping tools or robots are generally of the resistance-type, using grids of about 10 electrode wire cross-overs per cm^2 from which an average pressure force is determined acting on the gripper area; this is a much lower areal density than that of the skin sensors on human fingertips. Optical sensors offer 3D-force monitoring acting on a dome but are bulky, about 2.5×2.5 cm and generally rigid with not so good force sensitivity. Capacitive-type sensors have the ability to measure both transverse and in-plane stress (or force), using the formula for the capacitance, C, $C = \varepsilon_o \varepsilon_r A/d$ (where is ε_o the vacuum permittivity, ε_r is the relative permittivity or dielectric constant of the medium between two electrodes, A is the electrode area and d is the distance between the electrodes), so that a pressure decreases d and, hence, increases C, whereas an in-plane force or stress changes A and C accordingly. Lee et al. [6] used poly(dimethyl siloxane) (PDMS) as both the dielectric layer and the skin in which they embedded the capacitive-type force sensor, consisting of an array of 2×2 sensors of 2.3×2.3 mm and 100–200 fF each, with a PDMS dome of 0.7 mm diameter and 0.3 mm height at the array center on which the force is applied. These sensors measured a force range up to 20 mN in all three axes with sensitivities of 800 pF/N.

The aim of this study is to develop miniaturized capacitive-type sensors of much greater sensitivity than the sensors reported in literature so far so, when embedded in distributed format in a soft skin covering the gripper pads, they can sense the full range of forces, from the touch phase to the grasping and slipping phases. This is achieved by using highly porous electrodes which would increase overall capacitance values, hence, also sensitivity.

2 The Gripper

The first stage in this project was to design a robotic gripper which can act as a testing platform for different types of sensor skins that can be integrated with the control system of the gripper. The specifications for this gripper were: to be a two-finger gripper, able to lift up to 20 N, weigh less than 1 kg, be no longer than the human hand, have a maximum grasping width capacity of 100 mm, provide smooth operation, grasp objects of different shapes, and be housed in a mounting platform with legs. A literature search revealed that many of the grippers had a very small grasping capacity, and mostly used one motor to control both arms of the gripper.

This project intends to differ from these already developed grippers, and thus catered to a larger grasping capacity, with individual high torque motor control of each of the two arms. Servo motors have been selected due to their high torque to weight ratio, whilst harnessing their ease of control with the microcontroller and 180° position control. Figure 1 presents the CAD model of the gripper designed in this project and Fig. 2 presents its compliance with the set specifications.

Fig. 1. CAD model of the gripper

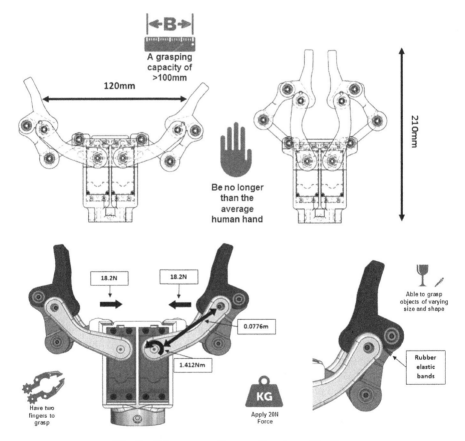

Fig. 2. Gripper compliance with set specifications

To keep costs minimal, and provide flexibility for maintenance and ease of repair, most components were 3D printed. As shown in Fig. 3(a), all joints are mounted on bearings to provide smooth operation. The combination of the gripper with motors weighs 790 g. The gripper and the electronics have been mounted on a four-leg standing structure presented in Fig. 3(b).

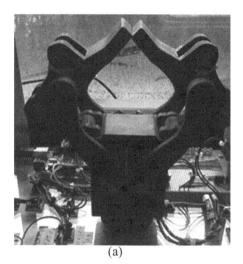

(a)   (b)

Fig. 3. (a) Gripper prototype and (b) fixed on a four-leg platform also with attached electronics

3 Capacitive-Type Sensor Grids

The first prototypes of the capacitive-type sensor grids had as electrodes carbon fiber tows of high porous area. Two such sensor grids were fabricated as arrays of 4×3 and 5×3 respectively as shown in Fig. 4. The electrodes were connected to an Arduino board via demultiplexer and a multiplexer. The board supplied AC pulses of 2 V which after passing through a resistor of 1500 Ω dropped to 0.5 V. The capacitors of 5×5 mm each were calibrated under different loads to the following relations for each sensor:

$$\text{Z-Force (pressure)}: \quad C/C_o = 0.19368\,F + 1 \tag{1}$$

$$\text{X - or Y - Force (in-plane)}: \quad C/C_o = -1.527F + 0.9997 \tag{2}$$

where F is force in Newton, C is capacitance of sensor under force F and C_o is sensor capacitance under no force.

Average sensitivities were 190 μF/N for the z-force (pressure) and 1.5 mF/N for the in-plane force which are over 2×10^5 and 1.8×10^6 times greater than the sensitivity of usual capacitors by Lee et al. [6]. This offers great opportunities for

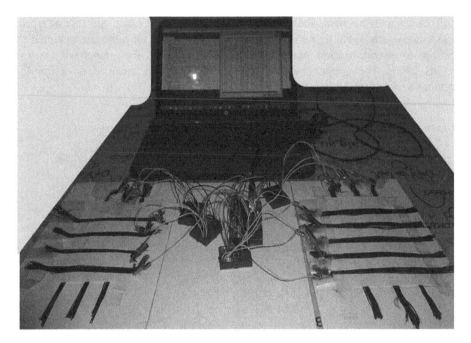

Fig. 4. First prototypes of innovative capacitive-type sensor grids of 4 × 3 and 5 × 3, operated via an Arduino board

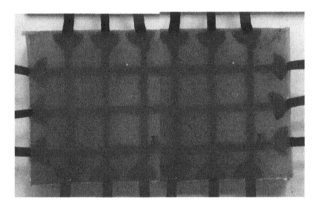

Fig. 5. Ecoflex skin of embedded sensor grid

miniaturization by 100× for example while the sensor sensitivity will still be maintained very high. The sensor grid was embedded in an Ecoflex layer as shown in Fig. 5.

The inner surface of each of the two "fingers" of the gripper has been coated with a sensor skin. The sensor grids have been integrated in the control system of the gripper. Figure 6 presents test cases of the gripper grasping relatively light or soft objects.

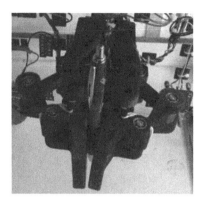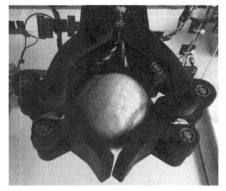

Fig. 6. The gripper grasping a pen and a ball

4 Conclusions

Two major stages of work were completed: (a) The design, manufacture and testing of a prototype two-"finger" gripper with two servomotors of high torque motor control, large capacity distance and a maximum lifting load of 18 N. (b) The development and testing of innovative capacitive-type sensors for normal pressure-type force and in-plane force with very high sensitivity of hundreds of thousands more than such sensors reported in the scientific literature so far. Work continues in the area of reactive control during grasping based on the feedback of the 3D force/stress sensor skin attached on the inner surface of each "finger" of the gripper.

References

1. Hsiao, K., Nangeroni, P., Huber, M., Saxena, A., Ng, A.Y.: Reactive grasping using optical proximity sensors. In: Proceedings of IEEE International Conference on Robotics and Automation, ICRA 2009, pp. 2098–2105. Institute of Electrical and Electronics Engineers, Kobe (2010)
2. Gunji, D., Mizoguchi, Y., Teshigawara, S., Ming, A., Namiki, A., Ishikawaand, M., Shimojo, M.: Grasping force control of multi-fingered robot hand based on slip detection using tactile sensor. In: Proceedings of IEEE International Conference on Robotics and Automation, ICRA 2008, pp. 2605–2610. Institute of Electrical and Electronics Engineers, Pasadena, CA (2008)
3. Liarokapis, M.V., Calli, B., Spiers, A.J., Dollar, A.M.: Unplanned, model-free, single grasp object classification with underactuated hands and force sensors. In: Proceedings of 2015 IEEE/RSJ International Conference on Intelligent Robots and Systems IROS 2015, pp. 5073–5080. Institute of Electrical and Electronics Engineers, Hamburg (2015)
4. Johansson, R.S., Flanagan, J.R.: Coding and use of tactile signals from the fingertips in object manipulation tasks. Nat. Rev. Neurosci. **10**, 345–359 (2009)
5. Gescheider, G.A., Wright, J.H., Verrillo, R.T.: Information Processing Channels in the Tactile Sensory System: A Psychophysical and Physiological Analysis. Taylor & Francis: Psychology Press, New York (2009)
6. Lee, H-K., Chung, J., Chang, S., Yoon, E.: Real-time measurement of the three-axis contact force distribution using a flexible capacitive polymer tactile sensor. J. Micromech. Microeng. **21**(3) (2011). Article No. 035010

Robotics Education for Children at Secondary School Level and Above

Anastasia Stone[1] and Ildar Farkhatdinov[2(✉)]

[1] London School of Mathematics and Programming, London, UK
[2] School of Electronic Engineering and Computer Science,
Queen Mary University of London, London, UK
i.farkhatdinov@qmul.ac.uk

Abstract. The present work describes the experience of teaching robotics for children at secondary school level. A set of exercises was designed and evaluated. The exercises were designed for teaching robotic systems, basic programming and control concepts, and the tasks included learning important mathematical and physical science definitions. The proposed robotics exercises were introduced to the curriculum of the London School of Mathematics and Programming and preliminary teaching and learning outcomes showed that the majority of the proposed robotics exercises were attractive to children independently of the tasks' difficulty.

Keywords: Robotics education · Children · Mobile robot · Programming

1 Introduction

The London School of Mathematics and Programming's (LSMP) goal is to develop problem solving skills and cultivate interest to science and engineering among children of ages 7–16. In 2016, LSMP has introduced robotics classes to the school's curriculum designed for secondary school level students. Teaching robotics was proven to be successful and complementary to classes in mathematics and computer programming. In the present paper the author's would like to share their experience and observations on introducing robotics to children education through providing examples on how teaching autonomous robotics contributes to learning science disciplines.

Nowadays, robotics classes, clubs and societies are typical in many secondary and high schools. The major reasons for rapid robotics education expansion are (1) decreasing costs of robotics teaching kits, (2) excitement of learning through interactive robotic systems and (3) general growth of interest to robotics and artificial intelligence in the society. Robotics education for children has been widely introduced and various teaching methodologies have been investigated [1–4,9]. In the majority of the cases wheeled mobile robots were used in teaching [6–8,10,11], but less popular applications included teaching humanoid robotics

© Springer International Publishing AG 2017
Y. Gao et al. (Eds.): TAROS 2017, LNAI 10454, pp. 576–585, 2017.
DOI: 10.1007/978-3-319-64107-2_47

for children [5], robotic manipulators [12] and aerial robotics [13]. In this work TRIK robotics mobile platform [14,16] was used to teach robotics to children. In contrast with the previous works we specifically address the challenges of formulating the robotics exercises for children. The goal of this work is to systematically present and evaluate a set of robotics problem for children which could be used to develop general analytical thinking, as well as more specific engineering and mathematical skills.

2 Educational Robotic Toolkit

The TRIK robotic set was used during robotics classes [14,16]. The set is composed of one embedded controller, various sensors and actuators, one battery with a charger and a system of *Meccano*-like assembling components. The TRIK set enables assembling different type of actuated mechanisms with controlled behaviour.

The behaviour of the robot is programmed with the help of a dedicated development environment [15]. The behaviour of the robot can be implemented with visual flow charts, as well as with JavaScript code. Designed behaviours can be first tested with built-in mobile robot software emulator. The emulated robot environment can be adjusted to have various type of obstacles (rigid immobile bodies) and guidance lines (visual markers on the ground). To test the programme with the physical robot the flow chart is translated into code and then uploaded to the robot controller via wireless network (WiFi).

The robot control diagrams are composed of interfacing and logical blocks. The primary interfacing blocks are used for applying voltage to the DC motors, stopping the DC motors, enabling the robot's sensors. Major logical blocks are used for control flow management and calculations. They are `if-then-else` statement, loop iterations and `goto` arrows, delay (wait) block and functional blocks to define variables and equations.

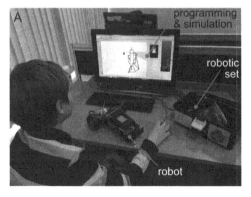 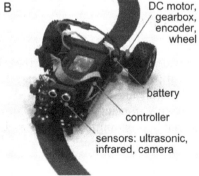

Fig. 1. A: programming the TRIK mobile robotic platform during the class; **B:** TRIK mobile robotic systems performing a line tracking task and its major components.

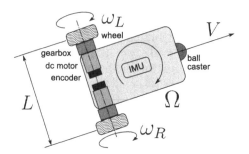

Fig. 2. Differential drive kinematics of the robot.

During the classes taught at LSMP the students assembled a mobile robot made of TRIK components with differential drive kinematics, as shown in Fig. 1. The differential kinematics of the robot is shown in Fig. 2. The robots kinematics is described as

$$V = \frac{r}{2}(\omega_L + \omega_R), \quad \Omega = \frac{r}{L}(\omega_R - \omega_L) \tag{1}$$

with the speed of the robot V and the robot's angular velocity Ω; the wheel's radius r; the distance between the wheels L; ω_L and ω_R the angular velocity of the left and right wheels, respectively. By varying the angular velocities of the two wheels, we can vary the trajectories that the robot takes. Therefore, to define the robots trajectory (translation and rotation in plane) angular velocity of the wheels needs to be controlled which was achieved by changing the voltage applied to the corresponding DC-motors:

$$\omega_{L/R} = kU_{L/R} \tag{2}$$

with the voltage applied to left/right DC motors $U_{L/R}$ and constant scalar k assuming linear motor dynamics.

3   Teaching Methodology

3.1   Students

Robotics classes at LSMP were organised in 10×1.5 h weekly sessions with a 2 weeks break in the middle for the school vacation. The age of the students varied from 9 to 14. In 2016, 9 students have attended the robotics classes. Majority of the students were not exposed to robotics, while some of the students had experience in using robotics sets from Lego. Most of the students have attended computer programming course at LSMP (Scratch and basics of Python) prior to attending the robotics classes.

3.2   Robotics Exercises

In this subsection we describe typical exercises which were used during the classes.

E1. Motion and timing. The goal of this exercise was to program the robot to move around a given rectangular obstacle and return to initial position as shown in Fig. 3(E1). The rectangular obstacle was defined by each student in the beginning of the class. There are two ways students can approach the problem: (1) activating and deactivating the motors' power for a given time, and (2) activating the motors and stopping them when the wheel's encoders reached the required values. In both cases, the students had to define required motor activation timing or encoder counting using trial and error method. However, the students were explained that they can calculate the required final encoder values if the wheel's geometry and gearbox ratio is known. Students also learn how to steer the robot by changing the control inputs (voltage) applied to the wheel's actuators. At this stage they were taught the differential drive kinematics which is typical for many wheeled robotics systems. Other topics explained during the class include work principles of DC actuators, optical encoders, and kinematic relations between speed, distance and time. Once the exercise is complete, the students were asked to check the defined motor power, timing (or encoder values) for turning parts of their flow charts. In an ideal case, the turning parameters should be same, as the code should contain of four identical corner turns. The students were asked to find the common turn parameters, if this was not the case. As a final stage of the exercise, the students were taught the concepts of functional programming: they were required to create a turning function (subprogram block) and replace all the turning commands with this new block.

E2. Simple collision avoidance. The task was to drive the robot towards an obstacle (a wall), stop at a given distance, which was then followed by a right turn (approx. 90°, using the subprogram block from *E1*) and motion towards the next wall if any (Fig. 3(E2)). In this exercise students learned how to use the ultrasonic sensors and `if-then` statement to develop the collision avoidance behaviour.

E3. Collision avoidance and navigating. This exercise is an extension of *E2*. Students were asked to draw an arbitrary labyrinth in the emulation software. The robot should find the exit without collisions with the wall as shown in example in Fig. 3(E3). Loops were introduced in this exercise to enable moving forward and turning left or right if there was a wall in front of the robot. An extension to this exercise was implementing alternating left/right turn, hence providing more flexible robot behaviour. In this task students learned how to program loops and `if-then-else` statements to implement simple navigation algorithms. They also learned how to use variables, implement loop iteration counters and use them to adjust the robots behaviour (i.e. checking if the loop counter's even or odd to decide which turn to take).

E4. Wall following and line following. This exercise is typical for robotics education and competitions. An example is shown in Fig. 3(E4). In comparison to *E3* the behaviour of the robot was defined through a system of control equations,

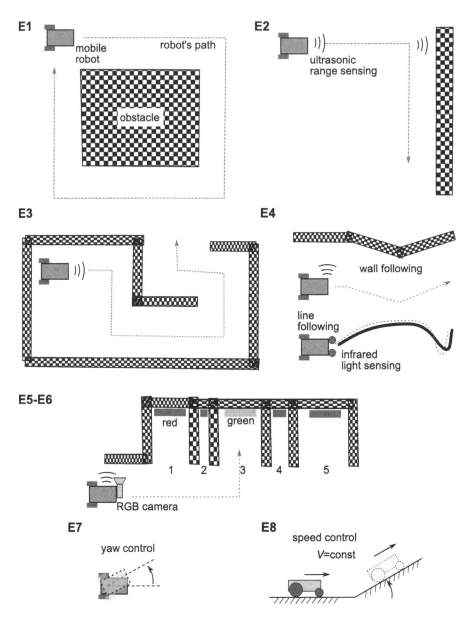

Fig. 3. Schematic diagrams of the exercises.

rather then by using `if-then-else` statements. The following equations were used for the wall following behaviour

$$U_L = k_w(d - \tilde{d}) + U_o, \quad U_R = -k_w(d - \tilde{d}) + U_o \qquad (3)$$

with controller gain k_w; reference distance to the wall d; measured distance to the wall $\tilde{d}$ and voltage defining the speed of the robot U_o. In the line following algorithm two light sensors (attached to the front corners of the robot's frame) are used to track the line. The following control law was used

$$U_L = k_l(s_L - s_R) + U_o, \quad U_R = -k_l(s_L - s_R) + U_o, \tag{4}$$

with the controller gain k_l, and left and right light intensity sensor measurements s_L and s_R, respectively. In this exercise students learned how to implement control laws for specific tracking tasks and how to use the light sensors. Importantly, the task introduced linear control concepts, as in the both tracking tasks proportional error based feedback control was used.

E5. Parking. The task for this exercise was to park the robot as shown in Fig. 3(E5–E6). In the first part of the exercise the robot should park in the $n - th$ slot of the parking space, where $n = 1, 2, 3$, etc. In the second part, the robot should park only if the slot was large enough for parking. Ultrasonic sensor installed on the side of the robot was used to count the parking slots and estimate their size. Here students learned how to use ultrasonic sensor measurements, timer and robot's speed to estimate distances (width of parking slots) and how to use loop iteration counters triggered by ultrasonic sensor measurements to count the parking slots.

E6. Parking with vision based control. This is an extension of *E5* parking task with additional RGB-camera based control. Parking was initiated only if a green coloured parking sign was presented to the robot as shown in Fig. 3(E5–E6). In this exercise students learned about RGB colour coding and principles of video camera operation for robot vision.

E7. Angular orientation control. In this exercise the robot should orient itself to a predefined angle in horizontal plane as shown in Fig. 3(E7). This was implemented with the help of yaw estimation using built-in gyrometer and proportional feedback controller. First, students learned how to use gyrometer to measure angular velocity of the robot, which was followed by implementing one step numerical integration to calculate the angular orientation (yaw) of the robot. A discrete-time linear proportional control law was introduced to turn the robot to desired location:

$$\varphi_i = \tilde{\Omega}T + \varphi_{i-1}, \tag{5}$$
$$e_i = \varphi_{ref} - \varphi_i,$$
$$U_{L,i} = k_\varphi e_i,$$
$$U_{R,i} = -k_\varphi e_i,$$

with the current loop iteration i; the sampling time T; calculated yaw angle of the robot φ; measured angular velocity of the robot in the horizontal plane $\tilde{\Omega}$ and the controller gain k_φ. The derivative component was not introduced to the controller to keep the exercise relatively simple. It was also tested experimentally, that friction and damping in the robot's mechanism was sufficient to keep the proportional feedback controller stable.

E8. Speed control. In this exercise students learned how to maintain the speed of the robot, so that the robot could move on inclined surfaces and automatically adjust the voltage applied to the motors. A simple example is shown in Fig. 3(E8). Students learned how to compute the velocity of the robot from the onboard accelerometer measurements using one-step time integration. Based on the calculated linear velocity of the robot the feedback control was implemented as follows:

$$V_i = \tilde{a}T + V_{i-1}, \tag{6}$$
$$e_i = V_{ref} - V_i,$$
$$U_{L,i} = U_{R,i} = k_V e_i,$$

with the current loop iteration number i; the sampling time T; calculated speed of the robot V; measured forward acceleration of the robot $\tilde{a}$ and the controller gain k_V. The designed controller was tested directly on the robotic platform because the simulator supports only the movements in the horizontal plane. In the exercise the students compared two control options for the robot driving on an inclined surface: constant voltage applied to the motors (conventional approach) and feedback controlled voltage based on velocity estimation from the accelerometer. Using acceleration in feedback control loop enabled automatic adjustment of the speed, as the calculated speed of the robot decreased when the robot climbed the inclined surfaces. In the exercise *E8*, as well as in the exercise *E7* the students were explained the advantages of inertial measurements with respect to wheel's encoder based control, which was less efficient due to slippage and friction of the mechanisms.

4   Results

The proposed exercises have been taught during one semester at LSMP. For each exercise difficulty, time required for completion and interest of students were evaluated. Difficulty and interest in the task were evaluated subjectively by the class teacher based on the students' response. Three levels were used to define the complexity and the interest: low (L), medium (M), high (H). The results are summarised in Table 1. Additionally, Table 1 summarises the skills and knowledge acquired by the students during their classes at LSMP.

Overall feedback from the students was positive and all students were interested in the exercises. The exercises which drew the most attention from the students were *E3*, *E4*, *E5* and *E6*. Navigation exercises *E3* and *E4* caught higher interest because the students were able to implement relatively complex behaviour of the robots and test them in various environments such as in emulated or real maze in comparison to the tasks in *E1* and *E2* when simple robot's activity was observed. Similarly, in the parking exercise *E5*, a real world application

Table 1. Summary of the exercises evaluation

Task	Difficulty	Interest	Completion time, h	Skills and knowledge
E1	L	M	1–2	**Hardware:** robot's structure, electric motors, encoders
				Software: timing, command sequences,subprogrammes
				Maths/physics: wheel kinematics,speed-distance-time relations
E2	L	L	0.5-1	**Hardware:** ultrasonic sensor
				Software: `if-then-else` statement
				Maths/physics: principle of ultrasonic sensor
E3	M/H	H	2	**Software:** control loops, loop counters, `if` statements in the loop
				Maths/physics: checking even/odd numbers
E4	M	H	1–2	**Hardware:** light sensor
				Software: variables, control laws and equation blocks
				Maths/physics: principles of light detection, equations
E5	H	H	2–4	**Software:** counters based on sensor's triggers
				Maths/physics: kinematics of robot and range measurements to calculate distances
E6	L	H	1–2	**Hardware:** RGB-camera
				Maths/physics: principles of colour coding
E7	H	L	2–3	**Hardware:** gyrometer
				Software: control error, feedback control
				Maths/physics: definition of angular velocity, one-step integration
E8	H	M	2–3	**Hardware:** accelerometer
				Software: control error, feedback control
				Maths/physics: definition of speed, acceleration, one-step integration, trigonometry to calculate tilting

was taken as the task model, which made the overall exercise more attractive to the students. Lastly, vision based parking task *E6* was popular as well due to the employment of an RGB-camera and a simple computer vision technique to modify the robot's parking controller. The orientation and speed control exercises were less attractive to the students, as they did not involve complex robot movements. The interest level for the orientation control exercise *E7* was low, while it was slightly higher for the speed control task. First reason for the low interest in these tasks was relatively high complexity, as both of them involved operations with equations and elements of numerical integration. However, in our opinion, one-step numerical integration can be well-explained if simple examples are introduced to the students. One of the major difficulties at this level was understanding how storage of previous and current values of the robot's states (speed, acceleration) can be implemented within the control loop. Nevertheless, all students were able to complete these tasks. Importantly, they were able to understand the application of feedback control as they were asked to compare the robot's performance with open loop and feedback loop control. For instance, for the exercise *E8*, the students compared how the robot could climb on inclined surfaces when a constant voltage is supplied to the motors, and when the speed-based feedback control was implemented. In terms of difficulty, only the first two exercises were assessed as simple. Exercises with the highest interest were characterised by medium and high complexity, except for *E6* when the RGB-camera was used because only minor modifications to the control algorithm from *E5* were required.

Informal communication with the students and their parents indicated the significant increase of children interest in robotics in particular and in science and technology in general. This result was achieved by careful planning of the robotics exercises and systematic inclusion of additional teaching material enabling the students to broaden and deepen their knowledge in mathematics and physical sciences, as well. The results reported in present work are promising, however they are initial and based on the observations from the first semester of robotics education at LSMP. In future, more detailed analysis of the learning outcomes over a longer period of time will be required.

Acknowledgments. The authors would like to thank E. Galuzo, I. Kirilenko, I. Shirokolobov, R. Luchin and D. Deliya for fruitful discussions and technical assistance.

References

1. Johnson, J.: Children, robotics, and education. Artif. Life Robot. **7**(1–2), 16–21 (2003)
2. Petre, M., Price, B.: Using robotics to motivate back door learning. Educ. Inf. Technol. **9**(2), 147–158 (2004)
3. Ruiz-del-Solar, J., Aviles, R.: Robotics courses for children as a motivation tool: the Chilean experience. IEEE Trans. Educ. **47**(4), 474–480 (2004)
4. Benitti, F.B.V.: Exploring the educational potential of robotics in schools: a systematic review. Comput. Educ. **58**(3), 978–988 (2012)

5. Robins, B., Dautenhahn, K., Te Boekhorst, R., Billard, A.: Robotic assistants in therapy and education of children with autism: can a small humanoid robot help encourage social interaction skills? Univ. Access Inf. Soc. **4**(2), 105–120 (2005)
6. Jojoa, E.M.J., Bravo, E.C., Cortes, E.B.B.: Tool for experimenting with concepts of mobile robotics as applied to children's education. IEEE Trans. Educ. **53**(1), 88–95 (2010)
7. Nourbakhsh, I.R., Crowley, K., Bhave, A., Hamner, E., Hsiu, T., Perez-Bergquist, A., Richards, S., Wilkinson, K.: The robotic autonomy mobile robotics course: robot design, curriculum design and educational assessment. Auton. Robots **18**(1), 103–127 (2005)
8. Mataric, M.J., Koenig, N.P., Feil-Seifer, D.: Materials for Enabling Hands-On Robotics and STEM Education. In: AAAI Spring Symposium: Semantic Scientific Knowledge Integration, pp. 99–102 (2007)
9. Mubin, O., Stevens, C.J., Shahid, S., Al Mahmud, A., Dong, J.J.: A review of the applicability of robots in education. J. Technol. Educ. Learn. **1**, 209–215 (2013)
10. Kulich, M., Chudoba, J., Kosnar, K., Krajnik, T., Faigl, J., Preucil, L.: SyRoTek Distance teaching of mobile robotics. IEEE Trans. Educ. **56**(1), 18–23 (2013)
11. Magnenat, S., Shin, J., Riedo, F., Siegwart, R., Ben-Ari, M.: Teaching a core CS concept through robotics. In: Proceedings of the 2014 Conference on Innovation & Technology in Computer Science Education, pp. 315–320. ACM (2014)
12. Cook, A.M., Bentz, B., Harbottle, N., Lynch, C., Miller, B.: School-based use of a robotic arm system by children with disabilities. IEEE Trans Neural Syst. Rehabil. Eng. **13**(4), 452–460 (2005)
13. Gaponov, I., Razinkova, A.: Quadcopter design and implementation as a multidisciplinary engineering course. In: Proceedings of IEEE International Conference on Teaching, Assessment and Learning for Engineering, pp. H2B–16 (2012)
14. Terekhov, A., Litvinov, Y., Bryksin, T.: Robots an environment for teaching computer science and robotics in schools. In: Proceedings of the 9th Central & Eastern European Software Engineering Conference in Russia p. 10. ACM (2013)
15. Sedov, B., Pakharev, S., Syschikov, A., Ivanovva, V.: Domain-specific approach to software development for microcontrollers. In: 17th Conference of Open Innovations Association (FRUCT), pp. 179–185. IEEE (2015)
16. Terekhov, A.N., Luchin, R.M., Filippov, S.A.: Educational cybernetical construction set for schools and universities. IFAC Proc. Vol. **45**(11), 430–435 (2012)

Formal Method for Mission Controller Generation of a Mobile Robot

Silvain Louis[1,2], Karen Godary-Dejean[1(✉)], Lionel Lapierre[1(✉)],
Thomas Claverie[2,3(✉)], and Sébastien Villéger[2,3(✉)]

[1] LIRMM, University of Montpellier, Montpellier, France
{silvain.louis,karen.godary-dejean,lionel.lapierre}@lirmm.fr
[2] MARBEC, CUFR Mayotte, Dembéni, Mayotte, France
thomas.claverie@univ-mayotte.fr
[3] MARBEC, CNRS, Montpellier, France
sebastien.villeger@cnrs.fr

Abstract. This article presents a methodology for generating a real-time mission controller of a submarine robot. The initial description of the mission considers the granularity constraints associated with the actors defining the mission. This methodology incorporates a formal analysis of the different possibilities for success of the mission from the models of each component involved in the description of the mission. This article ends illustrating this methodology with the generation of a real robotic mission for marine biodiversity assessment.

Keywords: Formal analysis · Mission controller · Mobile robot

1 Introduction and Context

One of the current major challenges of ecology, is to protect biodiversity against increasing threats from human activities (e.g. climate change, fishing). Towards this aim the first, and critical, step is to be able to assess biodiversity in as many places and as often as possible. Compared to terrestrial ecosystems, marine ecosystems are still poorly known because underwater observation of marine organisms by divers is a demanding task. Indeed, divers could not operate for more than one hour especially in deep habitats (i.e. >20 m) while counting mobile, abundant and diverse animals such as fishes required a long training. In addition presence of divers could affect the behavior of animals (attractive or repulsive interactions) which could ultimately bias biodiversity assessments.

MARBEC laboratory aims to address the challenge of assessing marine biodiversity in temperate and tropical coastal areas to ultimately provide conservation guidelines for their sustainable exploitation. Roboticians from LIRMM have been working for several years on the design of a semiautonomous robot named `Ulysse` able of performing underwater missions as video-recording missions. `Ulysse` is a submarine robot with 12 vector thrusters so that it is holonomic. It is autonomous in energy and carries its control architecture on an

© Springer International Publishing AG 2017
Y. Gao et al. (Eds.): TAROS 2017, LNAI 10454, pp. 586–600, 2017.
DOI: 10.1007/978-3-319-64107-2_48

embedded computer. It receives remote orders through a cable connected to a surface computer. It incorporates multiple sensors such as an inertial unit (IMU) and a Doppler loop sensor (DVL). It has a front live-camera for help with piloting and 2 front-top cameras for recording stereo-videos of marine organisms.

Researchers from LIRMM and MARBEC laboratories start an interdisciplinary scientific collaboration to improve observation techniques of marine biodiversity. The aim is to transpose live-census diver-operated protocols commonly used to monitor fish biodiversity, to a video-recording robot-based approach. Transect protocol [1] consists in censusing all fishes along a virtual segments of 50 m length at a constant depth. Localized observation consists in observing an habitat of interest (e.g. coral patch) from different angles. From a robotic point of view, we defined the 2 protocols as operating modes, each with different control algorithms. The robot is co-controlled, with some actions autonomously controlled while others are remotely driven by human operator. In the case of the Transect, the robot is controlled by a linear path (given depth and orientation) along which it is allowed to rotate around a vertical axis (to simulate the rotation of the diver head). In the case of localized observation, the robot control performs centering around the point of interest and the robot can only rotate at a fixed distance around it (i.e. on a sphere).

Therefore, a robot must be able to perform complex, modular and easily constructable missions. Such missions includes different users with very different skills, with different point of view and different needs. On the robotic side, each element of the mission must contain, to face with complex and unknown environment, functional, algorithmic, sensory or actuating redundancy. The construction of the mission controller and its formal verification must take all these aspects into account. To achieve this, we present in this article a methodology of generation and verification of the mission controller, based on a semi-formal language for mission description.

We will begin by presenting the needs of modularity and granularity for biologists and how this impacts the description of the architecture. Then, we present the mission description, voluntarily simplified to suit our partners. Then, we present the associated formal models and the methodology of generation and validation of the mission controller. Finally, we illustrate the methodology on a real example of mission.

2   Control Architecture Levels

The main concern of our architectural description in the context of the collaboration between roboticians and on-the-field experts (here, biologists) is that each actor can best exercise his competences at an appropriate level of abstraction. Thus the biologists could need two different views. First, on the field, responsible for the mission, they must have the vision of the whole mission and the possibility to change of protocols at any time. Here, they do not need knowing the technical details of the protocols implementation. But before that, the biological protocols must be stated more precisely into several high level robotic tasks. Studying the effectiveness of protocols, biologists also need to modify the mission parameters and to create new protocols without having to rewrite the robotic control laws, and without being dependent on the missions using these protocols. Then, automaticians, in charge of the control laws, must be able to write the appropriated control laws of the robotic tasks without being constrained by the utilization context of these laws. In the lowest level of abstraction, programmers, in charge of the implementation of the control architecture on the execution target, do not need to have a global vision of the missions, but must precisely manage the implementation constraints. These different levels of abstraction can be summarized in Fig. 1.

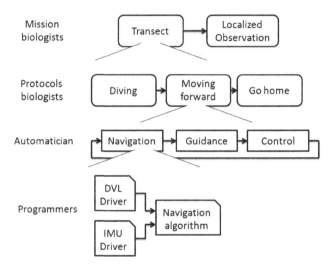

Fig. 1. Abstraction levels of the mission description

The integration of a mission into an architecture must consider 3 main parts: a decisional part, an automatic algorithmic part and a specific part to the implementation on the middleware. In this article, we will concentrate particularly on the decisional part of our methodology without neglecting the constraints related to the algorithm part and the implementation.

3   State of the Art

To answer our problematic, we have sought in the literature, a formal modeling language, allowing a hierarchical and modular description. It must also be complete but simple. This formalism should also be easily interfaced with the current architecture of our experimental platform.

We can find UML [2], composed of 13 diagrams (The package diagram, the use case diagram, the activity diagram ...) depending on the desired modeling but UML is not formal. We must also mention the Battle Management Language (BML) used to command and control forces and equipment conducting military operations [3] but BML is not modular enough in our context. We can find Language grammar, explain in [4] and partially used in [2] but which are hierarchically not simple. There is also XML, use in [5] (with XPath query language) and that we also use in the high-level description of our description for its simplicity of utilization and its great description flexibility. The XML language is not formal, but we use it only for the mission description and not for the verification.

We have also turned to programming languages since our mission will have to be executed on a real robot. In the synchronous languages, we quote the Esterel language [6], which is imperative and modular, allowing the instantaneous diffusion of signals. We will cite the RMPL (Reactive Model-Based Programming Language) [7] which allows model-based programming, used by NASA (DS1 probe). I would also quote the Signal [8,9], Luster [10] and StateChart [11] language. All these synchronous languages do not allow a formal verification with a hierarchical description. In asynchronous languages, I will quote the BIP (Behavior Interaction Priority) language of the LAAS architecture based on the use of component and allowing the formal validation [12,13]. The dataflow associated with the BIP language allows to generate code executing on their architecture (`Realtime BIP Engine`) but which is incompatible with the architecture of our `Ulysse` robot.

There is very often the use of several representations within the same structure, it is also our case, as explained below.

4   Mission Description

These works are in collaboration with those of Benoit Ropars on the hierarchization within an architecture [14] as well as those of Lotfi Jaiem on an approach for hardware and software resources management [15].

To answer the needs expressed in Sect. 2, we have defined a hierarchical description of the mission through 3 elements described in XML: Objective blocks, Parallel blocks and Activities.

4.1   Objective Block

The Objective block (Fig. 2) has an entry point and two exit points (Success and Failure). The block is activated when a token arrives at its entry point. If the objective succeeds, it sends a token on its success exit point. If the objective fails, the token go on the failure exit point. There are 2 types of objectives: Recursive objectives and Elementary objectives. Recursive objectives are encapsulations of a series of lower level objectives. It is therefore possible to build a complex mission using objective decomposition. The elementary objectives are the lowest level of decomposition. The highest objective block is the stand alone block named Mission block. The entry point of the Mission block is activated at the start of the robot.

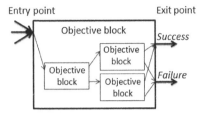

Fig. 2. Objective block

4.2 Parallel Block

The Parallel block (Fig. 3) allows several objectives to be performed at the same time (for example, a motion objective and a measurement objective). It has the same entry and exit points as the objective block. The parallel block has an objectives list that may be mandatory or optional. There is necessarily at least one mandatory objective per Parallel block. When activated, the Parallel block activates all its internal objectives. When all the internal objectives are completed, the choice of the final exit point value (`Success` or `Failure`) follows these rules: the success of all mandatory objectives drives the success of the Parallel block, conversely a failure of a mandatory objective causes its failure.

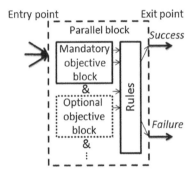

Fig. 3. Parallel block

4.3 Activity, Alternative and Resource

The activities are present in the Elementary objectives. They allow to carry out the basic robotic tasks (e.g. Location, Control, Guidance ...). An activity comes in several alternatives which are the different possibilities to perform the associated robotic task. For example, in our robot, the Localisation activity can have 2 alternatives: Location by GPS (active when the robot is on the surface) and Location by IMU integration (always possible). All the alternatives of a unique activity are ordered by priority. For example, the 2 location alternatives have a priority order which corresponds to the location accuracy. Activities provide resources (e.g. the `Location` value) and consume resources, which may be different depending on the selected alternative (`GPS position` in the case where the alternative `GPS localisation alternative` is selected or `IMU position` in the case where the alternative `IMU localisation alternative` is selected, in the example of Fig. 4).

For example, in Fig. 4 we see a `Manual control` objective with 5 activities and 7 resources. All activities have only one alternative, except the `Localisation` activity, which has 2. The `GpsDr` activity will only be active if the `GPS localisation` alternative of the `Localisation` activity is selected (same principle for the activity `ImuDr`). There are therefore two functioning modes for the architecture to achieve the `Manual control` objective.

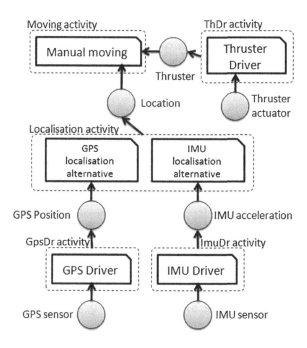

Fig. 4. Activities of the `Manual control` objective

Resources are divided into 2 categories: software resources and hardware resources. The software resources are produced by the activities. They are generally data carrier (for example the coordinates X and Y of the robot location resource). The hardware resources represent a real object in virtual form in the robot architecture, mostly associated to a sensor (for example the acoustic space around the robot) or a actuator (for example a thruster).

For a given elementary objective, all the possible combination of alternatives, with their associated resources production and consumption, form the different possible control schemes of the robot to perform this objective. The sequences of all the combination of all the objectives of a mission are called **functioning modes** (detailed below).

5   Methodology

When the mission is completely defined through the description of the objectives blocks, we apply the methodology summarized below to generate the mission controller embedded on the robot. All these steps are automatically performed by the generation program, except the formal analysis (see below).

5.1   Objectives Graph

At this point in the description of the mission, we have objectives on several levels of description. The first step consists in replacing all recursive objective blocks and parallel blocks with their contents to get a single level with only elementary objectives. The result of this flattening is called the Objectives Graph. An example of such a graph is given Fig. 5.

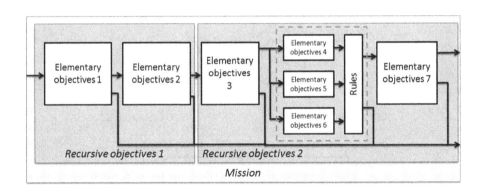

Fig. 5. Mission flattening

5.2   Alternatives Graph

It is necessary to generate the mission controller, which will pilot the control algorithms of the robot. To do this, we must deduce all the possible combinations of control according to the different activities, alternatives and resources presented in the model of the mission. To extract these combinations, it is necessary to be able to represent the links between all these elements. To do this, we have decided to use a formal language representation in order to study all the possible state space and thus the possible states of our controller.

There are several modeling languages as SMV (Symbolic model checking) [16], timed automata [17] or Petri net [5]. In our methodology, we will use the

Petri network. Indeed, this validation language is particularly adapted for the discrete event system as our mission description. The possibility of modeling the parallelism of two subsystems and their synchronization is adapted to model the resources, the activities, the objectives and the connections between them.

6   Petri Net Models

We describe the internal behavior and the interface of each block in Petri nets. We also model the activities and their resources, and the links of production/consumption. Then we can rewrite the whole mission as a complete Petri nets model.

6.1   Resources Models

In both the software (Fig. 7) and hardware (Fig. 6) Petri net models of resources, the internal structure (i.e. the common states Rx_free and Rx_busy) is represented by places (in red on the figures). In addition, hardware resources have an internal state Rx_OOS corresponding to the out-of-service (OOS in this article) state of this resource. Software resources have an internal state Rx_notAvailable when the activity that produces this resource is not in execution.

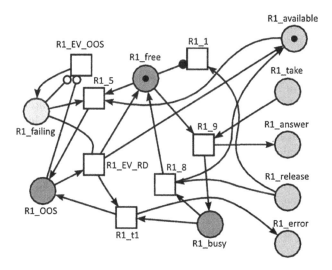

Fig. 6. Hardware resource Petri net model (Color figure online)

The transition represent the evolution between these states, either because all the input places of the transition are marked with a token, or if a specific event occurs (Rx_EV_yy). Resource models also represent temporary states of resources (in orange on the figures). In the hardware resource model, there is

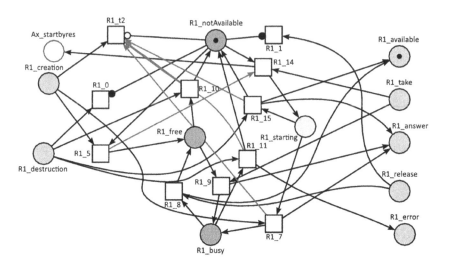

Fig. 7. Software resource Petri net model (Color figure online)

a failing temporary state triggered by the Rx_EV_OOS event. Conversely, there is the event Rx_EV_RD if the resource is available again. The resources do not have the Rx_EV_OOS and Rx_EV_RD events because they are conditioned only by their activity which produces them and therefore can not be physically OOS.

Unlike hardware resources, software resources do not exist when the activity that produces is not in execution. The resource must be created (activation place) and destroyed (deactivation place) on the order of the activity. It must wait for the activity to start (waiting place). All possible states of waiting, activation and deactivation of the producing resource are represented by internal states.

Places could also represent the production/consumption interface (in green on the figures). The interface of resources is divided into 5 places. The place Rx_available indicates to the activity that wants to consume the resource that the resource is available. The place Rx_take allows the request to reserve the resource. The place Rx_answer allows the consuming activity to know that the resource has answered to the request, whereas the place Rx_release allows to release the resource. Finally, the place Rx_error allows to notify the consuming activity if the producing activity stops producing the resource. This happens after the occurrence of the Rx_EV_OOS event.

6.2   Activities Models

We also model the activities by Petri net with the alternatives that compose it. There are 2 ways to start an activity. Either directly from the Start interface which comes from the modeling of the objectives. In this case, the stop is made by the interface Stop. Or from the StartByRes interface when a resource, produced by the activity, is requested. In this case, the stop is performed when no resource produced by this activity is requested.

Once the activity is launched, all the conditions (consumed resources available) of the alternatives will be evaluated according to their priority orders. If all the conditions are good, then the alternative is selected, the consumed resources are reserved and the produced resources are activated. An alternative stops when the activity is stopped or when a resource error occurs, in which case all alternatives are re-evaluated. See Fig. 8, the model of a single alternative branch. If no alternative is possible, then the activity generates an error to the mission controller.

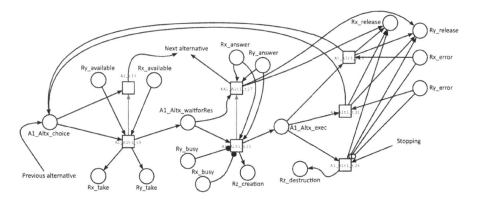

Fig. 8. Alternative branch Petri net model

6.3   Mission Models

We transform the objectives graph into Petri net. The events OBJx_EV_OK and OBJx_EV_FAIL are issued by the activities within the objective. In addition to the

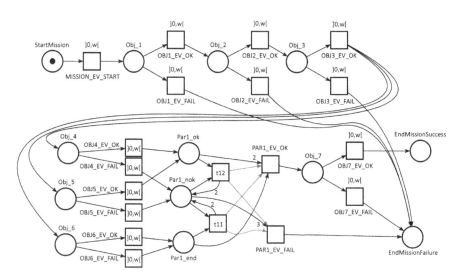

Fig. 9. Example of a mission Petri net model

places corresponding to the objectives, there is an initial place corresponding to the beginning of the mission with a transition on the event MISION_EV_START as well as 2 final places in case of success or failure of the mission. We have modeled the parallel blocks differently than the objectives to comply with the output rules, see Sect. 4.2. In Fig. 9, the transformation of the objective graph (Fig. 5) into a Petri net is shown.

7   Mission Controller

7.1   Controller Generation

Once the models of the different blocks are integrated and linked together, we perform an analysis to construct the markings graph. It represents the entire state space of the Petri net. In our case, it represents all the combinations (i.e. all the functioning modes) for each objective throughout the mission.

We see in Fig. 10 the markings graph of a hardware resource (i.e. of the Petri net of Fig. 6). The states contains the marking of the system at a given instant. In the example of Fig. 10, consider that the system is in its initial state with two marked places: Rx_available and Rx_free. The reservation of this hardware resource will be represented by the modification of the marking of the places of its interface. To simulate that, we add here a transition, associated to the event Rx_EV_TAKE, which consumes the token of the place R1_available and marked the place Rx_take[1]. Firing this transition Rx_EV_TAKE, the system moves to the state with the marking free/take. Then, from this state, the transition Rx_9 place the system in the state answer/busy. And so on, constructing the entire marking graph. In all models, transitions associated with events are given lower priority than other transitions.

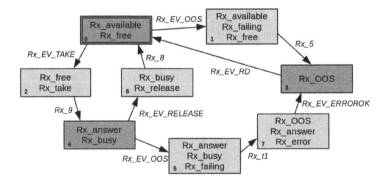

Fig. 10. Markings graph of a hardware resource

---

[1] The events Rx_EV_RELEASE and Rx_EV_ERROROK are also only present in the example to simulate the release of the resource.

In this graph, we observe two types of states: the stable states (in red on the figure) which are the states really achievable by the system, and the transient states (in orange on the figure) which are only present in the graph due to the modelling process, which could need extra transitions firing to represent a change of states. Considering again the preceding example, States 0, 3 and 4 are real states of the resource, whereas states 1, 2, 5, 6 and 7 are only due to internal evolution of the model. Stable states are identified because they have always and exclusively exit transitions with events (*_EV_*). Also, due to the construction of the Petri net models, the firing from a state of one event always leads to a deterministic stable state. Thus, if we are interested only on the real resource possible states, we could simplify the markings graph by keeping only the stable states. The simplified graph of the markings graph of Fig. 10 is given Fig. 11.

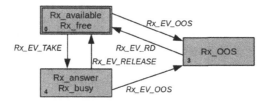

Fig. 11. Simplified marking graph of a hardware resource

On the same principle as the previous example of the resource, we generate the markings graph of the global Petri net model, i.e. all the models of the activities (with their alternatives), resources, mission objectives (from the objective graph) and all the connections between them. The stable states of the markings graph give the robot's functioning modes throughout the mission with the resources state and the alternatives selected of each activity.

7.2   Feasibility Analysis

From the markings graph, we can perform formal analyzes. We can analyze that the system is live (no deadlock in the mission) and bounded (no modeling mistake leading to an infinite state space). We can also verify specific functional properties, as for example that the place corresponding to the success of the mission is reachable. These analysis are done using a model checker on the states space of the system, here the markings graph. It is thus possible to do advanced analyzes, for example studying the resource events that force the mission into a branch leading to failure.

7.3   Controller Implementation

Robot architecture is based on the real-time middleware ContrACT. ContrACT is composed of synchronous modules (ordered in a control loop), a scheduler and asynchronous modules (execute on events). Activities are coded in synchronous modules. The alternatives are segments of code in the synchronous modules (executed according to a parameter input). The mission controller is encoded in an asynchronous module. The mission controller receives the events *_EV_* and reads in the graph of the alternatives the actions he must perform (alternative change, activation/deactivation of activity). The mission controller is automatically generated from the alternatives graph as a finite state machine.

8   Application Example

We have applied this methodology for a realistic mission planned by our biologist partners. The mission is the study of a coral zone, first performing a localized observation of a specific coral head and then performing a transect from the coral head to a given heading. The localized observation has 2 lower level elementary objectives: Manual moving, to go to the head of coral, followed by Isopheric observation. The transect begins with the objective Diving, then Filming, Advancing and Measuring temperature in parallel and ending with Going up to the surface. This mission is similar to the one shown Fig. 5, with 7 elementary objectives, 3 of which are in parallel. The whole mission comprises 11 activities (thruster_driver, gps_driver, imu_driver, localisation, manual_moving, isopheric_observation, diving, filming, advancing, temperature, go_surface). The activity localisation has 2 alternatives (gps_localisation, imu_localisation). There are 7 resources: 3 hardware (GPS_sensor, IMU_sensor, thruster_actuator) and 4 software (GPS_position, IMU_acceleration, location, thruster). We consider that all the hardware resources may be faulty, but the software resources can not.

First we have generated the whole Petri nets model of the mission. The model a too complex to be shown here, but its size in terms of numbers of places and

Table 1. Model and graphs generation results

Petri nets	
Generation time	0.24 s
Places no	133
Transitions no	150
Markings graph	
Generation time	116 s
States no	819111
Transitions no	1907422
Alternatives graph	
Generation time	191 s
States no	765
Transitions no	3602

transition is given in the column 1 of Table 1, as well as the duration necessary for this generation. Once the mission model has been generated, we have generated the markings graph using the tool Tina [18], a classical tool used for the generation of the state space of (possibly time) Petri net models. The toolbox tina also contains, among others useful tools, a model checker which allows LTL property verification. The markings graph generation results (size and generation duration) for our example model are given column 2 of Table 1. Finally, we have simplified the markings graph (automatically done by our program) to generate the alternatives graph and the mission controller. The results are given in the 3rd column of Table 1.

Thanks to this methodology, we have generated a mission controller (from the alternatives graph) ready to operate. This controller could react to the failure of a resource, managing the expected changing of functioning mode.

9   Conclusion

In this article, we have presented an architecture allowing different actors to define their part of the mission with an adapted level of abstraction. We have provided the necessary blocks for the description of the mission, in a semi-formal language automatically translated into a formal model (using Petri nets). We have presented the formal methodology related to this architecture allowing to study the accessibility properties of the success of the mission. This methodology also allows the study of the different functioning modes ensuring the control of the robot to fulfill the objectives. Finally, we have generated the mission controller that allow the online control of the robot at the decisional level.

The rest of this work will study how to reduce the alternatives graph to limit the risk of combinatorial explosion in case of complex architecture and mission. One idea could be to locally consider the objectives, or the parallel sections, generating local graph dedicated to each objective instead of generating a complete graph for the whole mission. We are also working on more reliable dependability methods (FMECA, risk analysis, fault tolerance..) and thus refining the fault models, their detection and the recovery after a failure.

Acknowledgment. The authors graciously thank the CUFR, FEDER, NUMEV and Agglo Beziers Mediterranee for their support to this work.

References

1. Edgar, G.J., Barrett, N.S., Morton, A.J.: Biases associated with the use of underwater visual census techniques to quantify the density and size-structure of fish populations. J. Exp. Mar. Biol. Ecol. **308**(2), 269–290 (2004)
2. Adolf, F., Andert, F.: Onboard mission management for a VTOL UAV using sequence and supervisory control. Cutting Edge Robot. **2010**, 301–317 (2010)
3. NATO and RTO, Coalition Battle Management Language (C-BML), Technical report (2012)

4. Meduna, A.: Formal Languages and Computation: Models and Their Applications. CRC Press, Boca Raton (2014)
5. Fernández-Perdomo, E., Cabrera-Gómez, J., Domínguez-Brito, A.C., Hernández-Sosa, D.: Mission specification in underwater robotics. J. Phys. Agents 4(1), 25–34 (2010)
6. Berry, G., Gonthier, G.: The esterel synchronous programming language: design, semantics, implementation. Sci. Comput. Program. 19, 87–152 (1992)
7. Ingham, M., Ragno, R., Williams, B.C.: A reactive model-based programming language for robotic space explorers. In: Proceedings of ISAIRAS-01 (2001)
8. Marchand, H., Rutten, É., Le Borgne, M., Samaan, M.: Formal verification of programs specified with signal: application to a power transformer station controller. Sci. Comput. Program. 41(1), 85–104 (2001)
9. Marchand, H., Bournai, P., Le Borgne, M., Le Guernic, P.: Synthesis of discrete controllers based on the signal environment. In: Boel, R., Stremersch, G. (eds.) Discrete Event Systems. ECC, vol. 569, pp. 479–480. Springer, Boston (2000)
10. Halbwachs, N., Caspi, P., Raymond, P., Pilaud, D.: The synchronous data flow programming language LUSTRE. Proc. IEEE 79(9), 1305–1320 (1991)
11. Harel, D.: Statecharts: a visual formalism for complex systems. Sci. Comput. Program. 8(3), 231–274 (1987)
12. Basu, A., Bensalem, S., Bozga, M., Combaz, J., Jaber, M., Thanh-Hung, N., Sifakis, J.: Rigorous component-based system design using the BIP framework. IEEE Softw. 28, 41–48 (2011)
13. Basu, A., Mounier, L., Poulhiès, M., Pulou, J., Sifakis, J.: Using BIP for modeling and verification of networked systems - a case study on TinyOS-based networks. In: Proceedings of the 6th IEEE International Symposium on Network Computing and Applications, NCA 2007, pp. 257–260 (2007)
14. Ropars, B., Lasbouygues, A., Lapierre, L., Andreu, D.: Thruster's dead-zones compensation for the actuation system of an underwater vehicle. In: ECC: European Control Conference, Linz, Austria, July 2015
15. Jaiem, L., Lapierre, L., GodaryDejean, K., Crestani, D.: Toward performance guarantee for autonomous mobile robotic mission: an approach for hardware and software resources management. In: TAROS 2016, Sheffield, UK (2016)
16. Burch, J.R., Clarke, E.M., McMillan, K.L., Dill, D.L., Hwang, L.J.: Symbolic model checking: 1020 states and beyond. Inf. Comput. 98(2), 142–170 (1992)
17. Alur, R.: Timed Automata. University of Pennsylvania, Technical report (1998)
18. Berthomieu, B., Ribet, P.O., Vernadat, F.: The tool tina-construction of abstract state spaces for petri nets and time petri nets. Int. J. Prod. Res. 42(14), 2741–2756 (2004)

Towards Camera Based Navigation in 3D Maps by Synthesizing Depth Images

Stefan Schubert[⊠], Peer Neubert, and Peter Protzel

TU Chemnitz, 09126 Chemnitz, Germany
{stefan.schubert,peer.neubert,peter.protzel}@etit.tu-chemnitz.de

Abstract. This paper presents a novel approach to localize a robot equipped with an omnidirectional camera within a given 3D map. The pose estimate builds upon the synthesis of panoramic depth images, which are compared to the current view of the camera. We present an algorithmic approach to compute the similarity between these synthetic depth images and visual images, and show how to utilize this image matching for mobile robot navigation tasks, i.e. heading estimation, global localization, and navigation towards a target position. The presented method requires neither additional colour nor laser intensity information in the map. We provide a first evaluation of the involved image processing pipeline and a set of proof-of-concept experiments on a mobile robot. The presented approach supports different use cases like map sharing for heterogeneous robotics teams, or the usage of external sources of 3D maps like extruded floor plans.

Keywords: Camera-based localization · Visual compass · Visual homing · 3D map · Omnidirectional camera

1 Introduction

In this paper, we present a novel approach to combine the advantages of powerful sensors that create 3D maps and cheap and lightweight cameras for mobile robot localization. Prerequisite is a 3D map of the world which has to be given or built in advance, and a camera which is moving around in this world/map (in our experiments, we use a panoramic camera). The map could be built by a 3D laserscanner, which makes this world representation very accurate, and gives metric information for an exact and global localization, however, the map could also be given by other sources like computer models, etc. Once the map is available, a camera which is cheap, light, and with potentially high frame rate moves around in this world. The 3D map is used as a world model which enables the system to synthesize images at arbitrary positions. Subsequently, in order to determine the current position in the world, the synthesized images are compared to the current visual camera view. We want to emphasize that our approach does not require additional information in the 3D map, i.e., there is no need to add colour or intensity information to the 3D points.

Y. Gao et al. (Eds.): TAROS 2017, LNAI 10454, pp. 601–616, 2017.
DOI: 10.1007/978-3-319-64107-2_49

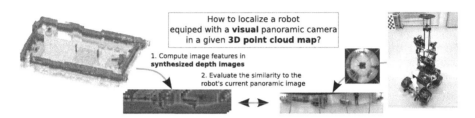

Fig. 1. We present an approach to localize a robot with a panoramic camera in a known 3D point cloud map based on synthesized depth images.

Our proposed system borrows a biological inspiration from a theory about the navigation mechanisms of the dessert ant [1]. Since the heat in the dessert prevents the ant from leaving a pheromone trace, desert ants developed an alternative method to find back to their nest: Before they leave their nest's location, they first take a 360° snapshot of their surroundings as a *home view*. Then, they walk around for foraging. When they want to find back to their nest, they start to acquire new 360° views of their current position. Such current views are then compared to their *home view* which they still remember. By relating both images' content, they can then finally determine a rough home direction. Details on a technical realization of the *ant algorithm* on mobile robots are provided by Möller [2]. His algorithm can be used to implement, e.g., a visual compass, visual homing, visual teach & repeat, or exploration.

Figure 1 illustrates our key idea to adapt this biologically plausible theory of visual navigation for cross sensor modality localization. We replace the ant's *home views* with depth images that are synthesized from a 3D map. We further provide an image processing pipeline, that can match these depth images to the current visual camera view of the robot. Based on this, we are able to solve navigation tasks, e.g., to determine the motion direction ("home direction") to arbitrary positions in the 3D map. In contrast to the dessert ant's approach, there is no need that we visited this place beforehand - all we need is the 3D information.

There are several use-cases for such a system: For instance, a heterogeneous robotics team consisting of one big robot equipped with a heavy (and expensive) 3D laserscanner, and one or more small robots (solely) equipped with cameras. The big robot maps the world and thus defines a reference frame for all small robots which can then manoeuvre afterwards or in parallel to the big robot. Moreover, if the scan rate of the big robot is low (i.e., if the robot has to stop to acquire a new scan [3]), the proposed system can be used to localize the robot between consecutive scans. In contrast to visual odometry, our approach is anchored to the previous laserscan which prevents drift. Another use-case of the proposed system is to preset the 3D map from other sources like CAD models, floor plans, or even from an extruded hand-drawn sketch.

In this paper, we

- present a novel approach for a camera-based localization in 3D maps that might be useful for a variety of navigation problems. As the approach builds upon synthesized depth images, an additional data augmentation with colour or intensity is not necessary.
- show a proof-of-concept implementation for a set of robot navigation tasks.
- provide preliminary experiments which first evaluate the visual pipeline for the comparison of colour and depth images, and second shows its potential for navigation tasks.

In the next section, we give an overview over the related work. The subsequent Sect. 3 gives then a detailed explanation about how to realize our proposed approach from an algorithmic point of view. Then, proof-of-concept experiments are shown in Sect. 4 which prove the applicability of our proposed approach. Finally, a conclusion and a discussion of future work are given in Sect. 5.

2   Related Work

Figure 2 provides a coarse taxonomy of approaches to camera based localization in 3D maps. A prerequisite for the presented problem is a given or previously built map. In [4] the map is given as a textured model, however, in most cases this map is rather generated in advance by active depth sensors like laserscanners or RGB-D cameras [5–13]. Furthermore, this geometrical data can be enhanced either by intensity or colour information. For the most common case of using a laserscanner for map generation, intensity data can be acquired directly with the range measurements as reflectance information [12–14], whereas colour information has to be added by additional sensors like mono- or omni-cameras [4,9–11]. It should be mentioned that RGB-D or stereo-camera could also be used as they measure the range and colour of an obstacle concurrently, however, this approach is less suited due to their low range and bad accuracy compared to laserscanners.

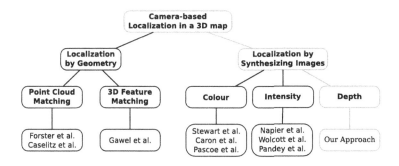

Fig. 2. Taxonomy of the camera-based localization approach in 3D maps including the corresponding related work.

As soon as an initial map is present, the goal is to localize a system equipped with a camera within this 3D map. Basically, there are two ways to achieve a localization: either the geometrical information of the map is used directly, or the map is used to generate synthetic views in the world with a suited projection/camera model. In the first case, the vision information is used to reconstruct the environment's geometrical structure. Therefore, [5,8] are using the Visual SLAM system ORB-SLAM [15] to build a semi-dense point cloud of their environment, whereas [7] builds a dense reconstruction. With both 3D representations given by the map and the visual reconstruction, the position of the camera can be determined either directly with a point cloud registration approach like ICP (Iterative Closest Point) [5–7], or with a 3D feature matching approach like in [8].

The second approach uses the map information to synthesize views close to the actual camera. Subsequently, the synthetic and the real images can be used to compute a transformation between both images. In [4,9–11], they synthesize the images with colour information, which requires a more expensive map generation in advance. In contrast, [12,14] showed that the intensity information of a laserscanner is sufficient to determine the current camera pose in the map. Finally, a transformation between both images has to be computed. The most common approach to compute this transformation is a Mutual Information Maximization based approach (e.g. see [4]) which maximizes the Shannon entropy between both images.

Napier et al. [13] presented a system which is similar to our approach but requires additionally intensity data. They first compute edges in both images with a subsequent patch normalization. Then as a brute force search, they simply sample synthetic images around an initial pose guess of the actual camera pose in order to find a best match which corresponds to the actual camera pose.

3   Algorithmic Approach

We aim at solving navigation tasks using an RGB or grey level camera and a given 3D map that is used for synthesizing depth images. Due to the challenges that raise when comparing images across such different modalities (visual and depth images), we focus on a holistic image comparison in contrast to feature-based methods (e.g., building on local keypoints). The following Sect. 3.1 presents our applied depth image synthesis followed by an explanation of the image processing part of our approach in Sect. 3.2 and a description of how this can be applied to mobile robot navigation tasks in Sect. 3.3.

3.1   Synthesizing Depth Images

Since we focus on the comparison between depth and visual image, we implemented a straightforward approach to generate a synthetic spherical depth image at an requested camera pose in the map. Given the map as point cloud and a requested pose, each point's distance is projected onto a unit sphere centred at this pose. The azimuthal and polar angles are discretised to the target image resolution. By keeping only the minimal distance values for each direction, this spherical grid corresponds to the depth image. Pixels without projected 3D points are set to NaN values. This preliminary approach is easy to implement but its runtime is linear in the number of 3D points. Presumably, the runtime could be improved by the usage of computer graphics techniques including ray tracing algorithms and efficient data structures like k-d trees or octrees.

3.2   Comparing Visual and Depth Images

A key component of the proposed system is the ability to compare visual grey level or colour images with depth images. Figure 3 provides an overview of the algorithmic steps. The input depth and visual images are first processed independently to obtain gradient based image features for both modalities which are combined in the final stage of the algorithm. The processing of the **depth image** involves the following steps:

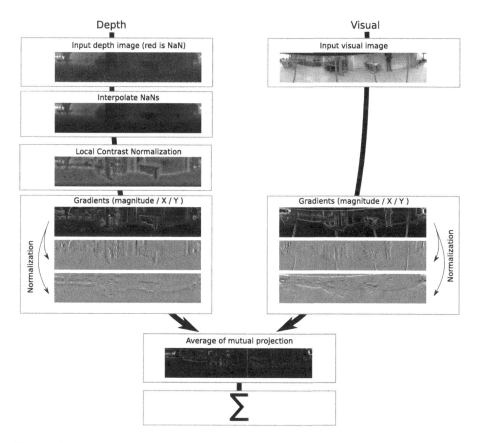

Fig. 3. Overview of the image processing pipeline to compute the similarity between depth and visual images. See text for details. (Color figure online)

1. **Interpolate not-a-number (NaN) values.** Our synthesized depth images, and also depth images from other sources like RGB-D cameras, include a considerable number of NaN pixels for which no depth information is provided. In the input depth image in Fig. 3, they are shown in red. To reduce their influence on subsequent processing steps, they are interpolated from their surrounding non-NaN values.

2. **Local contrast normalization.** The underlying thesis for matching depth and visual images is that those parts in the scene that create depth changes are also likely to create visual features. However, this likelihood is not directly proportional to the magnitude of the depth change: E.g., think of the depth change between a door frame and the wall where it is mounted. Although the absolute change in depth is rather small, it might be as clearly visible in the camera image as the depth edge from the frame to the room behind the door when the door is open. Both sides of the door frame might provide useful features in both modalities.

   To utilize small and large depth steps in an image, we perform a local contrast normalization. The goal is to scale depth changes dependent on the amount of change in their local surrounding. The first step is to smooth the image with a Gaussian kernel (e.g., with standard deviation 2). Then, for each depth pixel $D(i, j)$, we collect the depth information in a $[(2k+1) \times (2k+1)]$ image neighbourhood centralized at this pixel (e.g., k being 2.5% of the image width). Finally, we compute mean μ and standard deviation σ of this data and modify the initial central pixel by

   $$D(i,j) \leftarrow \frac{D(i,j) - \mu}{\sigma} \tag{1}$$

   To avoid spurious edges at patch boundaries, we do not apply a patch normalization to zero mean and unit standard deviation to the whole $[(2k+1) \times (2k+1)]$ neighbourhood in one step, but process each pixel independently with its own neighbourhood. To keep this computational feasible, we utilize integral images and the Steiner translation theorem to compute the means and standard deviations.

3. **Gradients.** To detect depth changes, we compute image gradients on the output of the local contrast normalization. Vertical and horizontal central differences are computed by convolving with Sobel filters. The resulting oriented gradients $\overrightarrow{G}_{depth}$ are additionally normalized to have a total magnitude sum of one for the whole image.

For the **visual image**, we directly compute the gradients $\overrightarrow{G}_{visual}$ by smoothing and central difference computation using Sobel filters and also normalize to a total gradient magnitude sum of one.

To obtain the similarity s between visual and depth images, we evaluate the mutual projections of these gradients by

$$s = \sum_{pixels} \left\| \frac{\overrightarrow{G}_{visual} \cdot \overrightarrow{G}_{depth}}{\|\overrightarrow{G}_{depth}\|^2} \cdot \overrightarrow{G}_{depth} \right\| + \sum_{pixels} \left\| \frac{\overrightarrow{G}_{depth} \cdot \overrightarrow{G}_{visual}}{\|\overrightarrow{G}_{visual}\|^2} \cdot \overrightarrow{G}_{visual} \right\| \tag{2}$$

The later Sect. 4.1 will provide experimental results on this similarity computation including an evaluation of the influence of individual parts of the processing pipeline. While this pipeline can be used with standard cameras (as is done in Sect. 4.1), the following section applies this approach to panoramic images from an omnidirectional camera to solve navigation tasks.

3.3   How to Apply This Approach to Navigation Tasks?

The application to navigation tasks is inspired by the theory of the dessert ant's navigation mechanisms [2] outlined in the introduction. Since we are not able to estimate the underlying camera motion directly from the comparison of depth and visual images, we require to sample possible transformations to find reasonable transformations. In the following, we want to discuss how this can be feasibly applied to three mobile robotics navigation tasks: visual compass, global localization, and navigation towards a goal location.

Visual Compass. Given a local 3D map (e.g., a single 3D laserscan from a nearby location) or a global 3D map and a rough estimate of the current position of the robot, we want to estimate the heading direction of the robot relative to this map based on a panoramic image from the current position.

Based on the comparison of visual and depth images from the previous section, we propose the following approach:

1. Inputs are a panoramic image I and a 3D map.
2. Synthesize a depth image D from the 3D map at the given estimated position. The orientation for synthesis is aligned to the coordinate system (i.e., yaw equals zero).
3. For a discrete set of possible orientations α (e.g., each $10°$), create the rotated panoramic image I_α. This can be efficiently done by circularly shifting the columns.
4. Compute the similarity between each rotated image I_α and D using Eq. 2. For an efficient implementation, Eq. 2 allows to precompute the image gradients and then rotate this feature image instead of computing features for each rotated input image.
5. The estimated robot orientation corresponds to the rotation α^* of the most similar image I_{α^*}.

The evaluation in Sect. 4.2 will show that the quality of the heading estimation is robust to errors in the initial pose estimate.

Global Localization. Given a global 3D map, we want to estimate the absolute pose of the robot in the map. The image similarity computation of Sect. 3.2 seamlessly integrates into Monte Carlo localization. For each sample robot position, a depth image is synthesized and compared to the current panoramic image based on the above described scheme for heading estimation. If only a single panoramic image is given, we can sample all possible robot locations and estimate their likelihood directly from the image similarities (example results are given in Fig. 6). If a sequence of images is available, the similarity from Eq. 2 can be used for computing the resampling weights in a particle filter for successive pose estimation.

Navigating Towards a Goal Location. Given a global 3D map, a rough initial guess of the current robot pose and a nearby target location X, we want to estimate the motion direction towards X. If the rough estimate of the current pose is far away from the target location, it may be sufficient to compute a (accordingly rough estimated) motion direction directly from the geometric relation between the initial guess for the current pose and the target. However, the closer we are to the target location, the higher is the relative error due to the only roughly known current robot pose.

In such cases, we can estimate the motion direction towards the target based on similarities between the current visual panoramic image of the robot and synthesized depth images around the target location. Therefore, we sample possible motion directions ψ and motion distances d. The sample values for ψ and d should be selected based on the geometric relation of the robot pose estimate and the target location. The more uncertain the pose estimate is, the more samples are required. In the results presented in Sect. 4.2, we sample ψ each $10°$ and use $d \in \{0.5\,\text{m}, 1\,\text{m}\}$.

Each sample is used to create a transformed *target location* $X_{\psi,d}$ and to synthesize a depth image from the 3D map at this pose. Again, the above scheme for heading estimation can be used to evaluate the accordance of this sample pose with the current image. The best motion direction can be obtained from the sample motion direction ψ^* that created the most similar synthetic depth image.

4   Experimental Results

This section is divided into two parts: an evaluation of the image processing pipeline and a proof-of-concept experiment on a navigation task with our mobile robot depicted in Fig. 5.

4.1   Image Processing Pipeline Evaluation

Experimental Setup. To answer the question whether we are able to compute a reasonable similarity measure between depth and visual images at all, we first evaluate the image processing pipeline of Sect. 3.2 on an RGB-D dataset. We collected a sequence of 300 image pairs with a hand held Asus Xtion sensor. This RGB-D camera provides pairs of visual and depth images that are (almost) pixel aligned. The sequence was captured in several rooms, a staircase and a hallway of our university building. A typical distance between consecutive images

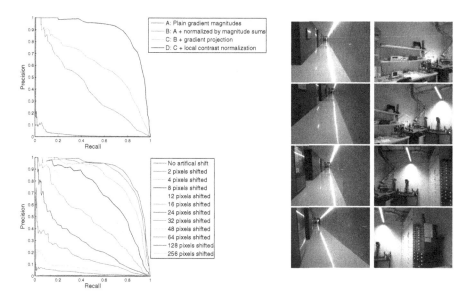

Fig. 4. (*left*) Evaluation results of the image processing pipeline on the RGB-D dataset. See text for details. (*right*) Two example sequence parts of the RGB-D dataset. (Color figure online)

is one meter walking distance and/or 25° rotation mainly around vertical axis. Example images can be seen in Fig. 4.

Based on this dataset, we pose the following place recognition problem: Given a visual image from this dataset, decide which depth images show the same place. This experiment is evaluated by computing precision-recall curves. We use the algorithm of Sect. 3.2 to compute similarities between all possible pairs of visual and depth images, and apply a threshold t to this similarity to obtain binary decisions about matchings. A true-positive (TP) matching is a visual image that is matched to the single correct depth image. A false-positive (FP) is every matching between non corresponding images. There can be one TP and multiple FP matchings for each image. All pairs of corresponding images that are not recognized as matchings are counted for false-negatives (FN). From these values, we compute:

$$recall = \frac{TP}{TP + FN} \qquad precision = \frac{TP}{TP + FP} \qquad (3)$$

The threshold t is varied to compute curves in the precision-recall graph.

Results. Figure 4 provides results of the image processing pipeline of Sect. 3.2 on this task. The similarities computed from the whole described pipeline (the black curve D) showed to be well suited to approach this task. A simple image evaluation, whether there are high gradients at the same parts of the images or not (by element-wise multiplication of the gradient magnitude images), is not sufficient to solve this task (the blue curve A). Normalizing the total sum of gradients in each image before the element-wise multiplication yields the improved red curve (B). Incorporating the direction of the gradients by mutually projecting them on each other further improves the results (the green curve C). Finally, the application of the described local contrast normalization results in an additional significant improvement.

While the images from the RGB-D camera are reasonably well pixel-aligned, for the target robotics application we want the similarity measure to be robust against small deviations. The second graph in Fig. 4 shows an evaluation of the influence of a misalignment between pixels in the visual and depth images. Therefore, we artificially applied a horizontal offset on the depth images before computation of the similarity (we shift the image columns and refill with NaNs). The resulting precision-recall curves show that the performance gradually decreases with increasing amount of misalignment. This behaviour is well suited for application in the navigation approaches described in Sect. 3.3: We don't want the similarity measure to be invariant against such misalignments since this would, e.g., prevent from determining the motion direction close to a target or even the application for a visual compass at all. On the other hand, robustness to reasonable misalignments reduces the required number of pose samples and increases robustness to small errors in the 3D map or the camera calibration.

Although there are significant differences between these RGB-D image pairs and the comparison of panoramic images and synthesized depth image, the good performance of the image processing pipeline on this experiment encourages its application for the navigation task of Sect. 3.3.

4.2   Proof-of-Concept Real-World Experiment

Experimental Setup. This proof-of-concept real-world experiment is conducted for an investigation of the performance of our proposed algorithm for a camera-based localization in a 3D world. As experimental environment we choose a lab (see Fig. 6) in which we mark eight points **A-H** in a 3×1 m grid for which our robot captures omnidirectional camera snapshots.

We use a skid-steering mobile robot[1] which is equipped with both a 3D laserscanner and an omni-camera (see Fig. 5). Our custom-made 3D laserscanner [16] consists of a spinning *Hokuyo UTM-30LX* 2D laserscanner, which achieves higher resolutions than typical ready-to-use 3D laserscanners. It provides $0.25°$ vertical resolution which enables us to acquire dense laserscans of an environment. For the navigation task, we create a 3D Point Cloud map of our room by matching multiple 360° laserscans with the point cloud registration algorithm ICP (Iterative Closest Point). Figure 6 shows the resulting 3D map; note that the ceiling was removed for visualization.

---

[1] A full description of the robot including hardware and software setup can be found in [3].

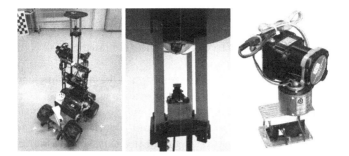

Fig. 5. The used hardware for the proof-of-concept real-world experiment. Our robot (see [3] for a system overview) is equipped with an omni-camera (middle), and a custom-made 3D laserscanner [16] (right).

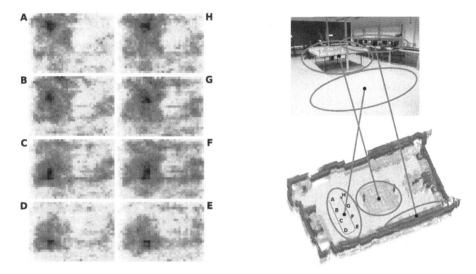

Fig. 6. Visualization of the result of our proof-of-concept real-world experiment. The left side shows heat maps (top view of the room) representing the similarity of depth images synthesized all over the room to the eight omni-camera images at the positions **A-H** (darker colour corresponds to higher similarity). The right 3D map is the model of the room (shown above), and was used to generate depth images at arbitrary positions. (Color figure online)

The used omnidirectional camera consists of a wide-angle camera which points at a curved concentric mirror. The omni-camera has an aperture angle of approx. 185°, and acquires images with a resolution of 480 × 752 pixels. The returned images are rectified with the *OCamCalib Toolbox* by Scaramuzza et al. [17] in order to get 360° panoramic images.

Given the full 3D map of our experimental environment, our robot performs a run along the points **A-H** (see Fig. 6). Meanwhile, it records omnidirectional images at the locations **A** to **H** for the subsequent evaluation (see results below).

Results. To evaluate the localization performance of our proposed approach we synthesize depth images in a regular grid all over the room, and use the algorithmic approach of Sect. 3 to compute their similarity to all eight real omni-images at the positions **A-H** separately.

Figure 6 shows the result of this evaluation: Our algorithm performs quite well as it shows the highest similarities for positions which are close to the actual positions. All maxima approximately correspond to the actual positions of the respective omni-image; this illustrates that our algorithm is able to perform a global localization, this is to estimate global positions in the world. As can be seen, positions close to the maximum show also higher values, and their similarity decreases with higher range. Such a continuous decrease with higher distance to the actual position is advantageous for tasks in which we want to navigate to a target position, as we could simply follow close high-similarity values until we reach our actual target position.

Figure 7 shows the result of a performance measure which investigates the heading estimation error as well as the image feature distance as a function of the range to the actual position. The heading estimation error (Fig. 7, left) represents the difference between the actual orientation of the omni-image and the estimated orientation of the synthesized depth images in the room. An ideal curve would be a horizontal line which remains at zero, however, such a behaviour is impossible since the amount of occlusions and perspective differences increases with a higher range. Therefore, the behaviour of the heading estimation error with increasing range is reasonable: for the first part, it remains relatively flat; this indicates the heading estimation works fine even for a difference to the actual position. The continuous increase for higher ranges is also desirable; it shows that the heading estimation performance does not rapidly drop for small occlusions.

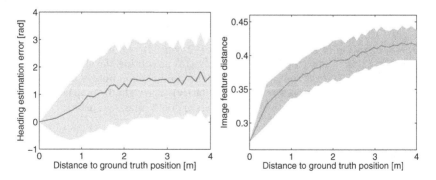

Fig. 7. (*left*) Evaluation of the heading estimation error between omni-image and synthesized depth image as a function of the distance between both images. (*right*) Evaluation of the image feature distance $\frac{1}{1+s}$ between omni-image and synthesized depth images as a function of the distance between both images.

The interpretation of the behaviour of the image distance with respect to the actual position distance in the world (Fig. 7, right) depends on the use case: A very rapid increase of the error value, even for small distances to the ground-truth location, might be advantageous for global localization tasks as we could determine the actual position more exactly, whereas a gradual increase might be more desirable for navigation tasks as we could follow the gradient to reach a target position. Since the curve shows a higher increase for lower values and a more continuous increase for medium distances, it seems to be a good combination for both a global localization and navigation.

Figure 8 shows a vector field which is intended to investigate the performance of an actual navigation task. Here, we use a localization approach as described in Sect. 3 which compares synthesized depth images with the actual omni-image in order to estimate the camera's orientation in the world, and the required movement direction to get to the target position. Given a current panoramic view, we illustrate the estimated motion direction (red lines) for a set of possible target locations (red circles; in a practical application, we would expect only a single target at a time). Each target is evaluated by sampling and evaluating synthetic depth images at angle ψ and motion distance d. The two concentric black circles illustrate the two resulting circles for one of the targets. As can be seen, for most of the target locations, the resulting motion directions connect

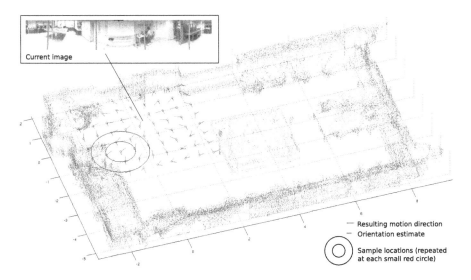

Fig. 8. Estimation of motion direction from the current pose to each of the target locations shown as red circles. For each of the targets, we sample depth images from the local neighbourhood at angles ψ on two circles with radius d of 0.5 and 1.0 m that are centred at the target. For one example target, these circles are shown in black. The red lines indicate the estimated motion direction between the current pose and target. The short blue lines show the estimated orientation of the current view (this should point parallel to the short dimension of the room). (Color figure online)

the target pose and the current view location. In particular, for many target locations whose distance is larger than d from the current image (i.e., the current image location is not on the black circles), there are reasonable motion direction estimates as well.

5   Conclusion and Future Work

In this paper, we dealt with the problem of camera-based localization in a given 3D map. Our presented approach builds upon synthesized depth images which are compared to real omnidirectional images in order to determine the current pose of the camera. We discussed how this image matching can be applied for navigation tasks like visual compass, global localization, or navigation towards a target position. The evaluation of the image processing part on an RGB-D dataset showed that the algorithm is able to provide reasonable similarity measures between visual and depth images. The final set of proof-of-concept experiments on mobile robot navigation tasks also showed promising results and revealed plenty of open questions for future work.

Our aim is to investigate the applicability of this algorithm for real-world indoor scenes like office environments, but also for outdoor scenarios like in the SpaceBot Cup; a German national contest on a moon-like surface which we attended in 2013 and 2015 (see [3] for details). For this outdoor navigation task, we intend to use a heterogeneous robot team which consists of a bigger robot, like in our real-world experiment in this work, and a smaller robot, which is not equipped with an on-board 3D laserscanner, so that it has to use the camera to localize itself in the bigger robot's 3D map which is acquired with a 3D laserscanner.

During our experiments we encountered problems with the calibration of our omni-camera. The camera-mirror alignment and consequently our intrinsic calibration is sensitive to mechanical strains. Hence, the applicability of our approach has to be investigated for fish-eye cameras, or even standard field-of-view cameras, which are less sensitive for mechanical strain. Furthermore, the system is also sensitive to its extrinsic calibration, i.e. the orientation of the vertical camera axis in the map has to be known. In uneven outdoor terrain, this could be addressed by combination with an IMU.

The current system is not runtime optimized and completely implemented in Matlab, which slows down the computation time. Beside a more efficient computational implementation, algorithmic improvements can particularly address the number of required depth-image samplings. This could be achieved by different techniques: First, a particle filter could be applied which reduces the number of possible locations in the world. Second, more sophisticated techniques for a reduction of depth-image sampling could be developed like the usage of image warping techniques which are applied in the mentioned *ant algorithm* by Möller [2].

Currently, the features of our synthesized depth images are computed in the 2D image space. In our future work, we want to compare this approach to a projection of 3D features onto our synthesized images. Our current colour-depth-image comparison is a hand-designed approach; we believe that the usage of learning techniques could contribute to a performance improvement of our approach as it could learn more sophisticated features.

In future work, we will also evaluate the benefit from enhancing the synthesized depth images with intensity and/or colour information and include a comparisons of our system to other existing approaches which encounter the problem of a camera-based localization in 3D maps.

References

1. Möller, R.: A model of ant navigation based on visual prediction. J. Theor. Biol. **305**, 118–130 (2012)
2. Möller, R.: Local visual homing by warping of two-dimensional images. Robot. Auton. Syst. **57**(1), 87–101 (2009)
3. Lange, S., Wunschel, D., Schubert, S., Pfeifer, T., Weissig, P., Uhlig, A., Truschzinski, M., Protzel, P.: Two autonomous robots for the dlr spacebot cup - lessons learned from 60 minutes on the moon. In: Proceedings of ISR 2016: 47th International Symposium on Robotics, pp. 1–8, June 2016
4. Caron, G., Dame, A., Marchand, E.: Direct model based visual tracking and pose estimation using mutual information. Image Vis. Comput. **32**(1), 54–63 (2014)
5. Caselitz, T., Steder, B., Ruhnke, M., Burgard, W.: Monocular camera localization in 3D lidar maps. In: 2016 IEEE/RSJ International Conference on Intelligent Robots and Systems (IROS), pp. 1926–1931, October 2016
6. Caselitz, T., Steder, B., Ruhnke, M., Burgard, W.: Matching geometry for long-term monocular camera localization. In: ICRA Workshop: AI for Long-Term Autonomy (2016)
7. Forster, C., Pizzoli, M., Scaramuzza, D.: Air-ground localization and map augmentation using monocular dense reconstruction. In: 2013 IEEE/RSJ International Conference on Intelligent Robots and Systems, pp. 3971–3978, November 2013
8. Gawel, A., Cieslewski, T., Dubé, R., Bosse, M., Siegwart, R., Nieto, J.: Structure-based vision-laser matching. In: 2016 IEEE/RSJ International Conference on Intelligent Robots and Systems (IROS), pp. 182–188, October 2016
9. Pascoe, G., Maddern, W., Newman, P.: Direct visual localisation and calibration for road vehicles in changing city environments. In: 2015 IEEE International Conference on Computer Vision Workshop (ICCVW), pp. 98–105, December 2015
10. Pascoe, G., Maddern, W., Stewart, A.D., Newman, P.: Farlap: fast robust localisation using appearance priors. In: 2015 IEEE International Conference on Robotics and Automation (ICRA), pp. 6366–6373, May 2015
11. Stewart, A.D., Newman, P.: Laps - localisation using appearance of prior structure: 6-dof monocular camera localisation using prior pointclouds. In: IEEE International Conference on Robotics and Automation, pp. 2625–2632, May 2012
12. Wolcott, R.W., Eustice, R.M.: Visual localization within lidar maps for automated urban driving. In: 2014 IEEE/RSJ International Conference on Intelligent Robots and Systems, pp. 176–183, September 2014
13. Napier, A., Corke, P., Newman, P.: Cross-calibration of push-broom 2d lidars and cameras in natural scenes. In: 2013 IEEE International Conference on Robotics and Automation, pp. 3679–3684, May 2013
14. Pandey, G., McBride, J.R., Savarese, S., Eustice, R.M.: Automatic extrinsic calibration of vision and lidar by maximizing mutual information. J. Field Robot. **32**(5), 696–722 (2015)

15. Mur-Artal, R., Montiel, J.M.M., Tardós, J.D.: ORB-SLAM: a versatile and accurate monocular SLAM system. IEEE Trans. Robot. **31**(5), 1147–1163 (2015)
16. Schubert, S., Neubert, P., Protzel, P.: How to build and customize a high-resolution 3D laserscanner using off-the-shelf components. In: Alboul, L., Damian, D., Aitken, J.M.M. (eds.) TAROS 2016. LNCS, vol. 9716, pp. 314–326. Springer, Cham (2016). doi:10.1007/978-3-319-40379-3_33
17. Scaramuzza, D., Martinelli, A., Siegwart, R.: A toolbox for easily calibrating omnidirectional cameras. In: 2006 IEEE/RSJ International Conference on Intelligent Robots and Systems, pp. 5695–5701, October 2006

Real-World, Real-Time Robotic Grasping with Convolutional Neural Networks

Joe Watson, Josie Hughes[(⊠)], and Fumiya Iida

Bio-Inspired Robotics Lab, Department of Engineering,
University of Cambridge, Cambridge, UK
joewatson125@gmail.com, jaeh2@cam.ac.uk, fi224@cam.ac.uk

Abstract. Adapting to uncertain environments is a key obstacle in the development of robust robotic object manipulation systems, as there is a trade-off between the computationally expensive methods of handling the surrounding complexity, and the real-time requirement for practical operation. We investigate the use of Deep Learning to develop a real-time scheme on a physical robot. Using a Baxter Research Robot and Kinect sensor, a convolutional neural network (CNN) was trained in a supervised manner to regress grasping coordinates from RGB-D data. Compared to existing methods, regression via deep learning offered an efficient process that learnt generalised grasping features and processed the scene in real-time. The system achieved a successful grasp rate of 62% and a successful detection rate of 78% on a diverse set of physical objects across varying position and orientation, executing grasp detection in 1.8 s on a CPU machine and a complete physical grasp and move in 60 s on the robot.

Keywords: Grasping · Deep learning · Convolution Neural Networks · Manipulation

1   Introduction

Operating in an unstructured environments is a prevailing challenge in robotics. The inherent stochasticity which exists in natural settings opposes the deterministic assumption that is often the foundation of robotic design. One key challenge to achieving robotic manipulation in unstructured environments is visuomotor control for object manipulation; the process of observing and grasping an object. The key challenge here is the translation of visual perception into physical motion and the ability to robustly infer grasping points of an object to enable successful picking. Grasping points are difficult to assess due to the continuous array of viable solutions which depend on geometry, mass distribution, material and object function. The sensing and decision making should be robust to environmental disturbances. For humans, grasping objects is an instantaneous and intuitive process, but algorithmic approaches are typically search-based, either through analysing the scene or leveraging a knowledge-base.

© Springer International Publishing AG 2017
Y. Gao et al. (Eds.): TAROS 2017, LNAI 10454, pp. 617–626, 2017.
DOI: 10.1007/978-3-319-64107-2_50

The field of Deep Learning has yielded several significant advances for robotics, particularly in scene understanding and motor control [17]. The general neural network architecture has been shown repeatedly to be able learn general, complex relationships from data; and that their levels of performance validate the computational and data intensive requirements.

This paper investigates the use of vision-based learning for robotic grasping, specifically using Convolutional Neural Networks (CNNs) to infer grasping coordinates from vision and depth. The approach will use a Kinect sensor and will infer the grasping points from vision using regression, reproducing the work of Redmon and Angelova [14]. This approach achieved impressive results, but was never implemented on a robotic platform or tested outside the dataset. This research implements this approach in real-time using the Baxter robot platform.

1.1   Literature Review

Deterministic, object-orientated grasping was an early approach to robotic grasping, using CAD models and simulation to find the optimal grasping configuration based on the object and manipulator. GraspIt was devised in 2011 [13], with a large repository of 3D models of objects developed [11]. This used a deterministic, grasp-orientated approach, using an algorithm to search and extract cylindrical templates from a raw point cloud feed. This appears to work well for cluttered scenes, but is biased towards cylindrical objects and handles. Probabilistic approaches were pioneered at Cornell, initially using filter banks, search and logistic regression trained on synthetic data [6], the machine learning approach was eventually extended to the field of deep learning. Lenz [9] devised a two-stage neural network, using a sliding window to detect viable grasping rectangles and a second neural network to select the best. Although a costly search approach, it achieved impressive results, generalising well to new objects and able to sort cluttered scenes. This approach was extended to training a single convolutional neural network to regress the grasping coordinates directly [14]. Using fast GPU libraries, the system was able to operate in real-time, however this was not physically implemented on a robot. Since this research was undertaken, several new approaches have been developed. One is 'self-supervision', where a trained network is used to generate a larger dataset autonomously, which is then used for further training. Pinto [12] first explored this approach, using the network to classify viable grasps via the wrist camera as the arm moved around the scene, an approach similar to Lenz. Levine [10] developed self-supervision further with multiple robots training in unison, and integrating the CNN as a visual servoing controller from just a single monocular camera. Johns [7] used a CNN as a *grasp function* that learns to classify a 'score' (discretized success rate from experience) for each location in the input image, and was trained on synthetic data.

2   System and Model

2.1   Experimental Setup

The Baxter research robot [1] has been used to demonstrate the grasping capabilities. The robot has two seven degrees of freedom arms, each with an embedded camera and parallel gripper with a travel of 35 mm. The robot is controlled using ROS (Robot Operating System) [2], an open-source software framework designed for robotic systems and provides an inverse kinematics solver for position control. A Kinect sensor mounted on top of Baxter is used to stream RGB-Depth (RGB-D) data for the surrounding environment. The experimental setup is illustrated in Fig. 1.

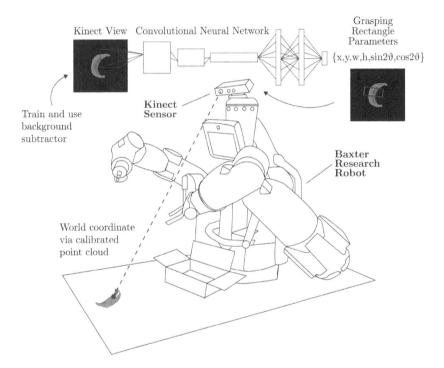

Fig. 1. Illustration of the robotic grasping process, from processing the Kinect feed to inferring the spatial location of the grasping point.

2.2   Grasping Procedure

The scene is preprocessed from the RGB-D stream into an RGD stream with background subtraction, using the popular Gaussian Mixture Model approach [19]. Applying the subtractor to the training data and real-time feed reduces possible variations between the two from the CNN's perspective. The image is then cropped to 224×224 and passed through the CNN, which produces a estimate of the grasping rectangle for the parallel gripper in pixel-space. These coordinates are converted to the robot's world frame of reference by using the disparity view in the Kinect's frame of reference and the geometrical transform between the two, which was found through calibration. Baxer's prepackaged inverse kinematics and position control are then used for motor control. As with the trend in previous literature, the grasping is tackled in a planar manner, with the wrist generally perpendicular to the surface. The five-dimensional parameterization of the grasping rectangle is illustrated in Fig. 9. Following Redmon [14], the sine and cosine of the orientation are used as the network's output, in order to encapsulate the 180° symmetry of the rectangle.

2.3   Online Evaluation

To properly assess the grasping estimate in the real world without extensive hand-labelling, a novel automatic approach was devised using markers. With the planar approach, viable grasping rectangles can be assumed to exist perpendicular to set of paths (such as ridges, handles, etc.). By placing markers and detecting them using computer vision, these paths could be piecewise-linearly approximated and used to generate a viable set of approximate ground-truth grasping rectangles. The closest match was then used to evaluate the CNN's output. An illustration of this process, and example of it in action, can be seen in Fig. 2.

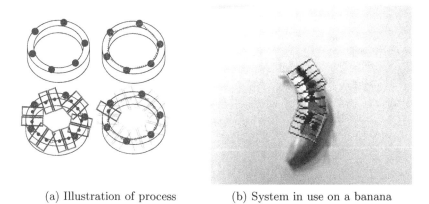

(a) Illustration of process   (b) System in use on a banana

Fig. 2. Marker-based method of online grasping rectangle ground truth generation for evaluation.

2.4   Deep Learning

The convolutional neural network is based on the model developed by Redmon [14] but trained from scratch using the Caffe library [5] rather than the CUDNN library [4] used in their work. The architecture takes advantage of Transfer Learning [3] to speed up training of the convolutional layers, so it is trained using a variant of the popular AlexNet network [8] pretrained on the large ImageNet image classification dataset. The fully connected layers were adapted to regress to the six-dimensional grasping rectangle parameters, using the batch-mean squared error cost function and initialised using Caffe's Xavier distribution. To stabilise regression, the pixel intensities of the input were scaled to the range [0,1], and the pixel labels were scaled down by 224, making them a fraction of the input dimension. Like Redmon, to make use of the pretrained three channel input and the four channel RGB-D data, the blue channel is arbitrarily removed and RGD data is passed to the network input.

The Cornell grasping dataset contains 280 everyday items hand-labelled with a variable number of correct and incorrect grasping rectangles. Only the single rectangle estimator from Redmon's work was replicated, and was trained on the first positive label from the dataset to avoid averaging of the positive labels. The data was randomly augmented x27 times via translation and rotation, to reduce overfitting (Fig. 3).

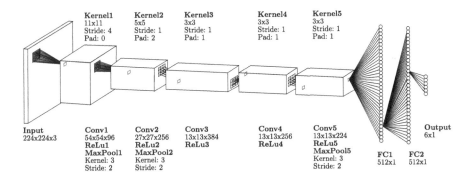

Fig. 3. Schematic of AlexNet-based CNN architecture for estimating a single grasp

The network was trained to 26 epochs over 42 h on an AWS EC2 2.2 × large server. The base learning rate was 0.0005, and scaled by 0.8 every three epochs. Momentum and weight decay were used, with weights of 0.8 and 0.001 respectively. Dropout was used [16], with probability of 0.5 applied to the fully connected units, to reduce overfitting.

3   Results

3.1   Deep Learning

The network was assessed by single-fold cross-validation. As with Lenz and Redmon, the rectangles are evaluated using the Jacquard Index between the areas of the estimate and ground-truth rectangle, which incorporates an allowable spatial variation in the position.

$$\text{For A and B, Jacquard Index } J(A,B)|\& = \frac{|A \cap B|}{|A \cup B|} \text{ so } 0 \leq J(A,B) \leq 1 \quad (1)$$

Lenz outlined a rectangle metric [9] for evaluating viable grasp, where by the Jacquard Index should be greater than 0.25 and the orientation error less than 30° in comparison to the ground truth (Table 1).

Table 1. Statistics of CNN evaluation

Dataset	Jacquard Index	Orientation error (°)		Rectangle metric
	Mean	Mean	St. Dev.	Success (%)
Training	0.61	−0.95	31.4	81
Testing	0.35	−4.4	36.9	50

3.2 Visualisation

To understand what the networks' learning process and ensure it behaves as expected, the units of the last fully connected layer were visualised using the Deep Visualisation Toolbox [18] and compared to the ImageNet-trained classification model used as a base for transfer learning. The visualisation works by optimising white noise at the input to maximise the response of the intended unit. A comparison between responses can be seen in Fig. 5, and shows that the network has learnt subtle grasping features - typically orientated features and edges. To aid generalisation, each unit has also learnt a variety of features across the input space. The difference between regression and classification is also clear, with the classification having a strong, textural response while with regression the activations are far more subtle (Figs. 4 and 6).

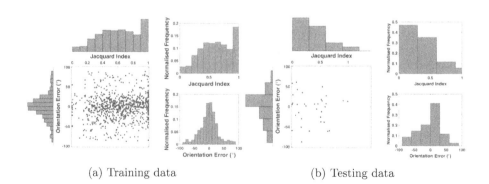

(a) Training data   (b) Testing data

Fig. 4. Scatter plot and marginal histograms of training results

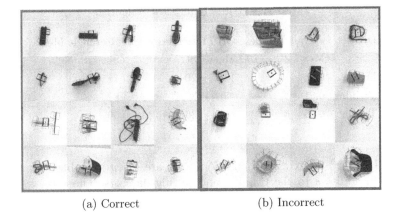

(a) Correct   (b) Incorrect

Fig. 5. Visual results on training data

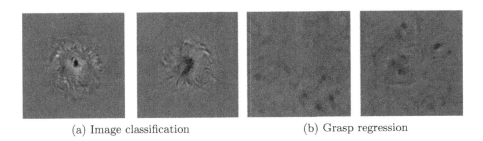

(a) Image classification   (b) Grasp regression

Fig. 6. Visualisations of the activations of the nal fully connected layer units for two AlexNet-based architectures.

3.3   Physical Grasping

For a physical grasping system, it is difficult to evaluate performance beyond pass or fail. For this system, it felt important to separate the performance of the grasp detection subsystem (incorporating the image processing and CNN) and the kinematic subsystem (involving the calibrated point cloud, inverse kinematics and gripper). Assessing the grasp detection would involve generating a new ground truth data set for the experimental set-up, and labelling each object consistently and thoroughly would be immensely time-consuming work. The online evaluation method outlined in Sect. 2.3 was used to efficiently evaluate the CNN in a real-world setting. The physical system was assessed in a pass/fail manner, across multiple varied everyday objects in a variety of positions and orientations. A workspace was divided into a 3×3 grid $45\,cm^2$, with each object randomly placed within each cell at two perpendicular orientations. Rotationally symmetric objects were tested in only one orientation.

Table 2. Statistics of physical evaluation

| Dataset | Jacquard Index | Orientation error (°) | | Rectangle Metric |
	Mean	Mean	St. Dev.	Success (%)
Live	0.63	15.7	20	78
Training	0.61	−0.95	31.4	81
Testing	0.25	−4.4	36.9	50

The Jacquard index and orientation error are given in Table 2 for the live datasets in addition to the training and testing datasets. The success rate for determining viable grasping rectangles and for physical grasping of objects are given in Figs. 7 and 8.

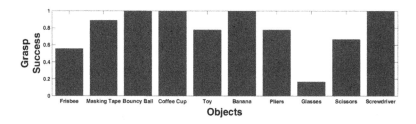

Fig. 7. Success rate of viable grasping rectangle estimates over objects for physical grasping

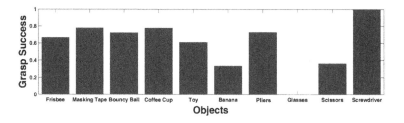

Fig. 8. Success rate for physical grasping over objects

The grasping system was implemented successfully, with each grasp executing within around 60 s. Figure 8 shows that the system is reasonably consistent, with the physical aspect only reducing the expected success rate (based on the rectangle estimates) by a small amount (comparing Figs. 7 and 8). The weakness to the frisbee, glasses and scissors was down to the CNN, while the weakness due to the physical system was primarily seen in the ball and banana. The ball requires precise positioning, which Baxter and the inverse kinematics cannot provide. Despite a correct rectangle and only a small placement error, the grasp

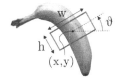

Fig. 9. Illustration of parameterization of grasping rectangle

was not successful. Interestingly, the interpolation problem can be observed with the pliers, but the handles are close enough to still enable a good grasp. A link to videos of the system in use can be found in the Appendix A.

The use of Background Subtraction became a significant issue in the system, with background variation increasing over time and affecting performance of the network. Shadows were also an issue, as they interpreted as part of the object.

4 Discussion and Conclusion

The results offer an initial demonstration that a robotic grasping system which uses a regression-based CNN can be used as a functional real-time grasping point estimator. The physical implementation has successfully integrated a range of robotic paradigms. The system was found to successfully grasp a range of items, across orientation and workspace location. The novel method of ground truth approximation for evaluation, using markers and image processing, was found to produce results consistent with the actual ground truth assessment.

Acknowledgements. Thanks to Lenz [9] and Saxena [15] for producing training dataset used, Pinot and Gupta [10] for helpful discussion, and Dr. Ankur Handa for support and encouragement.

A Appendix

Videos of the grasping system may be found at tiny.cc/birlDeepGrasp. Full training and testing results may be found at tiny.cc/birlTraining and tiny.cc/birlTesting. The ROS-related code may be found at tiny.cc/birlGraspCode.

References

1. Baxter—redening robotics and manufacturing—rethink robotics. http://www.rethinkrobotics.com/baxter/. Accessed 19 May 2016
2. Ros.org—powering the world's robots. http://www.ros.org/. Accessed 22 May 2016
3. Bengio, Y.: Deep learning of representations for unsupervised and transfer learning. In: Guyon, I., Dror, G., Lemaire, V., Taylor, G.W., Silver, D.L. (eds.) ICML Unsupervised and Transfer Learning. JMLR Proceedings, vol. 27, pp. 17–36. JMLR.org (2012). http://dblp.uni-trier.de/db/journals/jmlr/jmlrp27.html#Bengio12

4. Chetlur, S., Woolley, C., Vandermersch, P., Cohen, J., Tran, J., Catanzaro, B., Shelhamer, E.: CUDNN: efficient primitives for deep learning. CoRR abs/1410.0759 (2014). http://arxiv.org/abs/1410.0759
5. Jia, Y., Shelhamer, E., Donahue, J., Karayev, S., Long, J., Girshick, R., Guadarrama, S., Darrell, T., Eecs, U.C.B.: Caffe: convolutional architecture for fast feature embedding (2014)
6. Jiang, Y., Amend, J.R., Lipson, H., Saxena, A.: Learning hardware agnostic grasps for a universal jamming gripper. In: ICRA, pp. 2385–2391. IEEE (2012)
7. Johns, E., Leutenegger, S., Davison, A.J.: Deep learning a grasp function for grasping under gripper pose uncertainty. CoRR abs/1608.02239 (2016). http://arxiv.org/abs/1608.02239
8. Krizhevsky, A., Sutskever, I., Hinton, G.E.: ImageNet classification with deep convolutional neural networks. In: Advances In Neural Information Processing Systems, pp. 1–9 (2012)
9. Lenz, I., Lee, H., Saxena, A.: Deep learning for detecting robotic grasps. Int. J. Robot. Res. **34**(4–5), 705–724 (2015)
10. Levine, S., Pastor, P., Krizhevsky, A., Quillen, D.: Learning hand-eye coordination for robotic grasping with deep learning and large-scale data collection. CoRR abs/1603.02199 (2016). http://arxiv.org/abs/1603.02199
11. Pas, A., Platt, R.: Localizing handle-like grasp affordances in 3D point clouds. In: International Symposium on Experimental Robotics (2014)
12. Pinto, L., Gupta, A.: Supersizing self-supervision: learning to grasp from 50K tries and 700 robot hours (2015). http://arxiv.org/abs/1509.06825
13. Popovic, M., Kootstra, G., Jorgensen, J.A., Kragic, D., Kruger, N., Jørgensen, J.A., Krueger, N.: Grasping unknown objects using an Early Cognitive Vision system for general scene understanding. In: 2011 IEEE/RSJ International Conference on Intelligent Robots and Systems (IROS), pp. 987–994 (2011)
14. Redmon, J., Angelova, A.: Real-time grasp detection using convolutional neural networks. In: Proceedings of IEEE International Conference on Robotics and Automation, vol. 36(2), pp. 1316–1322 (2015)
15. Saxena, A., Wong, L., Quigley, M., Ng, A.Y.: A vision-based system for grasping novel objects in cluttered environments. In: Kaneko, M., Nakamura, Y. (eds.) Robotics Research, vol. 66. Springer, Heidelberg (2010)
16. Srivastava, N., Hinton, G., Krizhevsky, A., Sutskever, I., Salakhutdinov, R.: Dropout: a simple way to prevent neural networks from overfitting. J. Mach. Learn. Res. **15**(1), 1929–1958 (2014). http://dl.acm.org/citation.cfm?id=2627435.2670313
17. Tai, L., Liu, M.: Deep-learning in mobile robotics - from perception to control systems: a survey on why and why not. CoRR abs/1612.07139 (2016). http://arxiv.org/abs/1612.07139
18. Yosinski, J., Clune, J., Nguyen, A., Fuchs, T., Lipson, H.: Understanding neural networks through deep visualization. In: Deep Learning Workshop, International Conference on Machine Learning (ICML) (2015)
19. Zivkovic, Z.: Improved adaptive Gaussian mixture model for background subtraction. In: 17th International Conference on Proceedings of the Pattern Recognition, (ICPR 2004), vol. 2, pp. 28–31 (2004). http://dx.doi.org/10.1109/ICPR.2004.479

3D Printed Sensorized Soft Robotic Manipulator Design

Josie Hughes[(✉)] and Fumiya Iida

Bio-Inspired Robotics Lab, Department of Engineering,
University of Cambridge, Cambridge, UK
{jaeh2,fi224}@cam.ac.uk

Abstract. Anthropomorphic soft robotics systems which replicate the stiffness and range of human joints can be challenging to develop and fabricate. By using 3D printing it is possible to create flexible joints which can have the mechanical impedance and joint range determined by the physical parameters; this allows compliant manipulators to be produced from rigid materials in a single 3D print. The dexterity of the fingers developed using rapid prototyping methods has been demonstrated by using the approach with soft manipulators to handle chopsticks to grip objects.

Keywords: Manipulation · Soft robotics · 3D printing

1 Introduction

The ability to interact with the environment through manipulation is key for many robotic applications [14] with robots increasingly required to work in complex, non-deterministic human environments [18]. Soft robotic manipulators offer a compliance and adaptability, enabling safer, softer interactions with the environment and increases the ability of the manipulator to deal with uncertainty in the environment. There are many challenges associated with the development of soft robotics, one of which is develop manipulators that are easy to manufacture, control and customise whilst still enabling reliability and repeatability in movement [9]. There has been a wide range of soft body manipulators developed, including soft continuum body manipulators such as the universal gripper, [1]. Although such continuum body manipulators allow for 'universal' gripping using the principle of jamming to alter the stiffness and rigidity of the gripper, the design does not allow for any 'in-hand' manipulation of objects which could be required for some applications. More bio-inspired muscular hydrostat type manipulators, such as octopus arms or elephant trunks still has much of the behaviour of a continuum body, whilst still being able to achieve some 'in hand' manipulation [3,12]. However such approached lack the dexterity of multiple limbed manipulators such as the human hand, which could be considered as a 'hybrid' manipulator on the soft to rigid scale. The hand has a rigid bone structure which enables significant force to be applied and in-hand manipulation to be

© Springer International Publishing AG 2017
Y. Gao et al. (Eds.): TAROS 2017, LNAI 10454, pp. 627–636, 2017.
DOI: 10.1007/978-3-319-64107-2_51

performed, but also has a soft compliant outer skin and tissues layer combined with elastic tendons and ligaments which offer compliance and adaptability [10]. There have been a number of soft bio-inspired robotic hands which have adopted different approaches. Many pneumatic limbed manipulators use the expansion of chambers to cause actuation and do not have a joint structure [11] whereas more anthropomorphic based robotic hands, which have integrated soft ligaments and tendons, enable the compliance of the human hand to be replicated [5]. The construction of bio-inspired anthropomorphic soft manipulators can often be extremely time consuming requiring many parts and stages of construction and is often not repeatable or reliable. Therefore the ability to reliably produce soft manipulators with rapid prototyping methods, which require a reduced number of actuators whilst still providing the range and dexterity of movement that can be achieved using complex systems is highly useful.

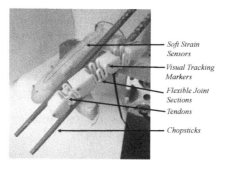

Fig. 1. Experimental setup developed using sensorized flexible finger design which enables chopsticks to be used to manipulate objects and detect size when grasped.

3D printing is a technology which has enabled robotics designs to be rapidly developed, tested and also tailored to a specific application. There has been some development of entirely 3D printed joints, however many of these are highly rigid ball and socket joints [2,13]. This paper presents a method for 3D printing joints and manipulators which have variable flexibility and compliance, such that a single print can be used to develop a single manipulator. The hybrid design is created from a flexible 3D printed inner structure and a silicone outer 3D structure which offers compliance and adaptability (Fig. 1). The 3D printed structure has joints which reflect that of a human hand and are elastic, such that antagonistic pairs of tendons are not required. Soft sensors have been added to the structure to enable the deformation and position of the hybrid manipulator to be determined. The capabilities and compliant nature of this manipulator have been demonstrated by creating a robotic hand which can use chop sticks to grasp objects.

2   Materials and Methods

2.1   3D Printing Flexible Joints

The flexible joint designed has two parallel thin rotation spring sections printed between more rigid 'bone' type sections (Fig. 2). This allows flexing in the X and Z directions as required for finger joints, whilst offering limited movement in the other degrees of freedom of the joint. The joints are 3D printed in ABS plastic, with the flexible sections printed parallel to the print bed.

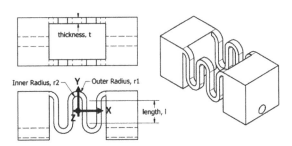

Fig. 2. CAD drawing of the 3D printed flexible joint showing the reference system and the parameters which can be varied.

Within 3D-space the joint (Fig. 2) has 6 degrees of freedom and has four key tunable design characteristics: length of flexures, inner radius, outer radius and thickness. There are three degrees of freedom corresponding to movement along an axis as shown in Fig. 3 and the torsional moments around these axes. The joint has been simulated in Finite Element Analysis (FEA) software. Forces are applied in the X, Y, Z directions are shown in Fig. 3 with the relevant displacement measured. It can be seen that (Fig. 4) there is a close agreement with real and simulation results; in each case displacement increase linearly with the force applied. The displacement is most significant in the y-direction which is the direction in which displacement is required. In the x direction this can be considered negligible, and although present in the z-direction considerably smaller to that in the x direction. Corresponding results are observed for the three axes when moments are applied. There are two tunable characteristics, the range of movement of the joint in the X and Z axis and also the stiffness of the joint. By understanding the effects the parameters of the joint have on the tunable characteristics, a finger can be designed with joints with the correct range for that specific joint and have a stiffness or mechanical impedance which matches that of the biological system being modelled, which itself has a stiffness resulting from the ligaments, tendons and other tissues within fingers.

The range of movement of the joint can be determined by setting the joint parameters to physically limit the joint movement; this is predominantly determined by the joint outer radius and length of the spring section of the joint. Another characteristics which can be determined by the design parameters is

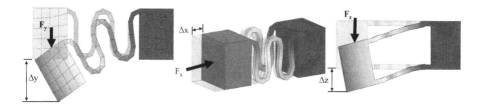

Fig. 3. FEA simulation of the joint showing the three main degrees of freedom (DOF) (x, y, z), the forces which can be applied and the resulting displacement.

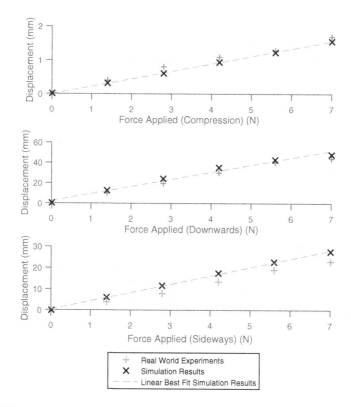

Fig. 4. FEA simulation results and real world experiment results when force is applied to the three different DOF (in order x, y, z) with no rotational moments. Joint parameters: l = 8 mm, r1 = 3 mm, r2 = 5 mm.

the joint stiffness and compliance. The human hand has inherent mechanical impedance as a result of the structure and the ligament and tendon system. The ability to determine this stiffness or impedance allows replication of the hand mechanics. This mechanical impedance of the finger describes the relationship between externally applied force and the motion of the body; this impedance considers the damping and inertia which relates the applied force to the velocity and acceleration of the body. The passive impedance assists the human hand in dealing with changes in grasping conditions [7]. The stiffness of a finger increases linearly with the force applied, with a strong grasping requiring greater stiffness to apply a greater force [8] and is typically in the region of 50–200 N/mm [17].

Using FEA the effects of varying a joint parameter on the stiffness can be investigated, with theoretical and experimental displacement determined for when a 5 N load is applied via the tendon (Fig. 5). There is a close correspondence between experimental and simulation results. Varying the length causes a linear increase in the downwards deflection and increasing the thickness of the spring sections reduces the deflection. Increasing the outer radius increases the deflection, however, the rate of increase of this displacement varies with the thickness of this section.

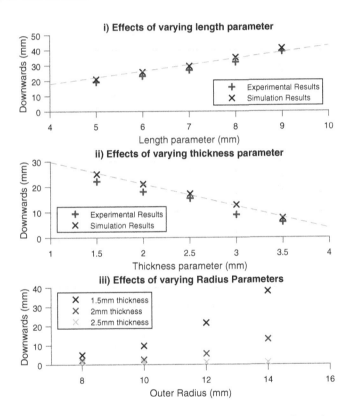

Fig. 5. Varying deflection when a 5 N load is applied for joints of varying parameters.

2.2 Hybrid Finger Development

The dimensions, range of movement and stiffness of the finger joints have been designed to match that of a human. To add a skin type structure to the manipulator to achieve a closer match the mechanical impedance and compliance of fingers, the 3D printed finger and tendons are cast in a finger shaped mould using EcoFlex 00-20 Silicone. To control the position of the finger, the tendons are each attached to a DC motor, which are controlled via a microcontroller using a speed controller.

2.3   Soft Sensing

To detect the 3D position of the manipulator, soft conductive thermoplastic elastomer (CTPE) sensors have been added to the finger. Conductive Thermoplastic Elastomer (CTPE) is a thermoplastic elastic matrix which is homogeneously mixed with carbon black powder under high pressure and temperature [16]. This process produces an electrically conductive material with a resistivity which varies linearly with the strain applied [15] and can be extruded into fibres. The sensors have previously been demonstrated in wearable applications by integrating into clothing [15] and gloves [6]. These fibres can undergo strains of over 100% without reaching their tensile limit (Fig. 6).

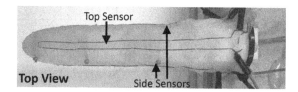

Fig. 6. The sensorized finger showing the three integrated sensors; the top sensor to detect flexing and the two side sensors the side to side movement.

Three sensors have been attached to the silicone; one sensor placed across the top of the sensor and others on the two sides of the sensors. The sensors are connected to a potential divider to provide an analog output before being connected to a microcontroller. The top sensor are used to give an indication of the strain of the outer finger and the flex/unflex motion of the finger with the side sensors allowing sideways deflection to be determined.

3   Results

To test the sensors visual markers were placed on a sensorized finger; this allows the distance moved by the finger tip and the sensor response to be determined with respect to the sensor response. The results show a linear relationship between sensor response and distance moved; allowing the position to be determined. By considering the difference in response between the two side sensors, the side to side movement can be detected. When the finger is moving up and down the two side sensors experience the same response such that the difference between the two sensors is fixed. However, when moving side to side the sensors have the opposite responses such that the responses is doubled (Fig. 7).

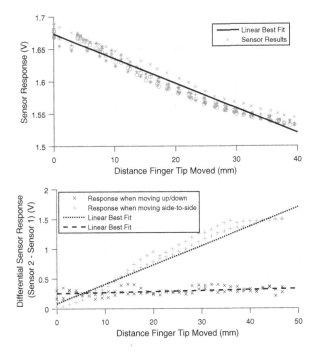

Fig. 7. (a) Varying sensors response with the distance the finger tip is moved (measured using visual markers and camera) when repeated 5 times. (b) Response of the differential response (difference between the two side sensors) to side-to-side movement

3.1   Demonstration: Chopstick Gripping Results

One challenge which requires considerable dexterity and utilises compliance in finger joints is the use of chopsticks. There has been some initial attempts to make robot hands which can use chopsticks [4], however this required the attachment of chopsticks to the hand. A three fingered hand (Fig. 8) which can hold and use chopsticks has been developed to show how the compliance of the fingers allows fine, dexterous control.

The top sensor on the actuated finger is used to detect when an object is gripped by when the sensor value plateaus which is the response to the chopsticks grasping objects and the fingers no longer move. By detecting the magnitude of the change of sensor response, the size of the object gripped can be estimated. The relationship between sensor response and object diameter is shown in Fig. 9.

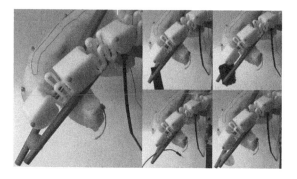

Fig. 8. Images of different objects which can be grasped.

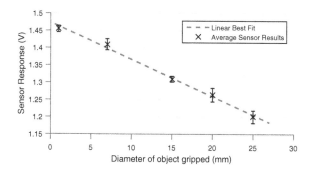

Fig. 9. Magnitude of sensor response plotted when gripping objects of different diameter. The objects were gripped five times with the average and standard deviation of the results determined.

4   Discussion and Conclusions

In summary, a method by which a single 3D printed finger can be created has presented. Joint analysis has shown how varying the parameters of the joint can affect the range of movement of the joint. The design parameters can be used to determine the mechanical impedance and range of movement of the joint so it can be designed for a given application. Rapid prototyping can be used to produce the flexible manipulator which is fast and cost-effective allowing rapid development of manipulators.

The compliance and dexterity of the fingers has been demonstrated by developing a three fingered system which allows the manipulation of chopsticks which allows objects to be gripped. Soft sensors have been added which allow the position of the finger to be detected, and hence when the chopsticks have gripped an object allows for simple feedback control of the actuator.

Acknowledgments. Thanks to Frank Clemens (EMPA) for providing assistance and CTPE. This project was funded by the EPSRC CDT in Sensor Technologies (Grant EP/L015889/1).

References

1. Brown, E., Rodenberg, N., Amend, J., Mozeika, A., Steltz, E., Zakin, M.R., Lipson, H., Jaeger, H.M.: Universal robotic gripper based on the jamming of granular material. Proc. Natl. Acad. Sci. **107**(44), 18809–18814 (2010)
2. Calì, J., Calian, D.A., Amati, C., Kleinberger, R., Steed, A., Kautz, J., Weyrich, T.: 3d-printing of non-assembly, articulated models. ACM Trans. Graph. (TOG) **31**(6), 130 (2012)
3. Calisti, M., Arienti, A., Renda, F., Levy, G., Hochner, B., Mazzolai, B., Dario, P., Laschi, C.: Design and development of a soft robot with crawling and grasping capabilities. In: 2012 IEEE International Conference on Robotics and Automation (ICRA), pp. 4950–4955, May 2012
4. Chepisheva, M., Culha, U., Iida, F.: A biologically inspired soft robotic hand using chopsticks for grasping tasks. In: Tuci, E., Giagkos, A., Wilson, M., Hallam, J. (eds.) SAB 2016. LNCS, vol. 9825, pp. 195–206. Springer, Cham (2016). doi:10.1007/978-3-319-43488-9_18
5. Çulha, U., Iida, F.: Enhancement of finger motion range with compliant anthropomorphic joint design. Bioinspiration and Biomimetics **11**(2), 026001 (2016)
6. Culha, U., Wani, U., Nurzaman, S.G., Clemens, F., Iida, F.: Motion pattern discrimination for soft robots with morphologically flexible sensors. In: 2014 IEEE/RSJ International Conference on Intelligent Robots and Systems, pp. 567–572. IEEE (2014)
7. Friedman, J., Flash, T.: Task-dependent selection of grasp kinematics and stiffness in human object manipulation. Cortex **43**(3), 444–460 (2007)
8. Höppner, H., Lakatos, D., Urbanek, H., Castellini, C., van der Smagt, P.: The grasp perturbator: Calibrating human grasp stiffness during a graded force task. In: 2011 IEEE International Conference on Robotics and Automation (ICRA), pp. 3312–3316. IEEE (2011)
9. Iida, F., Laschi, C.: Soft robotics: challenges and perspectives. Procedia Comput. Sci. **7**, 99–102 (2011)
10. Ilievski, F., Mazzeo, A.D., Shepherd, R.F., Chen, X., Whitesides, G.M.: Soft robotics for chemists. Angew. Chem. Int. Ed. **50**(8), 1890–1895 (2011)
11. Jamone, L., Natale, L., Metta, G., Sandini, G.: Highly sensitive soft tactile sensors for an anthropomorphic robotic hand. IEEE Sens. J. **15**(8), 4226–4233 (2015)
12. Laschi, C., Mazzolai, B., Mattoli, V., Cianchetti, M., Dario, P.: Design of a biomimetic robotic octopus arm. Bioinspiration and Biomimetics **4**(1), 015006 (2009)
13. Ma, R.R., Odhner, L.U., Dollar, A.M.: A modular, open-source 3D printed underactuated hand. In: 2013 IEEE International Conference on Robotics and Automation (ICRA), pp. 2737–2743. IEEE (2013)
14. Majidi, C.: Soft robotics: a perspective-current trends and prospects for the future. Soft Robot. **1**(1), 5–11 (2014)
15. Mattmann, C., et al.: Recognizing upper body postures using textile strain sensors. In: 2007 11th IEEE International Symposium on Wearable Computers, pp. 29–36 (2007)

16. Mattmann, C., et al.: Sensor for measuring strain in textile. Sensors **8**, 3719–3732 (2008)
17. Milner, T.E., Franklin, D.W.: Characterization of multijoint finger stiffness: dependence on finger posture and force direction. IEEE Trans. Biomed. Eng. **45**(11), 1363–1375 (1998)
18. Yousef, H., Boukallel, M., Althoefer, K.: Tactile sensing for dexterous in-hand manipulation in robotics-a review. Sens. Actuators, A **167**(2), 171–187 (2011)

Reinforcement Learning for Bio-Inspired Target Seeking

James Gillespie[1]([⊠]), Iñaki Rañó[1], Nazmul Siddique[1], José Santos[1],
and Mehdi Khamassi[2]

[1] Intelligent Systems Research Centre, Ulster University, Northern Ireland, UK
gillespie-j10@email.ulster.ac.uk,
{i.rano,nh.siddique,ja.santos}@ulster.ac.uk
[2] Institute des Sistèmes Intelligents et de Robotique,
University Pierre et Marie Curie, Paris, France
mehdi.khamassi@isir.upmc.fr

Abstract. Because animals are extremely effective at moving in their natural environments they represent an excellent model to implement robust robotic movement and navigation. Braitenberg vehicles are bio-inspired models of animal navigation widely used in robotics. Tuning the parameters of these vehicles to generate appropriate behaviour can be challenging and time consuming. In this paper we present a Reinforcement Learning methodology to learn the sensori-motor connection of Braitenberg vehicle 3a, a biological model of source seeking. We present simulations of different stimuli and reward functions to illustrate the feasibility of this approach.

Keywords: Braitenberg vehicles · Reinforcement learning · Source seeking

1 Introduction

Everyday experience shows that animals are extremely effective at moving in their natural environments which makes them an excellent model to implement robust robotic movement and navigation [4]. Bio-inspiration has played an important role in robotics for the design of locomotive systems [11], locomotion control [8], and control of steering [20]. This paper focuses on learning animal-like steering behaviour using Braitenberg vehicles, a well known model of insect tropotaxis [3], i.e. movement of insects towards or away from a stimulus [5]. While previous works used experimentally tuned models or relied on time consuming evolutionary strategies [2,12,17], this work investigates how robots can learn these tropotaxis controllers from experience using Reinforcement Learning techniques.

How animals navigate in the presence of stimuli has been a subject of research for several decades [5,7], yet the mechanisms generating these behaviours are not fully understood even for very simple animals. One natural mechanism to

© Springer International Publishing AG 2017
Y. Gao et al. (Eds.): TAROS 2017, LNAI 10454, pp. 637–650, 2017.
DOI: 10.1007/978-3-319-64107-2_52

control movement is tropotaxis, which relies on sampling the stimulus in the environment at two symmetrically placed sensing organs (eyes, ears...), and can be exploited to control robot movement. The values of the stimulus are used by the animal to steer or control its navigation, via some neural wiring between the sensing organs and the motor effectors. The concrete internal wiring defines the behaviour of the animal generating positive or negative taxis (movement towards or away from a stimulus), as captured in the seminal work of Valentino Braitenberg [3], where taxes are modelled through simple vehicles.

Braitenberg vehicles have been used in robotics for several decades from their most basic formulation [10], to extensions with fuzzy controllers [21] or neural networks [6]. Therefore, they are widely used to implement bio-inspired robotic behaviours, especially when the motion relies on unconventional sensors, for example sensors which are not providing distance readings [9,10,18]. Early research in the field aiming at enabling learning of animal-like movement relied on techniques like evolution strategies [17] and genetic algorithms [12]. These works obtained neural architectures of Braitenberg vehicles to navigate environments with no collisions through an iterative approach to optimise a fitness functions of the distance to obstacles and forward speed. A big drawback of these strategies is the amount of time necessary for the algorithms to find the optimal weights of the neural network to control the velocity of the wheels. Moreover, having such a neural controller makes the analysis of the sensori-motor connection extremely difficult. Another early approach to bio-inspired robotic steering used the Dynamical Systems Approach to behaviour generation for obstacle avoidance combined with a Braitenberg vehicle for target seeking [2]. Although the work presented is highly effective for robot navigation, the parameters of the control mechanism are selected experimentally, which means they might not generate the best possible behaviour.

Interestingly, recent works using Braitenberg vehicles have also developed models which do not use learning techniques to achieve their target seeking behaviour and can be sub-optimal. For instance, a basic implementation of Braitenberg vehicles to determine the speed of the wheels of a smelling robot [10] was used with a simple dynamical normalisation of the measured values of the sensors. All these works rely on experimental results, and while mathematical models of Braitenberg vehicles have been presented in [14,18], it can be challenging to tune the internal parameters of the vehicle, i.e. the controller, as formal proofs of stability are missing. Moreover, an outstanding open question in Braitenberg vehicles is how to define the relationship between sensors and motors in an optimal way. The main contribution of this paper is presenting a reinforcement learning based methodology to perform learning in bio-inspired steering, as a way to answer the question of optimal Braitenberg vehicle design. Obtaining an optimal controller depends on the selected definition of optimality, but also on the stimulus the vehicle perceives. We present results for two common families of stimuli, namely following the inverse square law, and the inverse distance law. As we will see, known theoretical results of Braitenberg vehicles help analysing and interpreting the results from the reinforcement learning process. The rest of the paper is organised as follows. Section 2 presents a brief introduction to the model of Braitenberg vehicle 3a, and states the problem of tuning the sensori-motor connection as a reinforcement learning problem. Section 3 presents the experimental results obtained for the simulation of these vehicles using the types of stimuli mentioned and several reward functions defining optimality criteria. The paper ends presenting some conclusions and future work in Sect. 4.

2 Reinforcement Learning in Braitenberg Vehicles

Braitenberg vehicles are well known models of animal behaviour, used in robotics as a simple way of implementing avoidance and target seeking behaviours. The lack of a mathematical formalism for the vehicles did not hamper their usage but made their implementation a trial and error process, where intuition and experience played a big role. The development of a mathematical model of the closed-loop system of Braitenberg vehicle 3a [13] as a non-linear differential equation allowed using dynamical systems theory to analyse characteristics of the solution trajectories. Oscillatory [15] and unstable [13] trajectories can be found among the solutions of this non-linear dynamical system. Moreover, their formalisation and the model equations allow to get a deeper understanding of how these controllers work, and enable making better informed guesses on the parameters without the need for experimentation. However, as we already stated, one outstanding open question is finding under which conditions the behaviour of Braitenberg vehicle 3a is stable close to a given equilibrium point, since the linear stability test provides no information [15], while finding a Lyapunov function is a non-trivial problem. Therefore, our goal with this work is learning a stable non-linear controller that achieves target seeking for a Braitenberg vehicle 3a.

Figure 1 shows Braitenberg vehicle 3a in the proximity of a light source (although to derive its mathematical model the stimulus can be of any nature and does not need to come from a source). The wheels of the vehicle are used to abstract the locomotive systems of animals focusing on the steering level of motion [1]. In fact, similar steering models have been used to understand human motion. As shown in the figure, the vehicle has two sensors connected to the ipsilateral wheel (the same side wheel) in a decreasing (inhibitory) way, i.e. in the sense the higher the stimulus value, the slower the wheel turns. Intuitively the vehicle turns towards, and approaches, the light source, performing a 'hill-climbing' on the stimulus. The closer the vehicle gets to the source, or maximum, the lower its velocity, and it will eventually stop near the peak when the speed of both wheels is zero. Because intuitively the motion converges to the maximum, these vehicles were used in real robots and simulated artificial agents without mathematical formalisation of their behaviour. These works assumed the vehicle converged regardless of the stimulus provided, if the connection between the sensors and the wheels was appropriately tuned.

We will present the steps to model the vehicle shown in Fig. 1, with a wheelbase d and distance between the sensors δ. Assuming the vehicle is immersed in a stimulus that does not change over time, the stimulus itself can be modelled

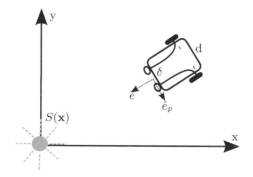

Fig. 1. Braitenberg vehicle 3a.

as a non negative function $S(\mathbf{x})$ of the position in the environment or the vehicle workspace $\mathbf{x} = (x, y) \in \mathcal{W} \subseteq R^2$. The stimulus is considered to simply be a position dependant scalar function, like light or sound intensity, for instance. Furthermore, we will assume $S(\mathbf{x})$ is of type C^∞ in $\mathcal{W}$, i.e. its value changes smoothly in the environment. If the stimulus is originated by a point-like source located at $\mathbf{x}_S \in \mathcal{W}$ the function $S(\mathbf{x})$ will reach a maximum at this point as the stimulus intensity decays with distance, i.e. $S(\mathbf{x}_S) \geq S(\mathbf{x}) \forall \mathbf{x} \in \mathcal{W}$, which also implies $\nabla S(\mathbf{x}_S) = \mathbf{0}$ and $\mathbf{y}^T D^2 S(\mathbf{x}_S)\mathbf{y} < 0 \forall \mathbf{y} \in R^2$ because the function is smooth, i.e. the gradient of $S(\mathbf{x})$ vanishes and the Hessian is a negative definite matrix at $\mathbf{x}_S$. Without loss of generality, as Fig. 1 shows, we can assume the source is located at the origin of a reference system, i.e. $\mathbf{x}_S = \mathbf{0}$, and the position of the vehicle is referred to that coordinate system.

According to the qualitative model proposed by Braitenberg, the connection between the sensor readings 's' and the left and right wheel velocities $v_{L/R}$ is direct (ipsilateral) and inhibitory. We will model this connection as a smooth function $F(s)$, fulfilling the following criteria: (i) the motion of the vehicle is never backwards, i.e. $F : \Re^+ \cup \{0\} \rightarrow \Re^+ \cup \{0\}$; (ii) the vehicle stops at the source, i.e. $F(S(\mathbf{0})) = 0$; and (iii) an inhibitory connection implies that the derivative of $F(s)$ is negative for all stimulus values s, i.e. $F'(s) < 0$. In the literature of Braitenberg vehicles for source seeking the function is selected to be an experimentally tuned linear function, or an Artificial Neural Network, however it can be any function fulfilling these conditions. Under the above conditions, the behaviour of the vehicle can be approximated as:

$$\dot{x} = F(S(\mathbf{x})) \cos \theta$$
$$\dot{y} = F(S(\mathbf{x})) \sin \theta$$
$$\dot{\theta} = -\frac{\delta}{d} \nabla_{\mathbf{x}} F(S(\mathbf{x})) \cdot \hat{e}_p \tag{1}$$

where $\mathbf{x} = (x, y)$ is the midpoint between the sensors, $\nabla_{\mathbf{x}} F(S(\mathbf{x}))$ is the gradient of the function composition, '·' represents the dot product, and $\hat{e}_p = [-\sin \theta, \cos \theta]$ is a unit vector perpendicular to the vehicle direction. While condition (ii) forces the dynamical system to have an equilibrium point, condition (*iii*) is related to the stability of the equilibrium point. Therefore the functions sought using Reinforcement Learning should fulfil these conditions for the vehicle to perform positive taxis, i.e. it should have negative slope and it should be zero when the vehicle is at the source.

2.1 Simulations of Vehicle Stimulus and Connection

The mathematical model introduced above is the tool to obtain analytic results on the behaviour of the vehicle, like stability analysis, features of the trajectories, et cetera. However, because its application in a reinforcement learning set-up would require computing the derivative of the function to learn $F(s)$, we opted for a simpler statement of the learning problem. Hence, in our simulations we use the straightforward implementation of vehicle 3a, i.e. evaluating the stimulus at two points and computing the speeds for the left and right wheels. Given the position of the right and left sensors $\mathbf{x}_r$ and $\mathbf{x}_l$, respectively, we can compute the velocities for the right and left wheel as $v_r = F(S(\mathbf{x}_r))$ and $v_l = F(S(\mathbf{x}_l))$, where $F(s)$ is the sought function and $S(\mathbf{x})$ is a selected stimulus function. The left and right sensor positions can be easily computed from the vehicle pose, i.e. the midpoint between the sensors, $\mathbf{x}$ and the orientation of the vehicle, θ, as $\mathbf{x}_r = \mathbf{x} - \frac{\delta}{2}\hat{e}_p$ and $\mathbf{x}_l = \mathbf{x} + \frac{\delta}{2}\hat{e}_p$, where the $\hat{e}_p = [-\sin\theta, \cos\theta]$ is obtained from the vehicle orientation θ. The velocities of the wheels can be converted into forward speed v and turning rate ω of the vehicle as:

$$v = \frac{F(S(\mathbf{x}_r)) + F(S(\mathbf{x}_l))}{2}$$

$$\omega = \frac{F(S(\mathbf{x}_r)) - F(S(\mathbf{x}_l))}{d} \tag{2}$$

where it is worth remembering that the positions of the sensors depend on the vehicle pose, i.e. $\mathbf{x}_r = \mathbf{x}_r(\mathbf{x}, \theta)$ and $\mathbf{x}_l = \mathbf{x}_l(\mathbf{x}, \theta)$, and, therefore, the movement of the vehicle depends on its pose $(\mathbf{x}, \theta)$ through the stimulus function and the sensori-motor connecting function $F(s)$. Given these velocities, the trajectory of the vehicle can be obtained as the solution of the system of non-linear differential equations:

$$\begin{bmatrix} \dot{x} \\ \dot{y} \\ \dot{\theta} \end{bmatrix} = \begin{bmatrix} \cos\theta & 0 \\ \sin\theta & 0 \\ 0 & 1 \end{bmatrix} \begin{bmatrix} v(\mathbf{x}, \theta) \\ \omega(\mathbf{x}, \theta) \end{bmatrix} \tag{3}$$

which has to be integrated numerically, and in our experiments we used the Euler method with a fixed time step of 0.05. It is worth remembering that the connection function $F(s)$ must be decreasing for the vehicle to be of type 3a, otherwise instead of target seeking the vehicle will move away from the source (ipsilateral increasing connection corresponds to vehicle 3b, negative taxis). However, as we will see in the next section this constraint cannot be imposed in the learning process, but good solutions are found using appropriate reward functions.

2.2   The Reinforcement Learning Problem

The problem of learning the target seeking behaviour for Braitenberg vehicle 3a given a stimulus function can be casted into finding a non-increasing function of the stimulus to compute the velocities. Given the stimulus $S(\mathbf{x})$ defined in some environment $\mathcal{W} \subseteq \Re^2$ and an initial pose of the vehicle $(x_0, \theta_0) \in \mathcal{W} \times S^1$ the trajectory followed depends on the connection function $F(s)$. Since the trajectory unfolds in time $(\mathbf{x}(t), \theta(t))$ but also depends on the initial pose and $F(s)$ we will write $(\mathbf{x}(t, \mathbf{x}_0, \theta_0, F), \theta(t, \mathbf{x}_0, \theta_0, F))$. For each pose of the vehicle we can define a scalar reward function $r(\mathbf{x}, \theta)$ measuring how good being at that state is, and because the trajectory depends on the initial pose and the connecting function, the reward along a given trajectory is therefore a function of the initial pose and the connecting function too, that is $r(\mathbf{x}, \theta) = r(t, \mathbf{x}_0, \theta_0, F)$. Theoretically, the function $F(s)$ can be approximated using any type of function approximation, however, for this work we opted to use a Radial Basis Function neural network of the form:

$$F(s) = \sum_{i=1}^{N} w_i \phi_i(s) \tag{4}$$

where N is the number of basis functions, w_i is the weight of the i-th neuron, and the radial basis functions $\phi_i(s)$ were Gaussian kernel functions centred at fixed equidistant positions s_i within the range of the stimulus (from $s = 0$ to $s = S(\mathbf{0})$). If we denote the weight vector of the network by $\Phi = (w_i)$, the reinforcement learning problem can be stated as maximising the following total return:

$$R[\Phi] = \int_{(x_0, \theta_0) \in \mathcal{W} \times S^1} dx_0 d\theta_0 \int_0^\infty r(t, \mathbf{x}_0, \theta_0, \Phi) dt \tag{5}$$

where we need to integrate for all the initial conditions, i.e. the points in the workspace $\mathbf{x}_0$ and all orientations in the unit circle $\theta_0 \in S^1$, but we also need to integrate over the whole trajectory. Because this total return function depends on the solution of a non-linear dynamical system it is impossible to evaluate these integrals. Moreover, integrating over the whole trajectory is obviously not feasible, so we defined a finite time t_f to run the simulations, changing the upper integration limit in Eq. (5). This does not solve the problem of evaluating the return, however we can use the sampling trick to estimate through simulations the value of the integral by randomly sampling the space of poses of the vehicle. We can use roll-outs from random initial poses to estimate the gradient $\nabla_\Phi R[\Phi]$ and perform a hill climbing on the return to find the optimal weight vector of the RBF network using:

$$\Phi_{k+1} = \Phi_k + \alpha_k \nabla_\Phi R[\Phi_k] \tag{6}$$

where $a_k = \frac{a_0}{k}$, a_0 is the initial learning rate, and, as already stated, the gradient was estimated using roll-outs through small random perturbations of the parameters Φ using central finite differences.

Although in our case the environment of the vehicle was the whole plane $\mathcal{W} = \Re^2$, to simplify things further the domain of the integral in Eq. (5), i.e. the domain in which the initial conditions are selected for the sampling process, was defined to be a square region around the origin. Moreover, the initial angular directions of the vehicle were selected to be pointing towards the source within a $\pm 90°$ range, i.e. $\theta_0 \in [\theta_t - \pi/2, \theta_t + \pi/2]$, where $\theta_t = \arctan \left[\frac{y_0}{x_0} \right] - \pi$.

3   Experimental Results

To learn the sensori-motor connection for a Braitenberg vehicle using Reinforcement Learning we defined and tested several reward functions. Because the goal of the vehicle is to reach the source of a stimulus, i.e. where it takes its highest value, an immediate candidate for the reward function would be the stimulus itself. Provided the vehicle has access to its pose, and knowing that the source is at the origin of the reference system, an alternative reward would be a function of the distance from the vehicle to the source and its relative heading. We simulated four different reward functions, two dependent on the stimulus and two on the pose of the vehicle, and to fulfil assumption (i) in Sect. 2 the reward was given only when the movement of the vehicle was in the forward direction. The reward functions used are:

1. The stimulus itself, and because the vehicle obtains readings from both sensors, we use as reward their sum, i.e. $r = S_L + S_R$.
2. The previous reward tries to maximise the stimulus value, but for a stimulus source it is important that the vehicle heads in the right direction. We defined a second stimulus based reward that accounts for the heading direction by trying to make the value in both sensors identical. The reward function accounts for the value but penalises directions perpendicular to the source $r = \frac{S_L + S_R}{1 + (S_L - S_R)^2}$.
3. In the simulations we have access to the pose of the vehicle, $(\mathbf{x}, \theta)$, which allows us to define additional reward functions. Using the pose this reward function consists of a linear combination of terms accounting for the proximity of the vehicle to the source and its heading. The selected function was $r = \frac{a}{1 + \alpha(\theta, \theta_T)^2} + \frac{1}{1 + \|\mathbf{x}\|^2}$, where $a = 3$ represents the relative importance of heading vs. the distance, $\|\mathbf{x}\|$ is the distance to the source, and $\alpha(\theta, \theta_T)$ is the angular distance in the range $[-\pi; \pi]$ between the robot heading (θ) and the desired heading $\theta_t = \arctan \left[\frac{y}{x} \right] - \pi$.
4. Our early experiments with the reward functions defined above showed the vehicle's trajectories stopped way before reaching the source. We thought it was due to the limited/bounded rate of growth of these reward functions close to the source. Therefore, we included as a reward function $r = \frac{1}{\|\mathbf{x}\|^2}$, but since it is singular at $\mathbf{x} = \mathbf{0}$, we defined an threshold distance ϵ such that if $\|\mathbf{x}\| < \epsilon$, $r = \frac{1}{\epsilon^2}$.

These four reward functions were used for the two general types of stimulus defined below. It is worth noting that in all the simulations the robot initial heading was randomly selected within $\pm\pi/2$ radians in the direction of the stimulus.

3.1   Inverse-Square Law Stimulus

Probably the best known example of Braitenberg vehicles is the one implementing phototaxis using light sensors. With a light source placed at some height h_0 above the origin of a reference systems of a ground plane, and since light intensity follows the inverse-square law, the stimulus as a function of the position $\mathbf{x}$ will be $S(\mathbf{x}) = \frac{I_0}{h_0^2 + ||\mathbf{x}||^2}$, where I_0 is the intensity of the light at the source. This function can be rewritten as $S(\mathbf{x}) = \frac{g_0}{1 + \eta ||\mathbf{x}||^2}$ where $\eta = \frac{1}{h_0^2}$ and $g_0 = \frac{I_0}{h_0^2}$. We selected in all the light-like simulations this last functional form and used $g_0 = 4$ and $\eta = 0.25$.

In our first set of simulations we used the stimulus sum reward function, and the results are shown in Fig. 2. We ran 10 learning experiments per reward function with random initialisations of an RBF network. Only results of the successful simulations are shown in the figures: Fig. 2 depicts simulated trajectories on the left and the corresponding $F(s)$ functions approximated by the RBF networks while Fig. 3 shows an example of the evolution of the reward as a function of time. The successful simulations are those which fulfil the conditions stated above, i.e. taking positive values (the vehicle moves forward), having a negative slope (the behaviour is positive taxis), and they become zero close to the stimulus maximum (in our case $S(\mathbf{0}) = 4$). The trajectories are shown in the $x - y$ coordinates, with a red star at the origin (where the source is). While Fig. 2 shows the vehicle successfully learns to reach the stimulus source in 9 out of the 10 trials, the degree to which it approaches the source changes across trials varies. All of the successful simulations stop relatively close to the source. Looking at the figure showing the RBF Network outputs we can see where the movement of the vehicle converges to, by looking at the zero crossings of the function. For instance the RBF network corresponding to the black dashed graph makes the vehicle stop when the stimulus $S(\mathbf{x})$ reaches a stimulus value of 3, and $F(s)$ is negative for larger values of the stimulus, which does not completely fulfil the conditions imposed for the sensori-motor connection function. The RBF network corresponding to the cyan graph, on the other hand, makes the vehicle stop when

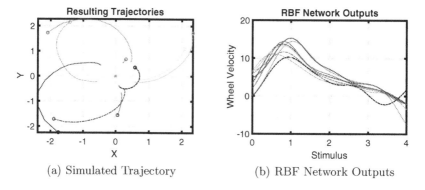

(a) Simulated Trajectory   (b) RBF Network Outputs

Fig. 2. Results from phototaxis simulations using reward function 1.

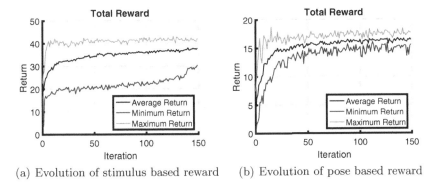

(a) Evolution of stimulus based reward   (b) Evolution of pose based reward

Fig. 3. On the left, an example from the phototaxis simulations of the evolution of a stimulus based reward (using reward function 1), and on the right, an example from the phonotaxis simulations of the evolution of a pose based reward (using reward function 3).

the stimulus $S(\mathbf{x})$ reaches 3.5, which is much closer to the source. On the other hand, as the figure on the right shows, most of the RBF networks approximate functions with a negative slope, and it is positive for points not experienced during the training. In general, the attractor of the Braitenberg vehicle on the workspace can be obtained by solving $S(\mathbf{x}) = s_0$, where s_0 is the value at the zero crossing of the RBF network.

In our second set of simulations we used the stimulus sum reward function which penalises perpendicular directions, results of which are shown in Fig. 4. For this experiment 8 out of the 10 trials successfully located the stimulus, again with varying degrees of success. However, it should be noted that still most of the RBF networks generate attractors around the maximum, not at the maximum.

In our third set of simulations we used a pose based reward, consisting of the proximity of the vehicle to the source and its heading. Figure 5 shows the results

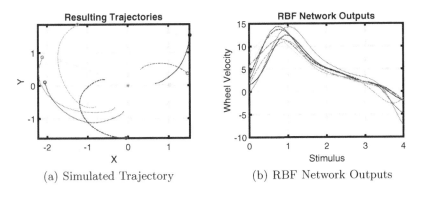

(a) Simulated Trajectory   (b) RBF Network Outputs

Fig. 4. Results from phototaxis simulations using reward function 2.

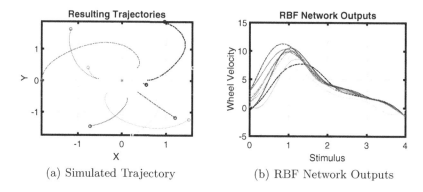

(a) Simulated Trajectory   (b) RBF Network Outputs

Fig. 5. Results from phototaxis simulations using reward function 3.

of this simulation. As can be seen from the RBF network, the functions that have been approximated are more accurate, allowing the robot to get much closer to the source before stopping, i.e. before the attractor set of the dynamical system. Using the pose based reward function proved to be advantageous as shown by this set of simulations, with a 100% learning success rate across the 10 trajectories.

In our fourth and final set of simulations we used an altered pose based reward to try to get the vehicle to reach the stimulus source, detailed in Fig. 6. As can be seen from the RBF network output, this is the first experiment whereby the RBF networks make the vehicle reach the maximum, i.e. the attractor is at the source. The results of this can be observed with the successful trajectories plotted, where each vehicle easily finds it's way to the stimulus source regardless of where it starts and gets very close to it in the simulated time.

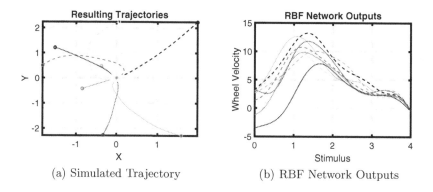

(a) Simulated Trajectory   (b) RBF Network Outputs

Fig. 6. Results from phototaxis simulations using reward function 4.

3.2   Inverse Distance Stimulus

Another common example of Braitenberg vehicles is the one implementing phonotaxis through microphones [19], for instance with a sound source placed at some height h_0 above the ground. It can be seen that, according to the inverse-distance law, the sound intensity will fulfil the conditions for the stimulus function. Furthermore, if the emission pattern of the sound source is isotropic, the stimulus $S(\mathbf{x})$ will be such that $S(\mathbf{x}) \propto \frac{1}{\sqrt{h_0^2 + x^2 + y^2}}$.

This section presents the results obtained for a stimulus source following the inverse distance law, i.e. a stimulus of the form $S(\mathbf{x}) = \frac{g_0}{\sqrt{1 + \eta ||\mathbf{x}||^2}}$. We selected in all the sound-like simulations this last functional form and used $g_0 = 4$ and $\eta = 0.25$. The same experiments were repeated to test whether changing the stimulus affects the performance of the learned controller, i.e. whether some stimulus might be more difficult to follow. As can be seen from the figures below, generally the performance was similar in these sets of simulations compared to the ones above using the inverse-square law stimulus. Like in the phototaxis experiments the RBF networks approximate a function which crosses the zero velocity before reaching the maximum stimulus, meaning the vehicles stop before they reach the stimulus source. The stimulus sum reward function (Fig. 7) has the same number of successful trials while the stimulus sum reward function which penalises perpendicular directions (Fig. 8) has 10 successful trials, 2 more than the phototaxis counterpart. This proves that, when a sound-like stimulus is used, including a penalty for perpendicular directions helps the Reinforcement Learning algorithm.

Interestingly, although the learning functions display a shape different from the previous results (and seem to have a smaller basin of attraction) the connection function $F(s)$ for reward function 3 and 4 generate a point attractor at the stimulus source. Figure 9 shows 10 successful trials using the first pose based reward, based on the proximity of the vehicle to the source and its heading (see Fig. 3 for the evolution of this reward), while Fig. 10 shows 7 successful trials of the altered pose reward function. Although Fig. 10 has less successful trials, the function it approximates is clearly more accurate as the vehicle trajectory is

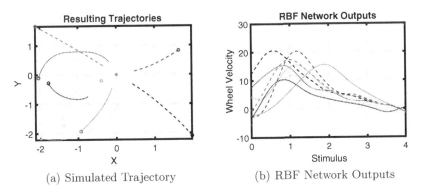

(a) Simulated Trajectory   (b) RBF Network Outputs

Fig. 7. Results from phonotaxis simulations using reward function 1.

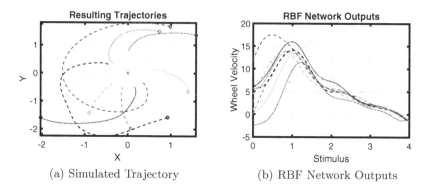

(a) Simulated Trajectory   (b) RBF Network Outputs

Fig. 8. Results from phonotaxis simulations using reward function 2.

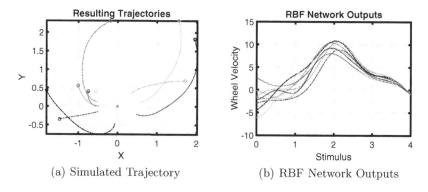

(a) Simulated Trajectory   (b) RBF Network Outputs

Fig. 9. Results from phonotaxis simulations using reward function 3.

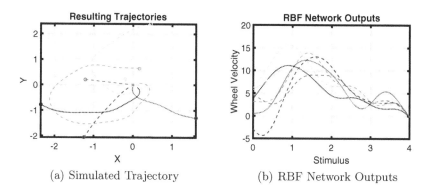

(a) Simulated Trajectory   (b) RBF Network Outputs

Fig. 10. Results from phonotaxis simulations using reward function 4.

closer to a shortest path trajectory compared to the results that can be seen in Fig. 9.

4   Conclusions and Future Work

This paper presents the first application of Reinforcement Learning to Braitenberg vehicles, a model of insect navigation. Previous robotic works implementing this taxis strategy used hand tuned parameters, or evolutionary strategies [2,12,17] to optimise some cost function dependent on the parameters of a neural controller. We used a reinforcement learning framework to adjust the weights of a radial basis function network to control the vehicle. The presented approach has two main advantages over existing techniques. First, it allows us to define an objective function instead of relying on the perception of the resulting behaviour by the developer. Second, the optimal solution is reached several orders of magnitude faster than the evolutionary approach. On the other hand, the analytic model of Braitenberg vehicles allows to draw conclusions about the stability of the learnt RBF controller.

The results obtained here are limited to computer simulations of the vehicles. In the future we plan to test this framework in real robots performing different types of target reaching behaviours. As an intermediate step, however, we plan to introduce noise in the simulated sensors, i.e. add noise to the stimulus function. This will turn the motion equation of the vehicle into a stochastic differential equation, and theoretical results on deterministic systems might not be applicable. Some early results on the behaviour of vehicle 3a under noise conditions exist [16] that can help interpreting the results of (or simplifying) the learning problem.

Acknowledgements. This work was partially supported by the Royal Society International Exchange Scheme under grant IE151293.

References

1. Arechavaleta, G., Laumond, J.P., Hicheur, H., Berthoz, A.: An optimality principle governing human walking. IEEE Trans. Robot. **24**(1), 5–14 (2008)
2. Bicho, E., Schöner, G.: The dynamic approach to autonomous robotics demonstrated on a low-level vehicle platform. Robot. Auton. Syst. **21**, 23–35 (1997)
3. Braitenberg, V.: Vehicles. Experiments in Synthetic Psychology. The MIT Press, Cambridge (1984)
4. Floreano, D., Ijspeert, A.J., Schaal, S.: Robotics and neuroscience. Curr. Biol. **24**, R910–R920 (2014)
5. Fraenkel, G.S., Gunn, D.L.: The Orientation of Animals: Kineses, Taxes and Compass Reactions. Dover Publications, New York (1961)
6. French, R., Cañamero, L.: Introducing neuromodulation to a braitenberg vehicle. In: Proceedings of the 2005 IEEE International Conference on Robotics and Automation, pp. 4188–4193 (2005)

7. Gallistel, C.: Navigation: whence our sense of direction? Curr. Biol. **27**(3), 108–110 (2017)
8. Ijspeert, A., Crespi, A., Ryczko, D., Cabelguen, J.: From swimming to walking with a salamander robot driven by a spinal cord model. Science **315**(5817), 1416–1420 (2007)
9. Lebastard, V., Boyer, F., Chevallereau, C., Servagent, N.: Underwater electro-navigation in the dark. In: Proceedings of the International Conference on Robotics and Automation (ICRA), pp. 1155–1160 (2012)
10. Lilienthal, A.J., Duckett, T.: Experimental analysis of smelling braitenberg vehicles. In: Proceedings of the IEEE International Conference on Advanced Robotics (ICAR 2003). IEEE (2003)
11. Menciassi, A., Dario, P.: Bio-inspired solutions for locomotion in the gastrointestinal tract: background and perspectives. Philos. Trans. A Math. Phys. Eng. Sci. **361**, 2287–2298 (2003). The Royal Society – Biologically Inspired Robots
12. Mondada, F., Floreano, D.: Evolution of neural control structures: some experiments on mobile robots. Robot. Auton. Syst. **16**, 183–195 (1995)
13. Rañó, I.: A steering taxis model and the qualitative analysis of its trajectories. Adapt. Behav. **17**(3), 197–211 (2009)
14. Rañó, I.: A model and formal analysis of braitenberg vehicles 2 and 3. In: IEEE International Conference on Robotics and Automation (2012)
15. Rañó, I.: Results on the convergence of braitenberg vehicle 3a. Artif. Life **20**(2), 223–235 (2014)
16. Rañó, I., Wong-Lin, K., Khamassi, M.: A drift diffusion model of biological source seeking for mobile robots. In: Proceedings of the IEEE International Conference on Robotics and Automation (2017)
17. Salomon, R.: Evolving and optimising braitenberg vehicles by means of evolution strategies. Int. J. Smart Eng. Syst. Des. **2**, 69–77 (1999)
18. Salumäe, T., Rañó, I., Akanyeti, O., Kruusmaa, M.: Against the flow: a braitenberg controller for a fish robot. In: IEEE International Conference on Robotics and Automation (2012)
19. Shaikh, D., Hallam, J., Christensen-Dalsgaard, J.: From ear to there: a review of biorobotic models of auditory processing in lizards. Biol. Cybern. **110**(4), 303–317 (2016)
20. Webb, B.: A Spiking Neuron Controller for Robot Phonotaxis, pp. 3–20. The MIT/AAAI Press, Cambridge (2001)
21. Yang, X., Patel, R., Moallem, M.: A fuzzy-braitenberg navigation strategy for differential drive mobile robots. J. Intell. Robot. Syst. **47**, 101–124 (2006)

Mobile Manipulators for Cooperative Transportation of Objects in Common

Jessica S. Ortiz$^{(\boxtimes)}$, José Varela Aldás, and Víctor H. Andaluz

Universidad de las Fuerzas Armadas ESPE, Sangolquí, Ecuador
{jsortiz4,vhandaluz1}@espe.edu.ec, jazjose@hotmail.es

Abstract. This work proposes a kinematic control scheme for the coordinated transport of an object by two anthropomorphic mobile manipulator robots. The proposed control scheme is based on a cascade system formed by three subsystems that treats a specific part as the problem of coordination and cooperation, thus giving greater flexibility to the proposed system. The stability of the proposed controller for tracking trajectories is demonstrated analytically using the Lyapunov method, obtaining that the control is asymptotically stable. Finally, results are shown, where it is demonstrate that the evolution of the configuration of the system converges to the desired formation according to the theoretical design planned.

Keywords: Cooperative transportation · Mobile manipulator · Kinemtic control · Cooperative

1 Introduction

A mobile manipulator nowadays is a broad term referring to robots constituted of a robotic arm, mounted on a mobile platform. This system, which is generally characterized by a high degree of redundancy, combines the manipulation of a fixed base manipulator with the mobility of a wheeled platform. These systems allow to perform the most common missions of robotic systems which require both *locomotion* and *manipulation*. Mobile manipulators offer multiple applications in different industrial and productive areas such as mining and construction or for the assistance of people [1–3].

Coordinated control of multiple robots has attracted the attention of researchers [4–7]. El interés en tales sistemas deriva de su capacidad para llevar a cabo tareas complejas o peligrosas que es difícil o inconveniente realizar con un solo robot. On the other hand, from the point of view of security, multiple small mobile manipulators are better suited for carrying out various tasks in the human environment than a large and heavy mobile manipulator.

The main coordination schemes among mobile manipulators in the literature are: (1) *Leader follower control* for mobile manipulators, when one or a group of mobile manipulators play the role of leader, following a planned path in advance, and the rest of the mobile manipulators form the group of followers that move in relation to the leading mobile manipulator [5–9]. The work of Liang *et al.*, proposes a method to transport an object with little manipulation. A leader follower controller is done, in which follower robots estimate the leader's trajectory using the interacting forces

© Springer International Publishing AG 2017
Y. Gao et al. (Eds.): TAROS 2017, LNAI 10454, pp. 651–660, 2017.
DOI: 10.1007/978-3-319-64107-2_53

between the robot and the object during its transport; and *(2) Position-force hybrid control* for centralized/decentralized schemes, where the position of the object is controlled in a given direction in the working space, and the internal force of the object is controlled in a small range of origin [8–13]. Zyada *et al.*, Presents the coupled dynamics of two mobile manipulators that manipulate an object in the presence of perturbations, an adaptive and robust control is proposed to guarantee the movement and the trajectories of the forces of the object. The results are validated by simulation.

For the above, this work proposes a multi-layer control scheme for coordinated and cooperative control between two mobile manipulators for the transfer of a common object. The proposed control scheme conceptualizes the object and the two mobile manipulator robots as a single system, *i.e.*, the desired motions are specified according to the attributes of the system: *(i) position* in the axis $\mathcal{X}$–$\mathcal{Y}$–$\mathcal{Z}$ of a referential system $<R>$; *(ii) orientation* about the axis $\mathcal{Z}$ of $<R>$; y *(iii) geometry* that corresponds to the distance where the operative ends of the movable manipulators can fasten, manipulate and move the object to a desired position or trajectory. These attributes allow the adequate selection of an independent set of state variables for specification, control and monitoring. The design of the coordinated cooperative controller for tracking trajectories allows the transport of a common object, for this system the control is developed by the Lyapunov method, which eliminates the inherent errors of kinematics. The experiments through a virtual structure allow to demonstrate that the controller is appropriate for the solution of movement problems.

The article is organized in V Sections including the Introduction. Section 2 presents the modeling and kinematic transformation of cooperative control between two mobile manipulators. The design of the proposed control scheme is presented in Sect. 3. While the results are shown in Sect. 4. Finally, the conclusions are presented in Sect. 5.

2   Kinematic Models

This section presents in general form the kinematic modelation of mobile manipulator robots and the kinematic transformation of a virtual structure for cooperative and coordinated control between two mobile manipulators of different configurations.

2.1   Mobile Manipulator Kinematic Model

The *instantaneous kinematic model of a mobile manipulator* gives the derivative of its end-effector location as a function of the derivatives of both the robotic arm configuration and the location of the mobile platform,

$$\dot{\mathbf{h}} = \frac{\partial f}{\partial \mathbf{q}}\left(\mathbf{q}_a, \mathbf{q}_p\right)\mathbf{v}$$

where, $\dot{\mathbf{h}} = \begin{bmatrix} \dot{h}_1 \ \dot{h}_2 \dots \dot{h}_m \end{bmatrix}^T$ is the vector of the end-effector velocity, $\mathbf{v} = [v_1 \ v_2 \dots v_{\delta_n}]^T = \begin{bmatrix} v_p^T \ v_a^T \end{bmatrix}^T$ is the control vector of mobility of the mobile manipulator. Its dimension is

$\delta_n = \delta_{np} + \delta_{na}$, where δ_{np} and δ_{na} are respectively the dimensions of the control vector of mobility associated to the robotic arm and the mobile platform. Now, after replacing $\mathbf{J}(\mathbf{q}) = \frac{\partial f}{\partial \mathbf{q}}(\mathbf{q}_p, \mathbf{q}_a)$ in the above equation, we obtain $\dot{\mathbf{h}}(t) = \mathbf{J}(\mathbf{q}_p, \mathbf{q}_a)\mathbf{v}(t)$ where, $\mathbf{J}(\mathbf{q}_p, \mathbf{q}_a)$ is the Jacobian matrix that defines a linear mapping between the vector of the mobile manipulator velocities $\mathbf{v}(t)$ and the vector of the end-effector velocity $\dot{\mathbf{h}}(t)$. The *i-th* mobile manipulator work team members can be represented by the following kinematic model,

$$\dot{\mathbf{h}}_i(t) = \mathbf{J}_i(\mathbf{q}_{pi}, \mathbf{q}_{ai})\mathbf{v}_i(t) \tag{1}$$

where, $\dot{\mathbf{h}}_i(t) = \begin{bmatrix} \dot{h}_{i1} \ \dot{h}_{i2} \dots \dot{h}_{im} \end{bmatrix}^T$, $\mathbf{q}_i(t) = \begin{bmatrix} \mathbf{q}_{ip}^T \ \mathbf{q}_{ia}^T \end{bmatrix}^T$ and $\mathbf{v}_i(t) = \begin{bmatrix} v_{ip}^T \ v_{ia}^T \end{bmatrix}^T$. In [14, 15] the kinematic model for a mobile manipulator 6-DOF is presented.

2.2   Kinematic Transformation

The kinematic model of a mobile manipulator with two robotic arms gives the location of the final effector h according to the configuration of the virtual point created by the mean value of the robotic arms and the location of the platform (or their operational coordinates as functions of the Generalized coordinates of the robotic arm with virtual midpoint and the operative coordinates of the mobile platform).

$$f : N_{a1} \times N_{a2} \times \mathcal{M}_{\mathcal{P}} \to \mathcal{M}$$

$$(\mathbf{q}_{a1}, \mathbf{q}_{a2}, \mathbf{q}_p) \mapsto \mathbf{h} = f(\mathbf{q}_{a1}, \mathbf{q}_{a2}, \mathbf{q}_p)$$

where, N_{a1} and N_{a2} are the *configuration space* of the robotic arms; $\mathcal{M}_{\sqrt{}}$ is the *operational space* of the mobile platform.

In this context, the proposed coordinated cooperative control method considers two robotic arms mounted on a mobile platform. In this case the control method is based on creating a virtual structure defined by the position of the end-effector of each mobile manipulator. The location of the upper side of the virtual structure in the plane *X-Y-Z* of the global framework is defined by $\mathbf{P_F} = [x_F \ y_F \ z_F]$, where (x_F, y_F, z_F) represents the position of its centroid on the inertial frame $<\mathcal{R}>$. The structure shape of the virtual structure is defined by $\mathbf{S_F} = [d_F \ \beta_F \ \phi_F]$, where, d_F represents the distance between the position of the end-effector $\mathbf{h}_1$ and $\mathbf{h}_2$; β_F and ϕ_F represents its orientation with respect to the global *Y*-axis and *X*-axis, respectability on the inertial frame $<\mathcal{R}>$. This situation is illustrated in the Fig. 1.

Remark 1: $\mathbf{h}_i$ represents the position the end-effector of the *i-th* mobile manipulator.

The relationship between the virtual structure pose-orientation-shape and the end-effector positions of the mobile manipulators is given by the forward and inverse kinematics transformation, *i.e.*, $\mathbf{r} = f(\mathbf{x})$ and $\mathbf{x} = f^{-1}(\mathbf{r})$, where $\mathbf{r} = \begin{bmatrix} \mathbf{P_F} & \mathbf{S_F} \end{bmatrix}^T$ and $\mathbf{x} = \begin{bmatrix} \mathbf{h}_1^T & \mathbf{h}_2^T \end{bmatrix}^T$.

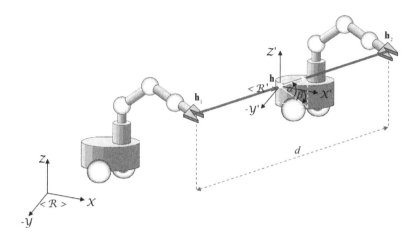

Fig. 1. Structure variables

The forward kinematic transformation $f(.)$, as shown in the Eq. 2, is given by

$$\mathbf{P_F} = \begin{bmatrix} \frac{1}{2}(x_1 + x_2) \\ \frac{1}{2}(y_1 + y_2) \\ \frac{1}{2}(z_1 + z_2) \end{bmatrix}^T ; \mathbf{S_F} = \begin{bmatrix} \sqrt{(x_1 - x_2)^2 + (y_1 - y_2)^2 + (z_1 - z_2)^2} \\ \arctan \frac{x_1 + x_2}{z_1 + z_2} \\ \arctan \frac{y_1 + y_2}{x_1 + x_2} \end{bmatrix}^T \tag{2}$$

In turn, for the inverse kinematic transformation $f^{-1}(.)$ it denoted $\mathbf{x} = f_{R_1 R_2}^{-1}(\mathbf{r})$ as, (R_i represents the i-th mobile manipulator robot)

$$\mathbf{x} = \begin{bmatrix} \mathbf{h}_1 \\ \mathbf{h}_2 \end{bmatrix} = \begin{bmatrix} x_F + \frac{1}{2}d_F \cos \beta_F \cos \phi_F \\ y_F + \frac{1}{2}d_F \cos \beta_F \sin \phi_F \\ z_F + \frac{1}{2}d_F \sin \beta_F \\ x_F - \frac{1}{2}d_F \cos \beta_F \cos \phi_F \\ y_F - \frac{1}{2}d_F \cos \beta_F \sin \phi_F \\ z_F - \frac{1}{2}d_F \sin \beta_F \end{bmatrix} \tag{3}$$

Taking the time derivative of the forward and the inverse kinematics transformations we can obtain the relationship between the time variations of $\mathbf{x}(t)$ and $\mathbf{r}(t)$, represented by the Jacobian matrix $\mathbf{J_F}$, which is given by

$$\mathbf{r} = \mathbf{J_F}(\mathbf{x})\dot{\mathbf{x}}, \tag{4}$$

and in the inverse way is given by

$$\dot{\mathbf{x}} = \mathbf{J_F}^{-1}(\mathbf{r})\dot{\mathbf{r}} \tag{5}$$

3 Controllers Design

In this section it is presented the design of the controllers for the following layers control: Formation Control, Mobile Manipulators Kinematic Control. It is worth remark that both the kinematic is performed separately for each mobile manipulator robot.

3.1 Formation Controller

The Control Layer receives from the upper layer the desired formation pose and shape $\mathbf{r}_d = \begin{bmatrix} \mathbf{P}_{Fd} & \mathbf{S}_{Fd} \end{bmatrix}^T$ and its desired variations $\dot{\mathbf{r}}_d = \begin{bmatrix} \dot{\mathbf{P}}_{Fd} & \dot{\mathbf{S}}_{Fd} \end{bmatrix}^T$. It generates the pose and shape variation references $\dot{\mathbf{r}}_{ref} = \begin{bmatrix} \dot{\mathbf{P}}_{Fref} & \dot{\mathbf{S}}_{Fref} \end{bmatrix}^T$, where the subscripts d and ref represent the desired and reference signals, respectively.

Defining the formation error as $\tilde{\mathbf{r}}(t) = \mathbf{r}_d(t) - \mathbf{r}(t)$ and taking its first time derivative, the following expression is obtained,

$$\dot{\tilde{\mathbf{r}}} = \dot{\mathbf{r}}_d - \dot{\mathbf{r}}. \tag{6}$$

Defining $\tilde{\mathbf{r}}(t) = \mathbf{0}$ as the control objective (an equilibrium point of the system), in order to prove its stability, it is proposed a controller in the sense of Lyapunov as following. Defining the positive definite candidate function $V(\tilde{\mathbf{r}}) = \frac{1}{2}\tilde{\mathbf{r}}^T\tilde{\mathbf{r}} > 0$, taking its first time derivative and replacing (6) and $\dot{\mathbf{r}}_{ref} = \mathbf{J}_F\dot{\mathbf{x}}_d$, assuming perfect velocity tracking, $i.e.$, $\dot{\mathbf{r}} \equiv \dot{\mathbf{r}}_{ref}$, one gets $\dot{V}(\tilde{\mathbf{r}}) = \tilde{\mathbf{r}}^T\dot{\mathbf{r}} = \tilde{\mathbf{r}}^T(\dot{\mathbf{r}}_d - \mathbf{J}_F\dot{\mathbf{x}}_d)$.

Now, the proposed formation control law is defined as

$$\dot{\mathbf{x}}_d = \mathbf{J}_F^{-1}(\dot{\mathbf{r}}_d + \mathcal{K}_1 \tanh(\mathcal{K}_2\tilde{\mathbf{r}})) = \mathbf{J}_F^{-1}\dot{\mathbf{r}}_{ref} \tag{7}$$

where $\mathcal{K}_1$ and $\mathcal{K}_2$ are diagonal positive gain matrix. Introducing (6.4) into the time derivative of V, it is obtained

$$\dot{V}(\tilde{\mathbf{r}}) = -\tilde{\mathbf{r}}^T\mathcal{K}_1 \tanh(\mathcal{K}_2\tilde{\mathbf{r}}) < 0. \tag{8}$$

Thus, the equilibrium point is asymptotically stable, $i.e.$ $\tilde{\mathbf{r}}(t) \to 0$ asymptotically.

3.2 Kinematic Controller

The controller is based on a minimal norm solution, which means that, at any time, the mobile manipulator will attain its navigation target with the smallest number of possible movements [13–15]. The following control law is proposed for the $i\text{-}th$ mobile manipulator,

$$\mathbf{v}_i = \mathbf{J}_i^{\#}\left(\dot{\mathbf{h}}_{\mathbf{d}i} + \mathbf{L}_i \tanh\left(\mathbf{L}_i\,\tilde{\mathbf{h}}_i\right)\right) \tag{9}$$

where, $\mathbf{J}_i^{\#} = \mathbf{W}_i^{-i}\mathbf{J}_i^{T}\left(\mathbf{J}_i\mathbf{W}_i^{-1}\mathbf{J}_i^{T}\right)^{-1}$, being $\mathbf{W}_i$ a definite positive matrix that weighs the control actions of the system; $\dot{\mathbf{h}}_{\mathbf{d}i} = \begin{bmatrix}\dot{h}_{xdi} & \dot{h}_{ydi} & \dot{h}_{zdi}\end{bmatrix}^{T}$ is the desired velocities vector of the end-effector of the i-th robot; $\tilde{\mathbf{h}}_i$ is the vector of control errors with $\tilde{\mathbf{h}}_i = \mathbf{h}_{\mathbf{d}i} - \mathbf{h}_i$; $\mathbf{L}$ is definite positive diagonal matrix that weigh the error vector $\tilde{\mathbf{h}}$; finality $\mathbf{v}(t) = \begin{bmatrix}u_l & u_m & \omega & \dot{q}_{11}\dots\dot{q}_{na1} & \dot{q}_{12}\dots\dot{q}_{na2}\end{bmatrix}^{T}$ represents the vector of maneuverability to achieve the desired operational motion.

On the other hand, the behaviour of the control error of the i-th end-effector $\tilde{\mathbf{h}}_i$ is now analysed assuming perfect velocity tracking. By substituting (9) in (3) it is obtained

$$\dot{\tilde{\mathbf{h}}}_i + \mathbf{L}\tanh\left(\tilde{\mathbf{h}}_i\right) = \mathbf{0}. \tag{10}$$

For the stability analysis the following Lyapunov candidate function is considered $V\left(\tilde{\mathbf{h}}_i\right) = \frac{1}{2}\tilde{\mathbf{h}}_i^{T}\tilde{\mathbf{h}}_i > 0$. Its time derivative on the trajectories of the system is

$$\dot{V}\left(\tilde{\mathbf{h}}_i\right) = -\tilde{\mathbf{h}}_i^{T}\mathbf{L}\tanh\left(\mathbf{L}\,\tilde{\mathbf{h}}_i\right) < 0, \tag{11}$$

which implies that the equilibrium point of the closed-loop (11) is asymptotically stable, thus the position error of the i-th end-effector verifies $\tilde{\mathbf{h}}_i(t) \to \mathbf{0}$ asymptotically with $t \to \infty$.

4   Results and Discussion

In order to assess and discuss the performance of the proposed coordinated cooperative controller, it was developed a simulation platform for multi-mobile manipulators with Matlab interface, see the Fig. 2. It is important mention that, in the simulator developed

Fig. 2. Mobile manipulator robot used by simulation platform developed

has incorporated the dynamic model of the robot. This is an online simulator, which allows users to view three-dimensional environment navigation of mobile manipulators. Ours simulation platform is based in MRSiM platform presents by [16]

The simulation experiments consist of two mobile manipulator tracking a desired trajectory while carrying a payload cooperatively. The mobile manipulators used in the simulation are composed by a non holonomic mobile platform and a 3 DOF robotic arm mounted on it.

Hence, the desired trajectory for the virtual structure centroid is described by: $x_{Fd} = 3\sin(t)$, $y_{Fd} = 3\cos(t) - 4$ and $z_{Fd} = 0.8$ [m]; While, the desired virtual structure is selected as, $d_{Fd} = 1$ [m], $\beta_{Fd} = \frac{\pi}{6}$ [rad], and $\alpha_{Fd} = \frac{2\pi}{9}$ [rad]. It is worth noting that this trajectory was chosen in order to excite the dynamics of the robots by changing their acceleration.

Figures 3, 4, 5 and 6 show the results of the simulation experiment. Figure 3 shows the stroboscopic movement on the plane X-Y-Z of the global framework $< \mathcal{R} >$. It can be seen that the proposed controller works correctly, where the mobile manipulators

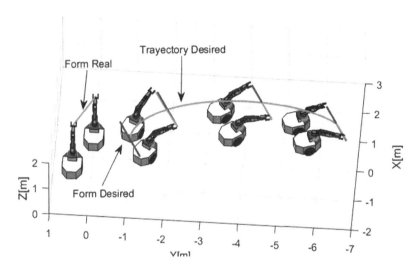

Fig. 3. Cooperative coordinated control of mobile manipulators

work in coordinated and cooperative form while transporting a common object. The Fig. 4 shows the path described by the operative ends of the robots and the point of interest of the virtual structure.

Figure 5 show that the formation control errors of the point of interest of the virtual structure formed by the ends of the mobile manipulators, control errors tend to zero when $t \to \infty$, for which it is comprobed that the proposed controller is asymptotically stable.

Finally the errors of the operative ends of the mobile manipulators are illustrated in Fig. 6, likewise these errors tend to zero when $t \to \infty$.

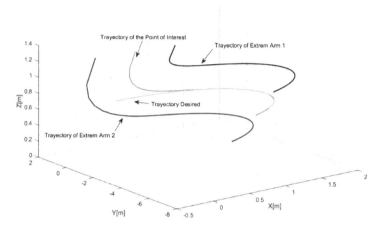

Fig. 4. Trajectory described by the operative ends of the robots.

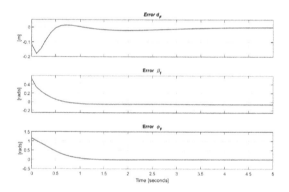

Fig. 5. Errors of position and form of the desired point of interest.

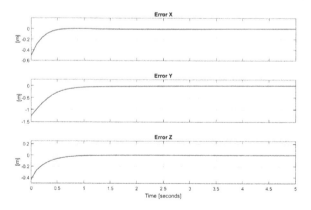

Fig. 6. Errors of position of the operative end of the robots

5 Conclusions

The design of a coordinated cooperative controller for trajectory tracking that allows transporting a common object was presented in this work. The design of the controller is based on kinematic control in cascade based on a virtual structure formed between the operative ends of the mobile manipulator robots. Stability is tested by the Lyapunov method. For the simulation experiments, a 3D platform was used in order to evaluate the performance of the proposed control scheme for different movement problems through an adequate selection of the control references.

References

1. Andaluz, V., Carelli, R., Salinas, L., Toibero, J., Roberti, F.: Visual control with adaptive dynamical compensation for 3D target tracking by mobile manipulators. Mechatronics **22**(4), 491–502 (2012)
2. Andaluz, V., Salinas, L., Roberti, F., Toibero, J., Carelli, R.: Switching control signal for bilateral tele-operation of a mobile manipulator. In: 2011 9th IEEE International Conference on Control and Automation (ICCA) (2011)
3. Andaluz, V.H., Quevedo, W.X., Chicaiza, F.A., Varela, J., Gallardo, C., Sánchez, J.S., Arteaga, O.: Transparency of a bilateral tele-operation scheme of a mobile manipulator robot. In: Paolis, L.T., Mongelli, A. (eds.) AVR 2016. LNCS, vol. 9768, pp. 228–245. Springer, Cham (2016). doi:10.1007/978-3-319-40621-3_18
4. Xidias, E., Paliotta, C., Aspragathos, N., Pettersen, K.: Path planning for formation control of autonomous vehicles. In: Rodić, A., Borangiu, T. (eds.) RAAD 2016. AISC, vol. 540, pp. 302–309. Springer, Cham (2017). doi:10.1007/978-3-319-49058-8_33
5. Simetti, E., Casalino, G.: Manipulation and trasnportation with cooperative underwater vehicle manipulator systems. IEEE J. Ocean. Eng. 1–18 (2016)
6. Andaluz, V., Roberti, F., Toibero, J., Carelli, R.: Adaptive unified motion control of mobile manipulators. Control Eng. Pract. **20**(12), 1337–1352 (2012)
7. Tsai, C., Wu, H., Tai, F., Chen, Y.: Decentralized cooperative transportation with obstacle avoidance using fuzzy wavelet neural networks for uncertain networked omnidirectional multi-robots. In: IEEE International Conference Control and Automation (ICCA), pp 978–983 (2016)
8. Zhang, Y., Zou, M., Xiao, H., Wen, J., Wang, Y.: Cooperative-manipulation scheme of routh-hurwitz type for simultaneous repetitive motion planning of two-manipulator robotic systems. In: Conference Contro and Decesion (CCDC), pp. 4409–4414 (2016)
9. Petitti, A., Franchi, A., Di Paola, D., Rizzo, A.: Decentralized motion control for cooperative manipulation with a team of networked mobile manipulators. In: IEEE International Conference on Robotics and Automation (ICRA), pp. 441–446 (2016)
10. Noohi, E., Zefran, M.: Modeling the interaction force during a haptically-coupled cooperative manipulation. In: 25th IEEE International Symposium on Robot and Human Interactive Communication (RO-MAN), pp. 119–124 (2016)
11. Liang, Y., Lee, H.: Decentralized formation control and obstacle avoidance for multiple robots with nonholonomic constraints. In: American Control Conference, (2006)
12. Zyada, Z., Hayakawa, Y., Hosoe, S.: Model-based control for nonprehensile manipulation of a two-rigid-link object by two cooperative arms. In: IEEE International Conference on Robotics and Biomimetics, pp. 472–477 (2010)

13. He, W., Ge, W., Li, Y., Liu, Y., Yang, C., Sun, C.: Model identification and control design for a humanoid robot. IEEE Trans. Syst. Man Cybern. Syst. Chin. **47**, 45–57 (2016)
14. Andaluz, V., Canseco, P., Rosales, A., Roberti, F., Carelli, R.: Multilayer scheme for the adaptive cooperative coordinated control of mobile manipulators. In: 38th Annual Conference on IEEE Industrial Electronics Society, IECON 2012 (2012)
15. Andaluz, V., Ortiz, J., Perez, M., Roberti, F., Carelli, R.: Adaptive cooperative control of multi-mobile manipulators. In: 40th Annual Conference of the IEEE Industrial Electronics Society, IECON 2014 (2014)
16. Brandao, A.S., Carelli, R., Sarcinelli-Filho, M., BastosFilho, T.F.: MRSiM: an environment for simulating mobile robots navigation. In: Jornadas Argentinas de Robótica (2008). (in Spanish)

Navigation and Dynamic Control
of Omnidirectional Platforms

Víctor H. Andaluz$^{(\boxtimes)}$, Christian P. Carvajal$^{(\boxtimes)}$, Alex Santana G.$^{(\boxtimes)}$,
Víctor D. Zambrano$^{(\boxtimes)}$, and José A. Pérez$^{(\boxtimes)}$

Universidad de Las Fuerzas Armadas ESPE, Sangolquí, Ecuador
{vhandaluz1,amsantana,vdzambrano}@espe.edu.ec,
chriss2592@hotmail.com, joansl1@hotmail.com

Abstract. This work proposes a Path Planning method using the virtual potential field, which provides a parameterized path in the space so that the omnidirectional mobile platform to reach the desired point and kinematic modeling of the platform to propose a Nonlinear Controller, that's used to execute the path-following by means of Linear Algebra, for to correct the desired position and orientation of the omnidirectional platform use a dynamic compensation.

Keywords: Path Planning · Kinematic modeling · Dynamic · Nonlinear Controller

1 Introduction

Robotics over the years has evolved, providing better benefits for users, using robots that are used to solve various tasks in the bodywork industry, medicine, military field, space exploration, agriculture among other areas [1, 2]. However, their efficiency depends on the mobility that they present in work environments with limited space or in situations where the movement requires spatial conditions, for them the systems must be versatile enough for their displacement in any direction [3].

The autonomy of a mobile robot to move from an initial point to desired destination, it's delimited by collision problems with fixed and mobile objects in both structured and unstructured environments [4, 5]. In this context the planning algorithms generate collision-free paths, considering aspects such as the dimensions of the robot, latency of the system, energy consumption, among others. Path planning can be classified into two main methods *(i)* path-free collision *i.e.* plans a road without considering obstacles in the work space; *(ii)* and path planning with avoidance of obstacles consisting of avoiding the obstacles that occur in the path of the robot, while it continues to reach the goal [6]. In order for a robot to reach a desired goal, random methods such as RPP (Random Path Planning), and PPP (Probabilistic Path Planning) [7] have been proposed.

In spite of the advantages of robotics it is necessary to emphasize the way in which it fulfills the proposed objectives, i.e., the control or algorithms implemented in each prototype, the methods proposed by several articles [8–10] emphasize Such as

© Springer International Publishing AG 2017
Y. Gao et al. (Eds.): TAROS 2017, LNAI 10454, pp. 661–672, 2017.
DOI: 10.1007/978-3-319-64107-2_54

Feedforward Nonlinear control, Fuzzy PD control, predictive control based on the linear model, among others. In the last decades, mathematics has become a fundamental tool for technological development by means of: plane and Spatial Geometry, Calculus and Linear Algebra; Within the Linear Algebra, research in the area of robotics has been the trend for the development of control algorithms, in order to execute specific tasks in structured or partially structured environments. Advanced control based on linear algebra doesn't require complex calculations to obtain the control signal [11, 12]. It's easy to understand and implement, it can easily adapt to a microcontroller without using an advanced computer [13], this algorithm saves processing time and energy at the time of executing the desired task.

These methods allow introducing concepts of Path Planning in mobile robots based on the potential field, where it's considered a force of attraction towards the target configuration, and a series of repulsion forces intended to avoid collision with obstacles [14].

For the above, this work is based on the planning of trajectories in work spaces in a structured way for omnidirectional mobile robots, based on the potential field, where it is considered a force of attraction towards the destination configuration, and a series of repulsion forces destined to avoid collision with obstacles [15]. This application has as a disadvantage the local minimums and to reduce we seek to use a movement gradient associated with the field that calculates the path based on the highest potential line, thus avoiding local minimum problems [16]. For the study is used an omnidirectional platform in AB configuration [17, 18], together with its dynamic and kinematic analysis [19], the control platform is based on the kinematics and redundancy of the omnidirectional platform, the structure of the proposed control law *(i)* meets the objective of the task and *(ii)* provides a homogeneous solution that allows one or more secondary objectives to be met.

This project have 6 Sections including the Introduction. The Sect. 2 presents the Kinematic studio of the omnidirectional móvil platform. The Sect. 3 describes Potential Field Path Planning. The Sect. 4 describe the design and stability analysis of the nolineal control algorithm based on the linear algebra. The Sect. 5 shows the experimental results, discussion and analysis of control scheme proposed. Finally, the conclusions are presented in the Sect. 6.

2 Kinematic Modeling

An omnidirectional robot is conformed by two lineal velocities u_l, u_m and one angular velocity ω such as shown in Fig. 1.

Each linear velocity is directed as one of the axes of the frame $<\chi>$ attached to the center of gravity of the omnidirectional robot: u_l points to the frontal direction and u_m points to the left-lateral direction. The angular velocity ω rotates the referential system $<\chi>$ counterclockwise, around the axis z' (considering the top view) then the kinematics model is describe by:

$$\begin{bmatrix} \dot{\chi}_x \\ \dot{\chi}_y \\ \dot{\chi}_\psi \end{bmatrix} = \begin{bmatrix} \cos(\psi) & -\sin(\psi) & 0 \\ \sin(\psi) & \cos(\psi) & 0 \\ 0 & 0 & 1 \end{bmatrix} \begin{bmatrix} u_l \\ u_m \\ \omega \end{bmatrix} \tag{1}$$

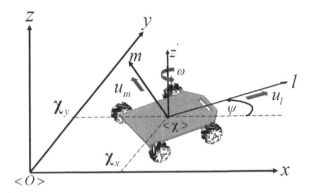

Fig. 1. Schematic representation of the omnidirectional robot.

where $\dot{\chi}_x$, $\dot{\chi}_y$ and $\dot{\chi}_\psi$ are all measured velocities with respect to the inertial frame $< O >$, also the equation system (1) can be written in compact form as show in Fig. 2:

$$\dot{\chi}(t) = \mathbf{J}(\psi)\boldsymbol{\mu}(t) \tag{2}$$

where, $\mathbf{J}(\psi) \in \Re^{m \times n}$ with $m = n = 3$ represents the Jacobian matrix that defines a linear mapping between the velocity vector of the omnidirectional mobile platform, $\boldsymbol{\mu} \in \Re^n$ with $\boldsymbol{\mu} = [u_l\, u_m\, \omega]^T$ and the velocity vector of the operative point $\dot{\chi} \in \Re^m$ where $\dot{\chi} = [\dot{\chi}_x\ \dot{\chi}_y\ \dot{\chi}_\psi]^T$. For determine the angular velocities correspondents to each wheel Fig. 7 of the omnidirectional robot is used the next system:

$$\begin{bmatrix} W_{d1} \\ W_{d2} \\ W_{d3} \\ W_{d4} \end{bmatrix} = \frac{1}{R}\begin{bmatrix} 1 & -1 & -(a+b) \\ 1 & 1 & (a+b) \\ 1 & 1 & -(a+b) \\ 1 & -1 & (a+b) \end{bmatrix}\begin{bmatrix} u_l \\ u_m \\ \omega \end{bmatrix} \tag{3}$$

this equation system can be defined as:

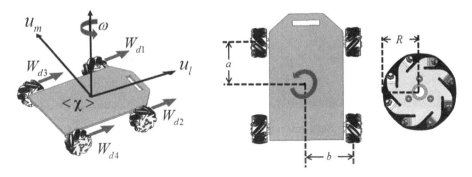

Fig. 2. Configuration of the omnidirectional robot.

$$\mathbf{W}_d(t) = \mathbf{J_T}(a,b)\boldsymbol{\mu}(t) \qquad (4)$$

where $\mathbf{W}_d$ is the vector of angular velocities of the each wheels of the omnidirectional mobile platform and $\mathbf{J_T} \in \mathbb{R}^{4\times3}$ is a constant transformation matrix, which was obtained from the inverse kinematics of platform velocities and $\boldsymbol{\mu}$ represents the mobility velocities of the omnidirectional robot.

3   Potential Field Path Planning

Path Planning by the potential field method is inspired by the physical property of the particles to attract and repel, where the robot is considered as a point electric charge within a potential field located in the space. In robotics it is possible to simulate the navigation of loads due to the existence of local minimums and global minimums within a function, in this context the algorithm emulates a potential well as the desired destination.

In this way the robot is considered a particle with electric charge in the free space defined as a potential field, where the obstacles have electric charge of the same sign of the robot, to obtain a repulsion force while the target is associated with a load of sign opposite the robot that results in an attractive force (5). Finally, by means of an associated movement gradient to the field, the path is calculated with criteria of the highest potential line avoiding problems of local minimums, indicated in Fig. 3.

$$\vec{\mathbf{F}}_{\text{total}} = \vec{\mathbf{F}}_{\text{att}} + \vec{\mathbf{F}}_{\text{rep}} \qquad (5)$$

In addition, the solution of the gradient decrease leads to three specific cases shown in Figs. 4, 5 and 6, where the response tends asymptotically to infinity by falling into a

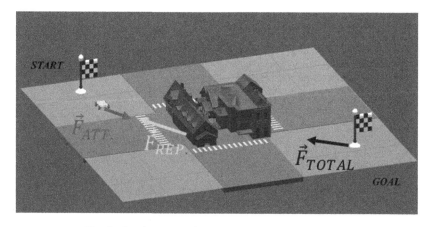

Fig. 3. Semi-structured environment represented in 3D.

potential well, thus generating a variation in the algorithm of virtual potential fields to find an exit of these critical conditions, thus the descent of gradient always looks for local minimums of the function.

Case I

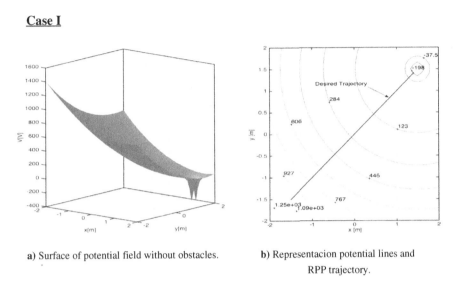

a) Surface of potential field without obstacles.

b) Representacion potential lines and
   RPP trajectory.

Fig. 4. Representation of the virtual potential fields surface and desired trajectory without obstacles.

Case II

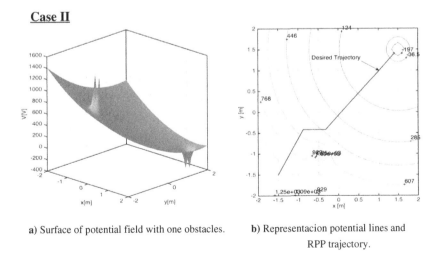

a) Surface of potential field with one obstacles.

b) Representacion potential lines and
   RPP trajectory.

Fig. 5. Representation of the virtual potential fields surface and desired trajectory with one obstacle.

Case III

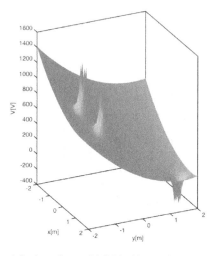

a) Surface of potential field with two obstacles.

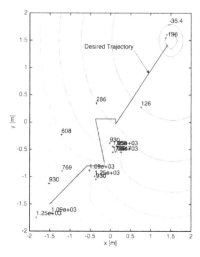

b) Representacion potential lines and
RPP trajectory.

Fig. 6. Representation of the virtual potential fields surface and desired trajectory with two obstacles.

4 Kinematic Controller

4.1 Design Controller

Through the Euler's approximation of the kinematic model of the mobile manipulator (2), the following kinematic model discrete is obtained

$$\chi(k+1) = \chi(k) + T_0 \mathbf{J}(\psi)\boldsymbol{\mu}(k) \tag{6}$$

where, values χ of at the discrete time $t = kT_0$ will be denoted as $\chi(k)$, T_0 is the sample time, and $k \in \{0, 1, 2, 3, 4, 5 \ldots\}$. On this way the discrete model for the robot could be expressed by:

$$
\begin{bmatrix}
\chi_x(k+1) \\
\chi_y(k+1) \\
\chi_\psi(k+1)
\end{bmatrix} =
\begin{bmatrix}
\chi_x(k) \\
\chi_y(k) \\
\chi_\omega(k)
\end{bmatrix} + T_0
\begin{bmatrix}
\cos(\psi) & -\sin(\psi) & 0 \\
\sin(\psi) & \cos(\psi) & 0 \\
0 & 0 & 1
\end{bmatrix}
\begin{bmatrix}
u_l(k) \\
u_m(k) \\
\omega(k)
\end{bmatrix} \tag{7}
$$

In order that the tracking error tends to zero the following expression is used

$$
\begin{bmatrix}
\chi_x(k+1) \\
\chi_y(k+1) \\
\chi_\psi(k+1)
\end{bmatrix} =
\begin{bmatrix}
\chi_{xd}(k+1) \\
\chi_{yd}(k+1) \\
\chi_{\psi d}(k+1)
\end{bmatrix} -
\begin{bmatrix}
\Phi_x & 0 & 0 \\
0 & \Phi_y & 0 \\
0 & 0 & \Phi_\psi
\end{bmatrix}
\left(
\begin{bmatrix}
\chi_{xd}(k+1) \\
\chi_{yd}(k+1) \\
\chi_{\psi d}(k+1)
\end{bmatrix} -
\begin{bmatrix}
\chi_x(k+1) \\
\chi_y(k+1) \\
\chi_\psi(k+1)
\end{bmatrix}
\right) \tag{8}
$$

where, $0 < (\Phi_x, \Phi_y, \Phi_\psi) < 1$ and $(\chi_{xd}, \chi_{yd}, \chi_{yd})$ is the desired trajectory. Using (7) and (8) we obtain:

$$
\underbrace{\begin{bmatrix} \cos(\psi_{(k)}) & -\sin(\psi_{(k)}) & 0 \\ \sin(\psi_{(k)}) & \cos(\psi_{(k)}) & 0 \\ 0 & 0 & 1 \end{bmatrix}}_{\mathbf{J}} \underbrace{\begin{bmatrix} u_{l(k)} \\ u_{m(k)} \\ \omega_{(k)} \end{bmatrix}}_{\mu} = \underbrace{\frac{1}{T_0} \left(\begin{bmatrix} \chi_{xd(k+1)} \\ \chi_{yd(k+1)} \\ \chi_{\psi d(k+1)} \end{bmatrix} - \Phi \left(\begin{bmatrix} \chi_{xd(k+1)} \\ \chi_{yd(k+1)} \\ \chi_{\psi d(k+1)} \end{bmatrix} - \begin{bmatrix} \chi_{x(k+1)} \\ \chi_{y(k+1)} \\ \chi_{\psi(k+1)} \end{bmatrix} \right) - \begin{bmatrix} \chi_{x(k)} \\ \chi_{y(k)} \\ \chi_{\psi(k)} \end{bmatrix} \right)}_{\mathbf{b}}
$$

then you can express $\mathbf{J}\mu = \mathbf{b}$ and the particular solution is:

$$\mu = \mathbf{J}^{-1}\mathbf{b} \tag{9}$$

4.2   Stability Analysis

In kinematics is fulfilled $\mathbf{v}_{\mathrm{ref}} = \mu$, therefore the closed-loop equation is given by,

$$\chi(k+1) - \chi(k) = T_0\mathbf{J}(\mathbf{J}^{-1}\mathbf{b}) \tag{10}$$

where $\mathbf{J}\mathbf{J}^{-1} = \mathbf{I}_m$ then (10) is reduced to,

$$\chi(k+1) - \chi(k) = T_0\mathbf{I}_m\mathbf{b} \tag{11}$$

Through the properties of the identity matrix have

$$\chi(k+1) - \chi(k) = (\chi_\mathbf{d}(k+1) - \Phi(\chi_\mathbf{d}(k) - \chi(k)) - \chi(k)) \tag{12}$$

Reducing terms and grouping them you have that the error in the following state $\chi_d(k+1) - \chi(k+1)$ depends only on the previous error by a gain $\Phi(\chi_\mathbf{d}(k) - \chi(k))$

$$
\begin{bmatrix} \chi_x(k+1) \\ \chi_y(k+1) \\ \chi_\omega(k+1) \end{bmatrix} = \begin{bmatrix} \chi_{xd}(k+1) - \Phi_x(e_x) \\ \chi_{yd}(k+1) - \Phi_y(e_y) \\ \chi_{\omega d}(k+1) - \Phi_\omega(e_\omega) \end{bmatrix} \text{ and } \begin{bmatrix} e_x(k+1) \\ e_y(k+1) \\ e_\omega(k+1) \end{bmatrix} = \begin{bmatrix} \Phi_x(e_x(k)) \\ \Phi_y(e_y(k)) \\ \Phi_\omega(e_\omega(k)) \end{bmatrix} \tag{13}
$$

The error on the following states comes by

$$
\begin{aligned}
e_i(k+1) &= \Phi_i e_i(k) \\
e_i(k+2) &= \Phi_i e_i(k+1) = \Phi_i^2 e(k) \\
e_i(k+3) &= \Phi_i e_i(k+2) = \Phi_i^3 e(k) \\
&\vdots \\
e_i(k+n) &= \Phi_i e_i(k+n-1) = \Phi_i^n e(k)
\end{aligned}
$$

Them i-esimo error approaches asymptotically to zero when $0 < \Phi_i < 1$ and $n \to \infty$.

4.3   Dynamic Compensation

Additionally, an Inner Velocity Controller is implemented to compensate for the dynamics of the omnidirectional robot, thus reducing the velocity tracking error. This controller receives as inputs the desired angular velocities $\mathbf{W}_d(t)$ calculated by the kinematic controller using the (4), and obtain the angular velocities $\mathbf{W}_g(t)$ from the omnidirectional robot. Hence, if there is no perfect velocity tracking, the velocity error is defined as $\tilde{\mathbf{W}}(t) = \mathbf{W}_d(t) - \mathbf{W}_g(t)$. This velocity error motivates the dynamic compensation process, which should be able to independently track four velocity commands: forward, lateral, and rotation, see Fig. 7.

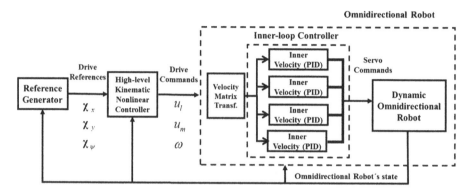

Fig. 7. Block diagram of the inner-loop controller of the omnidirectional robot.

with this aim, the following control law is proposed as:

$$\mathbf{W}_{di}(t) = k_{pj}\tilde{\mathbf{W}}_i(t) + k_{ij} \int_0^t \tilde{\mathbf{W}}_i(t)dt + k_{dj}\frac{d}{dt}\tilde{\mathbf{W}}_i(t) \qquad (14)$$

where, $\tilde{\mathbf{W}}_i(t) = \mathbf{W}_{di}(t) - \mathbf{W}_{ri}(t)$ with $i = 1,2,3,4$ is the angular velocities error, while that k_{pi}, k_{iji}, k_{di} with $i = 1,2,3,4$ are positive gain that weigh the control errors.

5   Results and Discussions

In order to demonstrate the performance of the control proposed in this article for Path Planning by potential fields, several experiments were carried out for trajectory tracking after the control of an omnidirectional mobile platform. The most representative results are presented in this section, for the experimental test was implemented an OMNIBEE Robot, which supports the respective angular velocities to each test as input reference signals, see Fig. 8.

Fig. 8. "OMNIBEE" omnidirectional mobile robot.

The test corresponds to Case II and Case III (Figs. 5b and 6b) of Path Planning where you have an obstacle, then the method gives the desired path for the robot to move. The desired velocity of the mobile robot depends of the error, then the reference velocity for the path in this case is expressed as, $\left|\mathbf{v}_{\chi d}\right| = \upsilon_P/(1 + k\rho)$, where υ_P is the constant velocity defined by de user, k is a positive constant that weigh the control and ρ is the error module. Also, the desired location is defined as the closest point on the path to the mobile robot.

For the Case II of Path Planning Figs. 9, 10 and 11 show the results of the experiment. Where Fig. 9 shows the stroboscopic movement on the $<\mathrm{x,y,z}>$ space. It can be seen that the proposed controller works correctly Fig. 10 the error $\rho(t)$ remains close to zero; and Fig. 11 illustrate the velocities of control.

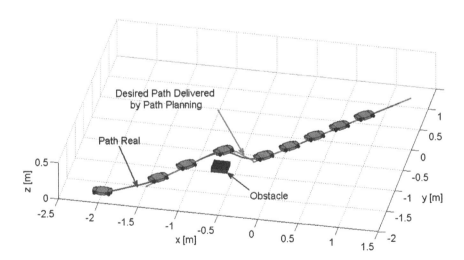

Fig. 9. Stroboscopic movement of the Omnidirectional mobile platform in the path.

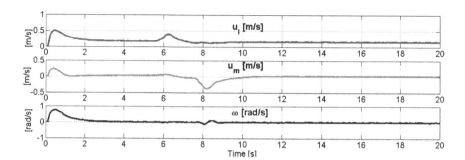

Fig. 10. Control velocities of the mobile platform.

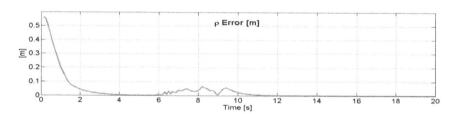

Fig. 11. Distance between the mobile platform position and the closest point on the path.

For the Case III of Path Planning the Figs. 12, 13 and 14 show the results of the experiment. Where Fig. 12 shows the stroboscopic movement on the $<x,y,z>$ space. It can be seen that the proposed controller works correctly Fig. 13 the error $\rho(t)$ remains close to zero; and Fig. 14 illustrate the velocities of control.

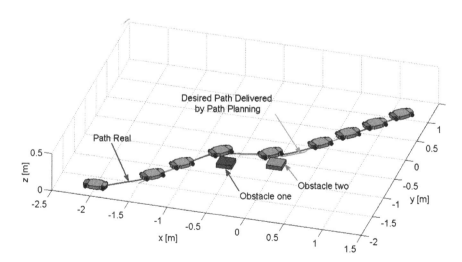

Fig. 12. Stroboscopic movement of the omnidirectional mobile platform in the path.

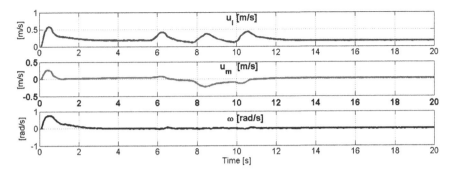

Fig. 13. Control velocities of the mobile platform.

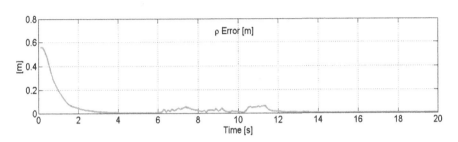

Fig. 14. Distance between the mobile platform position and the closest point on the path.

6   Conclusions

Path Planning by virtual potential fields manages to generate trajectories with evasion of obstacles in the way, where with the dynamical and kinematic analysis that accepts as reference velocities, corresponding to the angular velocities of each wheel, it was proposed a nonlinear controller by Linear Algebra. Finally the performance of the proposed controller was presented by means of experimental tests for each case of Path Planning and it was observed that the trajectories given to the robot, it was performed with what was planned.

References

1. Carrillo, A., Pelayo, S., Pelayo, J.: Development of a mobile service robot for classify objects and place them in containers. In: Power, Electronics and Computing (ROPEC) (2016)
2. Andaluz, V.H., Chicaiza, F.A., Gallardo, C., Quevedo, W.X., Varela, J., Sánchez, J.S., Arteaga, O.: Unity3D-MatLab simulator in real time for robotics applications. In: Paolis, L. T., Mongelli, A. (eds.) AVR 2016, Part I. LNCS, vol. 9768, pp. 246–263. Springer, Cham (2016). doi:10.1007/978-3-319-40621-3_19
3. Shenoy, P., Miller, K.J., Crawford, B., Rao, R.P.N.: Online electromyographic control of a robotic prosthesis. IEEE Trans. Biomed. Eng. **55**, 1128–1135 (2008). doi:10.1109/TBME. 2007.909536

4. Barraquand, J., Kavraki, L., Motwani, R., Latombe, J., Li, T., Raghavan, P.: A random sampling scheme for path planning. In: International Symposium on Robotics Research, vol. 6, pp. 249–264 (1996)
5. Andaluz, V.H., Ortiz, J.S., Chicaiza, F.A., Varela, J., Espinosa, E.G., Canseco, P.: Adaptive control of the human-wheelchair system through brain signals. In: Kubota, N., Kiguchi, K., Liu, H., Obo, T. (eds.) ICIRA 2016, Part II. LNCS, vol. 9835, pp. 223–234. Springer, Cham (2016). doi:10.1007/978-3-319-43518-3_22
6. Andaluz, V.H., Roberti, F., Toibero, J.M., Carelli, R., Wagner, B.: Adaptive dynamic path following control of an unicycle-like mobile robot. In: Jeschke, S., Liu, H., Schilberg, D. (eds.) ICIRA 2011, Part I. LNCS, vol. 7101, pp. 563–574. Springer, Heidelberg (2011). doi:10.1007/978-3-642-25486-4_56
7. Overmars, M., Svestka, P.: A probabilistic learning approach to motion planning. In: Workshop in Algorithmic Foundations of Robotics, vol. 32, pp. 1–25 (1994)
8. Karray, A., Feki, M.: Tracking control of a mobile manipulator with fuzzy PD controller. In: IEEE Conference Publications: 2015 World Congress on Information Technology and Computer Applications (WCITCA), pp. 1–5 (2015)
9. Karray, A., Feki, M.: Control de seguimiento de un manipulador móvil con un controlador de PD difuso. In: Publicaciones de la Conferencia IEEE: Congreso Mundial de Tecnología de la Información y Aplicaciones Informáticas 2015 (WCITCA), pp. 1–5 (2015)
10. Wieber, P.: Trajectory free linear model predictive control for stable walking in the presence of strong perturbations. In: 6th IEEE-RAS International Conference on Humanoid Robots, Genova, pp. 137–142 (2006)
11. Rosales, A., Scaglia, G., Mut, V., Sciascio, F.D.: Seguimiento de trayectorias de robots móviles en entornos dinámicos-un enfoque de álgebra lineal, vol. 27, pp. 981–997. Universidad de Cambridge (2009)
12. Rómoli, S., Serrano, M.E., Ortiz, O.A., Vega, J.R.: Control de seguimiento de los perfiles de concentración en un bioreactor fed-batch usando metodología de álgebra lineal, pp. 162–171. Elsevier (2015)
13. Scaglia, G., Rosales, A., Quintero, L., Mut, V., Agarwal, R.: A linear-interpolation-based controller design for trajectory tracking of mobile robots. Elsevier Control Eng. Pract. **18**, 318–329 (2010). https://doi.org/10.1016/j.conengprac.2009.11.011
14. Boyuan, L., Haiping, D., Weihua, L.: A potential field approach-based trajectory control for autonomous electric vehicles with in-wheel motors. IEEE Intell. Transp. Syst. Soc. **PP**(99),1–12 (2016)
15. Stentz, A.: Optimal and efficient path planning for partially-known environments. In: Proceedings of the 1994 IEEE International Conference on Robotics and Automation, pp. 3310–3317 (1994)
16. Veslin, E., Slama, J., Dutra, M.S., Slama, J.: Motion planning on mobile robots using differential flatness. IEEE Latin Am. Trans. **9**, 1006–1011 (2011)
17. Watanabe, K.: Control of an omnidirectional mobile robot. In: Proceedings of the 1998 Second International Conference on Knowledge-Based Intelligent Electronic Systems, KES 1998, Adelaide, pp. 51–60 (1998)
18. Jae, H.C., Byung-Ju, Y., Whee, K.K., Hogil, L.: The dynamic modeling and analysis for an omnidirectional mobile robot with three caster wheels. In: 2003 IEEE International Conference on Robotics and Automation, pp. 521–527 (2003)
19. Andaluz, G.M., Andaluz, V.H., Terán, H.C., Arteaga, O., Chicaiza, F.A., Varela, J., Ortiz, J. S., Pérez, F., Rivas, D., Sánchez, J.S., Canseco, P.: Modeling dynamic of the human-wheelchair system applied to NMPC. In: Kubota, N., Kiguchi, K., Liu, H., Obo, T. (eds.) ICIRA 2016, Part II. LNCS, vol. 9835, pp. 179–190. Springer, Cham (2016). doi:10.1007/978-3-319-43518-3_18

Unified Dynamic Control of Omnidirectional Robots

Víctor H. Andaluz[1](✉), Christian P. Carvajal[1], Oscar Arteaga[1],
José A. Pérez[1], Franklin S. Valencia[2], and Leonardo A. Solís[1]

[1] Universidad de las Fuerzas Armadas ESPE, Sangolquí, Ecuador
{vhandaluz1,obarteaga}@espe.edu.ec,
chriss2592@hotmail.com, joans11@hotmail.com,
leonardosolisc@gmail.com
[2] Universidad Técnica de Ambato, Ambato, Ecuador
franknejoss2011@hotmail.com

Abstract. This work is focused on the proposal of a kinematic modeling and kinematic nonlinear controller to solve problems such as point stabilization, trajectory tracking and path following about of dynamic omnidirectional robot for which will be synthesized in an unified controller. The dynamic compensation controller is considered through of omnidirectional robot-inner-loop system to independently track three velocity commands: front, lateral and angular. This controller is proved in the simulation and with the experimental test with the construction of the robot with mecanum wheels in AB configuration.

Keywords: Omnidirectional robot · Mecanum wheel · Asymptotically · Nonlinear controller and unified controller

1 Introduction

The development of the industry creates the necessity of getting access to dangerous or complex places for the human being [1], and at the same time to have faster mobility or transfer of objects to different places in most of the cases [2]. The omnidirectional robot is an alternative of solution to the mentioned problem; this can play the function of a conveyor, inspected in remote or explosive areas, supervising different tasks and as support or base for other robots or manipulators [3, 4]. The guiades vehicles automatically for the different applications are an important reason for a scientific and educational research, many studies like this one have been done in wheelchairs and unicycles, drones and others [5].

The omnidirectional robot due to its configuration can move in the desired direction from any initial position [6], once the movement system ensures a perfect mobility in any narrow, curved, diagonal or any other space [7], through its type Mecanum wheels [8]. Therefore, due to all these features, it is increases the demand in the use of omnidirectional robots [9].

While time has gone on, several control algorithms have been developed to solve certain tasks of positioning *(i)*, where the robot from an any initial position χ, it should

© Springer International Publishing AG 2017
Y. Gao et al. (Eds.): TAROS 2017, LNAI 10454, pp. 673–685, 2017.
DOI: 10.1007/978-3-319-64107-2_55

moved to a desired position χ_d, several control algorithms have been developed for this purpose, which comply with a target end, *(ii)* trajectory tracking, the robot should follow a determined path by the user, [10, 11] Besides that, algorithms have been developed for trajectory tracking and *(iii)* path following, which considered a path $\mathcal{P}(f)$ that is parameterized in the time, the robot should follow the path to a desired velocity wherever can be its initial position, for this the robot will find the point closest to it the same, in this type of problem have been implemented control algorithms in [12–14], as you can see in the above articles these control laws are performed to run an action to the time *i.e.* the different strategies of control consider that the robot is governed only to accomplish only one task and not several tasks with a single law of control.

This paper proposes to perform a law of unified based control in the kinematics of the omnidirectional robot, for the execution of positioning, trajectory tracking and path following, this law of control will solve these three types of problems which are detailed in this paper, only with performing small changes in its references of control. The strategy of unified control will be analyzed by simulation and experimental tests, for this reason was built an omnidirectional robot in configuration AB with Mecanum wheels.

The paper is organized in the follow way: in Sect. 2 the omnidirectional robot construction is presented; the problem formulation, including the positioning, trajectory tracking and path following are presented in Sect. 3; while the control and kinematics modeling are presented in Sect. 4. The results are presented and discussed in Sect. 5. Finally, conclusions are given in Sect. 6.

2   Omnidirectional Robot Construction

2.1   Hardware

This section describes the construction of omnidirectional mobile robot in which the hardware is divided in four modules, as is shown in Fig. 1.

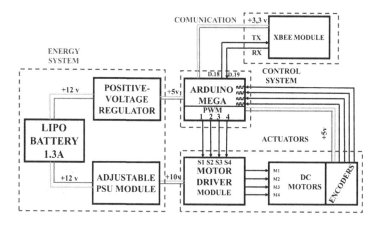

Fig. 1. Block diagram of hardware of omnidirectional robot.

A. **Energy system:** Consists on one LIPO 3S battery(1.3A), *i.e.* it has three load cells. Also are considered the voltage regulators for the control system and for the actuators module.

B. **Control system:** This is formed by one Arduino Mega, which *(i)* receives and transmits signal of the kinematics control implemented, *(ii)* performs the internal control of the actuators, this control compensates the dynamics of the omnidirectional robot, as inputs it have the desired angular velocities $W_d(t)$ and $W_q(t)$ that are the angular velocities obtained from de robot, the velocities errors are defined as $\tilde{W}(t) = W_d(t) - W_q(t)$, this error is compensated by the inner loop controller as shown in Fig. 2.

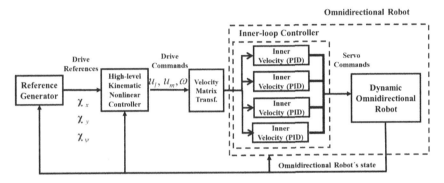

Fig. 2. Block diagram of the control system.

With this aim, the following control law is proposed:

$$W_{dj}(t) = k_{pj}\tilde{W}_j(t) + k_{ij}\int_0^t \tilde{W}_j(t)dt + k_{dj}\frac{d}{dt}\tilde{W}_j(t) \tag{1}$$

where, $\tilde{W}_j(t) = W_{dj}(t) - W_{qj}(t)\ldots$ with $j = 1,2,3,4$ is the angular velocities error, while that k_{pj}, k_{ij}, k_{dj} with $j = 1,2,3,4$ are positive gain that weigh the control errors.

C. **Actuators:** It consists on DC motors, encoders and their respective motor drivers that support a constant current of 1.2 A by channel.

D. **Communication:** It manages the communication between the robot and the computer system of kinematic control. Considering the transmission velocity and the distance that was based on the IEEE 802.15.4 standard of Zigbee wireless networks.

2.2 Software

This section describes the interface for the interaction of the omnidirectional robot and the operator, which is implemented in MATLAB by the facility of performing the experimental tests, simulations and validations of the controllers. This interface has two types of operation on the robot.

A. **Drive Implementation Mode:** Figure 3, in this mode is established the communication between the computer control system and omnidirectional robot. The computer system transmits the desired angular velocities $W_d(t)$ that will be delivered by the unified controller. Thus, the reconstruction of movement is performed by the information provided by the movement of the omnidirectional robot, allowing to verify if comply with the implemented algorithm control. At the end of the proposed task to the robot, the stroboscopic movement of the robot is automatically plotted on the plane $\mathcal{X}, \mathcal{Y}$ and rotation with respect to the axis of the reference system $<O>$.

B. **Tele-operation Mode:** Figure 4, in this mode is applied the navigation of omnidirectional robot in which commands are generated by pressing the interface buttons, with which you can realize vertical linear/backward, horizontal right/left movements, rotate on your own axis right/left and diagonal displacements in 45°. The interface sends these commands, updating the value of the velocities for each motor, which produces the movements expected by the user with a constant velocity set by the operator.

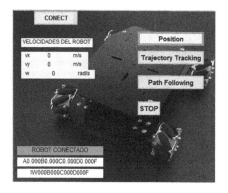 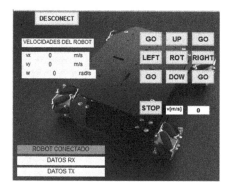

Fig. 3. Interface of drive implementation mode.

Fig. 4. Interface of Tele-operation mode

3 Problem Formulation

The fundamental problems of the control of omnidirectional robots are divided into three types which are detailed to continue:

3.1   Positioning

The problem of positioning with a desired orientation is to lead the omnidirectional robot to a desired position and orientation. The control problem is presented in Fig. 5a in which the target point is defined by χ_d that represents the desired final position of the omnidirectional robot in the work reference plane $<O>$, where the location and desired velocity are defined as: $\chi_d(t, \chi) = \chi_d = cte$ and $\mathbf{V}_{hd}(t, \chi) = \dot{\chi}_d = 0$. Here the problem is to determine the feedback $\mathbf{V}_{ref} = f(\tilde{\chi}(t))$ where $\tilde{\chi}(t) = \chi_d - \chi(t)$ that represent the error of the desired position, must reach to comply that $\lim_{t \to \infty} \tilde{\chi}(t) = 0$.

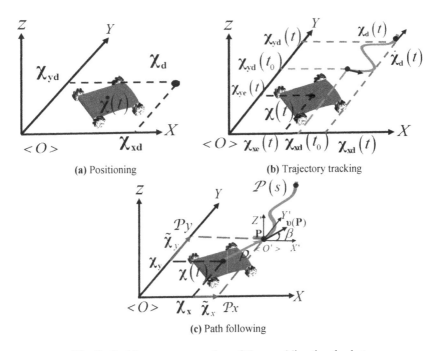

(a) Positioning   (b) Trajectory tracking

(c) Path following

Fig. 5. Problems representaction of the omnidirectional robot.

3.2   Trajectory Tracking

The problem of an omnidirectional robot consist on following a trajectory $\chi_d(t)$ where $\dot{\chi}_d(t)$ is the desired velocity of the trajectory and $\ddot{\chi}_d(t)$ represents the desired acceleration *i.e.* the trajectory of the omnidirectional robot does not depend on the instant position of the omnidirectional robot, but is only defined as a variable in time, for this control problem the desired velocity of the robot is defined which becomes the instant derivative of the trajectory $\mathbf{V}_d(t) = \dot{\chi}_d(t)$ such as is indicated in Fig. 5b *i.e.* the problem of the trajectory tracking of an omnidirectional robot is to find the control actions in function of the control error of the position and the desired velocity of the robot $\mathbf{V}_{ref} = f(\tilde{\chi}(t), \chi_d(t))$ for which $\lim_{t \to \infty} \tilde{\chi}(t) = 0$.

3.3   Path Following

The problem of path following is presented in Fig. 5c where is considered a path $\mathcal{P}$, the position of the robot with respect to the closest point **P**, ρ represents the distance between the position of the omnidirectional robot $\chi(t)$ and the closest point to the desired path and $\tilde{\beta}$ is the error vector of the robot orientation with respect to $\chi(t)$ y **P**. Then, the desired position and velocity are given by $\chi_d(t, \chi) = \mathbf{P}(t, \chi)$ and $\mathbf{V_{hd}}(t, \chi) = \mathbf{v}(\chi)$ respectively, the problem is to determine a control law for feedback $\mathbf{V}_{ref} = f\left(\mathbf{v}, \rho, \tilde{\beta}\right)$. Where the error of the position of the robot is given by $\tilde{\chi} = \chi_d - \chi(t)$, *i.e.* if $\lim_{t \to \infty} \tilde{\chi}(t) = 0$ then $\lim_{t \to \infty} \rho(t) = 0$ and $\lim_{t \to \infty} \tilde{\beta}(t) = 0$

The solution to these three described problems is based on desing a unified controller in which the robot complies with *(i)* stabilization at a desired point, *(ii)* trajectory tracking, and *(iii)* path following, by means of an appropriate selection of control references as $\mathbf{h_d}(t, \mathbf{h})$ and $\mathbf{V_{hd}}(t, \mathbf{h})$.

4   Control and Kinematic Modeling

An omnidirectional robot is conformed by *(i)* two linear velocities u_l and u_m and *(ii)* an angular velocity ω such as shown in Fig. 6.

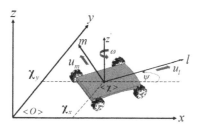

Fig. 6. Schematic representaction of the omnidirectional robot.

Each linear velocity is directed as one of the axes of the frame $<\chi>$ attached to the center of gravity of the omnidirectional robot: u_l points to the frontal direction and u_m points to the left-lateral direction. The angular velocity ω rotates the referential system $<\chi>$ counterclockwise, around the axis Z' (considering the top view).

$$\begin{bmatrix} \dot{\chi}_x \\ \dot{\chi}_y \\ \dot{\psi} \end{bmatrix} = \begin{bmatrix} \cos(\psi) & -\sin(\psi) & 0 \\ \sin(\psi) & \cos(\psi) & 0 \\ 0 & 0 & 1 \end{bmatrix} \begin{bmatrix} u_l \\ u_m \\ \omega \end{bmatrix} \tag{2}$$

where $\dot{\chi}_x$, $\dot{\chi}_y$ and $\dot{\chi}_\psi$ are all measured based on inertial frame $<O>$. Also the equation system (2) can be written in compact form as,

$$\dot{\chi}(t) = \mathbf{J}(\psi)\boldsymbol{\mu}(t) \tag{3}$$

where, $\mathbf{J}(\psi) \in \Re^{m \times n}$ with $m = n = 3$ represents the Jacobian matrix that defines a linear mapping between the velocity vector of the omnidirectional robot $\boldsymbol{\mu} \in \Re^n$ where $\boldsymbol{\mu} = [u_l \, u_m \, \omega]^T$ and the velocity vector of the operative end $\dot{\chi} \in \Re^m$ where $\dot{\chi} = [\dot{\chi}_x \, \dot{\chi}_y \, \dot{\chi}_\psi]^T$.

To determine the angular velocities correspondents to each wheel Fig. 7 of the omnidirectional robot is used the next system:

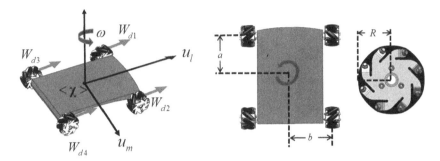

Fig. 7. Configuration of the omnidirectional robot.

$$\begin{bmatrix} W_{d1} \\ W_{d2} \\ W_{d3} \\ W_{d4} \end{bmatrix} = \frac{1}{R} \begin{bmatrix} 1 & -1 & -(a+b) \\ 1 & 1 & (a+b) \\ 1 & 1 & -(a+b) \\ 1 & -1 & (a+b) \end{bmatrix} \begin{bmatrix} u_l \\ u_m \\ \omega \end{bmatrix}$$

this equation system can be defined as:

$$\mathbf{W}_d(t) = \mathbf{J_T}(a, b)\boldsymbol{\mu}(t) \tag{4}$$

where $\mathbf{W}_d$ is the vector of angular velocities of the wheels of the omnidirectional robot and $\mathbf{J_T} \in \mathbb{R}^{4 \times 3}$ is a transformation matrix, which was obtained from the inverse kinematics of robot velocities and $\boldsymbol{\mu}$ represents the mobility velocities of the omnidirectional robot.

4.1 Controller Design

The purpose of the controller design is to solve the problems described in this article (*i*) stabilization of a point, (*ii*) trajectory tracking, and (*iii*) path following, with only simply specifying the control references as were indicated in the formulation of the problem.

The proposed unified controller aim is to calculate the position error at any time point and use these values to move the omnidirectional robot in a direction that decreases control errors. This unified controller is based on the kinematic model of the omnidirectional robot type Mecanum in AB configuration which is proposed as:

$$\mu(t) = \mathbf{J}^{\#}\left(\upsilon_{ref} + \mathbf{L_K}\tanh\left(\mathbf{L_K^{-1}K}\,\tilde{\chi}\right)\right) \tag{5}$$

where υ_{ref} represents the reference velocity of input of the omnidirectional robot for the controller, $\mathbf{J}^{\#}$ come to be the matrix of inverse Kinematic of the robot, while that the matrix $\mathbf{L_K}$ contain the gains that compensate the control errors based on reference system $<O>$ and the $\tanh(.)$ represents to the saturation function of the velocities of the omnidirectional robot.

The analysis of control error $\tilde{\chi}(t)$ in the interest point is done assuming a perfect following of the velocity therefore replacing (5) in (4) is obtained the equation of closed control loop,

$$\left(\upsilon_{ref} - \dot{\chi}\right) + \mathbf{L}\tanh\left(\mathbf{L_K^{-1}K}\,\tilde{\chi}\right) = \mathbf{0} \tag{6}$$

Taking something into account that the desired velocity υ_{ref} is different to the temporal derivate of the location of the omnidirectional robot $\dot{\chi}_d$ *i.e.* it defines a signal difference $\Upsilon = \dot{\chi}_d - \upsilon_{ref}$ and remembers that $\dot{\tilde{\chi}} = \dot{\chi}_d - \dot{\chi}$ the Eq. (6) can be written the next way

$$\dot{\tilde{\chi}} + \mathbf{L_K}\tanh\left(\mathbf{L_K^{-1}K}\,\tilde{\chi}\right) = \Upsilon \tag{7}$$

Remark: the kinematic characteristics of the Mecanum wheels of a robot Omnidirectional let to control in an independent way the robot orientation by means of the maneuverability velocity, *i.e.* that $\tilde{\chi}_\varphi(t) \to 0$ asymptotically independent of the errors in $\tilde{\chi}_x$ y $\tilde{\chi}_y$.

To apply this control law, the following specifications must be taken into account:
Case 1: Positioning $\upsilon_{ref} = \dot{\chi}_d \equiv 0 \therefore \Upsilon = 0$
Case 2: Trajectory tracking: $\upsilon_{ref} = \dot{\chi}_d \therefore \Upsilon = 0$ and the error $\tilde{\chi}(t) \to 0$ asymptotically.
Case 3: Path following: $\upsilon_{ref} = \dot{\chi}_d - \Upsilon$ and one time that the control error $\tilde{\chi}$ east in a suitable range is evaluated $\mathbf{L_K}\tanh\left(\mathbf{L_K^{-1}K}\,\tilde{\chi}\right)$ with small values.

5 Results and Discussions

The controllers proposed were implemented in omnidirectional robot with four Mecanum wheels with AB configuration as is shown in the Fig. 8, which receives as input the two lineal velocities and an angular velocity. Some of the most representative results are presented in this Section. Three experiments are executed in order to evaluate the performance of the proposed scheme.

The first experiment addressed in this Section corresponds to the point stabilization control. In this experiment, the mobile platform starts at $\chi = \begin{bmatrix} 0\ \mathrm{m} & 0\ \mathrm{m} & \frac{\pi}{3}\ \mathrm{rad} \end{bmatrix}^T$ and

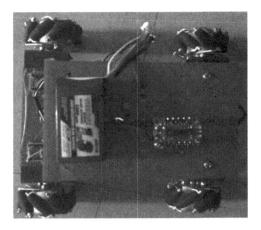

Fig. 8. Structure of the omnidirectional robot.

the desired final position of the robot is $\chi_\delta = [\,2\ \mathrm{m}\quad 2.5\ \mathrm{m}\quad \frac{\pi}{4}\ \mathrm{rad}\,]^{\mathrm{T}}$. Figures 9, 10 and 11 show the results of the first experiment. Figure 9 represents the stroboscopic movement of the omnidirectional robot. Figure 10 shows that the control errors $\tilde{\chi}(t)$ converge to values close to zero asymptotically and Fig. 11 represent the control actions of the robot.

The performance of the control structure for trajectory tracking is tested in the second experiment. The desired trajectory for the end-effector is described by

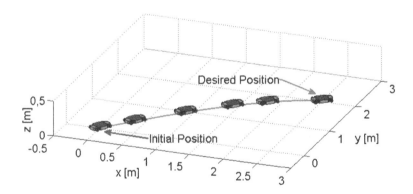

Fig. 9. Stroboscopic movement of the omnidirectional robot in the positioning problem.

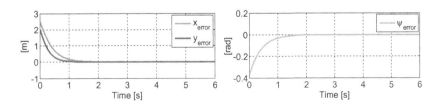

Fig. 10. Control errors: $\tilde{\chi}_x$, $\tilde{\chi}_y$ and $\tilde{\chi}_\varphi$.

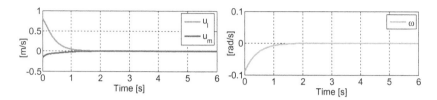

Fig. 11. Velocity commands to the mobile platform.

$\chi_{d} = \begin{bmatrix} \chi_{xd} & \chi_{yd} & \chi_{\psi d} \end{bmatrix}^{T}$,   where, $\chi_{xd} = 2 + \frac{1}{2}\cos\left(\frac{3}{25}t\right) + \frac{1}{2}t$, $\chi_{yd} = \frac{1}{5} + \frac{7}{100}t$ and $\chi_{\psi d} = \tan^{-1}\left(\frac{\chi_{yd}}{\chi_{xd}}\right)$. It is important to mention that this trajectory was chosen in order to excite the dynamics of the mobile platform by changing its acceleration. Recall that for trajectory tracking, it is chosen $\upsilon_{ref}(t) \equiv \dot{\chi}_{d}(t)$. Figures 12, 13 and 14, represent the experimental results. Figure 12, shows the desired trajectory and the current trajectory of the robot. It can be seen that the proposed controller presents a good performance. Figure 13, shows the evolution of the tracking errors $\tilde{\chi}(t)$, which remains close to zero and Fig. 14 represents the control actions of the robot.

Now, the next experiment corresponds to the path following control. Note that for the path following problem, the desired velocity of omnidirectional robot will depend

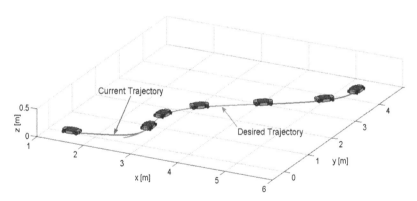

Fig. 12. Stroboscopic movement of the omnidirectional robot in the trajectory tracking experiment.

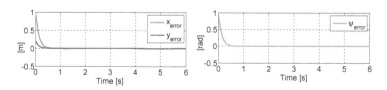

Fig. 13. Control errors: $\tilde{\chi}_{x}$, $\tilde{\chi}_{y}$ and $\tilde{\chi}_{\varphi}$.

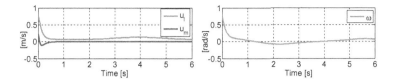

Fig. 14. Velocity commands to the mobile platform.

on the task, the control error, the velocity of the mobile robot, etc. In this experiment, it is considered that the reference velocity module depends on the control errors. Then, reference velocity in this experiment is expressed as $|v_{ref}| = v_{max}/(1 + k_1|\tilde{\chi}|)$ where k_1 is a positive constant that weigh the control error module. Also, the desired location is defined as the closest point on the path to the robot of the experimental system. Figure 15 shows the stroboscopic movement on the X-Y-Z space. It can be seen that the proposed controller works correctly. Figure 16 shows that $|\tilde{\chi}|$ is ultimately bounded close to zero and Fig. 17 represent the control actions of the robot.

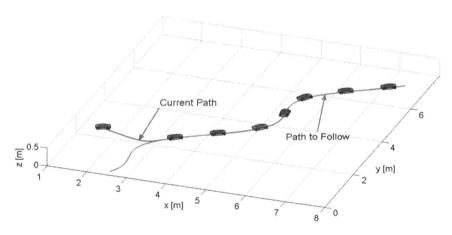

Fig. 15. Stroboscopic movement of the omnidirectional robot in the path following problem.

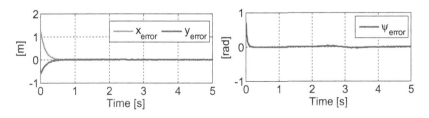

Fig. 16. Control errors: $\tilde{\chi}_x$, $\tilde{\chi}_y$ and $\tilde{\chi}_\varphi$.

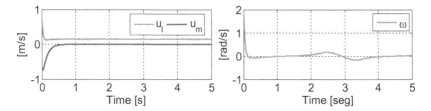

Fig. 17. Velocity commands to the mobile platform

6 Conclusions

The unified controller achieve to calculate the position error at any time point and use these values obtained to move the omnidirectional robot following the direction, where decreases control errors and resolving so the problems the positioning, trajectory|-tracking and path following. This control accomplish with the condition in each problems in the simulation and also in the omnidirectional robot with mecanum wheels in AB configuration implemented obtaining, so a controller unified is easy to implement and available in the literature.

References

1. Andaluz, V., Carelli, R., Salinas, L., Toibero, J., Roberti, F.: Visual control with adaptive dynamical compensation for 3D target tracking by mobile manipulators. Mechatronics, **22** (4), 491–502 (2012)
2. Carrillo, A., Pelayo, S., Pelayo, J.: Development of a mobile service robot for classify objects and place them in containers. In: Power, Electronics and Computing (ROPEC) (2016)
3. Wang, D., Yi, J., Zhao, D.: Teleoperation system of the internet-based omnidirectional mobile robot with a mounted manipulator. In: International Conference on Mechatronics and Automation, pp. 1799–1804, Harbin, China (2007)
4. Pepe, A., Chiaravalli, D., Melchiorri, C.: A hybrid teleoperation control scheme for a single-arm mobile manipulator with omnidirectional wheels. In: IEEE/RSJ International Conference on Intelligent Robots and Systems (IROS) (2016)
5. Costa, P., Moreira, N., Campos, D.: Localization and navigation of an omnidirectional mobile robot: the Robot@Factory case study. In: IEEE Revista Iberoamericana de Tecnologias del Aprendizaje (2016)
6. Jia, Q., Wang, M., Liu, S.: Research and development of Mecanum-wheeled omnidirectional mobile robot implemented by multiple control methods. In: 23rd International Conference on Mechatronics and Machine Vision in Practice (M2VIP) (2016)
7. Kang, W., Kim, S., Chung, J.: Development of omni-directional mobile robots with Mecanum wheels assisting the disabled in a factory environment. In: International Conference on Control, Automation and Systems (2008)
8. Diegel, O., Badve, A., Bright, G.: Improved Mecanum wheel design for omni-directional robots. In: Australasian Conference on Robotics and Automation (2002)

9. Yunan, Z., Shuangshuang, W., Jian, Z.: Research on motion characteristic of omnidirectional robot based on Mecanum wheel. In: Digital Manufacturing and Automation (ICDMA) (2010)
10. Chao, R., Shugen, M.: Trajectory tracking control of an omnidirectional mobile robot with friction compensation. In: Intelligent Robots and Systems (IROS) (2016)
11. Veer, A., Shital, S.: Design of robust adaptive controller for a four wheel omnidirectional mobile robot. In: Advances in Computing, Communications and Informatics (ICACCI) (2015)
12. Jian, W., Sergey, A., Aleksandr, J.: Geometric path following control for an omnidirectional mobile robot. In: 21st International Conference on Methods and Models in Automation and Robotics (MMAR) (2016)
13. Kanjanawanishkul, K., Zell, A.: Path following for an omnidirectional mobile robot based on model predictive control. In: IEEE International Conference on Robotics and Automation (2009)
14. Andaluz, V., Ortiz, J., Chicaiza, F., Varela, J., Espinosa, E., Canseco, P.: Adaptive control of the human-wheelchair system through brain signals. In: Kubota, N., Kiguchi, K., Liu, H., Obo, T. (eds.) Intelligent Robotics and Applications, pp. 223–234. Springer, Heidelberg (2016)

Mechanics of Continuum Manipulators, a Comparative Study of Five Methods with Experiments

S.M. Hadi Sadati[1]([⌧]), Seyedeh Elnaz Naghibi[2], Ali Shiva[1],
Ian D. Walker[3], Kaspar Althoefer[2], and Thrishantha Nanayakkara[1,4]

[1] Department of Informatics, Centre for Robotics Research (CoRe),
King's College London, London, UK
{seyedmohammadhadi.sadati,ali.shiva}@kcl.ac.uk
[2] School of Engineering and Materials Science, Queen Mary,
University of London, London, UK
{s.e.naghibi,k.althoefer}@qmul.ac.uk
[3] Department of Electrical and Computer Engineering, Clemson University,
Clemson, USA
iwalker@g.clemson.edu
[4] Dyson School of Design Engineering, Imperial College London, London, UK
t.nanayakkara@imperial.ac.uk

Abstract. Investigations on control and optimization of continuum manipulators have resulted in a number of kinematic and dynamic modeling approaches each having their own advantages and limitations in various applications. In this paper, a comparative study of five main methods in the literature for kinematic, static and dynamic modeling of continuum manipulators is presented in a unified mathematical framework. The five widely used methods of Lumped system dynamic model, Constant curvature, two-step modified constant curvature, variable curvature Cosserat rod and beam theory approach, and series solution identification are re-viewed here with derivation details in order to clarify their methodological differences. A comparison between computer simulations and experimental results using a STIFF-FLOP continuum manipulator is presented to study the advantages of each modeling method.

Keywords: Continuum manipulator · Dynamic · Lumped system · Constant curvature · Variable curvature · Cosserat · Beam theory · Series solution · Experiments

1 Introduction

Traditional limitations posed by conventional rigid linked robots, such as vast occupied space, rigidity, and relatively low dexterity, has resulted in an emerging trend during these recent years for scientists to show increasing interest in the concept of continuum robots. Taking inspiration from biological examples such as octopus tentacles, chameleon tongue and elephant trunk, researchers are looking into the possibility of replicating similar navigational and grasping characteristics by harnessing the

© Springer International Publishing AG 2017
Y. Gao et al. (Eds.): TAROS 2017, LNAI 10454, pp. 686–702, 2017.
DOI: 10.1007/978-3-319-64107-2_56

hyper-redundancy demonstrated in nature [1]. This class of robots promises considerable performance improvements in different areas which currently witness the presence of traditional robots, such as surgical applications, underwater manipulation, rehabilitation, repair, etc. [2–4]. As a natural by-product of this trend, kinematic and dynamic modeling and analysis of these types of robots have gained similar attention within the research community. However, the inherent nature of continuum robots being highly deformable has put forward new challenges in this regard.

The most popular kinematic model for a bent continuum manipulator is provided by the Constant Curvature (CC) model. The CC model simplifies the kinematics of a continuum manipulator by assuming that the backbone kinematics in a planar deformed state can be expressed by a CC profile. In [3], Webster and Jones deliver a thorough discussion on this subject and reviewed several methods for kinematic modelling of continuum robots using two separate sub-mappings: a robot-specific map relating the mechanics of the loads with the system material strains, and a general map to relate these strains to the spatial kinematic configuration of the manipulator. The general robot-independent mapping might suffer from singularity, as discussed in [5], where a new shape function approach suggested by Godage can handle this limitation. Although being commonly used as a simplifying assumption, the CC assumptions are usually not accurate in the presence of external forces. The recent dynamic models to address this limitation can be categorized into four groups: (1) Lumped model elements using Lagrangian demonstration, which approximates the continuum manipulator with a number of rigid-link pieces combined with springs and dampers in-between [6]. The total kinetic energy of the system as the degrees of freedom goes to infinity is similar to that of a continuum manipulator. (2) The Euler-Bernoulli beam model [7, 8] and/or the Principle of Virtual Work (PVW) [9, 10] using CC kinematic. (3) Variable Curvature (VC) kinematics [11] with Cosserat rod model (or equivalent beam theory method), as explained in [12, 13] which leads to an optimization boundary value problem (BVP). Tunay presented an approximate solution for the weak-form integral equations resulting from this BVP in a finite element discretized form [14]. (4) Approximate solutions based on the identification of the system with a polynomial [15], or shape function based series solutions [5] which construct a setup-specific model. These identified models are similar to single direct shooting methods in solving BVPs in mechanics of material community. The approximate solutions, appropriate for control purposes, are more precise and faster in terms of computation but do not ac-count for the structural characteristics, while the lumped model elements and Cost-rat rod model suffer from heavy calculations despite being suitable for design and optimization. In most of these methods, numerical inaccuracy and singularities in deriving the inverse kinematics are inevitable. We have recently introduced a new analytical method to model compound continuum manipulators in presence of external forces utilizing the principle of virtual work and experimental observation of the deformed system in which the CC is an initial but not essential assumption for the kinematic map. This can be categorized as an approximate solution which incorporates the compound structural characteristics of a continuum manipulator and provides a deformation map for the manipulator cross section.

In this paper, a comparative study between five modeling approaches for kinematic, static and dynamic of a continuum manipulator is presented and their accuracy, advantages and limitations are discussed in comparison to experimental results using a STIFF-FLOP continuum actuator module [2, 16] (Fig. 1.I and II). In the process; simple mathematic derivation of the manipulator deformation energy for the body and braided actuator chambers and mechanical maps based on Neo-Hookean assumptions are discussed; a comparison between different models for a braided extensile pneumatic actuator is presented and a novel tow-step modified solution is presented based on CC kinematics and Castigliano's method for beam deflections to enable using of CC assumption in the presence of high body and external loading.

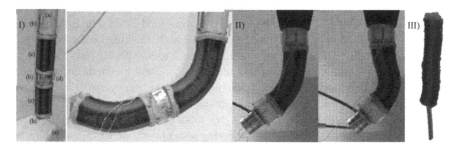

Fig. 1. Experiment with body loads: (a) base, (b) magnetic trackers, (c) STIFF-FLOP module, (d) force sensor, (e) Aurora tracker (I), experiments with extensive external force (II), a pneumatic braided extensile chamber (III).

In Sect. 2 a review of derivation and implementation of the five modelling methods for continuum manipulators (Lumped system dynamic model, CC, two-step modified CC, VC Cosserat rod and beam theory approach, and series solution identification) are presented. The models' applications are discussed based on our simulation result performance and accuracy in Sect. 3 followed by conclusion and discussion.

2   Modelling, Simulation and Experimental Framework

The spatial orientation of a continuum manipulator as the system control outputs can be derived based on CC or VC kinematics. This general map can be used as the system control model by relating the actuator chambers' length and manipulator tip position and orientation; however, a more precise model should consider the mechanical properties of the manipulator too [12]. Slenderness and softness of most continuum manipulators make external and body forces important in the modeling of their behavior. Body specific static and dynamic map models are used to relate these loads with the kinematic parameters of a continuum manipulator as are discussed in this section.

The simulation results are based on experimental setup dimensions (Table 1) and compared with the results from three set of experiments; (1) random pressurization of a STIFF-FLOP module in a two-module manipulator to study 3D deformation under extensive body weight (Fig. 1.I); (2) planar deformation of a module with extensive external load at the tip (Fig. 1.II); and (3) actuation of a pneumatic braided extensile

Table 1. Experiment parameters.

Par.	Value
r_{p1} [mm]	2.5
r_{p2} [mm]	3
r_o [mm]	8.5
γ_0 [deg]	89
r_1 [mm]	4.5
r_2 [mm]	12.5
l [mm]	44.0
E [KPa]	100
m_b [Kg]	0.0245
m_e [Kg]	0.011
g [m/s^2]	9.81
μ_t [Ns/m]	0.1
μ_r [Ns/m]	5e-4

Algorithm. 1. Sample "AutoTMTDyn" input code for lumped model of planar motion

```
body(i).type = 'rigid' ;   body type of disk i
body(i).m = mₑ/n ;   disk i mass, n: number of disks
body(i).l = lₑ/n ;   disk i length
body(i).l_com = [ 0 0 l/(2n) ] ;   disk i COM position
joint(i).first = i-1 ;   joint i 1ˢᵗ body
joint(i).second = i ;   joint i 2ⁿᵈ body
joint(i).tr(1).trans = [ 0 0 lₑ/n ] ;   joint i 1ˢᵗ translation
joint(i).tr(1).rot = [ 0 0 ] ;   joint i 1ˢᵗ rotation
joint(i).tr(2).trans = [ 0 0 inf ] ;   joint i 2ⁿᵈ translation, inf: for DOF
joint(i).tr(2).rot = [ 2 inf ] ;   joint i 2ⁿᵈ translation
joint(i).dof(1).init = 0 ;   1ˢᵗ DOF initial condition
joint(i).dof(2).init = 1e-5 ;   2ⁿᵈ DOF initial condition
joint(i).dof(1).spring = [ kₜ, 0 ] ;   1ˢᵗ DOF spring coeff. & initial value
joint(i).dof(1).damp = [ μₜ, 0 ] ;   1ˢᵗ DOF viscous & Coulomb damping
joint(i).dof(1).spring = [ kᵣ, 0 ] ;   2ⁿᵈ DOF spring coeff. & initial value
joint(i).dof(1).damp = [ μᵣ, 0 ] ;   2ⁿᵈ DOF viscous & Coulomb damping
exload(1).body = n ;   external load reference body
exload(1).tr(1).trans = [ 0 0 l/n ] ;   tip external load relative position
exload(1).tr(1).rot = [ 0 0 ] ;   tip external load relative orientation
```

chamber (Fig. 1.III). The error is defined as the difference in the length of the tip position vector in simulation and experiments and the error percentage is the ratio of the error to the experimental value of the tip position vector length.

Equivalent Lumped System Model

– *Kinematics:* A continuum manipulator can be assumed as a highly articulated rigid link system with an infinite number of disks connected through spring-damper supported spherical joints [6, 17] (Fig. 2.II). We used an axial transformation (ρ) followed by a 3-2-1 Euler angle set (η, ζ, ξ),

$$R_{ri} = R_z(\eta_i).R_y(\zeta_i).R_x(\xi_i) \rightarrow \Gamma_{ri} = \begin{bmatrix} R_{ri} & \rho_i \\ 0 & 1 \end{bmatrix}, R_j = \prod_{i=1}^{j} R_{ri}, \Gamma_j = \prod_{i=1}^{j} \Gamma_{ri,} \quad (1)$$

where R_a is the rotation matrix around a axis in the local frame, Γ is the transformation matrix, ρ is the axial transformation vector, subscript r denotes the relative rotation matrix between each two disks, i denotes the disk number and j denotes the segment number. We use C_x for cos(x) and S_x for sin(x). Centre of masses (COM) position vector ($\rho_i = \Gamma_i \rho_{ri}$), linear velocity ($\rho_i$) and angular velocity ($[\omega_{ci}]_\times = R_{i,t} \cdot R_i^T$) in Cartesian coordinates and w.r.t the spatial frame can be found afterward. $[\omega]_\times$ is the skew-symmetric matrix of the vector ω and subscript comma (_,) means derivative w.r.t. the following parameter. The axial linear transformation and Euler angle rotations of all joints can be assumed to be equal to model a uniformly deforming link [18] while assuming separate free DOFs results in a VC kinematic model. Joints' stiffness and

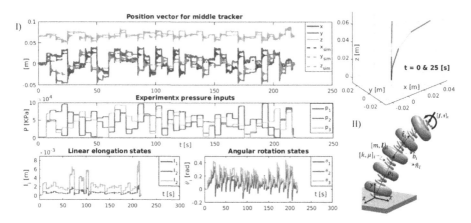

Fig. 2. Lumped system dynamic model results for a model with three rigid links and independent joints compared to the experimental results with body loads (I), Lumped system model diagram (II).

damping values can be identified from experimental results or can be derived using deformation energy of elastic material [6]. We left these two values to be constant. Cross-sectional deformation can be considered as a change in the inertia and diameter of the rigid links.

– *Dynamic Model:* Having the stiffness values and the gravitational potential energy function based on the initial shape of the manipulator, principle of virtual work (PVW) in static case and Lagrange method in the dynamic case can be used to model the system mechanics [6]. A high DOF BVP is formed in the static case and can be solved by a numerical optimization method. The dynamic equations are more efficient to be solved using a forward Runge-Kutta numerical integration method. A matrix form of equation of motion (EOM) using TMT method is presented to derive the dynamic model [19]. TMT method is a simple and clear method which eliminates the highest order derivatives in each step and results in a simplified matrix form of unconstrained Lagrange EOM, ideal for numerical simulation of complex large dynamic systems as

$$
T_{(q)} = [\,\rho_i \;\; \cdots\,]^{\mathrm{T}}_{[3n_i \times 1]}, \; \omega_{ci} = \bar{\omega}_{ci} q_{,t}, \quad M = \mathrm{diag}\big[m_1 m_1 m_1 I_{1[3\times3]} \;\cdots\big], \bar{T} = \left[\begin{bmatrix} T_{(q),q} \\ \bar{\omega}_c \\ \vdots \end{bmatrix}_i \right],
$$

$$
d = \big(\bar{T} q_{,t}\big)_{,q} q_{,t}, \overline{M} = \bar{T}^{\mathrm{T}} M \bar{T}, d_{\mathrm{EOM}} = \bar{T}^{\mathrm{T}}\Big[\sum f_{\mathrm{C}} - Md\Big] + f_q, \; \overline{M} q_{,tt} = d_{\mathrm{EOM},} \tag{2}
$$

where q is the generalized state vector, T is the transformation matrix for multi body links' COM position and rotation in terms of generalized coordinates, M is the system's mass and inertia matrix, m_i and I_i are the ith link mass and inertia matrices, f_{C} and f_q are the external conservative and non-conservative forces in Cartesian (i.e. gravitational forced) and joint space (i.e. joint inputs) respectively, n_i is the number of bodies and n_q

is the number of states. $\overline{\omega}_{ci}$ is a $3 \times n_q$ coefficient matrix derived by collecting $q_{,t}$ elements in ω_{ci}. The actuator forces are considered as concentrated force and torque acting uniformly on all DOFs. The translational and rotational stiffness are found from Euler-Bernoulli relation for each segment and by considering a symmetric deformation for the cross-section assuming an incompressible beam, where $\sum \lambda_i = 1$ and λ_i is the principle deformation rate vector in i direction [12] as explained later, $k_t = nEa/(\lambda_l^2 l)$ and $k_r = nEJ_d/(\lambda_l^3 l)$, where n is the number of segments, E is the modules of elasticity, a is the segment initial area, J_d is the initial second moment of area around the d axis and λ_l is the axial elongation of each link as $\lambda_l = 1 + n\varepsilon/l$.

We used "AutoTMTDyn", a software package in Matlab programming language that drives the TMT vector form of the Lagrange EOM using simple inputs about the kinematics of the system [19], to simulate a three-segment lumped model of a STIFF-FLOP manipulator module (Fig. 2.II). A sample input code for planar motion is presented in Algorithm 1. The model can capture transient behavior of the manipulator with high accuracy and good performance [6]. Despite the static models, the role of proper identification or modeling of the damping coefficient is important to capture an accurate dynamic model for the system. The model may become unstable and hard to simulate for higher number of links without the uniform deformation assumption, however shows to be accurate even for a small number of DOFs. The forward dynamics of the system is easier to solve and this method is suitable for dynamic control design purposes using traditional control theories for rigid body systems. Although some structural characteristics of the system is considered in the modeling procedure, this method cannot provide insight in the material property for structural design and optimization purposes. Simulation results are presented in Fig. 2.I showing 22% mean error compared to the dynamic experimental results with body loads.

Constant Curvature Kinematics and Mechanics

Kinematic Model: As the most common used model for the kinematic representation, the manipulator is considered as a continuous CC curve as in Fig. 3.I [3]. Here, a geometric map (f_G) and a structural specific map (f_S) describe the system mechanics. f_G maps the curvature parameters (l_m: central axis length, κ: curvature, ϕ: polar orientation angle) to curve tip position (ρ_{tip}) which can be found from CC assumptions using a set of transformations given by $R_y(\phi)$-$R_z(\kappa l)$-ρ_{xy}-$R_y(-\phi)$ [3], where $\rho_{xy} = [(1 - C_{\kappa l})/\kappa \quad S_{\kappa l}/\kappa 0]^T$ and,

$$f_G(l, \kappa, \phi) = \begin{bmatrix} R_y(\phi) & 0 \\ 0 & 1 \end{bmatrix} \begin{bmatrix} R_z(\theta) & \rho_{xy} \\ 0 & 1 \end{bmatrix} \begin{bmatrix} R_y(-\phi) & 0 \\ 0 & 1 \end{bmatrix} \begin{bmatrix} 0 \\ 1 \end{bmatrix}, 0 = [0 \quad 0 \quad 0]^T, \quad (3)$$

This map suffers from inherent singularity for $\kappa = 0$. An effective method to overcome this singularity is using the actuator lengths as the system states in the differential inversion method to find the system model [3, 5].

f_S maps the input parameters space (actuator lengths (l_C) for hydraulic and tendon driven models) to curvature parameters space. For a module with three actuators we have [3],

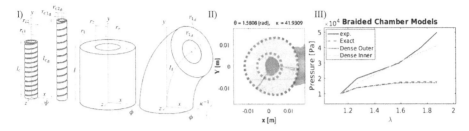

Fig. 3. CC and axial deformation parameters (I), deformed cross section predicted by the general geometry deformation method (II), braided pneumatic chamber models (For E = 45 [Kpa]) compared to experimental results (III).

$$
f_S = \begin{cases}
\phi = tan^{-1}\left(\sqrt{3}/3(l_{C2}+l_{C3}-2l_{C1})/(l_{C2}-l_{C3})\right) - \pi/2 \\
\kappa = 2\sqrt{\left(l_{C1}^2+l_{C2}^2+l_{C3}^2 - l_{C1}l_{C2} - l_{C1}l_{C3} - l_{C2}l_{C3}\right)/(d_C(l_{C1}+l_{C2}+l_{C3}))}, \\
l_m = l_{C1}+l_{C2}+l_{C3}
\end{cases}
$$

(4)

– *Euler-Bernoulli Beam Model:* For pneumatic actuators, a second step is needed to map the pressure inputs to actuator length. In the case of the well-known "OCT-Arm" series of continuum robots [20] where the modules are created from actuators without a supporting shell, a map between the actuator pressure and elongation is needed. A simple model can be derived by assuming the manipulator deformation as superposing of the elongation and bending of an Euler-Bernoulli beam in the ϕ direction (Eq. 5) due to the static balance between the axial force (f_{EB}) and bending moment (τ_{EB}) of the actuator at the tip, external loads and the body loads. The axial elongation is $\lambda_l = 1 + f_{EB}l/(Ea)$ or more precisely, by considering the cross section symmetric deformation of an incompressible material ($\sum \lambda_i = 1$) as explained later and solving $\lambda_l = 1 + f_{EB}\lambda_l^2 l/(Ea)$ for λ_l and the curvature is $\kappa = \tau_{EB}/EJ_\phi$ or more precisely, $\kappa = \tau_{EB}\lambda_l^2/EJ_\phi$ by considering the cross section deformation after elongation. The simulation results assuming fixed cross-section for pneumatic chambers in comparison to experiments with body loads (Fig. 1.I) is presented in Fig. 4.I and II.

– *Geometry Deformation Model for Compound Structure:* A more accurate model can be derived by considering the compound structure consisting of the body shell and braided actuators. A supporting body shell is usually used to prevent the actuator chambers from bulking, i.e. STIFF-FLOP [2, 16], f_S need to be derived by considering the body deformation energy (w_S). A simple solution for w_S can be found by only considering the body axial deformation and neglecting the bending and twisting as in the simple model for braided actuators. A more accurate but complex solution can be derived by extending our previous work [10] where the geometry deformation method is used as follows for the bending and elongation case,

$$I_1 = (\lambda(2 + \lambda^3) - 2\kappa x \sqrt{\lambda}(1 - \lambda^3))/(1 - 2\kappa x \sqrt{\lambda}), w_S = E/6 \oint I_1 dx. \quad (5)$$

This method predicts the cross-sectional deformation as in Fig. 3.II. Then the principle of virtual energy becomes $w_{C,q} + w_{G,q} + w_{S,q} + w_{B,q} = 0$, where $q = [\ l_m,\ \kappa,\ \varphi]$ is the curvature parameters vector and w_B is for external load and body forces. This can be solved for $p = f_S^{-1}(q)$. Simulation results in comparison to experiments for a STIFF-FLOP manipulator section are presented in Fig. 4.I and II. The model has an average of 28% error mainly because of CC assumption errors; however, it increases the model accuracy by 3% compared to a simple Euler-Bernoulli beam method.

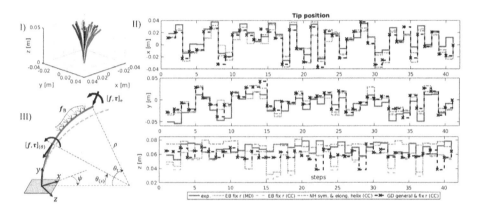

Fig. 4. Simulation results for CC and two-step modified CC (MD) models compared to the experiments with body loads for a STIFF-FLOP module (I,II), two-step modified CC (MD) model diagram (III).

– *Braided Pneumatic Actuator Exact Mechanics:* For pneumatic braided extensible actuators two analytical solutions are presented based on principle of virtual work ($\sum w_{i,q} = 0$), incompressibility assumption ($\sum \lambda_i = 1$) and Neo-Hookean deformation energy relation ($u_d = E/6 \left(\sum_{i=1}^{3} \lambda_i - 3 \right)$) [9, 12], where w is the virtual work or energy and q is the vector of system states. The principle of virtual energy for a chamber is $w_{C,\lambda} + w_{G,\lambda} = 0$, where w_C is the chamber body deformation energy, w_G is the air pressure work, $\lambda = l/l0$ (considered as the only system state) is the axial deformation rate, l_i and l_d are the module axis initial and deformed length. This can be solved for $p = f_S^{-1}(q)$. The most famous model to incorporate the braiding effect, used by Trivedi for the first time for continuum manipulators, assumes the outer surface of a constant volume cylindrical chamber is constrained to the helical braids deformation as $\lambda_3^2 S_{\gamma_i}^2 + \lambda^2 C_{\gamma_i}^2 = 1$, where λ_3 is the radial deformation rate [12, 21]. His presentation of this formula in his paper, [12], has some errors which are corrected here,

$$p = E(r_{c2}^2 - r_{c1}^2)(\lambda_{lc}^2 - 1)/6\lambda_{lc}^4 r_{c1}^2(1 - \lambda_{lc}^2 C_\gamma^2)^3 \times (\lambda_{lc}^6(-2S_\gamma^6 + 5S_\gamma^4 - 4S_\gamma^2 + 1)$$
$$+ \lambda_{lc}^4(7S_\gamma^6 - 16S_\gamma^4 + 11S_\gamma^2 - 2) + \lambda_{lc}^2(7S_\gamma^6 - 4S_\gamma^4 - 3S_\gamma^2 + 1) + 3S_\gamma^4) \tag{6}$$

Where γ is the initial thread helix angle, r_{20} and r_{10} are the chamber outer and inner initial radius, E is the module of elasticity and subscript 0 denotes values measured in the initial unreformed state while all other terms represent the current deformed states.

- *Braided Pneumatic Actuator Simplified Mechanics:* For a dense threaded chamber, as in most actuators of this type, where $\gamma \approx \pi/2$ and the chamber deformation does not change γ significantly, the thread helix radius change becomes negligible ($\lambda_3 \approx 1, r_c \approx r_{c0}$) and the relation simplifies to $p = E(r_{c2}^2 - r_{c1}^2)(\lambda_{lc}^2 - 1)(\lambda_{lc}^2 + 3)/6\lambda_{lc}^4 r_{c1}^2$. We have recently used a new so-called geometry deformation method inspired by Rivlin's work on the "Problem of Flexure" [22] with the same assumption as Trivedi [12] resulting in a new more complex way to reach the same results [9]. In both derivations, the braiding is on the outer surface of the chamber. If the manipulator has no shell as in OctArm [12], this gives the map f_S between the pressure and chamber length.

A third simpler model is possible to drive by assuming a dense thread ($\gamma \approx \pi/2 \rightarrow r_c \approx r_{c0}$) constraint on the inner body of the chamber. For the gas work, we have, $w_G = p a_{p0} l_{C0}(\lambda - 1)$, where a_{p0} is the initial internal area of the chamber. The outer radius of the chamber shrinks as the actuator extends. A homogeneous incompressible cylinder undergoing axial elongation with axial deformation ration λ, experiences radial and circumferential deformation with deformation rate $1/\sqrt{\lambda}$ to satisfy incompressibility criteria [23]. The Neo-Hookean model suggests that the deformation energy of body becomes $w_S = E a_{t0} l_0 (\lambda^2 + 2/\lambda - 3)/6$ as in [23], where a_{t0} is the initial chamber thickness area. From the principle of virtual work, the pressure can be found as, $p = E a_{t0}(\lambda - 1/\lambda^2)/(3a_{p0})$. A comparison between the results of these methods for one actuator from STIFF-FLOP manipulator is presented in Fig. 3. III. The figure shows the good accuracy of the inner dense thread model in predicting the values and overall behavior. Trivedi's exact and dense thread models have almost the same result with high error despite the results reported in [12]. We believe that this is due to the very small size and thickness of STIFF-FLOP actuators compared to OCTArm ones. The inner dense thread method is used to model the STIFF-FLOP manipulator using CC approach in the next sections.

- *Simple Compound Model:* Neglecting the bending in the body shell and the actuator chamber deformation energy (w_C), we can assume the braids are on the inner surface of the chambers. Then we simply have $w_G = \sum p\pi r_{10}^2(l_{Ci} - l_{Ci0})$ and $w_{G,q} + w_{S,q} + w_{B,q} = 0$ as the system static model where l_{Ci} is the ith chamber axial length as in [3],

$$l_{C1} = l_m(1 - \kappa d_C C_{(-\phi)}/2), l_{C2|3} = l_m(1 - \kappa d_C C_{(-\phi \pm 2\pi/3)}/2). \tag{7}$$

A careful choice of the combination of models for the actuator and body shell is important to achieve the best accuracy as well as comprehensiveness. The simulation results for the forward model compared to the experimental results with body loads (Fig. 1.I) show 28% error for the general deformation method (GD) and fix cross section actuator (fix r), 31% for the Euler-Bernoulli model (EB) with fix cross section and 28% for the Neo-Hookean symmetric elongation (NH sym.) model and extensile braided actuator (elong. helix) model, showing 3% increase in the accuracy of compound models as well as their comprehensive modeling ability (Fig. 4.I and II).

Two-Step Modified Constant Curvature Model

To compensate high modeling error related to CC assumption, Mahvash et al. used a two-step approximate model where the CC map is being used for non-contact map of an eccentric tube catheter and a modifying map based on beam theory is used to model the deflections from the CC geometry due external and body loadings [24]. Here we investigate a similar solution for continuum manipulators. Any change in the input pressures or actuator lengths results in a CC geometry. Then the resulted curved beam undergoes small deformations due to body and external loads assuming a linear stress-strain relation (Euler-Bernoulli beam model) (Fig. 4.III). Castigliano's method for a linear-elastic structures is used [25] to find an analytical solution for the modifying deformation at the tip and the middle of the manipulator,

$$
\begin{aligned}
f_{y(\theta)} &= (\rho f_{B_Y}(\theta_t - \theta) + f_{e_Y})C_{(\theta)} + (\rho f_{B_X}(\theta_t - \theta) + f_{e_X})S_{(\theta)}, \\
\tau_{x(\theta)} &= -\rho^2 f_{B_Z}(C_{(\theta_t - \theta)} - 1) + \rho f_{e_Z}S_{(\theta)}(\theta_t - \theta) - \tau_{e_Y}S_{(\theta)} + \tau_{e_X}C_{(\theta)}, \\
\tau_{y(\theta)} &= \rho^2 f_{B_Z}(\theta - \theta_t + S_{(\theta_t - \theta)}) - \rho f_{e_Z}(1 - C_{(\theta_t - \theta)}) + \tau_{e_Y}C_{(\theta)} + \tau_{e_X}S_{(\theta)}, \\
\tau_{z(\theta)} &= \rho^2 c f_{B_Y}(C_{(\theta_t)} - C_{(\theta)}) + \tau_{e_Z} + \rho f_{e_X}(S_{(\theta)} - S_{(\theta_t)}) + \rho^2 c((mg - f_{B_Y}l_d)(S_{(\theta_t)} - S_{(\theta)}) \quad (8) \\
&\quad + (\theta - \theta_t)C_{(\theta)}))/l_d + \rho^2 f_{B_X}(C_{(\theta_t)} - C_{(\theta)} - (\theta - \theta_t)S_{(\theta)}), \\
w_E &= \int_0^{\theta_t}(\tau_x^2/(2EI_{xx}) + \tau_z^2/(2EI_{zz}) + \tau_y^2/(2GJ_{yy}) + f_y^2/(2EA))d\theta
\end{aligned}
$$

where the shear strains are neglected, $\rho = 1/\kappa$, $\theta_t = l_d/\kappa$, $f_{B_{X/Y/Z}}$ is the external uniform load, $f_{e_{X/Y/Z}}$ and $\tau_{e_{X/Y/Z}}$ are the external load and torque vector at the tip, $I_{xx} = I_{zz} = \pi r_{s0}^4/(4\lambda^2)$ and $J_{yy} = \pi r_{s0}^4/(2\lambda^2)$ are the cross section first and second moment of inertias neglecting, G is the shear module, subscript x,y,z is the local curvilinear frame attached to COM and tangent to backbone curve and subscript X,Y,Z are for the main inertial frame. A correction factor ($c = 0.01$) is used for the forces in y direction in calculating $\tau_{z(\theta)}$ to adjust for the change in the moment arm in the static equilibrium compared to the initial CC configuration which should be identified for each loading condition from experiments. While this is a limiting factor, without this correction factor the formula results in a large error if the loading condition in the CC initial state is considerably different with the final equilibrium state. The final tip deflection from the constant curve geometry we have, $\epsilon_X = w_{E,f_{e_X}}, \epsilon_Y = w_{E,f_{e_Y}}, \epsilon_Z = w_{E,f_{e_Z}}$ which can be derived analytically, not presented here due to the limitation of space. The actuator forces are not mentioned as they have been considered to find the initial CC geometry. The modified model improves the accuracy by %1 for all the CC models to preserves the accuracy of CC model in the presence of small external and body forces (Fig. 4.II); however, it is not enough for precise control design. CC based models suffer from inaccuracy in presence of external and body forces and singularity at the straight orientations. However, they provide a simple solution to the continuous behavior of the manipulators being used for real-time or simple path planning and control applications [3]. Use of principle of virtual work or the introduced two-step modified model enables this method to preserve its accuracy in the presence of small body and external loads and to account for the structural characteristics of the manipulator which helps with the design optimization problems [8]. Lagrange dynamic method can be used for dynamic modeling of a continuum manipulator with CC assumption which mostly suffers from singularities and low accuracy.

Variable Curvature Kinematics and Mechanics
The VC model assumes the backbone consists of a series of infinitesimal CC curves [11, 12, 25, 26] to improve the accuracy of the modeling as the most important factor to increase the model accuracy.

- *Variable Curvature Kinematics*: VC kinematics presents the relation between the local curvilinear frames with unit vectors d_i along the manipulator backbone curve tangential ($\hat{t}$), normal ($\hat{n}$) and binormal ($\hat{b}$) axes (Fig. 5.III) and the curve spatial configuration usually expressed in inertial Cartesian coordinates. A set of rotation matrices (R_s) gives the relation between the local transnational strains ($\rho_{(s),s}$) and the deformation rates of the manipulator spatial geometry ($\rho_{(s),s}$) as $\rho_{(s),s} = R_{(s)} \cdot \left(v + [0,1,0]^T \right)$, where v is the linear strain rate vector in the local curvilinear frame which the rotation matrix R_s rotates to be expressed in the inertial reference frame. This rotation representation is equal to the variation of the position vector from a local frame to the next one ($\rho_{(s),s}$) along the backbone unit length (s). The variation of $R(s)$ along the curve length is found from the local rotational strain rates (u) as $R_{(s),s} = [u]_\times R_{(s)}$. Cosserat rod or beam theory methods are used to find v and u based on the system loads. Euler-Bernoulli equations for a rod is a special case of these methods with infinite shear modulus (G). Integrating to find ρ_s and $R(s)$ results in the system VC kinematics [12].

- *Cosserat Rod Method:* Cosserat rod model derive the equilibrium between the forces on each infinitesimal element of a continuum media using free body diagram of each element [26, 27] (Fig. 5.III) as $n_{,s} + f_{(s)} = ba_b \rho_{(s),tt}$ and $m_{,s} + \rho_{(s),s} \times n + \tau_{(s)} = J\omega_{(s),t}$, where the time dependent terms on the right side are dropped for static solutions. Hooke's law is been used to relate the variation of the boundary forces to the strain rates as $n_{(s)} = K_l v_{(s)}$ and $m_{(s)} = K_b u_{(s)}$, where $K_l = \text{diag}(Ga_b, Ea_b, Ga_b)$ and $K_b = \text{diag}(EJ_1, GJ_2, EJ_3)$ are the stiffness diagonal matrices. A simple version of this relation in the planar case is presented in [12]. Rearranging the derivations to find $v_{,s}$ and $u_{,s}$ based on the loads, results in the static mechanic map.

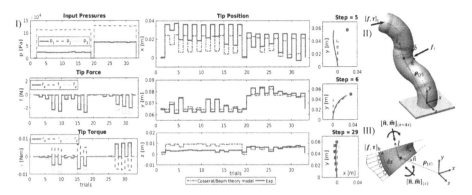

Fig. 5. Cosserat/beam theory model results vs. experiments with extensive external loads (I), Variable curvature kinematics (II), free body diagram for one element (III).

- *BVP Solution*: The static and kinematic map form a BVP for the strain and position vector rates [26] that needs to be integrated over the volume and time. One can use finite element approaches [28]. Alternatively, for a forward integration method, the system four states (u,v,ρ,R) should be known at the start point. An optimization based method is needed to guess and update the base point strain rates where the initial position ad orientation are known. The problem of finding proper initial guesses is simplified by finding the base strain rates based on beam theory.
- *Beam Theory Approach:* Beam theory method can be used instead of the Cosserat rod method to find the static map where a combination of a holistic and an element-wise view of the system is considered. Both methods result in the same set of equations and identical in the simulation results. The loads at each cross section are derived from writing a static equilibrium between the element internal stress vector and all the forces and moments acting on the cross-section that is located between the element section and the beam free end. This is different from Cosserat model where the equilibrium is considered between the element boundary forces. Here we need to know the geometry of the manipulator at the equilibrium state and finding the acting loads on the cross sections usually needs an integration over the manipulator length between the element position and the free end. These limit the application of this method especially for finite element implementation, however, it simplifies the BVP by eliminating the strain rates (we work with the strains in this method) and provides the opportunity to solve the forward integration method using approximate series solutions (concatenation, direct single and multiple shooting). The beam theory method results in the following static map for a continuum manipulator in the static case

$$v = K_l^{-1}.\left(R^{\mathrm{T}}.(f_{\mathrm{L}} + f_{\mathrm{b}}) + f_{p_{\mathrm{d}}}\right), u = K_{\mathrm{b}}^{-1}.\left(R^{\mathrm{T}}.(\tau_{\mathrm{b_d}} + \tau_{\mathrm{L_d}}) + \tau_{p_{\mathrm{d}}}\right), \tag{9}$$

where $f_{\mathrm{b}(s)} = ba(l-s)g$ is the body weight force, $f_{p_{\mathrm{d}}} = \sum_{i=1}^{3} p_i a_{\mathrm{c}}.d_i$ is the pneumatic pressure force assuming fix cross section (a dense thread), $\tau_{\mathrm{L_d}} = \left(\rho_{\mathrm{L_d}} - \rho_{\mathrm{d}_{(s)}}\right) \times f_{\mathrm{L}}$ is the external load moment, $\tau_{b_d} = ba \int_s^l \left(\rho_{d(s)} - \rho_{d(\varepsilon)} \right) d\varepsilon \times g$ is the body weight moment,

$\tau_{p_d} = a_p r_{0_d} \left(p \cdot \left[C_{(-\phi)}, C_{(-\phi+2\pi/3)}, C_{(-\phi-2\pi/3)} \right]^T \right) d_{\hat{b}}$ is the pneumatic pressure moment

exerting at the manipulator tip and $r_{0_d} = r_0/\sqrt{\lambda}$ is the deformed placement radius for the pneumatic chambers, all in deformed state. The deformed values in each element are found by using the local curvature parameters $\lambda_l = v_i + 1$ and $\kappa = u_{\hat{b}}/(v_i + 1)$.

– *Single Shooting Optimization Based Solution:* We can approximate the solution to the BVP with a series of finite terms, i.e. a polynomial of order n as a function of s, and investigating the equilibrium condition. This is considered as a special case of separation of variable method for Partial Differential Equation (PDE) systems that provides a weak form solution. The terms are consisting of separate space dependent shape functions and time dependent coefficients where the time dependent part is constant in static cases. The constants are being optimized so the guessed series solution represents the static equilibrium of the system. We fit a curve to seven points using Matlab "interp1" function and then use Matlab "fsolve" function for optimization of these points' positions in the plane starting from a straight configuration as the initial guess. The algorithm usually needs only two trials to find the equilibrium configuration for a single-curve formation and three trials for a double-curve formation, i.e. in presence of high external force (Fig. 5.I) showing the possibility of real-time implementation of this method. A similar result can be achieved by haven a polynomial of order at least three to model the "S" shape configuration of a single module under high external loads with good accuracy. As observed in previous research [13], the overall accuracy of the Cosserat rod model is about 16% better than the CC models with a 12% mean error in comparison to the experimental results with extensive external loads. It is relatively hard to model the dynamics of a system using Cosserat and beam theory methods; however, they are the best in terms of accuracy to find the manipulator configuration in static equilibrium points.

Identification Based Series Solutions
Coefficients of a series solution can be identified based on the experimental results [5, 15]. Godage presented an identification based Taylor series solution for the kinematic map of a continuum manipulator (the relation between actuator chamber length and manipulator geometry) and later implemented the resulted identified solution in the Lagrange EOM for dynamic modeling of a continuum manipulator [5]. The spatial geometry is described using a time-dependent coefficient vector $(\gamma(t))$ and a shape function matrix $(\Psi(\epsilon))$ as $r(\epsilon, t) = [x(\epsilon,t) \quad y(\epsilon,t) \quad z(\epsilon,t)]^T = \Psi(\epsilon)\gamma(t)$, where $\epsilon \in [0, 1]$ is a scalar variable defining the position of each point on the manipulator axis with 0 for the base and 1 for the tip. The final model can be as simple as a polynomial of order five [5]. Godage used three equations each with 56 shape functions of the form $A_1 l_1^{A_2} \epsilon^{A_3 + 1} R^{-A_3}$ where A_1, A_2 and A_3 are integers to be identified based on optimization and $A_1 \& A_2 \in [0, 1]$ and $A_3 \in [0, 5]$ [5]. Choice of the shape function and time-dependent coefficient can be based on observation, guessed solution or completely arbitrary. Similar to other weak approximation solutions, they should satisfy the boundary and initial conditions and the convergence should be investigated for

increasing the number of terms. Here we introduce a simpler series with eight time dependent coefficients (C_{ij}) to be identified using Least Square Value optimization as,

$$\Psi = C_{3\times8}.\text{diag}\begin{bmatrix} \epsilon & \epsilon & \epsilon & \epsilon & \epsilon^2 & \epsilon^2 & \epsilon^2 & \epsilon^3 \end{bmatrix}, \tag{10}$$

where $\gamma(t) = \begin{bmatrix} 1 & l_{C1} & l_{C2} & l_{C3} & l_{C1}l_{C2} & l_{C1}l_{C3} & l_{C2}l_{C3} & l_{C1}l_{C2}l_{C3} \end{bmatrix}^T$ is for a system with kinematic inputs and $\gamma(t) = \begin{bmatrix} 1 & p_1 & p_2 & p_3 & p_1p_2 & p_1p_3 & p_2p_3 & p_1p_2p_3 \end{bmatrix}^T$ for a system with pressure inputs. To satisfy boundary conditions we have $\begin{bmatrix} C_{11} & C_{21} & C_{31} \end{bmatrix} = \begin{bmatrix} x_0 & y_0 & z_0 \end{bmatrix}_{\text{tip}}$. The model trains and performs very fast, suitable for real-time and precise control purposes. The simulation results show 11% mean error which is the most accurate results in predicting the static behavior of the manipulator with body loads after being trained with 30% of the experimental points (Fig. 6). However, the structural information which is necessary for design optimization is not incorporated in the model. Besides the complexity of the series solution make any further analytical analysis such as dynamic modeling, controller design and stability analysis a hard task. This method incorporates the same level of structural parameters as the Cosserat method and can be assumed as a basis for both optimization and control frameworks.

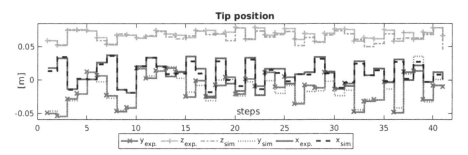

Fig. 6. Identification based series model results compared to experiments with body loads

3 Discussion and Comparison

In Table 2, a comparison between the different modeling methods is presented based on the derivation and implementation complexity, the level of structural characteristics in the model, sensitivity to model parameters, computation cost, overall accuracy and suggested applications. It worth mentioning that the information in Table 2 is provided based on the feasibility, ease and popularity of the model usage for a specific purpose; however, all the methods can be used for different purposes after some modification.

Table 2. Comparisons of different modelling approaches.

	Lumped sys.	CC & Euler-Bernoulli	CC & virt. energy	Modified CC	Cosserat/beam theory	Series id.
Spec.s	Dynamic, Forward/Inverse	Static, Forward/Inverse	Static, Inverse	Static, Forward	Static, Forward	Static, Forward/Inverse
Complexity	Hard	Easy	Medium	Medium	Hard	Medium
Struct. details	Medium	Low	High	Low/Medium	Medium	Low
Param. sensitive	Medium/High	Low	High	Medium	Medium	Low
Comp. cost	High	Low	Medium	Low	High	Low/Medium
Accuracy (error,%)	Medium (22%)	Low (31%)	Low–Med. (28%)	Low–Med. (27%)	High (12%)	High (11%)
app.	Simulation, Control	Non-accurate Control	Design	Non-accurate Control	Simulation	Control

4   Conclusion

In this paper, a review on derivation and implementation of five different approaches for modeling of continuum manipulators is presented. Lumped system dynamic model, Constant curvature, two-step modified constant curvature, variable curvature Cosserat rod and beam theory approach and series solution identification are derived and the modeling results are compared with experimental data using a STIFF-FLOP continuum manipulator section. Our study shows the competency of the identification based model in comparison to the other methods in accuracy and performance. From a different perspective, we conclude that dynamic behavior prediction and control method implementation are streamlined in lumped system model. Different CC models based on the principle of virtual work show less accuracy but the better incorporation of structural characteristics which makes them suitable for design optimization purposes. Furthermore, through the sections of this paper, simple mathematical derivations of the manipulator deformation energy are discussed; a comparison between different models for a braided extensile pneumatic actuator is presented and a novel two-step modified CC solution using Castigliano's method is suggested to simplify the design optimization, control and path planning problems of continuum manipulators.

Acknowledgement. This work is supported in part by the U.K. Engineering and Physical Sciences Research Council (EPSRC) under MOTION Grant: EP/N03211X/2, and European Union H2020 project FourByThree code 637095.

References

1. Hirose, S., Mori, M.: Biologically inspired snake-like robots. In: Proceedings of IEEE International Conference Robotics and Biomimetics, pp. 1–7 (2004)
2. Cianchetti, M., Ranzani, T., Gerboni, G., Nanayakkara, T., Althoefer, K., Dasgupta, P., Menciassi, A.: Soft robotics technologies to address shortcomings in today's minimally invasive surgery: the STIFFFLOP approach. Soft Robot. **1**(2), 122–131 (2014)

3. Webster, R.J., Jones, B.A.: Design and kinematic modeling of CC continuum robots: a review. Int. J. Rob. Res. **29**(13), 1661–1683 (2010)
4. Mehling, J.S., Diftler, M., Chu, M., et al.: A minimally invasive tendril robot for in-space inspection. In: The First IEEE/RAS-EMBS International Conference on Biomedical Robotics and Biomechatronics, BioRob 2006, pp. 690–695 (2006)
5. Godage, I.S., Branson, D.T., Guglielmino, E., et al.: Shape function-based kinematics and dynamics for variable length continuum robotic arms. In: 2011 IEEE International Conference on Robotics and Automation (ICRA), pp. 452–457 (2011)
6. Godage, I.S., Wirz, R., Walker, I.D., Webster III, R.J.: Accurate and efficient dynamics for variable-length continuum arms: a center of gravity approach. Soft Robot. **2**(3), 96–106 (2015)
7. Shapiro, Y., Wolf, A., Gabor, K.: Bi-bellows: pneumatic bending actuator. Sens. Actuators, A **167**(2), 484–494 (2011)
8. Fraś, J., Czarnowski, J., Maciaś, M., Główka, J.: Static modeling of multisection soft continuum manipulator for stiff-flop project. In: Szewczyk, R., Zieliński, C., Kaliczyńska, M. (eds.) Recent Advances in Automation, Robotics and Measuring Techniques. AISC, vol. 267, pp. 365–375. Springer, Cham (2014). doi:10.1007/978-3-319-05353-0_35
9. Sadati, S.M.H., Shiva, A., Ataka, A., et. al.: A Geometry deformation model for compound continuum manipulators with external loading. In: 2016 IEEE International Conference on Robotics and Automation (ICRA) (2016)
10. Sadati, S.M.H., et al.: A geometry deformation model for braided continuum manipulators. Front. Robot. AI **4**, June 2017
11. Mahl, T., Mayer, A.E., Hildebrandt, A., Sawodny, O.: A variable curvature modeling approach for kinematic control of continuum manipulators. In: 2013 American Control Conference, pp. 4945–4950 (2013)
12. Trivedi, D., Lotfi, A., Rahn, C.: Geometrically exact models for soft robotic manipulators. IEEE Trans. Robot. **4**(24), 773–780 (2008)
13. Walker, I.D.: Continuous backbone 'Continuum' robot manipulators. Int. Sch. Res. Not. (ISRN Robot.) **2013**, e726506 (2013)
14. Tunay, I.: Spatial continuum models of rods undergoing large deformation and inflation. IEEE Trans. Robot. **29**(2), 297–307 (2013)
15. Chen, G., Pham, M.T., Redarce, T.: sensor-based guidance control of a continuum robot for a semi-autonomous colonoscopy. Rob. Auton. Syst. **57**(6–7), 712–722 (2009)
16. Fraś, J., Czarnowski, J., Maciaś, M., Główka, J., Cianchetti, M., Menciassi, A.: New STIFF-FLOP module construction idea for improved actuation and sensing. In: 2015 IEEE International Conference on Robotics and Automation (ICRA), pp. 2901–2906 (2015)
17. Conrad, B., Zinn, M.: Closed loop task space control of an interleaved continuum-rigid manipulator. In: 2015 IEEE International Conference on Robotics and Automation (ICRA), pp. 1743–1750 (2015)
18. Jung, J., Penning, R.S., Zinn, M.R.: A modeling approach for robotic catheters: effects of nonlinear internal device friction. Adv. Robot. **28**(8), 557–572 (2014)
19. Sadati, S., Naghibi, S., Naraghi, M.: An automatic algorithm to derive linear vector form of lagrangian equation of motion with collision and constraint. Procedia Comput. Sci. **76**, 217–222 (2015)
20. Trivedi, D., Rahn, C.D.: Model-based shape estimation for soft robotic manipulators: the planar case. J. Mech. Robot. **6**(2), 021005 (2014)
21. Liu, W., Rahn, C.: Fiber-reinforced membrane models of McKibben actuators. J. Appl. Mech. **70**(6), 853–859 (2003)
22. Rivlin, R.S.: Large elastic deformations of isotropic materials. V. the problem of flexure. Proc. Roy. Soc. A: Math., Phy. Eng. Sci. **195**(1043), 463–473 (1949)

23. Gent, A.N.: Engineering with rubber: how to design rubber components. Carl Hanser Verlag, GmbH Co KG (2012)
24. Mahvash, M., Dupont, P.E.: Stiffness control of a continuum manipulator in contact with a soft environment. In: 2010 IEEE/RSJ International Conference on Intelligent Robots and Systems (IROS), pp. 863–870 (2010)
25. Juvinall, R.C., Marshek, K.M.: Fundamentals of Machine Component Design, vol. 83. Wiley, New York (2006)
26. Neumann, M., Burgner-Kahrs, J.: Considerations for follow-the-leader motion of extensible tendon-driven continuum robots (2016)
27. Burgner-Kahrs, J., Rucker, D.C., Choset, H.: Continuum robots for medical applications: a survey. IEEE Trans. Robot. **31**(6), 1261–1280 (2015)
28. Duriez, C., Bieze, T.: Soft robot modeling, simulation and control in real-time. In: Laschi, C., Rossiter, J., Iida, F., Cianchetti, M., Margheri, L. (eds.) Soft Robotics: Trends, Applications and Challenges. Biosystems & Biorobotics, vol. 17, pp. 103–109. Springer, Cham (2017), doi:10.1007/978-3-319-46460-2_13

Author Index